D1316665

ST. PAUL'S
EPISTLES
TO THE
COLOSSIANS
AND TO
PHILEMON

ST. PAUL'S EPISTLES TO THE COLOSSIANS AND TO PHILEMON

A REVISED TEXT
WITH
Introduction, Notes
and Dissertations

J.B. LIGHTFOOT, D.D.,D.C.L.,LL.D.

HENDRICKSON
PUBLISHERS
PEABODY, MASSACHUSETTS 01961-3473

Third Printing March, 1987
Printed In The United States of America

Dr. Joseph Barber Lightfoot was born in England in 1828. He was educated at Oxford and Cambridge, returning later to Cambridge as Professor of Divinity. He served the Church of England as Lord Bishop of Durham, and was a minister at St. Paul's Cathedral in London.

The commentaries of J.B. Lightfoot on Galatians, Philippians, Colossians and Philemon have long been hailed as among the finest ever written on these epistles. These volumes, complete with Greek Text, reflect the respected scholarship of Dr. Lightfoot, and are invaluable for thorough exegetical study as well as general reference.

TO THE

RIGHT REV. EDWARD HAROLD BROWNE, D.D.,

LORD BISHOP OF WINCHESTER,

IN SINCERE ADMIRATION

OF

HIS PERSONAL CHARACTER AND EPISCOPAL WORK

AND IN

GRATEFUL RECOGNITION

OF

THE PRIVILEGES OF A PRIVATE FRIENDSHIP.

ΜΙΜΗΤΑΊ ΜΟΥ ΓΊΝΕϹΘΕ ΚἀΘὼϹ ΚἀΓὼ ΧΡΙϹΤΟΥ

Παῦλος γενόμενος μέγιστος ὑπογραμμός.

CLEMENT.

Οὐχ ὡς Παῦλος διατάσσομαι ὑμῖν· ἐκεῖνος ἀπόστολος,
ἐγὼ κατάκριτος· ἐκεῖνος ἐλεύθερος, ἐγὼ δὲ μέχρι νῦν δοῦλος.

IGNATIUS.

Οὔτε ἐγὼ οὔτε ἄλλος ὅμοιος ἐμοὶ δύναται κατακολουθῆσαι
τῇ σοφίᾳ τοῦ μακαρίου καὶ ἐνδόξου Παύλου.

POLYCARP.

PREFACE TO THE FIRST EDITION.

On the completion of another volume of my commentary, I wish again to renew my thanks for the assistance received from previous labourers in the same field. Such obligations must always be great; but it is not easy in a few words to apportion them fairly, and I shall not make the attempt. I have not consciously neglected any aid which might render this volume more complete; but at the same time I venture to hope that my previous commentaries have established my claim to be regarded as an independent worker, and in the present instance more especially I have found myself obliged to diverge widely from the treatment of my predecessors, and to draw largely from other materials than those which they have collected.

In the preface to a previous volume I expressed an intention of appending to my commentary on the Colossian Epistle an essay on 'Christianity and Gnosis.' This intention has not been fulfilled in the letter; but the subject enters largely into the investigation of the Colossian heresy, where it receives as much attention as, at all events for the present, it seems to require. It will necessarily come under discussion again, when the Pastoral Epistles are taken in hand.

The question of the genuineness of the two epistles contained in this volume has been deliberately deferred. It could not be discussed with any advantage apart from the Epistle to the Ephesians, for the three letters are inseparably bound together. Meanwhile however the doctrinal and historical discussions will, if I mistake not, have furnished answers to the main objections which have been urged; while the commentary will have shown how thoroughly natural the language and thoughts are, if conceived as arising out of an immediate emergency. More especially it will have been made apparent that the Epistle to the Colossians hangs together as a whole, and that the phenomena are altogether adverse to any theory of interpolation such as that recently put forward by Professor Holtzmann.

In the commentary, as well as in the introduction, it has been a chief aim to illustrate and develope the theological conception of the Person of Christ, which underlies the Epistle to the Colossians. The Colossian heresy for instance owes its importance mainly to the fact that it throws out this conception into bolder relief. To this portion of the subject therefore I venture to direct special attention.

I cannot conclude without offering my thanks to Mr A. A. VanSittart, who, as on former occasions, has given his aid in correcting the proof sheets of this volume; and to the Rev. J. J. Scott, of Trinity College, who has prepared the index. I wish also to express my obligations to Dr Schiller-Szinessy, of whose talmudical learning I have freely availed myself in verifying Frankel's quotations and in other ways. I should add however that he is not in any degree responsible for my conclusions, and has not even seen what I have written.

Trinity College,
April 30, 1875.

CONTENTS.

EPISTLE TO THE COLOSSIANS.

I.

THE CHURCHES OF THE LYCUS.

LYING in, or overhanging, the valley of the Lycus, a Situation of the three cities. tributary of the Mæander, were three neighbouring towns, Laodicea, Hierapolis, and Colossæ[1]. The river flows,

[1] The following are among the most important books of travel relating to this district; Pococke *Description of the East and Some Other Countries*, Vol. II, Part II, London 1745; Chandler *Travels in Asia Minor* etc., Oxford 1775; Leake *Tour in Asia Minor*, London 1824; Arundell *Discoveries in Asia Minor*, London 1834; Hamilton *Researches in Asia Minor, Pontus, and Armenia*, London 1842; Fellows *Asia Minor*, London 1839, *Discoveries in Lycia*, London 1840; Davis *Anatolica*, London 1874; Tchihatcheff *Asie Mineure, Description Physique, Statistique et Archéologique*, Paris 1853 etc., with the accompanying Atlas (1860); Laborde *Voyage de l'Asie Mineure* (the expedition itself took place in 1826, but the date on the title-page is 1838, and the introduction was written in 1861); Le Bas *Voyage Archéologique en Grèce et en Asie Mineure*, continued by Waddington and not yet completed; Texier *Description de l'Asie Mineure*, Vol. I (1839). It is hardly necessary to add the smaller works of Texier and Le Bas on *Asie Mineure* (Paris 1862, 1863) in Didot's series *L'Univers*, as these have only a secondary value. Of the books enumerated, Hamilton's work is the most important for the topography, etc.; Tchihatcheff's for the physical features; and Le Bas and Waddington's for the inscriptions, etc. The best maps are those of Hamilton and Tchihatcheff: to which should be added the *Karte von Klein-Asien* by v. Vincke and others, published by Schropp, Berlin 1844.

Besides books on Asia Minor generally, some works relating especially to the Seven Churches may be mentioned. Smith's *Survey of the Seven Churches of Asia* (1678) is a work of great merit for the time, and contains the earliest description of the sites of these Phrygian cities. It was published in Latin first, and translated by its author afterwards. Arundell's *Seven Churches* (1828) is a well-known book. Allom and Walsh's *Constantinople and the Scenery of the Seven Churches of Asia Minor illustrated* (1850) gives some views of this district. Svoboda's *Seven Churches of Asia* (1869) contains 20 photographs and an introduction by the Rev. H. B. Tristram. This is a selection from a larger series of Svoboda's photographs, published separately.

roughly speaking, from east to west; but at this point, which is some few miles above its junction with the Mæander, its direction is more nearly from south-east to north-west[1]. Laodicea and Hierapolis stand face to face, being situated respectively on the southern and northern sides of the valley, at a distance of six miles[2], and within sight of each other, the river lying in the open plain between the two. The site of Colossæ is somewhat higher up the stream, at a distance of perhaps ten or twelve miles[3] from the point where the road between Laodicea and Hierapolis crosses the Lycus. Unlike Laodicea and Hierapolis, which overhang the valley on opposite sides, Colossæ stands immediately on the river-bank, the two parts of the town being divided by the stream. The three cities lie so near to each other, that it would be quite possible to visit them all in the course of a single day.

Their neighbourhood and intercourse. Thus situated, they would necessarily hold constant intercourse with each other. We are not surprised therefore to find them so closely connected in the earliest ages of Christianity. It was the consequence of their position that they owed their knowledge of the Gospel to the same evangelist, that the same phases of thought prevailed in them, and that they were exposed to the same temptations, moral as well as intellectual.

Physical forces at work. The physical features of the neighbourhood are very striking. Two potent forces of nature are actively at work to change the face of the country, the one destroying old landmarks, the other creating fresh ground.

On the one hand, the valley of the Lycus was and is

---

[1] The maps differ very considerably in this respect, nor do the statements of travellers always agree. The direction of the river, as given in the text, accords with the maps of Hamilton and Tchihatcheff, and with the accounts of the most accurate writers.

[2] *Anton. Itin.* p. 337 (Wesseling) gives the distance as 6 miles. See also

Fellows *Asia Minor* p. 283, Hamilton I. p. 514. The relative position of the two cities appears in Laborde's view, pl. xxxix.

[3] I do not find any distinct notice of the distance; but, to judge from the maps and itineraries of modern travellers, this estimate will probably be found not very far wrong.

especially liable to violent earthquakes. The same danger Frequent indeed extends over large portions of Asia Minor, but this earthquakes. district is singled out by ancient writers[1] (and the testimony of modern travellers confirms the statement[2]), as the chief theatre of these catastrophes. Not once or twice only in the history of Laodicea do we read of such visitations laying waste the city itself or some flourishing town in the neighbourhood[3].

Though the exterior surface of the earth shows no traces of recent volcanoes, still the cavernous nature of the soil and the hot springs and mephitic vapours abounding here indicate the presence of those subterranean fires which from time to time have manifested themselves in this work of destruction.

But, while the crust of the earth is constantly broken up Deposits by these forces from beneath, another agency is actively em- of travertine. ployed above ground in laying a new surface. If fire has its fitful outbursts of devastation, water is only less powerful in its gradual work of reconstruction. The lateral streams which swell the waters of the Lycus are thickly impregnated with calcareous matter, which they deposit in their course. The travertine formations of this valley are among the most remarkable in the world, surpassing even the striking phenomena of Tivoli and Clermont[4]. Ancient monuments are buried, fertile lands overlaid, river-beds choked up and streams diverted, fantastic grottoes and cascades and archways of stone formed, by this strange capricious power, at once destructive and creative, working silently and relentlessly through long ages. Fatal to vegetation, these incrustations spread like a stony shroud over the ground. Gleaming like glaciers on the hill-side they attract the eye of the traveller at a distance

---

[1] Strabo xii. 8 (p. 578) τὸ πολύτρητον τῆς χώρας καὶ τὸ εὔσειστον· εἰ γάρ τις ἄλλη, καὶ ἡ Λαοδίκεια εὔσειστος, καὶ τῆς πλησιοχώρου δὲ Κάρουρα, Ioann. Lyd. p. 349 (ed. Bonn.) πυκνότερον σείεται, οἷα τὰ περὶ τὴν Φρυγίας Λαοδίκειαν καὶ τὴν παρ᾽ αὐτῇ Ἱερὰν πόλιν.

[2] Thus Pococke (p. 71) in 1745 writes

of Denizli, which is close to Laodicea, 'The old town was destroyed about 25 years past by an earthquake, in which 12,000 people perished.'

[3] See below, p. 38.

[4] Tchihatcheff P. 1. Geogr. Phys. Comp. p. 344 sq., esp. p. 353. See the references below, pp. 9 sq., 15.

of twenty miles[1], and form a singularly striking feature in
scenery of more than common beauty and impressiveness.

Produce
and manu-
factures of
the dis-
trict. At the same time, along with these destructive agencies,
the fertility of the district was and is unusually great. Its
rich pastures fed large flocks of sheep, whose fleeces were of
a superior quality; and the trade in dyèd woollen goods was
the chief source of prosperity to these towns. For the bounty
of nature was not confined to the production of the material,
but extended also to the preparation of the fabric. The
mineral streams had chemical qualities, which were highly
valued by the dyer[2]. Hence we find that all the three towns,
with which we are concerned, were famous in this branch of
trade. At Hierapolis, as at Thyatira, the guild of the dyers
appears in the inscriptions as an important and influential
body[3]. Their colours vied in brilliancy with the richest
scarlets and purples of the farther East[4]. Laodicea again was
famous for the colour of its fleeces, probably a glossy black,
which was much esteemed[5]. Here also we read of a guild
of dyers[6]. And lastly, Colossæ gave its name to a peculiar

[1] Fellows *Asia Minor* p. 283.

[2] See note 4.

[3] Boeckh no. 3924 (comp. *Anatolica*
p. 104) τοῦτο τὸ ἡρῶον Στεφάνῳ ἡ ἐργα-
σία τῶν βαφέων, at Hierapolis. See
Laborde, pl. xxxv. In another inscription too (Le Bas and Waddington, no.
1687) there is mention of the purple-
dyers, πορφυραβαφεῖς.

[4] Strabo xiii. 4. 14 (p. 630) ἔστι δὲ
καὶ πρὸς βαφὴν ἐρίων θαυμαστῶς σύμ-
μετρον τὸ κατὰ τὴν Ἱερὰν πόλιν ὕδωρ,
ὥστε τὰ ἐκ τῶν ῥιζῶν βαπτόμενα ἐνά-
μιλλα εἶναι τοῖς ἐκ τῆς κόκκου καὶ τοῖς
ἀλουργέσιν.

[5] Strabo xii. 8. 16 (p. 578) φέρει δ' ὁ
περὶ τὴν Λαοδίκειαν τόπος 'άτων
ἀρετὰς οὐκ εἰς μαλακότητα μόνον τῶν
ἐρίων, ἦ καὶ τῶν Μιλησίων διαφέρει,
ἀλλὰ καὶ εἰς τὴν κοραξὴν χρόαν, ὥστε
καὶ προσοδεύονται λαμπρῶς ἀπ' αὐτῶν,
ὥσπερ καὶ οἱ Κολοσσηνοὶ ἀπὸ τοῦ ὁμω-

νύμου χρώματος, πλησίον οἰκοῦντες. For
this strange adjective κοραξός (which
seems to be derived from κόραξ and to
mean 'raven-black') see the passages
in Hase and Dindorf's *Steph. Thes.*
In Latin we find the form *coracinus*,
Vitruv. viii. 3 § 14 'Aliis coracino co-
lore,' Laodicea being mentioned in the
context. Vitruvius represents this as
the natural colour of the fleeces, and
attributes it to the water drunk by the
sheep. See also Plin. *N. H.* viii. 48
§ 73. So too Hieron. *adv. Jovin.* ii.
21 (ii. p. 358) 'Laodiceæ indumentis
ornatus incedis.' The ancient accounts
of the natural colour of the fleeces in
this neighbourhood are partially confirmed by modern travellers; e.g. Pococke p. 74, Chandler p. 228.

[6] Boeckh *Corp. Inscr.* 3938 [ἡ ἐρ-
γασία] τῶν γναφέ[ων καὶ βαφέων τῶν]
ἀλουργ[ῶ]ν.

dye, which seems to have been some shade of purple, and from which it derived a considerable revenue[1].

I. Of these three towns LAODICEA, as the most important, deserves to be considered first. Laodice was a common name among the ladies of the royal house of the Seleucidæ, as Antiochus was among the princes. Hence Antiochia and Laodicea occur frequently as the designations of cities within the dominions of the Syrian kings. Laodicea on the Lycus[2], as it was surnamed to distinguish it from other towns so called, and more especially perhaps from its near neighbour Laodicea Catacecaumene, had borne in succession the names of Diospolis and Rhoas[3]; but when refounded by Antiochus Theos (B.C. 261—246), it was newly designated after his wife Laodice[4]. It is situated[5] on an undulating hill, or group of hills, which overhangs the valley on the south, being washed on either side by the streams of the Asopus and the Caprus, tributaries of the Lycus[6]. Behind it rise the snow-capped

I. LAODICEA. Its name and history.

---

[1] See the passage of Strabo quoted p. 4, note 5. The place gives its name to the colour, and not conversely, as stated in Blakesley's Herod. vii. 113. See also Plin. N. H. xxi. 9 § 27, 'In vepribus nascitur cyclaminum ... flos ejus colossinus in coronas admittitur,' a passage which assists in determining the colour.

[2] ἐπὶ Λύκῳ, Boeckh Corp. Inscr. no. 3938, Ptol. Geogr. v. 2, Tab. Peut. 'laudicium pilycum'; πρὸς [τῷ] Λύκῳ, Eckhel Num. Vet. III. p. 166, Strabo l.c., Boeckh C.I. 5881,5893; πρὸς Λύκον, Boeckh 6478. A citizen was styled Λαοδικεὺς ἀπὸ Λύκου, Diog. Laert. ix. 12 § 116; C.I.L. VI. 374; comp. περὶ τὸν Λύκον Appian. Mithr. 20.

[3] Plin. N. H. v. 29.

[4] Steph. Byz. s. v., who quotes the oracle in obedience to which (ὡς ἐκέλευ-σε Ζεὺς ὑψιβρεμέτης) it was founded.

[5] For descriptions of Laodicea see Smith p. 250 sq., Pococke p. 71 sq., Chandler p. 224 sq., Arundell Seven

Churches p. 84 sq., Asia Minor II. p. 180 sq., Fellows Asia Minor 280 sq., Hamilton I. p. 514 sq., Davis Anatolica p. 92 sq., Tchihatcheff P. I. p. 252 sq., 258 sq. See also the views in Laborde, pl. xxxix, Allom and Walsh II. p. 86, and Svoboda phot. 36—38.

The modern Turkish name is Eskihissar, 'the Old Castle,' corresponding to the modern Greek, Paleókastro, a common name for the sites of ancient cities; Leake p. 251. On the ancient site itself there is no town or village; the modern city Denizli is a few miles off.

[6] The position of Laodicea with respect to the neighbouring streams is accurately described by Pliny N. H. v. 29 'Imposita est Lyco flumini, latera affluentibus Asopo et Capro'; see Tchihatcheff P. I. p. 258. Strabo xii. (l. c.) is more careless in his description (for it can hardly be, as Tchihatcheff assumes, that he has mistaken one of these two tributaries

heights of Cadmus, the lofty mountain barrier which shuts in the south side of the main valley[1]. A place of no great importance at first, it made rapid strides in the last days of the republic and under the earliest Cæsars, and had become, two or three generations before St Paul wrote, a populous and thriving city[2]. Among its famous inhabitants are mentioned the names of some philosophers, sophists, and rhetoricians, men renowned in their day but forgotten or almost forgotten now[3]. More to our purpose, as illustrating the boasted wealth and prosperity of the city, which appeared as a reproach and a stumblingblock in an Apostle's eyes[4], are the facts, that one of its citizens, Polemo, became a king and a father of kings, and that another, Hiero, having accumulated enormous wealth, bequeathed all his property to the people and adorned the city with costly gifts[5]. To the good fortune of her principal sons, as well as to the fertility of the country around, the geographer Strabo ascribes the increase and prosperity of Laodicea. The ruins of public buildings still bear testimony by their number and magnificence to the past greatness of the city[6].

for the Lycus itself), ἐνταῦθα δὲ καὶ ὁ Κάπρος καὶ ὁ Λύκος συμβάλλει τῷ Μαιάνδρῳ ποταμῷ ποταμὸς εὐμεγέθης, where ἐνταῦθα refers to ὁ περὶ τὴν Λαοδίκειαν τόπος, and where by the junction of the stream with the Mæander must be intended the junction of the *combined* stream of the Lycus and Caprus. On the coins of Laodicea (Eckhel III. p. 166, Mionnet IV. p. 330, ib. Suppl. VII. p. 587, 589) the Lycus and Caprus appear together, being sometimes represented as a wolf and a wild boar. The Asopus is omitted, either as being a less important stream or as being less capable of symbolical representation. Of modern travellers, Smith (p. 250), and after him Pococke (p. 72), have correctly described the position of the streams. Chandler (p. 227), misled by Strabo, mistakes the Caprus for the

Lycus and the Lycus for the Mæander. The modern name of the Lycus is Tchoruk Sú.

[1] The modern name of Cadmus is Baba-Dagh, 'The father of mountains.'

[2] Strabo xii. 1. c. ἡ δὲ Λαοδίκεια μικρὰ πρότερον οὖσα αὔξησιν ἔλαβεν ἐφ' ἡμῶν καὶ τῶν ἡμετέρων πατέρων, καίτοι κακωθεῖσα ἐκ πολιορκίας ἐπὶ Μιθριδάτου τοῦ Εὐπάτορος. Strabo flourished in the time of Augustus and the earlier years of Tiberius. The growing importance of Laodicea dates from before the age of Cicero : see p. 7.

[3] Strabo 1. c.; Diog. Laert. ix. 11 § 106, 12 § 116; Philostr. *Vit. Soph.* i. 25; Eckhel *Doctr. Num. Vet.* III. p. 162, 163 sq.

[4] Rev. iii. 17; see below p. 43.

[5] Strabo 1. c. On this family see *Ephemeris Epigraphica* I. p. 270 sq.

[6] The ruins of Laodicea have formed

Not less important, as throwing light on the Apostolic Its politi-
history, is the political status of Laodicea. Asia Minor as the
under the Romans was divided into districts, each compris- capital of a
ing several towns and having its chief city, in which the *conventus.*
courts were held from time to time by the proconsul or
legate of the province, and where the taxes from the subordinate towns were collected[1]. Each of these political ag-
gregates was styled in Latin *conventus*, in Greek διοίκησις—
a term afterwards borrowed by the Christian Church, being
applied to a similar ecclesiastical aggregate, and thus naturalised in the languages of Christendom as *diocese*. At the
head of the most important of these political dioceses, the
'Cibyratic convention' or 'jurisdiction,' as it was called, comprising not less than twenty-five towns, stood Laodicea[2].
Here in times past Cicero, as proconsul of Cilicia, had held
his court[3]; hither at stated seasons flocked suitors, advo-

the quarry out of which the modern
town of Denizli is built. Yet notwithstanding these depredations they are
still very extensive, comprising an
amphitheatre, two or three theatres,
an aqueduct, etc. The amphitheatre
was built by the munificence of a
citizen of Laodicea only a few years
after St Paul wrote, as the inscription
testifies; Boeckh *C. I.* no. 3935. See
especially Hamilton I. p. 515 sq., who
describes these ruins as 'bearing the
stamp of Roman extravagance and
luxury, rather than of the stern and
massive solidity of the Greeks.'

[1] See Becker and Marquardt *Röm.
Alterth.* III. I. p. 136 sq.

[2] See Cic. *ad Att.* v. 21, 'Idibus
Februariis ... forum institueram agere
Laodiceæ Cibyraticum,' with the references in the next note: comp. also
Plin. *N. H.* v. 29 'Una (jurisdictio)
appellatur Cibyratica. Ipsum (i. e.
Cibyra) oppidum Phrygiæ est. Con-
veniunt eo xxv civitates, celeberrima
urbe Laodicea.'

Besides these passages, testimony is
borne to the importance of the Cibyratic 'conventus' by Strabo, xiii. 4
§ 17 (p. 631), ἐν ταῖς μεγίσταις ἐξετάζε-
ται διοικήσεσι τῆς Ἀσίας ἡ Κιβυρατική.
It will be remembered also that Ho-
race singles out the *Cibyratica negotia*
(*Epist.* i. 6. 33) to represent Oriental
trade generally. The importance of
Laodicea may be inferred from the fact
that, though the union was named after
Cibyra, its head-quarters were from the
first fixed at or soon afterwards transferred to Laodicea.

[3] See *ad Fam.* ii. 17, iii. 5, 7, 8,
ix. 25, xiii. 54, 67, xv. 4; *ad Att.* v. 16,
17, 20, 21, vi. 1, 2, 3, 7. He visited
Laodicea on several occasions, sometimes making a long stay there, and
not a few of his letters are written
thence. See especially his account of
his work there, *ad Att.* vi. 2, 'Hoc foro
quod egi ex Idibus Februariis Laodiceæ
ad Kalendas Maias omnium dioece-
sium, præter Ciliciæ, mirabilia quædam efficimus; ita multæ civitates,

cates, clerks, sheriffs'-officers, tax-collectors, pleasure-seekers, courtiers—all those crowds whom business or leisure or policy or curiosity would draw together from a wealthy and populous district, when the representative of the laws and the majesty of Rome appeared to receive homage and to hold his assize[1]. To this position as the chief city of the Cibyratic union the inscriptions probably refer, when they style Laodicea the 'metropolis[2].' And in its metropolitan rank we see an explanation of the fact, that to Laodicea, as to the centre of a Christian diocese also, whence their letters would readily be circulated among the neighbouring brotherhoods, two Apostles addressed themselves in succession, the one writing from his captivity in Rome[3], the other from his exile at Patmos[4].

Its religious worship.

On the religious worship of Laodicea very little special information exists. Its tutelary deity was Zeus, whose guardianship had been recognised in Diospolis, the older name of the city, and who, having (according to the legend) commanded its rebuilding, was commemorated on its coins with the surname Laodicenus[5]. Occasionally he is also called Aseis, a title which perhaps reproduces a Syrian epithet of this deity, 'the mighty.' If this interpretation be correct, we have a link of connexion between Laodicea and the religions of the farther East—a connexion far from improbable, considering that Laodicea was

etc.' Altogether Laodicea seems to have been second in importance to none of the cities in his province, except perhaps Tarsus. See also the notice, in Verr. Act. ii. 1. c. 30.

[1] The description which Dion Chrysostom gives in his eulogy of Celænæ (Apamea Cibotus), the metropolis of a neighbouring ' dioececis,' enables us to realise the concourse which gathered together on these occasions : Orat. xxxv (II. p. 69) ξυνάγεται πλῆθος ἀνθρώπων δικαζομένων, δικαζόντων, ἡγεμόνων, ὑπηρετῶν, οἰκετῶν, κ.τ.λ.

[2] On this word see Becker and Mar-

quardt l. c. p. 138 sq. It had lost its original sense, as the mother city of a colony. Laodicea is styled ' metropolis' on the coins, Mionnet IV. p. 321.

[3] Col. iv. 16 with the notes. See also below p. 37, and the introduction to the Epistle to the Ephesians.

[4] Rev. iii. 14.

[5] See Eckhel III. p. 159 sq. (passim), Mionnet IV. p. 315 sq., ib. Suppl. VII. p. 578 sq. (passim). In the coins commemorating an alliance with some other city Laodicea is represented by Zeus ; e. g. Mionnet IV. pp. 320, 324, 331 sq., Suppl. VII. pp. 586, 589.

refounded by a Syrian king and is not unlikely to have adopted some features of Syrian worship[1].

2. On the north of the valley, opposite to the sloping hills which mark the site of Laodicea, is a broad level terrace jutting out from the mountain side and overhanging the plain with almost precipitous sides. On this plateau are scattered the vast ruins of HIERAPOLIS[2].

2. HIERA-POLIS. Its situation.

The mountains upon which it abuts occupy the wedge of ground between the Mæander and the Lycus; but, as the Mæander above its junction with the Lycus passes through a narrow ravine, they blend,

[1] ΛϹΕΙϹ or ΛϹΕΙϹ ΛΛΟΔΙΚΕШΝ. See Waddington *Voyage en Asie Mineure au point de vue Numismatique* (Paris 1853) pp. 25, 26 sq. Mr Waddington adopts a suggestion communicated to him by M. de Longpérier that this word represents the Aramaic עַזִיז 'the strong, mighty,' which appears also in the Arabic 'Aziz.' This view gains some confirmation from the fact, not mentioned by Mr Waddington, that Ἄζιϛος was an epithet of the Ares of Edessa: Julian *Orat.* iv; comp. Cureton *Spic. Syr.* p. 80, and see Lagarde *Gesamm. Abhandl.* p. 16. On the other hand this Shemitic word elsewhere, when adopted into Greek or Latin, is written Ἄζιϛος or Azizus: see Garrucci in the *Archæologia* XLIII. p. 45 'Tyrio Septimio Azizo,' and Boeckh *Corp. Inscr.* 9893 Ἄζιϛος Ἀγρίπα Σύρος. M. de Longpérier offers the alternative that ΛϹΕΙϹ, i. e. Ἀσίς, is equivalent to Ἀσιατικός. An objection to this view, stronger than those urged by Mr Waddington, is the fact that Ἀσίς seems only to be used as a feminine adjective. M. Renan points to the fact that this ΖΕΥϹ ΛϹΕΙϹ is represented with his hand on the horns of a goat, and on the strength of this coincidence would identify him with 'the Azazel of the Semites' (*Saint Paul*, p. 359), though tradition and orthography alike point to some other derivation of Azazel (עֲזָאזֵל).

[2] For descriptions of Hierapolis, see Smith p. 245 sq., Pococke p. 75 sq., Chandler 229 sq., Arundell *Seven Churches* p. 79 sq., Hamilton p. 517 sq., Fellows *Asia Minor* p. 283 sq. For the travertine deposits see especially the description and plates in Tchihatcheff P. I. p. 345, together with the views in Laborde (pl. xxxii—xxxviii), and Svoboda (photogr. 41 —47). Tchihatcheff repeatedly calls the place Hieropolis; but this form, though commonly used of other towns (see Steph. Byz. s. v. Ἱεραπόλις, Leake *Num. Hell.* p. 67), appears not to occur as a designation of the Phrygian city, which seems always to be written Hierapolis. The citizens however are sometimes called Ἱεροπολῖται on the coins.

The modern name is given differently by travellers. It is generally called Pambouk-Kalessi, i.e. 'cotton-castle,' supposed to allude to the appearance of the petrifactions, though cotton is grown in the neighbourhood (Hamilton I. p. 517). So Smith, Pococke, Chandler, Arundell, Tchihatcheff, Waddington, and others. M. Renan says '*Tambouk*, et non *Pambouk, Kalessi*' (*S. Paul* p. 357). Laborde gives the word *Tambouk* in some places and *Pambouk* in others; and Leake says 'Hierapolis, now called *Tabûk-Kale* or *Pambuk-Kale*' (p. 252).

when seen from a distance, with the loftier range of the
Mesogis which overhangs the right bank of the Mæander
almost from its source to its embouchure, and form with it
the northern barrier to the view, as the Cadmus range does
the southern, the broad valley stretching between. Thus
Hierapolis may be said to lie over against Mesogis, as Laodicea
lies over against Cadmus[1].

Remarkable physical features.

It is at Hierapolis that the remarkable physical features
which distinguish the valley of the Lycus display themselves
in the fullest perfection. Over the steep cliffs which support
the plateau of the city, tumble cascades of pure white stone,
the deposit of calcareous matter from the streams which, after
traversing this upper level, are precipitated over the ledge
into the plain beneath and assume the most fantastic shapes
in their descent. At one time overhanging in cornices fringed
with stalactites, at another hollowed out into basins or broken
up with ridges, they mark the site of the city at a distance,
glistening on the mountain-side like foaming cataracts frozen
in the fall.

Their relation to the Apostolic history.

But for the immediate history of St Paul's Epistles the
striking beauty of the scenery has no value. It is not
probable that he had visited this district when the letters
to the Colossians and Laodiceans were written. Were it
otherwise, we can hardly suppose that, educated under widely
different influences and occupied with deeper and more absorb-

---

[1] Strabo xiii. 4. 14 (p. 629) says
ὑπερβαλοῦσι δὲ τὴν Μεσωγίδα...πόλεις
εἰσὶ πρὸς μὲν τῇ Μεσωγίδι καταντικρὺ
Λαοδικείας Ἱερὰ πόλις, κ.τ.λ. He cannot mean that Hierapolis was situated
immediately in or by the Mesogis (for
the name does not seem ever to be applied to the mountains between the
Lycus and Mæander), but that with
respect to Laodicea it stood over a-
gainst the Mesogis, as I have explained it in the text. The view in Laborde
(pl. xxxix) shows the appearance of
Hierapolis from Laodicea. Strabo

had himself visited the place and
must have known how it was situated.
Some modern travellers however (e.g.
Chandler and Arundell) speak of the
plateau of Hierapolis as part of the
Mesogis. Steiger (Kolosser p. 33)
gets over the difficulty by translating
Strabo's words, 'near the Mesogis but
on the opposite side (i.e. of the Mæander) is the Laodicean Hierapolis'
(to distinguish it from others of the
name); but καταντικρὺ cannot be
separated from Λαοδικείας without
violence.

ing thoughts, he would have shared the enthusiasm which this
scenery inspires in the modern traveller. Still it will give
a reality to our conceptions, if we try to picture to ourselves
the external features of that city, which was destined before
long to become the adopted home of Apostles and other
personal disciples of the Lord, and to play a conspicuous part—
second perhaps only to Ephesus—in the history of the Church
during the ages immediately succeeding the Apostles.

Like Laodicea, Hierapolis was at this time an important Hierapolis
and a growing city, though not like Laodicea holding metro- a famous
watering-
politan rank[1]. Besides the trade in dyed wools, which it place.
shared in common with the neighbouring towns, it had another
source of wealth and prosperity peculiar to itself. The streams,
to which the scenery owes the remarkable features already
described, are endowed with valuable medicinal qualities,
while at the same time they are so copious that the ancient
city is described as full of self-made baths[2]. An inscription,
still legible among the ruins, celebrates their virtues in heroic
verse, thus apostrophizing the city :

> Hail, fairest soil in all broad Asia's realm;
> Hail, golden city, nymph divine, bedeck'd
> With flowing rills, thy jewels[3].

Coins of Hierapolis too are extant of various types, on which
Æsculapius and Hygeia appear either singly or together[4].
To this fashionable watering-place, thus favoured by nature,
seekers of pleasure and seekers of health alike were drawn.

To the ancient magnificence of Hierapolis its extant ruins The magnificence
bear ample testimony. More favoured than Laodicea, it has of its
not in its immediate neighbourhood any modern town or ruins.
village of importance, whose inhabitants have been tempted
to quarry materials for their houses out of the memorials of

---

[1] On its *ecclesiastical* title of metropolis, see below, p. 69.

[2] Strabo l. c. οὕτω δ' ἐστὶν ἄφθονον
τὸ πλῆθος τοῦ ὕδατος ὥστε ἡ πόλις μεστὴ
τῶν αὐτομάτων βαλανείων ἐστί.

[3] Boeckh *Corp. Inscr.* 3909, 'Ασίδος

εὐρείης προφερέστατον οὖδας ἁπάντων,
χαίροις, χρυσόπολι Ἱεράπολι, πότνια Νυμ-
φῶν, νάμασιν, ἀγλαΐῃσι, κεκασμένη.

[4] Mionnet IV. p. 297, 306, 307,
ib. Suppl. VII. p. 567; Waddington
Voyage etc. p. 24.

its former greatness. Hence the whole plateau is covered with ruins, of which the extent and the good taste are equally remarkable; and of these the palæstra and the thermæ, as might be expected, are among the more prominent.

Its religious worship.

A city, which combined the pursuit of health and of gaiety, had fitly chosen as its patron deity Apollo, the god alike of medicine and of festivity, here worshipped especially as 'Archegetes,' the Founder[1]. But more important, as illustrating the religious temper of this Phrygian city, is another fact connected with it. In Hierapolis was a spot called the

The Plutonium.

Plutonium, a hot well or spring, from whose narrow mouth issued a mephitic vapour immediately fatal to those who stood over the opening and inhaled its fumes. To the mutilated priests of Cybele alone (so it was believed) an immunity was given from heaven, which freed them from its deadly effects[2]. Indeed this city appears to have been a chief centre of the passionate mystical devotion of ancient Phrygia. But indications are not wanting, that in addition to this older worship religious rites were borrowed also from other parts

[1] Boeckh Corp. Inscr. 3905, 3906; Mionnet IV. pp. 297, 301, 307, ib. Suppl. VII. p. 568, 569, 570. In coins struck to commemorate alliances with other cities, Hierapolis is represented by Apollo Archegetes : Mionnet IV. p. 303, ib. Suppl. VII. 572, 573, 574; Waddington Voyage etc. p. 25; and see Eckhel III. p. 156. On the meaning of Archegetes, under which name Apollo was worshipped by other cities also, which regarded him as their founder, see Spanheim on Callim. Hymn. Apoll. 57.

[2] Strabo l. c. He himself had seen the phenomenon and was doubtful how to account for the immunity of these priests, εἴτε θείᾳ προνοίᾳ...εἴτε ἀντιδό-τοις τισὶ δυνάμεσι τούτου συμβαίνοντος. See also Plin. N. H. ii. 93 § 95 'locum...matris tantum magnæ sacerdoti innoxium.' Dion Cass. (Xiphil.) lxviii.

27, who also witnessed the phenomenon, adds οὐ μὴν καὶ τὴν αἰτίαν αὐτοῦ συννοῆ-σαι ἔχω, λέγω δὲ ἅ τε εἶδον ὡς εἶδον καὶ ἃ ἤκουσα ὡς ἤκουσα. Ammian. Marc. xxiii. 6. 18 also mentions this marvel, but speaks cautiously, 'ut asse-runt quidam,' and adds 'quod qua causa eveniat, rationibus physicis per-mittatur.' Comp. Anthol. VII. p. 190 Εἴ τις ἀπάγξασθαι μὲν ὀκνεῖ θανάτου δ' ἐπιθυμεῖ, ἐξ Ἱερᾶς πόλεως ψυχρὸν ὕδωρ πιέτω; Stobæus Ecl. i. 34, p. 680. La-borde states (p. 83) that he discovered by experiment that the waters are sometimes fatal to animal life and sometimes perfectly harmless; and if this be substantiated, we have a solu-tion of the marvel. Other modern travellers, who have visited the Pluto-nium, are Cockerell (Leake p. 342), and Svoboda. In Svoboda's work a chemical analysis of the waters is given.

of the East, more especially from Egypt[1]. By the multitude of her temples Hierapolis established her right to the title of the 'sacred city,' which she bore[2].

Though at this time we have no record of famous citizens at Hierapolis, such as graced the annals of Laodicea, yet a gene- *The birth-place of Epictetus.* ration or two later she numbered among her sons one nobler far than the rhetoricians and sophists, the millionaires and princes, of whom her neighbour could boast. The lame slave Epictetus, the loftiest of heathen moralists, must have been growing up to manhood when the first rumours of the Gospel reached his native city. Did any chance throw him across the path of Epaphras, who first announced the glad-tidings there? Did he ever meet the great Apostle himself, while *Epictetus and Chris-* dragging out his long captivity at Rome, or when after his *tianity.* release he paid his long-promised visit to the valley of the Lycus? We should be glad to think that these two men met together face to face—the greatest of Christian, and the greatest of heathen preachers. Such a meeting would solve more than one riddle. A Christian Epictetus certainly was not: his Stoic doctrine and his Stoic morality are alike apparent; but nevertheless his language presents some strange coincidences with the Apostolic writings, which would thus receive an explanation[3]. It must be confessed however, that of any outward intercourse between the Apostle and the philosopher history furnishes no hint.

3. While the sites of Laodicea and Hierapolis are con- *3. Colos-* spicuous, so that they were early identified by their ruins, *sæ.* *Difficulty* the same is not the case with COLOSSÆ. Only within the *of deter-* *mining its* present generation has the position of this once famous city *site.* been ascertained, and even now it lacks the confirmation of any

[1] On a coin of Hierapolis, Pluto-Serapis appears seated, while before him stands Isis with a sistrum in her hand; Waddington *Voyage* etc. p. 24. See also Mionnet IV. pp. 296, 305; Leake *Num. Hell.* p. 66.

The worship of Serapis appears else-where in this neighbourhood. At Chonæ (Colossæ) is an inscription recording a vow to this deity; Le Bas *Asie Mineure* inscr. 1693 b.

[2] Steph. Byz. s. v. ἀπὸ τοῦ ἱερὰ πολ-λὰ ἔχειν.

[3] See *Philippians*, pp. 312, 313.

inscription found *in situ* and giving the name[1]. Herodotus states that in Colossæ the river Lycus disappears in a subterranean cave, emerging again at a distance of about five stades[2]; and this very singular landmark—the underground passage of a stream for half a mile—might be thought to have placed the site of the city beyond the reach of controversy. But this is not the case. In the immediate neighbourhood of the only ruins which can possibly be identified with Colossæ, no such subterranean channel has been discovered. But on the other hand the appearance of the river at this point suggests that at one time the narrow gorge through which it runs, as it traverses the ruins, was overarched for some distance with incrustations of travertine, and that this natural bridge was broken up afterwards by an earthquake, so as to expose the channel of the stream[3]. This explanation seems satisfactory. If it be

---

[1] See however a mutilated inscription (Boeckh *Corp. Inscr.* 3956) with the letters...ΗΝѠΝ, found near Chonæ.

[2] Herod. vii. 30 ἀπίκετο ἐς Κολοσσάς, πόλιν μεγάλην Φρυγίης, ἐν τῇ Λύκος ποταμὸς ἐς χάσμα γῆς ἐσβάλλων ἀφανίζεται, ἔπειτα διὰ σταδίων ὡς πέντε μάλιστά κη ἀναφαινόμενος ἐκδιδοῖ καὶ οὗτος ἐς τὸν Μαίανδρον.

[3] This is the explanation of Hamilton (I. p. 509 sq.), who (with the doubtful exception of Laborde) has the merit of having first identified and described the site of Colossæ. It stands on the Tchoruk Sú (Lycus) at the point where it is joined by two other streams, the Bounar Bashi Sú and the Ak-Sú. In confirmation of his opinion, Hamilton found a tradition in the neighbourhood that the river had once been covered over at this spot (p. 522). He followed the course of the Lycus for some distance without finding any subterranean channel (p. 521 sq.). It is difficult to say whether the following account in Strabo xii. 8 § 16 (p. 578) refers to the Lycus or not;

ὄρος Κάδμος ἐξ οὗ καὶ ὁ Λύκος ῥεῖ καὶ ἄλλος ὁμώνυμος τῷ ὄρει· τὸ πλέον δ' οὗτος ὑπὸ γῆς ῥυεὶς εἶτ' ἀνακύψας συνέπεσεν εἰς ταὐτὸ τοῖς ἄλλοις ποταμοῖς, ἐμφαίνων ἅμα καὶ τὸ πολύτρητον τῆς χώρας καὶ τὸ εὔσειστον. If the Lycus is meant, may not συνέπεσεν imply that this remarkable feature had changed before Strabo wrote?

Laborde (p. 103), who visited the place before Hamilton, though his account was apparently not published till later, fixes on the same site for Colossæ, but thinks that he has discovered the subterranean course of the Lycus, to which Herodotus refers, much higher up a stream, close to its source ('à dix pas de cette source'), which he describes as 'à deux lieues au nord de Colossæ.' Yet in the same paragraph he says 'Or il [Hérodote, exact cicerone] savait que *le Lycus disparait près de Colossæ, ville considérable de la Phrygie*' (the italics are his own). He apparently does not see the vast difference between his *près de Colossæ* thus widely interpreted and

rejected, we must look for the underground channel, not within the city itself, as the words of Herodotus strictly interpreted require, but at some point higher up the stream. In either case there can be little doubt that these are the ruins of Colossæ. The fact mentioned by Pliny[1], that there is in this city a river which turns brick into stone, is satisfied by a side stream flowing into the Lycus from the north, and laying large deposits of calcareous matter; though in this region, as we have seen, such a phenomenon is very far from rare. The site of Colossæ then, as determined by these considerations, lies two or three miles north of the present town of Chonos, the mediæval Chonæ, and some twelve miles east of Laodicea. The Lycus traverses the site of the ruins, dividing the city into two parts, the necropolis standing on the right or northern bank, and the town itself on the left.

Petrifying stream.

Commanding the approaches to a pass in the Cadmus range, and standing on a great high-way communicating between Eastern and Western Asia, Colossæ at an early date appears as a very important place. Here the mighty host of Xerxes halted on its march against Greece; it is mentioned on this occasion as 'a great city of Phrygia[2].' Here too Cyrus remained seven days on his daring enterprise which terminated so fatally; the Greek captain, who records the expedition, speaks of it as 'a populous city, prosperous and great[3].' But after this time its glory seems to wane. The political supremacy

Its ancient greatness

---

the precise ἐν τῇ of Herodotus himself. Obviously no great reliance can be placed on the accuracy of a writer, who treats his authorities thus. The subterranean stream which Laborde saw, and of which he gives a view (pl. xl), may possibly be the phenomenon to which Herodotus alludes; but if so, Herodotus has expressed himself very carelessly. On the whole Hamilton's solution seems much more probable. See however *Anatolica* p. 117 sq.

Arundell's account (*Seven Churches* p. 98 sq., *Asia Minor* p. 160 sq.) is

very confused and it is not clear whether he has fixed on the right site for Colossæ; but it bears testimony to the existence of two subterranean courses of rivers, though neither of them is close enough to the city to satisfy Herodotus' description.

[1] Plin. *N. H.* xxxi. 2 § 20. This is the Ak-Sú, which has strongly petrifying qualities.

[2] Herod. vii. 30. See p. 14, note 2.

[3] Xen. *Anab.* i. 2. 6 ἐξελαύνει διὰ Φρυγίας...εἰς Κολοσσάς, πόλιν οἰκουμένην, εὐδαίμονα καὶ μεγάλην.

and later decline.

of Laodicea and the growing popularity of Hierapolis gradually drain its strength; and Strabo, writing about two generations before St Paul, describes it as a 'small town[1]' in the district' of which Laodicea was the capital. We shall therefore be prepared to find that, while Laodicea and Hierapolis both hold important places in the early records of the Church, Colossæ disappears wholly from the pages of history. Its comparative insignificance is still attested by its ruins, which are few and meagre[2], while the vast remains of temples, baths, theatres, aqueducts, gymnasia, and sepulchres, strewing the extensive sites of its more fortunate neighbours, still bear witness to their ancient prosperity and magnificence. It is not even mentioned by Ptolemy, though his enumeration of towns includes several inconsiderable places[3]. Without doubt Colossæ was the least important church to which any epistle of St Paul was addressed.

Uncertain orthography of the name.

And perhaps also we may regard the variation in the orthography of the name as another indication of its comparative obscurity and its early extinction. Are we to write *Colossæ* or *Colassæ*? So far as the evidence goes, the conclusion would seem to be that, while Colossæ alone occurs during the classical period and in St Paul's time, it was afterwards supplanted by Colassæ, when the town itself had either disappeared altogether or was already passing out of notice[4].

---

[1] πόλισμα, Strabo xii. 8. 13 (p. 576). Plin. *N. H.* v. 32. § 41 writes 'Phrygia ...oppida ibi celeberrima præter jam dicta, Ancyra, Andria, Celænæ, Colossæ,' etc. The commentators, referring to this passage, overlook the words 'præter jam dicta,' and represent Pliny as calling Colossæ 'oppidum celeberrimum.' Not unnaturally they find it difficult to reconcile this expression with Strabo's statement. But in fact Pliny has already exhausted all the considerable towns, Hierapolis, Laodicea, Apamea, etc., and even much less important places than these (see

v. 28, 29 § 29), so that only decayed and third-rate towns remain. The Ancyra here mentioned is not the capital of Galatia, but a much smaller Phrygian town.

[2] Laborde p. 102 'De cette grande célébrité de Colossæ il ne reste presque rien : ce sont des substructions sans suite, des fragments sans grandeur; les restes d'un théâtre de médiocre dimension, une acropole sans hardiesse,' etc.; comp. *Anatolica* p. 115.

[3] *Geogr.* v. 2.

[4] All Greek writers till some centuries after the Christian era write it

Considered ethnologically, these three cities are generally Ethnologi-
regarded as belonging to Phrygia. But as they are situated cal rela-
on the western border of Phrygia, and as the frontier line the three
separating Phrygia from Lydia and Caria was not distinctly cities.

Κολοσσαί: so Herod. vii. 30, Xen.
Anab. i. 2. 6, Strabo xii. 8. 13, Diod.
xiv. 80, Polyæn. Strat. vii. 16. 1;
though in one or more MSS of some
of these authors it is written Κολασσαί,
showing the tendency of later scribes.
Colossæ is also the universal form in
Latin writers. The coins moreover, even
as late as the reign of Gordian (A.D. 238
—244) when they ceased to be struck,
universally have ΚΟΛΟCCHNOI (or ΚΟ-
ΛΟCHNOI); Mionnet IV. p. 267 sq.:
see Babington Numismatic Chronicle
New series III. p. 1 sq., 6. In Hierocles (Synecd. p. 666, Wessel.) and
in the Apostolic Constitutions (vii. 46)
Κολασσαί seems to be the original reading of the text, and in later Byzantine writers this form is common. If
Prof. Babington (p. 3) were right in
supposing that it is connected with
κολοσσός, the question of the correct
spelling might be regarded as settled;
but in a Phrygian city over which so
many Eastern nations swept in succession, who shall say to what language the name belonged, or what are
its affinities?

Thus, judging from classical usage,
we should say that Κολοσσαί was the
old form and that Κολασσαί did not
supplant it till some time after St
Paul's age. This view is confirmed
by a review of the authorities for the
different readings in the New Testament.

In the opening of the epistle (i. 1)
the authorities for ἐν Κολοσσαῖς are
overwhelming. It is read by ℵBDFGL
(A is obliterated here and C is wanting); and in the Old Latin, Vulgate,
and Armenian Versions. On the other

hand ἐν Κολασσαῖς is read by KP. 17.
37. 47, and among the versions by the
Memphitic and the Philoxenian Syriac
(ܩܘܠܣܝܐ, though the marg.
gives ΚΟΛCCΑΙC). In the Peshito also
the present reading represents Κολασσαῖς, but as the vowel was not expressed originally and depends on the later
pointing, its authority can hardly be
quoted. The Thebaic is wanting here.
In the heading of the epistle however there is considerably more authority for the form in α. Κολασσαεις
is the reading of AB* KP . 37 (Κολα-
σαεις) . 47. C is wanting here, but has
Κολασσαεις in the subscription. On
the other hand Κολοσσαεις (or Κολοσ-
σαις) appears in ℵB¹ (according to
Tregelles, but B³ Tisch.; see his introd.
p. xxxviii) DFG (but G has left Κολασσαεις in the heading of one page,
and Κολασσαεις in another) L. 17 (Κο-
λοσαεις), in the Latin Version, and in
the margin of the Philoxenian Syriac.
The readings of both Peshito and
Philoxenian (text) here depend on the
vocalisation; and those of other versions are not recorded. In the subscription the preponderance of authority is even more favourable to
Κολασσαεις.

Taking into account the obvious
tendency which there would be in
scribes to make the title πρὸς Κολοσ-
σαεῖς or πρὸς Κολασσαεῖς conform to
the opening ἐν Κολοσσαῖς or ἐν Κολασσαῖς, as shown in G, we seem to
arrive at the conclusion that, while ἐν
Κολοσσαῖς was indisputably the original
reading in the opening, πρὸς Κολασσαεῖς was probably the earlier reading
in the title. If so, the title must have

traced, this designation is not persistent[1]. Thus Laodicea is sometimes assigned to Caria, more rarely to Lydia[2]; and again, Hierapolis is described as half Lydian, half Phrygian[3]. On the other hand I have not observed that Colossæ is ever regarded as other than Phrygian[4], partly perhaps because the notices relating to it belong to an earlier date when these several names denoted political as well as ethnological divisions, and their limits were definitely marked in consequence, but chiefly because it lies some miles to the east of the other cities, and therefore farther from the doubtful border land.

Their political relations.

Phrygia however ceased to have any political significance, when this country came under the dominion of the Romans. Politically speaking, the three cities with the rest of the

been added at a somewhat later date; which is not improbable.

Connected with this question is the variation in the adjectival form, -ηνός or -αεύς. Parallels to this double termination occur in other words; e. g. Δοκιμηνός, Δοκιμεύς; Λαοδικηνός, Λαοδικεύς; Νικαηνός, Νικαεύς; Σαγαλασσηνός, Σαγαλασσεύς, etc. The coins, while they universally exhibit the form in o, are equally persistent in the termination -ηνός, ΚΟΛΟϹϹΗΝѠΝ; and it is curious that to the form Κολοσσηνοί in Strabo xii. 8 § 16 (p. 578) there is a various reading Κολασσαεῖς. Thus, though there is no necessary connexion between the two, the termination -ηνός seems to go with the o form, and the termination -αεύς with the 'a form.

For the above reasons I have written confidently ἐν Κολοσσαῖς in the text, and with more hesitation πρὸς Κολασσαεῖς in the superscription.

[1] Strabo, xiii. 4. 12 (p. 628) τὰ δ' ἑξῆς ἐπὶ τὰ νότια μέρη τοῖς τόποις τούτοις ἐμπλοκὰς ἔχει μέχρι πρὸς τὸν Ταῦρον, ὥστε καὶ τὰ Φρύγια καὶ τὰ Καρικὰ καὶ τὰ Λύδια καὶ ἔτι τὰ τῶν Μυσῶν δυσδιάκριτα εἶναι παραπίπτοντα εἰς ἄλληλα·

εἰς δὲ τὴν σύγχυσιν ταύτην οὐ μικρὰ συλλαμβάνει τὸ τοὺς Ῥωμαίους μὴ κατὰ φῦλα διελεῖν αὐτούς κ.τ.λ.

[2] To Phrygia, Strabo xii. 8. 13 (p. 576), Polyb. v. 57, and so generally; to Caria, Orac. Sibyll. iii. 472 Καρῶν ἀγλαὸν ἄστυ, Ptol. v. 2, Philostr. Vit. Soph. i. 25 (though in the context Philostratus adds that at one time τῇ Φρυγίᾳ ξυνετάττετο); to Lydia, Steph. Byz. s. v. On the coins the city is sometimes represented as seated between two female figures ΦΡΥΓΙΑ and ΚΑΡΙΑ; Eckhel iii. p. 160, comp. Mionnet iv. p. 329. From its situation on the confines of the three countries Laodicea seems to have obtained the surname Trimitaria or Trimetaria, by which it is sometimes designated in later times : see below, p. 65, note 4, and comp. Wesseling, Itin. p. 665.

[3] Steph. Byz. s. v. says μεταξὺ Φρυγίας καὶ Λυδίας πόλις. But generally Hierapolis is assigned to Phrygia: e. g. Ptol. v. 2, Vitruv. viii. 3 § 10.

[4] Colossæ is assigned to Phrygia in Herod. vii. 30, Xen. Anab. i. 2. 6, Strabo xii. 8. 13, Diod. xiv. 80, Plin. N. H. v. 32 § 41, Polyæn. Strat. vii. 16. 1.

Cibyratic union belonged at this time to Asia, the proconsular province[1]. As an *Asiatic* Church accordingly Laodicea is addressed in the Apocalyptic letter. To this province they had been assigned in the first instance; then they were handed over to Cilicia[2]; afterwards they were transferred and retransferred from the one to the other; till finally, before the Christian era, they became a permanent part of Asia, their original province. Here they remained, until the close of the fourth century, when a new distribution of the Roman empire was made, and the province of Phrygia Pacatiana created with Laodicea as its capital[3].

The Epistle to the Colossians supposes a powerful Jewish colony in Laodicea and the neighbourhood. We are not however left to draw this inference from the epistle alone, but the fact is established by ample independent testimony. When, with the insolent licence characteristic of Oriental kings, Antiochus the Great transplanted two thousand Jewish families from Babylonia and Mesopotamia into Lydia and Phrygia[4], we can hardly doubt that among the principal stations of these new colonists would be the two most thriving cities of Phrygia, which were also the two most important settlements of the Syrian kings, Apamea and Laodicea, the one founded by his grandfather Antiochus the First, the other by his father Antiochus the Second. If the commercial importance of Apamea at this time was greater (for somewhat later it was reckoned second only to Ephesus among the cities of Asia Minor

Important Jewish settlement in this neighbourhood.

Colony of Antiochus the Great.

---

[1] After the year B. C. 49 they seem to have been permanently attached to 'Asia': before that time they are bandied about between Asia and Cilicia. These alternations are traced by Bergmann *de Asia provincia* (Berlin, 1846) and in *Philologus* II. 4 (1847) p. 641 sq. See Becker and Marquardt *Röm. Alterth.* III. 1. p. 130 sq. Laodicea is assigned to 'Asia' in Boeckh *Corp. Inscr.* 6512, 6541, 6626.

The name 'Asia' will be used throughout this chapter in its political

sense, as applying to the Roman province.

[2] Cic. *ad Fam.* xiii. 67 'ex provincia mea Ciliciensi, cui scis τρεῖς διοικήσεις Asiaticas [i. e. Cibyraticam, Apamensem, Synnadensem] attributas fuisse'; *ad Att.* v. 21 'mea expectatio Asiæ nostrarum diœcesium' and 'in hac mea Asia.' See also above, p. 7, notes 2, 3.

[3] Hierocles *Synecd.* p. 664 sq. (Wessel.): see below, p. 69.

[4] Joseph. *Antiq.* xii. 3, 4.

as a centre of trade), the political rank of Laodicea stood higher[1]. When mention is made of Lydia and Phrygia[2], this latter city especially is pointed out by its position, for it stood near the frontier of the two countries. A Jewish settlement once established, the influx of their fellow-countrymen would be rapid and continuous. Accordingly under the Roman domination we find them gathered here in very large numbers.

Confiscations of Flaccus.

When Flaccus the proprætor of Asia (B.C. 62), who was afterwards accused of maladministration in his province and defended by Cicero, forbade the contributions of the Jews to the temple-worship and the consequent exportation of money to Palestine, he seized as contraband not less than twenty pounds weight in gold in the single district of which Laodicea was the capital[3]. Calculated at the rate of a half-shekel for each man, this sum represents a population of more than eleven thousand adult freemen[4]: for women, children, and slaves were exempted. It must be remembered however, that this is only the sum which

---

[1] Strabo xii. 8. 13 (p. 576) εἶτα Ἀπάμεια ἡ Κιβωτὸς λεγομένη καὶ Λαοδίκεια αἵπερ εἰσὶ μέγισται τῶν κατὰ τὴν Φρυγίαν πόλεων. Below § 15 (p. 577) he says Ἀπάμεια δ᾽ ἐστὶν ἐμπόριον μέγα τῆς ἰδίως λεγομένης Ἀσίας δευτερεῦον μετὰ τὴν Ἔφεσον. The relative importance of Apamea and Laodicea two or three generations earlier than St Paul may be inferred from the notices in Cicero; but there is reason for thinking that Laodicea afterwards grew more rapidly than Apamea.

[2] In Josephus l. c. the words are τὰ κατὰ τὴν Φρυγίαν καὶ Λυδίαν, the two names being under the vinculum of the one article: while immediately afterwards Lydia is dropped and Phrygia alone named, πέμψαι τινὰς ... εἰς Φρυγίαν.

[3] Cic. pro Flacc. 28 'Sequitur auri illa invidia Judaici...Quum aurum Judæorum nomine quotannis ex Italia et ex omnibus provinciis Hierosolyma

exportari soleret, Flaccus sanxit edicto ne ex Asia exportari liceret...multitudinem Judæorum, flagrantem nonnumquam in concionibus, pro republica contemnere gravitatis summæ fuit...Apameæ manifesto comprehensum ante pedes prætoris in foro expensum est auri pondo centum paullo minus...Laodiceæ viginti pondo paullo amplius.'

Josephus (Antiq. xiv. 7. 2), quoting the words of Strabo, πέμψας δὲ Μιθριδάτης εἰς Κῶ ἔλαβε...τὰ τῶν Ἰουδαίων ὀκτακόσια τάλαντα, explains this enormous sum as composed of the temple-offerings of the Jews which they sent to Cos for safety out of the way of Mithridates.

[4] This calculation supposes (1) That the half-skekel weighs 110 gr.; (2) That the Roman pound is 5050 gr.: (3) That the relation of gold to silver was at this time as 12 : 1. This last estimate is possibly somewhat too high.

the Roman officers succeeded in detecting and confiscating; and that therefore the whole Jewish population would probably be much larger than this partial estimate implies. The amount seized at Apamea, the other great Phrygian centre, was five times as large as this[1]. Somewhat later we have a document purporting to be a decree of the Laodiceans, in which they thank the Roman Consul for a measure granting to Jews the liberty of observing their sabbaths and practising other rites of their religion[2]; and though this decree is probably spurious, yet it serves equally well to show that at this time Laodicea was regarded as an important centre of the dispersion in Asia Minor. To the same effect may be quoted the extravagant hyperbole in the Talmud, that when on a certain occasion an insurrection of the Jews broke out in Cæsarea the metropolis of Cappadocia, which brought down upon their heads the cruel vengeance of king Sapor and led to a massacre of 12,000, 'the wall of Laodicea was cloven with the sound of the harpstrings' in the fatal and premature merriment of the insurgents[3]. This place was doubtless singled

Other evidence.

---

[1] The coinage of Apamea affords a striking example of Judaic influence at a later date. On coins struck at this place in the reigns of Severus, Macrinus, and the elder Philip, an ark is represented floating on the waters. Within are a man and a woman: on the roof a bird is perched; while in the air another bird approaches bearing an olive-branch in its claws. The ark bears the inscription ΝΩΕ. Outside are two standing figures, a man and a woman (apparently the same two who have been represented within the ark), with their hands raised as in the attitude of prayer. The connexion of the ark of Noah with Apamea is explained by a passage in one of the Sibylline Oracles (i. 261 sq.), where the mountain overhanging Apamea is identified with Ararat, and the ark (κιβωτός) is

stated to have rested there. Whether this Apamea obtained its distinctive surname of Cibotus, the Ark or Chest, from its physical features or from its position as the centre of taxation and finance for the district, or from some other cause, it is difficult to say. In any case this surname might naturally suggest to those acquainted with the Old Testament a connexion with the deluge of Noah; but the idea would not have been adopted in the coinage of the place without the pressure of strong Jewish influences. On these coins see Eckhel Doctr. Num. Vet. III. p. 132 sq., and the paper of Sir F. Madden in the Numismatic Chronicle N. S. VI. p. 173 sq. (1866), where they are figured.

[2] Joseph. Ant. xiv. 10. 21.

[3] Talm. Babl. Moëd Katon 26 a, quoted by Neubauer, La Géographie du

out, because it had a peculiar interest for the Jews, as one of their chief settlements[1]. It will be remembered also, that Phrygia is especially mentioned among those countries which furnished their quota of worshippers at Jerusalem, and were thus represented at the baptism of the Christian Church on the great day of Pentecost[2].

Mention has already been made of the traffic in dyed wools, which formed the staple of commerce in the valley of the Lycus[3]. It may be inferred from other notices that this branch of trade had a peculiar attraction for the Jews[4]. If so, their commercial instincts would constantly bring fresh recruits to a colony which was already very considerable. But the neighbourhood held out other inducements besides this. Hierapolis, the gay watering place, the pleasant resort of idlers, had charms for them, as well as Laodicea the busy commercial city. At least such was the complaint of stricter patriots at home. 'The wines and the baths of Phrygia,' writes a Talmudist bitterly, 'have separated the ten tribes from Israel[5].'

Special attractions of Hierapolis.

Talmud p. 319, though he seems to have misunderstood the expression quoted in the text, of which he gives the sense, 'Cette ville tremblait au bruit des flèches qu'on avait tirées.' It is probably this same Laodicea which is meant in another Talmudical passage, Talm. Babl. *Baba Metziah* 84 a (also quoted by Neubauer, p. 311), in which Elijah appearing to R. Ishmael ben R. Jose, says 'Thy father fled to Asia; flee thou to Laodicea,' where Asia is supposed to mean Sardis.

[1] An inscription found at Rome in the Jewish cemetery at the Porta Portuensis (Boeckh *Corp. Inscr.* 9916) runs thus; ΕΝΘΑ . ΚΙΤΕ . ΑΜΜΙΑ . [Ε]ΙΟΥΔΕΑ . ΑΠΟ . ΛΑΔΙΚΙΑC. κ.τ.λ., i. e. ἔνθα κεῖται Ἀμμία Ἰουδαία ἀπὸ Λαοδικείας. Probably Laodicea on the Lycus is meant. Perhaps also we may refer another inscription (6478), which mentions one Trypho from Lao-

dicea on the Lycus, to a Jewish source.

[2] Acts ii. 10.

[3] See p. 4.

[4] Acts xvi. 14. Is there an allusion to this branch of trade in the message to the Church of Laodicea, Rev. iii. 17 οὐκ οἶδας ὅτι σὺ εἶ ὁ...γυμνός· συμβουλεύω σοι ἀγοράσαι ... ἱμάτια λευκὰ ἵνα περιβάλῃ, κ.τ.λ.? The only other of the seven messages, which contains an allusion to the white garments, is addressed to the Church of Sardis, where again there might be a reference to the βάμμα Σαρδιανικόν (Arist. *Pax* 1174, *Acharn.* 112) and the φοινικίδες Σαρδιανικαί (Plato Com. in Athen. II. p. 48 E) of the comic poets.

[5] Talm. Babl. *Sabbath* 147 b, quoted by Neubauer *La Géographie du Talmud* p. 317: see Wiesner *Schol. zum Babyl. Talm.* p. 259 sq., and p. 207 sq. On the word translated 'baths,' see Rapoport's *Erech Millin* p. 113, col. 1.

There is no ground for supposing that, when St Paul wrote St Paul
had not
visited the
district
when he
wrote. his Epistle to the Colossians, he had ever visited the church in which he evinces so deep an interest. Whether we examine the narrative in the Acts, or whether we gather up the notices in the epistle itself, we find no hint that he had ever been in this neighbourhood; but on the contrary some expressions indirectly exclude the suppōsition of a visit to the district.

It is true that St Luke more than once mentions Phrygia What is
meant by
Phrygia in
St Luke? as lying on St Paul's route or as witnessing his labours. But Phrygia was a vague and comprehensive term; nor can we assume that the valley of the Lycus was intended, unless the direction of his route or the context of the narrative distinctly points to this south-western corner of Phrygia. In neither of the two passages, where St Paul is stated to have travelled through Phrygia, is this the case.

1. On his second missionary journey, after he has revisited 1. St Paul's
visit to
Phrygia on
his second
mission-
ary jour-
ney. and confirmed the churches of Pisidia and Lycaonia founded on his first visit, he passes through 'the Phrygian and Galatian country[1].' I have pointed out elsewhere that this expression must be used to denote the region which might be called indifferently Phrygia or Galatia—the land which had originally belonged to the Phrygians and had afterwards been colonised by the Gauls; or the parts of either country which lay in the immediate neighbourhood of this debatable ground[2]. This region lies considerably north and east of the valley of the Lycus. Assuming that the last of the Lycaonian and Pisidian towns at which St Paul halted was Antioch, he would not on any probable supposition approach nearer to Colossæ than Apamea Cibotus on his way to 'the Phrygian and Galatian country,' nor indeed need he have gone nearly so far west-

---

[1] Acts xvi. 6 τὴν Φρυγίαν καὶ Γαλατικὴν χώραν, the correct reading. For this use of Φρυγίαν as an adjective comp. Mark i. 5 πᾶσα ἡ Ἰουδαία χώρα, Joh. iii. 22 εἰς τὴν Ἰουδαίαν γῆν, Luke iii. 1 τῆς Ἰτουραίας καὶ Τραχωνίτιδος χώρας, Acts xiii. 14 Ἀντιόχειαν τὴν Πισιδίαν (the correct reading).

[2] See *Galatians*, p. 18 sq., 22.

ward as this. And again on his departure from this region he journeys by Mysia to Troas, leaving 'Asia' on his left hand and Bithynia on his right. Thus the notices of his route conspire to show that his path on this occasion lay far away from the valley of the Lycus.

2. His visit on his third missionary journey.

2. But if he was not brought into the neighbourhood of Colossæ on his second missionary journey, it is equally improbable that he visited it on his third. So far as regards Asia Minor, he seems to have confined himself to revisiting the churches already founded; the new ground which he broke was in Macedonia and Greece. Thus when we are told that during this third journey St Paul after leaving Antioch 'passed in order through the Galatian country and Phrygia, confirming all the disciples [1],' we can hardly doubt that 'the Galatian country and Phrygia' in this latter passage denotes essentially the same region as 'the Phrygian and Galatian country' in the former. The slight change of expression is explained by the altered direction of his route. In the first instance his course, as determined by its extreme limits—Antioch in Pisidia its starting-point, and Alexandria Troas its termination— would be northward for the first part of the way, and thus would lie on the border land of Phrygia and Galatia; whereas on this second occasion, when he was travelling from Antioch in Syria to Ephesus, its direction would be generally from east to west, and the more strictly Galatian district would be traversed before the Phrygian. If we suppose him to leave Galatia at Pessinus on its western border, he would pass along the great highway—formerly a Persian and at this time a Roman road—by Synnada and Sardis to Ephesus, traversing the heart of Phrygia, but following the valleys of the Hermus and Cayster, and separated from the Mæander and Lycus by the high mountain ranges which bound these latter to the north [2].

---

[1] Acts xviii. 23.

[2] M. Renan (*Saint Paul* pp. 51 sq., 126, 313) maintains that the Galatia of St Paul and St Luke is not the country properly so called, but that they are speaking of the Churches of Pisidian

Thus St Luke's narrative seems to exclude any visit of The inference from
the Apostle to the Churches of the Lycus before his first

Antioch, Iconium, Lystra, and Derbe, which lay within the *Roman province* of Galatia. This interpretation of Galatia necessarily affects his view of St Paul's routes (pp. 126 sq., 331 sq.); and he supposes the Apostle on his third missionary journey to have passed through the valley of the Lycus, without however remaining to preach the Gospel there (pp. 331 sq., 356 sq., 362). As Antioch in Pisidia would on this hypothesis be the farthest church in 'Galatia and Phrygia' which St Paul visited, his direct route from that city to Ephesus (Acts xviii. 23, xix. 1) would naturally lie by this valley. I have already (*Galatians* pp. 18 sq., 22) stated the serious objections to which this interpretation of 'Galatia' is open, and (if I mistake not) have answered most of M. Renan's arguments by anticipation. But, as this interpretation nearly affects an important point in the history of St Paul's dealings with the Colossians, it is necessary to subject it to a closer examination.

Without stopping to enquire whether this view is reconcilable with St Paul's assertion (Col. ii. 1) that these churches in the Lycus valley 'had not seen his face in the flesh,' it will appear (I think) that M. Renan's arguments are in some cases untenable and in others may be turned against himself. The three heads under which they may be conveniently considered are: (i) The use of the name 'Galatia'; (ii) The itinerary of St Paul's travels; (iii) The historical notices in the Epistle to the Galatians.

(i) On the first point, M. Renan states that St Paul was in the habit of using the *official* name for each district, and therefore called the country which extends from Antioch in Pisidia

to Derbe 'Galatia,' supporting this view by the Apostle's use of Asia, Macedonia, and Achaia (p. 51). The answer is that the names of these elder provinces had very generally superseded the local names, but this was not the case with the other districts of Asia Minor where the provinces had been formed at a comparatively late date. The usage of St Luke is a good criterion. He also speaks of Asia, Macedonia, and Achaia; but at the same time his narrative abounds in historical or ethnographical names which have no official import; e.g. Lycaonia, Mysia, Pamphylia, Pisidia, Phrygia. Where we have no evidence, it is reasonable to assume that St Paul's usage was conformable to St Luke's. And again, if we consider St Luke's account alone, how insuperable are the difficulties which this view of Galatia creates. The part of Asia Minor, with which we are immediately concerned, was comprised officially in the provinces of Asia and Galatia. On M. Renan's showing, St Luke, after calling Antioch a city of Pisidia (xiii. 14) and Lystra and Derbe cities of Lycaonia (xiv. 6), treats all the three, together with the intermediate Iconium, as belonging to Galatia (xvi. 6, xviii. 23). He explains the inconsistency by saying that in the former case the narrative proceeds in detail, in the latter in masses. But if so, why should he combine a historical and ethnological name Phrygia with an official name Galatia in the same breath, when the two are different in kind and cannot be mutually exclusive? 'Galatia and Asia,' would be intelligible on this supposition, but not 'Galatia and Phrygia.' Moreover the very form of the expression in xvi. 6, 'the

Roman captivity. And this inference is confirmed by St Paul's own language to the Colossians.

Phrygian and Galatian country' (according to the correct reading which M. Renan neglects), appears in its studied vagueness to exclude the idea that St Luke means the province of Galatia, whose boundaries were precisely marked. And even granting that the Christian communities of Lycaonia and Pisidia could by a straining of language be called Churches of Galatia, is it possible that St Paul would address them personally as 'ye foolish Galatians' (Gal. iii. 1)? Such language would be no more appropriate than if a modern preacher in a familiar address were to appeal to the Poles of Warsaw as 'ye Russians,' or the Hungarians of Pesth as 'ye Austrians,' or the Irish of Cork as 'ye Englishmen.'

(ii) In the itinerary of St Paul several points require consideration. (a) M. Renan lays stress on the fact that in Acts xvi. 6, xviii. 23, the order in which the names of Phrygia and Galatia occur is inverted. I seem to myself to have explained this satisfactorily in the text. He appears to be unaware of the correct reading in xvi. 6, τὴν Φρυγίαν καὶ Γαλατικὴν χώραν (see Galatians p. 22), though it has an important bearing on St Paul's probable route. (b) He states that Troas was St Paul's aim ('l'objectif de Saint Paul') in the one case (xvi. 6), and Ephesus in the other (xviii. 23): consequently he argues that Galatia, properly so called, is inconceivable, as there was no reason why he should have made 'this strange detour towards the north.' The answer is that Troas was not his 'objectif' in the first instance, nor Ephesus in the second. On the first occasion St Luke states that the Apostle set out on his journey with quite different intentions, but that after he had got well to the north of Asia Minor he was driven by a series of divine intimations to proceed first to Troas and thence to cross over into Europe (see Philippians p. 48). This narrative seems to me to imply that he starts for his further travels from some point in the western part of Galatia proper. When he comes to the borders of Mysia, he designs bearing to the left and preaching in Asia; but a divine voice forbids him. He then purposes diverging to the right and delivering his message in Bithynia; but the same unseen power checks him again. Thus he is driven forward, and passes by Mysia to the coast at Troas (Acts xvi. 6—8). Here all is plain. But if we suppose him to start, not from some town in Galatia proper such as Pessinus, but from Antioch in Pisidia, why should Bithynia, which would be far out of the way, be mentioned at all? On the second occasion, St Paul's primary object is to revisit the Galatian Churches which he had planted on the former journey (xviii. 23), and it is not till after he has fulfilled this intention that he goes to Ephesus. (c) M. Renan also calls attention to the difficulty of traversing 'the central steppe' of Asia Minor. 'There was probably,' he says, 'at this epoch no route from Iconium to Ancyra,' and in justification of this statement he refers to Perrot, de Gal. Rom. prov. p. 102, 103. Even so, there were regular roads from either Iconium or Antioch to Pessinus; and this route would serve equally well. Moreover the Apostle, who was accustomed to 'perils of rivers, perils of robbers, perils in the wilderness' (2 Cor. xi. 26), and who preferred walking from Troas to Assos (Acts xx.

He represents his knowledge of their continued progress, borne out by St Paul's own language. and even of their first initiation, in the truths of the Gospel, as derived from the report of others. He describes himself

13) while his companions sailed, would not be deterred by any rough or unfrequented paths. But the facts adduced by Perrot do not lend themselves to any such inference, nor does he himself draw it. He cites an inscription of the year A.D. 82 which speaks of A. Cæsennius Gallus, the legate of Domitian, as a great roadmaker throughout the Eastern provinces of Asia Minor, and he suggests that the existing remains of a road between Ancyra and Iconium may be part of this governor's work. Even if the suggestion be adopted, it is highly improbable that no road should have existed previously, when we consider the comparative facility of constructing a way along this line of country (Perrot p. 103) and the importance of such a direct route. (d) 'In the conception of the author of the Acts,' writes M. Renan, 'the two journeys across Asia Minor are journeys of confirmation and not of conversion (Acts xv. 36, 41, xvi. 5, 6, xviii. 23).' This statement seems to me to be only partially true. In both cases St Paul *begins* his tour by confirming churches already established, but in both he advances beyond this and breaks new ground. In the former he starts with the existing churches of Lycaonia and Pisidia and extends his labours to Galatia: in the latter he starts with the then existing churches of Galatia, and carries the Gospel into Macedonia and Achaia. This, so far as I can discover, was his general rule.

(iii) The notices in the Galatian Epistles, which appear to M. Renan to favour his view, are these: (a) St Paul appears to have 'had intimate relations with the Galatian Church, at least as intimate as with the Corinthians and Thessalonians,' whereas St Luke disposes of the Apostle's preaching in Galatia very summarily, unless the communities of Lycaonia and Pisidia be included. But the Galatian Epistle by no means evinces the same close and varied personal relations which we find in the letters to these other churches, more especially to the Corinthians. And again ; St Luke's history is more or less fragmentary. Whole years are sometimes dismissed in a few verses. The stay in Arabia which made so deep an impression on St Paul himself is not even mentioned : the three months' sojourn in Greece, though doubtless full of stirring events, only occupies a single verse in the narrative (Acts xx. 3). St Luke appears to have joined St Paul after his visit to Galatia (xvi. 10); and there is no reason why he should have dwelt on incidents with which he had no direct acquaintance. (b) M. Renan sees in the presence of emissaries from Jerusalem in the Galatian Churches an indication that Galatia proper is not meant. 'It is improbable that they would have made such a journey.' But why so? There were important Jewish settlements in Galatia proper (*Galatians* p. 9 sq.); there was a good road through Syria and Cilicia to Ancyra (*Itin. Anton.* p. 205 sq., *Itin. Hierosol.* p. 575 sq. ed. Wessel.) ; and if we find such emissaries as far away from Jerusalem as Corinth (2 Cor. xi. 13, etc.), there is at least no improbability that they should have reached Galatia. (c) Lastly; M. Renan thinks that the mention of Barnabas (Gal. ii. 1, 9, 13) implies that he was personally known to the churches addressed,

as *hearing* of their faith in Christ and their love to the saints[1]. He recals the day when he first *heard* of their Christian pro-

Silence of St Paul.

fession and zeal[2]. Though opportunities occur again and again where he would naturally have referred to his direct personal relations with them, if he had been their evangelist, he abstains from any such reference. He speaks of their being instructed in the Gospel, of his own preaching the Gospel, several times in the course of the letter, but he never places the two in any direct connexion, though the one reference stands in the immediate neighbourhood of the other[3]. Moreover, if he had actually visited Colossæ, it must appear strange that he should not once allude to any incident occurring during his sojourn there, for this epistle would then be the single exception to his ordinary practice. And lastly; in one passage at least, if interpreted in its natural sense, he declares that the Colossians were personally unknown to him: 'I would have you know,' he writes, 'how great a conflict I have for you and them that are in Laodicea and as many as have not seen my face in the flesh[4].'

---

and therefore points to Lycaonia and Pisidia. But are we to infer on the same grounds that he was personally known to the Corinthians (1 Cor. ix. 6), and to the Colossians (Col. iv. 10)? In fact the name of Barnabas, as a famous Apostle and an older disciple even than St Paul himself, would not fail to be well known in all the churches. On the other hand one or two notices in the Galatian Epistle present serious obstacles to M. Renan's view. What are we to say for instance to St Paul's statement, that he preached the Gospel in Galatia δι' ἀσθένειαν τῆς σαρκός (iv. 13), i. e. because he was detained by sickness (see *Galatians* pp. 23 sq., 172), whereas his journey to Lycaonia and Pisidia is distinctly planned with a view to missionary work? Why again is there no mention of Timothy, who was much in St Paul's company about

this time, and who on this showing was himself a Galatian? Some mention would seem to be especially suggested where St Paul is justifying his conduct respecting the attempt to compel Titus to be circumcised.

[1] Col. i. 4.

[2] i. 9 διὰ τοῦτο καὶ ἡμεῖς, ἀφ' ἧς ἡμέρας ἠκούσαμεν, οὐ παυόμεθα κ.τ.λ. This corresponds to ver. 6 καθὼς καὶ ἐν ὑμῖν, ἀφ' ἧς ἡμέρας ἠκούσατε καὶ ἐπέγνωτε τὴν χάριν τοῦ Θεοῦ ἐν ἀληθείᾳ. The day when they first heard the preaching of the Gospel, and the day when he first heard the tidings of this fact, are set against each other.

[3] e.g. i. 5—8, 21—23, 25, 28, 29. ii. 5, 6.

[4] ii. 1 θέλω γὰρ ὑμᾶς εἰδέναι ἡλίκον ἀγῶνα ἔχω ὑπὲρ ὑμῶν καὶ τῶν ἐν Λαοδικείᾳ καὶ ὅσοι οὐχ ἑώρακαν τὸ πρόσωπόν μου ἐν σαρκί, ἵνα παρακληθῶσιν αἱ καρ-

But, if he was not directly their evangelist, yet to him Epaphras was the they were indirectly indebted for their knowledge of the truth. evangelist of this Epaphras had been his delegate to them, his representative district. in Christ. By Epaphras they had been converted to the Gospel. This is the evident meaning of a passage in the opening of the epistle, which has been much obscured by misreading and mistranslation, and which may be paraphrased thus: 'The Gospel, which has spread and borne fruit throughout the rest of the world, has been equally successful among yourselves. This fertile growth has been manifested in you from the first day when the message of God's grace was preached to you, and accepted by you—preached not as now with adulterations by these false teachers, but in its genuine simplicity by Epaphras our beloved fellowservant; he has been a faithful minister of Christ and a faithful representative of us, and from him we have received tidings of your love in the Spirit[1].'

δίαι αὐτῶν, συμβιβασθέντες κ.τ.λ. The question of interpretation is whether the people of Colossæ and Laodicea belong to the same category with the ὅσοι, or not. The latter view is taken by one or two ancient interpreters (e.g. Theodoret in his introduction to the epistle), and has been adopted by several modern critics. Yet it is opposed alike to grammatical and logical considerations. (1) The grammatical form is unfavourable; for the preposition ὑπὲρ is not repeated, so that all the persons mentioned are included under a vinculum. (2) No adequate sense can be extracted from the passage, so interpreted. For in this case what is the drift of the enumeration? If intended to be exhaustive, it does not fulfil the purpose; for nothing is said of others whom he had seen besides the Colossians and Laodiceans. If not intended to be exhaustive, it is meaningless; for there is no reason why the Colossians and Laodiceans

especially should be set off against those whom he had not seen, or indeed why in this connexion those whom he had not seen should be mentioned at all. The whole context shows that the Apostle is dwelling on his spiritual communion with and interest in those with whom he has had no personal communications. St Jerome (*Ep.* cxxx. ad Demetr. § 2) has rightly caught the spirit of the passage; 'Ignoti ad ignotam scribimus, dumtaxat juxta faciem corporalem. Alioquin interior homo pulcre sibi cognitus est illa notitia qua et Paulus apostolus Colossenses multosque credentium noverat quos ante non viderat.' For parallels to this use of καὶ ὅσοι, see the note on the passage.

[1] i. 6 ἐν παντὶ τῷ κόσμῳ ἐστὶν καρποφορούμενον καὶ αὐξανόμενον, καθὼς καὶ ἐν ὑμῖν, ἀφ' ἧς ἡμέρας ἠκούσατε καὶ ἐπέγνωτε τὴν χάριν τοῦ Θεοῦ ἐν ἀληθείᾳ, καθὼς ἐμάθετε ἀπὸ Ἐπαφρᾶ τοῦ ἀγαπητοῦ συνδούλου ἡμῶν, ὅς ἐστιν πιστὸς

St Paul's
residence
atEphesus
instru-
mental in
their con-
version.

A. D.
54—57.

How or when the conversion of the Colossians took place,
we have no direct information. Yet it can hardly be wrong
to connect the event with St Paul's long sojourn at Ephesus.
Here he remained preaching for three whole years. It is
possible indeed that during this period he paid short visits to
other neighbouring cities of Asia: but if so, the notices in the
Acts oblige us to suppose these interruptions to his residence
in Ephesus to have been slight and infrequent[1]. Yet, though
the Apostle himself was stationary in the capital, the Apostle's
influence and teaching spread far beyond the limits of the city
and its immediate neighbourhood. It was hardly an exaggeration when Demetrius declared that 'almost throughout
all Asia this Paul had persuaded and turned away much
people[2].' The sacred historian himself uses equally strong
language in describing the effects of the Apostle's preaching;
'All they which dwelt in Asia heard the word of the Lord,
both Jews and Greeks[3].' In accordance with these notices
the Apostle himself in an epistle written during this sojourn
sends salutations to Corinth, not from the Church of Ephesus
specially, as might have been anticipated, but from the

ὑπὲρ ἡμῶν διάκονος τοῦ Χριστοῦ, ὁ καὶ
δηλώσας ἡμῖν τὴν ὑμῶν ἀγάπην ἐν πνεύματι.

The various readings which obscure
the meaning are these. (i) The received text for καθὼς ἐμάθετε has καθὼς
καὶ ἐμάθετε. With this reading the
passage suggests that the instructions
of Epaphras were *superadded to*, and
so distinct from, the original evangeli-
zation of Colossæ; whereas the correct
text identifies them. (ii) For ὑπὲρ ἡμῶν
the received reading is ὑπὲρ ὑμῶν.
Thus the fact that St Paul did not
preach at Colossæ in person, but
through his representative, is obliterated. In both cases the authority for
the readings which I have adopted
against the received text is overwhelming.

The obscurity of rendering is in

καθὼς [καὶ] ἐμάθετε ἀπὸ 'Επαφρᾶ, translated in our English Version by the
ambiguous expression, ' as ye also
learned of Epaphras.' The true force
of the words is, ' according as ye were
taught by Epaphras,' being an explanation of ἐν ἀληθείᾳ. See the notes
on the passage.

[1] See especially xx. 18 'Ye know,
from the first day when I set foot on
Asia, how I was with you *all the time*,'
and ver. 31 'For three years *night and
day I ceased not* warning every one
with tears.' As it seems necessary to
allow for a brief visit to Corinth (2 Cor.
xii. 14, xiii. 1) during this period, other
interruptions of long duration should
not be postulated.

[2] Acts xix. 26.

[3] Acts xix. 10.

'Churches of Asia' generally[1]. St Luke, it should be observed, ascribes this dissemination of the Gospel, not to journeys undertaken by the Apostle, but to his preaching at Ephesus itself[2]. Thither, as to the metropolis of Western Asia, would flock crowds from all the towns and villages far and near. Thence they would carry away, each to his own neighbourhood, the spiritual treasure which they had so unexpectedly found.

Among the places thus represented at the Asiatic metropolis would doubtless be the cities lying in the valley of the Lycus. The bonds of amity between these places and Ephesus appear to have been unusually strong. The *Concord of the Laodiceans and Ephesians,* the *Concord of the Hierapolitans and Ephesians,* are repeatedly commemorated on medals struck for the purpose[3]. Thus the Colossians, Epaphras and Philemon, the latter with his household[4], and perhaps also the Laodicean Nymphas[5], would fall in with the Apostle of the Gentiles and hear from his lips the first tidings of a heavenly life.

Close alliance of these cities with Ephesus.

The work of Philemon and Nymphas,

But, whatever service may have been rendered by Philemon at Colossæ, or by Nymphas at Laodicea, it was to Epaphras especially that all the three cities were indebted for their knowledge of the Gospel. Though he was a Colossian by birth, the fervency of his prayers and the energy of his love are represented as extending equally to Laodicea and Hierapolis[6]. It is obvious that he looked upon himself as responsible for the spiritual well-being of all alike.

but especially Epaphras.

[1] 1 Cor. xvi. 19 ἀσπάζονται ὑμᾶς αἱ ἐκκλησίαι τῆς Ἀσίας. In accordance with these facts it should be noticed that St Paul himself alluding to this period speaks of 'Asia,' as the scene of his ministry (2 Cor. i. 8, Rom. xvi. 5).

[2] Acts xix. 10 'disputing daily in the School of Tyrannus; and this continued for two years, so that all they which dwelt in Asia, etc.'

[3] ΛΑΟΔΙΚΕωΝ . ΕΦΕϹΙωΝ . ΟΜΟΝΟΙΑ, Eckhel III. p. 165, Mionnet IV.

p. 324, 325, 331, 332, *Suppl.* VII. p. 583, 586, 589; ΙΕΡΑΠΟΛΕΙΤωΝ . ΕΦΕϹΙωΝ . ΟΜΟΝΟΙΑ, Eckhel III. p. 155, 157, Mionnet IV. p. 299, 300, 307, *Suppl.* VII. p. 569, 571, 572, 574, 575. See Steiger *Kolosser* p. 50, and comp. Krause *Civitat. Neocor.* § 20.

[4] Philem. 1, 2, 19.

[5] Col. iv. 15. On the question whether the name is *Nymphas* or *Nympha*, see the notes there.

[6] iv. 12, 13.

St Paul
still a
stranger to
this dis-
trict.
We pass over a period of five or six years. St Paul's
first captivity in Rome is now drawing to a close. During
this interval he has not once visited the valley of the Lycus.
He has, it is true, skirted the coast and called at Miletus,
which lies near the mouth of the Mæander; but, though the
elders of Ephesus were summoned to meet him there[1], no
mention is made of any representatives from these more distant towns.

His
imprison-
ment at
Rome.
I have elsewhere described the Apostle's circumstances
during his residence in Rome, so far as they are known to
us[2]. It is sufficient to say here, that though he is still a
prisoner, friends new and old minister freely to his wants.
Meanwhile the alienation of the Judaic Christians is complete.
Three only, remaining faithful to him, are commemorated as
honourable exceptions in the general desertion[3].

Colossæ
brought
before his
notice by
two inci-
dents.
We have seen that Colossæ was an unimportant place, and
that it had no direct personal claims on the Apostle. We
might therefore feel surprise that, thus doubly disqualified,
it should nevertheless attract his special attention at a critical
moment, when severe personal trials were superadded to 'the
care of all the churches.' But two circumstances, the one
affecting his public duties, the other private and personal,
happening at this time, conspired to bring Colossæ prominently
before his notice.

I. The
mission of
EPAPHRAS.
I. He had received a visit from EPAPHRAS. The dangerous
condition of the Colossian and neighbouring churches had
filled the mind of their evangelist with alarm. A strange
form of heresy had broken out in these brotherhoods—a combination of Judaic formalism with Oriental mystic speculation—and was already spreading rapidly. His distress was
extreme. He gratefully acknowledged and reported their faith
in Christ and their works of love[4]. But this only quickened
his anxiety. He had 'much toil for them'; he was 'ever

---

[1] Acts xx. 16, 17.
[2] See *Philippians* p. 6 sq.
[3] Col. iv. 10, 11. See *Philippians* p. 17 sq.
[4] i. 4, 8.

wrestling in his prayers on their behalf,' that they might stand fast and not abandon the simplicity of their earlier faith [1]. He came to Rome, we may suppose, for the express purpose of laying this state of things before the Apostle and seeking his counsel and assistance.

2. But at the time when Epaphras paid this visit, St Paul was also in communication with another Colossian, who had visited Rome under very different circumstances. ONESIMUS, the runaway slave, had sought the metropolis, the common sink of all nations [2], probably as a convenient hiding place, where he might escape detection among its crowds and make a livelihood as best he could. Here, perhaps accidentally, perhaps through the intervention of Epaphras, he fell in with his master's old friend. The Apostle interested himself in his case, instructed him in the Gospel, and transformed him from a good-for-nothing slave [3] into a 'faithful and beloved brother [4].'

2. ONESI-
MUS a fu-
gitive in
Rome.

This combination of circumstances called the Apostle's attention to the Churches of the Lycus, and more especially to Colossæ. His letters, which had been found 'weighty and powerful' in other cases, might not be unavailing now; and in this hope he took up his pen. Three epistles were written and despatched at the same time to this district.

The Apo-
stle de-
spatches
three let-
ters simul-
taneously.

1. He addresses a special letter to the COLOSSIANS, written in the joint names of himself and Timothy, warning them against the errors of the false teachers. He gratefully acknowledges the report which he has received of their love and zeal [5]. He assures them of the conflict which agitates him on their behalf [6]. He warns them to be on their guard against the delusive logic of enticing words, against the vain deceit of a false philosophy [7]. The purity of their Christianity is endangered by two errors, recommended to them by their heretical leaders—the one theological, the other practical—

1. The
EPISTLE
TO THE
COLOS-
SIANS.

The theo-
logical and
the practi-
cal error of
the Colos-
sians.

---

[1] iv. 12, 13.
[2] Tac. *Ann.* xv. 44.
[3] Philem. 11 τὸν ποτέ σοι ἄχρηστον κ.τ.λ.

[4] Col. iv. 9; comp. Philem. 16.
[5] i. 3—9, 21 sq.
[6] ii. 1 sq.
[7] ii. 4, 8, 18.

but both alike springing from the same source, the conception of matter as the origin and abode of evil. Thus, regarding God and matter as directly antagonistic and therefore apart from and having no communication with each other, they sought to explain the creation and government of the world by interposing a series of intermediate beings, emanations or angels, to whom accordingly they offered worship. At the same time, since they held that evil resided, not in the rebellious spirit of man, but in the innate properties of matter, they sought to overcome it by a rigid ascetic discipline, which failed after all to touch the springs of action. As both errors flowed from the same source, they must be corrected by the application of the same remedy, the Christ of the Gospel. In the Person of Christ, the one mediator between heaven and earth, is the true solution of the theological difficulty. Through the Life in Christ, the purification of the heart through faith and love, is the effectual triumph over moral evil[1]. St Paul therefore prescribes to the Colossians the true teaching of the Gospel, as the best antidote to the twofold danger which threatens at once their theological creed and their moral principles; while at the same time he enforces his lesson by the claims of personal affection, appealing to the devotion of their evangelist Epaphras on their behalf[2].

The proper corrective to both lies in the Christ of the Gospel.

References to Epaphras.

Of Epaphras himself we know nothing beyond the few but significant notices which connect him with Colossæ[3]. He did not return to Colossæ as the bearer of the letter, but remained

---

[1] i. 1—20, ii. 9, iii. 4. The two threads are closely interwoven in St Paul's refutation, as these references will show. The connexion of the two errors, as arising from the same false principle, will be considered more in detail in the next chapter.

[2] i. 7, iv. 12.

[3] For the reasons why Epaphras cannot be identified with Epaphroditus, who is mentioned in the Philippian letter, see *Philippians* p. 61,

note 4. The later tradition, which makes him bishop of Colossæ, is doubtless an inference from St Paul's language and has no independent value. The further statement of the martyrologies, that he suffered martyrdom for his flock, can hardly be held to deserve any higher credit. His day is the 19th of July in the Western Calendar. His body is said to lie in the Church of S. Maria Maggiore at Rome.

behind with St Paul[1]. As St Paul in a contemporary epistle designates him his fellow-prisoner[2], it may be inferred that his zeal and affection had involved him in the Apostle's captivity, and that his continuance in Rome was enforced. But however this may be, the letter was placed in the hands of Tychicus, a native of proconsular Asia, probably of Ephesus[3], who was entrusted with a wider mission at this time, and in its discharge would be obliged to visit the valley of the Lycus[4]. At the same time he was accompanied by Onesimus, whom the Colossians had only known hitherto as a worthless slave, but who now returns to them with the stamp of the Apostle's warm approval. St Paul says very little about himself, because Tychicus and Onesimus would be able by word of mouth to communicate all information to the Colossians[5]. But he sends one or two salutations which deserve a few words of explanation. Epaphras of course greets his fellow-townsmen and children in the faith. Other names are those of Aristarchus the Thessalonian, who had been with the Apostle at Ephesus[6] and may possibly have formed some personal connexion with the Colossians at that time: Mark, against whom apparently the Apostle fears that a prejudice may be entertained (perhaps the fact of his earlier desertion, and of St Paul's dissatisfaction in consequence[7], may have been widely known), and for whom therefore he asks a favourable reception at his approaching visit to Colossæ, according to instructions which they had already received; and Jesus the Just, of whose relations with the

Margin notes: Tychicus and Onesimus accompany the letter.

The salutations.

---

[1] Col. iv. 12.

[2] Philem. 23 ὁ συναιχμάλωτός μου. The word may possibly have a metaphorical sense (see *Philippians* p. 11); but the literal meaning is more probable. St Jerome on Philem. 23 (VII. p. 762) gives the story that St Paul's parents were natives of Giscala and, when the Romans invaded and wasted Judæa, were banished thence with their son to Tarsus. He adds that Epaphras may have been St Paul's fellow-prisoner at this time, and have been removed with his parents to Colossæ. It is not quite clear whether this statement respecting Epaphras is part of the tradition, or Jerome's own conjecture appended to it.

[3] Acts xx. 4, 2 Tim. iv. 12.

[4] See below, p. 37.

[5] Col. iv. 7—9.

[6] Acts xix. 29.

[7] Acts xiii. 13, xv. 37—39.

Colossians we know nothing, and whose only claim to a mention may have been his singular fidelity to the Apostle at a critical juncture. Salutations moreover are added from Luke and from Demas; and here again their close companionship with the Apostle is, so far as we know, the sole cause of their names appearing[1].

Charge respecting Laodicea.

Lastly, the Laodiceans were closely connected with the Colossians by local and spiritual ties. To the Church of Laodicea therefore, and to the household of one Nymphas who was a prominent member of it, he sends greeting. At the same time he directs them to interchange letters with the Laodiceans; for to Laodicea also he had written. And he closes his salutations with a message to Archippus, a resident either at Colossæ or at Laodicea (for on this point we are left to conjecture), who held some important office in the Church, and respecting whose zeal he seems to have entertained a misgiving[2].

2. The LETTER TO PHILEMON.

2. But, while providing for the spiritual welfare of the whole Colossian Church, he did not forget the temporal interests of its humblest member. Having attended to the solicitations of the evangelist Epaphras, he now addressed himself to the troubles of the runaway slave Onesimus. The mission of Tychicus to Colossæ was a favourable opportunity of restoring him to Philemon; for Tychicus, well known as the Apostle's friend and fellow-labourer, might throw the shield of his protection over him and avert the worst consequences of Philemon's anger. But, not content with this measure of precaution, the Apostle himself writes to PHILEMON on the offender's behalf, recommending him as a changed man[3], and claiming forgiveness for him as a return due from Philemon to himself as to his spiritual father[4].

The salutations in this letter are the same as those in the Epistle to the Colossians with the exception of Jesus

[1] Col. iv. 10—14.
[2] iv. 15—17.
[3] Philem. 11, 16.
[4] ver. 19.

Justus, whose name is omitted [1]. Towards the close St Paul declares his hope of release and intention of visiting Colossæ, and asks Philemon to 'prepare a lodging' for him [2].

3. But at the same time with the two letters destined especially for Colossæ, the Apostle despatched a third, which had a wider scope. It has been already mentioned that Tychicus was charged with a mission to the Asiatic Churches. It has been noticed also that the Colossians were directed to procure and read a letter in the possession of the Laodiceans. These two facts are closely connected. The Apostle wrote at this time a circular letter to the Asiatic Churches, which got its ultimate designation from the metropolitan city and is consequently known to us as the Epistle to the EPHESIANS [3]. It was the immediate object of Tychicus' journey to deliver copies of this letter at all the principal centres of Christianity in the district, and at the same time to communicate by word of mouth the Apostle's special messages to each [4]. Among these centres was Laodicea. Thus his mission brought him into the immediate neighbourhood of Colossæ. But he was not charged to deliver another copy of the circular letter at Colossæ itself, for this Church would be regarded only as a dependency of Laodicea; and besides he was the bearer of a special letter from the Apostle to them. It was sufficient therefore to provide that the Laodicean copy should be circulated and read at Colossæ.

Thus the three letters are closely related. Tychicus is the personal link of connexion between the Epistles to the Ephesians and to the Colossians; Onesimus between those to the Colossians and to Philemon.

For reasons given elsewhere [5], it would appear that these three letters were written and despatched towards the close of the Apostle's captivity, about the year 63. At some time not

Marginal notes: 3. The CIRCULAR LETTER, of which a copy is sent to LAODICEA.

Personal links connecting the three letters.

---

[1] vv. 23, 24.

[2] ver. 22.

[3] See the introduction to the epistle.

[4] Ephes. vi. 21, 22.

[5] See *Philippians* p. 30 sq.; where reasons are given for placing the Philippian Epistle at an earlier, and the others at a later stage in the Apostle's captivity.

very distant from this date, a great catastrophe overtook the cities of the Lycus valley. An earthquake was no uncommon occurrence in this region[1]. But on this occasion the shock had been unusually violent, and Laodicea, the flourishing and populous, was laid in ruins. Tacitus, who is our earliest authority for this fact, places it in the year 60 and is silent about the neighbouring towns[2]. Eusebius however makes it subse-

[1] See above, p. 3. Laodicea was visited by the following earthquakes in the ages preceding and subsequent to the Christian era.

(1) Before about B.C. 125, *Orac. Sibyll.* iii. 471, if the date now commonly assigned to this Sibylline Oracle be correct, and if the passage is to be regarded as a prophecy after the event. In iii. 347 Hierapolis is also mentioned as suffering in the same way; but it may be questioned whether the Phrygian city is meant.

(2) About B.C. 12, Strabo xii. 8, p. 579, Dion Cass. liv. 30. Strabo names only Laodicea and Tralles, but Dion Cassius says ἡ Ἀσία τὸ ἔθνος ἐπικουρίας τινὸς διὰ σεισμοὺς μάλιστα ἐδεῖτο.

(3) A.D. 60 according to Tacitus (*Ann.* xiv. 27); A.D. 64 or 65 according to Eusebius (*Chron.* s.a.), who includes also Hierapolis and Colossæ. To this earthquake allusion is made in a Sibylline Oracle written not many years after the event; *Orac. Sibyll.* iv. 107 (see also v. 289, vii. 23).

(4) Between A.D. 222 and A.D. 235, in the reign of Alexander Severus, as we learn from another Sibylline Oracle (xii. 280). On this occasion Hierapolis also suffered.

This list will probably be found not to have exhausted all these catastrophes on record.

The following earthquakes also are mentioned as happening in the neighbouring towns or in the district generally: at an uncertain date, *Carura* (Strabo xii. 8, p. 578); A.D. 17 *the*

twelve cities, *Sardis* being the worst sufferer (Tac. *Ann.* ii. 7, Plin. *N. H.* ii. 86, Dion Cass. lvii. 17, Strabo xii. 8, p. 579); A.D. 23 *Cibyra* (Tac. *Ann.* iv. 13); A.D. 53 *Apamea* (Tac. *Ann.* xii. 58): about A.D. 138—142, under Antoninus Pius, 'Rhodiorum et *Asiæ* oppida' (Capitol. *Anton. Pius* 9, Aristid. *Or.* xliv); A.D. 151 or 152, under the same emperor, *Mitylene* and other places (Aristid. *Or.* xxv); A.D. 180, under M. Aurelius, *Smyrna* (*Chron. Pasch.* I. p. 489, ed. Dind., Aristid. *Or.* xx, xxi, xli; see Clinton *Fast. Rom.* I. p. 176 sq., Hertzberg *Griechenland* etc. II. pp. 371, 410, and esp. Waddington *Mémoire sur la Chronologie du Rhéteur Ælius Aristide* pp. 242 sq., 267, in *Mém. de l'Acad. des Inscr.* xxvi, 1867, who has corrected the dates); A.D. 262, under Gallienus II (Trebell. *Gallien.* 5 'Malum tristius in *Asiæ* urbibus fuit ...hiatus terræ plurimis in locis fuerunt, cum aqua salsa in fossis appareret,' ib. 6 'vastatam *Asiam*...elementorum concussionibus'). Strabo says (p. 579) that *Philadelphia* is more or less shaken daily (καθ᾽ ἡμέραν), and that *Apamea* has suffered from numerous earthquakes.

[2] Tac. *Ann.* xiv. 27 'Eodem anno ex inlustribus Asiæ urbibus Laodicea, tremore terræ prolapsa, nullo a nobis remedio propriis opibus revaluit.' The year is given 'Nerone iv, Corn. Cosso consulibus' (xiv. 20). Two different writers, in *Smith's Dictionary of Geography* and *Smith's Dictionary of the Bible*, s.v. Laodicea, place the destruc-

quent to the burning of Rome (A.D. 64), and mentions Hiera- Its proba-
ble date.
polis and Colossæ also as involved in the disaster[1]; while later
writers, adopting the date of Eusebius and including the three
cities with him, represent it as one of a series of divine judg-
ments on the heathen world for the persecution of the Christians which followed on the fire[2]. Having no direct knowledge
of the source from which Eusebius derived his information, we
should naturally be disposed to accept the authority of Tacitus
for the date, as more trustworthy. But, as indications occur
elsewhere that Eusebius followed unusually good authorities in
recording these earthquakes[3], it is far from improbable that he

---

tion of Laodicea in the reign of Tiberius, confusing this earthquake with
an earlier one (*Ann.* ii. 47). By this
earlier earthquake 'duodecim celebres
Asiæ urbes conlapsæ,' but their names
are given, and not one is situated in
the valley of the Lycus.

[1] Euseb. *Chron.* Ol. 210 (II. p. 154
sq., ed. Schöne) 'In Asia tres urbes
terræ motu conciderunt Laodicea Hierapolis Colossæ.' The Armenian version and Jerome agree in placing it
the next event in order after the fire
at Rome (A.D. 64), though there is a
difference of a year in the two texts.
If the Sibylline Oracle, v. 317, refers to
this earthquake, as seems probable,
we have independent testimony that
Hierapolis was involved in the catastrophe; comp. *ib.* v. 289.

[2] This is evidently the idea of Oro-
sius, vii. 7.

[3] I draw this inference from his
account of the earthquake in the reign
of Tiberius. Tacitus (*Ann.* ii. 47) states
that *twelve* cities were ruined in one
night, and records their names. Pliny
also, who mentions this earthquake as
'the greatest within the memory of
man' (*N. H.* ii. 86), gives the same
number. Eusebius however, *Chron.*
Ol. 198 (II. p. 146 sq., ed. Schöne),
names *thirteen* cities, coinciding with

Tacitus as far as he goes, but including
Ephesus also. Now a monument was
found at Puteoli (see Gronov. *Thes.
Græc. Ant.* VII. p. 433 sq.), and is now
in the Museum at Naples (*Museo
Borbonico* XV, Tav. iv, v), dedicated
to Tiberius and representing *fourteen*
female figures with the names of fourteen Asiatic cities underneath; these
names being the same as those mentioned by Tacitus with the addition of
Ephesus and Cibyra. There can be
no doubt that this was one of those
monuments mentioned by Apollonius
quoted in Phlegon (*Fragm.* 42, Müller's
Fragm. Hist. Græc. III. p. 621) as
erected to commemorate the liberality
of Tiberius in contributing to the restoration of the ruined cities (see Eckhel
Doct. Num. Vet. VI. 192 sq.). But no
earthquake at Ephesus is mentioned
by Tacitus. He does indeed speak of
such a catastrophe as happening at
Cibyra (*Ann.* iv. 13) six years later
than the one which ruined the twelve
cities, and of the relief which Tiberius
afforded on this latter occasion as on
the former. But we owe to Eusebius
alone the fact that Ephesus also was
seriously injured by an earthquake in
the same year—perhaps not on the
same night—with the twelve cities:
and this fact is necessary to explain

gives the correct date[1]. In this case the catastrophe was subsequent to the writing of these letters. If on the other hand the year named by Tacitus be adopted, we gain a subsidiary confirmation of the comparatively late date which I have ventured to assign to these epistles on independent grounds; for, if they had been written two years earlier, when the blow was recent, we might reasonably have expected to find some reference to a disaster which had devastated Laodicea and from which Colossæ cannot have escaped altogether without injury. The additional fact mentioned by the Roman historian, that Laodicea was rebuilt from her own resources without the usual assistance from Rome[2], is valuable as illustrating a later notice in the Apostolic writings[3].

It has been seen that, when these letters were written, St Mark was intending shortly to visit Colossæ, and that the Apostle himself, looking forward to his release, hoped at length to make a personal acquaintance with these churches, which hitherto he knew only through the report of others. Whether St Mark's visit was ever paid or not, we have no means of determining[4]. Of St Paul himself it is reasonable to assume,

the monument. It should be added that Nipperdey (on Tac. *Ann.* ii. 47) supposes the earthquake at Ephesus to have been recorded in the lost portion of the fifth book of the *Annals* which comprised the years A.D. 29—31; but this bare hypothesis cannot outweigh the direct testimony of Eusebius.

[1] Hertzberg (*Geschichte Griechenlands unter der Herrschaft der Römer* II. p. 96) supposes that Tacitus and Eusebius refer to two different events, and that Laodicea was visited by earthquakes twice within a few years, A.D. 60 and A.D. 65.

[2] Tac. *Ann.* xiv. 27, quoted above, p. 38, note 2. To this fact allusion is made in the feigned prediction of the Sibyllines, iv. 107 Τλῆμον Λαοδίκεια, σὲ δὲ τρώσει ποτὲ σεισμὸς πρηνίξας, στήσει δὲ πάλιν πόλιν εὐρυάγυιαν, where στήσει must be the 2nd person, 'Thou wilt rebuild thy city with its broad streets.' This Sibylline poem was written about the year 80. The building of the amphitheatre, mentioned above (p. 6, note 6), would form part of this work of reconstruction.

[3] See below, p. 43.

[4] Two notices however imply that St Mark had some personal connexion with Asia Minor in the years immediately succeeding the date of this reference: (1) St Peter, writing to the Churches of Asia Minor, sends a salutation from St Mark (1 Pet. v. 13); (2) St Paul gives charge to Timothy, who appears to be still residing at Ephesus, to take up Mark and bring him to Rome (2 Tim. iv. 11 Μάρκον ἀναλαβὼν ἄγε μετὰ σεαυτοῦ). Thus it

that in the interval between his first and second Roman cap- St Paul
tivity he found some opportunity of carrying out his design. probably
At all events we find him at Miletus, near to the mouth of Colossæ.
the Mæander[1]: and the journey between this place and Laodicea is neither long nor difficult.

At the time of this visit—the first and last, we may
suppose, which he paid to the valley of the Lycus—St Paul's
direction of the Asiatic Churches is drawing to a close. With St John
his death they pass into the hands of St John[2], who takes up in Asia
his abode in Asia Minor. Of Colossæ and Hierapolis we hear
nothing more in the New Testament: but from his exile in
Patmos the beloved disciple delivers his Lord's message to the The mes-
Church of Laodicea[3]; a message doubtless intended to be Laodicea.
communicated also to the two subordinate Churches, to which
it would apply almost equally well.

The message communicated by St John to Laodicea pro- Corres-
longs the note which was struck by St Paul in the letter to between
Colossæ. An interval of a very few years has not materially lypse and
altered the character of these churches. Obviously the same St Paul's
temper prevails, the same errors are rife, the same correction
must be applied.

1. Thus, while St Paul finds it necessary to enforce the 1. The
truth that Christ is the image of the invisible God, that in the Person
Him all the divine fulness dwells, that He existed before all of Christ,
things, that through Him all things were created and in Him
all things are sustained, that He is the primary source ($\dot{a}\rho\chi\dot{\eta}$)

seems fairly probable that St Mark's
projected visit to Colossæ was paid.

[1] 2 Tim. iv. 20. By a strange error
Lequien (*Oriens Christ.* I. p. 833)
substitutes Hierapolis for Nicopolis in
Tit. iii. 12, and argues from the passage that the Church of Hierapolis
was founded by St Paul.

[2] It was apparently during the interval between St Paul's first captivity
at Rome and his death, that St Peter
wrote to the Churches of Asia Minor
(1 Pet. i. 1). Whether in this interval

he also visited personally the districts
evangelized directly or indirectly by
St Paul, we have no means of deciding.
Such a visit is far from unlikely, but
it can hardly have been of long duration. A copy of his letters would probably be sent to Laodicea, as a principal centre of Christianity in Proconsular Asia, which is among the
provinces mentioned in the address of
the First Epistle.

[3] Rev. iii. 14—21.

and has the pre-eminence in all things[1]; so in almost identical language St John, speaking in the person of our Lord, declares that He is the Amen, the faithful and true witness, the primary source ($\dot{\alpha}\rho\chi\dot{\eta}$) of the creation of God[2]. Some lingering shreds of the old heresy, we may suppose, still hung about these Churches, and instead of 'holding fast the Head' they were even yet prone to substitute intermediate agencies, angelic mediators, as links in the chain which should bind man to God. They still failed to realise the majesty and significance, the *completeness*, of the Person of Christ.

and practical duties which follow upon it.

And the practical duty also, which follows from the recognition of the theological truth, is enforced by both Apostles in very similar language. If St Paul entreats the Colossians to seek those things which are above, where Christ is seated on the right hand of God[3], and in the companion epistle, which also he directs them to read, reminds the Churches that God raised them with Christ and seated them with him in heavenly places in Christ Jesus[4]; in like manner St John gives this promise to the Laodiceans in the name of his Lord: 'He that overcometh, I will grant to him to sit with me in my throne, even as I also overcame and did sit with my Father in His throne[5].'

2. Warning against lukewarmness.

2. But again; after a parting salutation to the Church of Laodicea St Paul closes with a warning to Archippus, apparently its chief pastor, to take heed to his ministry[6]. Some

---

[1] Col. i. 15—18.

[2] Rev. iii. 14. It should be observed that this designation of our Lord ($\dot{\eta}$ $\dot{\alpha}\rho\chi\dot{\eta}$ $\tau\hat{\eta}s$ $\kappa\tau\dot{\iota}\sigma\epsilon\omega s$ $\tauo\hat{\upsilon}$ $\Theta\epsilono\hat{\upsilon}$), which so closely resembles the language of the Colossian Epistle, does not occur in the messages to the other six Churches, nor do we there find anything resembling it.

[3] Col. iii. 1.

[4] Ephes. ii. 6 $\sigma\upsilon\nu\dot{\eta}\gamma\epsilon\iota\rho\epsilon\nu$ $\kappa\alpha\dot{\iota}$ $\sigma\upsilon\nu\epsilon$-$\kappa\dot{\alpha}\theta\iota\sigma\epsilon\nu$ $\kappa.\tau.\lambda.$

[5] Rev. iii. 21 $\delta\dot{\omega}\sigma\omega$ $\alpha\dot{\upsilon}\tau\hat{\omega}$ $\kappa\alpha\theta\dot{\iota}\sigma\alpha\iota$

$\mu\epsilon\tau'$ $\dot{\epsilon}\muo\hat{\upsilon}$, $\kappa.\tau.\lambda.$ Here again it must be noticed that there is no such resemblance in the language of the promises to the faithful in the other six Churches. This double coincidence, affecting the two ideas which may be said to cover the whole ground in the Epistle to the Colossians, can hardly, I think, be fortuitous, and suggests an acquaintance with and recognition of the earlier Apostle's teaching on the part of St John.

[6] Col. iv. 17.

signs of slackened zeal seem to have called forth this rebuke. It may be an accidental coincidence, but it is at least worthy of notice, that lukewarmness is the special sin denounced in the angel of the Laodiceans, and that the necessity of greater earnestness is the burden of the message to that Church[1]. As with the people, so it is with the priest. The community takes its colour from and communicates its colour to its spiritual rulers. The 'be zealous' of St John is the counterpart to the 'take heed' of St Paul.

3. Lastly; in the Apocalyptic message the pride of wealth is sternly condemned in the Laodicean Church: 'For that thou sayest I am rich and have gotten me riches and have need of nothing, and knowest not that thou art utterly wretched and miserable and beggarly and blind and naked, I counsel thee to buy gold of me refined with fire, that thou mayest have riches[2].' This proud vaunt receives its best illustration from a recent occurrence at Laodicea, to which allusion has already been made. Only a very few years before this date an earthquake had laid the city in ruins. Yet from this catastrophe she rose again with more than her former splendour. This however was not her chief title to respect. While other cities, prostrated by a like visitation, had sought relief from the concessions of the Roman senate or the liberality of the emperor's purse, it was the glory of Laodicea that she alone neither courted nor obtained assistance, but recovered by her own resources. 'Nullo a nobis remedio,' says the Roman historian, 'propriis opibus revaluit[3].' Thus she had asserted a proud independence, to which neither far-famed metropolitan Ephesus, nor old imperial Sardis, nor her prosperous commer-

3. The pride of wealth denounced.

The vaunt of Laodicea.

---

[1] Rev. iii. 19. If the common view, that by the angel of the Church its chief pastor is meant, were correct, and if Archippus (as is very probable) had been living when St John wrote, the coincidence would be still more striking; see Trench's *Epistles to the Seven Churches in Asia* p. 180. But for reasons given elsewhere (*Philippians* p. 199 sq.), this interpretation of the angels seems to me incorrect.

[2] Rev. iii. 17, 18, where the correct reading with the repetition of the definite articles, ὁ ταλαίπωρος καὶ ὁ ἐλεινός, signifies the type, the embodiment of wretchedness, etc.

[3] Tac. *Ann.* xiv. 27.

cial neighbours, Apamea and Cibyra, could lay claim[1].   No
one would dispute her boast that she 'had gotten riches and
had need of nothing.'

Pride of intellectual wealth.   But is there not a second and subsidiary idea underlying
the Apocalyptic rebuke?   The pride of intellectual wealth,
we may well suspect, was a temptation at Laodicea hardly less
strong than the pride of material resources.   When St Paul
wrote, the theology of the Gospel and the comprehension of
the Church were alike endangered by a spirit of intellectual
exclusiveness[2] in these cities.   He warned them against a vain
philosophy, against a show of wisdom, against an intrusive
mystic speculation, which vainly puffed up the fleshly mind[3].
He tacitly contrasted with this false intellectual wealth 'the
riches of the glory of God's mystery revealed in Christ[4],' the
riches of the full assurance of understanding, the genuine treasures of wisdom and knowledge[5].   May not the same contrast
be discerned in the language of St John?   The Laodiceans
boast of their enlightenment, but they are blind, and to cure
their blindness they must seek eye-salve from the hands of the
great Physician.   They vaunt their wealth of knowledge, but
they are wretched paupers, and must beg the refined gold of
the Gospel to relieve their wants[6].

This is the last notice in the Apostolic records relating to
the Churches in the valley of the Lycus; but during the succeeding ages the Christian communities of this district play
a conspicuous part in the struggles and the development of the
Church.   When after the destruction of Jerusalem St John

---

[1] In all the other cases of earthquake which Tacitus records as happening in these Asiatic cities, *Ann.*
ii. 47 (the twelve cities), iv. 13 (Cibyra), xii. 58 (Apamea), he mentions
the fact of their obtaining relief from
the Senate or the Emperor. On an
earlier occasion Laodicea herself had
not disdained under similar circumstances to receive assistance from Augustus: Strabo, xii. p. 579.

[2] See the next chapter of this introduction.

[3] Col. ii. 8, 18, 23.

[4] i. 27.

[5] ii. 2, 3.

[6] Comp. Eph. i. 18 'The *eyes of
your understanding being enlightened*,
that ye may know what is the hope
of his calling, what the *riches of the
glory of his inheritance* in the saints.'

fixed his abode at Ephesus, it would appear that not a few of The early disciples settle in proconsular Asia the oldest surviving members of the Palestinian Church accompanied him into 'Asia,' which henceforward became the head-quarters of Apostolic authority. In this body of emigrants Andrew[1] and Philip among the twelve, Aristion and John the presbyter[2] among other personal disciples of the Lord, are especially mentioned.

Among the chief settlements of this Christian dispersion was and especially at Hierapolis. Hierapolis. This fact explains how these Phrygian Churches assumed a prominence in the ecclesiastical history of the second century, for which we are hardly prepared by their antecedents as they appear in connexion with St Paul, and which they failed to maintain in the history of the later Church.

Here at all events was settled Philip of Bethsaida[3], the

---

[1] *Canon Murator.* fol. 1, l. 14 (p. 17, ed. Tregelles), Cureton's *Ancient Syriac Documents* pp. 32, 34. Comp. Papias in Euseb. *H. E.* iii. 39.

[2] Papias in Euseb. *H. E.* iii. 39.

[3] Polycrates in Euseb. *H. E.* iii. 31, v. 24 Φίλιππον [τὸν] τῶν δώδεκα ἀποστόλων, ὃς κεκοίμηται ἐν Ἱεραπόλει, καὶ δύο θυγατέρες αὐτοῦ γεγηρακυῖαι παρθένοι, καὶ ἡ ἑτέρα αὐτοῦ θυγάτηρ ἐν ἁγίῳ πνεύματι πολιτευσαμένη, ἣ ἐν Ἐφέσῳ ἀναπαύεται. To this third daughter the statement of Clement of Alexandria must refer, though by a common looseness of expression he uses the plural number (Euseb. *H. E.* iii. 30) ἢ καὶ τοὺς ἀποστόλους ἀποδοκιμάσουσι· Πέτρος μὲν γὰρ καὶ Φίλιππος ἐπαιδοποιήσαντο, Φίλιππος δὲ καὶ τὰς θυγατέρας ἀνδράσιν ἐξέδωκε. On the other hand in the *Dialogue between Gaius and Proclus*, Philip the Evangelist was represented as residing at Hierapolis (Euseb. *H. E.* iii. 31) μετὰ τοῦτον δὲ προφήτιδες τέσσαρες αἱ Φιλίππου γεγένηνται ἐν Ἱεραπόλει τῇ κατὰ τὴν Ἀσίαν· ὁ τάφος αὐτῶν ἐστιν ἐκεῖ, καὶ ὁ τοῦ πατρὸς αὐτῶν, where the mention of the *four* daughters *prophesying* iden-

tifies the person meant (see Acts xxi. 8). Nothing can be clearer than that St Luke distinguishes Philip the Evangelist from Philip the Apostle; for (1) When the Seven are appointed, he distinctly states that this new office is created to relieve the Twelve of some onerous duties (Acts vi. 2—5). (2) After Philip the Evangelist has preached in Samaria, two of the Twelve are sent thither to convey the gifts of the Spirit, which required the presence of an Apostle (viii. 14—17). (3) When St Paul and his companions visit Philip at Cæsarea, he is carefully described as 'the Evangelist, being one of the Seven' (xxi. 8). As St Luke was a member of the Apostle's company when this visit was paid, and stayed 'many days' in Philip's house, the accuracy of his information cannot be questioned. Yet Eusebius (*H. E.* iii. 31) assumes the identity of the Apostle with the Evangelist, and describes the notice in the *Dialogue of Gaius and Proclus* as being 'in harmony with (συνᾴδων)' the language of Polycrates. And accordingly in another passage (*H. E.* iii. 39), when he has occasion

early friend and fellow-townsman of St John, and the first Apostle who is recorded to have held communication with the Gentiles[1]. Here he died and was buried; and here after

to mention the conversations of Papias with Philip's daughters at Hierapolis, he again supposes them to be the same who are mentioned in the Acts.

My reasons for believing that the Philip who lived at Hierapolis was not the Evangelist, but the Apostle, are as follows. (1) This is distinctly stated by the earliest witness, Polycrates, who was bishop of Ephesus at the close of the second century, and who besides claimed to have and probably had special opportunities of knowing early traditions. It is confirmed moreover by the notice in Clement of Alexandria, who is the next in order of time, and whose means of information also were good, for one of his earliest teachers was an Ionian Greek (*Strom.* I. 1, p. 322). (2) The other view depends solely on the authority of the *Dialogue of Gaius and Proclus*. I have given reasons elsewhere for questioning the separate existence of the Roman presbyter Gaius, and for supposing that this dialogue was written by Hippolytus bishop of Portus (*Journal of Philology* I. p. 98 sq., Cambridge, 1868). But however this may be, its author was a Roman ecclesiastic, and probably wrote some quarter of a century at least after Polycrates. In all respects therefore his authority is inferior. Moreover it is suspicious in form. It mentions four daughters instead of three, makes them all virgins, and represents them as prophetesses, thus showing a distinct aim of reproducing the particulars as given in Acts xxi. 9; whereas the account of Polycrates is divergent in all three respects. (3) A life-long friendship would naturally draw Philip the Apostle of Bethsaida after John,

as it also drew Andrew. And, when we turn to St John's Gospel, we can hardly resist the impression that incidents relating to Andrew and Philip had a special interest, not only for the writer of the Gospel, but also for his hearers (John i. 40, 43—46, vi. 5—8, xii. 20—22, xiv. 8, 9). Moreover the Apostles Andrew and Philip appear in this Gospel as inseparable companions. (4) Lastly; when Papias mentions collecting the sayings of the Twelve and of other early disciples from those who heard them, he gives a prominent place to these two Apostles τί Ἀνδρέας ... εἶπεν ἢ τί Φίλιππος, but there is no reference to Philip the Evangelist. When therefore we read later that he conversed with the daughters of Philip, it seems natural to infer that the Philip intended is the same person whom he has mentioned previously. It should be added, though no great value can be assigned to such channels of information, that the Acts of Philip place the Apostle at Hierapolis; Tischendorf, *Act. Apost. Apocr.* p. 75 sq.

On the other hand, those who suppose that the Evangelist, and not the Apostle, resided at Hierapolis, account for the other form of the tradition by the natural desire of the Asiatic Churches to trace their spiritual descent directly from the Twelve. This solution of the phenomenon might have been accepted, if the authorities in favour of Philip the Evangelist had been prior in time and superior in quality. There is no improbability in supposing that both the Philips were married and had daughters.

[1] John xii. 20.

his decease lived his two virgin daughters, who survived to a very advanced age and thus handed down to the second century the traditions of the earliest days of the Church. A third daughter, who was married, had settled in Ephesus, where her body rested[1]. It was from the two daughters who resided at Hierapolis, that Papias heard several stories of the first preachers of the Gospel, which he transmitted to posterity in his work[2].

Their traditions collected by Papias.

This Papias had conversed not only with the daughters of Philip, but also with at least two personal disciples of the Lord, Aristion and John the presbyter. He made it his business to gather traditions respecting the sayings of the Saviour and His Apostles; and he published a work in five books, entitled *An Exposition of Oracles of the Lord*, using the information thus collected to illustrate the discourses, and perhaps the doings, of Christ as recorded in the Gospels[3]. Among other stories he related, apparently on the authority of these daughters of Philip, how a certain dead man had been restored to life in his own day, and how Justus Barsabas, who is mentioned in the Acts, had drunk a deadly poison and miraculously escaped from any evil effects[4].

[1] See above p. 45, note 3.

[2] Euseb. *H. E.* iii. 39. This is the general reference for all those particulars respecting Papias which are derived from Eusebius.

[3] See Westcott, *Canon* p. 63. On the opinions of Papias and on the nature of his work, I may perhaps be allowed to refer to articles in the *Contemporary Review* Aug. 1867, Aug. and Sept. 1875, where I have investigated the notices of this father. The object of Papias' work was not to construct a Gospel narrative, but to interpret and illustrate those already existing. I ought to add that on two minor points, the martyrdom of Papias and the identity of Philip with the Evangelist, I have been led to modify my views since the first article was written.

[4] Euseb. l. c. ὡς δὲ κατὰ τοὺς αὐτοὺς ὁ Παπίας γενόμενος διήγησιν παρειλη-φέναι θαυμασίαν ὑπὸ [ἀπὸ?] τῶν τοῦ Φιλίππου θυγατέρων μνημονεύει, τὰ νῦν σημειωτέον· νεκροῦ γὰρ ἀνάστασιν κατ' αὐτὸν γεγονυῖαν ἱστορεῖ, καὶ αὖ πάλιν ἕτερον παράδοξον περὶ Ἰοῦστον τὸν ἐπι-κληθέντα Βαρσαβᾶν γεγονός κ.τ.λ. The information respecting the raising of the dead man might have come from the daughters of Philip, as the context seems certainly to imply, while yet the event happened in Papias' own time (κατ' αὐτόν). It will be remembered that even Irenæus mentions similar miracles as occurring in his own age (*Hær.* ii. 32. 4). Eusebius does not say that the miraculous preservation of Justus Barsabas also occurred in the time of Papias.

If we may judge by his name, PAPIAS was a native of
Phrygia, probably of Hierapolis[1], of which he afterwards became bishop, and must have grown up to youth or early manhood before the close of the first century. He is said to have
suffered martyrdom at Pergamum about the year 165; but
there is good reason for distrusting this statement, independently of any chronological difficulty which it involves[2]. Other-

---

[1] Papias, or (as it is very frequently
written in inscriptions) Pappias, is a
common Phrygian name. It is found
several times at Hierapolis, not only
in inscriptions (Boeckh *Corp. Inscr.*
no. 3930, 3912 a add.) but even on
coins (Mionnet IV. p. 301). This is
explained by the fact that it was
an epithet of the Hierapolitan Zeus
(Boeckh 3817 Παπίᾳ Διὲ σωτῆρι), just as
in Bithynia this same god was called
Πάπας (Lobeck *Aglaoph.* p. 1048; see
Boeckh *Corp. Inscr.* III. p. 1051).
Hence as the name of a mortal it is
equivalent to the Greek Diogenes; e.g.
Boeckh no. 3912 a add., Παπίας τοῦ
Στράτωνος ὁ καλούμενος Διογένης. Galen
also mentions a physician of Laodicea,
bearing this name (*Op.* XII. p. 799, ed.
Kühn). In an inscription at Tra-
janopolis we meet with it in a curious
conjunction with other familiar names
(Boeckh no. 3865 i add.) Παππίας Τρο-
φίμου καὶ Τυχικῆς κ.τ.λ. (see Wad-
dington on Le Bas, Inscr. no. 718).
This last belongs to the year A.D. 199.
On other analogous Phrygian names
see the introduction to the Epistle to
Philemon.

Thus at Hierapolis the name Papias
is derived from heathen mythology,
and accordingly the persons bearing it
on the inscriptions and coins are all
heathens. It may therefore be presumed that our Papias was of Gentile
origin. The inference however is not
absolutely certain. A rabbi of this
name is mentioned in the Mishna
Shekalim iv. 7, *Edaioth* vii. 6. These

two references are given by Zunz *Namen
der Juden* p. 16.

[2] *Chron. Pasch.* sub. ann. 163 σὺν
τῷ ἁγίῳ δὲ Πολυκάρπῳ καὶ ἄλλοι θ' ἀπὸ
Φιλαδελφείας μαρτυροῦσιν ἐν Σμύρνῃ· καὶ
ἐν Περγάμῳ δὲ ἕτεροι, ἐν οἷς ἦν καὶ Παπίας καὶ ἄλλοι πολλοί, ὧν καὶ ἔγγραφα
φέρονται τὰ μαρτύρια. See also the
Syrian epitome of Euseb. *Chron.* (II.
p. 216 ed. Schöne) 'Cum persecutio in
Asia esset, Polycarpos martyrium subiit
et Papias, quorum martyria in libro
(scripta) extant,' but the Armenian
version of the *Chronicon* mentions only
Polycarp, while Jerome says 'Poly-
carpus et Pionius fecere martyrium.'
In his history (iv. 15) Eusebius, after
quoting the *Martyrdom of Polycarp* at
length, adds ἐν τῇ αὐτῇ δὲ περὶ αὐτοῦ
γραφῇ καὶ ἄλλα μαρτύρια συνῆπτο
... μεθ' ὧν καὶ Μητρόδωρος ... ἀνῄρηται·
τῶν γε μὴν τότε περιβοήτων μαρτύρων εἷς
τις ἐγνωρίζετο Πιόνιος ... ἑξῆς δὲ καὶ
ἄλλων ἐν Περγάμῳ πόλει τῆς Ἀσίας ὑπο-
μνήματα μεμαρτυρηκότων φέρεται, Κάρ-
που καὶ Παπύλου καὶ γυναικὸς Ἀγα-
θονίκης κ.τ.λ. He here apparently falls
into the error of imagining that Metrodorus, Pionius, Carpus, Papylus, and
the others were martyred under M.
Aurelius, whereas we know from their
extant Acts that they suffered in the
Decian persecution. For the Martyr-
doms of Pionius and Metrodorus see
Act. SS. Bolland. Feb. 1; for those of
Carpus, Papylus, and Agathonica, *ib.*
April 13. The Acts of the former,
which are included in Ruinart (*Act.
Sinc. Mart.* p. 120 sq., 1689) are appa-

wise he must have lived to a very advanced age. Eusebius, to Account of
Eusebius. whom chiefly we owe our information respecting him, was repelled by his millennarian views, and describes him as a man of mean intelligence[1], accusing him of misunderstanding the Apostolic sayings respecting the kingdom of Christ and thus interpreting in a material sense expressions which were intended to be mystical and symbolical. This disparaging account, though one-sided, was indeed not altogether undeserved, for his love of the marvellous seems to have overpowered his faculty of discrimination. But the adverse verdict of Eusebius must be corrected by the more sympathetic language of Irenæus[2], who possibly may have known him personally, and who certainly must have been well acquainted with his reputation and character.

Much has been written respecting the relation of this writer to the Canonical Gospels, but the discussion has no very direct bearing on our special subject, and may be dismissed here[3]. One question however, which has a real importance

rently the same which were seen by Eusebius. Those of the latter are a late compilation of the Metaphrast, but were perhaps founded on the earlier document. At all events the tradition of the persecution in which they suffered could hardly have been perverted or lost. Eusebius seems to have found their Acts bound up in the same volume with those of Polycarp, and without reading them through, to have drawn the hasty inference that they suffered at the same time. But notwithstanding the error, or perhaps owing to it, this passage in the Ecclesiastical History, by a confusion of the names Papias and Papylus, seems to have given rise to the statement respecting Papias in the Chronicon Paschale and in the Syrian epitome, as it obviously has misled Jerome respecting Pionius. This part of the Chronicon Paschale is plainly taken from Eusebius, as the coincidences of expres-

sion and the sequence of events alike show. The martyrdom of Papias therefore appears to be a fiction, and he may have died a natural death at an earlier date. Polycarp's martyrdom is shown by M. Waddington's investigations to have taken place A.D. 155 or 156; see *Mémoire sur la Chronologie du Rhéteur Ælius Aristide* p. 232 sq., in the *Mém. de l'Acad. des Inscr.* XXVI (1867).

[1] *H. E.* iii. 39 σφόδρα σμικρὸς τὸν νοῦν. In another passage (iii. 36), as commonly read, Eusebius makes partial amends to Papias by calling him ἀνὴρ τὰ πάντα ὅτι μάλιστα λογιώτατος καὶ τῆς γραφῆς εἰδήμων, but this passage is found to be a spurious interpolation (see *Contemporary Review*, August, 1867, p. 12), and was probably added by some one who was acquainted with the work of Papias and desired to do him justice.

[2] Iren. v. 33. 3, 4.

[3] See on this subject Westcott *Canon*

as affecting the progress of the Gospel in these parts, has been raised by modern criticism and must not be passed over in silence.

It has been supposed that there was an entire dislocation and discontinuity in the history of Christianity in Asia Minor at a certain epoch; that the Apostle of the Gentiles was ignored and his teaching repudiated, if not anathematized; and that on its ruins was erected the standard of Judaism, around which with a marvellous unanimity deserters from the Pauline Gospel rallied. Of this retrograde faith St John is supposed to have been the great champion, and Papias a typical and important representative[1].

The subject, as a whole, is too wide for a full investigation here. I must content myself with occupying a limited area, showing not only the historical baselessness, but the strong inherent improbability of the theory, as applied to Hierapolis and the neighbouring churches. As this district is its chief strong-hold, a repulse at this point must involve its ultimate defeat along the whole line.

Of St John himself I have already spoken[2]. It has been shown that his language addressed to these Churches is not only not opposed to St Paul's teaching, but presents remarkable coincidences with it. So far at least the theory finds no support; and, when from St John we turn to Papias, the case is not different. The advocates of the hypothesis in question lay the chief stress of their argument on the silence of Papias, or rather of Eusebius. Eusebius quotes a passage from Papias, in which the bishop of Hierapolis mentions collecting from trustworthy sources the sayings of certain Apostles and early disciples; but St Paul is not named among them. He also gives short extracts from Papias referring to the Gospels of St Matthew and St Mark, and mentions that this writer made

p. 64 sq.; *Contemporary Review*, August and September, 1875.

[1] The theory of the Tübingen school may be studied in Baur's *Christliche Kirche der drei ersten Jahrhunderte*

or in Schwegler's *Nachapostolisches Zeitalter*. It has been reproduced (at least as far as regards the Asiatic Churches) by Renan *S. Paul* p. 366 sq.

[2] See above p. 41 sq.

use of the first Epistle of St John and the first Epistle of St
Peter; but here again there is no allusion to St Paul's writings.
Whether referring to the personal testimony or to the Canonical writings of the Apostles, Papias, we are reminded, is
equally silent about St Paul.

On both these points a satisfactory answer can be given;
but the two cases are essentially different, and must be considered apart.

(1) The range of *personal testimony* which Papias would be
able to collect depended on his opportunities. Before he had
grown up to manhood, the personal reminiscences of St Paul
would have almost died out. The Apostle of the Gentiles had
not resided more than three years even at Ephesus, and seems
to have paid only one brief visit to the valley of the Lycus, even
if he visited it at all. Such recollections of St Paul as might
once have lingered here would certainly be overshadowed by
and forgotten in the later sojourn of St John, which, beginning
where they ceased, extended over more than a quarter of a century. To St John, and to those personal disciples of Christ who
surrounded him, Papias and his contemporaries would naturally
and almost inevitably look for the traditions which they so
eagerly collected. This is the case with the leading representative of the Asiatic school in the next generation, Irenæus,
whose traditions are almost wholly derived from St John and
his companions, while at the same time he evinces an entire
sympathy with the work and teaching of St Paul. But indeed,
even if it had been otherwise, the object which Papias had
directly in view did not suggest any appeal to St Paul's
authority. He was writing an 'Exposition of Oracles of the
Lord,' and he sought to supplement and interpret these by
traditions of our Lord's life, such as eyewitnesses only could
give. St Paul could have no place among those personal
disciples of Christ, of whom alone he is speaking in this preface
to his work, which Eusebius quotes.

(2) But, though we have no right to expect any mention
of St Paul where the appeal is to personal testimony, yet with

1. The
traditions
collected
by Papias.

2. His re-
ferences to

the Ca-
nonical
writings. quotations from or references to the *Canonical writings*
the case, it may be argued, is different.   Here at all events we
might look for some recognition of St Paul.   To this argument
it would perhaps be a sufficient reply, that St Paul's Epistles
do not furnish any matter which must necessarily have been
introduced into a work such as Papias composed.   But the
complete and decisive answer is this; that the silence of Eusebius, so far from carrying with it the silence of Papias, does not
No weight
to be at-
tached to
the silence
of Euse-
bius. even afford a presumption in this direction.   Papias may have
quoted St Paul again and again, and yet Eusebius would see
no reason to chronicle the fact.   His usage in other cases is
decisive on this point.   The Epistle of Polycarp which was
read by Eusebius is the same which we still possess.   Not
only does it teem with the most obvious quotations from St
Paul, but in one passage it directly mentions his writing to the
Philippians[1].   Yet the historian, describing its relation to the
Canonical Scriptures, contents himself with saying that it 'employs some testimonies from the former Epistle of Peter[2].'
Exactly similar is his language respecting Irenæus also.   Irenæus, as is well known, cites by name almost every one of St
Paul's Epistles; yet the description which Eusebius gives under
this same head, after quoting this writer's notices respecting
the history of the Gospels and the Apocalypse, is that 'he
mentions also the first Epistle of John, alleging very many
testimonies from it, and in like manner also the former Epistle
of Peter[3].'   There is every reason therefore to suppose that
Eusebius would deal with Papias as he has dealt with Polycarp
and Irenæus, and that, unless Papias had introduced some

---

[1] § 3.

[2] *H.E.* iv. 14 ὁ γέ τοι Πολύκαρπος
ἐν τῇ δηλωθείσῃ πρὸς Φιλιππησίους αὐτοῦ
γραφῇ φερομένῃ εἰς δεῦρο κέχρηταί τισι
μαρτυρίαις ἀπὸ τῆς Πέτρου προτέρας ἐπιστολῆς.   This is all that Eusebius
says with reference to Polycarp's knowledge of the Canonical writings.   It
so happens that in an earlier passage
(iii. 36) he has given an extract from

Polycarp, in which St Paul's name
is mentioned; but the quotation is
brought to illustrate the life of Ignatius, and the mention of the Apostle
there is purely accidental.

[3] *H. E.* v. 8 μέμνηται δὲ καὶ τῆς
Ἰωάννου πρώτης ἐπιστολῆς, μαρτύρια ἐξ
αὐτῆς πλεῖστα εἰσφέρων, ὁμοίως δὲ καὶ
τῆς Πέτρου προτέρας.

curious fact relating to St Paul, it would not have occurred to him to record mere quotations from or references to this Apostle's letters. It may be supposed that Eusebius records with a fair amount of attention references to the Catholic Epistles in early writers, because the limits of the Canon in this part were not accurately fixed. On the other hand the Epistles of St Paul were universally received and therefore did not need to be accredited by any such testimony. But whatever may be the explanation, the fact is patent, and it furnishes a complete answer to the argument drawn from his silence in the case of Papias[1].

But, if the assumption has been proved to be baseless, have we any grounds for saying that it is also highly improbable ? Here it seems fair to argue from the well-known to the unknown. Of the opinions of Papias respecting St Paul we know absolutely nothing; of the opinions of Polycarp and Irenæus ample evidence lies before us. *Noscitur a sociis* is a sound maxim to apply in such a case. Papias was a companion of Polycarp, and he is quoted with deference by Irenæus[2]. Is it probable that his opinions should be diametrically opposed to those of his friend and contemporary on a cardinal point affecting the very conception of Christianity (for the rejection of St Paul must be considered in this light)? or that this vital heterodoxy, if it existed, should have escaped an intelligent critic of the next generation who had the five books of his work before him, who himself had passed his early life in Asia

The views of Papias inferred from his associates.

---

[1] It is necessary to press this argument, because though it has never been answered and (so far as I can see) is quite unanswerable, yet thoughtful men, who have no sympathy with the Tübingen views of early Christian history, still continue to argue from the silence of Eusebius, as though it had some real significance. To illustrate the omissions of Eusebius I have given only the instances of Polycarp and Irenæus, because they are historically connected with Papias; but his silence is even more remarkable in other cases. Thus, when speaking of the epistle of the Roman Clement (*H. E.* iii. 38), he alludes to the coincidences with the Epistle to the Hebrews, but omits to mention the direct references to St Paul's First Epistle to the Corinthians which is referred to by name. I have discussed the whole subject in the *Contemporary Review,* January, 1875, p. 169 sq.

[2] Iren. *Hær.* v. 33. 4.

Minor, and who yet appeals to Papias as preserving the doctrinal tradition which had been handed down from the Apostles themselves to his own time ? I say nothing of Eusebius himself, who, with a distinct prejudice against Papias, accuses him of no worse heresy in his writings than entertaining millennarian views.

Millennarian views consistent with the recognition of St Paul.

It may indeed be confessed that a man like Papias, whose natural bent, assisted by his Phrygian education, was towards sensuous views of religion, would not be likely to appreciate the essentially spiritual teaching of St Paul; but this proves nothing. The difference between unconscious want of sympathy and conscious rejection is all-important for the matter in hand. The same charge might be brought against numberless theologians, whether in the middle ages or in more modern times, into whose' minds it never entered to question the authority of the Apostle and who quote his writings with the utmost reverence. Neither in the primitive days of Christianity nor in its later stages has the profession of Chiliastic views been found inconsistent with the fullest recognition of St Paul's Apostolic claims. In the early Church Irenæus and Tertullian are notable instances of this combination; and in our own age and country a tendency to millennarian speculations has been commonly associated with the staunchest adherence to the fundamental doctrines of St Paul.

As the successor of Papias and the predecessor of Claudius Apollinaris in the see of Hierapolis, we may perhaps name ABERCIUS or AVIRCIUS[1]. His legendary Acts assign his epi-

ABERCIUS

---

[1] The life of this Abercius is printed in the Bollandist *Acta Sanctorum* Oct. 22. It may safely be pronounced spurious. Among other incidents, the saint goes to Rome and casts out a demon from Lucilla, the daughter of M. Aurelius and Faustina, at the same time compelling the demon to take up an altar from Rome and transport it through the air to Hierapolis. But these Acts, though legendary themselves, contain an epitaph which has the ring of genuineness and which seems to have suggested the story to the pious forger who invented the Acts. This very interesting memorial is given and discussed at length by Pitra, *Spicil. Solesm.* III. p. 532 sq. It is inscribed by one Abercius of Hierapolis on his tomb, which he erected during his life-time. He declares himself a disciple of the good shepherd, who

scopate to the reign of Marcus Aurelius; and, though they probably his succes-
are disfigured by extravagant fictions, yet the date may perhaps sor.
be accepted, as it seems to be confirmed by other evidence.
An inscription on his tombstone recorded how he had paid one

taught him trustworthy writings (γράμ- μᾱτᾱ πιστᾱ́) and sent him to visit queenly Rome, where he saw a people sealed with the bright seal [of baptism]. He recounts also a journey to Syria and the East, when he crossed the Euphrates. He says that faith served up to him as a banquet the ΙΧΘΥC from the fountain, giving him bread and wine. He states that he has reached his 72nd year. And he closes by threatening with severe penalties those who disturb his tomb. The resemblance of this inscription to others found *in situ* in the cemetery at Hierapolis, after allowance made for the Christian element, is very striking. The commencement Ἐκλεκτῆς πόλεως closely resembles the form of another Hierapolitan inscription, Boeckh *Corp. Inscr.* 3906; the enumeration of foreign tours has a counterpart in the monument of one Flavius Zeuxis which states that the deceased had made 72 voyages round the promontory of Malea to Italy (*ib.* 3920); and lastly, the prohibition against putting another grave upon his, and the imposition of fines to be paid to the treasury and the city if this injunction is violated, are echos of language which occurs again and again on tombstones in this city (*ib.* 3915, 3916, 3922, 3923, etc.). Out of this epitaph, which he found probably at Hierapolis, and which, as he himself tells us (§ 41), was in a much mutilated condition, the legend-writer apparently created his story, interpreting the queen, by which Abercius himself probably meant the city of Rome, to be the empress Faustina, with whom the saint is represented as having an interview, M. Aurelius himself being

absent at the time on his German campaign. This view, that the epitaph is genuine and gave rise to the Acts, is also maintained by Garrucci (*Civiltà Cattolica* 1856, I. p. 683, II. p. 84, quoted in the *Acta Sanct.* l. c.), whose criticisms however are not always sound; and indeed as a whole it bears every mark of authenticity, though possibly it may contain some interpolations, which its mutilated condition would encourage. The name Aburcius occurs in *Corp. Inscr. Lat.* VI. 127.

The inscription itself however does not tell us what office Abercius held or when he lived. There was a person of this name, bishop of Hierapolis, present at the Council of Chalcedon A.D. 451 (Labb. *Conc.* IV. 862, 1204, 1341, 1392, 1496, 1744, ed. Coleti). But a chief pastor of the Church at this late date would have declared his office plainly; and the inscription points to a more primitive age, for the expressions are archaic and the writer seems to veil his profession of Christianity under language studiously obscure. The open profession of Christianity on inscriptions occurs at an earlier date in these parts than elsewhere. Already the word ΧΡΙCΤΙΑΝΟC or ΧΡΗCΤΙΑΝΟC is found on tombstones of the third century; Boeckh *Corp. Inscr.* 3857 g, 3857 p, 3865 l; see Renan *Saint Paul* p. 363. Thus we are entirely at fault unless we accept the statement in the Acts.

And it is not unreasonable to suppose that, so far as regards the date and office of Abercius, the writer of these Acts followed some adequate historical tradition. Nor indeed is his statement altogether without confirmation. We have evidence that a

visit to the city of Rome, and another to the banks of the
Euphrates. These long journeys are not without parallels in
the lives of contemporary bishops. Polycarp of Smyrna visited
Rome, hoping to adjust the Paschal controversy; Melito of

person bearing this name lived in these
parts of Asia Minor, somewhere about
this time. An unknown writer of a
polemical tract against Montanism dedicates his work to one Avircius Marcellus, at whose instigation it was
written. Eusebius (*H. E.* v. 16), who
is our authority for this fact, relates
that Montanism found a determined
and formidable opponent in Apollinaris at Hierapolis and 'several other
learned men of that day with him,'
who left large materials for a history of the movement. He then goes
on to say; ἀρχόμενος γοῦν τῆς κατ'
αὐτῶν γραφῆς τῶν εἰρημένων δή τις
...προοιμιάζεται...τοῦτον τὸν τρόπον· Ἐκ
πλείστου ὅσου καὶ ἱκανωτάτου χρόνου,
ἀγαπητὲ Ἀουίρκιε Μάρκελλε, ἐπιταχθεὶς
ὑπὸ σοῦ συγγράψαι τινὰ λόγον κ.τ.λ.,
i.e. 'One of the aforesaid writers at
the commencement of his treatise
against them (the Montanists) etc.'
May not the person here addressed be
the Abercius of the epitaph?

But if so, who is the writer that
addresses him, and when did he live?
Some MSS omit δή τις, and others substitute ἤδη, thus making Apollinaris
himself the writer. But the words
seem certainly to have been part of
the original text, as the sense requires
them; for if they are omitted, τῶν εἰρημένων must be connected with κατ'
αὐτῶν, where it is not wanted. Thus
Eusebius quotes the writer anony-
mously; and those who assign the
treatise to Apollinaris cannot plead
the authority of the original text of
the historian himself.

But after all may it not have been
written by Apollinaris, though Euse-

bius was uncertain about the authorship? He quotes in succession three
συγγράμματα or treatises, speaking of
them as though they emanated from
the same author. The first of these,
from which the address to Avircius
Marcellus is quoted, might very well
have been composed soon after the
Montanist controversy broke out (as
Eusebius himself elsewhere states was
the case with the work of Apollinaris,
iv. 27 κατὰ τῆς τῶν Φρυγῶν αἱρέσεως
...ὥσπερ ἐκφύειν ἀρχομένης); but the
second and third distinctly state that
they were written some time after the
death of Montanus. May not Eusebius have had before him a volume
containing a collection of tracts against
Montanism 'by Claudius Apollinaris
and others,' in which the authorship
of the several tracts was not distinctly
marked? This hypothesis would explain the words with which he prefaces his extracts, and would also account for his vague manner of quotation. It would also explain the omission of δή τις in some texts (the
ancient Syriac version boldly substitutes the name of Apollinaris), and
would explain how Rufinus, Nicepho-
rus, and others, who might have had
independent information, ascribed the
treatise to this father. I have already pointed out how Eusebius was
led into a similar error of connecting
together several martyrologies and
treating them as contemporaneous, because they were collected in the same
volume (p. 48, note 2). Elsewhere
too I have endeavoured to show that
he mistook the authorship of a tract
which was bound up with others,

Sardis went as far as Palestine, desiring to ascertain on the spot the facts relating to the Canon of the Old Testament Scriptures. These or similar motives may have influenced Abercius to undertake his distant journeys. If we may assume the identification of this bishop with one Avircius Marcellus who is mentioned in a contemporary document, he took an active interest in the Montanist controversy, as from his position he was likely to do.

The literary character of the see of Hierapolis, which had been inaugurated by Papias, was ably sustained by CLAUDIUS APOLLINARIS. His surname, which seems to have been common in these parts[1], may have been derived from the patron

CLAUDIUS APOLLINARIS bishop of Hierapolis.

owing to the absence of a title (*Caius or Hippolytus?* in the *Journal of Philology* I. p. 98 sq.).

On this hypothesis, Claudius Apollinaris would very probably be the author of the first of these treatises. If so, it would appear to have been written while he was still a presbyter, at the instigation of his bishop Avircius Marcellus whom he succeeded not long after in the see of Hierapolis.

If on the other hand Eusebius has correctly assigned the first treatise to the same writer as the second and third, who must have written after the beginning of the third century, Avircius Marcellus to whom it is addressed cannot have held the see of Hierapolis during the reign of M. Aurelius (A.D. 161—180); and, if he was ever bishop of this city, must have been a successor, not a predecessor, of Claudius Apollinaris. In this case we have the alternative of abandoning the identification of this Avircius with the Hierapolitan bishop of the same name, or of rejecting the statement of the Acts which places his episcopate in this reign.

The occurrence of the name Abercius in the later history of the see of Hierapolis (see p. 55) is no argument

against the existence of this earlier bishop. It was no uncommon practice for the later occupants of sees to assume the name of some famous predecessor who lived in primitive or early times. The case of Ignatius at Antioch is only one of several examples which might be produced.

There is some ground for supposing that, like Papias and Apollinaris, Abercius earned a place in literary history. Baronio had in his hands an epistle to M. Aurelius, purporting to have been written by this Abercius, which he obviously considered genuine and which he describes as 'apostolicum redolens spiritum,' promising to publish it in his Annals (*Martyr. Rom.* Oct. 22). To his great grief however he afterwards lost it ('doluimus vehementer e manibus nostris elapsam nescio quomodo'), and was therefore unable to fulfil his promise (*Annal.* s.a. 163, n. 15). A $\beta\iota\beta\lambda o\varsigma$ $\delta\iota\delta a\sigma\kappa a\lambda\iota a\varsigma$ by Abercius is mentioned in the Acts (§ 39); but this, if it ever existed, was doubtless spurious.

[1] Some of the family, as we may infer from the monuments, held a high position in another Phrygian town. On a tablet at Æzani, on which

deity of Hierapolis[1] and suggests a Gentile origin. His intimate acquaintance with heathen literature, which is mentioned by more than one ancient writer, points in the same direction. During the reign of M. Aurelius he had already made himself a name by his writings, and seems to have been promoted to the see of Hierapolis before the death of that emperor[2].

His literary works.

Of his works, which were very numerous, only a few scanty fragments have survived[3]. The imperfect lists however, which have reached us, bear ample testimony both to the literary activity of the man, and to the prominence of the Church over which he presided, in the great theological and ecclesiastical controversies of the age.

He takes part in the two chief controversies of the day.

The two questions, which especially agitated the Churches of Asia Minor during the last thirty years of the first century, were the celebration of the Easter festival and the pretensions of the Montanist prophets. In both disputes Claudius Apollinaris took an active and conspicuous part.

1. The Paschal controversy, after smouldering long both

is inscribed a letter from the emperor Septimius Severus in reply to the congratulations of the people at the elevation of Caracalla to the rank of Augustus (A.D. 198), we find the name of ΚΛΑΥΔΙΟC . ΑΠΟΛΛΙΝΑΡΙΟC . ΑΥΡΗΛΙΑΝΟC, Boeckh 3837 (see III. p. 1066 add.). In another inscription at the same place, the same or another member of the family is commemorated as holding the office of prætor for the second time, CTPATHГOYNTOC . ΤΟ . Β . ΚΛ . ΑΠΟΛΛΙΝΑΡΙΟΥ ; Boeckh 3840, *ib.* p. 1067. See also the inscriptions 3842 c, 3846 z (*ib.* pp. 1069, 1078) at the same place, where again the name Apollinarius occurs. It is found also at Appia no. 3857 b (*ib.* p. 1086). At an earlier date one Claudius Apollinaris appears in command of the Roman fleet at Misenum (Tac. *Hist.* iii. 57, 76, 77). The name occurs also at Hierapolis itself, Boeckh, no. 3915, Π .

ΑΙΛΙΟC . Π . ΑΙΛΙΟΥ . ΑΠΟΛΛΙΝΑΡΙΟΥ . ΙΟΥΛΙΑΝΟ[Υ] . ΥΙΟC . CΕ[...]. ΑΠΟΛΛΙΝΑΡΙC . ΜΑΚΕΔΩΝ . κ.τ.λ., which shows that both the forms, *Apollinaris* and *Apollinarius*, by which the bishop of Hierapolis is designated, are legitimate. The former however is the correct Latin form, the latter being the Greek adaptation.

More than a generation later than our Apollinaris, Origen in his letter to Africanus (*Op.* I. 30, Delarue) sends greeting to a bishop bearing this name (τὸν καλὸν ἡμῶν πάπαν 'Απολινάριον), of whom nothing more is known.

[1] Apollo Archegetes; see above p. 12, note 1.

[2] Euseb. *H. E.* iv. 26, *Chron.* s. a. 171, 172, 'Apollinaris Asianus, Hierapolitanus episcopus, insignis habetur.'

[3] Collected in Routh's *Reliquiæ Sacræ* I. p. 159 sq., and more recently in Otto's *Corp. Apol. Christ.* IX. p. 479 sq.

here and elsewhere, first burst into flames in the neighbouring 1. The Paschal question. Church of Laodicea[1]. An able bishop of Hierapolis therefore must necessarily have been involved in the dispute, even if he had been desirous of avoiding it. What side Apollinaris took in the controversy the extant fragments of his work do not by themselves enable us to decide; for they deal merely with a subsidiary question which does not seriously affect the main issue[2]. But we can hardly doubt that with Polycarp of Smyrna and Melito of Sardis and Polycrates of Ephesus he defended the practice which was universal in Asia[3], observing the Paschal anniversary on the 14th Nisan whether it fell on a Friday or not, and invoking the authority of St John at Ephesus, and of St Philip at his own Hierapolis[4], against the divergent usage of Alexandria and Palestine and the West.

2. His writings on the Montanist controversy were still 2. Montanism. more famous, and are recommended as an authority on the subject by Serapion of Antioch a few years after the author's death[5]. Though later than many of his works[6], they were written soon after Montanus had divulged the extravagance of his pretensions and before Montanism had attained its complete development. If a later notice may be trusted, Apollinaris was not satisfied with attacking Montanism in writing, but summoned at Hierapolis a council of twenty-six bishops besides

---

[1] See below, p. 63.

[2] The main point at issue was whether the exact day of the month should be observed, as the Quartodecimans maintained, irrespective of the day of the week. The fragments of Apollinaris (preserved in the *Chron. Pasch.* p. 13) relate to a discrepancy which some had found in the accounts of St Matthew and St John.

[3] Eusebius represents the dioceses of 'Asia' and the neighbourhood, as absolutely unanimous; *H. E.* v. 23 τῆς Ἀσίας ἁπάσης αἱ παροικίαι, v. 24 τῆς Ἀσίας πάσης ἅμα ταῖς ὁμόροις ἐκκλησίαις τὰς παροικίας. 'Asia' includes all this district, as appears from Polycrates, *ib.*

[4] See Polycrates of Ephesus in Euseb. *H. E.* v. 24.

[5] In Euseb. *H. E.* v. 19.

[6] Eusebius (*H. E.* iv. 27) at the close of his list of the works of Apollinaris gives καὶ ἃ μετὰ ταῦτα συνέγραψε κατὰ τῆς [τῶν] Φρυγῶν αἱρέσεως μετ' οὐ πολὺν καινοτομηθείσης χρόνον, τότε γε μὴν ὥσπερ ἐκφύειν ἀρχομένης, ἔτι τοῦ Μοντανοῦ ἅμα ταῖς αὐτοῦ ψευδοπροφήτισιν ἀρχὰς τῆς παρεκτροπῆς ποιουμένου, *i. e.* the vagaries of Montanus and his followers had already begun when Apollinaris wrote, but Montanism assumed a new phase shortly after.

himself, where this heresy was condemned and sentence of
excommunication pronounced against Montanus together with
his adherent the pretended prophetess Maximilla[1].

His other
hæresiolo-
gical writ-
ings.

Nor were his controversial writings confined to these two
topics. In one place he refuted the Encratites[2]; in another he
upheld the orthodox teaching respecting the true humanity of
Christ[3]. It is plain that he did not confine himself to questions
especially affecting Asia Minor; but that the doctrine and the

[1] Included in the *Libellus Synodi-
cus* published by Pappus; see Labb.
Conc. I. 615, ed. Coleti. Though this
council is not mentioned elsewhere,
there is no sufficient ground for questioning its authenticity. The important part taken by Apollinaris against
the Montanists is recognised by Eusebius *H. E.* v. 16, πρὸς τὴν λεγομένην
κατὰ Φρύγας αἵρεσιν ὅπλον ἰσχυρὸν καὶ
ἀκαταγώνιστον ἐπὶ τῆς Ἱεραπόλεως τὸν
Ἀπολινάριον.

After mentioning the council the
compiler of this Synodicon speaks thus
of the false prophets; οἳ καὶ βλασφή-
μως, ἤτοι δαιμονῶντες, καθώς φησιν ὁ
αὐτὸς πατήρ [*i.e.* Ἀπολινάριος], τὸν βίον
κατέστρεψαν, σὺν αὐτοῖς δὲ κατέκρινε
καὶ Θεόδοτον τὸν σκυτέα. He evidently
has before him the fragments of the
anonymous treatises quoted by Eusebius (*H. E.* v. 16), as the following
parallels taken from these fragments
show: ὡς ἐπὶ ἐνεργουμένῳ καὶ δαιμο-
νῶντι...βλασφημεῖν διδάσκοντος τοῦ
ἀπηνθαδισμένου πνεύματος...τὸν βίον
καταστρέψαι Ἰούδα προδότου δίκην
...οἷον ἐπίτροπόν τινα Θεόδοτον πολὺς
αἱρεῖ λόγος...τετελευτήκασι Μοντανός τε
καὶ Θεόδοτος καὶ ἡ προειρημένη γυνή.
Thus he must have had before him a
text of Eusebius which omitted the
words δή τις at the commencement, as
they are omitted in some existing
MSS (see above, p. 56, note); and accordingly he ascribed all the treatises
to Apollinaris. The parallels are

taken from the first and second treatises; the first might have been written
by Apollinaris, but the second was
certainly not by his hand, as it refers to much later events (see above,
p. 56).

Hefele (*Conciliengeschichte* I. p. 71)
places the date of this council before A.D. 150. But if the testimony
of Eusebius is worth anything, this is
impossible; for he states that the
writings of Claudius Apollinaris a-
gainst the Montanists were later than
his Apology to M. Aurelius (see p. 59,
note 6), and this Apology was not
written till after A.D. 174 (see p. 61,
note 1). The chronology of Montanism
is very perplexing, but Hefele's dates
appear to be much too early. The
Chronicon of Eusebius gives the rise
of Montanism under A.D. 172 or 173,
and this statement is consistent with
the notices in his History. But if
this date be correct, it most probably
refers to Montanism as a distinct
system; and the fires had probably
been smouldering within the Church
for some time before they broke out.
It will be observed that the writer
of the Synodicon identifies Theodotus
the Montanist (see Euseb. *H. E.* v. 3)
with Theodotus the leather-seller who
was a Monarchian. There is no authority for this identification in Eusebius.

[2] Theodoret. *H. F.* i. 21.
[3] Socr. *H. E.* iii. 7.

practice of the Church generally found in him a vigorous advocate, who was equally opposed to the novelties of heretical teaching and to the rigours of overstrained asceticism.

Nor again did Apollinaris restrict himself to controversies carried on between Christian and Christian. He appears alike as the champion of the Gospel against attacks from without, and as the promoter of Christian life and devotion within the pale of the Church. On the one hand he was the author of an apology addressed to M. Aurelius[1], of a controversial treatise in five books against the Greeks, and of a second in two books against the Jews[2]; on the other we find mentioned among his writings a work in two books *on Truth*, and a second *on Piety*, besides several of which the titles have not come down to us[3]. He seems indeed to have written on almost every subject which interested the Church of his age. He was not only well versed in the Scriptures, but showed a wide acquaintance with secular

His apologetic

and didactic works.

---

[1] Euseb. *H. E.* iv. 26, 27. He referred in this Apology to the incident of the so-called Thundering Legion, which happened A. D. 174; and as reported by Eusebius (*H. E.* v. 5), he stated that the legion was thus named by the emperor in commemoration of this miraculous thunderstorm. As a contemporary however, he must probably have known that the title *Legio Fulminata* existed long before; and we may conjecture that he used some ambiguous expression implying that it was fitly so named (*e.g. ἐπώνυμον τῆς συντυχίας*), which Eusebius and later writers misunderstood; just as Eusebius himself (v. 24) speaks of Irenæus as *φερώνυμός τις ὢν τῇ προσηγορίᾳ αὐτῷ τε τῷ τρόπῳ εἰρηνοποιός*. Of the words used by Eusebius, *οἰκείαν τῷ γεγονότι πρὸς τοῦ βασιλέως εἰληφέναι προσηγορίαν*, we may suspect that *οἰκείαν τῷ γεγονότι προσηγορίαν* is an expression borrowed from Apollinaris himself, while *πρὸς τοῦ βασιλέως εἰληφέναι* gives Eusebius' own erroneous

interpretation of his author's meaning.

The name of this legion was *Fulminata*, not *Fulminatrix*, as it is often carelessly written out, where the inscriptions have merely FVLM.; see Becker and Marquardt *Röm. Alterth.* III. 2, p. 353.

[2] The words *καὶ πρὸς Ἰουδαίους πρῶτον καὶ δεύτερον* are omitted in some MSS and by Rufinus. They are found however in the very ancient Syriac version, and are doubtless genuine. Their omission is due to the homœoteleuton, as they are immediately preceded by *καὶ περὶ ἀληθείας πρῶτον καὶ δεύτερον*.

[3] A list of his works is given by Eusebius (*H. E.* iv. 27), who explains that there were many others which he had not seen. This list omits the work on the Paschal Feast, which is quoted in the *Chronicon Paschale* p. 13 (ed. Dind.), and the treatise *on Piety*, of which we know from Photius *Bibl.* 14.

literature also[1]. His style is praised by a competent judge[2], and his orthodoxy was such as to satisfy the dogmatic precision of the post-Nicene age[3].

These facts are not unimportant in their bearing on the question which has already been discussed in relation to Papias. *Important bearing of these facts on the history of Christianity.* If there had been such a discontinuity of doctrine and practice in the Church of Hierapolis as the theory in question assumes, if the Pauline Gospel was repudiated in the later years of the first century and rank Judaism adopted in its stead, how can we explain the position of Apollinaris? Obviously a counter-revolution must have taken place, which undid the effects of the former. One dislocation must have been compensated by another. And yet Irenæus knows nothing of these religious convulsions which must have shaken the doctrine of the Church to its foundations, but represents the tradition as one, continuous, unbroken, reaching back through the elders of the Asiatic Churches, through Papias and Polycarp, to St John himself— Irenæus who received his Christian education in Asia Minor, who throughout life was in communication with the churches there, and who had already reached middle age when this second revolution is supposed to have occurred. The demands on our credulity, which this theory makes, are enormous. And its improbability becomes only the more glaring, as we extend our view. *Solidarity of the Church in the second century.* For the *solidarity* of the Church is the one striking fact unmistakably revealed to us, as here and there the veil which shrouds the history of the second century is lifted. Anicetus and Soter and Eleutherus and Victor at Rome, Pantænus and Clement at Alexandria, Polycrates at Ephesus, Papias and Apollinaris at Hierapolis, Polycarp at Smyrna, Melito at Sardis, Ignatius and Serapion at Antioch, Primus and Dionysius at Corinth, Pothinus and Irenæus in Gaul, Philippus

---

[1] Theodoret. *Hær. Fab.* iii. 2 ἀνὴρ ἀξιέπαινος καὶ πρὸς τῇ γνώσει τῶν θείων καὶ τὴν ἔξωθεν παιδείαν προσειληφώς. So too Jerome, *Ep.* 70 (I. p. 428, ed. Vallarsi), names him among those who were equally versed in sacred and pro-

fane literature.

[2] Photius l. c., ἀξιόλογος δὲ ὁ ἀνὴρ καὶ φράσει ἀξιολόγῳ κεχρημένος.

[3] Euseb. *H. E.* iv. 21, Jerome l. c., Theodoret. l. c., Socr. *H. E.* iii. 7.

and Pinytus in Crete, Hegesippus and Narcissus in Palestine, all are bound together by the ties of a common organization and the sympathy of a common creed. The Paschal controversy is especially valuable, as showing the limits of divergence consistent with the unity of the Church. The study of this controversy teaches us to appreciate with ever-increasing force the pregnant saying of Irenæus that the difference of the usage establishes the harmony of the faith[1].

Though Laodicea cannot show the same intellectual activity as Hierapolis, yet in practical energy she is not wanting. *Activity of Laodicea.*

One of those fitful persecutions, which sullied the rule of the imperial Stoic, deprived Laodicea of her bishop Sagaris[2]. The exact date of his martyrdom is not known; but we cannot be far wrong in assigning it to an early year in the reign of M. Aurelius[3]. His name appears to have been held in great honour[4]. *Martyrdom of Sagaris. c. A.D. 165.*

But while the Church of Laodicea was thus contending against foes without, she was also torn asunder by feuds within. Coincident with the martyrdom of Sagaris was the outburst of the Paschal controversy, of which mention has been already made, and which for more than a century and a half disturbed the peace of the Church, until it was finally laid at rest by the *Outbreak of the Paschal controversy.*

---

[1] Iren. in Euseb. *H. E.* v. 24 ἡ διαφωνία τῆς νηστείας (the fast which preceded the Paschal festival) τὴν ὁμόνοιαν τῆς πίστεως συνίστησι.

[2] Melito in Euseb. *H. E.* iv. 26 ἐπὶ Σερουιλλίου Παύλου ἀνθυπάτου τῆς Ἀσίας, ᾧ Σάγαρις καιρῷ ἐμαρτύρησεν, ἐγένετο ζήτησις πολλὴ ἐν Λαοδικείᾳ περὶ τοῦ πάσχα ἐμπεσόντος κατὰ καιρὸν ἐν ἐκείναις ταῖς ἡμέραις, καὶ ἐγράφη ταῦτα (*i. e.* Melito's own treatise on the Paschal festival).

[3] The proconsulate of Paullus, under whom this martyrdom took place, is dated by Borghesi (*Œuvres* viii. p. 507) somewhere between A.D. 163—168; by Waddington (*Fastes des Provinces Asiatiques* p. 731, in Le Bas and Waddington *Voyage Archéologique etc.*) probably

A.D. 164—166. This rests on the assumption that the *Servillius Paullus* here named must be identified with *L. Sergius Paullus* of the inscriptions. The name *Sergius* is elsewhere confounded with *Servius* (*Servillius*) (see Borghesi iv. p. 493, viii. p. 504, Mommsen *Röm. Forsch.* i. p. 8, *Ephem. Epigr.* ii. p. 338.). The mistake must have been introduced very early into the text of Eusebius. All the Greek mss have *Servillius* (*Servilius*), and so it is given in the Syriac Version. Ruffinus however writes it correctly *Sergius*.

[4] Besides Melito (l. c.), Polycrates of Ephesus refers to him with respect; Euseb. *H. E.* v. 24, τί δὲ δεῖ λέγειν Σάγαριν ἐπίσκοπον καὶ μάρτυρα, ὃς ἐν Λαοδικείᾳ κεκοίμηται.

Council of Nicæa.   The Laodiceans would naturally regulate their festival by the Asiatic or Quartodeciman usage, strictly observing the day of the month and disregarding the day of the week.   But a great commercial centre like Laodicea must have attracted large crowds of foreign Christians from Palestine or Egypt or Rome or Gaul, who were accustomed to commemorate the Passion always on a Friday and the Resurrection on a Sunday according to the western practice; and in this way probably the dispute arose.   The treatise *on the Paschal Festival* by Melito of Sardis was written on this occasion to defend the Asiatic practice.   The fact that Laodicea became the head-quarters of the controversy is a speaking testimony to the prominence of this Church in the latter half of the second century.

Hierapolis and Laodicea in later history.

At a later date the influence of both Hierapolis and Laodicea has sensibly declined.   In the great controversies of the fourth and fifth centuries they take no conspicuous part.   Among their bishops there is not one who has left his mark on history.   And yet their names appear at most of the great Councils, in which

The *Arian* heresy. NICÆA A.D. 325.

they bear a silent part.   At Nicæa Hierapolis was represented by Flaccus[1], Laodicea by Nunechius[2].   They both acquiesced in its decrees, and the latter as metropolitan published them throughout the Phrygian Churches[3].   Soon after, both sees

Philippopolis A.D. 347.

lapsed into Arianism.   At the synod of Philippopolis, composed of bishops who had seceded from the Council of Sardica, the representatives of these two sees were present and joined in the condemnation of the Athanasians.   On this occasion Hierapolis was still represented by Flaccus, who had thus turned traitor to his former faith[4].   On the other hand Laodicea had changed its bishop twice meanwhile.   Cecropius had won the

[1] Labb. *Conc.* II. 57, 62, ed. Coleti; Cowper's *Syriac Miscellanies* p. 11, 28. It is remarkable that after Papias all the early bishops of Hierapolis of whom we hear have Roman names; Avircius Marcellus (?), Claudius Apollinaris, Flaccus, Lucius, Venantius.

[2] Labb. *Conc.* II. 57, 62; Cowper's *Syriac Miscellanies* pp. 11, 28, 34.   He had also been present at the Synod of Ancyra held about A.D. 314 (see *Galatians* p. 34); *ib.* p. 41.

[3] Labb. *Conc.* II. 236.

[4] *ib.* 744.

imperial favour by his abuse of the orthodox party, and was first promoted to Laodicea, whence he was translated to Nicomedia[1]. He was succeeded by Nonnius, who signed the Arian decree at Philippopolis[2]. When these sees recovered their orthodoxy we do not know; but it is perhaps a significant fact, that neither is represented at the second general Council, held at Constantinople (A.D. 381)[3]. At the third general Council, which met at Ephesus, Laodicea is represented by Aristonicus, Hierapolis by Venantius[4]. Both bishops sign the decrees condemning Nestorius. Again in the next Christological controversy which agitated the Church the two sees bear their part. At the notorious Robbers' Synod, held also at Ephesus, Laodicea was represented by another Nunechius, Hierapolis by Stephanus. Both bishops committed themselves to the policy of Dioscorus and the opinions of the heretic Eutyches[5]. Yet with the fickleness which characterized these sees at an earlier date during the Arian controversy, we find their representatives two years later at the Council of Chalcedon siding with the orthodox party and condemning the Eutychian heresy which they had

[CONSTAN-
TINOPLE.
A.D. 381.]

The *Nestorian* and *Eutychian* heresies.
EPHESUS.
A.D. 431.

Latrocinium.
A.D. 449.

CHALCE-
DON.
A.D. 451.

---

[1] Athanas. *ad Episc. Ægypt.* 8 (*Op.* I. p. 219), *Hist. Arian. ad Mon.* 74 (*ib.* p. 307).

[2] Labb. *Conc.* II. 744.

[3] Cowper's *Syriac Miscell.* p. 39.

[4] Labb. *Conc.* III. 1085, 1222, Mans. *Conc.* IV. 1367. The name of this bishop of Hierapolis is variously written, but Venantius seems to be the true orthography. For some unexplained reason, though present in person, he signs by deputy. He had before subscribed the protest to Cyril against commencing the proceedings before the arrival of John of Antioch (Mans. *Conc.* V. 767), and perhaps his acquiescence in the decisions of the Council was not very hearty.

[5] Labb. *Conc.* IV. 892, 925, 928, 1107, 1170, 1171, 1185. In the Acts of this heretical council, as occasion-

ally in those of the Council of Chalcedon, Laodicea is surnamed *Trimitaria* (see above, p. 18, note 2). Following Le Quien (*Or. Christ.* I. p. 835), I have assumed the Stephanus who was present at the *Latrocinium* to have been bishop of the *Phrygian* Hierapolis, though I have not found any decisive indication which Hierapolis is meant. On the other hand the bishop of the *Syrian* Hierapolis at this time certainly bore the name Stephanus (Labb. *Conc.* IV. 727, 1506, [1550], 1644, 1836, v. 46); and the synod held under Stephanus A.D. 445, which Wiltsch (*Geography and Statistics of the Church* I. p. 170, Eng. Trans.) assigns to our Hierapolis, belongs to the Syrian city of the same name, as the connexion with Perrha shews: Labb. *Conc.* IV. 727, 1644.

so lately supported[1]. Nunechius is still bishop of Laodicea, and reverses his former vote. Stephanus has been succeeded at Hierapolis by Abercius, whose orthodoxy, so far as we know, had not been compromised by any previous expression of opinion[2].

Later vacillation of these sees.

The history of these churches at a later date is such as might have been anticipated from their attitude during the period of the first Four General Councils. The sees of Laodicea and Hierapolis, one or both, are represented at all the more important assemblies of the Church; and the same vacillation and infirmity of purpose, which had characterized their holders in the earlier councils, marks the proceedings of their later successors[3].

Their comparative unimportance.

But, though the two sees thus continue to bear witness to their existence by the repeated presence of their occupants at councils and synods, yet the real influence of Laodicea and Hierapolis on the Church at large has terminated with the close of the second century. On one occasion only did either community assume a position of prominence. About the middle of the fourth century a council was held at Laodicea[4]. It

COUNCIL OF LAODICEA an exception.

---

[1] Labb. *Conc.* IV. 853, 862, 1195, 1204, 1241, 1312, 1337, 1383, 1392, 1444, 1445, 1463, 1480, 1481, 1496, 1501, 1505, 1716, 1732, 1736, 1744, 1746, 1751.

[2] The bishops of both sees are addressed by the Emperor Leo in his letter respecting the Council of Chalcedon: but their replies are not preserved. Nunechius is still bishop of Laodicea; but Hierapolis has again changed hands, and Philippus has succeeded Abercius (Labb. *Conc.* IV. 1836 sq.). Nunechius of Laodicea was one of those who signed the decree against simony at the Council of Constantinople (A.D. 459): *Conc.* V. 50.

[3] See for instance the tergiversation of Theodorus of Laodicea and Ignatius of Hierapolis in the matter of Photius and the 8th General Council.

[4] This council cannot have been held earlier than the year 344, as the 7th canon makes mention of the Photinians, and Photinus did not attract notice before that year: see Hefele, *Conciliengesch.* I. p. 722 sq. In the ancient lists of Councils it stands after that of Antioch (A.D. 341), and before that of Constantinople (A.D. 381). Dr Westcott (*History of the Canon* p. 400) is inclined to place it about A.D. 363, and this is the time very generally adopted.

Here however a difficulty presents itself, which has not been noticed hitherto. In the Syriac MS *Brit. Mus.* Add. 14,528, are lists of the bishops present at the earlier councils, including Laodicea (see Wright's *Catalogue of the Syriac MSS in the British Museum,* DCCCVI, p. 1030 sq.). These lists have been published by Cowper (*Syriac Miscell.* p. 42 sq., *Analecta Nicæna*

was convened more especially to settle some points of ecclesi- Its decree
astical discipline; but incidentally the assembled bishops were on the Canon.
led to make an order respecting the Canon of Scripture[1]. As

p. 36), who however has transposed the lists of Antioch and Laodicea, so that he ascribes to the Antiochian Synod the names which really belong to the Laodicean. This is determined (as I am informed by Prof. Wright) by the position of the lists.

The Laodicean list then, which seems to be imperfect, contains twenty names; and, when examined, it yields these results. (1) At least three-fourths of the names can be identified with bishops who sat at Nicæa, and probably the exceptions would be fewer, if in some cases they had not been obscured by transcription into Syriac and by the errors of copyists. (2) When identified, they are found to belong in almost every instance to Cœlesyria, Phœnicia, Palestine, Cilicia, and Isauria, whereas apparently not one comes from Phrygia, Lydia, or the other western districts of Asia Minor.

Supposing that this is a genuine Laodicean list, we are led by the first result to place it as near in time as possible to the Council of Nicæa; and by the second to question whether after all the Syrian Laodicea may not have been meant instead of the Phrygian. On the other hand tradition is unanimous in placing this synod in the Phrygian town, and in this very Syriac MS the heading of the canons begins 'Of the Synod of Laodicea of Phrygia.' On the whole it appears probable that this supposed list of bishops who met at Laodicea belongs to some other Council. The Laodicean Synod seems to have been, as Dr Westcott describes it (l. c.), 'A small gathering of clergy from parts of Lydia and Phrygia.'

In a large mosaic work in the Church

at Bethlehem, in which all the more important councils are represented, we find the following inscription; ['H ἀγία σύνοδος ἡ ἐν Λαοδικείᾳ τῆς Φρυγίας τῶν κε ἐπισκόπων γέγονεν διὰ Μοντανὸν κὲ [τ]ὰ[ς] λοιπὰς ἐρέσεις· τού[τους] ὡς αἱρετικοὺς καὶ ἐχθροὺς τῆς ἀλεθείας ἡ ἀγία σύνοδος ἀνεθεμάτισεν (Ciampini de Sacr. Ædif. a Constant. constr. p. 156; comp. Boeckh Corp. Inscr. 8953). The mention of Montanus might suggest that this was one of those Asiatic synods held against Montanism at the end of the second or beginning of the third century. But no record of any such synod is preserved elsewhere, and, as all the other Councils commemorated in these mosaics are found in the list sanctioned by the Quinisextine Council, this can hardly have been an exception. The inscription must therefore refer to the well-known Council of Laodicea in the fourth century, which received this sanction. The description however is not very correct, for though Montanism is incidentally condemned in the eighth canon, yet this condemnation was not the main object of the council and occupies a very subordinate place. The Bethlehem mosaics were completed A.D. 1169. see Boeckh C. I. 8736.

[1] The canons of this Council, 59 in number, will be found in Labb. Conc. I. 1530 sq., ed. Coleti. The last of these forbids the reading of any but 'the Canonical books of the New and Old Testament.' To this is often appended (sometimes as a 60th canon) a list of the Canonical books; but Dr Westcott has shown that this list is a later addition and does not belong to the original decrees of the council (Canon p. 400 sq.).

this was the first occasion in which the subject had been brought formally before the notice of an ecclesiastical assembly, this Council of Laodicea secured a notoriety which it would not otherwise have obtained, and to which it was hardly entitled by its constitution or its proceedings. Its decrees were confirmed and adopted by later councils both in the East and in the West[1].

Its decrees illustrate the Epistle to the Colossians. More important however for my special purpose, than the influence of this synod on the Church at large, is the light which its canons throw on the heretical tendencies of this district, and on the warnings of St Paul in the Colossian Epistle. To illustrate this fact it will only be necessary to write out some of these canons at length:

Col. ii. 14, 16, 17. 29. 'It is not right for Christians to Judaize and abstain from labour on the sabbath, but to work on this same day. They should pay respect rather to the Lord's day, and, if possible, abstain from labour on it as Christians. But if they should be found Judaizers, let them be anathema in the sight of Christ.'

Col. ii. 18. 35. 'It is not right for Christians to abandon the Church of God and go away and invoke angels (ἀγγέλους ὀνομάζειν)[2]

---

[1] By the Quinisextine Council (A.D. 692) in the East (Labb. *Conc.* VII. 1345), and by the Synod of Aix-la-Chapelle (A.D. 789) in the West (*Conc.* IX. 10 sq.).

[2] Theodoret about a century after the Laodicean Council, commenting on Col. ii. 18, states that this disease (τὸ πάθος) which St Paul denounces 'long remained in Phrygia and Pisidia.' 'For this reason also,' he adds, 'a synod convened in Laodicea of Phrygia forbad by a decree the offering prayer to angels; and even to the present time oratories of the holy Michael may be seen among them and their neighbours.' See also below p. 70, note 3. A curious inscription, found in the theatre at Miletus (Boeckh *C. I.* 2895), illustrates this tendency. It is written in seven columns, each having a different planetary symbol, and a different permutation of the vowels with the same invocation, ΑΓΙΕ. ΦΥΛΑΤΟΝ. ΤΗΝ . ΠΟΛΙΝ . ΜΙΛΗCΙΩΝ . ΚΑΙ . ΠΑΝΤΑC · ΤΟΥC . ΚΑΤΟΙΚΟΥΝΤΑC, while at the common base is written ΑΡΧΑΓΓΕΛΟΙ . ΦΥΛΑCCΕΤΑΙ . Η . ΠΟΛΙC . ΜΙΛΗCΙΩΝ . ΚΑΙ . ΠΑΝΤΕC . ΟΙ . ΚΑΤ ... Boeckh writes, 'Etsi hic titulus Gnosticorum et Basilidianorum commentis prorsus congruus est, tamen potuit ab ethnicis Milesiis scriptus esse; quare nolui eum inter Christianos rejicere, quum praesertim publicae Milesiorum superstitionis docu-

and hold conventicles (συνάξεις ποιεῖν); for these things are forbidden. If therefore any one is found devoting himself to this secret idolatry, let him be anathema, because he abandoned our Lord Jesus Christ and went after idolatry.'

36. 'It is not right for priests or clergy to be magicians or enchanters or mathematicians or astrologers[1], or to make safeguards (φυλακτήρια) as they are called, for such things are prisons (δεσμωτήρια) of their souls[2]: and we have enjoined that they which wear them be cast out of the Church.'

37. 'It is not right to receive from Jews or heretics the festive offerings which they send about, nor to join in their festivals.'

38. 'It is not right to receive unleavened bread from the Jews or to participate in their impieties.'

It is strange, at this late date, to find still lingering in these churches the same readiness to be 'judged in respect of an holiday or a new moon or a sabbath,' with the same tendency to relinquish the hold of the Head and to substitute 'a voluntary humility and worshipping of angels,' which three centuries before had called forth the Apostle's rebuke and warning in the Epistle to the Colossians.

During the flourishing period of the Eastern Church, Laodicea appears as the metropolis of the province of Phrygia Pacatiana, counting among its suffragan bishoprics the see of Colossæ[3]. On the other hand Hierapolis, though only six miles distant, belonged to the neighbouring province of Phrygia Salutaris[4], whose metropolis was Synnada, and of which it was

Ecclesiastical status of Laodicea and Hierapolis.

---

mentum insigne sit.' The idea of the seven ἅγιοι, combined in the one ἀρχάγγελος, seems certainly to point to Jewish, if not Christian, influences: Rev. i. 4, iii. 1, iv. 5, v. 6.

[1] Though there is no direct mention of 'magic' in the letter to the Colossians, yet it was a characteristic tendency of this part of Asia: Acts xix. 19, 2 Tim. iii. 8, 13. See the note on Gal. v. 20. The term μαθη-

ματικοί is used in this decree in its ordinary sense of astrologers, soothsayers.

[2] A play on the double sense of φυλακτήριον (1) a safeguard or amulet, (2) a guard-house.

[3] A list of the bishoprics belonging to this province at the time of the Council of Chalcedon is given, Labb. Conc. IV. 1501, 1716.

[4] Conc. IV. 1716, 1744.

one of the most important sees. The stream of the Lycus
seems to have formed the boundary line between the two
ecclesiastical provinces. At a later date Hierapolis itself was
raised to metropolitan rank[1].

Obscurity
of Colossæ.

But while Laodicea and Hierapolis held the foremost place
in the records of the early Church, and continued to bear an
active, though inconspicuous part, in later Christian history,
Colossæ was from the very first a cipher. The town itself, as
we have seen, was already waning in importance, when the
Apostle wrote; and its subsequent decline seems to have been
rapid. Not a single event in Christian history is connected
with its name; and its very existence is only rescued from
oblivion, when at long intervals some bishop of Colossæ attaches his signature to the decree of an ecclesiastical synod.
The city ceased to strike coins in the reign of Gordian (A.D.

It is sup-
planted by
Chonæ.

238—244)[2]. It fell gradually into decay, being supplanted by
the neighbouring town Chonæ, the modern Chonos, so called
from the natural funnels by which the streams here disappear
in underground channels formed by the incrustations of travertine[3]. We may conjecture also that its ruin was hastened by

---

[1] At the 5th and 6th General Councils (A.D. 553 and A.D. 680) Hierapolis
is styled a metropolis (Labb. *Conc.* VI.
220, VII. 1068, 1097, 1117); and in the
latter case it is designated metropolis
of *Phrygia Pacatiana*, though this
same designation is still given to Laodicea. Synnada retains its position
as metropolis of *Phrygia Salutaris*.

From this time forward Hierapolis
seems always to hold metropolitan
rank. But no notice is preserved of
the circumstances under which the
change was made. In the *Notitiæ* it
generally occurs twice—first as a suffragan see of Phrygia Salutaris, and
secondly as metropolis of another
Phrygia Pacatiana (distinct from that
which has Laodicea for its metropolis):
Hieroclis Synecdemus et Notitiæ (ed.
Parthey) Not. 1, pp. 56, 57, 69, 73;

Not. 3, pp. 114, 124; Not. 7, pp. 152,
161; Not. 8, pp. 164, 176, 180; Not.
9, pp. 193, 197; Not. 10, pp. 212, 220.
In this latter position it is placed
quite out of the proper geographical
order, thus showing that its metropolitan jurisdiction was created comparatively late. The number of dioceses
in the province is generally given as
9; Nilus *ib.* p. 301. The name of the
province is variously corrupted from
Πακατιανῆς, e. g. Καππατιανῆς, Καππα-
δοκίας. Unless the ecclesiastical position of Hierapolis was altogether anomalous, as a province within a province, its double mention in the *Notitiæ* must be explained by a confusion
of its earlier and later status.

[2] See Mionnet IV. p. 269, Leake
Numism. Hellen. p. 45.

[3] Joannes Curopalata p. 686 (ed.

a renewed assault of its ancient enemy, the earthquake[1]. It is commonly said that Chonæ is built on the site of the ancient Colossæ; but the later town stands at some distance from the

Bonn.) φήμη ... τοὺς Τούρκους ἀπαγγέλλουσα τὴν ἐν Χώναις πολιτείαν καὶ αὐτὸν τὸν περιβόητον ἐν θαύμασι καὶ ἀναθήμασι τοῦ ἀρχιστρατήγου ναὸν καταλαβεῖν ἐν μαχαίρᾳ ... καὶ τὸ δὴ σχετλιώτερον, μηδὲ τὰς τοῦ χάσματος σήραγγας ἐν ᾧπερ οἱ παρρρέοντες ποταμοὶ ἐκεῖσε χωνευόμενοι διὰ τῆς τοῦ ἀρχιστρατήγου παλαιᾶς ἐπιδημίας καὶ θεοσημίας ὡς διὰ πρανοῦς ἀστατοῦν τὸ ῥεῦμα καὶ λιὰν εὐδρομοῦν ἔχουσι, τοὺς καταπεφευγότας διατηρῆσαι, κ.τ.λ.

The 'worship of angels' is curiously connected with the physical features of the country in the legend to which Curopalata refers. The people were in imminent danger from a sudden inundation of the Lycus, when the archangel Michael appeared and opened a chasm in the earth through which the waters flowed away harmlessly: Hartley's *Researches in Greece* p. 53. See another legend, or another version of the legend, in which the archangel interposes, in Laborde p. 103.

It was the birthplace of Nicetas Choniates, one of the most important of the Byzantine historians, who thus speaks of it (*de Manuel.* vi. 2, p. 230, ed. Bonn.); Φρυγίαν τε καὶ Λαοδίκειαν διελθὼν ἀφικνεῖται ἐς Χώνας, πόλιν εὐδαίμονα καὶ μεγάλην, πάλαι τὰς Κολασσάς, τὴν ἐμοῦ τοῦ συγγραφέως πατρίδα, καὶ τὸν ἀρχαγγελικὸν ναὸν εἰσιὼν μεγέθει μέγιστον καὶ κάλλει κάλλιστον ὄντα καὶ θαυμασίας χειρὸς ἅπαντα ἔργον κ.τ.λ., where a corrupt reading Παλασσὰς for Κολασσὰς had misled some. It will be remembered that the words πόλιν εὐδαίμονα καὶ μεγάλην are borrowed from Xenophon's description of Colossæ (*Anab.* i. 2. 6): see above, p. 15, note 3.

He again alludes to his native place, *de Isaac.* ii. 2, pp. 52, 3 τοὺς Λαοδικεῖς

δὲ Φρύγας μυριαχῶς ἐκάκωσεν, ὥσπερ καὶ τοὺς τῶν Χωνῶν τῶν ἐμῶν οἰκήτορας, and *Urbs Capta* 16, p. 842, τὸ δὲ ἦν ἐμοῦ τοῦ συγγραφέως Νικήτα πατρὶς αἱ Χῶναι καὶ ἡ ἀγχιτέρμων ταύτῃ Φρυγικὴ Λαοδίκεια.

[1] We may conjecture that it was the disastrous earthquake under Gallienus (A.D. 262) which proved fatal to Colossæ (see above p. 38, note 1). This is consistent with the fact above mentioned that no Colossian coins later than Gordian are extant. We read indeed of an earthquake in the reign of Gordian himself 'eo usque gravis ut civitates etiam terræ hiatu deperirent' (Capitol. *Vit. Gord.* 26), but we are not informed of the localities affected by it. When St Chrysostom wrote, the city existed no longer, as may be inferred from his comment (XI. p. 323) Ἡ πόλις τῆς Φρυγίας ἦν· καὶ δῆλον ἐκ τοῦ τὴν Λαοδίκειαν πλησίον εἶναι.

On the other hand M. Renan (*L'Antechrist* p. 99) says of the earthquake under *Nero*, 'Colosses ne sut se relever; elle disparut presque du nombre des églises'; and he adds in a note 'Colosses n'a pas de monnaies impériales [Waddington].' For this statement there is, I believe, no authority; and as regards the coins it is certainly wrong.

Earthquakes have been largely instrumental in changing the sites of cities situated within the range of their influence. Of this we have an instance in the neighbourhood of Colossæ. Hamilton (I. p. 514) reports that an earthquake which occurred at Denizli about a hundred years ago caused the inhabitants to remove their residences to a different locality, where they have remained ever since.

earlier, as Salisbury does from Old Sarum. The episcopal
see necessarily followed the population; though for some time
after its removal to the new town the bishop still continued
to use the older title, with or without the addition of Chonæ
by way of explanation, till at length the name of this primitive
Apostolic Church passes wholly out of sight[1].

Turkish
conquest.
The Turkish conquest pressed with more than common
severity on these districts. When the day of visitation came,
the Church was taken by surprise. Occupied with ignoble
quarrels and selfish interests, she had no ear for the voice of
Him who demanded admission. The door was barred and
the knock unheeded. The long-impending doom overtook
her, and the golden candlestick was removed for ever from
the Eternal Presence[2].

[1] At the Council of Chalcedon (A.D.
451) Nunechius of Laodicea subscribes
'for the absent bishops under him,'
among whom is mentioned Ἐπιφανίου
πόλεως Κολασσῶν (Labb. *Conc.* IV. 1501,
ed. Coleti; comp. *ib.* 1745). At the
Quinisextine Council (A.D. 692) occurs
the signature of Κοσμᾶς ἐπίσκοπος πόλεως Κολασσᾶς (*sic*) Πακατιανῆς (*Conc.*
VII. 1408). At the 2nd Council of
Nicæa (A.D. 787) the name of the see
is in a transition state; the bishop
Theodosius (or Dositheus) signs himself sometimes Χωνῶν ἤτοι Κολασσῶν,
sometimes Χωνῶν simply (*Conc.* VIII.

689, 796, 988, 1200, 1222, 1357, 1378,
1432, 1523, 1533, in many of which
passages the word Χωνῶν is grossly
corrupted). At later Councils the see
is called Χῶναι; and this is the name
which it bears in the *Notitiæ* (pp. 97,
127, 199, 222, 303, ed. Parthey).

[2] For the remains of Christian
churches at Laodicea see Fellows *Asia
Minor* p. 282, Pococke p. 74. A description of three fine churches at
Hierapolis is given in Fergusson's *Illustrated Handbook of Architecture* II.
p. 967 sq.; comp. Texier *Asie Mineure*
I. p. 143.

II.

THE COLOSSIAN HERESY.

FROM the language of St Paul, addressed to the Church Two elements in the Colossian heresy. of Colossæ, we may infer the presence of two disturbing elements which threatened the purity of Christian faith and practice in this community. These elements are distinguishable in themselves, though it does not follow that they present the teaching of two distinct parties.

1. A mere glance at the epistle suffices to detect the 1. JUDAIC. presence of JUDAISM in the teaching which the Apostle combats. The observance of sabbaths and new moons is decisive in this respect. The distinction of meats and drinks points in the same direction[1]. Even the enforcement of the initiatory rite of Judaism may be inferred from the contrast implied in St Paul's recommendation of the spiritual circumcision[2].

2. On the other hand a closer examination of its language 2. GNOSTIC. shows that these Judaic features do not exhaust the portraiture of the heresy or heresies against which the epistle is directed. We discern an element of theosophic speculation, which is alien to the spirit of Judaism proper. We are confronted with a shadowy mysticism, which loses itself in the contemplation of the unseen world. We discover a tendency to interpose certain spiritual agencies, intermediate beings, between God and man, as the instruments of communication and the objects of worship[3]. Anticipating the result which will appear more clearly hereafter, we may say that along

---

[1] Col. ii. 16, 17, 21 sq.   [2] ii. 11.   [3] ii. 4, 8, 18, 23.

with its Judaism there was a GNOSTIC element in the false teaching which prevailed at Colossæ.

Are these combined or separate?

Have we then two heresies here, or one only? Were these elements distinct, or were they fused into the same system? In other words, Is St Paul controverting a phase of Judaism on the one hand, and a phase of Gnosticism on the other; or did he find himself in conflict with a Judæo-Gnostic heresy which combined the two[1]?

General reasons for supposing one heresy only, in which they are fused.

On closer examination we find ourselves compelled to adopt the latter alternative. The epistle itself contains no hint that the Apostle has more than one set of antagonists in view; and the needless multiplication of persons or events is always to be deprecated in historical criticism. Nor indeed does the hypothesis of a single complex heresy present any

---

[1] The Colossian heresy has been made the subject of special dissertations by SCHNECKENBURGER *Beiträge zur Einleitung ins N. T.* (Stuttgart 1832), and *Ueber das Alter der jüdischen Proselyten-Taufe, nebst einer Beilage über die Irrlehrer zu Colossä* (Berlin 1828); by OSIANDER *Ueber die Colossischen Irrlehrer* (*Tübinger Zeitschrift* for 1834, III. p. 96 sq.); and by RHEINWALD *De Pseudodoctoribus Colossensibus* (Bonn 1834). But more valuable contributions to the subject will often be found in introductions to the commentaries on the epistle. Those of BLEEK, DAVIES, MEYER, OLSHAUSEN, STEIGER, and DE WETTE may be mentioned. Among other works which may be consulted are BAUR *Der Apostel Paulus* p. 417 sq.; BOEHMER *Isagoge in Epistolam ad Colossenses*, Berlin 1829, p. 56 sq., p. 277 sq.; BURTON *Inquiry into the Heresies of the Apostolic Age*, Lectures IV, V; EWALD *Die Sendschreiben des Apostels Paulus* p. 462 sq.; HILGENFELD *Der Gnosticismus u. das Neue Testament* in the *Zeitschr. f. Wissensch.*

Theol. XIII. p. 233 sq.; R. A. LIPSIUS in *Schenkels Bibel-Lexicon*, s. v. Gnosis; MAYERHOFF *Der Brief an die Colosser* p. 107 sq.; NEANDER *Planting of the Christian Church* I. p. 319 sq. (Eng. Trans.); PRESSENSE *Trois Premiers Siècles* II. p. 194 sq.; STORR *Opuscula* II. p. 149 sq.; THIERSCH *Die Kirche im Apostolischen Zeitalter* p. 146 sq. Of all the accounts of these Colossian false teachers, I have found none more satisfactory than that of Neander, whose opinions are followed in the main by the most sober of later writers.

In the investigation which follows I have assumed that the Colossian false teachers were Christians in some sense. The views maintained by some earlier critics, who regarded them as (1) Jews, or (2) Greek philosophers, or (3) Chaldean magi, have found no favour and do not need serious consideration. See Meyer's introduction for an enumeration of such views. A refutation of them will be found in Bleek's *Vorlesungen* p. 12 sq.

real difficulty. If the two elements seem irreconcilable, or at least incongruous, at first sight, the incongruity disappears on further examination. It will be shown in the course of this investigation, that some special tendencies of religious thought among the Jews themselves before and about this time prepared the way for such a combination in a Christian community like the Church of Colossæ [1]. Moreover we shall find that the Christian heresies of the next succeeding ages exhibit in a more developed form the same complex type, which here appears in its nascent state [2]; this later development not only showing that the combination was historically possible in itself, but likewise presupposing some earlier stage of its existence such as confronts us at Colossæ.

But in fact the Apostle's language hardly leaves the question open. The two elements are so closely interwoven in his refutation, that it is impossible to separate them. He passes backwards and forwards from the one to the other in such a way as to show that they are only parts of one complex whole. On this point the logical connexion of the sentences is decisive: 'Beware lest any man make spoil of you through philosophy and vain deceit after the tradition of men, after the rudiments of the world...Ye were circumcised with a circumcision not made with hands...And you...did He quicken,...blotting out the handwriting of ordinances which was against you...Let no man therefore judge you in meat or drink, or in respect of a holy day or a new moon or a sabbath...Let no man beguile you of your prize in a self-imposed humility and service of angels...If ye died with Christ from the rudiments of the world, why...are ye subject to ordinances...which things have a show of wisdom in self-imposed service and humility and hard treatment of the body, but are of no value against indulgence of the flesh [3].' Here

S. Paul's language is decisive on this point.

---

[1] See below, p. 83 sq.
[2] See below, p. 107 sq.
[3] Col. ii. 8—23. Hilgenfeld (*Der Gnosticismus* etc. p. 250 sq.) contends strenuously for the separation of the two

elements. He argues that 'these two tendencies are related to one another as fire and water, and nothing stands in the way of allowing the author after the first side-glance at the Gnostics to

the superior wisdom, the speculative element which is characteristic of Gnosticism, and the ritual observance, the practical element which was supplied by Judaism, are regarded not only as springing from the same stem, but also as intertwined in their growth. And the more carefully we examine the sequence of the Apostle's thoughts, the more intimate will the connexion appear.

Gnosticism must be defined and described. Having described the speculative element in this complex heresy provisionally as Gnostic, I purpose enquiring in the first place, how far Judaism prior to and independently of Christianity had allied itself with Gnostic modes of thought; and afterwards, whether the description of the Colossian heresy is such as to justify us in thus classing it as a species of Gnosticism. But, as a preliminary to these enquiries, some definition of the word, or at least some conception of the leading ideas which it involves, will be necessary. With its complex varieties and elaborate developments we have no concern here: for, if Gnosticism can be found at all in the records of the

pass over with ver. 11 to the Judaizers, with whom Col. ii. 16 sq. is exclusively concerned.' He supposes therefore that ii. 8—10 refers to 'pure Gnostics,' and ii. 16—23 to 'pure Judaizers.' To this it is sufficient to answer (1) That, if the two elements be so antagonistic, they managed nevertheless to reconcile their differences; for we find them united in several Judæo-Gnostic heresies in the first half of the second century, ξυνώμοσαν γάρ, ὄντες ἔχθιστοι τὸ πρίν, πῦρ καὶ θάλασσα, καὶ τὰ πίστ᾽ ἐδειξάτην; (2) That the two passages are directly connected together by τὰ στοιχεῖα τοῦ κόσμου, which occurs in both vv. 8, 20; (3) That it is not a simple transition once for all from the Gnostic to the Judaic element, but the epistle passes to and fro several times from the one to the other; while no hint is given that two

separate heresies are attacked, but on the contrary the sentences are connected in a logical sequence (e.g. ver. 9 ὅτι, 10 ὅς, 11 ἐν ᾧ, 12 ἐν ᾧ, 13 καί, 16 οὖν). I hope to make this point clear in my notes on the passage.

The hypothesis of more than one heresy is maintained also by Heinrichs (Koppe N. T. VII. Part 2, 1803). At an earlier date it seems to be favoured by Grotius (notes on ii. 16, 21); but his language is not very explicit. And earlier still Calvin in his argument to the epistle writes, 'Putant aliqui duo fuisse hominum genera, qui abducere tentarent Colossenses ab evangelii puritate,' but rejects this view as uncalled for.

The same question is raised with regard to the heretical teachers of the Pastoral Epistles, and should probably be answered in the same way.

Apostolic age, it will obviously appear in a simple and elementary form. Divested of its accessories and presented in its barest outline, it is not difficult of delineation [1].

1. As the name attests [2], Gnosticism implies the possession of a superior wisdom, which is hidden from others. It makes a distinction between the select few who have this higher gift, and the vulgar many who are without it. Faith, blind faith, suffices the latter, while knowledge is the exclusive possession of the former. Thus it recognises a separation of intellectual *caste* in religion, introducing the distinction of an esoteric and an exoteric doctrine, and interposing an initiation of some kind or other between the two classes. In short it is animated by the exclusive *aristocratic* spirit [3], which distinguishes the ancient religions, and from which it was a main function of Christianity to deliver mankind.

1. Intellectual exclusiveness of Gnosticism.

2. This was its spirit; and the intellectual questions, on which its energies were concentrated and to which it professed to hold the key, were mainly twofold. How can the work of creation be explained? and, How are we to account for the existence of evil [4]? To reconcile the creation of the world and the existence of evil with the conception of God as the absolute Being, was the problem which all the Gnostic systems set themselves to solve. It will be seen that the two questions cannot be treated independently but have a very close and intimate connexion with each other.

2. Speculative tenets of Gnosticism.

Creation of the world, and existence of evil.

---

[1] The chief authorities for the history of Gnosticism are NEANDER *Church History* II. p. 1 sq.; BAUR *Die Christliche Gnosis* (Tübingen, 1835); MATTER *Histoire Critique du Gnosticisme* (2nd ed., Strasbourg and Paris, 1843); R. A. LIPSIUS *Gnosticismus* in Ersch u. Gruber *s. v.* (Leipzig, 1860); MANSEL *Gnostic Heresies of the First and Second Centuries* (London, 1875); and for Gnostic art, KING *Gnostics and their Remains* (London 1864).

[2] See esp. Iren. i. 6. 1 sq., Clem. Alex. *Strom.* ii. p. 433 sq. (Potter). On the words τέλειοι, πνευματικοί, by which they designated the possessors of this higher *gnosis*, see the notes on Col. i. 28, and Phil. iii. 15.

[3] See Neander l. c. p. 1 sq., from whom the epithet is borrowed.

[4] The fathers speak of this as the main question about which the Gnostics busy themselves; *Unde malum?* πόθεν ἡ κακία; Tertull. *de Præscr.* 7, adv. Marc. I. 2, Eus. *H. E.* v. 27; passages quoted by Baur *Christliche Gnosis* p. 19. On the leading conceptions of Gnosticism see especially Neander, l. c. p. 9 sq.

Existence of evil, how to be explained? The Gnostic argument ran as follows: Did God create the world out of nothing, evolve it from Himself? Then, God being perfectly good and creation having resulted from His sole act without any opposing or modifying influence, evil would have been impossible; for otherwise we are driven to the conclusion that God created evil.

Matter the abode of evil. This solution being rejected as impossible, the Gnostic was obliged to postulate some antagonistic principle independent of God, by which His creative energy was thwarted and limited. This opposing principle, the kingdom of evil, he conceived to be the world of matter. The precise idea of its mode of operation varies in different Gnostic systems. It is sometimes regarded as a dead passive resistance, sometimes as a turbulent active power. But, though the exact point of view may shift, the object contemplated is always the same. In some way or other evil is regarded as residing in the material, sensible world. Thus Gnostic speculation on the existence of evil ends in a dualism.

Creation, how to be explained? This point being conceded, the ulterior question arises: How then is creation possible? How can the Infinite communicate with the Finite, the Good with the Evil? How can God act upon matter? God is perfect, absolute, incomprehensible.

Doctrine of emana- tions. This, the Gnostic went on to argue, could only have been possible by some self-limitation on the part of God. God must express Himself in some way. There must be some evolution, some effluence, of Deity. Thus the Divine Being germinates, as it were; and the first germination again evolves a second from itself in like manner. In this way we obtain a series of successive emanations, which may be more or fewer, as the requirements of any particular system demand. In each successive evolution the Divine element is feebler. They sink gradually lower and lower in the scale, as they are farther removed from their source; until at length contact with matter is possible, and creation ensues. These are the emanations, æons, spirits, or angels, of Gnosticism, conceived as more or less concrete and personal according to the different aspects in which they are regarded in different systems.

3. Such is the bare outline (and nothing more is needed for my immediate purpose) of the speculative views of Gnosticism. But it is obvious that these views must have exerted a powerful influence on the ethical systems of their advocates, and thus they would involve important practical consequences. If matter is the principle of evil, it is of infinite moment for a man to know how he can avoid its baneful influence and thus keep his higher nature unclogged and unsullied.

3. Practical errors of Gnosticism.

To this practical question two directly opposite answers were given[1]:

Two opposite ethical rules.

(i) On the one hand, it was contended that the desired end might best be attained by a rigorous abstinence. Thus communication with matter, if it could not be entirely avoided, might be reduced to a minimum. Its grosser defilements at all events would be escaped. The material part of man would be subdued and mortified, if it could not be annihilated; and the spirit, thus set free, would be sublimated, and rise to its proper level. Thus the ethics of Gnosticism pointed in the first instance to a strict *asceticism*.

(i) Rigid asceticism.

(ii) But obviously the results thus attained are very slight and inadequate. Matter is about us everywhere. We do but touch the skirts of the evil, when we endeavour to fence ourselves about by prohibitive ordinances, as, for instance, when we enjoin a spare diet or forbid marriage. Some more comprehensive rule is wanted, which shall apply to every contingency and every moment of our lives. Arguing in this way, other Gnostic teachers arrived at an ethical rule directly opposed to the former. 'Cultivate an entire indifference,' they said, 'to the world of sense. Do not give it a thought one way or

(ii) Unrestrained license.

---

[1] On this point see Clem. *Strom.* iii. 5 (p. 529) εἰς δύο διελόντες πράγματα ἁπάσας τὰς αἱρέσεις ἀποκρινώμεθα αὐτοῖς· ἢ γάρ τοι ἀδιαφόρως ζῆν διδάσκουσιν, ἢ τὸ ὑπέρτονον ἄγουσαι ἐγκράτειαν διὰ δυσσεβείας καὶ φιλαπεχθη- μοσύνης καταγγέλλουσι, with the whole passage which follows. As examples of the one extreme may be instanced the Carpocratians and Cainites: of the other the Encratites.

the other, but follow your own impulses. The ascetic principle assigns a certain importance to matter. The ascetic fails in consequence to assert his own independence. The true rule of life is to treat matter as something alien to you, towards which you have no duties or obligations and which you can use or leave unused as you like[1].' In this way the reaction from rigid asceticism led to the opposite extreme of unrestrained *licentiousness*, both alike springing from the same false conception of matter as the principle of evil.

Original independence of Gnosticism and its subsequent connexion with Christianity. Gnosticism, as defined by these characteristic features, has obviously no necessary connexion with Christianity[2]. Christianity would naturally arouse it to unwonted activity, by leading men to dwell more earnestly on the nature and power of evil, and thus stimulating more systematic thought on the theological questions which had already arrested attention. After no long time Gnosticism would absorb into its system more or fewer Christian elements, or Christianity in some of its forms would receive a tinge from Gnosticism. But the thing itself had an independent root, and seems to have been

---

[1] See for instance the description of the Carpocratians in Iren. i. 25. 3 sq., ii. 32. 1 sq., Hippol. *Hær.* vii. 32, Epiphan. *Hær.* xxvii. 2 sq.; from which passages it appears that they justified their moral profligacy on the principle that the highest perfection consists in the most complete contempt of mundane things.

[2] It will be seen from the description in the text, that Gnosticism (as I have defined it) presupposes only a belief in one God, the absolute Being, as against the vulgar polytheism. All its *essential* features, as a speculative system, may be explained from this simple element of belief, without any intervention of specially Christian or even Jewish doctrine. Christianity added two new elements to it; (1) the idea of *Redemption*, (2) the person of *Christ*. To explain the former, and to find a place for the latter, henceforth become prominent questions which press for solution; and Gnosticism in its several developments undergoes various modifications in the endeavour to solve them. Redemption must be set in some relation to the fundamental Gnostic conception of the antagonism between God and matter; and Christ must have some place found for Him in the fundamental Gnostic doctrine of emanations.

If it be urged that there is no authority for the name 'Gnostic' as applied to these pre-Christian theosophists, I am not concerned to prove the contrary, as my main position is not affected thereby. The term 'Gnostic' is here used, only because no other is so convenient or so appropriate. See note 2, p. 81.

prior in time. The probabilities of the case, and the scanty
traditions of history, alike point to this independence of the
two[1]. If so, it is a matter of little moment at what precise
time the name 'Gnostic' was adopted, whether before or after
contact with Christianity; for we are concerned only with the
growth and direction of thought which the name represents[2].

If then Gnosticism was not an offspring of Christianity, *Its alliance with*
but a direction of religious speculation which existed indepen- *Judaism*
dently, we are at liberty to entertain the question whether it *before
Christi-*
did not form an alliance with Judaism, contemporaneously *anity.*
with or prior to its alliance with Christianity. There is at
least no obstacle which bars such an investigation at the out-

[1] This question will require closer
investigation when I come to discuss
the genuineness of the Epistle to the
Colossians. Meanwhile I content myself with referring to Baur *Christliche
Gnosis* p. 29 sq. and Lipsius *Gnosticismus* p. 230 sq. Both these writers
concede, and indeed insist upon, the
non-Christian basis of Gnosticism, at
least so far as I have maintained it in
the text. Thus for instance Baur
says (p. 52), 'Though Christian gnosis
is the completion of gnosis, yet the
Christian element in gnosis is not so
essential as that gnosis cannot still be
gnosis even without this element. But
just as we can abstract it from the
Christian element, so can we also go still
further and regard even the Jewish as
not strictly an essential element of
gnosis.' In another work (*Die drei ersten
Jahrhunderte* p. 167, 1st ed.) he expresses himself still more strongly to
the same effect, but the expressions
are modified in the second edition.

[2] We may perhaps gather from the
notices which are preserved that, though
the substantive γνῶσις was used with
more or less precision even before contact with Christianity to designate the
superior illumination of these opinions,

the adjective γνωστικοί was not distinctly applied to those who maintained
them till somewhat later. Still it is
possible that pre-Christian Gnostics
already so designated themselves.
Hippolytus speaks of the Naassenes
or Ophites as giving themselves this
name; *Hær.* v. 6 μετὰ δὲ ταῦτα ἐπε-
κάλεσαν ἑαυτοὺς γνωστικούς, φάσκοντες
μόνοι τὰ βάθη γινώσκειν; comp. §§ 8,
11. His language seems to imply
(though it is not explicit) that they
were the first to adopt the name. The
Ophites were plainly among the earliest
Gnostic sects, as the heathen element
is still predominant in their teaching,
and their Christianity seems to have
been a later graft on their pagan theosophy; but at what stage in their
development they adopted the name
γνωστικοί does not appear. Irenæus
(*Hær.* i. 25. 6) speaks of the name as
affected especially by the Carpocratians. For the use of the substantive
γνῶσις see 1 Cor. viii. 1, xiii. 2, 8, 1 Tim.
vi. 20, and the note on Col. ii. 3: comp.
Rev. ii. 24 οἵτινες οὐκ ἔγνωσαν τὰ βαθέα
τοῦ Σατανᾶ, ὡς λέγουσιν (as explained
by the passage already quoted from
Hippol. *Hær.* v. 6; see *Galatians*,
p. 309, note 3).

set. If this should prove to be the case, then we have a combination which prepares the way for the otherwise strange phenomena presented in the Epistle to the Colossians.

The three sects of the Jews. Those, who have sought analogies to the three Jewish sects among the philosophical schools of Greece and Rome, have compared the Sadducees to the Epicureans, the Pharisees to the Stoics, and the Essenes to the Pythagoreans. Like all historical parallels, this comparison is open to misapprehension : but, carefully guarded, the illustration is pertinent and instructive.

Sadducee-ism, pure-ly nega-tive. With the Sadducees we have no concern here. Whatever respect may be due to their attitude in the earlier stages of their history, at the Christian era at least they have ceased to deserve our sympathy ; for their position has become mainly *negative.* They take their stand on denials—the denial of the existence of angels, the denial of the resurrection of the dead, the denial of a progressive development in the Jewish Church. In these negative tendencies, in the materialistic teaching of the sect, and in the moral consequences to which it led, a very rough resemblance to the Epicureans will appear[1].

Pharisee-ism and Essenism compared. The two *positive* sects were the Pharisees and the Essenes. Both alike were strict observers of the ritual law ; but, while the Pharisee was essentially *practical,* the tendency of the Essene was to *mysticism ;* while the Pharisee was a man of the world, the Essene was a member of a brotherhood. In this respect the Stoic and the Pythagorean were the nearest counterparts which the history of Greek philosophy and social life could offer. These analogies indeed are suggested by Josephus himself[2].

Elusive features of Essenism. While the portrait of the Pharisee is distinctly traced and easily recognised, this is not the case with the Essene. The Essene is the great enigma of Hebrew history. Admired alike by Jew, by Heathen, and by Christian, he yet remains a dim vague outline, on which the highest subtlety of successive

---

[1] The name *Epicureans* seems to be applied to them even in the Talmud ; see Eisenmenger's *Entdecktes Judenthum* I. pp. 95, 694 sq.; comp. Keim *Geschichte Jesu von Nazara* I. p. 281.

[2] For the Pharisees see *Vit.* 2 παραπλήσιός ἐστι τῇ παρ' Ἕλλησι Στωϊκῇ λεγομένῃ: for the Essenes, *Ant.* xv. 10. 4 διαίτῃ χρώμενον τῇ παρ' Ἕλλησιν ὑπὸ Πυθαγόρου καταδεδειγμένῃ.

critics has been employed to supply a substantial form and an adequate colouring. An ascetic mystical dreamy recluse, he seems too far removed from the hard experience of life to be capable of realisation.

And yet by careful use of the existing materials the portrait of this sect may be so far restored, as to establish with a reasonable amount of probability the point with which alone we are here concerned. It will appear from the delineations of ancient writers, more especially of Philo and Josephus, that the characteristic feature of Essenism was a particular direction of mystic speculation, involving a rigid asceticism as its practical consequence. Following the definition of Gnosticism which has been already given, we may not unfitly call this tendency *Gnostic*.

A sufficiently distinct portrait of the sect attainable.

Having in this statement anticipated the results, I shall now endeavour to develope the main features of Essenism; and, while doing so, I will ask my readers to bear in mind the portrait of the Colossian heresy in St Paul, and to mark the resemblances, as the enquiry proceeds[1].

Main features of Essenism.

The Judaic element is especially prominent in the life and teaching of the sect. The Essene was exceptionally rigorous in his observance of the Mosaic ritual. In his strict abstinence

---

[1] The really important contemporary sources of information respecting the Essenes are JOSEPHUS, *Bell. Jud.* ii. 8. 2—13, *Ant.* xiii. 5. 9, xviii. 1. 5, *Vit.* 2 (with notices of individual Essenes *Bell. Jud.* i. 3. 5, ii. 7. 3, ii. 20. 4, iii. 2. 1, *Ant.* xiii. 11. 2, xv. 10. 4, 5); and PHILO, *Quod omnis probus liber* § 12 sq. (II. p. 457 sq.), *Apol. pro Jud.* (II. p. 632 sq., a fragment quoted by Eusebius *Præp. Evang.* viii. 11). The account of the Therapeutes by the latter writer, *de Vita Contemplativa* (II. p. 471 sq.), must also be consulted, as describing a closely allied sect. To these should be added the short notice of PLINY, *N. H.* v. 15. 17, as expressing the views of a Roman writer. His account, we may conjecture, was taken from Alexander Polyhistor, a contemporary of Sulla, whom he mentions in his prefatory elenchus as one of his authorities for this 5th book, and who wrote a work *On the Jews* (Clem. Alex. *Strom.* i. 21, p. 396, Euseb. *Præp. Ev.* ix. 17). Significant mention of the Essenes is found also in the Christian HEGESIPPUS (Euseb. *H. E.* iv. 22) and in the heathen DION CHRYSOSTOM (Synesius *Dion* 3, p. 39). EPIPHANIUS (*Hær.* pp. 28 sq., 40 sq.) discusses two separate sects, which he calls *Essenes* and *Ossæans* respectively. These are doubtless different names of the same persons. His account is, as usual, confused and inaccurate, but

from work on the sabbath he far surpassed all the other Jews.
He would not light a fire, would not move a vessel, would not
perform even the most ordinary functions of life[1]. The whole
day was given up to religious exercises and to exposition of the

has a certain value. All other authorities are secondary. HIPPOLYTUS, *Hær.* ix. 18—28, follows Josephus (*Bell. Jud.* ii. 8. 2 sq.) almost exclusively. PORPHYRY also (*de Abstinentia*, iv. 11 sq.) copies this same passage of Josephus, with a few unimportant exceptions probably taken from a lost work by the same author, πρὸς τοὺς Ἕλληνας, which he mentions by name. EUSEBIUS (*Præp. Evang.* viii. 11 sq., ix. 3) contents himself with quoting Philo and Porphyry. SOLINUS (*Polyh.* xxxv. 9 sq.) merely abstracts Pliny. TALMUDICAL and RABBINICAL passages, supposed to contain references to the Essenes, are collected by Frankel in the articles mentioned in a later paragraph; but the allusions are most uncertain (see the second dissertation on the Essenes). The authorities for the history of the Essenes are the subject of an article by W. Clemens in the *Zeitschr. f. Wiss. Theol.* 1869,p. 328 sq.

The attack on the genuineness of Philo's treatise *De Vita Contemplativa* made by Grätz (III. p. 463 sq.) has been met by Zeller (*Philosophie*, III. ii. p. 255 sq.), whose refutation is complete. The attack of the same writer (III. p. 464) on the genuineness of the treatise *Quod omnis probus liber* Zeller considers too frivolous to need refuting (*ib.* p. 235). A refutation will be found in the above-mentioned article of W. Clemens (p. 340 sq.).

Of modern writings relating to the Essenes the following may be especially mentioned; BELLERMANN *Ueber Essäer u. Therapeuten*, Berlin 1821; GFRÖRER *Philo* II. p. 299 sq.; DÄHNE *Ersch u. Gruber's Encyklopädie* s. v.; FRANKEL *Zeitschrift für die religiösen*

Interessen des Judenthums 1846 p. 441 sq., *Monatsschrift für Geschichte u. Wissenschaft des Judenthums* 1853, p. 30 sq., 61 sq.; BÖTTGER *Ueber den Orden der Essäer*, Dresden 1849; EWALD *Geschichte des Volkes Israel* IV. p. 420 sq., VII. p. 153 sq.; RITSCHL *Entstehung der Altkatholischen Kirche* p. 179 sq. (ed. 2, 1857), and *Theologische Jahrbücher* 1855, p. 315 sq.; JOST *Geschichte des Judenthums* I. p. 207 sq.; GRAETZ *Geschichte der Juden* III. p. 79 sq., 463 sq. (ed. 2, 1863); HILGENFELD *Jüdische Apocalyptik* p. 245 sq., and *Zeitschr. f. Wiss. Theol.* X. p. 97 sq., XI. p. 343 sq., XIV. p. 30 sq.; WESTCOTT *Smith's Dictionary of the Bible* s. v.; GINSBURG *The Essenes*, London 1864, and in *Kitto's Cyclopædia* s. v.; DERENBOURG *L'Histoire et la Géographie de la Palestine* p. 166 sq., 460 sq.; KEIM *Geschichte Jesu von Nazara* I. p. 282 sq.; HAUSRATH *Neutestamentliche Zeitgeschichte* I. p. 133 sq.; LIPSIUS *Schenkel's Bibel Lexikon* s. v.; HERZFELD *Geschichte des Volkes Israel* II. 368 sq., 388 sq., 509 sq. (ed. 2, 1863); ZELLER *Philosophie der Griechen* III. 2, p. 234 sq. (ed. 2, 1868); LANGEN *Judenthum in Palästina* p. 190 sq.; LÖWY *Kritisch-talmudisches Lexicon* s. v. (Wien 1863); WEISS *Zur Geschichte der jüdischen Tradition* p. 120 sq. (Wien).

[1] *B. J.* ii. 8. 9 φυλάσσονται ... ταῖς ἑβδόμασιν ἔργων ἐφάπτεσθαι διαφορώτατα Ἰουδαίων ἁπάντων· οὐ μόνον γὰρ τροφὰς ἑαυτοῖς πρὸ ἡμέρας μιᾶς παρασκευάζουσιν, ὡς μηδὲ πῦρ ἐναύοιεν ἐκείνῃ τῇ ἡμέρᾳ, ἀλλ' οὐδὲ σκεῦός τι μετακινῆσαι θαρροῦσιν κ.τ.λ. Hippolytus (*Hær.* ix. 25) adds that some of them do not so much as leave their beds on this day.

Scriptures[1]. His respect for the law extended also to the law-giver. After God, the name of Moses was held in the highest reverence. He who blasphemed his name was punished with death[2]. In all these points the Essene was an exaggeration, almost a caricature, of the Pharisee.

So far the Essene has not departed from the principles of normal Judaism; but here the divergence begins. In three main points we trace the working of influences which must have been derived from external sources. *External elements super-added.*

1. To the legalism of the Pharisee, the Essene added an asceticism, which was peculiarly his own, and which in many respects contradicted the tenets of the other sect. The honour-able, and even exaggerated, estimate of marriage, which was characteristic of the Jew, and of the Pharisee as the typical Jew, found no favour with the Essene[3]. Marriage was to him an abomination. Those Essenes who lived together as members of an order, and in whom the principles of the sect were carried to their logical consequences, eschewed it altogether. To secure the continuance of their brotherhood they adopted children, whom they brought up in the doctrines and practices of the community. There were others however who took a different view. They accepted marriage, as necessary for the preservation of the race. Yet even with them it seems to have been regard-ed only as an inevitable evil. They fenced it off by stringent rules, demanding a three years' probation and enjoining various *1. Rigid asceticism in respect to marriage,*

---

[1] Philo *Quod omn. prob. lib.* § 12. Of the Therapeutes see Philo *Vit. Cont.* § 3, 4.

[2] *B. J.* l. c. § 9 σέβας δὲ μέγιστον παρ' αὐτοῖς μετὰ τὸν Θεὸν τὸ ὄνομα τοῦ νομοθέτου, κἂν βλασφημήσῃ τις εἰς τοῦτον (i.e. τὸν νομοθέτην), κολάζεσθαι θανάτῳ: comp. § 10.

[3] *B. J.* l. c. § 2 γάμου μὲν ὑπεροψία παρ' αὐτοῖς ... τὰς τῶν γυναικῶν ἀσελγείας φυλασσόμενοι καὶ μηδεμίαν τηρεῖν πεπεισμένοι τὴν πρὸς ἕνα πίστιν, *Ant.* xviii. 1. 5; Philo *Fragm.* p. 633 γάμον παρῃτήσαντο μετὰ τοῦ διαφερόντως ἀσκεῖν

ἐγκράτειαν· Ἐσσαίων γὰρ οὐδεὶς ἄγεται γυναῖκα, διότι φίλαυτον ἡ γυνὴ καὶ ζηλότυπον οὐ μετρίως καὶ δεινὸν ἀνδρὸς ἤθη παρασαλεῦσαι, with more to the same purpose. This peculiarity astonished the heathen Pliny, *N. H.* v. 15, 'gens sola et in toto orbe præter ceteros mira, sine ulla femina, venere abdicata ... In diem ex æquo convenarum turba renascitur large frequentantibus ... Ita per sæculorum millia (incredibile dictu) gens æterna est, in qua nemo nascitur. Tam fœcunda illis aliorum vitæ pœnitentia est.'

purificatory rites[1]. The conception of marriage, as quickening and educating the affections and thus exalting and refining human life, was wholly foreign to their minds. Woman was a mere instrument of temptation in their eyes, deceitful, faithless, selfish, jealous, misled and misleading by her passions.

meats and drinks

But their ascetic tendencies did not stop here. The Pharisee was very careful to observe the distinction of meats lawful and unlawful, as laid down by the Mosaic code, and even rendered these ordinances vexatious by minute definitions of his own. But the Essene went far beyond him. He drank no wine, he did not touch animal food. His meal consisted of a piece of bread and a single mess of vegetables. Even this simple fare was prepared for him by special officers consecrated for the purpose, that it might be free from all contamination[2]. Nay, so stringent were the rules of the order on this point, that when an Essene was excommunicated, he often died of starvation, being bound by his oath not to take food prepared by defiled hands, and thus being reduced to eat the very grass of the field[3].

and oil for anointing.

Again, in hot climates oil for anointing the body is almost a necessary of life. From this too the Essenes strictly abstained. Even if they were accidentally smeared, they were careful at once to wash themselves, holding the mere touch to be a contamination[4].

---

[1] *B. J.* 1. c. § 13. Josephus speaks of these as ἕτερον Ἐσσηνῶν τάγμα, ὃ δίαιταν μὲν καὶ ἔθη καὶ νόμιμα τοῖς ἄλλοις ὁμοφρονοῦν, διεστὸς δὲ τῇ κατὰ γάμον δόξῃ. We may suppose that they corresponded to the third order of a Benedictine or Franciscan brotherhood; so that, living in the world, they would observe the rule up to a certain point, but would not be bound by vows of celibacy or subject to the more rigorous discipline of the sect.

[2] *B. J.* 1. c. § 5; see Philo's account of the Therapeutes, *Vit. Cont.* § 4 σιτοῦνται δὲ πολυτελὲς οὐδέν, ἀλλὰ ἄρτον εὐτελῆ· καὶ ὄψον ἅλες, οὓς οἱ ἁβροδιαιτότατοι παραρτύουσιν ὑσσώπῳ· ποτὸν ὕδωρ ναματιαῖον αὐτοῖς ἐστιν; and again more to the same effect in § 9: and compare the Essene story of St James in Hegesippus (Euseb. *H. E.* ii. 23) οἶνον καὶ σίκερα οὐκ ἔπιεν, οὐδὲ ἔμψυχον ἔφαγε. Their abstention from animal food accounts for Porphyry's giving them so prominent a place in his treatise: see Zeller, p. 243.

[3] *B. J.* 1. c. § 8.

[4] *B. J.* 1. c. § 3 κηλῖδα δὲ ὑπολαμβάνουσι τὸ ἔλαιον κ.τ.λ.; Hegesippus 1. c. ἔλαιον οὐκ ἠλείψατο.

From these facts it seems clear that Essene abstinence was Underlying principle of this asceticism. something more than the mere exaggeration of Pharisaic principles. The rigour of the Pharisee was based on his obligation of obedience to an absolute external law. The Essene introduced a new principle. He condemned in any form the gratification of the natural cravings, nor would he consent to regard it as moral or immoral only according to the motive which suggested it or the consequences which flowed from it. It was in itself an absolute evil. He sought to disengage himself, as far as possible, from the conditions of physical life. In short, in the asceticism of the Essene we seem to see the germ of that Gnostic dualism which regards matter as the principle, or at least the abode, of evil.

2. And, when we come to investigate the speculative tenets of the sect, we shall find that the Essenes have diverged appreciably from the common type of Jewish orthodoxy.

2. Speculative tenets.

(i) Attention was directed above to their respect for Moses and the Mosaic law, which they shared in common with the Pharisee. But there was another side to their theological teaching. Though our information is somewhat defective, still in the scanty notices which are preserved we find sufficient indications that they had absorbed some foreign elements of religious thought into their system. Thus at day-break they addressed certain prayers, which had been handed down from their forefathers, to the Sun, 'as if entreating him to rise[1].' They were careful also to conceal and bury all polluting substances, so as not 'to insult the rays of the god[2].' We can-

(i) Tendency to sun-worship.

---

[1] *B. J.* l. c. § 5 πρός γε μὴν τὸ θεῖον ἰδίως εὐσεβεῖς· πρὶν γὰρ ἀνασχεῖν τὸν ἥλιον οὐδὲν φθέγγονται τῶν βεβήλων, πατρίους δέ τινας εἰς αὐτὸν εὐχάς, ὥσπερ ἱκετεύοντες ἀνατεῖλαι. Compare what Philo says of the Therapeutes, *Vit. Cont.* § 3 ἡλίου μὲν ἀνίσχοντος εὐημερίαν αἰτούμενοι τὴν ὄντως εὐημερίαν, φωτὸς οὐρανίου τὴν διάνοιαν αὐτῶν ἀναπλησθῆναι, and *ib.* § 11. On the attempt of Frankel (*Zeitschr.* p. 458) to resolve this worship, which

Josephus states to be offered to the sun (εἰς αὐτόν), into the ordinary prayers of the Pharisaic Jew at day-break, see the second dissertation on the Essenes.

[2] *B. J.* l. c. § 9 ὡς μὴ τὰς αὐγὰς ὑβρίζοιεν τοῦ θεοῦ. There can be no doubt, I think, that by τοῦ θεοῦ is meant the 'sun-god'; comp. Eur. *Heracl.* 749 θεοῦ φαεσίμβροτοι αὐγαί, *Alc.* 722 τὸ φέγγος τοῦτο τοῦ θεοῦ, Appian *Præf.* 9 δυομένου τοῦ θεοῦ, *Lib.* 113 τοῦ θεοῦ

not indeed suppose that they regarded the sun as more than a
symbol of the unseen power who gives light and life ; but their
outward demonstrations of reverence were sufficiently prominent to attach to them, or to a sect derived from them, the
epithet of 'Sun-worshippers[1],' and some connexion with the
characteristic feature of Parsee devotion at once suggests itself.
The practice at all events stands in strong contrast to the
denunciations of worship paid to the 'hosts of heaven' in the
Hebrew prophets.

(ii) Resur-
rection of
the body
denied.

    (ii) Nor again is it an insignificant fact that, while the
Pharisee maintained the resurrection of the body as a cardinal
article of his faith, the Essene restricted himself to a belief in
the immortality of the soul. The soul, he maintained, was confined in the flesh, as in a prison-house. Only when disengaged
from these fetters would it be truly free. Then it would
soar aloft, rejoicing in its newly attained liberty[2]. This
doctrine accords with the fundamental conception of the
malignity of matter. To those who held this conception a

περὶ δείλην ἑσπέραν ὄντος, Civ. iv. 79
δύνοντος ἄρτι τοῦ θεοῦ: comp. Herod. ii.
24. Dr Ginsburg has obliterated this
very important touch by translating τὰς
αὐγὰς τοῦ θεοῦ 'the Divine rays' (Essenes
p. 47). It is a significant fact that
Hippolytus (Hær. ix. 25) omits the
words τοῦ θεοῦ, evidently regarding them
as a stumbling-block. How Josephus
expressed himself in the original Hebrew of the Bellum Judaicum, it is
vain to speculate: but the Greek translation was authorised, if not made, by
him.

[1] Epiphan. Hær. xix. 2, xx. 3 Ὀσ-
σηνοὶ δὲ μετέστησαν ἀπὸ Ἰουδαϊσμοῦ εἰς
τὴν τῶν Σαμψαίων αἵρεσιν, liii. 1, 2 Σαμ-
ψαῖοι γὰρ ἑρμηνεύονται Ἡλιακοί, from
the Hebrew שׁמשׁ 'the sun.' The
historical connexion of the Sampsæans
with the Essenes is evident from these
passages: though it is difficult to say
what their precise relations to each

other were. See below, p. 374.

[2] B. J. l. c. § 11 καὶ γὰρ ἔρρωται παρ'
αὐτοῖς ἥδε ἡ δόξα, φθαρτὰ μὲν εἶναι τὰ
σώματα καὶ τὴν ὕλην οὐ μόνιμον αὐτοῖς,
τὰς δὲ ψυχὰς ἀθανάτους ἀεὶ διαμένειν . . .
ἐπειδὰν δὲ ἀνεθῶσι τῶν κατὰ σάρκα δεσμῶν, οἷα δὴ μακρᾶς δουλείας ἀπηλλαγ-
μένας, τότε χαίρειν καὶ μετεώρους φέρεσ-
θαι κ.τ.λ. To this doctrine the teaching of the Pharisees stands in direct
contrast; ib. § 13: comp. also Ant.
xviii. 1. 3, 5.

Nothing can be more explicit than
the language of Josephus. On the other
hand Hippolytus (Hær. ix. 27) says of
them ὁμολογοῦσι γὰρ καὶ τὴν σάρκα
ἀναστήσεσθαι καὶ ἔσεσθαι ἀθάνατον ὃν
τρόπον ἤδη ἀθάνατός ἐστιν ἡ ψυχή κ.τ.λ.;
but his authority is worthless on this
point, as he can have had no personal
knowledge of the facts: see Zeller p.
251, note 2. Hilgenfeld takes a different view; Zeitschr. xiv. p. 49.

resurrection of the body would be repulsive, as involving a perpetuation of evil.

(iii) But they also separated themselves from the religious belief of the orthodox Jew in another respect, which would provoke more notice. While they sent gifts to the temple at Jerusalem, they refused to offer sacrifices there[1]. It would appear that the slaughter of animals was altogether forbidden by their creed[2]. It is certain that they were afraid of contracting some ceremonial impurity by offering victims in the temple. Meanwhile they had sacrifices, bloodless sacrifices, of their own. They regarded their simple meals with their accompanying prayers and thanksgiving, not only as devotional but even as sacrificial rites. Those who prepared and presided over these meals were their consecrated priests[3]. *(iii) Prohibition of sacrifices.*

(iv) In what other respects they may have departed from, or added to, the normal creed of Judaism, we do not know. But it is expressly stated that, when a novice after passing through the probationary stages was admitted to the full privileges of the order, the oath of admission bound him ' to conceal nothing from the members of the sect, and to report nothing concerning them to others, even though threatened with death ; not to communicate any of their doctrines to anyone otherwise than as he himself had received them ; but to abstain from robbery, and in like manner to guard carefully the books *(iv) Esoteric doctrine of angels.*

---

[1] *Ant.* xviii. 1. 5 εἰς δὲ τὸ ἱερὸν ἀναθήματά τε στέλλοντες θυσίας οὐκ ἐπιτελοῦσι διαφορότητι ἁγνειῶν, ἃς νομίζοιεν, καὶ δι' αὐτὸ εἰργόμενοι τοῦ κοινοῦ τεμενίσματος ἐφ' αὑτῶν τὰς θυσίας ἐπιτελοῦσι. So Philo *Quod omn. prob. lib.* § 12 describes them as οὐ ζῷα καταθύοντες ἀλλ' ἱεροπρεπεῖς· τὰς ἑαυτῶν διανοίας κατασκευάζειν ἀξιοῦντες.

[2] The following considerations show that their abstention should probably be explained in this way: (1) Though the language of Josephus may be ambiguous, that of Philo is unequivocal on this point; (2) Their abstention

from the temple-sacrifices cannot be considered apart from the fact that they ate no animal food: see above p. 86, note 2. (3) The Christianised Essenes, or Ebionites, though strong Judaizers in many respects, yet distinctly protested against the sacrifice of animals; see Clem. *Hom.* iii. 45, 52, and comp. Ritschl p. 224. On this subject see also Zeller p. 242 sq., and my second dissertation.

[3] *Ant.* xviii. 1. 5 ἱερεῖς τε [χειροτονοῦσι] διὰ ποίησιν σίτου τε καὶ βρωμάτων, *B. J.* ii. 8. 5 προκατεύχεται δὲ ὁ ἱερεὺς τῆς τροφῆς κ.τ.λ.; see Ritschl p.181.

of their sect, and *the names of the angels*[1].' It may be reasonably supposed that more lurks under this last expression than
meets the ear. This esoteric doctrine, relating to angelic beings,
may have been another link which attached Essenism to the
religion of Zoroaster[2]. At all events we seem to be justified
in connecting it with the self-imposed service and worshipping
of angels at Colossæ : and we may well suspect that we have
here a germ which was developed into the Gnostic doctrine of
æons or emanations.

(v) Specu-
lations on
God and
Creation.
(v) If so, it is not unconnected with another notice relating
to Essene peculiarities. The Gnostic doctrine of intermediate
beings between God and the world, as we have seen, was
intimately connected with speculations respecting creation.
Now we are specially informed that the Essenes, while leaving
physical studies in general to speculative idlers ($\mu\epsilon\tau\epsilon\omega\rho o$-
$\lambda\epsilon\sigma\chi\alpha\iota\varsigma$), as being beyond the reach of human nature, yet
excepted from their general condemnation that philosophy
which treats of the existence of God and the generation of the
universe[3].

(vi) Magic-
al charms.
(vi) Mention has been made incidentally of certain secret
books peculiar to the sect. The existence of such an apocryphal
literature was a sure token of some abnormal development in
doctrine[4]. In the passage quoted it is mentioned in relation to

---

[1] *B. J.* l. c. § 7 ὅρκους αὐτοῖς ὄμνυσι
φρικώδεις...μήτε κρύψειν τι τοὺς αἱρε-
τιστὰς μήτε ἑτέροις αὐτῶν τι μηνύσειν, καὶ
ἂν μέχρι θανάτου τις βιάζηται. πρὸς
τούτοις ὀμνύουσι μηδενὶ μὲν μεταδοῦναι
τῶν δογμάτων ἑτέρως ἢ ὡς αὐτὸς μετέ-
λαβεν· ἀφέξεσθαι δὲ λῃστείας καὶ συντηρήσειν ὁμοίως τά τε τῆς αἱρέσεως αὐτῶν
βιβλία καὶ τὰ τῶν ἀγγέλων ὀνόματα.
With this notice should be compared
the Ebionite διαμαρτυρία, or protest of
initiation, prefixed to the *Clementine
Homilies*, which shows how closely
the Christian Essenes followed the
practice of their Jewish predecessors
in this respect. See Zeller p. 254.

[2] See the second dissertation.

[3] Philo *Omn. prob. lib.* § 12 (p. 458)
τὸ δὲ φυσικὸν ὡς μεῖζον ἢ κατὰ ἀνθρωπί-
νην φύσιν μετεωρολέσχαις ἀπολιπόντες,
πλὴν ὅσον αὐτοῦ περὶ ὑπάρξεως Θεοῦ καὶ
τῆς τοῦ παντὸς γενέσεως φιλοσοφεῖται.

[4] The word *Apocrypha* was used
originally to designate the secret books
which contained the esoteric doctrine
of a sect. The secondary sense 'spurious' was derived from the general
character of these writings, which were
heretical, mostly Gnostic, forgeries.
See Prof. Plumptre's article *Apocrypha*
in Smith's *Dictionary of the Bible*,
and the note on ἀπόκρυφοι below, ii. 3.

some form of angelology. Elsewhere their skill in prediction, for which they were especially famous, is connected with the perusal of certain 'sacred books,' which however are not described[1]. But more especially, we are told that the Essenes studied with extraordinary diligence the writings of the ancients, selecting those especially which could be turned to profit for soul and body, and that from these they learnt the qualities of roots and the properties of stones[2]. This expres-

---

[1] B. J. ii. 8. 12 εἰσὶ δὲ ἐν αὐτοῖς οἳ καὶ τὰ μέλλοντα προγινώσκειν ὑπισχνοῦνται, βίβλοις ἱεραῖς καὶ διαφόροις ἁγνείαις καὶ προφητῶν ἀποφθέγμασιν ἐμπαιδοτριβούμενοι· σπάνιον δέ, εἴποτε, ἐν ταῖς προαγορεύσεσιν ἀστοχήσουσιν. Dr Ginsburg (p. 49) translates βίβλοις ἱεραῖς ' the sacred Scripture,' and προφητῶν ἀποφθέγμασιν ' the sayings of the prophets'; but as the definite articles are wanting, the expressions cannot be so rendered, nor does there seem to be any reference to the Canonical writings.

We learn from an anecdote in Ant. xiii. 11. 2, that the teachers of this sect communicated the art of prediction to their disciples by instruction. We may therefore conjecture that with the Essenes this acquisition was connected with magic or astrology. At all events it is not treated as a direct inspiration.

[2] B. J. ii. 8. 6 σπουδάζουσι δὲ ἐκτόπως περὶ τὰ τῶν παλαιῶν συγγράμματα, μάλιστα τὰ πρὸς ὠφέλειαν ψυχῆς καὶ σώματος ἐκλέγοντες· ἔνθεν αὐτοῖς πρὸς θεραπείαν παθῶν ῥίζαι τε ἀλεξιτήριοι καὶ λίθων ἰδιότητες ἀνερευνῶνται. This passage might seem at first sight to refer simply to the medicinal qualities of vegetable and mineral substances; but a comparison with another notice in Josephus invests it with a different meaning. In Ant. viii. 2, 5 he states that Solomon, having received by divine inspiration the art of defeating demons for the advantage and healing of man (εἰς ὠφέλειαν καὶ θεραπείαν τοῖς ἀνθρώποις), composed and left behind him charms (ἐπῳδάς) by which diseases were allayed, and diverse kinds of exorcisms (τρόπους ἐξορκώσεων) by which demons were cast out. 'This mode of healing,' he adds, ' is very powerful even to the present day'; and he then relates how, as he was credibly informed (ἱστόρησα), one of his countrymen, Eleazar by name, had healed several persons possessed by demons in the presence of Vespasian and his sons and a number of officers and common soldiers. This he did by applying to the nose of the possessed his ring, which had concealed in it one of the roots which Solomon had directed to be used, and thus drawing out the demon through the nostrils of the person smelling it. At the same time he adjured the evil spirit not to return, 'making mention of Solomon and repeating the charms composed by him.' On one occasion this Eleazar gave ocular proof that the demon was exorcized; and thus, adds Josephus, σαφὴς ἡ Σολομῶνος καθίστατο σύνεσις καὶ σοφία. On these books relating to the occult arts and ascribed to Solomon see Fabricius Cod. Pseud. Vet. Test. I. p. 1036 sq., where many curious notices are gathered together. See especially Origen In Matth. Comm. xxxv. § 110 (III. p. 910), Pseudo-Just. Quæst. 55.

This interpretation explains all the expressions in the passage. The λίθων

sion, as illustrated by other notices, points clearly to the study of occult sciences, and recalls the alliance with the practice of magical arts, which was a distinguishing feature of Gnosticism, and is condemned by Christian teachers even in the heresies of the Apostolic age.

3. Exclusive spirit of Essenism.

3. But the notice to which I have just alluded suggests a broader affinity with Gnosticism. Not only did the theological speculations of the Essenes take a Gnostic turn, but they guarded their peculiar tenets with Gnostic reserve. They too had their esoteric doctrine which they looked upon as the exclusive possession of the privileged few; their 'mysteries' which it was a grievous offence to communicate to the uninitiated. This doctrine was contained, as we have seen, in an apocryphal literature. Their whole organisation was arranged so as to prevent the divulgence of its secrets to those without. The long period of noviciate, the careful rites of initiation, the distinction of the several orders[1] in the community, the solemn oaths by which they bound their members, were so many safeguards against a betrayal of this precious deposit, which

ἰδιότητες naturally points to the use of charms or amulets, as may be seen e.g. from the treatise, Damigeron *de Lapidibus*, printed in the *Spicil. Solemn.* III. p. 324 sq.: comp. King *Antique Gems* Sect. IV, *Gnostics and their Remains.* The reference to 'the books of the ancients' thus finds an adequate explanation. On the other hand the only expression which seemed to militate against this view, ἀλεξιτήριοι ῥίζαι, is justified by the story in the *Antiquities;* comp. also Clem. Hom. viii. 14. It should be added also that Hippolytus (*Hær.* ix. 22) paraphrases the language of Josephus so as to give it this sense; πάνυ δὲ περιέργως ἔχουσι περὶ βοτάνας καὶ λίθους, περιεργότεροι ὄντες πρὸς τὰς τούτων ἐνεργείας, φάσκοντες μὴ μάτην ταῦτα γεγονέναι. The sense which περίεργος ('curiosus') bears in Acts xix.

19 and elsewhere, referring to magical arts, illustrates its use here.

Thus these Essenes were dealers in charms, rather than physicians. And yet it is quite possible that along with this practice of the occult sciences they studied the healing art in its nobler forms. The works of Alexander of Tralles, an eminent ancient physician, constantly recommend the use of such charms, of which some obviously come from a Jewish source and not improbably may have been taken from these Solomonian books to which Josephus refers. A number of passages from this and other writers, specifying charms of various kinds, are given in Becker and Marquardt *Rom. Alterth.* IV. p. 116 sq. See also Spencer's note on Orig. *c. Cels.* p. 17 sq.

[1] See especially *B. J.* ii. 8. 7, 10.

they held to be restricted to the inmost circle of the brother-hood.

In selecting these details I have not attempted to give a finished portrait of Essenism. From this point of view the delineation would be imperfect and misleading: for I have left out of sight the nobler features of the sect, their courageous endurance, their simple piety, their brotherly love. My object was solely to call attention to those features which distinguish it from the normal type of Judaism, and seem to justify the attribution of Gnostic influences. And here it has been seen The three that the three characteristics, which were singled out above as notes of Gnostic-distinctive of Gnosticism, reappear in the Essenes; though it ism found in the has been convenient to consider them in the reversed order. Essenes. This Jewish sect exhibits the same exclusiveness in the communication of its doctrines. Its theological speculations take the same direction, dwelling on the mysteries of creation, regarding matter as the abode of evil, and postulating certain intermediate spiritual agencies as necessary links of communication between heaven and earth. And lastly, its speculative opinions involve the same ethical conclusions, and lead in like manner to a rigid asceticism. If the notices relating to these points do not always explain themselves, yet read in the light of the heresies of the Apostolic age and in that of subsequent Judæo-Gnostic Christianity, their bearing seems to be distinct enough; so that we should not be far wrong, if we were to designate Essenism as Gnostic Judaism [1].

But the Essenes of whom historical notices are preserved How were inhabitants of the Holy Land. Their monasteries were widely were the situated on the shores of the Dead Sea. We are told indeed, Essenes that the sect was not confined to any one place, and that dispersed?

[1] I have said nothing of the Kabbala, as a development of Jewish thought illustrating the Colossian heresy: because the books containing the Kabbalistic speculations are comparatively recent, and if they contain ancient elements, it seems impossible to separate these from later additions or to assign to them even an approximate date. The Kabbalistic doctrine however will serve to show to what extent Judaism may be developed in the direction of speculative mysticism.

members of the order were found in great numbers in divers cities and villages[1]. But Judæa in one notice, Palestine and Syria in another, are especially named as the localities of the Essene settlements[2]. Have we any reason to suppose that they were represented among the Jews of the Dispersion? In Egypt indeed we find ourselves confronted with a similar ascetic sect, the Therapeutes, who may perhaps have had an independent origin, but who nevertheless exhibit substantially the same type of Jewish thought and practice[3]. But the Dispersion of Egypt, it may be argued, was exceptional; and we might expect to find here organisations and developments of Judaism hardly less marked and various than in the mother country.

Do they appear in Asia Minor? What ground have we for assuming the existence of this type in Asia Minor? Do we meet with any traces of it in the cities of the Lycus, or in proconsular Asia generally, which would justify the opinion that it might make its influence felt in the Christian communities of that district?

Now it has been shown that the colonies of the Jews in this neighbourhood were populous and influential[4]; and it might be argued with great probability that among these large numbers Essene Judaism could not be unrepresented.

How the term Essene is to be understood. But indeed throughout this investigation, when I speak of the Judaism in the Colossian Church as Essene, I do not assume a precise identity of origin, but only an essential

---

[1] Philo *Fragm.* p. 632 οἰκοῦσι δὲ πολλὰς μὲν πόλεις τῆς Ἰουδαίας, πολλὰς δὲ κώμας, καὶ μεγάλους καὶ πολυανθρώπους ὁμίλους; Joseph. *B. J.* ii. 8. 4 μία δὲ οὐκ ἔστιν αὐτῶν πόλις, ἀλλ' ἐν ἑκάστῃ κατοικοῦσι πολλοί. On the notices of the settlements and dispersion of the Essenes see Zeller p. 239.

[2] Philo names *Judæa* in *Fragm.* p. 632; *Palestine* and *Syria* in *Quod omn. prob. lib.* 12, p. 457. Their chief settlements were in the neighbourhood of the Dead Sea. This fact is mentioned by the heathen writers Pliny (*N. H.* v. 15) and Dion Chrysostom (Synesius *Dio* 3). The name of the

'Essene gate' at Jerusalem (*B. J.* v. 4. 2) seems to point to some establishment of the order close to the walls of that city.

[3] They are only known to us from Philo's treatise *de Vita Contemplativa*. Their settlements were on the shores of the Mareotic lake near Alexandria. Unlike the Essenes, they were not gathered together in convents as members of a fraternity, but lived apart as anchorites, though in the same neighbourhood. In other respects their tenets and practices were very similar to those of the Essenes.

[4] See above p. 19 sq.

affinity of type, with the Essenes of the mother country. As a matter of history, it may or may not have sprung from the colonies on the shores of the Dead Sea; but as this can neither be proved nor disproved, so also it is immaterial to my main purpose. All along its frontier, wherever Judaism became enamoured of and was wedded to Oriental mysticism, the same union would produce substantially the same results. In a country where Phrygia, Persia, Syria, all in turn had moulded religious thought, it would be strange indeed if Judaism entirely escaped these influences. Nor, as a matter of fact, are indications wanting to show that it was not unaffected by them. If the traces are few, they are at least as numerous and as clear as with our defective information on the whole subject we have any right to expect in this particular instance.

Probabilities of the case.

Direct indications.

When St Paul visits Ephesus, he comes in contact with certain strolling Jews, exorcists, who attempt to cast out evil spirits[1]. Connecting this fact with the notices of Josephus, from which we infer that exorcisms of this kind were especially practised by the Essenes[2], we seem to have an indication of their presence in the capital of proconsular Asia. If so, it is a significant fact that in their exorcisms they employed the name of our Lord: for then we must regard this as the earliest notice of those overtures of alliance on the part of Essenism, which involved such important consequences in the subsequent history of the Church[3]. It is also worth observing, that the next incident in St Luke's narrative is the burning of their magical books by those whom St Paul converted on this occasion[4]. As Jews are especially mentioned among these converts, and as books of charms are ascribed to the Essenes by Josephus, the two incidents, standing in this close

St Paul at Ephesus A.D. 54—57.

Exorcisms and

magical books.

---

[1] Acts xix. 13 τῶν περιερχομένων Ἰουδαίων ἐξορκιστῶν.

[2] See above p. 91, note 2.

[3] On the latter contact of Essenism with Christianity, see the third dissertation, and *Galatians* p. 322 sq.

[4] There is doubtless a reference to the charms called Ἐφέσια γράμματα

in this passage: see Wetstein ad loc., and the references in Becker and Marquardt *Rom. Alterth.* IV. p. 123 sq. But this supposition does not exclude the Jews from a share in these magical arts, while the context points to some such participation.

connexion, throw great light on the type of Judaism which thus appears at Ephesus [1].

Somewhat later we have another notice which bears in the same direction. The Sibylline Oracle, which forms the fourth book in the existing collection, is discovered by internal evidence to have been written about A.D. 80 [2]. It is plainly a product of Judaism, but its Judaism does not belong to the normal Pharisaic type. With Essenism it rejects sacrifices, even regarding the shedding of blood as a pollution [3], and with Essenism also it inculcates the duty of frequent washings [4]. Yet from other indications we are led to the conclusion, that this poem was not written in the interests of Essenism properly so called, but represents some allied though

---

[1] I can only regard it as an accidental coincidence that the epulones of the Ephesian Artemis were called *Essenes*, Pausan. viii. 13. 1 τοὺς τῇ ᾿Αρτέμιδι ἱστιάτορας τῇ ᾿Εφεσίᾳ γινομένους, καλουμένους δὲ ὑπὸ τῶν πολιτῶν ᾿Εσσῆνας: see Guhl *Ephesiaca* 106 sq. The *Etymol. Magn.* has ᾿Εσσήν· ὁ βασιλεὺς κατὰ ᾿Εφεσίους, and adds several absurd derivations of the word. In the sense of 'a king' it is used by Callimachus *Hymn. Jov.* 66 οὔ σε θεῶν ἐσσῆνα πάλιν θέσαν. It is probably not a Greek word, as other terms connected with the worship of the Ephesian Artemis (e.g. μεγάβυζος, a Persian word) point to an oriental or at least a non-Greek origin; and some have derived it from the Aramaic חסין *chasin* 'strong' or 'powerful.' But there is no sufficient ground for connecting it directly with the name of the sect ᾿Εσσηνοί or ᾿Εσσαῖοι, as some writers are disposed to do (e.g. Spanheim on *Callim.* l. c., Creuzer *Symbolik* IV. pp. 347, 349); though this view is favoured by the fact that certain ascetic practices were enjoined on these pagan 'Essenes.'

[2] Its date is fixed by the following allusions. The temple at Jerusalem has been destroyed by Titus (vv. 122 sq.), and the cities of Campania have been overwhelmed in fire and ashes (vv. 127 sq.). Nero has disappeared and his disappearance has been followed by bloody contests in Rome (vv. 116 sq.); but his return is still expected (vv. 134 sq.).

[3] See vv. 27—30 οἳ νηοὺς μὲν ἅπαντας ἀποστρέψουσιν ἰδόντες, καὶ βωμοὺς, εἰκαῖα λίθων ἱδρύματα κωφῶν αἵμασιν ἐμψύχων μεμιασμένα καὶ θυσίῃσι τετραπόδων κ.τ.λ. In an earlier passage vv. 8 sq. it is said of God, οὔτε γὰρ οἶκον ἔχει ναῷ λίθον ἱδρυθέντα κωφότατον νωδόν τε, βροτῶν πολυαλγέα λώβην.

[4] ver. 160 ἐν ποταμοῖς λούσασθε ὅλον δέμας ἀενάοισι. Another point of contact with the Essenes is the great stress on prayers before meals, ver. 26 εὐλογέοντες πρὶν πιέειν φαγέειν τε. Ewald (*Sibyll. Bücher* p. 46) points also to the prominence of the words εὐσεβεῖν, εὐσεβής, εὐσεβία (vv. 26, 35, 42, 45, 133, 148, 151, 162, 165, 181, 183) to designate the elect of God, as tending in the same direction. The force of this latter argument will depend mainly on the derivation which is given to the name *Essene*. See below, p. 349 sq.

independent development of Judaism. In some respects at
all events its language seems quite inconsistent with the purer
type of Essenism[1]. But its general tendency is clear: and
of its locality there can hardly be a doubt. The affairs of
Asia Minor occupy a disproportionate space in the poet's description of the past and vision of the future. The cities of
the Mæander and its neighbourhood, among these Laodicea,
are mentioned with emphasis[2].

And certainly the moral and intellectual atmosphere would Phrygia
not be unfavourable to the growth of such a plant. The same and Asia
congenial
district, which in speculative philosophy had produced a Thales to this
type of
and a Heraclitus[3], had developed in popular religion the wor- religion.
ship of the Phrygian Cybele and Sabazius and of the Ephesian Artemis[4]. Cosmological speculation, mystic theosophy,
religious fanaticism, all had their home here. Associated with
Judaism or with Christianity the natural temperament and the
intellectual bias of the people would take a new direction;

[1] Thus for instance, Ewald (l. c., p.
47) points to the tacit approval of marriage in ver. 33. I hardly think however
that this passage, which merely condemns adultery, can be taken to imply
so much. More irreconcilable with pure
Essenism is the belief in the resurrection of the body and the future life
on earth, which is maintained in vv.
176 sq.; though Hilgenfeld (*Zeitschr.*
xiv. p. 49) does not recognise the difficulty. See above p. 88. This Sibylline writer was perhaps rather a Hemerobaptist than an Essene. On the
relation of the Hemerobaptists and
Essenes see the third dissertation.
Alexandre, *Orac. Sibyll.* (ii. p. 323),
says of this Sibylline Oracle, 'Ipse
liber haud dubie Christianus est,' but
there is nothing distinctly Christian
in its teaching.

[2] vv. 106 sq., 145 sq.; see above p. 40,
note 2. It begins κλῦθι λεὼς 'Ασίης με-
γαλαυχέος Εὐρώπης τε.

[3] The exceptional activity of the

forces of nature in these districts of
Asia Minor may have directed the
speculations of the Ionic school towards
physics, and more especially towards
cosmogony. In Heraclitus there is
also a strong mystical element. But
besides such broader affinities, I venture to call attention to special dicta of
the two philosophers mentioned in the
text, which curiously recall the tenets
of the Judæo-Gnostic teachers. Thales
declared (Diog. Laert. i. 27) τὸν κόσμον
ἔμψυχον καὶ δαιμόνων πλήρη, or, as reported by Aristotle (*de An.* i. 5, p. 411),
πάντα πλήρη θεῶν εἶναι. In a recorded
saying of Heraclitus we have the very
language of a Gnostic teacher; Clem.
Alex. *Strom.* v. 13, p. 699, τὰ μὲν τῆς
γνώσιος βάθη κρύπτειν ἀπιστίη
ἀγαθή, καθ' 'Ηράκλειτον· ἀπιστίη γὰρ
διαφυγγάνει τὸ μὴ γινώσκεσθαι. See
above pp. 77, 92.

[4] For the characteristic features of
Phrygian religious worship see Steiger
Kolosser p. 70 sq.

but the old type would not be altogether obliterated. Phrygia reared the hybrid monstrosities of Ophitism[1]. She was the mother of Montanist enthusiasm[2], and the foster-mother of Novatian rigorism[3]. The syncretist, the mystic, the devotee, the puritan, would find a congenial climate in these regions of Asia Minor.

Previous results summed up.

It has thus been shown *first*, that Essene Judaism was Gnostic in its character; and *secondly*, that this type of Jewish thought and practice had established itself in the Apostolic age in those parts of Asia Minor with which we are more directly concerned. It now remains to examine the heresy of the Colossian Church more nearly, and to see whether it deserves the name, which provisionally was given to it, of Gnostic Judaism. Its Judaism all will allow. Its claim to be regarded as Gnostic will require a closer scrutiny. And in conducting this examination, it will be convenient to take the three notes of Gnosticism which have been already laid down, and to enquire how far it satisfies these tests.

Is the Colossian heresy Gnostic?

Three notes of Gnosticism.

1. Intellectual exclusiveness.

1. It has been pointed out that Gnosticism strove to establish, or rather to preserve, an *intellectual oligarchy* in religion. It had its hidden wisdom, its exclusive mysteries, its privileged class.

Now I think it will be evident, that St Paul in this epistle

---

[1] The prominence, which the Phrygian mysteries and Phrygian rites held in the syncretism of the Ophites, is clear from the account of Hippolytus *Hær.* v. 7 sq. Indeed Phrygia appears to have been the proper home of Ophitism. Yet the admixture of Judaic elements is not less obvious, as the name *Naassene*, derived from the Hebrew word for a serpent, shows.

[2] The name, by which the Montanists were commonly known in the early ages, was the sect of the 'Phrygians'; Clem. *Strom.* vii. 17, p. 900 αἱ δὲ [τῶν αἱρέσεων] ἀπὸ ἔθνους [προσαγορεύονται], ὡς ἡ τῶν Φρυγῶν (comp. Eus.

H. E. iv. 27, v. 16, Hipp. *Hær.* viii. 19, x. 25). From οἱ (or ἡ) κατὰ Φρυγάς (Eus. *H. E.* ii. 25, v. 16, 18, vi. 20) comes the solœcistic Latin name *Cataphryges*.

[3] Socrates (iv. 28) accounts for the spread of Novatianism in Phrygia by the σωφροσύνη of the Phrygian temper. If so, it is a striking testimony to the power of Christianity, that under its influence the religious enthusiasm of the Phrygians should have taken this direction, and that they should have exchanged the fanatical orgiasm of their heathen worship for the rigid puritanism of the Novatianist.

feels himself challenged to contend for the *universality* of the St Paul
Gospel. This indeed is a characteristic feature of the Apostle's contends
teaching at all times, and holds an equally prominent place in universal-
the epistles of an earlier date. But the point to be observed is, Gospel,
that the Apostle, in maintaining this doctrine, has changed the
mode of his defence; and this fact suggests that there has been
a change in the direction of the attack. It is no longer against
national exclusiveness, but against intellectual exclusiveness,
that he contends. His adversaries do not now plead ceremonial
restrictions, or at least do not plead these alone: but they erect
an artificial barrier of spiritual privilege, even more fatal to
the universal claims of the Gospel, because more specious and
more insidious. It is not now against the Jew as such, but
against the Jew become Gnostic, that he fights the battle of
liberty. In other words; it is not against Christian Pharisaism
but against Christian Essenism that he defends his position.
Only in the light of such an antagonism can we understand the
emphatic iteration with which he claims to 'warn *every* man
and teach *every* man in *every* wisdom, that he may present
every man perfect in Christ Jesus[1].' It will be remembered against
that 'wisdom' in Gnostic teaching was the exclusive possession of the pre-
the few; it will not be forgotten that 'perfection' was the term an aristo-
especially applied in their language to this privileged minority, intellect.
as contradistinguished from the common herd of believers;
and thus it will be readily understood why St Paul should go
on to say that this universality of the Gospel is the one object
of his contention, to which all the energies of his life are
directed, and having done so, should express his intense anxiety
for the Churches of Colossæ and the neighbourhood, lest they
should be led astray by a spurious wisdom to desert the true
knowledge[2]. This danger also will enable us to appreciate a

---

[1] i. 28 νουθετοῦντες πάντα ἄνθρωπον
καὶ διδάσκοντες πάντα ἄνθρωπον ἐν
πάσῃ σοφίᾳ ἵνα παραστήσωμεν πάντα
ἄνθρωπον τέλειον ἐν Χριστῷ κ.τ.λ. The
reiteration has offended the scribes;
and the first πάντα ἄνθρωπον is omitted

in some copies, the second in others.
For τέλειον see the note on the passage.

[2] The connexion of the sentences
should be carefully observed. After
the passage quoted in the last note
comes the asseveration that this is

novel feature in another passage of the epistle. While dwelling
on the obliteration of all distinctions in Christ, he repeats his
earlier contrasts, 'Greek and Jew,' 'circumcision and uncircumcision,' 'bondslave and free'; but to these he adds new words
which at once give a wider scope and a more immediate application to the lesson.   In Christ the existence of 'barbarian' and
even 'Scythian,' the lowest type of barbarian, is extinguished[1].
As culture, civilisation, philosophy, knowledge, are no conditions
of acceptance, so neither is their absence any disqualification in
the believer.   The aristocracy of intellectual discernment, which
Gnosticism upheld in religion, is abhorrent to the first principles
of the Gospel.

He con-
trasts the
true wis-
dom with
the false,

Hence also must be explained the frequent occurrence of
the words 'wisdom' ($\sigma o\phi ia$), 'intelligence' ($\sigma \acute{\nu}\nu\epsilon\sigma\iota s$), 'knowledge'
($\gamma\nu\hat{\omega}\sigma\iota s$), 'perfect knowledge' ($\acute{\epsilon}\pi\acute{\iota}\gamma\nu\omega\sigma\iota s$), in this epistle[2].   St
Paul takes up the language of his opponents, and translates it
into a higher sphere.   The false teachers put forward a 'philosophy,' but it was only an empty deceit, only a plausible display
of false reasoning[3].   They pretended 'wisdom,' but it was
merely the profession, not the reality[4].   Against these pretentions
the Apostle sets the true wisdom of the Gospel.   On its wealth,
its fulness, its perfection, he is never tired of dwelling[5].   The
true wisdom, he would argue, is essentially spiritual and yet
essentially definite; while the false is argumentative, is specu-

the one object of the Apostle's preach-
ing (i. 29) $\epsilon \grave{\iota}s$ $\grave{o}$ $\kappa a\grave{\iota}$ $\kappa o\pi\iota\hat{\omega}$ $\kappa.\tau.\lambda.$; then
the expression of concern on behalf
of the Colossians (ii. 1) $\theta\acute{\epsilon}\lambda\omega$ $\gamma\grave{a}\rho$ $\acute{\upsilon}\mu\hat{a}s$
$\epsilon \acute{\iota}\delta\acute{\epsilon}\nu a\iota$ $\grave{\eta}\lambda\acute{\iota}\kappa o\nu$ $\grave{a}\gamma\hat{\omega}\nu a$ $\acute{\epsilon}\chi\omega$ $\acute{\upsilon}\pi\grave{\epsilon}\rho$ $\acute{\upsilon}\mu\hat{\omega}\nu$
$\kappa.\tau.\lambda.$; then the desire that they may
be brought (ii. 2) $\epsilon \grave{\iota}s$ $\pi\hat{a}\nu$ $\pi\lambda o\hat{\upsilon}\tau os$ $\tau\hat{\eta}s$
$\pi\lambda\eta\rho o\phi o\rho\acute{\iota}as$ $\tau\hat{\eta}s$ $\sigma\upsilon\nu\acute{\epsilon}\sigma\epsilon\omega s$, $\epsilon \grave{\iota}s$ $\acute{\epsilon}\pi\acute{\iota}$-
$\gamma\nu\omega\sigma\iota\nu$ $\tau o\hat{\upsilon}$ $\mu\upsilon\sigma\tau\eta\rho\acute{\iota}o\upsilon$ $\tau o\hat{\upsilon}$ $\Theta\epsilon o\hat{\upsilon}$; then
the definition of this mystery (ii. 2, 3),
$X\rho\iota\sigma\tau o\hat{\upsilon}$ $\acute{\epsilon}\nu$ $\hat{\phi}$ $\epsilon \acute{\iota}\sigma\grave{\iota}\nu$ $\pi\acute{a}\nu\tau\epsilon s$ $o\grave{\iota}$ $\theta\eta\sigma a\upsilon\rho o\grave{\iota}$
$\kappa.\tau.\lambda.$; then the warning against the
false teachers (ii. 4) $\tau o\hat{\upsilon}\tau o$ $\lambda\acute{\epsilon}\gamma\omega$ $\acute{\iota}\nu a$
$\mu\eta\delta\epsilon\grave{\iota}s$ $\acute{\upsilon}\mu\hat{a}s$ $\pi a\rho a\lambda o\gamma\acute{\iota}\zeta\eta\tau a\iota$ $\kappa.\tau.\lambda.$

[1] Col. iii. 11 after $\pi\epsilon\rho\iota\tau o\mu\grave{\eta}$ $\kappa a\grave{\iota}$
$\grave{a}\kappa\rho o\beta\upsilon\sigma\tau\acute{\iota}a$ the Apostle adds $\beta\acute{a}\rho\beta a\rho os$,

$\Sigma\kappa\acute{\upsilon}\theta\eta s$. There is nothing corresponding to this in the parallel passage,
Gal. iii. 28.

[2] For $\sigma o\phi\acute{\iota}a$ see i. 9, 28, ii. 3, iii. 16,
iv. 5; for $\sigma\acute{\upsilon}\nu\epsilon\sigma\iota s$ i. 9, ii. 2; for $\gamma\nu\hat{\omega}\sigma\iota s$
ii. 3; for $\acute{\epsilon}\pi\acute{\iota}\gamma\nu\omega\sigma\iota s$ i. 9, 10, ii. 2,
iii. 10.

[3] ii. 4 $\pi\iota\theta a\nu o\lambda o\gamma\acute{\iota}a$, ii. 8 $\kappa\epsilon\nu\grave{\eta}$ $\grave{a}\pi\acute{a}\tau\eta$.

[4] ii. 23 $\lambda\acute{o}\gamma o\nu$ $\mu\grave{\epsilon}\nu$ $\acute{\epsilon}\chi o\nu\tau a$ $\sigma o\phi\acute{\iota}as$,
where the $\mu\grave{\epsilon}\nu$ suggests the contrast
of the suppressed clause.

[5] e.g. i. 9, 28, iii. 16 $\acute{\epsilon}\nu$ $\pi\acute{a}\sigma\eta$
$\sigma o\phi\acute{\iota}q$; ii. 2 $\tau\hat{\eta}s$ $\pi\lambda\eta\rho o\phi o\rho\acute{\iota}as$. For the
'wealth' of this knowledge compare
i. 27, ii. 2, iii. 16; and see above
p. 44.

lative, is vague and dreamy[1]. Again they had their rites of initiation. St Paul contrasts with these the one universal, com- *and dwells on the veritable mystery.* prehensive mystery[2], the knowledge of God in Christ. This mystery is complete in itself: it contains 'all the treasures of wisdom and of knowledge hidden' in it[3]. Moreover it is offered to all without distinction: though once hidden, its revelation is unrestricted, except by the waywardness and disobedience of men. The esoteric spirit of Gnosticism finds no countenance in the Apostle's teaching.

2. From the informing spirit of Gnosticism we turn to the *2. Speculative tenets.* speculative tenets—the cosmogony and the theology of the Gnostic. *Cosmogony and theology.*

And here too the affinities to Gnosticism reveal themselves in the Colossian heresy. We cannot fail to observe that the Apostle has in view the doctrine of intermediate agencies, re- *St Paul attacks the doctrine of angelic mediators,* garded as instruments in the creation and government of the world. Though this tenet is not distinctly mentioned, it is tacitly assumed in the teaching which St Paul opposes to it. Against the philosophy of successive evolutions from the Divine nature, angelic mediators forming the successive links in the chain which binds the finite to the Infinite, he sets the doctrine of the one Eternal Son, the Word of God begotten before the *setting against it the doctrine of the Word Incarnate,* worlds[4]. The angelology of the heretics had a twofold bearing; it was intimately connected at once with cosmogony and with religion. Correspondingly St Paul represents the mediatorial function of Christ as twofold: it is exercised in the natural creation, and it is exercised in the spiritual creation. In both these spheres His initiative is absolute, His control is universal, His action is complete. By His agency the world of matter was created and is sustained. He is at once the beginning and the

---

[1] ii. 4, 18.

[2] i. 26, 27, ii. 2, iv. 3.

[3] ii. 2 ἐν ᾧ εἰσὶν πάντες οἱ θησαυροὶ τῆς σοφίας καὶ τῆς γνώσεως ἀπόκρυφοι. For the meaning of ἀπόκρυφοι see above p. 90, and the note on the passage.

[4] The two great Christological pas-

sages are i. 15—20, ii. 9—15. They will be found to justify the statements in this and the following paragraphs of the text. For the meaning of individual expressions see the notes on the passages.

end of the material universe; 'All things have been created through Him and unto Him.' Nor is His office in the spiritual

as the re-
conciler of
heaven
and earth. world less complete. In the Church, as in the Universe, He is sole, absolute, supreme; the primary source from which all life proceeds and the ultimate arbiter in whom all feuds are reconciled.

His rela-
tions to
(1) Deity;
as God
mani-
fested. On the one hand, in relation to Deity, He is the visible image of the invisible God. He is not only the chief manifestation of the Divine nature: He exhausts the Godhead manifested. In Him resides the totality of the Divine powers and attributes. For this totality Gnostic teachers had a technical

The *plero-*
ma resides
in Him. term, the *pleroma* or *plenitude*[1]. From the pleroma they supposed that all those agencies issued, through which God has at any time exerted His power in creation, or manifested His will through revelation. These mediatorial beings would retain more or less of its influence, according as they claimed direct parentage from it or traced their descent through successive evolutions. But in all cases this pleroma was distributed, diluted, transformed and darkened by foreign admixture. They were only partial and blurred images, often deceptive caricatures, of their original, broken lights of the great central Light. It is not improbable that, like later speculators of the same school, they found a place somewhere or other in their genealogy of spiritual beings for the Christ. If so, St Paul's language becomes doubly significant. But this hypothesis is not needed to explain its reference. In contrast to their doctrine, he asserts and repeats the assertion, that the pleroma abides absolutely and wholly in Christ as the Word of God[2]. The entire light is concentrated in Him.

(2) Created
things; as
absolute
Lord. Hence it follows that, as regards created things, His supremacy must be absolute. In heaven as in earth, over things immaterial as over things material, He is king. Speculations on the nature of intermediate spiritual agencies—their names, their ranks, their offices—were rife in the schools of Judæo-Gnostic

---

[1] See the detached note on πλή-ρωμα.

[2] i. 19 ἐν αὐτῷ εὐδόκησεν πᾶν τὸ πλήρωμα κατοικῆσαι, ii. 9 ἐν αὐτῷ κατοικεῖ πᾶν τὸ πλήρωμα τῆς θεότητος σωματικῶς.

thought. 'Thrones, dominations, princedoms, virtues, powers'—these formed part of the spiritual nomenclature which they had invented to describe different grades of angelic mediators. Without entering into these speculations, the Apostle asserts that Christ is Lord of all, the highest and the lowest, whatever rank they may hold and by whatever name they are called[1], for they are parts of creation and He is the source of creation. Through Him they became, and unto Him they tend.

Hence the worship of angels, which the false teachers inculcated, was utterly wrong in principle. The motive of this angelolatry it is not difficult to imagine. There was a show of humility[2], for there was a confession of weakness, in this subservience to inferior mediatorial agencies. It was held feasible to grasp at the lower links of the chain which bound earth to heaven, when heaven itself seemed far beyond the reach of man. The successive grades of intermediate beings were as successive steps, by which man might mount the ladder leading up to the throne of God. This carefully woven web of sophistry the Apostle tears to shreds. The doctrine of the false teachers was based on confident assumptions respecting angelic beings of whom they could know nothing. It was moreover a denial of Christ's twofold personality and His mediatorial office. It follows from the true conception of Christ's Person, that He and He alone can bridge over the chasm between earth and heaven; for He is at once the lowest and the highest. He raises up man to God, for He brings down God to man. Thus the chain is reduced to a single link, this link being the Word made flesh. As the *pleroma* resides in Him, so is it communicated to us through Him[3]. To substitute allegiance to any other spiritual mediator is to sever

Angelolatry is therefore condemned

as a denial of His perfect mediation.

---

[1] See especially i. 16 εἴτε θρόνοι εἴτε κυριότητες εἴτε ἀρχαὶ εἴτε ἐξουσίαι κ.τ.λ., compared with the parallel passage in Eph. i. 21 ὑπεράνω πάσης ἀρχῆς καὶ ἐξουσίας καὶ δυνάμεως καὶ κυριότητος καὶ παντὸς ὀνόματος ὀνομαζομένου κ.τ.λ.

Compare also ii. 10 ἡ κεφαλὴ πάσης ἀρχῆς καὶ ἐξουσίας, and ii. 15 ἀπεκδυσάμενος τὰς ἀρχὰς καὶ τὰς ἐξουσίας κ.τ.λ.

[2] ii. 18 θέλων ἐν ταπεινοφροσύνῃ καὶ θρησκείᾳ τῶν ἀγγέλων κ.τ.λ.

[3] ii. 10; comp. i. 9.

the connexion of the limbs with the Head, which is the centre of life and the mainspring of all energy throughout the body[1].

The Apostle's practical inference. Hence follows the practical conclusion, that, whatever is done, must be done in the name of the Lord[2]. Wives must submit to their husbands 'in the Lord': children must obey their parents 'in the Lord': servants must work for their masters as working 'unto the Lord[3].' This iteration, 'in the Lord,' 'unto the Lord,' is not an irrelevant form of words; but arises as an immediate inference from the main idea which underlies the doctrinal portion of the epistle.

3. Moral results of Gnostic doctrine. 3. It has been shown that the speculative tenets of Gnosticism might lead (and as a matter of fact we know that they did lead) to either of two practical extremes, to rigid asceticism or to unbridled license. The latter alternative appears to some extent in the heresy of the Pastoral Epistles[4] and still more plainly in those of the Catholic Epistles[5] and the Apocalypse[6]. It is constantly urged by Catholic writers as a reproach against later Gnostic sects[7].

Asceticism of the Colossian heresy But the former and nobler extreme was the first impulse of the Gnostic. To escape from the infection of evil by escaping from the domination of matter was his chief anxiety. This appears very plainly in the Colossian heresy. Though the prohibitions to which the Apostle alludes might be explained in part by the ordinances of the Mosaic ritual, this explanation will not cover all the facts. Thus for instance drinks are mentioned as well as meats[8], though on the former the law of Moses is silent. Thus again the rigorous denunciation, 'Touch not, taste not, handle not[9],' seems to go very far beyond the Levitical enactments. And moreover the *motive* of these pro-

---

[1] ii. 18.

[2] iii. 17.

[3] iii. 18, 20, 23.

[4] At least in 2 Tim. iii. 1—7, where, though the most monstrous developments of the evil were still future, the Apostle's language implies that it had already begun. On the other hand in the picture of the heresy in 1 Tim.

iv. 2 the ascetic tendency still predominates.

[5] 2 Pet. ii. 10 sq., Jude 8.

[6] Apoc. ii. 14, 20—22.

[7] See the notes on Clem. Rom. *Ep.* ii. § 9.

[8] ii. 16.

[9] ii. 21.

hibitions is Essene rather than Pharisaic, Gnostic rather than Jewish. These severities of discipline were intended 'to check indulgence of the flesh[1].' They professed to treat the body with entire disregard, to ignore its cravings and to deny its wants. In short they betray a strong *ascetic* tendency[2], of which normal Judaism, as represented by the Pharisee, offers no explanation.

not explained by its Judaism.

And St Paul's answer points to the same inference. The difference will appear more plainly, if we compare it with his treatment of Pharisaic Judaism in the Galatian Church. This epistle offers nothing at all corresponding to his language on that occasion; 'If righteousness be by law, then Christ died in vain'; 'If ye be circumcised, Christ shall profit you nothing'; 'Christ is nullified for you, whosoever are justified by law; ye are fallen from grace[3].' The point of view in fact is wholly changed. With these Essene or Gnostic Judaizers the Mosaic law was neither the motive nor the standard, it was only the starting point, of their austerities. Hence in replying the Apostle no longer deals with law, as law; he no longer points the contrast of grace and works; but he enters upon the *moral* aspects of these ascetic practices. He denounces them, as concentrating the thoughts on earthly and perishable things[4]. He points out that they fail in their purpose, and are found valueless against carnal indulgences[5]. In their place he offers the true and only remedy against sin—the elevation of the inner life in Christ, the transference of the affections into a higher sphere[6], where the temptations of the flesh are powerless. Thus dying with Christ, they will kill *all* their earthly members[7]. Thus rising with Christ, they will be renewed in the image of God their Creator[8].

St Paul's reply shows its Gnostic bearing.

It is no longer the contrast of law and grace.

---

[1] ii. 23.

[2] Asceticism is of two kinds. There is the asceticism of dualism (whether conscious or unconscious), which springs from a false principle; and there is the asceticism of self-discipline, which is the training of the Christian athlete (1 Cor. ix. 27). I need not say that the remarks in the text apply only to the former.

[3] Gal. ii. 21, v. 2, 4.

[4] ii. 8, 20—22.

[5] ii. 23 οὐκ ἐν τιμῇ τινὶ πρὸς πλησμονὴν τῆς σαρκός: see the note on these words.

[6] iii. 1, 2.

[7] iii. 3, 5.

[8] iii. 10.

The truth of the above result tested by

In attempting to draw a complete portrait of the Colossian heresy from a few features accidentally exhibited in St Paul's epistle, it has been necessary to supply certain links; and some assurance may not unreasonably be required that this has not been done arbitrarily. Nor is this security wanting. In all such cases the test will be twofold. The result must be consistent with itself: and it must do no violence to the historical conditions under which the phenomena arose.

(1) Its inherent consistency and symmetry.

1. In the present instance the former of these tests is fully satisfied. The consistency and the symmetry of the result is its great recommendation. The postulate of a Gnostic type brings the separate parts of the representation into direct connexion. The speculative opinions and the practical tendencies of the heresy thus explain, and are explained by, each other. It is analogous to the hypothesis of the comparative anatomist, who by referring the fossil remains to their proper type restores the whole skeleton of some unknown animal from a few bones belonging to different extremities of the body, and without the intermediate and connecting parts. In the one case, as in the other, the result is the justification of the postulate.

(2) Its place in a historical sequence.

2. And again; the historical conditions of the problem are carefully observed. It has been shown already, that Judaism in the preceding age had in one of its developments assumed a form which was the natural precursor of the Colossian heresy. In order to complete the argument it will be necessary to show that Christianity in the generation next succeeding exhibited a perverted type, which was its natural outgrowth. If this can be done, the Colossian heresy will take its proper place in a regular historical sequence.

Continuance of this type of Judæo-Gnosticism in the district.

I have already pointed out that the language of St John in the Apocalypse, which was probably written within a few years of this epistle, seems to imply the continuance in this district of the same type of heresy which is here denounced by St Paul[1]. But the notices in this book are not more de-

---

[1] See above p. 41 sq.

finite than those of the Epistle to the Colossians itself; and
we are led to look outside the Canonical writings for some
more explicit evidence. Has early Christian history then preserved any record of a distinctly Gnostic school existing on the
confines of the Apostolic age, which may be considered a legitimate development of the phase of religious speculation that
confronts us here?

We find exactly the phenomenon which we are seeking in Heresy of
the heresy of Cerinthus[1]. The time, the place, the circum- Cerinthus.
stances, all agree. This heresiarch is said to have been originally a native of Alexandria[2]; but proconsular Asia is allowed His date
on all hands to have been the scene of his activity as a and place.
teacher[3]. He lived and taught at the close of the Apostolic
age, that is, in the latest decade of the first century. Some
writers indeed make him an antagonist of St Peter and St
Paul[4], but their authority is not trustworthy, nor is this very
early date at all probable. But there can be no reasonable
doubt that he was a contemporary of St John, who was related
by Polycarp to have denounced him face to face on one me-
morable occasion[5], and is moreover said by Irenæus to have
written his Gospel with the direct object of confuting his errors[6].

[1] The relation of Cerinthus to the
Colossian heresy is briefly indicated
by Neander *Planting of Christianity*
I. p. 325 sq. (Eng. Trans.). It has
been remarked by other writers also,
both earlier and later. The subject
appears to me to deserve a fuller
investigation than it has yet received.

[2] Hippol. *Hær.* vii. 33 Αἰγυπτίων
παιδείᾳ ἀσκηθείς, x. 21 ὁ ἐν Αἰγύπτῳ
ἀσκηθείς, Theodoret. *Hær. Fab.* ii. 3 ἐν
Αἰγύπτῳ πλεῖστον διατρίψας χρόνον.

[3] Iren. i. 26. 1 'et Cerinthus autem
quidam...in Asia docuit,' Epiphan.
Hær. xxviii. 1 ἐγένετο δὲ οὗτος ὁ Κή-
ρινθος ἐν τῇ 'Ασίᾳ διατρίβων, κἀκεῖσε
τοῦ κηρύγματος τὴν ἀρχὴν πεποιημένος,
Theodoret. l. c. ὕστερον εἰς τὴν 'Ασίαν
ἀφίκετο. The scene of his encounter

with St John in the bath is placed at
Ephesus: see below, note 5.

[4] Epiphanius (xxviii. 2 sq.) represents him as the ringleader of the
Judaizing opponents of the Apostles
in the Acts and Epistles to the Corinthians and Galatians. Philastrius
(*Hær.* 36) takes the same line.

[5] The well-known story of the encounter between St John and Cerinthus
in the bath is related by Irenæus
(iii. 3. 4) on the authority of Polycarp,
who appears from the sequence of
Irenæus' narrative to have told it at
Rome, when he paid his visit to Anicetus; ὃς καὶ ἐπὶ 'Ανικήτου ἐπιδημήσας
τῇ 'Ρώμῃ πολλοὺς ἀπὸ τῶν προειρημένων
αἱρετικῶν ἐπέστρεψεν...καὶ εἰσὶν οἱ ἀκη-
κοότες αὐτοῦ ὅτι 'Ιωάννης κ.τ.λ.

[6] Iren. iii. 11. 1.

Cerinthus a link between Judaism and Gnosticism.

'Cerinthus,' writes Neander, 'is best entitled to be considered as the intermediate link between the Judaizing and the Gnostic sects.' 'Even among the ancients,' he adds, 'opposite reports respecting his doctrines have been given from opposite points of view, according as the Gnostic or the Judaizing element was exclusively insisted upon: and the dispute on this point has been kept up even to modern times. In point of chronology too Cerinthus may be regarded as representing the principle in its transition from Judaism to Gnosticism[1].'

Judaism still prominent in his system

Of his Judaism no doubt has been or can be entertained. The gross Chiliastic doctrine ascribed to him[2], even though it may have been exaggerated in the representations of adverse writers, can only be explained by a Jewish origin. His conception of the Person of Christ was Ebionite, that is Judaic, in its main features[3]. He is said moreover to have enforced the rite of circumcision and to have inculcated the observance of sabbaths[4]. It is related also that the Cerinthians, like the Ebionites, accepted the Gospel of St Matthew alone[5].

though Gnosticism is already aggressive.

At the same time, it is said by an ancient writer that his adherence to Judaism was only partial[6]. This limitation is doubtless correct. As Gnostic principles asserted themselves more distinctly, pure Judaism necessarily suffered. All or nearly all the early Gnostic heresies were Judaic; and for a time a compromise was effected which involved more or less concession on either side. But the ultimate incompatibility of the two at length became evident, and a precarious alliance was exchanged for an open antagonism. This final result however was not reached till the middle of the second century: and meanwhile it was a question to what extent Judaism was pre-

---

[1] *Church History* II. p. 42 (Bohn's Trans.).

[2] See the *Dialogue of Gaius and Proclus* in Euseb. *H. E.* iii. 28, Dionysius of Alexandria, ib. vii. 25, Theodoret. 1. c., Augustin. *Hær.* 8.

[3] See below p. 111.

[4] Epiphan. *Hær.* xxviii. 4, 5, Philastr. *Hær.* 36, Augustin. 1. c. The

statements of these writers would not carry much weight in themselves; but in this instance they are rendered highly probable by the known Judaism of Cerinthus.

[5] Epiphan. *Hær.* xxviii. 5, xxx. 14, Philastr. *Hær.* 36.

[6] Epiphan. *Hær.* xxviii. 1 προσέχειν τῷ Ἰουδαϊσμῷ ἀπὸ μέρους.

pared to make concessions for the sake of this new ally. Even the Jewish Essenes, as we have seen, departed from the orthodox position in the matter of sacrifices; and if we possessed fuller information, we should probably find that they made still larger concessions than this. Of the Colossian heretics we can only form a conjecture, but the angelology and angelolatry attributed to them point to a further step in the same direction. As we pass from them to Cerinthus we are no longer left in doubt; for the Gnostic element has clearly gained the ascendant, though it has not yet driven its rival out of the field. Two characteristic features in his teaching especially deserve consideration, both as evincing the tendency of his speculations and as throwing back light on the notices in the Colossian Epistle.

Gnostic element in his teaching.

1. His cosmogony is essentially Gnostic. The great problem of creation presented itself to him in the same aspect; and the solution which he offered was generically the same. The world, he asserted, was not made by the highest God, but by an angel or power far removed from, and ignorant of, this Supreme Being[1]. Other authorities describing his system speak not of a single power, but of powers, as creating the universe[2]: but all alike represent this demiurge, or these

1. His Gnostic Cosmogony

---

[1] Iren. i. 26. 1 'Non a primo Deo factum esse mundum docuit, sed a virtute quadam valde separata et distante ab ea principalitate quæ est super universa, et ignorante eum qui est super omnia Deum'; Hippol. *Hær.* vii. 33 ἔλεγεν οὐχ ὑπὸ τοῦ πρώτου Θεοῦ γεγονέναι τὸν κόσμον, ἀλλ' ὑπὸ δυνάμεώς τινος κεχωρισμένης τῆς ὑπὲρ τὰ ὅλα ἐξουσίας καὶ ἀγνοούσης τὸν ὑπὲρ πάντα Θεόν, x. 21 ὑπὸ δυνάμεώς τινος ἀγγελικῆς, πολὺ κεχωρισμένης καὶ διεστώσης τῆς ὑπὲρ τὰ ὅλα αὐθεντίας καὶ ἀγνοούσης τὸν ὑπὲρ πάντα Θεόν.

[2] Pseudo-Tertull. *Hær.* 3 'Carpocrates præterea hanc tulit sectam: Unam esse dicit virtutem in superioribus principalem, ex hac prolatos angelos atque virtutes, quos distantes longe a superioribus virtutibus mundum istum in inferioribus partibus condidisse... Post hunc Cerinthus hæreticus erupit, similia docens. Nam et ipse mundum institutum esse ab illis dicit'; Epiphan. *Hær.* xxviii. 1 ἕνα εἶναι τῶν ἀγγέλων τῶν τὸν κόσμον πεποιηκότων; Theodoret. *II. F.* ii. 3 ἕνα μὲν εἶναι τὸν τῶν ὅλων Θεόν, οὐκ αὐτὸν δὲ εἶναι τοῦ κόσμου δημιουργόν, ἀλλὰ δυνάμεις τινὰς κεχωρισμένας καὶ παντελῶς αὐτὸν ἀγνοούσας; Augustin. *Hær.* 8. The one statement is quite reconcilable with the other. Among those angels by whose instrumentality the world was created, Cerinthus appears to have assigned a position of preeminence to one, whom

demiurges, as ignorant of the absolute God. It is moreover
stated that he held the Mosaic law to have been given not
by the supreme God Himself, but by this angel, or one of
these angels, who created the world[1].

**and conse-
quent an-
gelology.** From these notices it is plain that angelology had an important place in his speculations; and that he employed it
to explain the existence of evil supposed to be inherent in
the physical world, as well as to account for the imperfections
of the old dispensation. The 'remote distance' of his angelic
demiurge from the supreme God can hardly be explained except on the hypothesis of *successive* generations of these intermediate agencies. Thus his solution is thoroughly Gnostic.
At the same time, as contrasted with later and more sharply
defined Gnostic systems, the Judaic origin and complexion of
his cosmogony is obvious. His intermediate agencies still retain the name and the personality of angels, and have not
yet given way to those vague idealities which, as emanations
**Angels of
earlier and
æons of
later Gnos-
tics.** or æons, took their place in later speculations. Thus his theory
is linked on to the angelology of later Judaism founded on
the angelic appearances recorded in the Old Testament narrative. And again: while later Gnostics represent the demiurge and giver of the law as antagonistic to the supreme and
good God, Cerinthus does not go beyond postulating his ignorance. He went as far as he could without breaking entirely
with the Old Testament and abandoning his Judaic standing-
ground.

**Cerinthus
a link be-
tween the
Colossian
heresy and
later Gnos-
ticism.** In these respects Cerinthus is the proper link between the
incipient gnosis of the Colossian heretics and the mature
gnosis of the second century. In the Colossian epistle we
still breathe the atmosphere of Jewish angelology, nor is there
any trace of the *æon* of later Gnosticism[2]; while yet speculation
is so far advanced that the angels have an important function

he regarded as the demiurge in a
special sense and under whom the
others worked; see Neander *Church
History* II. p. 43.

[1] Pseudo-Tertull. l. c.; Epiphan.

Hær. xxviii. 4 τὸν δεδωκότα νόμον ἕνα
εἶναι τῶν ἀγγέλων τῶν τὸν κόσμον πεποιηκότων.

[2] I am quite unable to see any
reference to the Gnostic conception of

in explaining the mysteries of the creation and government of the world. On the other hand it has not reached the point at which we find it in Cerinthus. Gnostic conceptions respecting the relation of the demiurgic agency to the supreme God would appear to have passed through three stages. This relation was represented first, as imperfect appreciation; next, as entire ignorance; lastly, as direct antagonism. The second and third are the standing points of Cerinthus and of the later Gnostic teachers respectively. The first was probably the position of the Colossian false teachers. The imperfections of the natural world, they would urge, were due to the limited capacities of these angels to whom the demiurgic work was committed, and to their imperfect sympathy with the Supreme God; but at the same time they might fitly receive worship as mediators between God and man; and indeed humanity seemed in its weakness to need the intervention of some such beings less remote from itself than the highest heaven.

2. Again the Christology of Cerinthus deserves attention from this point of view. Here all our authorities are agreed. As a Judaizer Cerinthus held with the Ebionites that Jesus was only the son of Joseph and Mary, born in the natural way. As a Gnostic he maintained that the Christ first descended in the form of a dove on the carpenter's son at his baptism; that He revealed to him the unknown Father, and worked miracles through him: and that at length He took His flight and left him, so that Jesus alone suffered and rose, while the Christ remained impassible[1]. It would appear also, though this is

2. His Christo-logy.

---

an *æon* in the passages of the New Testament, which are sometimes quoted in support of this view, e. g., by Baur *Paulus* p. 428, Burton *Lectures* p. 111 sq.

[1] Iren. i. 26. 1, Hippol. *Hær.* vii. 33, x. 21, Epiphan. *Hær.* xxviii. 1, Theodoret. *H. F.* ii. 3. The arguments by which Lipsius (*Gnosticismus* pp. 245, 258, in Ersch u. Gruber; *Quellenkritik des Epiphanios* p. 118

sq.) attempts to show that Cerinthus did not separate the Christ from Jesus, and that Irenæus (and subsequent authors copying him) have wrongly attributed to this heretic the theories of later Gnostics, seem insufficient to outweigh these direct statements. It is more probable that the system of Cerinthus should have admitted some foreign elements not very consistent with his Judaic standing

not certain, that he described this re-ascension of the Christ as
a return 'to His own *pleroma*[1].'

Approach
towards
Cerinthian
Christo-
logy in the
Colossian
heresy.

Now it is not clear from St Paul's language what opinions
the Colossian heretics held respecting the person of our Lord;
but we may safely assume that he regarded them as inadequate
and derogatory. The emphasis, with which he asserts the
eternal being and absolute sovereignty of Christ, can hardly be
explained in any other way. But individual expressions tempt
us to conjecture that the same ideas were already floating in
the air, which ultimately took form and consistency in the
tenets of Cerinthus. Thus, when he reiterates the statement
that the *whole* pleroma abides *permanently* in Christ[2], he
would appear to be tacitly refuting some opinion which maintained only mutable and imperfect relations between the two.
When again he speaks of the true gospel first taught to the
Colossians as the doctrine of 'the Christ, *even* Jesus the Lord[3],'
his language might seem to be directed against the tendency
to separate the heavenly Christ from the earthly Jesus, as
though the connexion were only transient. When lastly he
dwells on the work of reconciliation, as wrought 'through the
blood of Christ's cross,' 'in the body of His flesh through
death[4],' we may perhaps infer that he already discerned a
disposition to put aside Christ's passion as a stumbling-block
in the way of philosophical religion. Thus regarded, the

point, than that these writers should
have been misinformed. Inconsistency
was a necessary condition of Judaic
Gnosticism. The point however is
comparatively unimportant as affecting my main purpose.

[1] Irenæus (iii. 11. 1), after speaking
of Cerinthus, the Nicolaitans, and
others, proceeds 'non, quemadmodum
illi dicunt, alterum quidem fabricatorem
(i.e. demiurgum), alium autem Patrem
Domini: et alium quidem fabricatoris
filium, alterum vero de superioribus
Christum, quem et impassibilem per-
severasse, descendentem in Jesum
filium fabricatoris, et iterum *revolasse*

in suum pleroma.' The doctrine is precisely that which he has before ascribed to Cerinthus (i. 26. 1), but the
mode of statement may have been
borrowed from the Nicolaitans or the
Valentinians or some other later Gnostics. There is however no improbability in the supposition that Cerinthus
used the word *pleroma* in this way. See
the detached note on πλήρωμα below.

[2] i. 19, ii. 9. See above p. 102, note 2.
On the force of κατοικεῖν see the note
on the earlier of the two passages.

[3] ii. 6 παρελάβετε τὸν Χριστόν, Ἰησοῦν τὸν Κύριον.

[4] i. 20, 22.

Apostle's language gains force and point; though no stress can be laid on explanations which are so largely conjectural.

But if so, the very generality of his language shows that these speculations were still vague and fluctuating. The difference which separates these heretics from Cerinthus may be measured by the greater precision and directness in the Apostolic counter-statement, as we turn from the Epistle to the Colossians to the Gospel of St John. In this interval, extending over nearly a quarter of a century, speculation has taken a definite shape. The elements of Gnostic theory, which were before held in solution, had meanwhile crystallized around the facts of the Gospel. Yet still we seem justified, even at the earlier date, in speaking of these general ideas as Gnostic, guarding ourselves at the same time against misunderstanding with the twofold caution, that we here employ the term to express the simplest and most elementary conceptions of this tendency of thought, and that we do not postulate its use as a distinct designation of any sect or sects at this early date. Thus limited, the view that the writer of this epistle is combating a Gnostic heresy seems free from all objections, while it appears necessary to explain his language; and certainly it does not, as is sometimes imagined, place any weapon in the hands of those who would assail the early date and Apostolic authorship of the epistle.

The Gnosticism of the Colossians being vague and undeveloped.

III.

CHARACTER AND CONTENTS OF THE EPISTLE.

The understanding of the heresy necessary. WITHOUT the preceding investigation the teaching of this epistle would be very imperfectly understood; for its direction was necessarily determined by the occasion which gave rise to it. Only when we have once grasped the nature of the doctrine which St Paul is combating, do we perceive that every sentence is instinct with life and meaning.

The errors though twofold sprang from one root. We have seen that the error of the heretical teachers was twofold. They had a false conception in theology, and they had a false basis of morals. It has been pointed out also, that these two were closely connected together, and had their root in the same fundamental error, the idea of matter as the abode of evil and thus antagonistic to God.

So the answer to both is in the same truth. As the two elements of the heretical doctrine were derived from the same source, so the reply to both was sought by the Apostle in the same idea, the conception of the Person of Christ as the one absolute mediator between God and man, the true and only reconciler of heaven and earth.

But though they are thus ultimately connected, yet it will be necessary for the fuller understanding of St Paul's position to take them apart, and to consider first the theological and then the ethical teaching of the epistle.

1. The theological teaching of the heretics. 1. This Colossian heresy was no coarse and vulgar development of falsehood. It soared far above the Pharisaic Judaism which St Paul refutes in the Epistle to the Galatians. The questions in which it was interested lie at the very root of our

religious consciousness. The impulse was given to its specu- Its lofty
lations by an overwhelming sense of the unapproachable motive,
majesty of God, by an instinctive recognition of the chasm
which separates God from man, from the world, from matter.
Its energy was sustained by the intense yearning after some
mediation which might bridge over this chasm, might establish
inter-communion between the finite and the Infinite. Up to
this point it was deeply religious in the best sense of the term.

The answer which it gave to these questions we have but com-
already seen. In two respects this answer failed signally. On failure.
the one hand it was drawn from the atmosphere of mystical
speculation. It had no foundation in history, and made no
appeal to experience. On the other hand, notwithstanding
its complexity, it was unsatisfactory in its results; for in this
plurality of mediators none was competent to meet the requirements of the case. God here and man there—no angel or
spirit, whether one or more, being neither God nor man, could
truly reconcile the two. Thus as regards credentials it was
without a guarantee; while as regards efficiency it was wholly
inadequate.

The Apostle pointed out to the Colossians a more excellent The
way. It was the one purpose of Christianity to satisfy those answer
very yearnings which were working in their hearts, to solve is in the
that very problem which had exercised their minds. In Christ of Christ.
they would find the answer which they sought. His life—His
cross and resurrection—was the guarantee; His Person—the The me-
Word Incarnate—was the solution. He alone filled up, He the world
alone could fill up, the void which lay between God and man, and in the
could span the gulf which separated the Creator and creation. Church.
This solution offered by the Gospel is as simple as it is adequate. To their cosmical speculations, and to their religious
yearnings alike, Jesus Christ is the true answer. In the
World, as in the Church, He is the one only mediator, the one
only reconciler. This twofold idea runs like a double thread
through the fabric of the Apostle's teaching in those passages
of the epistle where he is describing the Person of Christ.

It will be convenient for the better understanding of St Paul's teaching to consider these two aspects of Christ's mediation apart—its function in the natural and in the spiritual order respectively.

(i) The heresy of the Colossian teachers took its rise, as we saw, in their cosmical speculations. It was therefore natural that the Apostle in replying should lay stress on the function of the Word in the creation and government of the world. This is the aspect of His work most prominent in the first of the two distinctly Christological passages. The Apostle there predicates of the Word, not only prior, but absolute existence. All things were created through Him, are sustained in Him, are tending towards Him. Thus He is the beginning, middle, and end, of creation. This He is, because He is the very *image* of the Invisible God, because in Him dwells the *plenitude* of Deity.

This creative and administrative work of Christ the Word in the natural order of things is always emphasized in the writings of the Apostles, when they touch upon the doctrine of His Person. It stands in the forefront of the prologue to St John's Gospel: it is hardly less prominent in the opening of the Epistle to the Hebrews. His mediatorial function in the Church is represented as flowing from His mediatorial function in the world. With ourselves this idea has retired very much into the background. Though in the creed common to all the Churches we profess our belief in Him, as the Being 'through whom all things were created,' yet in reality this confession seems to exercise very little influence on our thoughts. And the loss is serious. How much our theological conceptions suffer in breadth and fulness by the neglect, a moment's reflexion will show. How much more hearty would be the sympathy of theologians with the revelations of science and the developments of history, if they habitually connected them with the operation of the same Divine Word who is the centre of all their religious aspirations, it is needless to say. Through the recognition of this idea with all the consequences which flow from it, as a living influence, more than in any other way, may we hope to strike the chords of that 'vaster music,' which results only from the harmony of knowledge and faith, of reverence and research.

It will be said indeed, that this conception leaves untouched the philosophical difficulties which beset the subject; that creation still remains as much a mystery as before. This may be allowed. But is there any reason to think that with our present limited capacities the veil which shrouds it ever will be or can be removed? The metaphysical speculations of twenty-five centuries have done nothing to raise it. The physical investigations of our own age from their very nature can do nothing; for, busied with the evolution of phenomena, they lie wholly outside this question, and do not even touch the fringe of the difficulty. But meanwhile revelation has interposed and thrown out the idea, which, if it leaves many questions unsolved, gives a breadth and unity to our conceptions, at once satisfying our religious needs and linking our scientific instincts with our theological beliefs. *notwithstanding difficulties yet unsolved.*

(ii) But, if Christ's mediatorial office in the physical creation was the starting point of the Apostle's teaching, His mediatorial office in the spiritual creation is its principal theme. The cosmogonies of the false teachers were framed not so much in the interests of philosophy as in the interests of religion; and the Apostle replies to them in the same spirit and with the same motive. If the function of Christ is unique in the Universe, so is it also in the Church. He is the sole and absolute link between God and humanity. Nothing short of His personality would suffice as a medium of reconciliation between the two. Nothing short of His life and work in the flesh, as consummated in His passion, would serve as an assurance of God's love and pardon. His cross is the atonement of mankind with God. He is the Head with whom all the living members of the body are in direct and immediate communication, who suggests their manifold activities to each, who directs their several functions in subordination *(ii) In the Church.* *Its absolute character.*

to the healthy working of the whole, from whom they individually receive their inspiration and their strength.

Hence angelic mediations are fundamentally wrong. And being all this He cannot consent to share His prerogative with others. He absorbs in Himself the whole function of mediation. Through Him alone, without any interposing link of communication, the human soul has access to the Father. Here was the true answer to those deep yearnings after spiritual communion with God, which sought, and could not find, satisfaction in the manifold and fantastic creations of a dreamy mysticism. The worship of angels might have the semblance of humility; but it was in fact a contemptuous defiance of the fundamental idea of the Gospel, a flat denial of the absolute character of Christ's Person and office. It was a severance of the proper connexion with the Head, an amputation of the disordered limb, which was thus disjoined from the source of life and left to perish for want of spiritual nourishment.

Christ's mediation in the Church justified by His mediation in the World. The language of the New Testament writers is beset with difficulties, so long as we conceive of our Lord only in connexion with the Gospel revelation: but, when with the Apostles we realise in Him the same Divine Word who is and ever has been the light of the whole world, who before Christianity wrought first in mankind at large through the avenues of the conscience, and afterwards more particularly in the Jews through a special though still imperfect revelation, then all these difficulties fall away. Then we understand the significance, and we recognise the truth, of such passages as these: 'No man cometh unto the Father, but by me': 'There is no salvation in any other'; 'He that disbelieveth the Son shall not see life, but the wrath of God abideth upon him[1].' The exclusive claims advanced in Christ's name have their full and perfect justification in the doctrine of the Eternal Word.

Relation of the doctrine of the Word The old dispensation is primarily the revelation of the absolute sovereignty of God. It vindicates this truth against two opposing forms of error, which in their extreme types are repre-

---

[1] Joh. xiv. 6, Acts iv. 12, Joh. iii. 36.

sented by Pantheism and Manicheism respectively. The Pantheist identifies God with the world : the Manichee attributes to the world an absolute existence, independent of God. With the Pantheist sin ceases to have any existence : for it is only one form of God's working. With the Manichee sin is inherent in matter, which is antagonistic to God. The teaching of the Old Testament, of which the key-note is struck in the opening chapters of Genesis, is a refutation of both these errors. God is distinct from the world, and He is the Creator of the world. Evil is not inherent in God, but neither is it inherent in the material world. Sin is the disobedience of intelligent beings whom He has created, and whom He has endowed with a free-will, which they can use or misuse. *to the monotheism of the Old Testament.*

The revelation of the New Testament is the proper complement to the revelation of the Old. It holds this position in two main respects. If the Old Testament sets forth the absolute unity of God—His distinctness from and sovereignty over His creatures—the New Testament points out how He holds communion with the world and with humanity, how man becomes one with Him. And again, if the Old Testament shows the true character of sin, the New Testament teaches the appointed means of redemption. On the one hand the monotheism of the Old Testament is supplemented by the theanthropism[1] of the New. Thus the *theology* of revelation is completed. On the other hand, the hamartiology of the Old Testament has its counterpart in the soteriology of the New. Thus the *economy* of revelation is perfected. *The New Testament is complementary to the Old.*

[1] I am indebted for the term *theanthropism*, as describing the substance of the new dispensation, to an article by Prof. Westcott in the *Contemporary Review* IV. p. 417 (December, 1867); but it has been used independently, though in very rare instances, by other writers. The value of terms such as I have employed here in fixing ideas is enhanced by their strangeness, and will excuse any appearance of affectation.

In applying the terms *theanthropism* and *soteriology* to the New Testament, as distinguished from the Old, it is not meant to suggest that the ideas involved in them were wholly wanting in the Old, but only to indicate that the conceptions, which were inchoate and tentative and subsidiary in the one, attain the most prominent position and are distinctly realised in the other.

2. The
ethical
error of
the here-
tics.

Their
practical
earnest-
ness,

but funda-
mental
miscon-
ception
and con-
sequent
failure.

St Paul
substi-
tutes a
principle
for ordi-
nances.

2.   When we turn from the theology of these Colossian heretics to their ethical teaching, we find it characterised by the same earnestness. Of them it might indeed be said that they did 'hunger and thirst after righteousness.' Escape from impurity, immunity from evil, was a passion with them. But it was no less true that notwithstanding all their sincerity they 'went astray in the wilderness'; 'hungry and thirsty, their soul fainted within them.' By their fatal transference of the abode of sin from the human heart within to the material world without, they had incapacitated themselves from finding the true antidote. Where they placed the evil, there they necessarily sought the remedy. Hence they attempted to fence themselves about, and to purify their lives by a code of rigorous prohibitions. Their energy was expended on battling with the physical conditions of human life. Their whole mind was absorbed in the struggle with imaginary forms of evil. Necessarily their character was moulded by the thoughts which habitually engaged them. Where the 'elements of the world,' the 'things which perish in the using[1],' engrossed all their attention, it could not fail but that they should be dragged down from the serene heights of the spiritual life into the cloudy atmosphere which shrouds this lower earth.

St Paul sets himself to combat this false tendency. For negative prohibitions he substitutes a positive principle; for special enactments, a comprehensive motive. He tells them that all their scrupulous restrictions are vain, because they fail to touch the springs of action. If they would overcome the evil, they must strike at the root of the evil. Their point of view must be entirely changed. They must transfer themselves into a wholly new sphere of energy. This transference is nothing less than a migration from earth to heaven—from the region of the external and transitory to the region of the spiritual and eternal[2]. For a code of rules they must substitute a principle of life, which is one in its essence but

---

[1] ii. 20, 22.   [2] iii. 1 sq.

infinite in its application, which will meet every emergency, will control every action, will resist every form of evil.

This principle they have in Christ. With Him they have died to the world; with Him they have risen to God. Christ, the revelation of God's holiness, of God's righteousness, of God's love, is light, is life, is heaven. With Him they have been translated into a higher sphere, have been brought face to face with the Eternal Presence. Let them only realise this translation. It involves new insight, new motives, new energies. They will no more waste themselves upon vexatious special restrictions: for they will be furnished with a higher inspiration which will cover all the minute details of action. They will not exhaust their energies in crushing this or that rising desire, but they will kill the whole body[1] of their earthly passions through the strong arm of this personal communion with God in Christ.

When we once grasp this idea, which lies at the root of St Paul's ethical teaching, the moral difficulty which is supposed to attach to his doctrine of faith and works has vanished. It is simply an impossibility that faith should exist without works. Though in form he states his doctrine as a relation of contrast between the two, in substance it resolves itself into a question of precedence. Faith and works are related as principle and practice. Faith—the repose in the unseen, the recognition of eternal principles of truth and right, the sense of personal obligations to an Eternal Being who vindicates these principles—must come first. Faith is not an intellectual assent, nor a sympathetic sentiment merely. It is the absolute surrender of self to the will of a Being who has a right to command this surrender. It is this which places men in personal relation to God, which (in St Paul's language) justifies them before God. For it touches the springs of their actions; it fastens not on this or that detail of conduct, but extends

Marginal notes: This principle is the heavenly life in Christ.

St Paul's doctrine of faith and works considered in the light of this principle.

---

[1] ii. 11 ἐν τῇ ἀπεκδύσει τοῦ σώματος τῆς σαρκός, iii. 5 νεκρώσατε οὖν τὰ μέλη with ver. 8 νυνὶ δὲ ἀπόθεσθε καὶ ὑμεῖς τὰ πάντα, and ver. 9 ἀπεκδυσάμενοι τὸν παλαιὸν ἄνθρωπον. See the notes on the several passages.

throughout the whole sphere of moral activity; and thus it
determines their character as responsible beings in the sight
of God.

The
Christ-
ology of
this epistle

From the above account it will have appeared that the distinctive feature of this epistle is its Christology. The doctrine
of the Person of Christ is here stated with greater precision
and fulness than in any other of St Paul's epistles. It is
therefore pertinent to ask (even though the answer must necessarily be brief) what relation this statement bears to certain
other enunciations of the same doctrine; to those for instance
considered which occur elsewhere in St Paul's own letters, to those which
in relation
to
are found in other Apostolic writings, and to those which
appear in the fathers of the succeeding generations.

1. The
Christo-
logy of St
Paul's
earlier
epistles

1. The Christology of the Colossian Epistle is in no way
different from that of the Apostle's earlier letters. It may
indeed be called a development of his former teaching, but only
as exhibiting the doctrine in fresh relations, as drawing new
deductions from it, as defining what had hitherto been left un-
defined, not as superadding any foreign element to it. The
doctrine is practically involved in the opening and closing words
of his earliest extant epistle: 'The Church which is in God
the Father and the Lord Jesus Christ'; 'The grace of our Lord
Jesus Christ be with you[1].' The main conception of the Person
of Christ, as enforced in the Colossian Epistle, alone justifies and
explains this language, which otherwise would be emptied of all
significance. And again: it had been enunciated by the Apostle
explicitly, though briefly, in the earliest directly doctrinal passage
which bears on the subject; 'One Lord Jesus Christ, through
whom are all things and we through Him[2].' The absolute
the same universal mediation of the Son is declared as unreservedly in
in sub-
stance but
this passage from the First Epistle to the Corinthians, as in any

[1] 1 Thess. i. 1, v. 28.
[2] 1 Cor. viii. 6 δι' οὗ τὰ πάντα καὶ
ἡμεῖς δι' αὐτοῦ. The expression δι' οὗ
implies the conception of the Logos,

even where the term itself is not
used. See the dissertation on the doctrine of the Logos in the Apostolic
writers.

later statement of the Apostle: and, if all the doctrinal and practical inferences which it implicitly involves were not directly emphasized at this early date, it was because the circumstances did not yet require explicitness on these points. New forms of error bring into prominence new aspects of the truth. The heresies of Laodicea and Colossæ have been invaluable to the later Church in this respect. The Apostle himself, it is not too much to say, realised with ever-increasing force the manifoldness, the adaptability, the completeness of the Christian idea, notwithstanding its simplicity, as he opposed it to each successive development of error. The Person of Christ proved the complete answer to false speculations at Colossæ, as it had been found the sovereign antidote to false practices at Corinth. All these unforeseen harmonies must have appeared to him, as they will appear to us, fresh evidences of its truth. *less fully developed.*

2. And when we turn from St Paul to the other Apostolic writings which dwell on the Person of Christ from a doctrinal point of view, we find them enunciating it in language which implies the same fundamental conception, though they may not always present it in exactly the same aspect. More especially in the Epistle to the Hebrews first, and in the Gospel of St John afterwards, the form of expression is identical with the statement of St Paul. In both these writings the universe is said to have been created or to exist *by* or *through* Him. This is the crucial expression, which involves in itself all the higher conceptions of the Person of Christ[1]. The Epistle to the Hebrews seems to have been written by a disciple of St Paul immediately after the Apostle's death, and therefore within some five or six years from the date which has been assigned to the Colossian letter. The Gospel of St John, if the traditional report may be accepted, dates about a quarter of a century later; but it is linked with our epistle by the fact that the readers for whom it was primarily intended belonged to the neighbouring districts of proconsular Asia. Thus it illustrates, *2. The Christ-ology of other Apostolic writings.*

Their fundamental identity.

---

[1] Joh. i. 3 πάντα δι' αὐτοῦ ἐγένετο κ.τ.λ., Heb. i. 2 δι' οὗ καὶ ἐποίησεν τοὺς αἰῶνας.

and is illustrated by, the teaching of St Paul in this letter. More especially by the emphatic use of the term *Logos*, which St Paul for some reason has suppressed, it supplies the centre round which the ideas gather, and thus gives unity and directness to the conception.

Firmness of the apostolic idea.

In the Christology of these Apostolic writings there is a firmness and precision which leaves no doubt about the main conception present to the mind of the writers. The idea of Christ as an intermediate being, neither God nor man, is absolutely and expressly excluded. On the one hand His humanity is distinctly emphasized. On the other He is represented as existing from eternity, as the perfect manifestation of the Father, as the absolute mediator in the creation and government of the world.

3. The Christology of the succeeding ages.

3. But, when we turn from these Apostolic statements to the writings of succeeding generations, we are struck with the contrast[1]. A vagueness, a flaccidity, of conception betrays itself in their language.

In the Apostolic Fathers and in the earlier Apologists we find indeed for the most part a *practical* appreciation of the Person of Christ, which leaves nothing to be desired; but as soon as they venture upon any directly dogmatic statement, we

Its looseness of conception.

miss at once the firmness of grasp and clearness of conception which mark the writings of the Apostles. If they desire to emphasize the majesty of His Person, they not unfrequently fall into language which savours of patripassianism[2]. If on the other hand they wish to present Him in His mediatorial capacity, they use words which seem to imply some divine being, who is God and yet not quite God, neither Creator nor creature[3].

---

[1] The remarks on the theology of the Apostolic Fathers, as compared with the Apostles, in Dorner's *Lehre von der Person Christi* i. p. 130 sq. seem to me perfectly just and highly significant. See also Pressensé *Trois Premiers Siècles* ii. p. 406 sq. on the unsystematic spirit of the Apostolic Fathers.

[2] See for instance the passages

quoted in the note on Clem. Rom. 2 τὰ παθήματα αὐτοῦ.

[3] The unguarded language of Justin for instance illustrates the statement in the text. On the one hand Petavius, *Theol. Dogm.* de Trin. ii. 3. 2, distinctly accuses him of Arianism: on the other Bull, *Def. Fid. Nic.* ii. 4. 1 sq., indignantly repudiates the charge and claims him as strictly orthodox. Peta-

The Church needed a long education, before she was fitted
to be the expositor of the true Apostolic doctrine. A conflict
of more than two centuries with Gnostics, Ebionites, Sabellians,
Arians, supplied the necessary discipline. The true successors *The Apo-*
of the Apostles in this respect are not the fathers of the second *stolic idea applied in*
century, but the fathers of the third and fourth centuries. In the *later ages.*
expositors of the Nicene age we find indeed technical terms
and systematic definitions, which we do not find in the Apostles
themselves; but, unless I have wholly misconceived the nature
of the heretical teaching at Colossæ and the purport of St Paul's
reply, the main idea of Christ's Person, with which he here
confronts this Gnostic Judaism, is essentially the same as that
which the fathers of these later centuries opposed to the Sabel-
lianism and the Arianism of their own age. If I mistake not,
the more distinctly we realise the nature of the heresy, the
more evident will it become that any conception short of the
perfect deity and perfect humanity of Christ would not have
furnished a satisfactory answer; and this is the reason why
I have dwelt at such length on the character of the Colossian
false teaching, and why I venture to call especial attention to
this part of my subject.

Of the style of the letter to the Colossians I shall have occa- *Style of*
sion to speak hereafter, when I come to discuss its genuine- *this epistle.*
ness. It is sufficient to say here, that while the hand of St Paul
is unmistakeable throughout this epistle, we miss the flow and
the versatility of the Apostle's earlier letters.

A comparison with the Epistles to the Corinthians and to the
Philippians will show the difference. It is distinguished from *Its rug-*
them by a certain ruggedness of expression, a 'want of finish' *gedness and com-*
often bordering on obscurity. What account should be given of *pression,*
this characteristic, it is impossible to say. The divergence of

vius indeed approaches the subject
from the point of view of later Western
theology and, unable to appreciate
Justin's doctrine of the Logos, does
less than justice to this father; but
nevertheless Justin's language is occasionally such as no Athanasian could
have used. The treatment of this
father by Dorner (*Lehre* I. p. 414 sq.)
is just and avoids both extremes.

style is not greater than will appear in the letters of any active-minded man, written at different times and under different circumstances. The epistles which I have selected for contrast suggest that the absence of all personal connexion with the Colossian Church will partially, if not wholly, explain the diminished fluency of this letter. At the same time no epistle of *but essential vigour.* St Paul is more vigorous in conception or more instinct with meaning. It is the very compression of the thoughts which creates the difficulty. If there is a want of fluency, there is no want of force. Feebleness is the last charge which can be brought against this epistle.

Analysis.   The following is an analysis of the epistle :

I.   INTRODUCTORY (i. 1—13).

    (1) i. 1, 2.   Opening salutation.

    (2) i. 3—8.   Thanksgiving for the progress of the Colossians hitherto.

    (3) i. 9—13.   Prayer for their future advance in knowledge and well-doing through Christ.

        [This leads the Apostle to speak of Christ as the only path of progress.]

II.   DOCTRINAL (i. 13—ii. 3).

    The Person and Office of Christ.

    (1) i. 13, 14.   Through the Son we have our deliverance, our redemption.

    (2) i. 15—19.   The *Preeminence* of the Son ;

        (i)   As the Head of the natural Creation, the Universe (i. 15—17) ;

        (ii)   As the Head of the new moral Creation, the Church (i. 18).

        Thus He is first in all things ; and this, because the *pleroma* has its abode in Him (i. 19).

    (3) i. 20—ii. 3.   The *Work* of the Son—a work of reconciliation ;

        (i)   Described generally (i. 20).

        (ii)   Applied specially to the Colossians (i. 21—23).

(iii) St Paul's own part in carrying out this work. His sufferings and preaching. The 'mystery' with which he is charged (i. 24—27).

His anxiety on behalf of all (i. 28, 29): and more especially of the Colossian and neighbouring Churches (ii. 1—3).

[This expression of anxiety leads him by a direct path to the next division of the epistle.]

III. POLEMICAL (ii. 4—iii. 4).

Warning against errors.

(1) ii. 4—8. The Colossians charged to abide in the truth of the Gospel as they received it at first, and not to be led astray by a strange philosophy which the new teachers offer.

(2) ii. 9—15. The truth stated first positively and then negatively.

[In the passage which follows (ii. 9—23) it will be observed how St Paul vibrates between the theological and practical bearings of the truth, marked a, β, respectively.]

(i) *Positively.*

(a) The *pleroma* dwells wholly in Christ and is communicated through Him (ii. 9, 10).

(β) The true circumcision is a spiritual circumcision (ii. 11, 12).

(ii) *Negatively.* Christ has

(β) annulled the law of ordinances (ii. 14);

(a) triumphed over all spiritual agencies, however powerful (ii. 15).

(3) ii. 16—iii. 4. Obligations following thereupon.

(i) Consequently the Colossians must not

(β) either submit to ritual prohibitions (ii. 16, 17),

(a) or substitute the worship of inferior beings for allegiance to the Head (ii. 18, 19).

(ii) On the contrary this must henceforth be their rule:

1. They have *died* with Christ; and with Him they have died to their old life, to earthly *ordinances* (ii. 20—23).

2. They have *risen* with Christ; and with Him they have risen to a new life, to heavenly *principles* (iii. 1—4).

IV. HORTATORY (iii. 5—iv. 6).

Practical application of this death and this resurrection.

(1) iii. 5—17.   *Comprehensive* rules.

  (i) What vices are to be put off, being mortified in this death (iii. 5—11).

  (ii) What graces are to be put on, being quickened through this resurrection (iii. 12—17).

(2) iii. 18—iv. 6.   *Special* precepts.

  (*a*) The obligations

     Of wives and husbands (iii. 18, 19);

     Of children and parents (iii. 20, 21);

     Of slaves and masters (iii. 22—iv. 1).

  (*b*) The duty of prayer and thanksgiving; with special intercession on the Apostle's behalf (iv. 2—4).

  (*c*) The duty of propriety in behaviour towards the unconverted (iv. 5, 6).

V. PERSONAL (iv. 7—18).

  (1) iv. 7—9.   Explanations relating to the letter itself.

  (2) iv. 10—14.   Salutations from divers persons.

  (3) iv. 15—17.   Salutations to divers persons. A message relating to Laodicea.

  (4) iv. 18.   Farewell.

ΠΡΟΣ ΚΟΛΑΣΣΑΕΙΣ.

WE SPEAK WISDOM AMONG THEM THAT ARE PERFECT.

YET NOT THE WISDOM OF THIS WORLD.

BUT WE SPEAK THE WISDOM OF GOD IN A MYSTERY.

Iste vas electionis
Vires omnes rationis
    Humanæ transgreditur :
Super choros angelorum
Raptus, cœli secretorum
    Doctrinis imbuitur.

De hoc vase tam fecundo,
Tam electo et tam mundo,
    Tu nos, Christe, complue ;
Nos de luto, nos de fœce,
Tua sancta purga prece,
    Regno tuo statue.

ΠΡΟΣ ΚΟΛΑΣΣΑΕΙΣ.

ΠΑΥΛΟΣ ἀπόστολος Χριστοῦ Ἰησοῦ διὰ θελήματος
Θεοῦ, καὶ Τιμόθεος ὁ ἀδελφός, ²τοῖς ἐν Κολοσσαῖς

1, 2. 'PAUL, an apostle of Christ
Jesus by no personal merit but by
God's gracious will alone, and TIMOTHY,
our brother in the faith, to the consecrated people of God in COLOSSÆ, the
brethren who are stedfast in their
allegiance and faithful in Christ. May
grace the well-spring of all mercies, and
peace the crown of all blessings, be
bestowed upon you from God our
Father.'

I. ἀπόστολος] On the exceptional
omission of this title in some of St
Paul's epistles see Phil. i. 1. Though
there is no reason for supposing that
his authority was directly impugned
in the Colossian Church, yet he interposes by virtue of his Apostolic commission and therefore uses his authoritative title.

διὰ θελήματος Θεοῦ] As in 1 Cor. i. 1,
2 Cor. i. 1, Ephes. i. 1, 2 Tim. i. 1.
These passages show that the words
cannot have a polemical bearing. If
they had been directed against those
who questioned his Apostleship, they
would probably have taken a stronger
form. The expression must therefore
be regarded as a renunciation of all
personal worth, and a declaration of
God's unmerited grace; comp. Rom.
ix. 16 ἄρα οὖν οὐ τοῦ θέλοντος οὐδὲ
τοῦ τρέχοντος ἀλλὰ τοῦ ἐλεῶντος Θεοῦ.
The same words διὰ θελήματος Θεοῦ are
used in other connexions in Rom. xv.
32, 2 Cor. viii. 5, where no polemical
reference is possible.

Τιμόθεος] The name of this disciple
is attached to the Apostle's own in

the heading of the Philippian letter,
which was probably written at an
earlier stage in his Roman captivity.
It appears also in the same connexion
in the Epistle to Philemon, but not in
the Epistle to the Ephesians, though
these two letters were contemporaneous with one another and with the
Colossian letter. For an explanation
of the omission, see the introduction
to that epistle.

In the Epistles to the Philippians
and to Philemon the presence of Timothy is forgotten at once (see Phil.
i. 1). In this epistle the plural is
maintained throughout the thanksgiving (vv. 3, 4, 7, 8, 9), but afterwards dropped, when the Apostle begins to speak in his own person (i. 23,
24), and so he continues to the end.
The exceptions (i. 28, iv. 3) are rather
apparent than real.

ὁ ἀδελφός] Timothy is again designated simply 'the brother' in 2 Cor.
i. 1, Philem. 1, but not in Heb. xiii. 23,
where the right reading is τὸν ἀδελφὸν
ἡμῶν. The same designation is used
of Quartus (Rom. xvi. 23), of Sosthenes
(1 Cor. i. 1), of Apollos (1 Cor. xvi. 12);
comp. 2 Cor. viii. 18, ix. 3, 5, xii. 18.
As some designation seemed to be
required, and as Timothy could not
be called an Apostle (see *Galatians*,
p. 96, note 2), this, as the simplest
title, would naturally suggest itself.

2. Κολοσσαῖς] For the reasons
why this form is preferred here, while
Κολασσαεῖς is adopted in the heading
of the epistle, see above, p. 16 sq.

ἁγίοις καὶ πιστοῖς ἀδελφοῖς ἐν Χριστῷ· χάρις ὑμῖν
καὶ εἰρήνη ἀπὸ Θεοῦ πατρὸς ἡμῶν.
³ Εὐχαριστοῦμεν τῷ Θεῷ [καὶ] πατρὶ τοῦ Κυρίου

ἁγίοις] 'saints,' i.e. the people consecrated to God, the Israel of the new
covenant; see the note on Phil. i. 1.
This mode of address marks the later
epistles of St Paul. In his earlier
letters (1, 2 Thess., 1, 2 Cor., Gal.) he
writes τῇ ἐκκλησίᾳ, ταῖς ἐκκλησίαις. The
change begins with the Epistle to the
Romans, and from that time forward
the Apostle always uses ἁγίοις in
various combinations in addressing
churches (Rom., Phil., Col., Ephes.).
For a similar phenomenon, serving as
a chronological mark, see the note on
ἡ χάρις, iv. 18. The word ἁγίοις must
here be treated as a substantive in
accordance with its usage in parallel
passages, and not as an adjective connected with ἀδελφοῖς. See the next
note.

καὶ πιστοῖς ἀδελφοῖς] This unusual
addition is full of meaning. Some
members of the Colossian Church were
shaken in their allegiance, even if they
had not fallen from it. The Apostle
therefore wishes it to be understood
that, when he speaks of the saints, he
means the true and stedfast members
of the brotherhood. In this way he
obliquely hints at the defection. Thus
the words καὶ πιστοῖς ἀδελφοῖς are a
supplementary explanation of τοῖς ἁ-
γίοις. He does not directly exclude
any, but he indirectly warns all. The
epithet πιστὸς cannot mean simply
'believing'; for then it would add nothing which is not already contained
in ἁγίοις and ἀδελφοῖς. Its passive
sense, 'trustworthy, stedfast, unswerv-
ing,' must be prominent here, as in
Acts xvi. 15 εἰ κεκρίκατέ με πιστὴν τῷ
Κυρίῳ εἶναι. See Galatians p. 155.

ἐν Χριστῷ] Most naturally connected
with both words πιστοῖς ἀδελφοῖς,
though referring chiefly to πιστοῖς;
comp. Ephes. vi. 21 πιστὸς διάκονος ἐν

Κυρίῳ, 1 Tim. i. 2 γνησίῳ τέκνῳ ἐν πίστει. For the expression πιστὸς ἐν
Χριστῷ, ἐν Κυρίῳ, see also 1 Cor. iv. 17,
Ephes. i. 1. The Apostle assumes
that the Colossian brethren are 'stedfast in Christ.' Their state thus contrasts with the description of the heretical teacher, who (ii. 19) οὐ κρατεῖ
τὴν κεφαλήν.

χάρις κ.τ.λ.] On this form of salutation see the note to 1 Thess. i. 1.

πατρὸς ἡμῶν] The only instance in
St Paul's epistles, where the name of
the Father stands alone in the opening benediction without the addition
of Jesus Christ. The omission was
noticed by Origen (Rom. I. § 8, IV. p.
467), and by Chrysostom (ad loc. XI. p.
324, Hom. in 2 Cor. xxx, x.p.651). But
transcribers naturally aimed at uniformity, and so in many copies we find
the addition καὶ Κυρίου Ἰησοῦ Χριστοῦ.
The only other exception to the Apostle's usual form is in 1 Thessalonians,
where the benediction is shorter still,
χάρις ὑμῖν καὶ εἰρήνη, and where likewise the copyists have supplied words
to lengthen it out in accordance with
St Paul's common practice.

3—8. 'We never cease to pour
forth our thanksgiving to God the
Father of our Lord Jesus Christ on
your account, whensoever we pray to
Him. We are full of thankfulness
for the tidings of the *faith* which ye
have in Christ Jesus, and the *love* which
ye show towards all the people of God,
while ye look forward to the *hope*
which is stored up for you in heaven
as a treasure for the life to come.
This hope was communicated to you
in those earlier lessons, when the Gospel was preached to you in its purity
and integrity—the one universal unchangeable Gospel, which was made
known to you, even as it was carried

ἡμῶν Ἰησοῦ Χριστοῦ πάντοτε περὶ ὑμῶν προσευχόμενοι· ⁴ἀκούσαντες τὴν πίστιν ὑμῶν ἐν Χριστῷ Ἰησοῦ, καὶ τὴν ἀγάπην [ἣν ἔχετε] εἰς πάντας τοὺς ἁγίους, ⁵διὰ τὴν

throughout the world, approving itself by its fruits wheresoever it is planted. For, as elsewhere, so also in you, these fruits were manifested from the first day when ye received your lessons in, and apprehended the power of, the genuine Gospel, which is not a law of ordinances but a dispensation of grace, not a device of men but a truth of God. Such was the word preached to you by Epaphras, our beloved fellow-servant in our Master's household, who in our absence and on our behalf has ministered to you the Gospel of Christ, and who now brings back to us the welcome tidings of the love which ye show in the Spirit.'

3. Εὐχαριστοῦμεν] See the notes on 1 Thess. i. 2.

πατρί] If the καὶ be omitted, as the balance of authorities appears to suggest, the form of words here is quite exceptional. Elsewhere it runs ὁ Θεὸς καὶ πατὴρ τοῦ Κυρίου, Rom. xv. 6, 2 Cor. i. 3, xi. 31, Ephes. i. 3 (v. l.), 1 Pet. i. 3; comp. Rev. i. 6: and in analogous cases, such as ὁ Θεὸς καὶ πατὴρ ἡμῶν, the rule is the same. See the note on Clem. Rom. § 7. In iii. 17 however we have τῷ Θεῷ πατρί, where the evidence is more decisive and the expression quite as unusual. On the authorities for the various readings here see the detached note.

πάντοτε κ.τ.λ.] We here meet the same difficulty about the connexion of the clauses, which confronts us in several of St Paul's opening thanksgivings. The words πάντοτε and περὶ ὑμῶν must clearly be taken together, because the emphasis of περὶ ὑμῶν would be inexplicable, if it stood at the beginning of a clause. But are they to be attached to the preceding or to the following sentence? The connexion with the previous words is fa-

voured by St Paul's usual conjunction of εὐχαριστεῖν πάντοτε (see the note on Phil. i. 3), and by the parallel passage οὐ παύομαι εὐχαριστῶν ὑπὲρ ὑμῶν in Ephes. i. 16. Thus the words will mean ' We give thanks for you always in our prayers.' For this absolute use of προσευχόμενοι see Matt. vi. 7, Acts xvi. 25.

4. ἀκούσαντες] 'having heard' from Epaphras (ver. 8); for the Apostle had no direct personal knowledge of the Colossian Church: see the introduction, p. 27 sq.

ἐν Χριστῷ Ἰησοῦ] To be connected with τὴν πίστιν ὑμῶν. The strict classical language would require τὴν ἐν Χ. Ἰ., but the omission of the article is common in the New Testament (e. g. ver. 8); see the note on 1 Thess. i. 1, and Winer § xx. p. 169 (ed. Moulton). The preposition ἐν here and in the parallel passage, Ephes. i. 15, denotes the sphere in which their faith moves, rather than the object to which it is directed (comp. 1 Cor. iii. 5); for, if the object had been meant, the natural preposition would have been ἐπὶ or εἰς (e. g. ii. 5). This is probably the case also in the passages where at first sight it might seem otherwise, e. g. 1 Tim. iii. 13, 2 Tim. iii. 15; for compare 2 Tim. i. 13 ἐν πίστει καὶ ἀγάπῃ τῇ ἐν Χριστῷ Ἰησοῦ, where the meaning is unambiguous. There is however authority in the LXX for the use of ἐν with πίστις, πιστεύειν, to denote the object, in Jer. xii. 6, Ps. lxxviii. 22, and perhaps in Mark i. 15, Rom. iii. 25, and (more doubtfully still) in Joh. iii. 15.

ἣν ἔχετε] See the detached note on the various readings.

5. διὰ τὴν ἐλπίδα] 'for the hope,' i.e. looking to the hope. The following reasons seem decisive in favour of con-

ἐλπίδα τὴν ἀποκειμένην ὑμῖν ἐν τοῖς οὐρανοῖς, ἣν προη-
κούσατε ἐν τῷ λόγῳ τῆς ἀληθείας τοῦ εὐαγγελίου, ⁶τοῦ
παρόντος εἰς ὑμᾶς, καθὼς καὶ ἐν παντὶ τῷ κόσμῳ ἐστὶν

necting διὰ τὴν ἐλπίδα, not with εὐχαριστοῦμεν, but with τὴν πίστιν κ.τ.λ.,
whether ἣν ἔχετε be retained or not.
(1) The great distance of εὐχαριστοῦμεν is against the former connexion;
(2) The following clause, ἣν προηκού-
σατε κ.τ.λ., suggests that the words
διὰ τὴν ἐλπίδα describe the motives of
the Colossians for well-doing, rather
than the reasons of the Apostle for
thanksgiving: (3) The triad of Christian graces, which St Paul delights to
associate together, would otherwise be
broken up. This last argument seems
conclusive; see especially the corresponding thanksgiving in 1 Thess. i. 3,
μνημονεύοντες ὑμῶν τοῦ ἔργου τῆς πίστεως καὶ τοῦ κόπου τῆς ἀγάπης καὶ
τῆς ὑπομονῆς τῆς ἐλπίδος κ.τ.λ., with
the note there. The order is the same
here, as there; and it is the natural
sequence. Faith rests on the past;
love works in the present; hope looks
to the future. They may be regarded as the efficient, material, and
final causes respectively of the spiritual life. Compare Polycarp Phil. 3
πίστιν ἥτις ἐστὶ μήτηρ πάντων ἡμῶν,
ἐπακολουθούσης τῆς ἐλπίδος, προαγούσης
τῆς ἀγάπης.

The hope here is identified with the
object of the hope: see the passages
quoted on Gal. v. 5. The sense of
ἐλπίς, as of the corresponding words
in any language, oscillates between the
subjective feeling and the objective
realisation; comp. Rom. viii. 24 τῇ
γὰρ ἐλπίδι ἐσώθημεν· ἐλπὶς δὲ βλεπο-
μένη οὐκ ἔστιν ἐλπίς· ὃ γὰρ βλέπει τις
κ.τ.λ., where it passes abruptly from
the one to the other.

τὴν ἀποκειμένην] 'which is stored
up.' It is the θησαυρὸς ἐν οὐρανῷ of
the Gospels (Matt. vi. 20, 21, Luke xii.
34, xviii. 22).

προηκούσατε] 'of which ye were

told in time past.' The preposition
seems intended to contrast their
earlier with their later lessons—the
true Gospel of Epaphras with the false
gospel of their recent teachers (see
the next note). The expression would
gain force, if we might suppose that
the heretical teachers obscured or
perverted the doctrine of the resurrection (comp. 2 Tim. ii. 18); and their
speculative tenets were not unlikely
to lead to such a result. But this is
not necessary; for under any circumstances the false doctrine, as leading
them astray, tended to cheat them of
their hope; see ver. 23. The common
interpretations, which explain προ- as
meaning either 'before its fulfilment'
or 'before my writing to you,' seem
neither so natural in themselves nor
so appropriate to the context.

τῆς ἀληθείας τοῦ εὐαγγελίου] 'the
truth of the Gospel,' i.e. the true and
genuine Gospel as taught by Epaphras,
and not the spurious substitute of
these later pretenders: comp. ver. 6
ἐν ἀληθείᾳ. See also Gal. ii. 5, 14,
where a similar contrast is implied in
the use of ἡ ἀλήθεια τοῦ εὐαγγελίου.

6. τοῦ παρόντος εἰς ὑμᾶς] 'which
reached you.' The expression παρεῖναι εἰς is not uncommon in classical
writers; comp. παρεῖναι πρὸς in Acts
xii. 20, Gal. iv. 18, 20. So also εὑρε-
θῆναι εἰς (Acts viii. 40), γενέσθαι εἰς
(e.g. Acts xxv. 15), and even εἶναι
εἰς (Luke xi. 7). See Winer § 1. p.
516 sq.

ἐν παντὶ τῷ κόσμῳ] For a similar
hyperbole see Rom. i. 8 ἐν ὅλῳ τῷ
κόσμῳ; comp. 1 Thess. i. 8, 2 Cor. ii. 14,
ἐν παντὶ τόπῳ. More lurks under these
words than appears on the surface. The
true Gospel, the Apostle seems to say,
proclaims its truth by its universality.
The false gospels are the outgrowths

καρποφορούμενον καὶ αὐξανόμενον, καθὼς καὶ ἐν ὑμῖν,
ἀφ᾽ ἧς ἡμέρας ἠκούσατε καὶ ἐπέγνωτε τὴν χάριν τοῦ

of local circumstances, of special idiosyncrasies; the true Gospel is the
same everywhere. The false gospels
address themselves to limited circles;
the true Gospel proclaims itself boldly
throughout the world. Heresies are
at best ethnic: truth is essentially
catholic. See ver. 23 μὴ μετακινούμενοι
ἀπὸ τῆς ἐλπίδος τοῦ εὐαγγελίου οὗ
ἠκούσατε, τοῦ κηρυχθέντος ἐν πάσῃ
κτίσει τῇ ὑπὸ τὸν οὐρανόν.

ἐστὶν καρποφορούμενον] 'is constantly
bearing fruit.' The fruit, which the
Gospel bears without fail in all soils
and under every climate, is its credential, its verification, as against the
pretensions of spurious counterfeits.
The substantive verb should here be
taken with the participle, so as to
express *continuity* of present action;
as in 2 Cor. ix. 12 οὐ μόνον ἐστὶν προσα
ναπληροῦσα κ.τ.λ., Phil. ii. 26 ἐπιποθῶν
ἦν. It is less common in St Paul
than in some of the Canonical writers,
e.g. St Mark and St Luke; but probably only because he deals less in
narrative.

Of the middle καρποφορεῖσθαι no
other instance has been found. The
voice is partially illustrated by κωδω
νοφορεῖσθαι, σιδηροφορεῖσθαι, τυμπα
νοφορεῖσθαι, though, as involving a
different sense of -φορεῖσθαι 'to wear,'
these words are not exact parallels.
Here the use of the middle is the
more marked, inasmuch as the active
occurs just below (ver. 10) in the
same connexion, καρποφοροῦντες καὶ
αὐξανόμενοι. This fact however points
to the force of the word here. The
middle is *intensive*, the active *extensive*. The middle denotes the inherent
energy, the active the external diffusion. The Gospel is essentially a reproductive organism, a plant whose
'seed is in itself.' For this 'dynamic'
middle see Moulton's note on Winer
§ xxxviii. p. 319.

καὶ αὐξανόμενον] The Gospel is not
like those plants which exhaust themselves in bearing fruit and wither
away. The external growth keeps
pace with the reproductive energy.
While καρποφορούμενον describes the
inner working, αὐξανόμενον gives the
outward extension of the Gospel. The
words καὶ αὐξανόμενον are not found
in the received text, but the authority in their favour is overwhelming.

καθὼς καὶ ἐν ὑμῖν] The comparison
is thus doubled back, as it were, on
itself. This irregularity disappears in
the received text, καὶ ἐστὶν καρποφο
ρούμενον καθὼς καὶ ἐν ὑμῖν, where the
insertion of καὶ before καρποφορούμε
νον straightens the construction. For
a similar irregularity see 1 Thess. iv.
1 παρακαλοῦμεν ἐν Κυρίῳ Ἰησοῦ ἵνα,
καθὼς παρελάβετε παρ᾽ ἡμῶν τὸ πῶς δεῖ
ὑμᾶς περιπατεῖν καὶ ἀρέσκειν Θεῷ, καθὼς
καὶ περιπατεῖτε, ἵνα περισσεύητε μᾶλλον,
where again the received text simplifies the construction, though in a different way, by omitting the first ἵνα
and the words καθὼς καὶ περιπατεῖτε.
In both cases the explanation of the
irregularity is much the same; the
clause reciprocating the comparison
(here καθὼς καὶ ἐν ὑμῖν, there καθὼς
καὶ περιπατεῖτε) is an afterthought
springing out of the Apostle's anxiety
not to withhold praise where praise
can be given.

For the appearance of καὶ in both
members of the comparison, καὶ ἐν
παντὶ τῷ κόσμῳ…καθὼς καί, comp.
Rom. i. 13 καὶ ἐν ὑμῖν καθὼς καὶ ἐν τοῖς
λοιποῖς ἔθνεσιν; and in the reversed
order below, iii. 13 καθὼς καὶ ὁ Κύριος
ἐχαρίσατο ὑμῖν, οὕτως καὶ ὑμεῖς (with
the note): see also Winer liii. p. 549
(ed. Moulton). The correlation of the
clauses is thus rendered closer, and
the comparison emphasized.

ἠκούσατε καὶ ἐπέγνωτε] The accusative is governed by both verbs equally,

Θεοῦ ἐν ἀληθείᾳ, ⁷καθὼς ἐμάθετε ἀπὸ Ἐπαφρᾶ τοῦ ἀγαπητοῦ συνδούλου ἡμῶν, ὅς ἐστιν πιστὸς ὑπὲρ ἡμῶν διάκονος τοῦ Χριστοῦ, ⁸ὁ καὶ δηλώσας ἡμῖν τὴν ὑμῶν ἀγάπην ἐν πνεύματι.

'Ye were instructed in and fully apprehended the grace of God.' For this sense of ἀκούειν see below, ver. 23. For ἐπιγινώσκειν as denoting 'advanced knowledge, thorough appreciation,' see the note on ἐπίγνωσις, ver. 9.

τὴν χάριν τοῦ Θεοῦ] St Paul's synonyme for the Gospel. In Acts xx. 24 he describes it as his mission to preach τὸ εὐαγγέλιον τῆς χάριτος τοῦ Θεοῦ. The true Gospel as taught by Epaphras was an offer of free grace, a message from God; the false gospel, as superposed by the heretical teachers, was a code of rigorous prohibitions, a system of human devising. It was not χάρις but δόγματα (ii. 14); not τοῦ Θεοῦ but τοῦ κόσμου, τῶν ἀνθρώπων (ii. 8, 20, 22). For God's power and goodness it substituted self-mortification and self-exaltation. The Gospel is called ἡ χάρις τοῦ Θεοῦ again in 2 Cor. vi. 1, viii. 9, with reference to the same leading characteristic which the Apostle delights to dwell upon (e.g. Rom. iii. 24, v. 15, Eph. ii. 5, 8), and which he here tacitly contrasts with the doctrine of the later intruders. The false teachers of Colossæ, like those of Galatia, would lead their hearers ἀθετεῖν τὴν χάριν τοῦ Θεοῦ (Gal. ii. 21); to accept their doctrine was ἐκπίπτειν τῆς χάριτος (Gal. v. 4).

ἐν ἀληθείᾳ] i.e. 'in its genuine simplicity, without adulteration': see the note on τῆς ἀληθείας τοῦ εὐαγγελίου, ver. 5.

7. καθὼς ἐμάθετε] 'even as ye were instructed in it,' the clause being an explanation of the preceding ἐν ἀληθείᾳ; comp. ii. 7 καθὼς ἐδιδάχθητε. On the insertion of καὶ before ἐμάθετε in the received text, and the consequent obscuration of the sense, see above, p. 29 sq. The insertion how-

ever was very natural, inasmuch as καθὼς καὶ is an ordinary collocation of particles and has occurred twice in the preceding verse.

Ἐπαφρᾶ] On the notices of Epaphras, and on his work as the evangelist of the Colossians see above, p. 29 sq., p. 34 sq., and the note on iv. 12.

συνδούλου] See iv. 7. The word does not occur elsewhere in St Paul.

ὑπὲρ ἡμῶν] As the evangelist of Colossæ, Epaphras had represented St Paul there and preached in his stead; see above, p. 30. The other reading ὑπὲρ ὑμῶν might be interpreted in two ways: either (1) It might describe the personal ministrations of Epaphras to St Paul as the representative of the Colossians (see a similar case in Phil. ii. 25, iv. 18), and so it might be compared with Philem. 13 ἵνα ὑπὲρ σοῦ μοι διακονῇ; but this interpretation is hardly consistent with τοῦ Χριστοῦ. Or (2) It might refer to the preaching of Epaphras for the good of the Colossians; but the natural construction in this case would hardly be ὑπὲρ ὑμῶν (of which there is no direct example), but either ὑμῶν (Rom. xv. 8) or ὑμῖν (1 Pet. i. 12). The balance of external authority however is against it. Partly by the accidental interchange of similar sounds, partly by the recurrence of ὑπὲρ ὑμῶν in the context (vv. 3, 9), and partly also from ignorance of the historical circumstances, ὑμῶν would readily be substituted for ἡμῶν. See the detached note on various readings.

8. ὁ καὶ δηλώσας] 'As he preached to you from us, so also he brought back to us from you the tidings, etc.'

ἐν πνεύματι] To be connected with τὴν ὑμῶν ἀγάπην. 'The fruit of the Spirit is love,' Gal. v. 22. For the

$$^9 \Delta\iota\grave{a} \ \tau o\hat{v}\tau o \ \kappa a\grave{\iota} \ \dot{\eta}\mu\epsilon\hat{\iota}s, \ \dot{a}\phi' \ \hat{\eta}s \ \dot{\eta}\mu\acute{\epsilon}\rho as \ \dot{\eta}\kappa o\acute{v}\sigma a\mu\epsilon\nu, \ o\dot{v}$$
$$\pi a\upsilon\acute{o}\mu\epsilon\theta a \ \dot{v}\pi\grave{\epsilon}\rho \ \dot{v}\mu\hat{\omega}\nu \ \pi\rho o\sigma\epsilon\upsilon\chi\acute{o}\mu\epsilon\nu o\iota \ \kappa a\grave{\iota} \ a\dot{\iota}\tau o\acute{v}\mu\epsilon\nu o\iota \ \ddot{\iota}\nu a$$
$$\pi\lambda\eta\rho\omega\theta\hat{\eta}\tau\epsilon \ \tau\grave{\eta}\nu \ \dot{\epsilon}\pi\acute{\iota}\gamma\nu\omega\sigma\iota\nu \ \tau o\hat{v} \ \theta\epsilon\lambda\acute{\eta}\mu a\tau os \ a\dot{v}\tau o\hat{v} \ \dot{\epsilon}\nu$$

omission of the article, τὴν ἐν πνεύματι, see the note on ver. 4.

9—14. 'Hearing then that ye thus abound in works of faith and love, we on our part have not ceased, from the day when we received the happy tidings, to pray on your behalf. And this is the purport of our petitions ; that ye may grow more and more in knowledge, till ye attain to the perfect understanding of God's will, being endowed with all wisdom to apprehend His verities and all intelligence to follow His processes, living in the mind of the Spirit—to the end that knowledge may manifest itself. in practice, that your conduct in life may be worthy of your profession in the Lord, so as in all ways to win for you the gracious favour of God your King. Thus, while ye bear fruit in every good work, ye will also grow as the tree grows, being watered and refreshed by this knowledge, as by the dew of heaven: thus ye will be strengthened in all strength, according to that power which centres in and spreads from His glorious manifestation of Himself, and nerved to all endurance under affliction and all long-suffering under provocation, not only without complaining, but even with joy : thus finally '(for this is the crown of all), so rejoicing ye will pour forth your thanksgiving to the Universal Father, who prepared and fitted us all—you and us alike—to take possession of the portion which His goodness has allotted to us among the saints in the kingdom of light. Yea, by a strong arm He rescued us from the lawless tyranny of Darkness, removed us from the land of our bondage, and settled us as free citizens in our new and glorious home, where His Son, the offspring and the representa-

tive of His love, is King; even the same, who paid our ransom and thus procured our redemption from captivity—our redemption, which (be assured) is nothing else than the remission of our sins.'

9. Διὰ τοῦτο] '*for this cause,*' i.e. 'by reason of your progressive faith and love,' referring not solely to ὁ καὶ δηλώσας κ.τ.λ. but to the whole of the preceding description. For διὰ τοῦτο καὶ ἡμεῖς in an exactly similar connexion, see 1 Thess. ii. 13 ; comp. Ephes. i. 15 διὰ τοῦτο κἀγὼ κ.τ.λ. In all these cases the καὶ denotes the *response* of the Apostle's personal feeling to the favourable character of the news ; 'we on our part.' This idea of correspondence is still further emphasized by the repetition of the same words : καὶ ἐν ὑμῖν ἀφ' ἧς ἡμέρας ἠκούσατε (ver. 6), καὶ ἡμεῖς ἀφ' ἧς ἡμέρας ἠκούσαμεν (ver. 9).

καὶ αἰτούμενοι] The words have an exact parallel in Mark xi. 24 (as correctly read) πάντα ὅσα προσεύχεσθε καὶ αἰτεῖσθε.

ἵνα] With words like προσεύχεσθαι, αἰτεῖσθαι, etc., the earlier and stronger force of ἵνα, implying *design*, glides imperceptibly into its later and weaker use, signifying merely *purport* or *result*, so that the two are hardly separable, unless one or other is directly indicated by something in the context. See the notes on Phil. i. 9, and comp. Winer § xliv. p. 420 sq.

τὴν ἐπίγνωσιν] A favourite word in the later epistles of St Paul ; see the note on Phil. i. 9. In all the four epistles of the first Roman captivity it is an element in the Apostle's opening prayer for his correspondents' well-being (Phil. i. 9, Ephes. i. 17, Philem. 6, and here). The greater stress which is thus laid on the contemplative aspects of the Gospel

πάσῃ σοφίᾳ καὶ συνέσει πνευματικῇ, ¹⁰περιπατῆσαι
ἀξίως τοῦ Κυρίου εἰς πᾶσαν ἀρέσκειαν· ἐν παντὶ ἔργῳ

may be explained partly by St Paul's
personal circumstances, partly by the
requirements of the Church. His enforced retirement and comparative
leisure would lead his own thoughts
in this direction, while at the same
time the fresh dangers threatening the
truth from the side of mystic speculation required to be confronted by
an exposition of the Gospel from a
corresponding point of view.

The compound ἐπίγνωσις is an advance upon γνῶσις, denoting a larger
and more thorough knowledge. So
Chrysostom here, ἔγνωτε, ἀλλὰ δεῖ τι
καὶ ἐπιγνῶναι. Comp. Justin Mart.
Dial. 3, p. 221 A, ἡ παρέχουσα αὐτῶν
τῶν ἀνθρωπίνων καὶ τῶν θείων γνῶσιν,
ἔπειτα τῆς τούτων θειότητος καὶ δικαιοσύνης ἐπίγνωσιν. So too St Paul
himself contrasts γινώσκειν, γνῶσις, with
ἐπιγινώσκειν, ἐπίγνωσις, as the partial with the complete, in two passages, Rom. i. 21, 28, 1 Cor. xiii. 12.
With this last passage (ἄρτι γινώσκω
ἐκ μέρους, τότε δὲ ἐπιγνώσομαι) compare Clem. Alex. Strom. i. 17, p. 369,
παρὰ τῶν Ἑβραϊκῶν προφητῶν μέρη
τῆς ἀληθείας οὐ κατ' ἐπίγνωσιν λα-
βόντες, where κατ' ἐπίγνωσιν is commonly but wrongly translated 'without
proper recognition' (comp. Tatian ad
Græc. 40). Hence also ἐπίγνωσις is
used especially of the knowledge of
God and of Christ, as being the perfection of knowledge : e.g. Prov. ii. 5,
Hos. iv. 1, vi. 6, Ephes. i. 17, iv. 13,
2 Pet. i. 2, 8, ii. 20, Clem. Alex. Pæd.
ii. 1, p. 173.

σοφίᾳ καὶ συνέσει] 'wisdom and intelligence.' The two words are frequently found together : e.g. Exod.
xxxi. 3, Deut. iv. 6, 1 Chron. xxii. 12,
2 Chron. i. 10 sq., Is. xi. 2, xxix. 14,
Dan. ii. 20, Baruch iii. 23, 1 Cor. i. 19,
Clem. Rom. 32. So too σοφοὶ καὶ
συνετοί, Prov. xvi. 21, Matt. xi. 25,
and elsewhere. In the parallel pas-

sage, Eph. i. 8, the words are ἐν πάσῃ
σοφίᾳ καὶ φρονήσει, and the substitution of φρόνησις for σύνεσις there is
instructive. The three words are
mentioned together, Arist. Eth. Nic.
i. 13, as constituting the intellectual
(διανοητικαὶ) virtues. Σοφία is mental
excellence in its highest and fullest
sense ; Arist. Eth. Nic. vi. 7 ἡ ἀκρι-
βεστάτη τῶν ἐπιστημῶν...ὥσπερ κεφαλὴν ἔχουσα ἐπιστήμη τῶν τιμιωτάτων
(see Waitz on Arist. Organ. II. p. 295
sq.), Cicero de Off. i. 43 'princeps omnium virtutum,' Clem. Alex. Pæd. ii. 2,
p. 181, τελεία...ἐμπεριλαβοῦσα τὰ ὅλα.
The Stoic definition of σοφία, as ἐπιστήμη θείων καὶ ἀνθρωπίνων καὶ τῶν
τούτων αἰτιῶν, is repeated by various
writers : e.g. Cic. de Off. ii. 5, Philo
Congr. erud. grat. 14, p. 530, [Joseph.]
Macc. 2, Clem. Alex. Pæd. ii. 2, p. 181,
Strom. i. 5, p. 333, Orig. c. Cels. iii. 72,
Aristob. in Eus. Præp. Ev. xiii. 12,
p. 667. And the glorification of σοφία
by heathen writers was even surpassed by its apotheosis in the Pro-
verbs and in the Wisdom of Solomon.
While σοφία 'wisdom' is thus primary
and absolute (Eth. Nic. vi. 7 μὴ μόνον
τὰ ἐκ τῶν ἀρχῶν εἰδέναι ἀλλὰ καὶ περὶ
τὰς ἀρχὰς ἀληθεύειν), both σύνεσις 'intelligence' and φρόνησις 'prudence'
are derivative and special (Eth. Nic
vi. 12 τῶν ἐσχάτων καὶ τῶν καθ' ἕκαστον).
They are both applications of σοφία
to details, but they work on different
lines ; for, while σύνεσις is critical,
φρόνησις is practical ; while σύνεσις
apprehends the bearings of things,
φρόνησις suggests lines of action : see
Arist. Eth. Nic. vi. 11 ἡ μὲν γὰρ φρόνησις ἐπιτακτική ἐστιν...ἡ δὲ σύνεσις κριτική. For σύνεσις see 2 Tim.
ii. 7 νόει ὃ λέγω, δώσει γάρ σοι ὁ Κύριος σύνεσιν ἐν πᾶσιν. This relation
of σοφία to σύνεσις explains why in
almost every case σοφία (σοφός) precedes σύνεσις (συνετός), where they

ἀγαθῷ καρποφοροῦντες καὶ αὐξανόμενοι τῇ ἐπιγνώσει
τοῦ Θεοῦ· ¹¹ἐν πάσῃ δυνάμει δυναμούμενοι κατὰ τὸ

are found together, and also why in Baruch iii. 23 οἱ ἐκζητηταὶ τῆς συνέσεως, ὁδὸν δὲ σοφίας οὐκ ἔγνωσαν, we find σύνεσις implying a tentative, partial, approach to σοφία. The relation of σοφία to φρόνησις will be considered more at length in the note on the parallel passage, Ephes. i. 8.

πνευματικῇ] The word is emphatic from its position. The false teachers also offered a σοφία, but it had only a show of wisdom (ii. 23); it was an empty counterfeit calling itself philosophy (ii. 8); it was the offspring of vanity nurtured by the mind of the *flesh* (ii. 18). See 2 Cor. i. 12 οὐκ ἐν σοφίᾳ σαρκικῇ, where a similar contrast is implied, and 1 Cor. i. 20, ii. 5, 6, 13, iii. 19, where it is directly expressed by σοφία τοῦ κόσμου, σοφία ἀνθρώπων, σοφία τοῦ αἰῶνος τούτου, ἀνθρωπίνη σοφία, etc.

10. περιπατῆσαι ἀξίως κ.τ.λ.] So 1 Thess. ii. 12, Ephes. iv. 1; comp. Phil. i. 27. The infinitive here denotes the consequence (not necessarily the purpose) of the spiritual enlightenment described in ἵνα πληρωθῆτε κ.τ.λ.; see Winer § xliv. p. 399 sq. With the received text περιπατῆσαι ὑμᾶς ἀξίως κ.τ.λ. the connexion might be doubtful; but this reading is condemned by external evidence. The emphasis of the sentence would be marred by the insertion of ὑμᾶς. The end of all knowledge, the Apostle would say, is conduct.

τοῦ Κυρίου] i. e. 'of Christ.' In 1 Thess. ii. 12 indeed we have περιπατεῖν ἀξίως τοῦ Θεοῦ; but St Paul's common, and apparently universal, usage requires us to understand ὁ Κύριος of Christ.

ἀρέσκειαν] i.e. 'to please *God* in all ways'; comp. 1 Thess. iv. 1 πῶς δεῖ ὑμᾶς περιπατεῖν καὶ ἀρέσκειν Θεῷ. As this word was commonly used to describe the proper attitude of men towards God, the addition of τοῦ Θεοῦ

would not be necessary: Philo *Quis rer. div. her.* 24 (I. p. 490) ὡς ἀποδεχομένου (τοῦ Θεοῦ) τὰς ψυχῆς ἑκουσίου ἀρεσκείας, *de Abrah.* 25 (II. p. 20) τὰς πρὸς ἀρέσκειαν ὁρμάς, *de Vict. Off.* 8 (II. p. 257) διὰ πασῶν ἰέναι τῶν εἰς ἀρέσκειαν ὁδῶν, with other passages quoted by Loesner. Otherwise it is used especially of ingratiating oneself with a sovereign or potentate, e. g. Polyb. vi. 2. 12; and perhaps in the higher connexion, in which it occurs in the text, the idea of a king is still prominent, as e. g. Philo *de Mund. Op.* 50 (I. p. 34) πάντα καὶ λέγειν καὶ πράττειν ἐσπούδαζεν εἰς ἀρέσκειαν τοῦ πατρὸς καὶ βασιλέως. Towards men this complaisance is always dangerous and most commonly vicious; hence ἀρέσκεια is a bad quality in Aristotle [?] (*Eth. Eud.* ii. 3 τὸ λίαν πρὸς ἡδονήν) as also in Theophrastus (*Char.* 5 οὐκ ἐπὶ τῷ βελτίστῳ ἡδονῆς παρασκευαστικῇ), but towards the King of kings no obsequiousness can be excessive. The ἀρέσκεια of Aristotle and Theophrastus presents the same moral contrast to the ἀρέσκεια here, as ἀνθρώποις ἀρέσκειν to Θεῷ ἀρέσκειν in such passages as 1 Thess. ii. 4, Gal. i. 10. Opposed to the ἀρέσκεια commended here is ἀνθρωπαρέσκεια condemned below, iii. 22.

ἐν παντὶ κ.τ.λ.] i. e. 'not only showing the fruits of your faith before men (Matt. vii. 16), but yourselves growing meanwhile in moral stature (Eph. iv. 13).'

τῇ ἐπιγνώσει] *by the knowledge.* The other readings, ἐν τῇ ἐπιγνώσει, εἰς τὴν ἐπίγνωσιν, are unsuccessful attempts to define the construction. The simple instrumental dative represents the knowledge of God as the dew or the rain which nurtures the growth of the plant; Deut. xxxii. 2, Hos. xiv. 5.

11. δυναμούμενοι] A word found more than once in the Greek versions of the Old Testament, Ps. lxvii (lxviii).

κράτος τῆς δόξης αὐτοῦ εἰς πᾶσαν ὑπομονὴν καὶ μακρο-
θυμίαν μετὰ χαρᾶς· ¹²εὐχαριστοῦντες τῷ πατρὶ τῷ ἱκα-

12. τῷ ἱκανώσαντι ὑμᾶς.

29 (LXX), Eccles. x. 10 (LXX), Dan. ix. 27 (Theod.), Ps. lxiv (lxv). 4 (Aq.), Job xxxvi. 9 (Aq.), but not occurring elsewhere in the New Testament, except in Heb. xi. 34 and as a various reading in Ephes. vi. 10. The compound ἐνδυναμοῦν however appears several times in St Paul and elsewhere.

κατὰ τὸ κράτος] The power communicated to the faithful corresponds to, and is a function of, the Divine might whence it comes. Unlike δύναμις or ἰσχύς, the word κράτος in the New Testament is applied solely to God.

τῆς δόξης αὐτοῦ] The 'glory' here, as frequently, stands for the majesty or the power or the goodness of God, as *manifested* to men; e.g. Eph. i. 6, 12, 17, iii. 16; comp. ver. 27, below. The δόξα, the bright light over the mercy-seat (Rom. ix. 4), was a symbol of such manifestations. God's revelation of Himself to us, however this revelation may be made, is the one source of all our highest strength (κατὰ τὸ κράτος κ.τ.λ.).

ὑπομονὴν καὶ μακροθυμίαν]'*endurance and long-suffering.*' The two words occur in the same context in 2 Cor. vi. 4, 6, 2 Tim. iii. 10, James v. 10, 11, Clem. Rom. 58 (64), Ign. *Ephes.* 3. They are distinguished in Trench *Synon.* § liii. p. 184 sq. The difference of meaning is best seen in their opposites. While ὑπομονή is the temper which does not easily succumb under suffering, μακροθυμία is the self-restraint which does not hastily retaliate a wrong. The one is opposed to *cowardice* or *despondency*, the other to *wrath* or *revenge* (Prov. xv. 18, xvi. 32; see also the note on iii. 12). While ὑπομονή is closely allied to *hope* (1 Thess. i. 3), μακροθυμία is commonly connected with *mercy* (e.g. Exod. xxxiv. 6). This distinction however, though it applies generally, is not true without exception. Thus in Is. lvii. 15 μακροθυμία is opposed to ὀλιγοψυχία, where we should rather have expected ὑπομονή; and μακροθυμεῖν is used similarly in James v. 7.

μετὰ χαρᾶς] So James i. 2, 3, πᾶσαν χαρὰν ἡγήσασθε...ὅταν πειρασμοῖς περιπέσητε ποικίλοις, γινώσκοντες ὅτι τὸ δοκίμιον ὑμῶν τῆς πίστεως κατεργάζεται ὑπομονήν κ.τ.λ.: comp. 1 Pet. iv. 13, and see below i. 24. This parallel points to the proper connexion of μετὰ χαρᾶς, which should be attached to the preceding words. On the other hand some would connect it with εὐχαριστοῦντες for the sake of preserving the balance of the three clauses, ἐν παντὶ ἔργῳ ἀγαθῷ καρποφοροῦντες, ἐν πάσῃ δυνάμει δυναμούμενοι, μετὰ χαρᾶς εὐχαριστοῦντες; and this seems to be favoured by Phil. i. 4 μετὰ χαρᾶς τὴν δέησιν ποιούμενος: but when it is so connected, the emphatic position of μετὰ χαρᾶς cannot be explained; nor indeed would these words be needed at all, for εὐχαριστία is in itself an act of rejoicing.

12. εὐχαριστοῦντες] Most naturally coordinated with the preceding participles and referred to the Colossians. The duty of thanksgiving is more than once enforced upon them below, ii. 7, iii. 17, iv. 2; comp. 1 Thess. v. 18. On the other hand the first person ἡμᾶς, which follows, has led others to connect εὐχαριστοῦντες with the primary verb of the sentence, οὐ παυόμεθα ver. 9. But, even if the reading ἡμᾶς be preferred to ὑμᾶς (which is perhaps doubtful), the sudden transition from the second to the first person is quite after St Paul's manner (see the note on ii. 13, 14, συνεζωοποίησεν ὑμᾶς... χαρισάμενος ἡμῖν), and cannot create any difficulty.

τῷ ἱκανώσαντι] '*who made us competent*'; comp. 2 Cor. iii. 6. On the

νώσαντι ἡμᾶς εἰς τὴν μερίδα τοῦ κλήρου τῶν ἁγίων ἐν
τῷ φωτί· ¹³ὃς ἐρύσατο ἡμᾶς ἐκ τῆς ἐξουσίας τοῦ

various readings see the detached
note.

τὴν μερίδα τοῦ κλήρου] 'the parcel
of the lot,' 'the portion which consists
in the lot,' τοῦ κλήρου being the
genitive of apposition: see Winer § lix.
p. 666 sq., and comp. Ps. xv (xvi). 5
Κύριος μερὶς τῆς κληρονομίας μου. In
Acts viii. 21 μερὶς and κλῆρος are co-
ordinated; in Gen. xxxi. 14, Num.
xviii. 20, Is. lvii. 6, μερὶς and κληρο-
νομία. The inheritance of Canaan, the
allotment of the promised land, here
presents an analogy to, and supplies
a metaphor for, the higher hopes of
the new dispensation, as in Heb. iii.
7—iv. 11. See also below, iii. 24 τὴν
ἀνταπόδοσιν τῆς κληρονομίας, and Ephes.
i. 18. St Chrysostom writes, διὰ τί
κλῆρον καλεῖ; δεικνὺς ὅτι οὐδεὶς ἀπὸ
κατορθωμάτων οἰκείων βασιλείας τυγχάνει, referring to Luke xvii. 10. It is
not won by us, but allotted to us.

ἐν τῷ φωτί] Best taken with the
expression τὴν μερίδα κ.τ.λ. For the
omission of the definite article, [τὴν]
ἐν τῷ φωτί, see above, vv. 2, 4, 8. The
portion of the saints is situated in the
kingdom of light. For the whole context compare St Paul's narrative in
Acts xxvi. 18 τοῦ ἐπιστρέψαι ἀπὸ
σκότους εἰς φῶς καὶ τῆς ἐξουσίας
τοῦ Σατανᾶ ἐπὶ τὸν Θεόν, τοῦ λαβεῖν
αὐτοὺς ἄφεσιν ἁμαρτιῶν καὶ κλῆρον
ἐν τοῖς ἡγιασμένοις, where all the
ideas and many of the expressions
recur. See also Acts xx. 32, in another
of St Paul's later speeches. As a classical parallel, Plato Resp. vii. p. 518 A,
ἔκ τε φωτὸς εἰς σκότος μεθισταμένων
καὶ ἐκ σκότους εἰς φῶς, is quoted.

13. 'We were slaves in the land of
darkness. God rescued us from this
thraldom. He transplanted us thence,
and settled us as free colonists and
citizens in the kingdom of His Son, in
the realms of light.'

ἐρύσατο] 'rescued, delivered us' by
His strong arm, as a mighty conquer-
or: comp. ii. 15 θριαμβεύσας. On the
form ἐρύσατο see A. Buttmann, p. 29:
comp. Clem. Rom. 55, and see the
note on ἐξερίζωσεν, ib. 6.

ἐξουσίας] Here 'arbitrary power, tyranny.' The word ἐξουσία properly signifies 'liberty of action' (ἔξεστι), and
thence, like the corresponding English word 'license,' involves two secondary ideas, of which either may be so
prominent as to eclipse the other; (1) 'authority,' 'delegated power' (e.g.
Luke xx. 2); or (2) 'tyranny,' 'law-
lessness,' 'unrestrained or arbitrary
power.' For this second sense comp.
e.g. Demosth. F. L. p. 428 τὴν ἄγαν
ταύτην ἐξουσίαν, Xenoph. Hiero 5
τῆς εἰς τὸ παρὸν ἐξουσίας ἕνεκα (speaking of tyrants), Plut. Vit. Eum. 13 ἀνά-
γωγοι ταῖς ἐξουσίαις καὶ μαλακοὶ ταῖς
διαίταις, Vit. Alex. 33 τὴν ἐξουσίαν
καὶ τὸν ὄγκον τῆς Ἀλεξάνδρου δυνάμεως,
Herodian ii. 4 καθαίρεσιν τῆς ἀνέτου
ἐξουσίας. This latter idea of a capricious unruly rule is prominent here.
The expression ἡ ἐξουσία τοῦ σκότους
occurs also in Luke xxii. 53, where
again the idea of disorder is involved.
The transference from darkness to
light is here represented as a transference from an arbitrary tyranny, an
ἐξουσία, to a well-ordered sovereignty,
a βασιλεία. This seems also to be
St Chrysostom's idea; for he explains
τῆς ἐξουσίας by τῆς τυραννίδος, adding
χαλεπὸν καὶ τὸ ἁπλῶς εἶναι ὑπὸ τῷ δια-
βόλῳ· τὸ δὲ καὶ μετ' ἐξουσίας, τοῦτο
χαλεπώτερον.

μετέστησεν] 'removed,' when they
were baptized, when they accepted
Christ. The image of μετέστησεν is
supplied by the wholesale transporta-
tion of peoples (ἀναστάτους or ἀνα-
σπάστους ποιεῖν), of which the history
of oriental monarchies supplied so

σκότους, καὶ μετέστησεν εἰς τὴν βασιλείαν τοῦ υἱοῦ τῆς

many examples. See Joseph. *Ant.* ix.
11. 1 τοὺς οἰκήτορας αἰχμαλωτίσας
μετέστησεν εἰς τὴν αὐτοῦ βασιλείαν,
speaking of Tiglath-Pileser and the
Transjordanic tribes.

τοῦ υἱοῦ] Not of inferior angels, as
the false teachers would have it (ii. 18),
but of His own Son. The same contrast between a dispensation of angels
and a dispensation of the Son underlies the words here, which is explicitly brought out in Heb. i. 1—ii. 8;
see especially i. 2 ἐλάλησεν ἡμῖν ἐν υἱῷ,
compared with ii. 5 οὐ γὰρ ἀγγέλοις
ὑπέταξεν τὴν οἰκουμένην τὴν μέλλουσαν.
Severianus has rightly caught the idea
underlying τοῦ υἱοῦ here ; ὑπὸ τὸν
κληρονόμον ἐσμέν, οὐχ ὑπὸ τοὺς οἰκέτας.

τῆς ἀγάπης αὐτοῦ] '*of His love.*' As
love is the essence of the Father (1 Joh.
iv. 8, 16), so is it also of the Son. The
mission of the Son is the revelation of
the Father's love; for as He is the
μονογενής, the Father's love is perfectly represented in Him (see 1 Joh.
iv. 9). St Augustine has rightly interpreted St Paul's words here, *de
Trin.* xv. 19 (VIII. p. 993) 'Caritas
quippe Patris...nihil est quam ejus
ipsa natura atque substantia...ac per
hoc filius caritatis ejus nullus est alius
quam qui de ejus substantia est genitus.' See also Orig. *c. Cels.* v. 11. Thus
these words are intimately connected
with the expressions which follow,
εἰκὼν τοῦ Θεοῦ τοῦ ἀοράτου (ver. 15),
and ἐν αὐτῷ εὐδόκησεν πᾶν τὸ πλήρωμα κατοικῆσαι (ver. 19). The loose
interpretation, which makes τοῦ υἱοῦ
τῆς ἀγάπης equivalent to τοῦ υἱοῦ τοῦ
ἠγαπημένου, destroys the whole force
of the expression.

In the preceding verses we have a
striking illustration of St Paul's teaching in two important respects. *First.*
The reign of Christ has already begun.
His kingdom is a present kingdom.
Whatever therefore is *essential* in the
kingdom of Christ must be capable of

realisation now. There may be some
exceptional manifestation in the world
to come, but this cannot alter its inherent character. In other words the
sovereignty of Christ is essentially a
moral and spiritual sovereignty, which
has begun now and will only be perfected hereafter. *Secondly.* Corresponding to this, and equally significant, is his language in speaking of
individual Christians. He regards
them as already rescued from the
power of darkness, as already put in
possession of their inheritance as
saints. They are *potentially* saved,
because the knowledge of God is itself
salvation, and this knowledge is within
their reach. Such is St Paul's constant mode of speaking. He uses the
language not of exclusion, but of comprehension. He prefers to dwell on
their potential advantages, rather than
on their actual attainments. He hopes
to make them saints by dwelling on
their calling as saints. See especially
Ephes. ii. 6 συνήγειρεν καὶ συνεκάθισεν
ἐν τοῖς ἐπουρανίοις ἐν Χριστῷ Ἰησοῦ κ.τ.λ.

14. ἔχομεν] For the reading ἔσχομεν, which is possibly correct here,
and which carries out the idea enforced in the last note, see the detached note on the various readings.
In the parallel passage, Ephes. i. 7,
there is the same variation of reading.

τὴν ἀπολύτρωσιν] '*ransom, redemption.*' The image of a captive and en-
slaved people is still continued : Philo
Omn. prob. lib. 17 (II. p. 463) αἰχμάλωτος ἀπήχθη...ἀπογνοὺς ἀπολύτρωσιν,
Plut. *Vit. Pomp.* 24 πόλεων αἰχμα-
λώτων ἀπολυτρώσεις. The metaphor
however has changed from the victor
who rescues the captive by force of arms
(ver. 13 ἐρύσατο) to the philanthropist
who releases him by the payment of a
ransom. The clause which follows in
the received text, διὰ τοῦ αἵματος αὐτοῦ, is interpolated from the parallel
passage, Ephes. i. 7.

ἀγάπης αὐτοῦ, ¹⁴ἐν ᾧ ἔχομεν τὴν ἀπολύτρωσιν, τὴν
ἄφεσιν τῶν ἁμαρτιῶν·

14. ἐν ᾧ ἔσχομεν.

τὴν ἄφεσιν τῶν ἁμαρτιῶν] So in the
parallel passage Ephes. i. 7 the Apostle defines τὴν ἀπολύτρωσιν as τὴν
ἄφεσιν τῶν παραπτωμάτων. May not
this studied precision point to some
false conception of ἀπολύτρωσις put
forward by the heretical teachers?
Later Gnostics certainly perverted the
meaning of the term, applying it to
their own formularies of initiation.
This is related of the Marcosians by
Irenæus i. 13. ὁ διὰ τὴν ἀπολύτρωσιν
ἀκρατήτους καὶ ἀοράτους γίνεσθαι τῷ
κριτῇ κ.τ.λ., i. 21. ͙ ὅσοι γάρ εἰσι
ταύτης τῆς γνώμης μυσταγωγοί, τοσαῦ-
ται καὶ ἀπολυτρώσεις, ib. § 4 εἶναι δὲ
τελείαν ἀπολύτρωσιν αὐτὴν τὴν ἐπίγνωσιν τοῦ ἀρρήτου μεγέθους (with the
whole context), and Hippolytus _Hær._
vi. 41 λέγουσί τι φωνῇ ἀρρήτῳ, ἐπιτι-
θέντες χεῖρα τῷ τὴν ἀπολύτρωσιν λα-
βόντι κ.τ.λ. (comp. ix. 13). In support of their nomenclature they perverted such passages as the text, Iren.
i. 21. 2 τὸν Παῦλον ῥητῶς φάσκουσι
τὴν ἐν Χριστῷ Ἰησοῦ ἀπολύτρωσιν πολλάκις μεμηνυκέναι. It seems not improbable that the communication of
similar mystical secrets, perhaps connected with their angelology (ii. 18),
was put forward by these Colossian
false teachers as an ἀπολύτρωσις. Compare the words in the baptismal formula of the Marcosians as given in
Iren. i. 21. 3 (comp. Theodt. _Hær._
Fab. i. 9) εἰς ἕνωσιν καὶ ἀπολύτρωσιν καὶ
κοινωνίαν τῶν δυνάμεων, where the last
words (which have been differently
interpreted) must surely mean 'communion with the (spiritual) powers.'
Thus it is a parallel to εἰς λύτρωσιν
ἀγγελικήν, which appears in an alternative formula of these heretics given
likewise by Irenæus in the context;
for this latter is explained in Clem.
Alex. _Exc. Theod._ p. 974, εἰς λύτρωσιν

ἀγγελικήν, τουτέστιν, ἣν καὶ ἄγγελοι
ἔχουσιν. Any direct historical connexion between the Colossian heretics
and these later Gnostics of the Valentinian school is very improbable; but
the passages quoted will serve to show
how a false idea of ἀπολύτρωσις would
naturally be associated with an esoteric doctrine of angelic powers. See
the note on i. 28 ἵνα παραστήσωμεν
πάντα ἄνθρωπον τέλειον.

15 sq. In the passage which follows St Paul defines the Person of
Christ, claiming for Him the absolute
supremacy,
(1) In relation to the _Universe_, the
Natural Creation (vv. 15—17);
(2) In relation to the _Church_, the
new _Moral_ Creation (ver. 18);
and he then combines the two, ἵνα
γένηται ἐν πᾶσιν αὐτὸς πρωτεύων, explaining this twofold sovereignty by the
absolute indwelling of the _pleroma_ in
Christ, and showing how, as a consequence, the reconciliation and harmony of all things must be effected
in Him (vv. 19, 20).

As the idea of the _Logos_ underlies
the whole of this passage, though the
term itself does not appear, a few
words explanatory of this term will be
necessary by way of preface. The
word λόγος then, denoting both 'reason' and 'speech,' was a philosophical
term adopted by Alexandrian Judaism before St Paul wrote, to express
the _manifestation_ of the Unseen God,
the Absolute Being, in the creation
and government of the World. It
included all modes by which God
makes Himself known to man. As
His _reason_, it denoted His purpose
or design; as His _speech_, it implied
His revelation. Whether this λόγος
was conceived merely as the divine
energy personified, or whether the

¹⁵ὅς ἐστιν εἰκὼν τοῦ Θεοῦ τοῦ ἀοράτου, πρωτότοκος

conception took a more concrete form, I need not stop now to enquire ; but I hope to give a fuller account of the matter in a later volume. It is sufficient for the understanding of what follows to say that Christian teachers, when they adopted this term, exalted and fixed its meaning by attaching to it two precise and definite ideas : (1) 'The Word is a Divine Person,' ὁ λόγος ἦν πρὸς τὸν Θεὸν καὶ Θεὸς ἦν ὁ λόγος ; and (2) 'The Word became incarnate in Jesus Christ,' ὁ λόγος σὰρξ ἐγένετο. It is obvious that these two propositions must have altered materially the significance of all the subordinate terms connected with the idea of the λόγος; and that therefore their use in Alexandrian writers, such as Philo, cannot be taken to *define*, though it may be brought to *illustrate*, their meaning in St Paul and St John. With 'these cautions the Alexandrian phraseology, as a providential preparation for the teaching of the Gospel, will afford important aid in the understanding of the Apostolic writings.

15—17. 'He is the perfect image, the visible representation, of the unseen God. He is the Firstborn, the absolute Heir of the Father, begotten before the ages; the Lord of the Universe by virtue of primogeniture, and by virtue also of creative agency. For in and through Him the whole world was created, things in heaven and things on earth, things visible to the outward eye and things cognisable by the inward perception. His supremacy is absolute and universal. All powers in heaven and earth are subject to Him. This subjection extends even to the most exalted and most potent of angelic beings, whether they be called Thrones or Dominations or Princedoms or Powers, or whatever title of dignity men may confer upon them. Yes : He is first and He is last. Through Him, as the

mediatorial Word, the universe has been created; and unto Him, as the final goal, it is tending. In Him is no before or after. He is pre-existent and self-existent before all the worlds. And in Him, as the binding and sustaining power, universal nature coheres and consists.'

15. ὅς ἐστιν κ.τ.λ.] The Person of Christ is described *first* in relation more especially to Deity, as εἰκὼν τοῦ Θεοῦ τοῦ ἀοράτου, and *secondly* in relation more especially to created things, as πρωτότοκος πάσης κτίσεως. The fundamental conception of the Logos involves the idea of *mediation* between God and creation. A perverted view respecting the nature of the mediation between the two lay, as we have seen, at the root of the heretical teaching at Colossæ (p. 34, p. 101 sq., p. 115 sq.), and required to be met by the true doctrine of Christ as the Eternal Logos.

εἰκών] '*the image.*' This expression is used repeatedly by Philo, as a description of the Logos; *de Mund. Op.* 8 (1. p. 6) τὸν ἀόρατον καὶ νοητὸν θεῖον λόγον εἰκόνα λέγει Θεοῦ, *de Confus. ling.* 20 (1. p. 419) τὴν εἰκόνα αὐτοῦ, τὸν ἱερώτατον λόγον, *ib.* § 28 (1. p. 427) τῆς ἀϊδίου εἰκόνος αὐτοῦ λόγου τοῦ ἱερωτάτου κ.τ.λ., *de Profug.* 19 (1. p. 561) ὁ ὑπεράνω τούτων λόγος θεῖος...αὐτὸς εἰκὼν ὑπάρχων Θεοῦ, *de Monarch.* ii. 5 (II. p. 225) λόγος δέ ἐστιν εἰκὼν Θεοῦ δι' οὗ σύμπας ὁ κόσμος ἐδημιουργεῖτο, *de Somn.* i. 41 (1. p. 656), etc. For the use which Philo made of the text Gen. i. 26, 27, κατ' εἰκόνα ἡμετέραν, κατ' εἰκόνα Θεοῦ, see the note on iii. 10. Still earlier than Philo, before the idea of the λόγος had assumed such a definite form, the term was used of the Divine σοφία personified in Wisd. vii. 26 ἀπαύγασμα γάρ ἐστι φωτὸς ἀϊδίου...καὶ εἰκὼν τῆς ἀγαθότητος αὐτοῦ. St Paul himself applies the term to our Lord in an earlier epistle, 2 Cor. iv. 4 τῆς δόξης τοῦ Χριστοῦ ὅς ἐστιν εἰκὼν τοῦ Θεοῦ (comp. iii. 18 τὴν αὐτὴν εἰκόνα μεταμορφούμεθα). Closely allied to εἰκών also is χαρακτήρ, which appears in the same connexion in Heb. i. 3 ὢν ἀπαύγασμα τῆς δόξης καὶ χαρακτὴρ τῆς ὑποστάσεως αὐτοῦ, a passage illustrated by Philo de Plant. 5 (I. p. 332) σφραγῖδι Θεοῦ ἧς ὁ χαρακτήρ ἐστιν ἀΐδιος λόγος. See also Phil. ii. 6 ἐν μορφῇ Θεοῦ ὑπάρχων.

Beyond the very obvious notion of *likeness*, the word εἰκών involves two other ideas ;

(1) *Representation.* In this respect it is allied to χαρακτήρ, and differs from ὁμοίωμα. In ὁμοίωμα the resemblance may be accidental, as one egg is like another; but εἰκών implies an archetype of which it is a *copy*, as Greg. Naz. *Orat.* 30 (I. p. 554) says αὕτη γὰρ εἰκόνος φύσις μίμημα εἶναι τοῦ ἀρχετύπου. So too Io. Damasc. *de Imag.* i. 9 (I. p. 311) εἰκών ἐστιν ὁμοίωμα χαρακτηρίζον τὸ πρωτότυπον ; comp. Philo de Mund. Op. 23 (I. p. 16). On this difference see Trench *N. T. Synon.* § xv. p. 47. The εἰκών might be the result of direct imitation (μιμητική) like the head of a sovereign on a coin, or it might be due to natural causes (φυσική) like the parental features in the child, but in any case it was *derived* from its prototype: see Basil. *de Spir. Sanct.* 18 § 45 (III. p. 38). The word itself however does not necessarily imply *perfect* representation. Thus man is said to be the image of God ; 1 Cor. xi. 7 εἰκὼν καὶ δόξα Θεοῦ ὑπάρχων, Clem. Rom. 33 ἄνθρωπον...τῆς ἑαυτοῦ εἰκόνος χαρακτῆρα. Thus again an early Judæo-Christian writer so designates the duly appointed bishop, as the representative of the Divine authority; *Clem. Hom.* iii. 62 ὡς εἰκόνα Θεοῦ προτιμῶντας. The idea of *perfection* does not lie in the word itself, but must be sought from the context (e.g. πᾶν τὸ πλήρωμα ver. 19). The use which was made of this expression, and especially of this passage, in the

Christological controversies of the fourth and fifth centuries may be seen from the patristic quotations in Petav. *Theol. Dogm.* de Trin. ii. 11. 9 sq., vi. 5. 6.

(2) *Manifestation.* This idea comes from the implied contrast to τοῦ ἀοράτου Θεοῦ. St Chrysostom indeed maintains the direct opposite, arguing that, as the archetype is invisible, so the image must be invisible also, ἡ τοῦ ἀοράτου εἰκὼν καὶ αὐτὴ ἀόρατος καὶ ὁμοίως ἀόρατος. So too Hilary c. *Const. Imp.* 21 (II. p. 378) 'ut imago invisibilis Dei, etiam per id quod ipse invisibilis est, invisibilis Dei imago esset.' And this was the view of the Nicene and post-Nicene fathers generally. But the underlying idea of the εἰκών, and indeed of the λόγος generally, is the manifestation of the hidden : comp. Philo *de Vit. Moys.* ii. 12 (II. p. 144) εἰκὼν τῆς ἀοράτου φύσεως ἐμφανής. And adopted into Christian theology, the doctrine of the λόγος expresses this conception still more prominently by reason of the Incarnation; comp. Tertull. *adv. Marc.* v. 19 'Scientes filium semper retro visum, si quibus visus est in Dei nomine, ut imaginem ipsius,' Hippol. c. *Noet.* 7 διὰ γὰρ τῆς εἰκόνος ὁμοίας τυγχανούσης εὔγνωστος ὁ πατὴρ γίνεται, *ib.* § 12, 13, Orig. *in Ioann.* vi. § 2 (IV. p. 104). Among the post-Nicene fathers too St Basil has caught the right idea, *Epist.* xxxviii. 8 (III. p. 121) ὁ τῆς εἰκόνος κατανοήσας κάλλος ἐν περινοίᾳ τοῦ ἀρχετύπου γίνεται...βλέπειν διὰ τούτου ἐκεῖνον...τὸ ἀγέννητον κάλλος ἐν τῷ γεννητῷ κατοπτεύσας. The Word, whether pre-incarnate or incarnate, is the revelation of the unseen Father : comp. John i. 18 Θεὸν οὐδεὶς ἑώρακεν πώποτε· μονογενὴς Θεός, ὁ ὢν εἰς τὸν κόλπον τοῦ πατρός, ἐκεῖνος ἐξηγήσατο, xiv. 9, 10 ὁ ἑωρακὼς ἐμὲ ἑώρακεν τὸν πατέρα· πῶς σὺ λέγεις, Δεῖξον ἡμῖν τὸν πατέρα ; (compared with vi. 46 οὐχ ὅτι τὸν πατέρα ἑώρακέν τις κ.τ.λ.). The epithet ἀοράτου however must not be confined to the ap-

prehension of the bodily senses, but will include the cognisance of the inward eye also.

πρωτότοκος πάσης κτίσεως] *the First-born of all creation.* The word πρωτότοκος has a twofold parentage:

(1) Like εἰκών it is closely connected with and taken from the Alexandrian vocabulary of the Logos. The word however which Philo applies to the λόγος is not πρωτότοκος but πρωτόγονος: *de Agric.* 12 (I. p. 308) προστησάμενος τὸν ὀρθὸν αὐτοῦ λόγον πρωτόγονον υἱόν, *de Somn.* i. 37 (I. p. 653) ὁ πρωτόγονος αὐτοῦ θεῖος λόγος, *de Confus. ling.* i. 28 (I. p. 427) σπουδαζέτω κοσμεῖσθαι κατὰ τὸν πρωτόγονον αὐτοῦ λόγον: comp. *ib.* i. 14 (I. p. 414) τοῦτον πρεσβύτατον υἱὸν ὁ τῶν ὄντων ἀνέτειλε πατήρ, ὃν ἑτέρωθι πρωτόγονον ὠνόμασε: and this designation πρεσβύτατος υἱὸς is several times applied to the λόγος. Again in *Quis rer. div. her.* § 24 (I. p. 489) the language of Exod. xiii. 2 ἁγίασόν μοι πᾶν πρωτότοκον πρωτογενές κ.τ.λ. is so interpreted as to apply to the Divine Word. These appellations, 'the first-begotten, the eldest son,' are given to the Logos by Philo, because in his philosophy it includes the original conception, the archetypal idea, of creation, which was afterwards realised in the material world. Among the early Christian fathers Justin Martyr again and again recognises the application of the term πρωτότοκος to the Word; *Apol.* i. 23 (p. 68) λόγος αὐτοῦ ὑπάρχων καὶ πρωτότοκος καὶ δύναμις, *ib.* § 46 (p. 83) τὸν Χριστὸν πρωτότοκον τοῦ Θεοῦ εἶναι .. λόγον ὄντα οὗ πᾶν γένος ἀνθρώπων μετέσχε, *ib.* § 33 (p. 75 c) τὸν λόγον ὃς καὶ πρωτότοκος τῷ Θεῷ ἐστι. So too Theophilus *ad Autol.* ii. 22 τοῦτον τὸν λόγον ἐγέννησεν προφορικόν, πρωτότοκον πάσης κτίσεως.

(2) The word πρωτοτοκος had also another not less important link of connexion with the past. The Messianic reference of Ps. lxxxix. 28, ἐγὼ πρωτότοκον θήσομαι αὐτὸν κ.τ.λ., seems to have been generally allowed. So

at least it is interpreted by R. Nathan in *Shemoth Rabba* 19, fol. 118. 4, 'God said, As I made Jacob a first-born (Exod. iv. 22), so also will I make king Messiah a first-born (Ps. lxxxix. 28).' Hence 'the first-born' ὁ πρωτότοκος (בכור) used absolutely, became a recognised title of Messiah. The way had been paved for this Messianic reference of πρωτότοκος by its prior application to the Israelites, as the prerogative race, Exod. iv. 22 'Israel is my son, my first-born': comp. Psalm. Salom. xviii. 4 ἡ παιδεία σου ἐφ' ἡμᾶς ὡς υἱὸν πρωτότοκον μονογενῆ, 4 Esdr. vi. 58 'nos populus tuus, quem vocasti primogenitum, unigenitum,' where the combination of the two titles applied in the New Testament to the Son is striking. Here, as elsewhere (see the note on Gal. iii. 16 καὶ τοῖς σπέρμασιν κ.τ.λ.), the terms are transferred from the race to the Messiah, as the representative, the embodiment, of the race.

As the Person of Christ was the Divine response alike to the philosophical questionings of the Alexandrian Jew and to the patriotic hopes of the Palestinian, these two currents of thought meet in the term πρωτότοκος as applied to our Lord, who is both the true Logos and the true Messiah. For this reason, we may suppose, as well as for others, the Christian Apostles preferred πρωτότοκος to πρωτόγονος, which (as we may infer from Philo) was the favourite term with the Alexandrians, because the former alone would include the Messianic reference as well.

The main ideas then which the word involves are twofold; the one more directly connected with the Alexandrian conception of the Logos, the other more nearly allied to the Palestinian conception of the Messiah.

(1) *Priority* to all creation. In other words it declares the absolute pre-existence of the Son. At first sight it might seem that Christ is here regarded as one, though the earliest, of created beings. This in-

terpretation however is not required
by the expression itself. The fathers
of the fourth century rightly called
attention to the fact that the Apostle
writes not πρωτόκτιστος, but πρωτότοκος ; e.g. Basil. *c. Eunom.* iv (I.
p. 292). Much earlier, in Clem. Alex.
Exc. Theod. 10 (p. 970), though without any direct reference to this passage, the μονογενὴς καὶ πρωτότοκος is
contrasted with the πρωτόκτιστοι, the
highest order of angelic beings; and
the word πρωτόκτιστος occurs more
than once elsewhere in his writings (e.g.
Strom. v. 14, p. 699). Nor again does
the genitive case necessarily imply that
the πρωτότοκος Himself belonged to
the κτίσις, as will be shown presently.
And if this sense is not required by the
words themselves, it is directly excluded by the context. It is inconsistent
alike with the universal agency in
creation which is ascribed to Him in
the words following, ἐν αὐτῷ ἐκτίσθη
τὰ πάντα, and with the absolute pre-
existence and self-existence which is
claimed for Him just below, αὐτὸς
ἔστιν πρὸ πάντων. We may add also
that it is irreconcilable with other
passages in the Apostolic writings,
while it contradicts the fundamental
idea of the Christian consciousness.
More especially the description πρωτότοκος πάσης κτίσεως must be interpreted in such a way that it is not inconsistent with His other title of μονογενής, *unicus*, alone of His kind and
therefore distinct from created things.
The two words express the same
eternal fact ; but while μονογενής
states it in itself, πρωτότοκος places it
in relation to the Universe. The
correct interpretation is supplied by
Justin Martyr, *Dial.* § 100 (p. 326
D) πρωτότοκον τοῦ Θεοῦ καὶ πρὸ πάντων τῶν κτισμάτων. He does not
indeed mention this passage, but it
was doubtless in his mind, for he elsewhere uses the very expression πρωτότοκος πάσης κτίσεως, *Dial.* § 85
(p. 311 B), § 138 (p. 367 D); comp. also
§ 84 (p. 310 B), where the words πρω-

τότοκος τῶν πάντων ποιημάτων occur.

(2) *Sovereignty* over all creation.
God's 'first-born' is the natural ruler,
the acknowledged head, of God's
household. The right of primogeniture appertains to Messiah over all
created things. Thus in Ps. lxxxix.
28 after πρωτότοκον θήσομαι αὐτὸν
the explanation is added, ὑψηλὸν
παρὰ τοῖς βασιλεῦσιν τῆς γῆς, i.e. (as
the original implies) 'above all the
kings of the earth.' In its Messianic
reference this secondary idea of
sovereignty predominated in the word
πρωτότοκος, so that from this point of
view πρωτότοκος πάσης κτίσεως would
mean 'Sovereign Lord over all creation by virtue of primogeniture.' The
ἔθηκεν κληρόνομον πάντων of the Apostolic writer (Heb. i. 2) exactly corresponds to the θήσομαι πρωτότοκον
of the Psalmist (lxxxix. 28), and
doubtless was tacitly intended as a
paraphrase and application of this
Messianic passage. So again in Heb.
xii. 23, ἐκκλησίᾳ πρωτοτόκων, the most
probable explanation of the word is
that which makes it equivalent to
'heirs of the kingdom,' all faithful
Christians being *ipso facto* πρωτότοκοι,
because all are kings. Nay, so com-
pletely might this idea of dominion by
virtue of priority eclipse the primary
sense of the term 'first-born' in some
of its uses, that it is given as a title to
God Himself by R. Bechai on the Pen-
tateuch, fol. 124. 4, 'Who is *primogenitus mundi*,' שהוא בכורו של עולם,
i.e ὅς ἐστιν πρωτότοκος τοῦ κόσμου, as
it would be rendered in Greek. In this
same work again, fol. 74. 4, Exod. xiii.
2 is falsely interpreted so that God is
represented as calling Himself 'primogenitus': see Schöttgen p. 922.
For other instances of secondary uses
of בכור in the Old Testament, where
the idea of 'priority of birth' is overshadowed by and lost in the idea of
'pre-eminence,' see Job xviii. 13 'the
first-born of death,' Is. xiv. 30 'the
first-born of the poor.'

πάσης κτίσεως] '*of all creation*,'

rather than '*of every created thing.*'
The three senses of κτίσις in the New
Testament are : (1) creation, as the
act of creating, e.g. Rom. i. 20 ἀπὸ
κτίσεως κόσμου : (2) creation, as the
aggregate of created things, Mark xiii.
19 ἀπ᾽ ἀρχῆς κτίσεως ἣν ἔκτισεν ὁ Θεός
(where the parallel passage, Matt.
xxiv. 21, has ἀπ᾽ ἀρχῆς κόσμου), Rom.
viii. 22 πᾶσα ἡ κτίσις συστενάζει : (3)
a creation, a single created thing, a
creature, e.g. Rom. viii. 39 οὔτε τις
κτίσις ἑτέρα, Heb. iv. 13 οὐκ ἔστιν
κτίσις ἀφανής. As κτίσις without the
definite article is sometimes used of
the created world generally (e. g. Mark
xiii. 19), and indeed belongs to the
category of anarthrous nouns like
κόσμος, γῆ, οὐρανός, etc. (see Winer
§ xix. p. 149 sq.), it is best taken so
here. Indeed πάσης κτίσεως, in the
sense of πάντος κτίσματος, would be
awkward in this connexion; for πρωτότοκος seems to require either a collective noun, or a plural πασῶν τῶν
κτίσεων. In ver. 23 the case is different (see the note there). The anarthrous πᾶσα κτίσις is found in Judith
ix. 12 βασιλεῦ πάσης κτίσεώς σου,
while πᾶσα ἡ κτίσις occurs in Judith
xvi. 14, Mark xvi. 15, Rom. viii. 22,
Clem. Rom. 19, *Mart. Polyc.* 14. For
πᾶς, signifying '*all,*' and not '*every,*'
when attached to this class of nouns,
see Winer § xviii. p. 137.

The genitive case must be interpreted so as to include the full meaning of πρωτότοκος, as already explained. It will therefore signify :
'He stands in the relation of πρωτότοκος to all creation,' i.e. 'He is the
Firstborn, and, as the Firstborn, the
absolute Heir and sovereign Lord, of
all creation.' The connexion is the
same as in the passage of R. Bechai
already quoted, where God is called
primogenitus mundi. Another explanation which would connect the
genitive with the first part of the compound alone (πρωτό-), comparing Joh.
i. 15, 30, πρῶτός μου ἦν, unduly strains
the grammar, while it excludes the

idea of 'heirship, sovereignty.'

The history of the patristic exegesis
of this expression is not without a pain-
ful interest. All the fathers of the
second and third centuries without
exception, so far as I have noticed,
correctly refer it to the Eternal
Word and not to the Incarnate Christ,
to the Deity and not to the humanity of our Lord. So Justin *l. c.*,
Theophilus *l. c.*, Clement of Alexandria *Exc. Theod.* 7, 8, 19 (pp. 967,
973), Tertullian *adv. Prax.* 7, *adv.*
Marc. v. 19, Hippolytus *Hær.* x. 33,
Origen *c. Cels.* vi. 47, 63, 64, etc., *in*
Ioann. i. § 22 (IV. p. 21), xix. § 5 (p.
305), xxviii. § 14 (p. 392), Cyprian
Test. ii. 1, Novatian *de Trin.* 16, and
the Synod of Antioch (Routh's *Rel.*
Sacr. III. pp. 290, 293). The Arian
controversy however gave a different turn to the exegesis of the
passage. The Arians fastened upon
the expression πρωτότοκος πάσης κτίσεως, and drew from it the inference
that the Son was a created being.
The great use which they made of
the text appears from the document
in Hilary, *Fragm. Hist. Op.* II. p.
644. The right answer to this false
interpretation we have already seen.
Many orthodox fathers however, not
satisfied with this, transferred the
expression into a new sphere, and
maintained that πρωτότοκος πάσης
κτίσεως describes the Incarnate Christ.
By so doing they thought to cut up
the Arian argument by the roots. As
a consequence of this interpretation,
they were obliged to understand the
κτίσις and the κτίζεσθαι in the context
of the new spiritual creation, the
καινὴ κτίσις of 2 Cor. v. 17, Gal. vi. 15.
Thus interpreted, πρωτότοκος πάσης
κτίσεως here becomes nearly equivalent to πρωτότοκος ἐν πολλοῖς ἀδελφοῖς
in Rom. viii. 29. The arguments alleged in favour of this interpretation
are mainly twofold : (1) That, if applied to the Divine nature, πρωτότοκος
would contradict μονογενὴς which elsewhere describes the nature of the

Eternal Son. But those who maintained, and rightly maintained, that πρωτότοκος (Luke ii. 7) did not necessarily imply that the Lord's mother had other sons, ought not to have been led away by this fallacy. (2) That πρωτότοκος in other passages (e. g. Rom. viii. 29, Rev. i. 5, and just below, ver. 18) is applied to the humanity of Christ. But elsewhere, in Heb. i. 6 ὅταν δὲ πάλιν εἰσαγάγῃ τὸν πρωτότοκον κ.τ.λ., the term must almost necessarily refer to the preexistence of the Son; and moreover the very point of the Apostle's language in the text (as will be seen presently) is the parallelism in the two relations of our Lord—His relation to the natural creation, as the Eternal Word, and His relation to the spiritual creation, as the Head of the Church— so that the same word (πρωτότοκος πάσης κτίσεως ver. 15, πρωτότοκος ἐκ τῶν νεκρῶν ver. 18) is studiously used of both. A false exegesis is sure to bring a nemesis on itself. Logical consistency required that this interpretation should be carried farther; and Marcellus, who was never deterred by any considerations of prudence, took this bold step. He extended the principle to the whole context, including even εἰκὼν τοῦ ἀοράτου Θεοῦ, which likewise he interpreted of our Lord's humanity. In this way a most important Christological passage was transferred into an alien sphere; and the strongest argument against Arianism melted away in the attempt to combat Arianism on false grounds. The criticisms of Eusebius on Marcellus are perfectly just: Eccl. Theol. i. 20 (p. 96) ταῦτα περὶ τῆς θεότητος τοῦ υἱοῦ τοῦ Θεοῦ, κἂν μὴ Μαρκέλλῳ δοκῇ, εἴρηται· οὐ γὰρ περὶ τῆς σαρκὸς εἶπεν ἂν τοσαῦτα ὁ θεῖος ἀπόστολος κ.τ.λ.; comp. ib. ii. 9 (p. 67), iii. 6 sq. (p. 175), c. Marcell. i. 1 (p. 6), i. 2 (p. 12), ii. 3 (pp. 43, 46 sq., 48). The objections to this interpretation are threefold : (1) It disregards the history of the terms in their connexion with the pre

Christian speculations of Alexandrian Judaism. These however, though directly or indirectly they were present to the minds of the earlier fathers and kept them in the right exegetical path, might very easily have escaped a writer in the fourth century. (2) It shatters the context. To suppose that such expressions as ἐν αὐτῷ ἐκτίσθη τὰ πάντα [τὰ] ἐν τοῖς οὐρανοῖς καὶ [τὰ] ἐπὶ τῆς γῆς, or τὰ πάντα δι' αὐτοῦ ...ἔκτισται, or τὰ πάντα ἐν αὐτῷ συνέστηκεν, refer to the work of the Incarnation, is to strain language in a way which would reduce all theological exegesis to chaos; and yet this, as Marcellus truly saw, is a strictly logical consequence of the interpretation which refers πρωτότοκος πάσης κτίσεως to Christ's humanity. (3) It takes no account of the cosmogony and angelology of the false teachers against which the Apostle's exposition here is directed (see above, pp. 101 sq., 110 sq., 115 sq.). This interpretation is given by St Athanasius c. Arian. ii. 62 sq. (I. p. 419 sq.) and appears again in Greg. Nyss. c. Eunom. ii. (II. pp. 451—453, 492), ib. iii. (II. p. 540—545), de Perf. (III. p. 290 sq.), Cyril Alex. Thes. 25, p. 236 sq., de Trin. Dial. iv. p. 517 sq., vi. p. 625 sq., Anon. Chrysost. Op. VIII. p. 223, appx. (quoted as Chrysostom by Photius Bibl. 277). So too Cyril expresses himself at the Council of Ephesus, Labb. Conc. III. p. 652 (ed. Colet). St Athanasius indeed does not confine the expression to the condescension (συγκατάβασις) of the Word in the Incarnation, but includes also a prior condescension in the Creation of the world (see Bull Def. Fid. Nic. iii. 9 § 1, with the remarks of Newman Select Treatises of S. Athanasius I. pp. 278, 368 sq.). This double reference however only confuses the exegesis of the passage still further, while theologically it might lead to very serious difficulties. In another work, Expos. Fid. 3 (I. p. 80), he seems to take a truer view of its meaning. St Basil,

πάσης κτίσεως· ¹⁶ὅτι ἐν αὐτῷ ἐκτίσθη τὰ πάντα, [τὰ]

who to an equally clear appreciation
of doctrine generally unites a sounder
exegesis than St Athanasius, while mentioning the interpretation which refers
the expression to Christ's human nature, himself prefers explaining it
of the Eternal Word; c. Eunom. iv. (1.
p. 292). Of the Greek commentators
on this passage, Chrysostom's view is
not clear; Severianus (Cram. Cat. p.
303) and Theodoret understand it
rightly of the Eternal Word ; while
Theodore of Mopsuestia (Cram. Cat.
pp. 306, 308, 309, Rab. Maur. Op. VI.
p. 511 sq. ed. Migne) expresses himself very strongly on the opposite
side. Like Marcellus, he carries the
interpretation consistently into the
whole context, explaining ἐν αὐτῷ to
refer not to the original creation (κτίσις) but to the moral re-creation
(ἀνάκτισις), and referring εἰκών to the
Incarnation in the same way. At a
later date, when the pressure of an
immediate controversy has passed
away, the Greek writers generally
concur in the earlier and truer interpretation of the expression. Thus
John Damascene (de Orthod. Fid. iv.
8, 1. p. 258 sq.), Theophylact (ad loc.),
and Œcumenius (ad loc.), all explain
it of Christ's Divine Nature. Among
Latin writers there is more diversity of interpretation. While Ma-
rius Victorinus (adv. Arium i. 24, p.
1058, ed. Migne), Hilary of Poictiers
(Tract. in ii Ps. § 28 sq., 1. p. 47 sq.; de
Trin. viii. 50, II. p. 248 sq.), and Hilary
the commentator (ad loc.), take it of
the Divine Nature, Augustine (Expos.
ad Rom. 56, III. p. 914) and Pelagius
(ad loc.) understand it of the Incarnate
Christ. This sketch of the history of
the interpretation of the expression
would not be complete without a reference to another very different explanation. Isidore of Pelusium, Epist.
iii. 31 (p. 268), would strike out a new
path of interpretation altogether (εἰ
καὶ δόξαιμί τισι καινοτέραν ἑρμηνείας

ἀνατέμνειν ὁδόν), and for the passive
πρωτότοκος suggests reading the active
πρωτοτόκος, alluding to the use of this
latter word in Homer (Il. xvii. 5 μήτηρ
πρωτοτόκος...οὐ πρὶν εἰδυῖα τόκοιο :
comp. Plat. Theæt. 151 ο ὥσπερ αἱ
πρωτότοκοι). Thus St Paul is made
to say that Christ πρῶτον τετοκέναι,
τουτέστι, πεποιηκέναι τὴν κτίσιν.

16. ὅτι κ.τ.λ.] We have in this sentence the justification of the title
given to the Son in the preceding
clause, πρωτότοκος πάσης κτίσεως. It
must therefore be taken to explain
the sense in which this title is used.
Thus connected, it shows that the
πρωτότοκος Himself is not included
in πᾶσα κτίσις ; for the expression
used is not τὰ ἄλλα or τὰ λοιπά, but
τὰ πάντα ἐκτίσθη—words which are
absolute and comprehensive, and will
admit no exception.

ἐν αὐτῷ] 'in Him,' as below ver.
17 ἐν αὐτῷ συνέστηκεν. For the preposition comp. Acts xvii. 28 ἐν αὐτῷ
γὰρ ζῶμεν καὶ κινούμεθα καί ἐσμεν.
All the laws and purposes which
guide the creation and government
of the Universe reside in Him, the
Eternal Word, as their meeting-point.
The Apostolic doctrine of the Logos
teaches us to regard the Eternal
Word as holding the same relation to
the Universe which the Incarnate
Christ holds to the Church. He is
the source of its life, the centre of all
its developments, the mainspring of
all its motions. The use of ἐν to
describe His relations to the Church
abounds in St Paul (e.g. Rom. viii. 1,
2, xii. 5, xvi. 3, 7, 9, etc., 1 Cor. i. 30,
iv. 15, 17, vii. 39, xv. 18, 22, etc.), and
more especially in the Epistles to the
Colossians and Ephesians (e.g. below
ii. 7, 10). In the present passage, as
in ver. 17, the same preposition is
applied also to His relations to the
Universe ; comp. Joh. i. 4 ἐν αὐτῷ
ζωὴ ἦν (more especially if we connect
the preceding ὁ γέγονεν with it)

ἐν τοῖς οὐρανοῖς καὶ [τὰ] ἐπὶ τῆς γῆς, τὰ ὁρατὰ καὶ τὰ

Thus it is part of the parallelism which runs through the whole passage, and to which the occurrence of πρωτότοκος in both relations gives the key. The Judæo-Alexandrian teachers represented the Logos, which in their view was nothing more than the Divine mind energizing, as the τόπος where the eternal ideas, the νοητὸς κόσμος, had their abode ; Philo *de Mund. Op.* 4 (I. p. 4) ὅσαπερ ἐν ἐκείνῳ νοητά, *ib.* § 5 (p. 4) οὐδὲ ὁ ἐκ τῶν ἰδεῶν κόσμος ἄλλον ἂν ἔχοι τόπον ἢ τὸν θεῖον λόγον τὸν ταῦτα διακοσμήσαντα, *ib.* § 10 (p. 8) ὁ ἀσώματος κόσμος... ἱδρυθεὶς ἐν τῷ θείῳ λόγῳ ; and see especially *de Migr. Abr.* 1 (I. p. 437) οἶκος ἐν ᾧ διαιτᾶται...ὅσα ἂν ἐνθυμήματα τέκῃ, ὥσπερ ἐν οἴκῳ τῷ λόγῳ διαθείς. The Apostolic teaching is an enlargement of this conception, inasmuch as the Logos is no longer a philosophical abstraction but a Divine Person : see Hippol. *Hær.* x. 33 αἴτιον τοῖς γινομένοις Λόγος ἦν, ἐν ἑαυτῷ φέρων τὸ θέλειν τοῦ γεγεννηκότος...ἔχει ἐν ἑαυτῷ τὰς ἐν τῷ πατρὶ προεννοηθείσας ἰδέας ὅθεν κελεύοντος πατρὸς γίνεσθαι κόσμον τὸ κατὰ ἓν Λόγος ἀπετελεῖτο ἀρέσκων Θεῷ : comp. Orig. *in Ioann.* i. § 22, IV. p. 21.

ἐκτίσθη] The aorist is used here ; the perfect below. Ἐκτίσθη describes the definite historical act of creation ; ἔκτισται the continuous and present relations of creation to the Creator : comp. Joh. i. 3 χωρὶς αὐτοῦ ἐγένετο οὐδὲ ἓν with *ib.* ὃ γέγονεν, I Cor. ix. 22 ἐγενόμην τοῖς ἀσθενέσιν ἀσθενής with *ib.* τοῖς πᾶσιν γέγονα πάντα, 2 Cor. xii. 17 μή τινα ὧν ἀπέσταλκα with ver. 18 καὶ συναπέστειλα τὸν ἀδελφόν, I Joh. iv. 9 τὸν μονογενῆ ἀπέσταλκεν ὁ Θεὸς εἰς τὸν κόσμον ἵνα ζήσωμεν δι' αὐτοῦ with ver. 10 ὅτι αὐτὸς ἠγάπησεν ἡμᾶς καὶ ἀπέστειλεν τὸν υἱὸν αὐτοῦ.

τὰ πάντα] 'the universe of things,' not πάντα 'all things severally,' but τὰ πάντα 'all things collectively.' With very few exceptions, wherever this

phrase occurs elsewhere, it stands in a similar connexion ; see below, vv. 17, 20, iii. 11, Rom. xi. 36, 1 Cor. viii. 6, xi. 12, xii. 6, xv. 27, 28, 2 Cor. v. 18, Eph. i. 10, 11, 23, iv. 10, Heb. i. 3, ii. 8, Rev. iv. 11. Compare Rom. viii. 32 τὰ πάντα ἡμῖν χαρίσεται, 2 Cor. iv. 15 τὰ πάντα δι' ὑμᾶς, with 1 Cor. iii. 22 εἴτε κόσμος...ὑμῶν ; and Phil. iii. 8 τὰ πάντα ἐζημιώθην with Matt. xvi. 26 ἐὰν τὸν κόσμον ὅλον κερδήσῃ. Thus it will appear that τὰ πάντα is nearly equivalent to 'the universe.' It stands midway between πάντα and τὸ πᾶν. The last however is not a scriptural phrase ; for, while with τὰ πάντα it involves the idea of connexion, it suggests also the unscriptural idea of *self-contained* unity, the great world-soul of the Stoic pantheist.

ἐν τοῖς οὐρανοῖς κ.τ.λ.] This division of the universe is not the same with the following, as if [τὰ] ἐν τοῖς οὐρανοῖς were equivalent to τὰ ἀόρατα and [τὰ] ἐπὶ τῆς γῆς to τὰ ὁρατά. It should rather be compared with Gen. i. 1 ἐποίησεν ὁ Θεὸς τὸν οὐρανὸν καὶ τὴν γῆν, ii. 1 συνετελέσθησαν ὁ οὐρανὸς καὶ ἡ γῆ καὶ πᾶς ὁ κόσμος αὐτῶν, xiv. 19 ὃς ἔκτισεν τὸν οὐρανὸν καὶ τὴν γῆν, Rev. x. 6 ὃς ἔκτισεν τὸν οὐρανὸν καὶ τὰ ἐν αὐτῷ καὶ τὴν γῆν καὶ τὰ ἐν αὐτῇ. It is a classification by *locality*, as the other is a classification by *essences*. Heaven and earth together comprehend all space ; and all things whether material or immaterial are conceived for the purposes of the classification as having their abode in space. Thus the sun and the moon would belong to ὁρατά, but they would be ἐν τοῖς οὐρανοῖς ; while the human soul would be classed among ἀόρατα but would be regarded as ἐπὶ τῆς γῆς ; see below ver. 20.

It is difficult to say whether τὰ...τὰ should be expunged or retained. The elements in the decision are ; (1) The facility either of omission or of addition in the first clause, owing to the

ἀόρατα, εἴτε θρόνοι εἴτε κυριότητες, εἴτε ἀρχαὶ εἴτε

termination of πάντα : (2) The much greater authority for the omission in the, first clause than in the second. These two combined suggest that τὰ was omitted accidentally in the first clause, and then expunged purposely in the second for the sake of uniformity. On the other hand there is (3) The possibility of insertion in both cases either for the sake of grammatical completeness or owing to the parallel passages, ver. 20, Ephes. i. 10. On the whole the reasons for their omission preponderate. At all events we can hardly retain the one without the other.

τὰ ὁρατὰ κ.τ.λ.] 'Things material and immaterial,' or, according to the language of philosophy, φαινόμενα and νούμενα : comp. Plato *Phæd.* 79 A θῶμεν οὖν, εἰ βούλει, ἔφη, δύο εἴδη τῶν ὄντων, τὸ μὲν ὁρατόν, τὸ δὲ ἀειδές, κ.τ.λ.

εἴτε κ.τ.λ.] '*whether they be thrones or lordships, etc.*' The subdivision is no longer exhaustive. The Apostle singles out those created beings that from their superior rank had been or might be set in rivalry with the Son.

A comparison with the parallel passage Ephes. i. 21, ὑπεράνω πάσης ἀρχῆς καὶ ἐξουσίας καὶ δυνάμεως καὶ κυριότητος καὶ παντὸς κ.τ.λ., brings out the following points :

(1) No stress can be laid on the sequence of the names, as though St Paul were enunciating with authority some precise doctrine respecting the grades of the celestial hierarchy. The names themselves are not the same in the two passages. While ἀρχή, ἐξουσία, κυριότης, are common to both, θρόνος is peculiar to the one and δύναμις to the other. Nor again is there any correspondence in the sequence. Neither does δύναμις take the place of θρόνος, nor do the three words common to both appear in the same order, the sequence being ἀρχ. ἐξ. [δύν.] κυρ. in Eph. i. 21, and [θρόν.] κυρ. ἀρχ. ἐξ. here.

(2) An expression in Eph. i. 21 shows the Apostle's *motive* in introducing these lists of names : for he there adds καὶ παντὸς ὀνόματος ὀνομαζομένου οὐ μόνον ἐν τῷ αἰῶνι τούτῳ ἀλλὰ καὶ ἐν τῷ μέλλοντι, i.e. 'of every dignity or title (whether real or imaginary) which is reverenced,' etc.; for this is the force of παντὸς ὀνόματος ὀνομαζομένου (see the notes on Phil. ii. 9, and Eph. *l.c.*). Hence it appears that in this catalogue St Paul does not profess to describe objective realities, but contents himself with repeating subjective opinions. He brushes away all these speculations without enquiring how much or how little truth there may be in them, because they are altogether beside the question. His language here shows the same spirit of impatience with this elaborate angelology, as in ii. 18.

(3) Some commentators have referred the terms used here solely to earthly potentates and dignities. There can be little doubt however that their chief and primary reference is to the orders of the celestial hierarchy, as conceived by these Gnostic Judaizers. This appears from the context; for the words τὰ ἀόρατα immediately precede this list of terms, while in the mention of πᾶν τὸ πλήρωμα and in other expressions the Apostle clearly contemplates the rivalry of *spiritual* powers with Christ. It is also demanded by the whole design and purport of the letter, which is written to combat the worship paid to angels. The names too, more especially θρόνοι, are especially connected with the speculations of Jewish angelology. But when this is granted, two questions still remain. First; are evil as well as good spirits included, demons as well as angels? And next; though the primary reference is to spiritual powers, is it not possible that the expression was intended to be compre-

hensive and to include earthly dignities
as well? The clause added in the
parallel passage, οὐ μόνον ἐν τῷ αἰῶνι
τούτῳ κ.τ.λ., encourages us thus to
extend the Apostle's meaning; and we
are led in the same direction by the
comprehensive words which have preceded here, [τὰ] ἐν τοῖς οὐρανοῖς
κ.τ.λ. Nor is there anything in the
terms themselves which bars such an
extension; for, as will be seen, the
combination ἀρχαὶ καὶ ἐξουσίαι is
applied not only to good angels but
to bad, not only to spiritual powers
but to earthly. Compare Ignat.
Smyrn. 6 τὰ ἐπουράνια καὶ ἡ δόξα τῶν
ἀγγέλων καὶ οἱ ἄρχοντες ὁρατοί τε καὶ
ἀόρατοι.

Thus guided, we may paraphrase
the Apostle's meaning as follows:
'You dispute much about the successive grades of angels; you distinguish
each grade by its special title; you
can tell how each order was generated
from the preceding; you assign to
each its proper degree of worship.
Meanwhile you have ignored or you
have degraded Christ. I tell you, it
is not so. He is first and foremost,
Lord of heaven and earth, far above
all thrones or dominations, all princedoms or powers, far above every
dignity and every potentate—whether
earthly or heavenly—whether angel
or demon or man—that evokes your
reverence or excites your fear.' See
above, pp. 103 sq.

Jewish and Judæo-Christian speculations respecting the grades of the
celestial hierarchy took various forms.
In the *Testaments of the Twelve
Patriarchs* (Levi 3), which as coming
near to the Apostolic age supplies a
valuable illustration (see *Galatians*
p. 307 sq.), these orders are arranged
as follows: (1) θρόνοι, ἐξουσίαι, these
two in the highest or seventh heaven;
(2) οἱ ἄγγελοι οἱ φέροντες τὰς ἀπο-
κρίσεις τοῖς ἀγγέλοις τοῦ προσώπου in
the sixth heaven; (3) οἱ ἄγγελοι τοῦ
προσώπου in the fifth heaven; (4) οἱ
ἅγιοι in the fourth heaven; (5) αἱ δυνά-

μεις τῶν παρεμβολῶν in the third
heaven; (6) τὰ πνεύματα τῶν ἐπαγωγῶν
(i.e. of visitations, retributions) in the
second heaven: or perhaps the denizens
of the sixth and fifth heavens, (2) and
(3), should be transposed. The lowest
heaven is not peopled by any spirits.
In Origen *de Princ.* i. 5. 3, *ib.* i. 6.
2, 1. pp. 66, 70 (comp. i. 8. 1, *ib.* p. 74),
we have five classes, which are given
in an ascending scale in this order;
(1) angels (*sancti angeli,* τάξις ἀγγε-
λική); (2) princedoms (*principatus,*
δύναμις ἀρχική, ἀρχαί); (3) powers (*po-
testates,* ἐξουσίαι); (4) thrones (*throni
vel sedes,* θρόνοι); (5) dominations
(*dominationes,* κυριότητες); though
elsewhere, *in Ioann.* i. § 34, IV. p. 34,
he seems to have a somewhat different classification in view. In Ephrem
Syrus *Op. Syr.* I. p. 270 (where the
translation of Benedetti is altogether
faulty and misleading) the ranks are
these: (1) θεοί, θρόνοι, κυριότητες; (2)
ἀρχάγγελοι, ἀρχαί, ἐξουσίαι; (3) ἄγγελοι,
δυνάμεις, χερουβίμ, σεραφίμ; these three
great divisions being represented by
the χιλίαρχοι, the ἑκατόνταρχοι, and the
πεντηκόνταρχοι respectively in Deut. i.
15, on which passage he is commenting. The general agreement between
these will be seen at once. This
grouping also seems to underlie the
conception of Basil of Seleucia *Orat.*
39 (p. 207), who mentions them in this
order; θρόνοι, κυριότητες, ἀρχαί, ἐξουσίαι, δυνάμεις, χερουβίμ, σεραφίμ.
On the other hand the arrangement of
the pseudo-Dionysius, who so largely
influenced subsequent speculations,
is quite different and probably later
(Dion. Areop. *Op.* I. p. 75, ed. Cord.);
(1) θρόνοι, χερουβίμ, σεραφίμ; (2) ἐξουσίαι, κυριότητες, δυνάμεις; (3) ἄγγελοι,
ἀρχάγγελοι, ἀρχαί. But the earlier
lists for the most part seem to
suggest as their common foundation a
classification in which θρόνοι, κυριότητες, belonged to the highest order, and
ἀρχαί, ἐξουσίαι to the next below
Thus it would appear that the Apostle takes as an illustration the titles

$$\dot{\epsilon}\xi o v \sigma i a\iota \cdot \ \ \tau \grave{a} \ \pi \acute{a} v \tau a \ \delta\iota' \ a\dot{v} \tau o \hat{v} \ \kappa a\grave{\iota} \ \dot{\epsilon}\iota s \ a\dot{v} \tau \grave{o} v \ \dot{\epsilon}\kappa \tau\iota\sigma\tau a\iota \cdot$$

assigned to the two highest grades in a system of the celestial hierarchy which he found current, and which probably was adopted by these Gnostic Judaizers. See also the note on ii. 18.

θρόνοι] In all systems alike these 'thrones' belong to the highest grade of angelic beings, whose place is in the immediate presence of God. The meaning of the name however is doubtful: (1) It may signify the *occupants of thrones* which surround the throne of God; as in the imagery of Rev. iv. 4 κύκλοθεν τοῦ θρόνου θρόνοι εἴκοσι τέσσαρες (comp. xi. 16, xx. 4). The imagery is there taken from the court of an earthly king: see Jer. lii. 32. This is the interpretation given by Origen *de Princ.* i. 5. 3 (p. 66), i. 6. 2 (p. 70) 'judicandi vel regendi... habentes officium.' Or (2) They were so called, as *supporting* or *forming the throne of God;* just as the chariot-seat of the Almighty is represented as resting on the cherubim in Ezek. i. 26, ix. 3, x. 1 sq., xi. 22, Ps. xviii. 10, 1 Chron. xxviii. 18. So apparently Clem. Alex. *Proph. Ecl.* 57 (p. 1003) θρόνοι ἂν εἶεν...διὰ τὸ ἀναπαύεσθαι ἐν αὐτοῖς τὸν Θεόν. From this same imagery of the prophet the later mysticism of the Kabbala derived its name 'wheels,' which it gave to one of its ten orders of Sephiroth. Adopting this interpretation, several fathers identify the 'thrones' with the cherubim : e.g. Greg. Nyss. *c. Eunom.* i (II. p. 349 sq.), Chrysost. *de Incompr. Nat.* iii. 5 (I. p. 467), Theodoret (*ad loc.*), August. *in Psalm.* xcviii. § 3 (IV. p. 1061). This explanation was adopted also by the pseudo-Dionysius *de Cœl. Hier.* 7 (I. p. 80), without however identifying them with the cherubim ; and through his writings it came to be generally adopted. The former interpretation however is more probable; for (1) The highly symbolical character of the latter accords better

with a later stage of mystic speculation, like the Kabbala ; and (2) It seems best to treat θρόνοι as belonging to the same category with κυριότητες, ἀρχαί, ἐξουσίαι, which are concrete words borrowed from different grades of human rank and power. As implying *regal* dignity, θρόνοι naturally stands at the head of the list.

κυριότητες] '*dominations,*' as Ephes. i. 21. These appear to have been regarded as belonging to the first grade, and standing next in dignity to the θρόνοι. This indeed would be suggested by their name.

ἀρχαί, ἐξουσίαι] as Ephes. i. 21. These two words occur very frequently together. In some places they refer to human dignities, as Luke xii. 11, Tit. iii. 1 (comp. Luke xx. 20); in others to a spiritual hierarchy. And here again there are two different uses : sometimes they designate good angels, e.g. below ii. 10, Ephes. iii. 10; sometimes evil spirits, e.g. ii. 15, Ephes. vi. 12 : while in one passage at least (1 Cor. xv. 24) both may be included. In Rom. viii. 38 we have ἀρχαὶ without ἐξουσίαι (except as a v. l.), and in 1 Pet. iii. 22 ἐξουσίαι without ἀρχαί, in connexion with the angelic orders.

δι' αὐτοῦ κ.τ.λ.] 'As all creation passed out from Him, so does it all converge again towards Him.' For the combination of prepositions see Rom. xi. 36 ἐξ αὐτοῦ καὶ δι' αὐτοῦ καὶ εἰς αὐτὸν τὰ πάντα. He is not only the ᴀ but also the ω, not only the ἀρχή but also the τέλος of creation, not only the first but also the last in the history of the Universe : Rev. xxii. 13. For this double relation of Christ to the Universe, as both the initial and the final cause, see Heb. ii. 10 δι' ὃν τὰ πάντα καὶ δι' οὗ τὰ πάντα, where δι' ὃν is nearly equivalent to εἰς αὐτὸν of the text.

In the Judaic philosophy of Alexandria the preposition διὰ with the

¹⁷καὶ αὐτός ἐστιν πρὸ πάντων, καὶ τὰ πάντα ἐν αὐτῷ

genitive was commonly used to describe the function of the Logos in the creation and government of the world; e.g. *de Cherub.* 35 (I. p. 162) where Philo, enumerating the causes which combine in the work of Creation, describes God as ὑφ᾽ οὗ, matter as ἐξ οὗ, and the Word as δι᾽ οὗ; comp. *de Mon.* ii. 5 (II. p. 225) λόγος... δι᾽ οὗ σύμπας ὁ κόσμος ἐδημιουργεῖτο. The Christian Apostles accepted this use of διὰ to describe the mediatorial function of the Word in creation; e.g. John i. 3 πάντα δι᾽ αὐτοῦ ἐγένετο κ.τ.λ., *ib.* ver. 10 ὁ κόσμος δι᾽ αὐτοῦ ἐγένετο, Heb. i. 2 δι᾽ οὗ καὶ ἐποίησεν τοὺς αἰῶνας. This mediatorial function however has entirely changed its character. To the Alexandrian Jew it was the work of a passive tool or instrument (*de Cherub.* l. c. δι᾽ οὗ, τὸ ἐργαλεῖον, ὄργανον...δι᾽ οὗ); but to the Christian Apostle it represented a cooperating agent. Hence the Alexandrian Jew frequently and consistently used the simple instrumental dative ᾧ to describe the relation of the Word to the Creator, e. g. *Quod Deus immut.* 12 (I. p. 281) ᾧ καὶ τὸν κόσμον εἰργάζετο, *Leg. All.* i. 9 (I p. 47) τῷ περιφανεστάτῳ καὶ τηλαυγεστάτῳ ἑαυτοῦ λόγῳ ῥήματι ὁ Θεὸς ἀμφότερα ποιεῖ, comp. *ib.* iii. 31 (I. p. 106) ὁ λόγος...ᾧ καθάπερ ὀργάνῳ προσχρησάμενος. This mode of speaking is not found in the New Testament.

εἰς αὐτόν] '*unto Him.*' As of the Father it is said elsewhere, 1 Cor. viii. 6 ἐξ οὗ τὰ πάντα καὶ ἡμεῖς εἰς αὐτόν, so here of the Son we read τὰ πάντα δι᾽ αὐτοῦ καὶ εἰς αὐτόν. All things must find their meeting-point, their reconciliation, at length in Him from whom they took their rise—in the Word as the mediatorial agent, and through the Word in the Father as the primary source. The Word is the final cause as well as the creative agent of the Universe. This ultimate goal of the present dispensation in

time is similarly stated in several passages. Sometimes it is represented as the birth-throe and deliverance of all creation through Christ; as Rom. viii. 19 sq. αὐτὴ ἡ κτίσις ἐλευθερωθήσεται, πᾶσα ἡ κτίσις...συνωδίνει. Sometimes it is the absolute and final subjection of universal nature to Him; as 1 Cor. xv. 28 ὅταν ὑποταγῇ αὐτῷ τὰ πάντα. Sometimes it is the reconciliation of all things through Him; as below, ver. 20 δι᾽ αὐτοῦ ἀποκαταλλάξαι τὰ πάντα. Sometimes it is the recapitulation, the gathering up in one head, of the Universe in Him; as Ephes. i. 10 ἀνακεφαλαιώσασθαι τὰ πάντα ἐν τῷ Χριστῷ. The image involved in this last passage best illustrates the particular expression in the text εἰς αὐτὸν ἔκτισται; but all alike enunciate the same truth in different terms. The Eternal Word is the goal of the Universe, as He was the starting-point. It must end in unity, as it proceeded from unity: and the centre of this unity is Christ. This expression has no parallel, and could have none, in the Alexandrian phraseology and doctrine.

17. καὶ αὐτὸς κ.τ.λ.] '*and HE IS before all things*': comp. Joh. viii. 58 πρὶν Ἀβραὰμ γενέσθαι, ἐγώ εἰμι (and perhaps also viii. 24, 28, xiii. 19). The imperfect ἦν might have sufficed (comp. Joh. i. 1), but the present ἔστιν declares that this pre-existence is absolute existence. The ΑΥΤΟΣ ΕΣΤΙΝ here corresponds exactly to the ΕΓΩ ΕΙΜΙ in St John, and this again is illustrated by Exod. iii. 14. The verb therefore is not an enclitic, but should be accentuated ἔστιν. See Basil *adv. Eunom.* iv (I. p. 294) ὁ ἀπόστολος εἰπών, Πάντα δι᾽ αὐτοῦ καὶ εἰς αὐτὸν ἔκτισται, ὤφειλεν εἰπεῖν, Καὶ αὐτὸς ἐγένετο πρὸ πάντων, εἰπὼν δέ, Καὶ αὐτὸς ἔστι πρὸ πάντων, ἔδειξε τὸν μὲν ἀεὶ ὄντα τὴν δὲ κτίσιν γενομένην. The αὐτός is as necessary for the completeness of the meaning,

συνέστηκεν. ¹⁸καὶ αὐτός ἐστιν ἡ κεφαλὴ τοῦ σώ-

as the ἔστιν. The one emphasizes the *personality*, as the other declares the *pre-existence*. For this emphatic αὐ-τός see again ver. 18; comp. Ephes. ii. 14, iv. 10, 11, 1 Joh. ii. 2, and esp. Rev. xix. 15 καὶ αὐτὸς ποιμανεῖ...καὶ αὐτὸς πατεῖ. The other interpretation which explains πρὸ πάντων of superiority in rank, and not of priority in time, is untenable for several reasons. (1) This would most naturally be expressed otherwise in Biblical language, as ἐπὶ πάντων (e.g. Rom. ix. 5, Eph. iv. 6), or ὑπὲρ πάντα (Eph. i. 22), or ὑπεράνω πάντων (Eph. i. 21, iv. 10). (2) The key to the interpretation is given by the analogous words in the context, esp. πρωτότοκος, vv. 15, 18. (3) Nothing short of this declaration of absolute pre-existence would be adequate to introduce the statement which follows, καὶ τὰ πάντα ἐν αὐτῷ συνέστηκεν.

πρὸ πάντων] *'before all things.'* In the Latin it was translated ' ante omnes,' i.e. thronos, dominationes, etc.; and so Tertullian *adv. Marc.* v. 19 'Quomodo enim ante omnes, si non ante omnia? Quomodo ante omnia, si non primogenitus conditionis?' But the neuter τὰ πάντα, standing in the context before and after, requires the neuter here also.

συνέστηκεν] *'hold together, cohere.'* He is the principle of cohesion in the universe. He impresses upon creation that unity and solidarity which makes it a cosmos instead of a chaos. Thus (to take one instance) the action of gravitation, which keeps in their places things fixed and regulates the motions of things moving, is an expression of His mind. Similarly in Heb. i. 3 Christ the Logos is described as φέρων τὰ πάντα (*sustaining* the Universe) τῷ ῥήματι τῆς δυνάμεως αὐτοῦ. Here again the Christian Apostles accept the language of Alexandrian Judaism, which describes the Logos as the δεσμὸς of the Universe; e.g.

Philo *de Profug.* 20 (I. p. 562) ὅ τε γὰρ τοῦ ὄντος λόγος δεσμὸς ὢν τῶν ἁπάντων...καὶ συνέχει τὰ μέρη πάντα καὶ σφίγγει καὶ κωλύει αὐτὰ διαλύεσθαι καὶ διαρτᾶσθαι, *de Plant.* 2 (I. p. 331) συνάγων τὰ μέρη πάντα καὶ σφίγγων· δεσμὸν γὰρ αὐτὸν ἄρρηκτον τοῦ παντὸς ὁ γεννήσας ἐποίει πατήρ, *Quis rer. div. her.* 38 (I. p. 507) λόγῳ σφίγγεται θείῳ· κόλλα γάρ ἐστι καὶ δεσμὸς οὗτος τὰ πάντα τῆς οὐσίας ἐκπεπληρωκώς : and for the word itself see *Quis rer. div. her.* 12 (I. p. 481) συνέστηκε καὶ ζωπυρεῖται προνοίᾳ Θεοῦ, Clem. Rom. 27 ἐν λόγῳ τῆς μεγαλωσύνης αὐτοῦ συνεστήσατο τὰ πάντα. In the same connexion σύγκειται is used, Ecclus. xliii. 26. The indices to Plato and Aristotle amply illustrate this use of συνέστηκεν. This mode of expression was common with the Stoics also.

18. 'And not only does He hold this position of absolute priority and sovereignty over the Universe—the natural creation. He stands also in the same relation to the Church—the new spiritual creation. He is its head, and it is His body. This is His prerogative, because He is the source and the beginning of its life, being the First-born from the dead. Thus in all things—in the spiritual order as in the natural—in the Church as in the World—He is found to have the pre-eminence.'

The elevating influence of this teaching on the choicest spirits of the subapostolic age will be seen from a noble passage in the noblest of early Christian writings, *Epist. ad Diogn.* § 7 τὸν λόγον τὸν ἅγιον...ἀνθρώποις ἐνίδρυσε...οὗ, καθάπερ ἄν τις εἰκάσειεν, ἀνθρώποις ὑπηρέτην τινὰ πέμψας ἢ ἄγγελον ἢ ἄρχοντα ἤ τινα τῶν διεπόντων τὰ ἐπίγεια ἤ τινα τῶν πεπιστευμένων τὰς ἐν οὐρανοῖς διοικήσεις, ἀλλ' αὐτὸν τὸν τεχνίτην καὶ δημιουργὸν τῶν ὅλων...ᾧ πάντα διατέτακται καὶ διώρισται καὶ ὑποτέτακται, οὐρανοὶ καὶ τὰ ἐν

ματος, τῆς ἐκκλησίας· ὅς ἐστιν ἀρχή, πρωτότοκος

τοῖς οὐρανοῖς, γῇ καὶ τὰ ἐν τῇ γῇ κ.τ.λ.
See the whole context.

καὶ αὐτός] 'and He,' repeated from
the preceding verse, to emphasize the
identity of the Person who unites in
Himself these prerogatives : see on
ver. 17, and comp. ver. 18 αὐτός, ver.
19 δι' αὐτοῦ. The Creator of the
World is also the Head of the Church.
There is no blind ignorance, no imperfect sympathy, no latent conflict, in
the relation of the demiurgic power
to the Gospel dispensation, as the
heretical teachers were disposed consciously or unconsciously to assume
(see above, p. 101 sq., p. 110 sq.), but
an absolute unity of origin.

ἡ κεφαλή] 'the head,' the inspiring,
ruling, guiding, combining, sustaining
power, the mainspring of its activity,
the centre of its unity, and the seat
of its life. In his earlier epistles the
relations of the Church to Christ are
described under the same image (1
Cor. xii. 12—27; comp. vi. 15, x. 17,
Rom. xii. 4 sq.); but the Apostle
there takes as his starting-point the
various functions of the members, and
not, as in these later epistles, the
originating and controling power of
the Head. Comp. i. 24, ii. 19, Eph.
i. 22 sq., ii. 16, iv. 4, 12, 15 sq., v. 23, 30.

τῆς ἐκκλησίας] in apposition with
τοῦ σώματος : comp. i. 24 τοῦ σώματος
αὐτοῦ, ὅ ἐστιν ἡ ἐκκλησία, Eph. i. 23.

ἀρχή] 'the origin, the beginning.'
The term is here applied to the Incarnate Christ in relation to the
Church, because it is applicable to
the Eternal Word in relation to the
Universe, Rev. iii. 14 ἡ ἀρχὴ τῆς κτίσεως τοῦ Θεοῦ. The parallelism of the
two relations is kept in view throughout. The word ἀρχή here involves
two ideas: (1) Priority in time; Christ
was the first-fruits of the dead, ἀπαρχή
(1 Cor. xv. 20, 23): (2) Originating
power; Christ was also the source of
life, Acts iii. 14 ὁ ἀρχηγὸς τῆς ζωῆς;
comp. Acts v. 31, Heb. ii. 10. He is

not merely the principium princi-
piatum but the principium princi-
pians (see Trench Epistles to the
Seven Churches p. 183 sq.). He rose
first from the dead, that others might
rise through Him.

The word ἀρχή, like πρῶτος (see
the note on Phil. i. 5), being absolute
in itself, does not require the definite
article. Indeed the article is most
commonly omitted where ἀρχή occurs
as a predicate, as will appear from
several examples to be gathered from
the extracts in Plut. Mor. p. 875 sq.,
Stob. Ecl. Phys. i. 10. 12 sq. Comp. also
Aristot. Met. x. 7, p. 1064, τὸ θεῖον...
ἂν εἴη πρώτη καὶ κυριωτάτη ἀρχή, Onatas
in Stob. Ecl. Phys. i. 2. 39 αὐτὸς γὰρ
[Θεὸς] ἀρχὰ καὶ πρᾶτον, Tatian. ad
Graec. 4 Θεὸς...μόνος ἄναρχος ὢν καὶ
αὐτὸς ὑπάρχων τῶν ὅλων ἀρχή, Clem.
Alex. Strom. iv. 25, p. 638, ὁ Θεὸς δὲ
ἄναρχος, ἀρχὴ τῶν ὅλων παντελής, ἀρχῆς
ποιητικός, Method. de Creat. 3 (p. 100,
ed. Jahn) πάσης ἀρετῆς ἀρχὴν καὶ πη-
γήν...ἡγῇ τὸν Θεόν, pseudo-Dionys.
de Div. Nom. v. § 6 ἀρχὴ γάρ ἐστι τῶν
ὄντων, § 10 πάντων οὖν ἀρχὴ καὶ τελευ-
τὴ τῶν ὄντων ὁ προών.

The text is read with the definite
article, ἡ ἀρχή, in one or two excellent authorities at least; but the obvious motive which would lead a
scribe to aim at greater distinctness
renders the reading suspicious.

πρωτότοκος] Comp. Rev. i. 5 ὁ πρωτότοκος τῶν νεκρῶν καὶ ὁ ἄρχων τῶν
βασιλέων τῆς γῆς. His resurrection
from the dead is His title to the
headship of the Church ; for 'the
power of His resurrection' (Phil. iii.
10) is the life of the Church. Such
passages as Gen. xlix. 3, Deut. xxi. 17,
where the πρωτότοκος is called ἀρχὴ
τέκνων and superior privileges are
claimed for him as such, must necessarily be only very faint and partial
illustrations of the connexion between
ἀρχὴ and πρωτότοκος here, where the
subject-matter and the whole context

ἐκ τῶν νεκρῶν, ἵνα γένηται ἐν πᾶσιν αὐτὸς πρωτεύων·
¹⁹ὅτι ἐν αὐτῷ εὐδόκησεν πᾶν τὸ πλήρωμα κατοικῆ-

point to a fuller meaning of the words. The words πρωτότοκος ἐκ τῶν νεκρῶν here correspond to πρωτότοκος πάσης κτίσεως ver. 15, so that the parallelism between Christ's relations to the Universe and to the Church is thus emphasized.

ἵνα γένηται κ.τ.λ.] As He *is* first with respect to the Universe, so it was ordained that He should *become* first with respect to the Church as well. The γένηται here answers in a manner to the ἔστιν of ver. 17. Thus ἔστιν and γένηται are contrasted as the absolute being and the historical manifestation. The relation between Christ's headship of the Universe by virtue of His Eternal Godhead and His headship of the Church by virtue of His Incarnation and Passion and Resurrection is somewhat similarly represented in Phil. ii. 6 sq. ἐν μορφῇ Θεοῦ ὑπάρχων...μορφὴν δούλου λαβών...γενόμενος ὑπήκοος μέχρι θανάτου...διὸ καὶ ὁ Θεὸς αὐτὸν ὑπερύψωσεν κ.τ.λ.

ἐν πᾶσιν] 'in all things,' not in the Universe only but in the Church also. Καὶ γάρ, writes Theodoret, ὡς Θεός, πρὸ πάντων ἐστὶ καὶ σὺν τῷ πατρί ἐστι, καὶ ὡς ἄνθρωπος, πρωτότοκος ἐκ τῶν νεκρῶν καὶ τοῦ σώματος κεφαλή. Thus ἐν πᾶσιν is neuter and not masculine, as it is sometimes taken. Either construction is grammatically correct, but the context points to the former interpretation here; and this is the common use of ἐν πᾶσιν, e. g. iii. 11, Eph. i. 23, Phil. iv. 12. For the neuter compare Plut. *Mor.* p. 9 σπεύδοντες τοὺς παῖδας ἐν πᾶσι τάχιον πρωτεῦσαι. On the other hand in [Demosth.] *Amat.* p. 1416 κράτιστον εἶναι τὸ πρωτεύειν ἐν ἅπασι the context shows that ἅπασι is masculine.

αὐτός] '*He Himself*'; see the note on καὶ αὐτὸς above.

19, 20. 'And this absolute supre-

macy is His, because it was the Father's good pleasure that in Him all the plenitude of Deity should have its home; because He willed through Him to reconcile the Universe once more to Himself. It was God's purpose to effect peace and harmony through the blood of Christ's cross, and so to restore all things, whatsoever and wheresoever they be, whether on the earth or in the heavens.'

19. ὅτι ἐν αὐτῷ κ.τ.λ.] The eternal indwelling of the Godhead explains the headship of the Church, not less than the headship of the Universe. The resurrection of Christ, whereby He became the ἀρχὴ of the Church, was the result of and the testimony to His deity; Rom. i. 4 τοῦ ὁρισθέντος υἱοῦ Θεοῦ...ἐξ ἀναστάσεως νεκρῶν.

εὐδόκησεν] sc. ὁ Θεός, the nominative being understood; see Winer § lviii. p. 655 sq., § lxiv. p. 735 sq.; comp. James i. 12 (the right reading), iv. 6. Here the omission is the more easy, because εὐδοκία, εὐδοκεῖν etc. (like θέλημα), are used absolutely of God's good purpose, e. g. Luke ii. 14 ἐν ἀνθρώποις εὐδοκίας (or εὐδοκία), Phil. ii. 13 ὑπὲρ τῆς εὐδοκίας, Clem. Rom. § 40 πάντα τὰ γινόμενα ἐν εὐδοκήσει; see the note on Clem. Rom. § 2. For the expression generally comp. 2 Macc. xiv. 35 σύ, Κύριε, εὐδόκησας ναὸν τῆς σῆς κατασκηνώσεως ἐν ἡμῖν γενέσθαι. The alternative is to consider πᾶν τὸ πλήρωμα personified as the nominative; but it is difficult to conceive St Paul so speaking, more especially as with εὐδόκησεν personification would suggest personality. The πλήρωμα indeed is personified in Clem. Alex. *Exc. Theod.* 43 (p. 979) συναινέσαντος καὶ τοῦ πληρώματος, and in Iren. i. 2. 6 βουλῇ μιᾷ καὶ γνώμῃ τὸ πᾶν πλήρωμα τῶν αἰώνων κ.τ.λ., i. 12. 4 πᾶν τὸ πλήρωμα ηὐδόκησεν [δι' αὐτοῦ δοξάσαι τὸν πατέρα]; but the phraseology of the

σαι, ²⁰καὶ δι᾽ αὐτοῦ ἀποκαταλλάξαι τὰ πάντα εἰς

Valentinians, to which these passages refer, cannot be taken as an indication of St Paul's usage, since their view of the πλήρωμα was wholly different. A third interpretation is found in Tertullian *adv. Marc.* v. 19, who translates ἐν αὐτῷ *in semetipso*, taking ὁ Χριστὸς as the nominative to εὐδόκησεν: and this construction is followed by some modern critics. But, though grammatically possible, it confuses the theology of the passage hopelessly.

τὸ πλήρωμα] '*the plenitude,*' a recognised technical term in theology, denoting the totality of the Divine powers and attributes; comp. ii. 9. See the detached note on πλήρωμα. On the relation of this statement to the speculations of the false teachers at Colossæ see the introduction, pp. 102, 112. Another interpretation, which explains τὸ πλήρωμα as referring to the Church (comp. Ephes. i. 22), though adopted by several fathers, is unsuited to the context and has nothing to recommend it.

κατοικῆσαι] '*should have its permanent abode.*' The word occurs again in the same connexion, ii. 9. The false teachers probably, like their later counterparts, maintained only a partial and transient connexion of the πλήρωμα with the Lord. Hence St Paul declares in these two passages that it is not a παροικία but a κατοικία. The two words κατοικεῖν, παροικεῖν, occur in the LXX as the common renderings of ישׁב and גור respectively, and are distinguished as the *permanent* and the *transitory;* e.g. Gen. xxxvi. 44 (xxxvii. 1) κατῴκει δὲ Ἰακὼβ ἐν τῇ γῇ οὗ παρῴκησεν ὁ πατὴρ αὐτοῦ ἐν γῇ Χαναάν (comp. Hos. x. 5), Philo *Sacr. Ab. et Ca.* 10 (1. p. 170 M) ὁ τοῖς ἐγκυκλίοις μόνοις ἐπανέχων παροικεῖ σοφίᾳ, οὐ κατοικεῖ, Greg. Naz. *Orat.* xiv (1. p. 271 ed. Caillau) τίς τὴν κάτω σκηνὴν καὶ τὴν ἄνω πόλιν; τίς παροικίαν καὶ κατοικίαν; comp. *Orat.* vii

(1. p. 200). See also the notes on Ephes. ii. 19, and on Clem. Rom. 1.

20. The false teachers aimed at effecting a partial reconciliation between God and man through the interposition of angelic mediators. The Apostle speaks of an absolute and complete reconciliation of universal nature to God, effected through the mediation of the Incarnate Word. Their mediators were ineffective, because they were neither human nor divine. The true mediator must be both human and divine. It was necessary that in Him all the plenitude of the Godhead should dwell. It was necessary also that He should be born into the world and should suffer as a man.

δι᾽ αὐτοῦ] i.e. τοῦ Χριστοῦ, as appears from the preceding ἐν αὐτῷ, and the following διὰ τοῦ αἵματος τοῦ σταυροῦ αὐτοῦ, δι᾽ αὐτοῦ. This expression δι᾽ αὐτοῦ has been already applied to the Preincarnate Word in relation to the Universe (ver. 16); it is now used of the Incarnate Word in relation to the Church.

ἀποκαταλλάξαι] sc. εὐδόκησεν ὁ Θεός. The personal pronoun αὐτόν, instead of the reflexive ἑαυτόν, is no real obstacle to this way of connecting the words (see the next note). The alternative would be to take τὸ πλήρωμα as governing ἀποκαταλλάξαι, but this mode of expression is harsh and improbable.

The same double compound ἀποκαταλλάσσειν is used below, ver. 21 and Ephes. ii. 16, in place of the usual καταλλάσσειν. It may be compared with ἀποκατάστασις, Acts iii. 21. Tertullian, arguing against the dualism of Marcion who maintained an antagonism between the demiurge and the Christ, lays stress on the compound, *adv. Marc.* v. 19 '*conciliari* extraneo possent, *reconciliari* vero non alii quam suo.' The word ἀποκαταλλάσσειν corresponds to ἀπηλλοτριωμένους

αὐτόν, εἰρηνοποιήσας διὰ τοῦ αἵματος τοῦ σταυροῦ
αὐτοῦ, δι' αὐτοῦ εἴτε τὰ ἐπὶ τῆς γῆς εἴτε τὰ ἐν τοῖς
οὐρανοῖς, ²¹καὶ ὑμᾶς ποτὲ ὄντας ἀπηλλοτριωμένους καὶ

here and in Ephes. ii. 16, implying a *restitution* to a state from which they had fallen, or which was potentially theirs, or for which they were destined. Similarly St Augustine on Gal. iv. 5 remarks that the word used of the υἱοθεσία is not *accipere* (λαμβάνειν) but *recipere* (ἀπολαμβάνειν). See the note there.

• τὰ πάντα] The whole universe of things, material as well as spiritual, shall be restored to harmony with God. How far this restoration of universal nature may be subjective, as involved in the changed perceptions of man thus brought into harmony with God, and how far it may have an objective and independent existence, it were vain to speculate.

εἰς αὐτόν] 'to Him,' i.e. 'to Himself.' The reconciliation is always represented as made to the Father. The reconciler is sometimes the Father Himself (2 Cor. v. 18, 19 ἐκ τοῦ Θεοῦ τοῦ καταλλάξαντος ἡμᾶς ἑαυτῷ διὰ Χριστοῦ...Θεὸς ἦν ἐν Χριστῷ κόσμον καταλλάσσων ἑαυτῷ), sometimes the Son (Ephes. ii. 16: comp. Rom. v. 10, 11). Excellent reasons are given (Bleek *Hebr.* II. p. 69, A. Buttmann *Gramm.* p. 97) for supposing that the reflexive pronoun ἑαυτοῦ etc. is never contracted into αὑτοῦ etc. in the Greek Testament. But at the same time it is quite clear that the oblique cases of the personal pronoun αὐτός are there used very widely, and in cases where we should commonly find the reflexive pronoun in classical authors: e.g. Ephes. i. 4, 5 ἐξελέξατο ἡμᾶς... εἶναι ἡμᾶς ἁγίους καὶ ἀμώμους κατενώπιον αὐτοῦ...προορίσας ἡμᾶς εἰς υἱοθεσίαν διὰ Ἰησοῦ Χριστοῦ εἰς αὐτόν. See also the instances given in A. Buttmann p. 98. It would seem indeed that αὐτοῦ etc. may be used for ἑαυ-

τοῦ etc. in almost every connexion, except where it is the direct object of the verb.

εἰρηνοποιήσας] The word occurs in the LXX, Prov. x. 10, and in Hermes in Stob. *Ecl. Phys.* xli. 45. The substantive εἰρηνοποιός (see Matt. v. 9) is found several times in classical writers.

δι' αὐτοῦ] The external authority for and against these words is nearly evenly balanced : but there would obviously be a tendency to reject them as superfluous. They are a resumption of the previous δι' αὐτοῦ. For other examples see ii. 13 ὑμᾶς, Rom. viii. 23 καὶ αὐτοί, Gal. ii. 15, 16 ἡμεῖς, Ephes. i. 13 ἐν ᾧ καί, iii. 1, 14 τούτου χάριν, where words are similarly repeated for the sake of emphasis or distinctness. In 2 Cor. xii. 7 there is a repetition of ἵνα μὴ ὑπεραίρωμαι, where again it is omitted in several excellent authorities.

21—23. 'And ye too—ye Gentiles—are included in the terms of this peace. In times past ye had estranged yourselves from God. Your hearts were hostile to Him, while ye lived on in your evil deeds. But now, in Christ's body, in Christ's flesh which died on the Cross for your atonement, ye are reconciled to Him again. He will present you a living sacrifice, an acceptable offering unto Himself, free from blemish and free even from censure, that ye may stand the piercing glance of Him whose scrutiny no defect can escape. But this can only be, if ye remain true to your old allegiance, if ye hold fast (as I trust ye are holding fast) by the teaching of Epaphras, if the edifice of your faith is built on solid foundations and not reared carelessly on the sands, if ye suffer not yourselves to be

ἐχθροὺς τῇ διανοίᾳ ἐν τοῖς ἔργοις τοῖς πονηροῖς, νυνὶ δὲ
ἀποκατηλλάγητε ²²ἐν τῷ σώματι τῆς σαρκὸς αὐτοῦ διὰ

21.   νυνὶ δὲ ἀποκατήλλαξεν.

shifted or shaken but rest firmly on the hope which ye have found in the Gospel—the one universal unchangeable Gospel, which was proclaimed to every creature under heaven, of which I Paul, unworthy as I am, was called to be a minister.'

21. ἀπηλλοτριωμένους] 'estranged,' not ἀλλοτρίους, 'strangers'; comp. Ephes. ii. 12, iv. 18. See the note on ἀποκαταλλάξαι, ver. 20.

ἐχθρούς] 'hostile to God,' as the consequence of ἀπηλλοτριωμένους, not 'hateful to God,' as it is taken by some. The active rather than the passive sense of ἐχθρούς is required by the context, which (as commonly in the New Testament) speaks of the sinner as reconciled to God, not of God as reconciled to the sinner : comp. Rom. v. 10 εἰ γὰρ ἐχθροὶ ὄντες κατηλλάγημεν τῷ Θεῷ κ.τ.λ. It is the mind of man, not the mind of God, which must undergo a change, that a reunion may be effected.

τῇ διανοίᾳ] 'in your mind, intent.' For the dative of the part affected compare Ephes. iv. 18 ἐσκοτωμένοι τῇ διανοίᾳ, Luke i. 51 ὑπερηφάνους διανοίᾳ καρδίας αὐτῶν. So καρδίᾳ, καρδίαις, Matt. v. 8, xi. 29, Acts vii. 51, 2 Cor. ix. 7, 1 Thess. ii. 17; φρεσίν, 1 Cor. xiv. 20.

ἐν τοῖς ἔργοις κ.τ.λ.] 'in the midst of, in the performance of your wicked works'; the same use of the preposition as e.g. ii. 23, iv. 2.

νυνί] Here, as frequently, νῦν (νυνί) admits an aorist, because it denotes not 'at the present moment,' but 'in the present dispensation, the present order of things': comp. e.g. ver. 26, Rom. v. 11, vii. 6, xi. 30, 31, xvi. 26, Ephes. ii. 13, iii. 5, 2 Tim. i. 10, 1 Pet. i. 10, ii. 10, 25. In all these passages there is a direct contrast between the old dispensation

and the new, more especially as affecting the relation of the Gentiles to God. The aorist is found also in Classical writers, where a similar contrast is involved; e.g. Plato Symp. 193 A πρὸ τοῦ, ὥσπερ λέγω, ἐν ἦμεν· νυνὶ δὲ διὰ τὴν ἀδικίαν διῳκίσθημεν ὑπὸ τοῦ θεοῦ, Isæus de Cleon. her. 20 τότε μέν...νυνὶ δὲ...ἐβουλήθη.

ἀποκατηλλάγητε] The reasons for preferring this reading, though the direct authority for it is so slight, are given in the detached note on the various readings. But, whether ἀποκατηλλάγητε or ἀποκατήλλαξεν be preferred, the construction requires explanation. If ἀποκατήλλαξεν be adopted, it is perhaps best to treat δὲ as introducing the apodosis, the foregoing participial clause serving as the protasis : 'And you, though ye were once estranged... yet now hath he reconciled,' in which case the first ὑμᾶς will be governed directly by ἀποκατήλλαξεν; see Winer Gramm. § liii. p. 553. If this construction be adopted, παραστῆσαι ὑμᾶς will describe the result of ἀποκατήλλαξεν, 'so as to present you'; but ὁ Θεὸς will still be the nominative to ἀποκατήλλαξεν as in 2 Cor. v. 19. If on the other hand ἀποκατηλλάγητε be taken, it is best to regard νυνὶ δὲ ἀποκατηλλάγητε as a direct indicative clause substituted for the more regular participial form νυνὶ δὲ ἀποκαταλλαγέντας for the sake of greater emphasis : see the note on ver. 26 τὸ ἀποκεκρυμμένον...νῦν δὲ ἐφανερώθη. In this case παραστῆσαι will be governed directly by εὐδόκησεν, and will itself govern ὑμᾶς ποτε ὄντας κ.τ.λ., the second ὑμᾶς being a repetition of the first; 'And you who once were estranged...but now ye have been reconciled...to present you, I say, holy and without blemish.' For the repetition of ὑμᾶς, which was

τοῦ θανάτου [αὐτοῦ], παραστῆσαι ὑμᾶς ἁγίους καὶ ἀμώμους καὶ ἀνεγκλήτους κατενώπιον αὐτοῦ, ²³εἴ γε ἐπιμέ-
νετε τῇ πίστει τεθεμελιωμένοι καὶ ἑδραῖοι καὶ μὴ μετα-

needed to disentangle the construction, see the note on δι' αὐτοῦ ver. 20.

22. τῆς σαρκὸς αὐτοῦ] It has been supposed that St Paul added these words, which are evidently emphatic, with a polemical aim either; (1) To combat docetism. Of this form of error however there is no direct evidence till a somewhat later date: or (2) To combat a false spiritualism which took offence at the doctrine of an atoning sacrifice. But for this purpose they would not have been adequate, because not explicit enough. It seems simpler therefore to suppose that they were added for the sake of greater clearness, to distinguish the natural body of Christ intended here from the mystical body mentioned just above, ver. 18. Similarly in Ephes. ii. 14 ἐν τῇ σαρκὶ αὐτοῦ is used rather than ἐν τῷ σώματι αὐτοῦ, because σῶμα occurs in the context (ver. 16) of Christ's mystical body. The same expression, τὸ σῶμα τῆς σαρκός, which we have here, occurs also below, ii. 11, but with a different emphasis and meaning. There the emphasis is on τὸ σῶμα, the contrast lying between the whole body and a single member (see the note); whereas here τῆς σαρκός is the emphatic part of the expression, the antithesis being between the material and the spiritual. Compare also Ecclus. xxiii. 16 ἄνθρωπος πόρνος ἐν σώματι σαρκὸς αὐτοῦ.

Marcion omitted τῆς σαρκὸς as inconsistent with his views, and explained ἐν τῷ σώματι to mean the Church. Hence the comment of Tertullian adv. Marc. v. 19, 'utique in eo corpore, in quo mori potuit per carnem, mortuus est, non per ecclesiam sed propter ecclesiam, corpus commutando pro corpore, carnale pro spiritali.'

παραστῆσαι] If the construction which I have adopted be correct, this is said of God Himself, as in 2 Cor. iv. 14 ὁ ἐγείρας τὸν Κύριον Ἰησοῦν καὶ ἡμᾶς σὺν Ἰησοῦ ἐγερεῖ καὶ παραστήσει σὺν ὑμῖν. This construction seems in all respects preferable to connecting παραστῆσαι directly with ἀποκατηλλάγητε and interpreting the words, ' Ye have been reconciled so that ye should present yourselves (ὑμᾶς)...before Him.' This latter interpretation leaves the καὶ ὑμᾶς ποτὲ ὄντας κ.τ.λ. without a government, and it gives to the second ὑμᾶς a reflexive sense (as if ὑμᾶς αὐτοὺς or ἑαυτούς), which is at least harsh.

ἀμώμους] 'without blemish,' rather than 'without blame,' in the language of the New Testament; see the note on Ephes. i. 4. It is a sacrificial word, like τέλειος, ὁλόκληρος, etc. The verb παριστάναι also is used of presenting a sacrifice in Rom. xii. 1 παραστῆσαι τὰ σώματα ὑμῶν θυσίαν ζῶσαν ἁγίαν κ.τ.λ., Lev. xvi. 7 (v. l.): comp. Luke ii. 2.

ἀνεγκλήτους] An advance upon ἀμώμους, 'in whom not only no blemish is found, but against whom no charge is brought': comp. 1 Tim. vi. 14 ἄσπιλον, ἀνεπίλημπτον. The word ἀνέγκλητος occurs again in 1 Cor. i. 8, 1 Tim. iii. 10, Tit. i. 6, 7.

κατενώπιον αὐτοῦ] 'before Him,' i. e. 'Himself,' as in the parallel passage, Ephes. i. 4; if the construction here adopted be correct. For this use of the personal pronoun instead of the reflexive see the note on εἰς αὐτόν, ver. 20. But does κατενώπιον αὐτοῦ refer to God's future judgment or His present approbation? The latter seems more probable, both because the expression certainly has this meaning in the parallel passage, Ephes. i. 4, and because κατενώπιον, ἐνώπιον,

κινούμενοι ἀπὸ τῆς ἐλπίδος τοῦ εὐαγγελίου οὗ ἠκούσατε,
τοῦ κηρυχθέντος ἐν πάσῃ κτίσει τῇ ὑπὸ τὸν οὐρανόν, οὗ
ἐγενόμην ἐγὼ Παῦλος διάκονος.

κατέναντι, etc., are commonly so used; e.g. Rom. xiv. 22, 1 Cor. i. 29, 2 Cor. ii. 17, iv. 2, vii. 12, xii. 19, etc. On the other hand, where the future judgment is intended, a different expression is found, 2 Cor. v. 10 ἔμπροσθεν τοῦ βήματος τοῦ Χριστοῦ. Thus God is here regarded, not as the judge who tries the accused, but as the μωμοσκόπος who examines the victims (Polyc. *Phil.* 4, see the note on Ephes. i. 4). Compare Heb. iv. 12, 13, for a closely allied metaphor. The passage in Jude 24, στῆσαι κατενώπιον τῆς δόξης αὐτοῦ ἀμώμους ἐν ἀγαλλιάσει, though perhaps referring to final approval, is too different in expression to influence the interpretation of St Paul's language here.

23. εἴ γε] On the force of these particles see Gal. iii. 4. They express a pure hypothesis in themselves, but the indicative mood following converts the hypothesis into a hope.

ἐπιμένετε] '*ye abide by, ye adhere to*,' with a dative; the common construction of ἐπιμένειν in St Paul: see the note on Phil. i. 24. In this connexion τῇ πίστει is perhaps '*your* faith,' rather than '*the* faith.'

τεθεμελιωμένοι κ.τ.λ.] '*built on a foundation and so firm*'; not like the house of the foolish man in the parable who built χωρὶς θεμελίου, Luke vi. 49. For τεθεμελιωμένοι comp. Ephes. iii. 17. The consequence of τεθεμελιωμένοι is ἑδραῖοι: Clem. Rom. 33 ἥδρασεν ἐπὶ τὸν ἀσφαλῆ τοῦ ἰδίου βουλήματος θεμέλιον. The words ἑδραῖος, ἑδράζω, etc., are not uncommonly applied to buildings, e.g. ἑδραίωμα 1 Tim. iii. 15. Comp. Ign. *Ephes.* 10 ὑμεῖς ἑδραῖοι τῇ πίστει.

μὴ μετακινούμενοι] '*not constantly shifting*,' a present tense; the same idea as ἑδραῖοι expressed from the negative side, as in 1 Cor. xv. 58 ἑδραῖοι

γίνεσθε, ἀμετακίνητοι, Polyc. *Phil.* 10 'firmi in fide et immutabiles.'

τῆς ἐλπίδος κ.τ.λ.] '*the hope held out by the Gospel*,' τοῦ εὐαγγελίου being a subjective genitive, as in Ephes. i. 18 ἡ ἐλπὶς τῆς κλήσεως (comp. iv. 4).

ἐν πάσῃ κτίσει] '*among every creature*,' in fulfilment of the Lord's last command, Mark xvi. 15 κηρύξατε τὸ εὐαγγέλιον πάσῃ τῇ κτίσει. Here however the definitive article, though found in the received text, ἐν πάσῃ τῇ κτίσει, must be omitted in accordance with the best authorities. For the meanings of πᾶσα κτίσις, πᾶσα ἡ κτίσις, see the note on ver. 15. The expression πᾶσα κτίσις must not be limited to man. The statement is given in the broadest form, all creation animate and inanimate being included, as in Rev. v. 13 πᾶν κτίσμα...καὶ τὰ ἐν αὐτοῖς πάντα ἤκουσα λέγοντα κ.τ.λ. For the hyperbole ἐν πάσῃ κτίσει compare 1 Thess. i. 8 ἐν παντὶ τόπῳ. To demand statistical exactness in such a context would be to require what is never required in similar cases. The motive of the Apostle here is at once to emphasize the universality of the genuine Gospel, which has been offered without reserve to all alike, and to appeal to its publicity, as the credential and guarantee of its truth: see the notes on ver. 6 ἐν παντὶ τῷ κόσμῳ and on ver. 28 πάντα ἄνθρωπον.

οὗ ἐγενόμην κ.τ.λ.] Why does St Paul introduce this mention of himself so abruptly? His motive can hardly be the assertion of his Apostolic authority, for it does not appear that this was questioned; otherwise he would have declared his commission in stronger terms. We can only answer that impressed with the dignity of his office, as involving the offer of grace to the Gentiles, he cannot

^{24} Νῦν χαίρω ἐν τοῖς παθήμασιν ὑπὲρ ὑμῶν, καὶ

refrain from magnifying it. At the
same time this mention enables him
to link himself in bonds of closer sympathy with the Colossians, and he
passes on at once to his relations with
them: comp. Ephes. iii. 2—9, 1 Tim.
i. 11 sq., in which latter passage the
introduction of his own name is
equally abrupt.

ἐγὼ Παῦλος] i.e. 'weak and unworthy as I am': comp. Ephes. iii. 8 ἐμοὶ
τῷ ἐλαχιστοτέρῳ πάντων ἁγίων.

24—27. 'Now when I see the full
extent of God's mercy, now when I
ponder over His mighty work of reconciliation, I cannot choose but rejoice in my sufferings. Yes, I Paul
the persecutor, I Paul the feeble and
sinful, am permitted to supplement—
I do not shrink from the word—to
supplement the afflictions of Christ.
Despite all that He underwent, He the
Master has left something still for me
the servant to undergo. And so my
flesh is privileged to suffer for His
body—His spiritual body, the Church.
I was appointed a minister of the
Church, a steward in God's household,
for this very purpose, that I might
administer my office on your behalf,
might dispense to you Gentiles the
stores which His bountiful grace has
provided. Thus I was charged to
preach without reserve the whole
Gospel of God, to proclaim the great
mystery which had remained a secret
through all the ages and all the generations from the beginning, but which
now in these last times was revealed
to His holy people. For such was His
good pleasure. God willed to make
known to them, in all its inexhaustible
wealth thus displayed through the
call of the Gentiles, the glorious revelation of this mystery—Christ not the
Saviour of the Jews only, but Christ
dwelling in you, Christ become to you
the hope of glory.'

24 Νῦν χαίρω] A sudden outburst
of thanksgiving, that he, who was less

than the least, who was not worthy to
be called an Apostle, should be allowed
to share and even to supplement the
sufferings of Christ. The relative ὅς,
which is found in some authorities, is
doubtless the repetition of the final
syllable of διάκονος; but its insertion
would be assisted by the anxiety of
scribes to supply a connecting link
between the sentences. The genuine
reading is more characteristic of St
Paul. The abruptness, which dis-
penses with a connecting particle, has
a parallel in 1 Tim. i. 12 χάριν ἔχω τῷ
ἐνδυναμώσαντί με Χριστῷ κ.τ.λ., where
also the common text inserts a link of
connexion, καὶ χάριν ἔχω κ.τ.λ. Compare also 2 Cor. vii. 9 νῦν χαίρω, οὐχ
ὅτι κ.τ.λ., where again there is no connecting particle.

The thought underlying νῦν seems to
be this: 'If ever I have been disposed
to repine at my lot, if ever I have felt
my cross almost too heavy to bear,
yet now—now, when I contemplate
the lavish wealth of God's mercy—
now when I see all the glory of bearing a part in this magnificent work—
my sorrow is turned to joy.'

ἀνταναπληρῶ] 'I fill up on my part,'
'I supplement.' The single compound
ἀναπληροῦν occurs several times (e.g.
1 Cor. xiv. 16, xvi. 17, Gal. vi. 2); another double compound προσαναπλη-
ροῦν twice (2 Cor. ix. 12, xi. 9; comp.
Wisd. xix. 4, v. l.); but ἀνταναπληροῦν
only here in the LXX or New Testament. For this verb compare Demosth. de Symm. p. 182 τούτων τῶν
συμμοριῶν ἑκάστην διελεῖν κελεύω πέντε
μέρη κατὰ δώδεκα ἄνδρας, ἀνταναπληροῦντας πρὸς τὸν εὐπορώτατον ἀεὶ
τοὺς ἀπορωτάτους (where τοὺς ἀπορωτάτους should be taken as the subject to
ἀνταναπληροῦντας), Dion Cass. xliv. 48
ἵν᾽ ὅσον...ἐνέδει, τοῦτο ἐκ τῆς παρὰ τῶν
ἄλλων συντελείας ἀνταναπληρωθῇ,
Clem. Alex. Strom. vii. 12 p. 878 οὕ-
τος...τὴν ἀποστολικὴν ἀπουσίαν
ἀνταναπληροῖ, Apollon. Constr. Or. i. 3

ἀνταναπληρῶ τὰ ὑστερήματα τῶν θλίψεων τοῦ Χρι-

(p. 13 sq.) ἡ ἀντωνυμία ἀνταναπλη-
ροῦσα καὶ τὴν θέσιν τοῦ ὀνόματος καὶ
τὴν τάξιν τοῦ ῥήματος, Ptol. *Math.
Comp.* vi. 9 (I. p. 435 ed. Halma) ἐπεὶ
δ᾽ ἡ μὲν ἐλλείπειν ἐποίει τὴν ἀπο-
κατάστασιν ἡ δὲ πλεονάζειν κατά
τινα συντυχίαν ἣν ἴσως καὶ ὁ ῞Ιπ-
παρχος ἀνταναπληρουμένην πως κατα-
νενόηκει κ.τ.λ. The substantive ἀντα-
ναπλήρωσις occurs in Diog. Laert. x.
48. So too ἀνταναπλήθειν Xen. *Hell.*
ii. 4. 11, 12 ξυνετάξαντο ὥστε ἐμπλῆ-
σαι τὴν ὁδόν...οἱ δὲ ἀπὸ τῆς φυλῆς
ἀντανέπλησαν...τὴν ὁδόν. Compare also
ἀντανισοῦν Themist. *Paraphr. Arist.*
43 B οὐδὲν κωλύει κατὰ ταὐτὸν ἄλλοθί
που μεταβάλλειν ἀέρα εἰς ὕδωρ καὶ
ἀντανισοῦσθαι τὸν σύμπαντα ὄγκον, and
ἀντανίσωμα Joseph. *Ant.* xviii. 9. 7.
The meaning of ἀντὶ in this compound
will be plain from the passages quoted.
It signifies that the supply comes *from
an opposite quarter* to the deficiency.
This idea is more or less definitely expressed in the context of all the passages, in the words which are spaced.
The force of ἀνταναπληροῦν in St Paul
is often explained as denoting simply
that the supply *corresponds in extent* to the deficiency. This interpretation practically deprives ἀντί of
any meaning, for ἀναπληροῦν alone
would denote as much. If indeed the
supply had been the subject of the
verb, and the sentence had run τὰ
παθήματά μου ἀνταναπληροῖ τὰ ὑστη-
ρήματα κ.τ.λ., this idea might perhaps
be reached without sacrificing the
sense of ἀντί; but in such a passage
as this, where one personal agent is
mentioned in connexion with the supply and another in connexion with
the deficiency, the one forming the
subject and the other being involved
in the object of the verb, the ἀντὶ can
only describe the antithesis of these
personal agents. So interpreted, it
is eminently expressive here. The
point of the Apostle's boast is that
Christ the sinless Master should have
left something for Paul the unworthy

servant to suffer. The right idea has
been seized and is well expressed by
Photius *Amphil.* 121 (I. p. 709 Migne)
οὐ γὰρ ἁπλῶς φησιν Ἀναπληρῶ, ἀλλ᾽
Ἀνταναπληρῶ; τουτέστιν, Ἀντὶ δεσπό-
του καὶ διδασκάλου ὁ δοῦλος ἐγὼ καὶ
μαθητὴς κ.τ.λ. Similar in meaning,
though not identical, is the expression in 2 Cor. i. 5, where the sufferings of Christ are said to 'overflow'
(περισσεύειν) upon the Apostle. The
theological difficulty which this plain
and natural interpretation of ἀνταναπληροῦν is supposed to involve will
be considered in the note on τῶν
θλίψεων.

τὰ ὑστερήματα] '*the things lack-
ing.*' This same word ὑστέρημα 'deficiency' occurs with ἀναπληροῦν 1 Cor.
xvi. 17, Phil. ii. 30, and with προσανα-
πληροῦν 2 Cor. ix. 12, xi. 9. Its direct
opposite is περίσσευμα 'abundance,
superfluity,' 2 Cor. viii. 13, 14 ; comp.
Luke xxi. 4. Another interpretation,
which makes ὑστέρημα an antithesis
to προτέρημα, explaining it 'the later'
as opposed to the earlier 'sufferings
of Christ,' is neither supported by the
usage of the word nor consistent with
ἀνταναπληρῶ.

τῶν θλίψεων τοῦ Χριστοῦ] '*of the
afflictions of Christ,*' i.e. which Christ
endured. This seems to be the only
natural interpretation of the words.
Others have explained them as meaning 'the afflictions imposed by Christ,'
or 'the afflictions endured for Christ's
sake,' or 'the afflictions which resemble those of Christ.' All such
interpretations put a more or less
forced meaning on the genitive. All
alike ignore the meaning of ἀντὶ in
ἀνταναπληρῶ· which points to a *distinction* of persons suffering. Others
again suppose the words to describe
St Paul's own afflictions regarded as
Christ's, because Christ suffers in His
suffering Church ; e.g. Augustine *in
Psalm.* cxlii. § 3 (IV. p. 1590) 'Patitur,
inquit, adhuc Christus pressuram, non
in carne sua in qua ascendit in cælum,

στοῦ ἐν τῇ σαρκί μου ὑπὲρ τοῦ σώματος αὐτοῦ, ὅ
ἐστιν ἡ ἐκκλησία· ²⁵ἧς ἐγενόμην ἐγὼ διάκονος κατὰ τὴν

sed in carne mea quæ adhuc laborat
in terra,' quoting Gal. ii. 20. This
last is a very favourite explanation,
and has much to recommend it. It
cannot be charged with wresting the
meaning of αἱ θλίψεις τοῦ Χριστοῦ.
Moreover it harmonizes with St Paul's
mode of speaking elsewhere. But, like
the others, it is open to the fatal objection that it empties the first preposition in ἀνταναπληρῶ of any force.
The central idea in this interpretation
is the *identification* of the suffering
Apostle with the suffering Christ,
whereas ἀνταναπληρῶ emphasizes the
distinction between the two. It is
therefore inconsistent with this context, however important may be the
truth which it expresses.

The theological difficulty, which
these and similar explanations are intended to remove, is imaginary and
not real. There is a sense in which
it is quite legitimate to speak of
Christ's afflictions as *incomplete*, a
sense in which they may be, and indeed must be, *supplemented*. For
the sufferings of Christ may be considered from two different points of
view. They are either *satisfactoriæ*
or *ædificatoriæ*. They have their
sacrificial efficacy, and they have their
ministerial utility. (1) From the
former point of view the Passion of
Christ was the one full perfect and
sufficient sacrifice, oblation, and satisfaction for the sins of the whole
world. In this sense there could
be no ὑστέρημα of Christ's sufferings;
for, Christ's sufferings being different
in kind from those of His servants,
the two are incommensurable. But
in this sense the Apostle would surely
have used some other expression
such as τοῦ σταυροῦ (i. 20, Eph. ii.
16 etc.), or τοῦ θανάτου (i. 22, Rom.
v. 10, Heb. ii. 14, etc.), but hardly
τῶν θλίψεων. Indeed θλίψις, 'afflic-

tion,' is not elsewhere applied in
the New Testament in any sense
to Christ's sufferings, and certainly
would not suggest a sacrificial act.
(2) From the latter point of view
it is a simple matter of fact that the
afflictions of every saint and martyr do supplement the afflictions of
Christ. The Church is built up by
repeated acts of self-denial in successive individuals and successive generations. They continue the work which
Christ began. They bear their part
in the sufferings of Christ (2 Cor. i. 7
κοινωνοὶ τῶν παθημάτων, Phil. iii. 10
κοινωνίαν τῶν παθημάτων); but St Paul
would have been the last to say that
they bear their part in the atoning
sacrifice of Christ. This being so, St
Paul does not mean to say that his
own sufferings filled up all the ὑστερήματα, but only that they *went towards* filling them up. The present
tense ἀνταναπληρῶ denotes an inchoate, and not a complete act. These
ὑστερήματα will never be fully supplemented, until the struggle of the
Church with sin and unbelief is
brought to a close.

Thus the idea of expiation or satisfaction is wholly absent from this
passage; and with it is removed the
twofold temptation which has beset
theologians of opposite schools. (1)
On the one hand Protestant commentators, rightly feeling that any interpretation which infringed the completeness of the work wrought by
Christ's death must be wrong, because it would make St Paul contradict himself on a cardinal point of his
teaching, have been tempted to wrest
the sense of the words. They have
emptied ἀνταναπληρῶ of its proper
force; or they have assigned a false
meaning to ὑστερήματα; or they have
attached a non-natural sense to the
genitive τοῦ Χριστοῦ. (2) On the

οἰκονομίαν τοῦ Θεοῦ τὴν δοθεῖσάν μοι εἰς ὑμᾶς, πληρῶσαι
τὸν λόγον τοῦ Θεοῦ, ²⁶τὸ μυστήριον τὸ ἀποκεκρυμμένον

other hand Romanist commentators, while protesting (as they had a right to do) against these methods of interpretation, have fallen into the opposite error. They have found in this passage an assertion of the merits of the saints, and (as a necessary consequence) of the doctrine of indulgences. They have not observed that, if the idea of vicarious satisfaction comes into the passage at all, the satisfaction of St Paul is represented here as the same in kind with the satisfaction of Christ, however different it may be in degree; and thus they have truly exposed themselves to the reproach which Estius indignantly repudiates on their behalf, 'quasi Christus non satis passus sit ad redemptionem nostram, ideoque supplemento martyrum opus habeat; quod impium est sentire, quodque Catholicos dicere non minus impie calumniantur hæretici.' It is no part of a commentator here to enquire generally whether the Roman doctrine of the satisfaction of the saints can in any way be reconciled with St Paul's doctrine of the satisfaction of Christ. It is sufficient to say that, so far as regards this particular passage, the Roman doctrine can only be imported into it at the cost of a contradiction to the Pauline doctrine. It is only fair to add however that Estius himself says, 'quæ quidem doctrina, etsi Catholica et Apostolica sit, atque aliunde satis probetur, ex hoc tamen Apostoli loco nobis non videtur admodum solide statui posse.' But Roman Catholic commentators generally find this meaning in the text, as may be seen from the notes of à Lapide.

τοῦ σώματος αὐτοῦ] An antithesis of the Apostle's own flesh and Christ's body. This antithetical form of expression obliges St Paul to explain what he means by the body of Christ,

ὅ ἐστιν ἡ ἐκκλησία; comp. ver. 18. Contrast the explanation in ver. 22 ἐν τῷ σώματι τῆς σαρκὸς αὐτοῦ, and see the note there.

25. τὴν οἰκονομίαν κ.τ.λ.] '*stewardship in the house of God.*' The word οἰκονομία seems to have two senses: (1) 'The actual administration of a household'; (2) 'The office of the administrator.' For the former meaning see the note on Ephes. i. 10; for the latter sense, which it has here, compare 1 Cor. ix. 17 οἰκονομίαν πεπίστευμαι, Luke xvi. 2—4, Isaiah xxii. 19, 21. So the Apostles and ministers of the Church are called οἰκονόμοι, 1 Cor. iv. 1, 2, Tit. i. 7: comp. 1 Pet. iv. 10.

εἰς ὑμᾶς] '*to youward,*' i.e. 'for the benefit of you, the Gentiles'; εἰς ὑμᾶς being connected with τὴν δοθεῖσάν μοι, as in Ephes. iii. 2 τὴν οἰκονομίαν τῆς χάριτος τοῦ Θεοῦ τῆς δοθείσης μοι εἰς ὑμᾶς; comp. Rom. xv. 16 διὰ τὴν χάριν τὴν δοθεῖσάν μοι ὑπὸ τοῦ Θεοῦ εἰς τὸ εἶναί με λειτουργὸν Χριστοῦ Ἰησοῦ εἰς τὰ ἔθνη.

πληρῶσαι] '*to fulfil,*' i.e. 'to preach fully,' 'to give its complete development to'; as Rom. xv. 19 ὥστε με ἀπὸ Ἰερουσαλὴμ καὶ κύκλῳ μέχρι τοῦ Ἰλλυρικοῦ πεπληρωκέναι τὸ εὐαγγέλιον τοῦ Χριστοῦ. Thus 'the word of God' here is 'the Gospel,' as in most places (1 Cor. xiv. 36, 2 Cor. ii. 17, iv. 2, etc.), though not always (e.g. Rom. ix. 6), in St Paul, as also in the Acts. The other interpretation, 'to accomplish the promise of God,' though suggested by such passages as 1 Kings ii. 27 πληρωθῆναι τὸ ῥῆμα Κυρίου, 2 Chron. xxxvi. 21 πληρωθῆναι λόγον Κυρίου, etc., is alien to the context here.

26. τὸ μυστήριον] This is not the only term borrowed from the ancient mysteries, which St Paul employs to describe the teaching of the Gospel

ἀπὸ τῶν αἰώνων καὶ ἀπὸ τῶν γενεῶν, νῦν δὲ ἐφανερώθη
τοῖς ἁγίοις αὐτοῦ, ²⁷οἷς ἠθέλησεν ὁ Θεὸς γνωρίσαι τί
τὸ πλοῦτος τῆς δόξης τοῦ μυστηρίου τούτου ἐν τοῖς

The word τέλειον just below, ver. 28, seems to be an extension of the same metaphor. In Phil. iv. 12 again we have the verb μεμύημαι: and in Ephes. i. 14 σφραγίζεσθαι is perhaps an image derived from the same source. So too the Ephesians are addressed as Παύλου συμμύσται in Ign. *Ephes.* 12. The Christian teacher is thus regarded as a ἱεροφάντης (see Epict. iii. 21. 13 sq.) who initiates his disciples into the rites. There is this difference however; that, whereas the heathen mysteries were strictly confined to a narrow circle, the Christian mysteries are freely communicated to all. There is therefore an intentional paradox in the employment of the image by St Paul. See the notes on πάντα ἄνθρωπον τέλειον below.

Thus the idea of *secresy* or *reserve* disappears when μυστήριον is adopted into the Christian vocabulary by St Paul: and the word signifies simply 'a truth which was once hidden but now is revealed,' 'a truth which without special revelation would have been unknown.' Of the nature of the truth itself the word says nothing. It may be transcendental, incomprehensible, mystical, mysterious, in the modern sense of the term (1 Cor. xv. 51, Eph. v. 32): but this idea is quite accidental, and must be gathered from the special circumstances of the case, for it cannot be inferred from the word itself. Hence μυστήριον is almost universally found in connexion with words denoting revelation or publication; e. g. ἀποκαλύπτειν, ἀποκάλυψις, Rom. xvi. 25, Ephes. iii. 3, 5, 2 Thess. ii. 7; γνωρίζειν Rom. xvi. 26, Ephes. i. 9, iii. 3, 10, vi. 19; φανεροῦν Col. iv. 3, Rom. xvi. 26, 1 Tim. iii. 16; λαλεῖν iv. 3, 1 Cor. ii. 7, xiv. 2; λέγειν, 1 Cor. xv. 51.

But the one special 'mystery' which

absorbs St Paul's thoughts in the Epistles to the Colossians and Ephesians is the free admission of the Gentiles on equal terms to the privileges of the covenant. For this he is a prisoner; this he is bound to proclaim fearlessly (iv. 3, Ephes, vi. 19); this, though hidden from all time, was communicated to him by a special revelation (Ephes. iii. 3 sq.); in this had God most signally displayed the lavish wealth of His goodness (ver. 27, ii. 2 sq., Ephes. i. 6 sq., iii. 8 sq.). In one passage only throughout these two epistles is μυστήριον applied to anything else, Ephes. v. 32. The same idea of the μυστήριον appears very prominently also in the thanksgiving (added apparently later than the rest of the letter) at the end of the Epistle to the Romans, xvi. 25 sq. μυστηρίου... εἰς ὑπακοὴν πίστεως εἰς πάντα τὰ ἔθνη γνωρισθέντος.

ἀπὸ τῶν αἰώνων κ.τ.λ.] The preposition is doubtless temporal here, being opposed to νῦν, as in the parallel passage, Ephes. iii. 9: comp. Rom. xvi. 25 κατὰ ἀποκάλυψιν μυστηρίου χρόνοις αἰωνίοις σεσιγημένου, 1 Cor. ii. 7 Θεοῦ σοφίαν ἐν μυστηρίῳ τὴν ἀποκεκρυμμένην ἣν προώρισεν ὁ Θεὸς πρὸ τῶν αἰώνων. So too ἀπ' αἰῶνος, Acts iii. 21, xv. 18, Ps. xcii. 3, etc.; ἀπὸ καταβολῆς κόσμου, Matt. xiii. 35, xxv. 34, etc.

τῶν γενεῶν] An αἰὼν is made up of many γενεαί; comp. Ephes. iii. 21 εἰς πάσας τὰς γενεὰς τοῦ αἰῶνος τῶν αἰώνων, Is. li. 9 ὡς γενεὰ αἰῶνος (where the Hebrew has the plural 'generations'). Hence the order here. Not only was this mystery unknown in remote periods of antiquity, but even in recent generations. It came upon the world as a sudden surprise. The moment of its revelation was the moment of its fulfilment.

ἔθνεσιν, ὅ ἐστιν Χριστὸς ἐν ὑμῖν, ἡ ἐλπὶς τῆς δόξης·
²⁸ ὅν ἡμεῖς καταγγέλλομεν νουθετοῦντες πάντα ἄνθρω-

27. ὅς ἐστιν.

νῦν δὲ κ.τ.λ.] An indicative clause is substituted for a participial, which would otherwise have been more natural, for the sake of emphasizing the statement; comp. ver. 22 νυνὶ δὲ ἀποκατηλλάγητε, and see Winer§lxiii.p.717.

27. ἠθέλησεν]'*willed*,'*'was pleased.*' It was God's grace: it was no merit of their own. See the note on i. 1 διὰ θελήματος Θεοῦ.

τὸ πλοῦτος] The '*wealth* of God,' as manifested in His dispensation of grace, is a prominent idea in these epistles: comp. ii. 2, Ephes. i. 7, 18, iii. 8, 16; comp. Rom. xi. 33. See above, p. 43 sq. St Paul uses the neuter and the masculine forms indifferently in these epistles (e.g. τὸ πλοῦτος Ephes. i. 7, ὁ πλοῦτος Ephes. i. 18), as in his other letters (e.g. τὸ πλοῦτος 2 Cor. viii. 2, ὁ πλοῦτος Rom. ix. 23). In most passages however there are various readings. On the neuter forms τὸ πλοῦτος, τὸ ζῆλος, etc., see Winer § ix. p. 76.

τῆς δόξης] i.e. 'of the glorious manifestation.' This word in Hellenistic Greek is frequently used of a bright light; e.g. Luke ii. 9 περιέλαμψεν, Acts xxii. 11 τοῦ φωτός, 1 Cor. xv. 41 ἡλίου, σελήνης, etc., 2 Cor. iii. 7 τοῦ προσώπου [Μωυσέως]. Hence it is applied generally to a divine *manifestation*, even where there is no physical accompaniment of light; and more especially to the revelation of God in Christ (e. g. Joh. i. 14, 2 Cor. iv. 4, etc.). The expression πλοῦτος τῆς δόξης occurs again, Rom. ix. 23, Ephes. i. 18, iii. 16. See above, ver. 11 with the note.

ἐν τοῖς ἔθνεσιν] i.e. 'as exhibited among the Gentiles.' It was just here that this 'mystery,' this dispensation of grace, achieved its greatest triumphs and displayed its transcendant glory; φαίνεται μὲν γὰρ καὶ ἐν ἐτέροις, writes Chrysostom, πολλῷ δὲ

πλέον ἐν τούτοις ἡ πολλὴ τοῦ μυστηρίου δόξα. Here too was its *wealth*; for it overflowed all barriers of caste or race. Judaism was 'beggarly' (Gal. iv. 9) in comparison, since its treasures sufficed only for a few.

ὅ ἐστιν] The antecedent is probably τοῦ μαστηρίου; comp. ii. 2 τοῦ μυστηρίου τοῦ Θεοῦ, Χριστοῦ ἐν ᾧ εἰσιν πάντες κ.τ.λ.

Χριστὸς ἐν ὑμῖν] '*Christ in you*,' i.e. 'you Gentiles.' Not Christ, but Christ given freely to the Gentiles, is the 'mystery' of which St Paul speaks; see the note on μυστήριον above. Thus the various reading, ὅς for ὅ, though highly supported, interferes with the sense. With Χριστὸς ἐν ὑμῖν compare μεθ' ἡμῶν Θεός Matt. i. 23. It may be a question however, whether ἐν ὑμῖν means '*within you*' or '*among you*.' The former is perhaps the more probable interpretation, as suggested by Rom. viii. 10, 2 Cor. xiii. 5, Gal. iv. 19; comp. Ephes. iii. 17 κατοικῆσαι τὸν Χριστὸν διὰ τῆς πίστεως ἐν ταῖς καρδίαις ὑμῶν.

ἡ ἐλπίς] Comp. 1 Tim. i. 2; so ἡ [κοινὴ] ἐλπὶς ἡμῶν Ign. *Eph.* 21, *Magn.* 11, *Philad.* 5, etc., applied to our Lord.

28, 29. 'This Christ we, the Apostles and Evangelists, proclaim without distinction and without reserve. We know no restriction either of persons or of topics. We admonish every man and instruct every man. We initiate every man in all the mysteries of wisdom. It is our single aim to present every man fully and perfectly taught in Christ. For this end I train myself in the discipline of self-denial; for this end I commit myself to the arena of suffering and toil, putting forth in the conflict all that energy which He inspires, and which works in me so powerfully.'

28. ἡμεῖς] '*we*,' the preachers; the same opposition as in 1 Cor. iv. 8, 10,

πον καὶ διδάσκοντες πάντα ἄνθρωπον ἐν πάσῃ σοφίᾳ,
ἵνα παραστήσωμεν πάντα ἄνθρωπον τέλειον ἐν Χριστῷ·

ix. 11, 2 Cor. xiii. 5 sq., 1 Thess. ii.
13 sq., etc. The Apostle hastens, as
usual, to speak of the part which he
was privileged to bear in this glorious
dispensation. He is constrained to
magnify his office. See the next note,
and comp. ver. 23.

ὃν ἡμεῖς κ.τ.λ.] As in St Paul's own
language at Thessalonica, Acts xvii. 3
ὃν ἐγὼ καταγγέλλω ὑμῖν, and at
Athens, Acts xvii. 23 τοῦτο ἐγὼ καταγγέλλω ὑμῖν, in both which passages, as here, emphasis is laid on the
person of the preacher.

νουθετοῦντες] 'admonishing.' The
two words νουθετεῖν and διδάσκειν present complementary aspects of the
preacher's duty, and are related the
one to the other, as μετάνοια to πίστις,
'warning to repent, instructing in
the faith.' For the relation of νουθετεῖν
to μετάνοια see Plut. Mor. p. 68 ἔνεστι
τὸ νουθετοῦν καὶ μετάνοιαν ἐμποιοῦν,
p. 452 ἡ νουθεσία καὶ ὁ ψόγος ἐμποιεῖ
μετάνοιαν καὶ αἰσχύνην. The two verbs
νουθετεῖν and διδάσκειν are connected
in Plato Protag. 323 D, Legg. 845 B,
Plut. Mor. p. 46 (comp. p. 39), Dion
Chrys. Or. xxxiii. p. 369; the substantives διδαχή and νουθέτησις in
Plato Resp. 399 B. Similarly νουθετεῖν and πείθειν occur together in
Arist. Rhet. ii. 18. For the two functions of the preacher's office, corresponding respectively to the two
words, see St Paul's own language in
Acts xx. 21 διαμαρτυρόμενος...τὴν εἰς
Θεὸν μετάνοιαν καὶ πίστιν εἰς τὸν
Κύριον ἡμῶν Ἰησοῦν.

πάντα ἄνθρωπον] Three times repeated for the sake of emphasizing
the universality of the Gospel. This
great truth, for which St Paul gave
his life, was now again endangered
by the doctrine of an intellectual exclusiveness taught by the Gnosticizers
at Colossæ, as before it had been
endangered by the doctrine of a

ceremonial exclusiveness taught by
the Judaizers in Galatia. See above,
pp. 77, 92, 98 sq. For the repetition
of πάντα compare especially 1 Cor. x.
1 sq., where πάντες is five times, and
ib. xii. 29, 30, where it is seven times
repeated; see also Rom. ix. 6, 7, xi.
32, 1 Cor. xii. 13, xiii. 7, xiv. 31, etc.
Transcribers have been offended at
this characteristic repetition here, and
consequently have omitted πάντα ἄνθρωπον in one place or other.

ἐν πάσῃ σοφίᾳ] The Gnostic spoke
of a blind faith for the many, of a
higher γνῶσις for the few. St Paul
declares that the fullest wisdom is
offered to all alike. The character of
the teaching is as free from restriction,
as are the qualifications of the recipients. Comp. ii. 2, 3 πᾶν πλοῦτος τῆς
πληροφορίας τῆς συνέσεως...πάντες οἱ
θησαυροὶ τῆς σοφίας καὶ γνώσεως.

παραστήσωμεν] See the note on
παραστῆσαι, ver. 22.

τέλειον] So 1 Cor. ii. 6, 7 σοφίαν δὲ
λαλοῦμεν ἐν τοῖς τελείοις...θεοῦ σοφίαν ἐν μυστηρίῳ τὴν ἀποκεκρυμμένην.
In both these passages the epithet
τέλειος is probably a metaphor borrowed from the ancient mysteries,
where it seems to have been applied
to the fully instructed, as opposed to
the novices: comp. Plato Phædr.
249 C τελέους ἀεὶ τελετὰς τελούμενος
τέλεος ὄντως μόνος γίγνεται...250 B, C
εἰδόν τε καὶ ἐτελοῦντο τελετῶν ἣν θέμις
λέγειν μακαριωτάτην...μυούμενοί τε καὶ
ἐποπτεύοντες ἐν αὐγῇ καθαρᾷ, Symp.
209 E ταῦτα...κἂν σὺ μυηθείης· τὰ δὲ
τέλεα καὶ ἐποπτικά...οὐκ οἶδ' εἰ οἷός τ'
ἂν εἴης, Plut. Fragm. de An. vi. 2
(v. p. 726 Wyttenb.) ὁ παντελὴς ἤδη
καὶ μεμυημένος (with the context),
Dion Chrys. Or. xii. p. 203 τὴν ὁλό-
κληρον καὶ τῷ ὄντι τελείαν τελετὴν
μυούμενον; see Valcknaer on Eurip.
Hippol. 25, and Lobeck Aglaoph. p. 33
sq., p. 126 sq. Somewhat similarly in

²⁹εἰς ὃ καὶ κοπιῶ ἀγωνιζόμενος κατὰ τὴν ἐνέργειαν αὐτοῦ τὴν ἐνεργουμένην ἐν ἐμοὶ ἐν δυνάμει.

the LXX, 1 Chron. xxv. 8 τελείων καὶ
μανθανόντων stands for 'the teachers
(or the wise) and the scholars.' So
also in 2 Pet. i. 16 ἐπόπται γενηθέντες
τῆς ἐκείνου μεγαλειότητος we seem to
have the same metaphor. As an illustration it may be mentioned that
Plato and Aristotle called the higher
philosophy ἐποπτικόν, because those
who have transcended the bounds
of the material, οἶον ἐντελῆ [l. ἐν τε-
λετῇ] τέλος ἔχειν φιλοσοφίαν [φιλοσο-
φίας] νομίζουσι, Plut. *Mor.* 382 D, E.
For other metaphorical expressions
in St Paul, derived from the mysteries, see above on μυστήριον ver. 26.
Influenced probably by this heathen
use of τέλειος, the early Christians
applied it to the baptized, as opposed
to the catechumens: e.g. Justin *Dial.*
8 (p. 225 C) πάρεστιν ἐπιγνόντι σοι τὸν
Χριστὸν τοῦ Θεοῦ καὶ τελείῳ γενομένῳ
εὐδαιμονεῖν, *Clem. Hom.* iii. 29 ὑποχω-
ρεῖν μοι κελεύσας, ὡς μήπω εἰληφότι τὸ
πρὸς σωτηρίαν βάπτισμα, τοῖς ἤδη τελείοις ἔφη κ.τ.λ., xi. 36 βαπτίσας...ἤδη
λοιπὸν τέλειον ὄντα κ.τ.λ.; and for
later writers see Suicer *Thes.* s. vv. τε-
λειόω, τελείωσις. At all events we
may ascribe to its connexion with the
mysteries the fact that it was adopted
by Gnostics at a later date, and most
probably by the Gnosticizers at this
time, to distinguish the possessors of
the higher γνῶσις from the vulgar
herd of believers: see the passages
quoted in the note on Phil. iii. 15.
While employing the favourite Gnostic
term, the Apostle strikes at the root
of the Gnostic doctrine. The language descriptive of the heathen mysteries is transferred by him to the
Christian dispensation, that he may
thus more effectively contrast the
things signified. The true Gospel also
has its mysteries, its hierophants, its
initiation: but these are open to all
alike. In Christ every believer is τέ-

λειος, for he has been admitted as
ἐπόπτης of its most profound, most
awful, secrets. See again the note
on ἀπόκρυφοι, ii. 3.

29. εἰς ὃ] i.e. εἰς τὸ παραστῆσαι πάντα
ἄνθρωπον τέλειον, 'that I may initiate
all mankind in the fulness of this mystery,' 'that I may preach the Gospel
to all without reserve.' If St Paul
had been content to preach an exclusive Gospel, he might have saved himself from more than half the troubles
of his life.

κοπιῶ] This word is used especially of the labour undergone by the
athlete in his training, and therefore
fitly introduces the metaphor of ἀγωνιζόμενος: comp. 1 Tim. iv. 10 εἰς τοῦτο γὰρ κοπιῶμεν καὶ ἀγωνιζόμεθα (the
correct reading), and see the passages
quoted on Phil. ii. 16.

ἀγωνιζόμενος] *'contending in the
lists,'* the metaphor being continued
in the next verse (ii. 1), ἡλίκον ἀγῶνα;
comp. iv. 12. These words ἀγών, ἀγωνία, ἀγωνίζεσθαι, are only found in St
Paul and the Pauline writings (Luke,
Hebrews) in the New Testament.
They occur in every group of St Paul's
Epistles. The use here most resembles
1 Thess. ii. 2 λαλῆσαι πρὸς ὑμᾶς τὸ
εὐαγγέλιον τοῦ Θεοῦ ἐν πολλῷ ἀγῶνι.

ἐνεργουμένην] Comp. Eph. iii. 20. For
the difference between ἐνεργεῖν and
ἐνεργεῖσθαι see the note on Gal. v. 6.

II. 1—3. 'I spoke of an *arena* and
a *conflict* in describing my apostolic
labours. The image was not lightly
chosen. I would have you know that my
care is not confined to my own direct
and personal disciples. I wish you to
understand the magnitude of the
struggle, which my anxiety for you
costs me—for you and for your neighbours of Laodicea, and for all who,
like yourselves, have never met me
face to face in the flesh. I am constantly wrestling in spirit, that the

II. ¹Θέλω γὰρ ὑμᾶς εἰδέναι, ἡλίκον ἀγῶνα ἔχω ὑπὲρ ὑμῶν καὶ τῶν ἐν Λαοδικίᾳ καὶ ὅσοι οὐχ ἑώρακαν τὸ πρόσωπόν μου ἐν σαρκί, ²ἵνα παρακληθῶσιν αἱ καρδίαι

hearts of all such may be confirmed and strengthened in the faith; that they may be united in love; that they may attain to all the unspeakable wealth which comes from the firm conviction of an understanding mind, may be brought to the perfect knowledge of God's mystery, which is nothing else than Christ—Christ containing in Himself all the treasures of wisdom and knowledge hidden away.'

1. Θέλω κ.τ.λ.] As in 1 Cor. xi. 3. The corresponding negative form, οὐ θέλω [θέλομεν] ὑμᾶς ἀγνοεῖν, is the more common expression in St Paul; Rom. i. 13, xi. 25, 1 Cor. x. 1, xii. 1, 2 Cor. i. 8, 1 Thess. iv. 13.

ἀγῶνα] The arena of the contest to which ἀγωνιζόμενος in the preceding verse refers may be either outward or inward. It will include the 'fightings without,' as well as the 'fears within.' Here however the inward struggle, the wrestling in prayer, is the predominant idea, as in iv. 12 πάντοτε ἀγωνιζόμενος ὑπὲρ ὑμῶν ἐν ταῖς προσευχαῖς ἵνα σταθῆτε κ.τ.λ.

τῶν ἐν Λαοδικίᾳ] The Laodiceans were exposed to the same doctrinal perils as the Colossians: see above, pp. 2, 41 sq. The Hierapolitans are doubtless included in καὶ ὅσοι κ.τ.λ. (comp. iv. 13), but are not mentioned here by name, probably because they were less closely connected with Colossæ (see iv. 15 sq.), and perhaps also because the danger was less threatening there.

καὶ ὅσοι κ.τ.λ.] 'and all who, like yourselves, have not seen, etc.'; where the καὶ ὅσοι introduces the whole class to which the persons previously enumerated belong; so Acts iv. 6 Ἄννας ὁ ἀρχιερεὺς καὶ Καϊάφας καὶ Ἰωάννης καὶ Ἀλέξανδρος καὶ ὅσοι ἦσαν ἐκ γένους ἀρχιερατικοῦ, Rev. xviii. 17 καὶ πᾶς κυβερνήτης καὶ πᾶς ὁ ἐπὶ τόπον πλέων καὶ

ναῦται καὶ ὅσοι τὴν θάλασσαν ἐργάζονται. Even a simple καὶ will sometimes introduce the general after the particular, e.g. Acts v. 29 ὁ Πέτρος καὶ οἱ ἀπόστολοι, Ar. Nub. 413 ἐν Ἀθηναίοις καὶ τοῖς Ἕλλησι, etc.; see Kühner Gramm. § 521, II. p. 791. On the other hand καὶ ὅσοι, occurring in an enumeration, sometimes introduces a different class from those previously mentioned, as e.g. in Herod. vii. 185. As a pure grammatical question therefore it is uncertain whether St Paul's language here implies his personal acquaintance with his correspondents or the contrary. But in all such cases the sense of the context must be our guide. In the present instance καὶ ὅσοι is quite out of place, unless the Colossians and Laodiceans also were personally unknown to the Apostle. There would be no meaning in singling out individuals who were known to him, and then mentioning comprehensively all who were unknown to him: see above, p. 28, note 4. Hence we may infer from the expression here, that St Paul had never visited Colossæ—an inference which has been already shown (p. 23 sq.) to accord both with the incidental language of this epistle elsewhere and with the direct historical narrative of the Acts.

ἑώρακαν] For this ending of the 3rd pers. plur. perfect in -αν see Winer § xiii. p. 90. The received text reads ἑωράκασι. In this passage the ω form has the higher support; but below in ver. 18 the preponderance of authority favours ἑόρακεν rather than ἑώρακεν. On the use of the form in ο see Buttmann Ausf. Griech. Sprachl. § 84, I. p. 325.

2. παρακληθῶσιν] 'encouraged, confirmed,' i.e. 'comforted' in the older and wider meaning of the word ('confortati'), but not with its mo-

αὐτῶν, συμβιβασθέντες ἐν ἀγάπῃ καὶ εἰς πᾶν πλοῦτος
τῆς πληροφορίας τῆς συνέσεως, εἰς ἐπίγνωσιν τοῦ μυστηρίου τοῦ Θεοῦ, Χριστοῦ ³ἐν ᾧ εἰσὶν πάντες οἱ θη-

dern and restricted sense: see παράκλησις Phil. ii. 1. For παρακαλεῖν τὰς
καρδίας comp. iv. 8, Ephes. vi. 22, 2
Thess. ii. 17.

αἱ καρδίαι] They met the Apostle
heart to heart, though not face to
face. We have here the same opposition of καρδία and πρόσωπον as in
1 Thess. ii. 17, though less directly
expressed; see ver. 5.

αὐτῶν] Where we should expect
ὑμῶν, but the substitution of the third
person for the second is suggested by
the immediately preceding καὶ ὅσοι.
This substitution confirms the interpretation of καὶ ὅσοι already given.
Unless the Colossians are included in
ὅσοι, they must be excluded by αὐτῶν.
Yet this exclusion is hardly conceivable in such a context.

συμβιβασθέντες] 'they being united,
compacted,' for συμβιβάζειν must here
have its common meaning, as it has
elsewhere in this and the companion
epistle : ver. 19 διὰ τῶν ἁφῶν καὶ
συνδέσμων...συμβιβαζόμενον, Ephes. iv.
16 πᾶν τὸ σῶμα συναρμολογούμενον καὶ
συμβιβαζόμενον. Otherwise we might
be disposed to assign to this verb here
the sense which it always bears in the
LXX (e.g. in Is. xl. 13, 14, quoted
in 1 Cor. ii. 16), 'instructed, taught,'
as it is rendered in the Vulgate. Its
usage in the Acts is connected with
this latter sense; e.g. ix. 22 συμβιβάζων
'proving,' xvi. 10 συμβιβάζοντες 'concluding'; and so in xix. 33 συνεβίβα-
σαν Ἀλέξανδρον (the best supported
reading) can only mean 'instructed
Alexander.' For the different sense
of the nominative absolute see the
note on iii. 16. The received text
substitutes συμβιβασθέντων here.

ἐν ἀγάπῃ] For love is the σύνδεσμος
(iii. 14) of perfection.

καὶ εἰς] 'and brought unto,' the
thought being supplied from the pre-

ceding συμβιβασθέντες, which involves
an idea of motion, comp. Joh. xx. 7
ἐντετυλιγμένον εἰς ἕνα τόπον.

πᾶν πλοῦτος] This reading is better
supported than either πᾶν τὸ πλοῦτος
or πάντα πλοῦτον, while, as the intermediate reading, it also explains the
other two.

τῆς πληροφορίας] 'the full assurance,' for such seems to be the
meaning of the substantive wherever
it occurs in the New Testament; 1
Thess. i. 5 ἐν πληροφορίᾳ πολλῇ, Heb.
vi. 11 πρὸς τὴν πληροφορίαν τῆς ἐλπίδος,
x. 22 ἐν πληροφορίᾳ πίστεως, comp.
Clem. Rom. 42 μετὰ πληροφορίας πνεύματος ἁγίου. With the exception of
1 Thess. i. 5 however, all the Biblical
passages might bear the other sense
'fulness': see Bleek on Heb. vi. 11.
For the verb see the note on πεπληροφορημένοι below, iv. 12.

ἐπίγνωσιν] See the note on i. 9.

τοῦ μυστηρίου κ.τ.λ.] 'the mystery
of God, even Christ in whom, etc.'
Χριστοῦ being in apposition with τοῦ
μυστηρίου; comp. i. 27 τοῦ μυστηρίου
τούτου...ὅ ἐστιν Χριστὸς ἐν ὑμῖν, 1 Tim.
iii. 16 τὸ τῆς εὐσεβείας μυστήριον, Ὃς
ἐφανερώθη κ.τ.λ. The reasons for adopting the reading τοῦ Θεοῦ Χριστοῦ are
given in the detached note on various
readings. Other interpretations of this
reading are; (1) 'the God Christ,'
taking Χριστοῦ in apposition with
Θεοῦ; or (2) 'the God of Christ,'
making it the genitive after Θεοῦ:
but both expressions are without a
parallel in St Paul. The mystery
here is not 'Christ,' but 'Christ as
containing in Himself all the treasures
of wisdom'; see the note on i. 27
Χριστὸς ἐν ὑμῖν. For the form of the
sentence comp. Ephes. iv. 15, 16 ἡ κεφαλή, Χριστὸς ἐξ οὗ πᾶν τὸ σῶμα κ.τ.λ.

3. πάντες] So πᾶν πλοῦτος ver. 2,
πάσῃ σοφίᾳ ii. 28. These repetitions

σαυροὶ τῆς σοφίας καὶ γνώσεως ἀπόκρυφοι. ⁴τοῦτο

serve to emphasize the character of the Gospel, which is as complete in itself, as it is universal in its application.

σοφίας καὶ γνώσεως] The two words occur together again Rom. xi. 33 ὦ βάθος πλούτου καὶ σοφίας καὶ γνώσεως Θεοῦ, 1 Cor. xii. 8. They are found in conjunction also several times in the LXX of Eccles. i. 7, 16, 18, ii. 21, 26, ix. 10, where חכמה is represented by σοφία and דעת by γνῶσις. While γνῶσις is simply *intuitive*, σοφία is *ratiocinative* also. While γνῶσις applies chiefly to the apprehension of truths, σοφία superadds the power of reasoning about them and tracing their relations. When Bengel on 1 Cor. xii. 8 sq. says, 'Cognitio [γνῶσις] est quasi visus; sapientia [σοφία] visus cum sapore,' he is so far right; but when he adds, 'cognitio, rerum agendarum; sapientia, rerum æternarum,' he is quite wide of the mark. Substantially the same, and equally wrong, is St Augustine's distinction *de Trin.* xii. 20, 25 (VIII. pp. 923, 926) 'intelligendum est ad contemplationem sapientiam [σοφίαν], ad actionem scientiam [γνῶσιν] pertinere...quod alia [σοφία] sit intellectualis cognitio æternarum rerum, alia [γνῶσις]rationalis temporalium'(comp. xiv. 3, p. 948), and again *de Div. Quæst. ad Simpl.* ii. 2 § 3 (VI. p. 114) 'ita discerni probabiliter solent, ut sapientia pertineat ad intellectum æternorum, scientia vero ad ea quæ sensibus corporis experimur.' This is directly opposed to usage. In Aristotle *Eth. Nic.* i. 1 γνῶσις is opposed to πρᾶξις. In St Paul it is connected with the apprehension of eternal mysteries, 1 Cor. xiii. 2 εἰδῶ τὰ μυστήρια πάντα καὶ πᾶσαν τὴν γνῶσιν. On the relation of σοφία to σύνεσις see above, i. 9.

ἀπόκρυφοι] So 1 Cor. i. 7 λαλοῦμεν Θεοῦ σοφίαν ἐν μυστηρίῳ, τὴν ἀποκεκρυμμένην. As before in τέλειος

(i. 28), so here again in ἀπόκρυφοι the Apostle adopts a favourite term of the Gnostic teachers, only that he may refute a favourite doctrine. The word *apocrypha* was especially applied to those esoteric writings, for which such sectarians claimed an *auctoritas secreta* (Aug. *c. Faust.* xi. 2, VIII. p. 219) and which they carefully guarded from publication after the manner of their Jewish prototypes the Essenes (see above, p. 89 sq.): comp. Iren. i. 20. 1 ἀμύθητον πλῆθος ἀποκρύφων καὶ νόθων γραφῶν, Clem. Alex. *Strom.* i. 15 (p. 357) βίβλους ἀποκρύφους τἀνδρὸς τοῦδε οἱ τὴν Προδίκου μετίοντες αἵρεσιν αὐχοῦσι κεκτῆσθαι, *ib.* iii. 4 (p. 524) ἐρρύη δὲ αὐτοῖς τὸ δόγμα ἔκ τινος ἀποκρύφου. See also the application of the text Prov. ix. 17 ἄρτων κρυφίων ἡδέως ἄψασθε to these heretics in *Strom.* i. 19 (p. 375). Thus the word *apocrypha* in the first instance was an honourable appellation applied by the heretics themselves to their esoteric doctrine and their secret books; but owing to the general character of these works the term, as adopted by orthodox writers, got to signify 'false,' 'spurious.' The early fathers never apply it, as it is now applied, to *deutero-canonical* writings, but confine it to *supposititious* and *heretical* works: see Smith's *Dictionary of the Bible* s. v. In the text St Paul uses it καταχρηστικῶς, as he uses μυστήριον. 'All the richest treasures of that secret wisdom,' he would say, 'on which you lay so much stress, are buried in Christ, and being buried there are accessible to all alike who seek Him.' But, while the term ἀπόκρυφος is adopted because it was used to designate the secret doctrine and writings of the heretics, it is also entirely in keeping with the metaphor of the 'treasure'; e.g. Is. xlv. 3 δώσω σοι θησαυροὺς σκοτεινοὺς ἀποκρύφους, 1 Macc. i. 23 ἔλαβε τοὺς θησαυροὺς τοὺς ἀποκρύφους, Dan. xi. 43 ἐν τοῖς

λέγω, ἵνα μηδεὶς ὑμᾶς παραλογίζηται ἐν πιθανολογίᾳ·
⁵εἰ γὰρ καὶ τῇ σαρκὶ ἄπειμι, ἀλλὰ τῷ πνεύματι σὺν

ἀποκρύφοις τοῦ χρυσοῦ καὶ τοῦ ἀργύρου: comp. Matt. xiii. 44.

The stress thus laid on ἀπόκρυφοι will explain its position. It is not connected with εἰσίν, but must be taken apart as a secondary predicate: comp. ver. 10 ἐστὲ ἐν αὐτῷ πεπληρωμένοι, iii. 1 οὗ ὁ Χριστός ἐστιν ἐν δεξιᾷ τοῦ Θεοῦ καθήμενος, James i. 17 πᾶν δώρημα τέλειον ἄνωθέν ἐστιν, καταβαῖνον κ. τ. λ.

4—7. 'I do not say this without a purpose. I wish to warn you against any one who would lead you astray by specious argument and persuasive rhetoric. For I am not an indifferent spectator of your doings. Although I am absent from you in my flesh, yet I am present with you in my spirit. I rejoice to behold the orderly array and the solid phalanx which your faith towards Christ presents against the assaults of the foe. I entreat you therefore not to abandon the Christ, as you learnt from Epaphras to know Him, even Jesus the Lord, but to walk still in Him as heretofore. I would have you firmly rooted once for all in Him. I desire to see you built up higher in Him day by day, to see you growing ever stronger and stronger through your faith, while you remain true to the lessons taught you of old, so that you may abound in it, and thus abounding may pour forth your hearts in gratitude to God the giver of all.'

4. τοῦτο λέγω κ.τ.λ.] 'I say all this to you, lest you should be led astray by those false teachers who speak of another knowledge, of other mysteries.' In other connexions τοῦτο λέγω will frequently refer to the words following (e.g. Gal. iii. 17, 1 Cor. i. 12); but with ἵνα it points to what has gone before, as in Joh. v. 34 ταῦτα λέγω ἵνα ὑμεῖς σωθῆτε.

The reference in τοῦτο λέγω extends over vv. 1—3, and involves two statements; (1) The declaration that all knowledge is comprehended in Christ, vv. 2, 3; (2) The expression of his own personal anxiety that they should remain stedfast in this conviction, vv. 1, 2. This last point explains the language which follows, εἰ γὰρ καὶ τῇ σαρκὶ κ.τ.λ.

παραλογίζηται] 'lead you astray by false reasoning,' as in Daniel xiv. 7 μηδείς σε παραλογιζέσθω (LXX): comp. James i. 22, Ign. Magn. 3. It is not an uncommon word either in the LXX or in classical writers. The system against which St Paul here contends professed to be a φιλοσοφία (ver. 8) and had a λόγον σοφίας (ver. 23).

ἐν πιθανολογίᾳ] The words πιθανολογεῖν (Arist. Eth. Nic. i. 1), πιθανολογία (Plat. Theæt. 162 E), πιθανολογικός (Epictet. i. 8. 7), occur occasionally in classical writers, but do not bear a bad sense, being most frequently opposed to ἀπόδειξις, as probable argument to strict mathematical demonstration. This contrast probably suggested St Paul's language in 1 Cor. ii. 4 οὐκ ἐν πειθοῖς σοφίας λόγοις ἀλλ' ἐν ἀποδείξει πνεύματος κ.τ.λ., and may possibly have been present to his mind here.

5. ἀλλά] Frequently introduces the apodosis after εἰ or εἰ καί in St Paul; e.g. Rom. vi. 5, 1 Cor. ix. 2, 2 Cor. iv. 16, v. 16, xi. 6, xiii. 4 (v. l.).

τῷ πνεύματι] 'in my spirit,' not 'by the Spirit.' We have here the common antithesis of flesh and spirit, or body and spirit: comp. 1 Cor. v. 3 ἀπὼν τῷ σώματι, παρὼν δὲ τῷ πνεύματι. St Paul elsewhere uses another antithesis, προσώπῳ and καρδίᾳ, to express this same thing; 1 Thess. ii. 17.

χαίρων καὶ βλέπων] 'rejoicing and beholding.' This must not be regarded as a logical inversion. The contemplation of their orderly array, though it might have been first the cause,

ὑμῖν εἰμί, χαίρων καὶ βλέπων ὑμῶν τὴν τάξιν καὶ τὸ
στερέωμα τῆς εἰς Χριστὸν πίστεως ὑμῶν. ⁶ὡς οὖν παρελάβετε τὸν Χριστόν, Ἰησοῦν τὸν Κύριον, ἐν αὐτῷ περι-

was afterwards the consequence, of the Apostle's rejoicing. He looked, because it gave him satisfaction to look.

τὴν τάξιν] 'your orderly array,' a military metaphor: comp. e.g. Xen. *Anab.* i. 2. 18 ἰδοῦσα τὴν λαμπρότητα καὶ τὴν τάξιν τοῦ στρατεύματος ἐθαύμασε, Plut. *Vit. Pyrrh.* 16 κατιδὼν τάξιν τε καὶ φυλακὰς καὶ κόσμον αὐτῶν καὶ τὸ σχῆμα τῆς στρατοπεδείας ἐθαύμασε. The enforced companionship of St Paul with the soldiers of the prætorian guard at this time (Phil. i. 13) might have suggested this image. At all events in the contemporary epistle (Ephes. vi. 14 sq.) we have an elaborate metaphor from the armour of a soldier.

τὸ στερέωμα] 'solid front, close phalanx,' a continuation of the metaphor: comp. 1 Macc. ix. 14 εἶδεν Ἰούδας ὅτι Βακχίδης καὶ τὸ στερέωμα τῆς παρεμβολῆς ἐν τοῖς δεξιοῖς. Somewhat similar are the expressions στερεοῦν τὸν πόλεμον 1 Macc. x. 50, κατὰ τὴν στερέωσιν τῆς μάχης Ecclus. xxviii. 10. For the connexion here compare 1 Pet. v. 9 ἀντίστητε στερεοὶ τῇ πίστει, Acts xvi. 5 ἐστερεοῦντο τῇ πίστει.

6. ὡς οὖν παρελάβετε κ.τ.λ.] i.e. 'Let your conviction and conduct be in perfect accordance with the doctrines and precepts of the Gospel as it was taught to you.' For this use of παρελάβετε 'ye received from your teachers, were instructed in,' comp. 1 Cor. xv. 1, 3, Gal. i. 9, Phil. iv. 9, 1 Thess. ii. 13, iv. 1, 2 Thess. iii. 6. The word παραλαμβάνειν implies either 'to receive as transmitted,' or 'to receive for transmission': see the note on Gal. i. 12. The ὡς of the protasis suggests a οὕτως in the apodosis, which in this case is unexpressed but must be understood. The meaning of ὡς

παρελάβετε here is explained by the καθὼς ἐμάθετε ἀπὸ Ἐπαφρᾶ in i. 7; see the note there, and comp. below, ver. 7 καθὼς ἐδιδάχθητε.

τὸν Χριστόν] 'the Christ,' rather than 'the Gospel,' because the central point in the Colossian heresy was the subversion of the true idea of the Christ.

Ἰησοῦν τὸν Κύριον] 'even Jesus the Lord,' in whom the true conception of the Christ is realised: comp. Ephes. iv. 20, 21, ὑμεῖς δὲ οὐχ οὕτως ἐμάθετε τὸν Χριστόν, εἴγε αὐτὸν ἠκούσατε καὶ ἐν αὐτῷ ἐδιδάχθητε, καθώς ἐστιν ἀλήθεια ἐν τῷ Ἰησοῦ, where the same idea is more directly expressed. The genuine doctrine of the Christ consists in (1) the recognition of the historical person *Jesus*, and (2) the acceptance of Him as *the Lord*. This doctrine was seriously endangered by the mystic theosophy of the false teachers. The same order which we have here occurs also in Ephes. iii. 11 ἐν τῷ Χριστῷ Ἰησοῦ τῷ Κυρίῳ ἡμῶν (the correct reading).

7. ἐρριζωμένοι] Two points may be noticed here; (1) The expressive change of tenses; ἐρριζωμένοι 'firmly rooted' *once for all*, ἐποικοδομούμενοι, βεβαιούμενοι, 'built up and strengthened' *from hour to hour*. (2) The rapid transition of metaphor, περιπατεῖτε, ἐρριζωμένοι, ἐποικοδομούμενοι, the path, the tree, the building: comp. Ephes. iii. 17 ἐρριζωμένοι καὶ τεθεμελιωμένοι. The metaphors of the plant and the building occur together in 1 Cor. iii. 9 Θεοῦ γεώργιον, Θεοῦ οἰκοδομή. The transition in this passage is made easier by the fact that ῥιζοῦν (Plut. *Mor.* 321 D), ἐκριζοῦν (Jer. i. 10, 1 Macc. v. 51), πρόρριζος (Jos. *B. J.* vii. 8. 7), etc., are not uncommonly used of cities and buildings.

πατεῖτε, ⁷ἐρριζωμένοι καὶ ἐποικοδομούμενοι ἐν αὐτῷ καὶ
βεβαιούμενοι τῇ πίστει, καθὼς ἐδιδάχθητε, περισσεύ-
οντες ἐν αὐτῇ ἐν εὐχαριστίᾳ.

ἐποικοδομούμενοι] 'being built up,'
as in 1 Cor. iii. 10—14. After this
verb we might have expected ἐπ'
αὐτῷ or ἐπ' αὐτόν (1 Cor. iii. 12)
rather than ἐν αὐτῷ; but in this
and the companion epistle Christ is
represented rather as the binding
element than as the foundation of the
building: e.g. Ephes. ii. 20 ἐποικοδο-
μηθέντες ἐπὶ τῷ θεμελίῳ τῶν ἀποστόλων
καὶ προφητῶν, ὄντος ἀκρογωνιαίου
αὐτοῦ Χριστοῦ Ἰησοῦ, ἐν ᾧ πᾶσα [ἡ]
οἰκοδομὴ αὔξει εἰς ναὸν ἅγιον ἐν Κυρίῳ,
ἐν ᾧ καὶ ὑμεῖς συνοικοδομεῖσθε. The
ἐπὶ in ἐποικοδομεῖν does not necessarily refer to the original foundation,
but may point to the continued progress of the building by successive
layers, as e.g. [Aristot.] Rhet. ad Alex.
4 (p. 1426) ἐποικοδομοῦντα τὸ ἕτερον ὡς
ἐπὶ τὸ ἕτερον αὔξειν. Hence ἐποικοδομεῖν is frequently used absolutely,
'to build up' (e.g. Jude 20, Polyb.
iii. 27. 4), as here. The repetition of
ἐν αὐτῷ emphasizes the main idea of
the passage, and indeed of the whole
epistle.

τῇ πίστει] 'by your faith,' the
dative of the instrument; comp. Heb.
xiii. 9 καλὸν γὰρ χάριτι βεβαιοῦσθαι
τὴν καρδίαν. Faith is, as it were, the
cement of the building: comp. Clem.
Rom. 22 ταῦτα πάντα βεβαιοῖ ἡ ἐν
Χριστῷ πίστις.

καθὼς ἐδιδάχθητε] i. e. 'remaining
true to the lessons which you received from Epaphras, and not led
astray by any later pretenders'; comp.
i. 6, 7 ἐν ἀληθείᾳ, καθὼς ἐμάθετε ἀπὸ
Ἐπαφρᾶ.

ἐν αὐτῇ κ.τ.λ.] The same ending
occurs in iv. 2. Thanksgiving is the
end of all human conduct, whether
exhibited in words or in works. For
the stress laid on thanksgiving in St
Paul's epistles generally, see the note

on Phil. iv. 6. The words εὐχάριστος,
εὐχαριστεῖν, εὐχαριστία, occur in St
Paul's writings alone of the Apostolic
epistles. In this epistle especially
the duty of thanksgiving assumes a
peculiar prominence by being made
a refrain, as here and in iii. 15, 17,
iv. 2: see also i. 12.

8—15. 'Be on your guard; do not
suffer yourselves to fall a prey to
certain persons who would lead you
captive by a hollow and deceitful
system, which they call philosophy.
They substitute the traditions of men
for the truth of God. They enforce
an elementary discipline of mundane
ordinances fit only for children. Theirs
is not the Gospel of Christ. In Christ
the entire fulness of the Godhead
abides for ever, having united itself
with man by taking a human body.
And so in Him—not in any inferior
mediators—ye have your life, your
being, for ye are filled from His
fulness. He, I say, is the Head over
all spiritual beings—call them principalities or powers or what you will.
In Him too ye have the true circumcision—the circumcision which is not
made with hands but wrought by
the Spirit—the circumcision which
divests not of a part only but of the
whole carnal body—the circumcision
which is not of Moses but of Christ.
This circumcision ye have, because ye
were buried with Christ to your old
selves beneath the baptismal waters,
and were raised with Him from those
same waters to a new and regenerate
life, through your faith in the powerful working of God who raised Him
from the dead. Yes, you—you Gentiles who before were dead, when ye
walked in your transgressions and in
the uncircumcision of your unchastened
carnal heathen heart—even you did

^{8} Βλέπετε μή τις ὑμᾶς ἔσται ὁ συλαγωγῶν διὰ

8. μή τις ἔσται ὑμᾶς.

God quicken into life together with Christ; then and there freely forgiving all of us—Jews and Gentiles alike—all our transgressions; then and there cancelling the bond which stood valid against us (for it bore our own signature), the bond which engaged us to fulfil all the law of ordinances, which was our stern pitiless tyrant. Aye, this very bond hath Christ put out of sight for ever, nailing it to His cross and rending it with His body and killing it in His death. Taking upon Him our human nature, He stripped off and cast aside all the powers of evil which clung to it like a poisonous garment. As a mighty conqueror He displayed these His fallen enemies to an astonished world, leading them in triumph on His cross.'

8. Βλέπετε κ.τ.λ.] The form of the sentence is a measure of the imminence of the peril. The usual construction with βλέπειν μὴ is a conjunctive; e.g. in Luke xxi. 8 βλέπετε μὴ πλανηθῆτε. Here the substitution of an indicative shows that the danger is real; comp. Heb. iii. 12 βλέπετε μήποτε ἔσται ἔν τινι ὑμῶν καρδία πονηρὰ ἀπιστίας. For an example of μὴ with a future indicative see Mark xiv. 2 μήποτε ἔσται θόρυβος; and comp. Winer § lvi. p. 631 sq.

τις] This indefinite τις is frequently used by St Paul, when speaking of opponents whom he knows well enough but does not care to name: see the note on Gal. i. 7. Comp. Ign. *Smyrn.* 5 ὅν τινες ἀγνοοῦντες ἀρνοῦνται...τὰ δὲ ὀνόματα αὐτῶν, ὄντα ἄπιστα, οὐκ ἔδοξέ μοι ἐγγράψαι.

συλαγωγῶν] 'makes you his prey, carries you off body and soul.' The word appears not to occur before St Paul, nor after him, independently of this passage, till a late date: e.g. Heliod. *Aeth.* x. 35 οὗτός ἐστιν ὁ τὴν ἐμὴν θυγατέρα συλαγωγήσας. In Tatian *ad Graec.* 22 ὑμεῖς δὲ ὑπὸ τούτων συλαγω-

γεῖσθε it seems to be a reminiscence of St Paul. Its full and proper meaning, as appears from the passages quoted, is not 'to despoil,' but 'to carry off as spoil,' in accordance with the analogous compounds, δουλαγωγεῖν, σκευαγωγεῖν. So too the closely allied word λαφυραγωγεῖν in Plut. *Mor.* p. 5 πόλεμος γὰρ οὐ λαφυραγωγεῖ ἀρετήν, *Vit. Galb.* 5 τὰ μὲν Γαλατῶν, ὅταν ὑποχείριοι γένωνται, λαφυραγωγήσεσθαι. The Colossians had been rescued from the bondage of darkness; they had been transferred to the kingdom of light; they had been settled there as free citizens (i. 12, 13); and now there was danger that they should fall into a state worse than their former slavery, that they should be carried off as so much booty. Comp. 2 Tim. iii. 6 αἰχμαλωτίζοντες γυναικάρια.

For the construction ἔσται ὁ συλαγωγῶν see the notes on Gal. i. 7, iii. 21. The former passage is a close parallel to the words here, εἰ μή τινές εἰσιν οἱ ταράσσοντες ὑμᾶς κ.τ.λ. The expression ὁ συλαγωγῶν gives a directness and individuality to the reference, which would have been wanting to the more natural construction ὃς συλαγωγήσει.

διὰ τῆς φιλοσοφίας κ.τ.λ.] '*through his philosophy which is an empty deceit.*' The absence of both preposition and article in the second clause shows that κενῆς ἀπάτης describes and qualifies φιλοσοφίας. Clement therefore (*Strom.* vi. 8, p. 771) had a right to contend that St Paul does not here condemn 'philosophy' absolutely. The φιλοσοφία καὶ κενὴ ἀπάτη of this passage corresponds to the ψευδώνυμος γνῶσις of 1 Tim. vi. 20.

But though 'philosophy' is not condemned, it is disparaged by the connexion in which it is placed. St Chrysostom's comment is not altogether wrong, ἐπειδὴ δοκεῖ σεμνὸν εἶναι τὸ

τῆς φιλοσοφίας καὶ κενῆς ἀπάτης, κατὰ τὴν παρά-

τῆς φιλοσοφίας, προσέθηκε καὶ κενῆς ἀπάτης. The term was doubtless used by the false teachers themselves to describe their system. Though essentially Greek as a name and as an idea, it had found its way into Jewish circles. Philo speaks of the Hebrew religion and Mosaic law as ἡ πάτριος φιλοσοφία (*Leg. ad Gai.* 23, II. p. 568, *de Somn.* ii. 18, I. p. 675) or ἡ Ἰουδαϊκὴ φιλοσοφία (*Leg. ad Gai.* 33, II. p. 582) or ἡ κατὰ Μωϋσῆν φιλοσοφία (*de Mut. Nom.* 39, I. p. 612). The system of the Essenes, the probable progenitors of the false teachers at Colossæ, he describes as ἡ δίχα περιεργείας Ἑλληνικῶν ὀνομάτων φιλοσοφία (*Omn. prob. lib.* 13, II. p. 459). So too Josephus speaks of the three Jewish sects as τρεῖς φιλοσοφίαι(*Ant.* xviii. 1. 2, comp. *B. J.* ii. 8. 2). It should be remembered also, that in this later age, owing to Roman influence, the term was used to describe practical not less than speculative systems, so that it would cover the ascetic life as well as the mystic theosophy of these Colossian heretics. Hence the Apostle is here flinging back at these false teachers a favourite term of their own, 'their vaunted *philosophy*, which is hollow and misleading.'

The word indeed could claim a truly noble origin; for it is said to have arisen out of the humility of Pythagoras, who called himself 'a lover of wisdom,' μηδένα γὰρ εἶναι σοφὸν ἄνθρωπον ἀλλ' ἢ Θεόν (Diog. Laert. Procem. § 12; comp. Cic. *Tusc.* v. 3). In such a sense the term would entirely accord with the spirit and teaching of St Paul; for it bore testimony to the insufficiency of the human intellect and the need of a revelation. But in his age it had come to be associated generally with the idea of subtle dialectics and profitless speculation; while in this particular instance it was combined with a mystic cosmogony and angelology which contributed a

fresh element of danger. As contrasted with the power and fulness and certainty of revelation, all such philosophy was 'foolishness' (1 Cor. i. 20). It is worth observing that this word, which to the Greeks denoted the highest effort of the intellect, occurs here alone in St Paul, just as he uses ἀρετή, which was their term to express the highest moral excellence, in a single passage only (Phil. iv. 8; see the note there). The reason is much the same in both cases. The Gospel had deposed the terms as inadequate to the higher standard, whether of knowledge or of practice, which it had introduced.

On the attitude of the fathers towards philosophy, while philosophy was a living thing, see Smith's *Dictionary of the Bible* s.v. Clement, who was followed in the main by the earlier Alexandrine fathers, regards Greek philosophy not only as a preliminary training (προπαιδεία) for the Gospel, but even as in some sense a covenant (διαθήκη) given by God to the Greeks (*Strom.* i. 5, p. 331, vi. 5, p. 761, *ib.* § 8, p. 771 sq.). Others, who were the great majority and of whom Tertullian may be taken as an extreme type, set their faces directly against it, seeing in it only the parent of all heretical teaching: e. g. *de Anim.* 2, 3, *Apol.* 46, 47. In the first passage, referring to this text, he says, ' Ab apostolo jam tunc philosophia concussio veritatis providebatur'; in the second he asks, 'Quid simile philosophus et Christianus?' St Paul's speech at Athens, on the only occasion when he is known to have been brought into direct personal contact with Greek philosophers (Acts xvii. 18), shows that his sympathies would have been at least as much with Clement's representations as with Tertullian's.

κατὰ κ.τ.λ.] The false teaching is described (1) As regards its source—

δοσιν τῶν ἀνθρώπων, κατὰ τὰ στοιχεῖα τοῦ κόσμου,

'the tradition of *men*'; (2) As regards its subject matter—'the rudiments of *the world*.'

τὴν παράδοσιν κ.τ.λ.] Other systems, as for instance the ceremonial mishna of the Pharisees, might fitly be described in this way (Matt. xv. 2 sq., Mark vii. 3 sq.): but such a description was peculiarly appropriate to a mystic theosophy like this of the Colossian false teachers. The teaching might be oral or written, but it was essentially esoteric, essentially traditional. It could not appeal to sacred books which had been before all the world for centuries. The Essenes, the immediate spiritual progenitors of these Colossian heretics, distinctly claimed to possess such a source of knowledge, which they carefully guarded from divulgence; *B. J.* ii. 8. 7 συντηρήσειν ὁμοίως τά τε τῆς αἱρέσεως αὐτῶν βιβλία καὶ τὰ τῶν ἀγγέλων ὀνόματα (see above pp. 89, 90 sq., 95). The various Gnostic sects, their direct or collateral spiritual descendants, almost without exception traced their doctrines to a similar source : o. g. Hippol. *Haer*.v. 7 ἃ φησὶ παραδεδωκέναι Μαριάμνῃ τὸν Ἰάκωβον τοῦ Κυρίου τὸν ἀδελφόν, vii. 20 φασὶν εἰρηκέναι Ματθίαν αὐτοῖς λόγους ἀποκρύφους οὓς ἤκουσε παρὰ τοῦ σωτῆρος, Clem. Alex. *Strom*. vii. 17 (p. 898) καθάπερ ὁ Βασιλείδης, κἂν Γλαυκίαν ἐπιγράφηται διδάσκαλον, ὡς αὐχοῦσιν αὐτοί, τὸν Πέτρου ἑρμηνέα· ὡσαύτως δὲ καὶ Οὐαλεντῖνον Θεοδᾶ διακηκοέναι φέρουσιν, γνώριμος δὲ οὗτος ἐγεγόνει Παύλου. So too a later mystic theology of the Jews, which had many affinities with the teaching of the Christianized Essenes at Colossæ, was self-designated *Kabbala* or 'tradition,' professing to have been handed down orally from the patriarchs. See the note on ἀπόκρυφοι, ii. 3.

τὰ στοιχεῖα] '*the rudiments, the elementary teaching*'; comp. ver. 20. The same phrase occurs again Gal. iv.

3 (comp. ver. 9). As στοιχεῖα signifies primarily 'the letters of the alphabet,' so as a secondary meaning it denotes 'rudimentary instruction.' Accordingly it is correctly interpreted by Clement *Strom*. vi. 8 (p.771)Παῦλος ... οὐκ ἔτι παλινδρομεῖν ἀξιοῖ ἐπὶ τὴν Ἑλληνικὴν φιλοσοφίαν, στοιχεῖα τοῦ κόσμου ταύτην ἀλληγορῶν, στοιχειωτικήν τινα οὖσαν. (i.e. elementary) καὶ προπαιδείαν τῆς ἀληθείας (comp. *ib*. vi. 15, p. 799), and by Tertullian *adv. Marc.* v. 19 '*secundum elementa mundi*, non secundum caelum et terram dicens, sed secundum litteras seculares.' A large number of the fathers however explained the expression to refer to the heavenly bodies (called στοιχεῖα), as marking the seasons, so that the observance of 'festivals and newmoons and sabbaths' was a sort of bondage to them. It would appear from Tertullian's language that Marcion also had so interpreted the words. On this false interpretation see the note on Gal. iv. 3. It is quite out of place here : for (1) The context suggests some *mode of instruction*, e.g. τὴν παράδοσιν τῶν ἀνθρώπων here, and δογματίζεσθε in ver. 20; (2) The keeping of days and seasons is quite subordinate to other external observances. The rite of circumcision (ver. 11), and the distinction of meats (ver. 21), respectively, are placed in close and immediate connexion with τὰ στοιχεῖα τοῦ κόσμου in the two places where it occurs, whereas the observance of days and seasons (ver. 16) stands apart from either.

τοῦ κόσμου] '*of the world*,' that is, 'belonging to the sphere of material and external things.' See the notes on Gal. iv. 3, vi. 14.

'In Christ,' so the Apostle seems to say, 'you have attained the liberty and the intelligence of manhood; do not submit yourselves again to a rudimentary discipline fit only for children (τὰ στοιχεῖα). In Christ you

καὶ οὐ κατὰ Χριστόν· ⁹ὅτι ἐν αὐτῷ κατοικεῖ πᾶν τὸ
πλήρωμα τῆς θεότητος σωματικῶς, ¹⁰καὶ ἐστὲ ἐν αὐτῷ

have been exalted into the sphere of
the Spirit: do not plunge yourselves
again into the atmosphere of material
and sensuous things (τοῦ κόσμου).'

οὐ κατὰ Χριστόν] ' *not after Christ.*'
This expression is wide in itself, and
should be interpreted so as to supply
the negative to both the preceding
clauses ; ' Christ is neither the author
nor the substance of their teaching :
not the author, for they listen to human traditions (κατὰ τὴν παράδοσιν
τῶν ἀνθρώπων); not the substance, for
they replace Him by formal ordinances
(κατὰ τὰ στοιχεῖα τοῦ κόσμου) and by
angelic mediators.'

9 sq. In explaining the true doctrine which is 'after Christ,' St Paul
condemns the two false principles,
which lay at the root of this heretical
teaching; (1) The *theological* error of
substituting inferior and created beings, angelic mediators, for the divine
Head Himself (vv. 9, 10); and (2) The
practical error of insisting upon ritual
and ascetic observances as the foundation of their moral teaching (vv. 11
—14). Their theological speculations
and their ethical code alike were at
fault. On the intimate connexion between these two errors, as springing
out of a common root, the Gnostic
dualism of these false teachers, see
the introduction, pp. 33 sq., 79, 87,
114 sq.

ὅτι κ.τ.λ.] The Apostle justifies the
foregoing charge that this doctrine
was not κατὰ Χριστόν; 'In Christ
dwells the whole pleroma, the entire
fulness of the Godhead, whereas they
represent it to you as dispersed among
several spiritual agencies. Christ is
the one fountain-head of all spiritual
life, whereas they teach you to seek it
in communion with inferior creatures.'
The same truths have been stated before (i. 14 sq.) more generally, and they
are now restated, with direct and im-

mediate reference to the heretical
teaching.

κατοικεῖ] '*has its fixed abode.*' On
the force of this compound in relation
to the false teaching, see the note on
i. 19.

πᾶν τὸ πλήρωμα] '*all the plenitude,*'
'the totality of the divine powers and
attributes.' On this theological term
see i. 19, and the detached note at the
end of the epistle.

τῆς θεότητος] '*of the Godhead.*'
'Non modo divinae virtutes, sed ipsa
divina natura,' writes Bengel. For
the difference between θεότης '*deitas,*'
the essence, and θειότης '*divinitas,*'
the quality, see Trench *N. T. Syn.*
§ ii. p. 6. The different force of
the two words may be seen by a
comparison of two passages in Plutarch, *Mor.* p. 857 A πᾶσιν Αἰγυπτίοις
θειότητα πολλὴν καὶ δικαιοσύνην μαρ-
τυρήσας (where it means a divine
inspiration or faculty, and where no
one would have used θεότητα), and
Mor. 415 C ἐκ δὲ ἡρώων εἰς δαίμονας αἱ
βελτίονες ψυχαὶ τὴν μεταβολὴν λαμβά-
νουσιν, ἐκ δὲ δαιμόνων ὀλίγαι μὲν ἔτι
χρόνῳ πολλῷ δι᾽ ἀρετῆς καθαρθεῖσαι
παντάπασι θεότητος μετέσχον (where
θειότητος would be quite out of place,
because all δαίμονες without exception
were θεῖοι, though they only became
θεοὶ in rare instances and after long
probation and discipline). In the
New Testament the one word occurs
here alone, the other in Rom. i. 20
alone. So also τὸ θεῖον, a very favourite expression in Greek philosophy, is
found once only, in Acts xvii. 29, where
it is used with singular propriety; for
the Apostle is there meeting the heathen philosophers on their own ground
and arguing with them in their own
language. Elsewhere he instinctively
avoids a term which tends to obscure
the idea of a personal God. In the
Latin versions, owing to the poverty of

πεπληρωμένοι, ὅς ἐστιν ἡ   κεφαλὴ πάσης ἀρχῆς καὶ

the language, both θεότης and θειότης are translated by the same term *divinitas;* but this was felt to be inadequate, and the word *deitas* was coined at a later date to represent θεότης: August. *de Civ. Dei* vii. § 1, VII. p. 162 (quoted in Trench) 'Hanc divinitatem vel, ut sic dixerim, *deitatem*: nam et hoc verbo uti jam nostros non piget, ut de Graeco expressius transferant id quod illi θεότητα appellant etc.'

σωματικῶς] '*bodily-wise,*' '*corporeally,*' i.e. 'assuming a bodily form, becoming incarnate.' This is an addition to the previous statement in i. 19 ἐν αὐτῷ εὐδόκησεν πᾶν τὸ πλήρωμα κατοικῆσαι. The indwelling of the pleroma refers to the Eternal Word, and not to the Incarnate Christ: but σωματικῶς is added to show that the Word, in whom the pleroma thus had its abode from all eternity, crowned His work by the Incarnation. Thus while the main statement κατοικεῖ πᾶν τὸ πλήρωμα τῆς θεότητος of St Paul corresponds to the opening sentence ὁ λόγος ἦν πρὸς τὸν Θεὸν καὶ Θεὸς ἦν ὁ λόγος of St John, the subsidiary adverb σωματικῶς of St Paul has its counterpart in the additional statement καὶ ὁ λόγος σὰρξ ἐγένετο of St John. All other meanings which have been assigned to σωματικῶς here, as 'wholly' (Hieron. *in Is.* xi. 1 sq., IV. p. 156; 'nequaquam per partes, ut in ceteris sanctis'), or 'really' (Aug. *Epist.* cxlix, II. p. 513 'Ideo corporaliter dixit, quia illi umbratiliter seducebant'), or 'essentially' (Hilar. *de Trin.* viii. 54, II. p. 252 'Dei ex Deo significat veritatem etc.,' Cyril. Alex. in Theodoret. *Op.* v. p. 34 τουτέστιν, οὐ σχετικῶς, Isid. Pelus. *Ep.* iv. 166 ἀντὶ τοῦ οὐσιωδῶς), are unsupported by usage. Nor again can the body be understood of anything else but Christ's human body; as for instance of the created World (Theod. Mops. in Rab. *Op.* VI. p. 522) or of the Church (Anon. in Chrysost. *ad loc.*). According to these two last interpretations τὸ πλήρωμα τῆς θεότητος is taken to mean the Universe ('universam naturam repletam ab eo') and the Church (τὴν ἐκκλησίαν πεπληρωμένην ὑπὸ τῆς θεότητος αὐτοῦ, see Ephes. i. 23) respectively, because either of these may be said to reside in Him, as the source of its life, and to stand to Him in the relation of the body to the head (σωματικῶς). But these forced interpretations have nothing to recommend them.

St Paul's language is carefully guarded. He does not say ἐν σώματι, for the Godhead cannot be confined to any limits of space; nor σωματοειδῶς, for this might suggest the unreality of Christ's human body; but σωματικῶς, 'in bodily wise,' 'with a bodily manifestation.' The relation of σωματικῶς to the clause which it qualifies will vary with the circumstances, e.g. Plut. *Mor.* p. 424 E τὸ μέσον οὐ τοπικῶς ἀλλὰ σωματικῶς λέγεσθαι, i.e. 'ratione corporis habita,' Athan. *Exp. Fid.* 4 (I. p. 81) σωματικῶς εἰς τὸν Ἰησοῦν γέγραπται, i.e. 'secundum corpus,' Ptolem. in Epiphan. *Haer.* xxxiii. 5 κατὰ μὲν τὸ φαινόμενον καὶ σωματικῶς ἐκτελεῖσθαι ἀνῃρέθη, Orig. *c. Cels.* ii. 69 ἀφανῆ γενέσθαι σωματικῶς, *ib.* vi. 68 καὶ σωματικῶς γε λαλούμενος, Macar. Magn. iii. 14 σωματικῶς χωρίζειν τῶν μαθητῶν.

10. καὶ ἐστὲ ἐν αὐτῷ] '*and ye are in Him,*' where ἐστὲ should be separated from the following πεπληρωμένοι; comp. John xvii. 21, Acts xvii. 28. True life consists in union with Him, and not in dependence on any inferior being; comp. ver. 19 οὐ κρατῶν τὴν κεφαλήν, ἐξ οὗ κ.τ.λ.

πεπληρωμένοι] '*being fulfilled,*' with a direct reference to the preceding πλήρωμα; 'Your fulness comes from His fulness; His πλήρωμα is transfused into you by virtue of your incorporation in Him.' So too John i. 16 ἐκ τοῦ πληρώματος αὐτοῦ ἡμεῖς πάντες ἐλάβομεν, Ephes. iii. 19 ἵνα πλη-

ἐξουσίας· ¹¹ἐν ᾧ καὶ περιετμήθητε περιτομῇ ἀχειρο-

ρωθῆτε εἰς πᾶν τὸ πλήρωμα τοῦ Θεοῦ, iv. 13 εἰς μέτρον ἡλικίας τοῦ πληρώμα-τος τοῦ Χριστοῦ, comp. Ign. *Ephes.* init. τῇ εὐλογημένῃ ἐν μεγέθει Θεοῦ πατρὸς πληρώματι. Hence also the Church, as ideally regarded, is called the πλήρωμα of Christ, because all His graces and energies are communicated to her; Ephes. i. 23 ἥτις ἐστὶν τὸ σῶμα αὐτοῦ, τὸ πλήρωμα τοῦ τὰ πάντα ἐν πᾶσιν πληρουμένου.

ὅς] For the various reading ὅ see the detached note. It was perhaps a correction made on the false supposition that ἐν αὐτῷ referred to the πλήρωμα. At all events it must be regarded as an impossible reading; for the image would be altogether confused and lost, if the πλήρωμα were represented as the head. And again ἡ κεφαλὴ is persistently said elsewhere of Christ; i. 18, ii. 19, Ephes. i. 22, iv. 15, v. 23. Hilary *de Trin.* ix. 8 (II. p. 264) explains the ὅ as referring to the whole sentence τὸ εἶναι ἐν αὐτῷ πεπληρωμένους, but this also is an inconceivable sense. Again it has been suggested that ὅ ἐστιν (like τουτέστιν) may be taken as equivalent to *scilicet* (comp. *Clem. Hom.* viii. 22); but this would require τῇ κεφαλῇ, even if it were otherwise admissible here.

ἡ κεφαλή] The image expresses much more than the idea of sovereignty: the head is also the centre of vital force, the source of all energy and life; see the note on ver. 19.

πάσης ἀρχῆς κ.τ.λ.] '*of every principality and power,*' and therefore of those angelic beings whom the false teachers adopted as mediators, thus transferring to the inferior members the allegiance due to the Head: comp. ver. 18 sq. For ἀρχῆς καὶ ἐξουσίας, see the note on i. 16.

11. The previous verses have dealt with the theological tenets of the false teachers. The Apostle now turns to their practical errors; 'You do not need the circumcision of the flesh;

for you have received the circumcision of the heart. The distinguishing features of this higher circumcision are threefold. (1) It is not external but inward, not made with hands but wrought by the Spirit. (2) It divests not of a part only of the flesh, but of the whole body of carnal affections. (3) It is the circumcision not of Moses or of the patriarchs, but of Christ.' Thus it is distinguished, as regards *first* its character, *secondly* its extent, and *thirdly* its author.

περιετμήθητε] The moment at which this is conceived as taking place is defined by the other aorists, συντα-φέντες, συνηγέρθητε, etc., as the time of their baptism, when they 'put on Christ.'

ἀχειροποιήτῳ] i.e. 'immaterial,' 'spiritual,' as Mark xiv. 58, 2 Cor. v. 1. So χειροποίητος, which is used in the N.T. of material temples and their furniture (Acts vii. 48, xvii. 24, Heb. ix. 11, 24, comp. Mark *l. c.*), and of the material circumcision (Ephes. ii. 11 τῆς λεγομένης περιτομῆς ἐν σαρκὶ χει-ροποιήτου). In the LXX χειροποίητα occurs exclusively as a rendering of idols (אֱלִילִים, e.g. Lev. xxvi. 1, Is. ii. 18, etc.), false gods (אֱלֹהִים Is. xxi. 9, where perhaps they read אֱלִילִים), or images (חַמָּנִים Lev. xxvi. 30), except in one passage, Is. xvi. 12, where it is applied to an idol's sanctuary. Owing to this association of the word the application which we find in the New Testament would sound much more depreciatory to Jewish ears than it does to our own; e.g. ἐν χειροποιήτοις κατοικεῖ in St Stephen's speech, where the force is broken in the received text by the interpolation of ναοῖς.

For illustrations of the typical significance of circumcision, as a symbol of purity, see the note on Phil. iii. 3. ἐν τῇ κ.τ.λ.] The words are chosen to express the *completeness* of the spiritual change. (1) It is not an ἔκδυσις nor an ἀπόδυσις, but an ἀπέκδυσις.

ποιήτῳ, ἐν τῇ ἀπεκδύσει τοῦ σώματος τῆς σαρκός,
ἐν τῇ περιτομῇ τοῦ Χριστοῦ, ¹²συνταφέντες αὐτῷ ἐν

The word ἀπέκδυσις is extremely rare, and no earlier instances of it are produced; see the note on ver. 15 ἀπεκδυσάμενος. (2) It is not a single member but the whole body, which is thus cast aside; see the next note. Thus the idea of completeness is brought out both in the energy of the action and in the extent of its operation, as in iii. 9 ἀπεκδυσάμενοι τὸν παλαιὸν ἄνθρωπον.

τοῦ σώματος κ.τ.λ.] 'the whole body which consists of the flesh,' i. e. 'the body with all its corrupt and carnal affections'; as iii. 5 νεκρώσατε οὖν τὰ μέλη. For illustrations of the expression see Rom. vi. 6 ἵνα καταργηθῇ τὸ σῶμα τῆς ἁμαρτίας, vii. 24 τοῦ σώματος τοῦ θανάτου τούτου, Phil. iii. 21 τὸ σῶμα τῆς ταπεινώσεως ἡμῶν. Thus τὸ σῶμα τῆς σαρκός here means 'the fleshly body' and not 'the entire mass of the flesh'; but the contrast between the whole and the part still remains. In i. 22 the same expression τὸ σῶμα τῆς σαρκός occurs, but with a different emphasis and meaning : see the note there.

The words τῶν ἁμαρτιῶν, inserted between τοῦ σώματος and τῆς σαρκός in the received text, are clearly a gloss, and must be omitted with the vast majority of ancient authorities.

12. Baptism is the grave of the old man, and the birth of the new. As he sinks beneath the baptismal waters, the believer buries there all his corrupt affections and past sins; as he emerges thence, he rises regenerate, quickened to new hopes and a new life. This it is, because it is not only the crowning act of his own faith but also the seal of God's adoption and the earnest of God's Spirit. Thus baptism is an image of his participation both in the death and in the resurrection of Christ. See *Apost. Const.* iii. 17 ἡ κατάδυσις τὸ

συναποθανεῖν, ἡ ἀνάδυσις τὸ συναναστῆναι. For this twofold image, as it presents itself to St Paul, see especially Rom. vi. 3 sq.

ἐν τῷ βαπτισμῷ] 'in the act of baptism.' A distinction seems to be observed elsewhere in the New Testament between βάπτισμα 'baptism' properly so called, and βαπτισμὸς 'lustration' or 'washing' of divers kinds, e. g. of vessels (Mark vii. 4, [8,] Heb. ix. 10). Even Heb. vi. 2 βαπτισμῶν διδαχῆς, which at first sight might seem to be an exception to this rule, is perhaps not really so (Bleek *ad loc.*). Here however, where the various readings βαπτισμῷ and βαπτίσματι appear in competition, the preference ought probably to be given to βαπτισμῷ as being highly supported in itself and as the less usual word in this sense. There is no *a priori* reason why St Paul should not have used βαπτισμὸς with this meaning, for it is so found in Josephus *Ant.* xviii. 5. 2 βαπτισμῷ συνιέναι (of John the Baptist). Doubtless the form βάπτισμα was more appropriate to describe the one final and complete act of Christian baptism, and it very soon obtained exclusive possession of the ground in Greek; but in St Paul's age the other form βαπτισμὸς may not yet have been banished. In the Latin Version *baptisma* and *baptismus* are used indiscriminately: and this is the case also with the Latin fathers. The substantive 'baptism' occurs so rarely in any sense in St Paul (only Rom. vi. 4, Eph. iv. 5, besides this passage), or indeed elsewhere in the N. T. of Christian baptism (only in 1 Pet. iii. 21), that we have not sufficient data for a sound induction. So far as the two words have any inherent difference of meaning, βαπτισμὸς denotes rather the act in process and βάπτισμα the result.

τῷ βαπτισμῷ, ἐν ᾧ καὶ συνηγέρθητε διὰ τῆς πίστεως
τῆς ἐνεργείας τοῦ Θεοῦ τοῦ ἐγείραντος αὐτὸν ἐκ [τῶν]

12. τῷ βαπτίσματι.

ἐν ᾧ] i.e. βαπτισμῷ. Others would
understand Χριστῷ for the sake of
the parallelism with ver. 11 ἐν ᾧ
καί...ἐν ᾧ καί. But this parallelism is
not suggested by the sense: while on
the other hand there is obviously a
very close connexion between συντα-
φέντες and συνηγέρθητε as the two
complementary aspects of baptism;
comp. Rom. vi. 4 sq. συνετάφημεν
αὐτῷ διὰ τοῦ βαπτίσματος ἵνα ὥσπερ
ἠγέρθη Χριστὸς...οὕτως καὶ ἡμεῖς...εἰ
γὰρ σύμφυτοι γεγόναμεν τῷ ὁμοιώματι
τοῦ θανάτου αὐτοῦ, ἀλλὰ καὶ τῆς
ἀναστάσεως ἐσόμεθα, 2 Tim. ii. 11
εἰ γὰρ συναπεθάνομεν, καὶ συνζή-
σομεν. In fact the idea of Χριστῷ
must be reserved for συνηγέρθητε
where it is wanted, 'ye were raised
together with Him.'

διὰ τῆς πίστεως κ.τ.λ.] 'through
your faith in the operation,' ἐνεργείας
being the objective genitive. So St
Chrysostom, πίστεως ὅλον ἐστίν· ἐπι-
στεύσατε ὅτι δύναται ὁ Θεὸς ἐγεῖραι,
καὶ οὕτως ἠγέρθητε. Only by a belief
in the resurrection are the benefits of
the resurrection obtained, because
only so are its moral effects produced.
Hence St Paul prays that he may
'know the power of Christ's resurrection' (Phil. iii. 10). Hence too he
makes this the cardinal article in the
Christian's creed, 'If thou...believest
in thy heart that God raised Him
from the dead, thou shalt be saved'
(Rom. x. 9). For the influence of
Christ's resurrection on the moral and
spiritual being, see the note on Phil.
l.c. Others take τῆς ἐνεργείας as the
subjective genitive, 'faith which comes
from the operation etc.,' arguing from
a mistaken interpretation of the parallel passage Ephes. i. 19 (where κατὰ
τὴν ἐνέργειαν should be connected, not
with τοὺς πιστεύοντας, but with τί τὸ

ὑπερβάλλον μέγεθος κ.τ.λ.). The former
explanation however yields a better
sense, and the genitive after πίστις
far more commonly describes the object than the source of the faith, e.g.
Rom. iii. 22, 26, Gal. iii. 22, Ephes. iii.
12, Phil. i. 27, iii. 9, 2 Thess. ii. 13.

13. In the sentence which follows
it seems necessary to assume a change
of subject. There can be little doubt
that ὁ Θεὸς is the nominative to συνεζωοποίησεν: for (1) The parallel passage Ephes. ii. 4, 5 directly suggests
this. (2) This is uniformly St Paul's
mode of speaking elsewhere. It is
always God who ἐγείρει, συνεγείρει,
ζωοποιεῖ, συνζωοποιεῖ, etc., with or in
or through Christ. (3) Though it might
be possible to assign σὺν αὐτῷ to the
subject of συνεζωοποίησεν (see the note
on i. 20), yet a reference to some other
person is more natural. These reasons
seem to decide the subject of συνεζωοποίησεν. But at the same time it
appears quite impossible to continue
the same subject, ὁ Θεός, to the end of
the sentence. No grammatical meaning can be assigned to ἀπεκδυσάμενος,
by which it could be understood of
God the Father. We must suppose
therefore that a new subject, ὁ Χριστός, is introduced meanwhile, either
with ἦρκεν or with ἀπεκδυσάμενος itself ; and of the two the former seems
the easier point of transition. For a
similar instance of abrupt transition,
which is the more natural owing to the
intimate connexion of the work of the
Son with the work of the Father, see
e.g. i. 17 sq.

καὶ ὑμᾶς] i.e. 'you Gentiles.' This
will appear from a study of the
parallel passages iii. 7, 8, Ephes. i. 13,
ii. 1 sq., 11, 13, 17, 22, iii. 2, iv. 17;
see the notes on Ephes. i. 13, and on
τῇ ἀκροβυστίᾳ just below.

νεκρῶν· ¹³καὶ ὑμᾶς νεκροὺς ὄντας τοῖς παραπτώμασιν
καὶ τῇ ἀκροβυστίᾳ τῆς σαρκὸς ὑμῶν, συνεζωοποίησεν

τοῖς παραπτώμασιν κ.τ.λ.] '*by reason
of your transgressions* etc.' The πα
ραπτώματα are the actual definite transgressions, while the ἀκροβυστία τῆς
σαρκὸς is the impure carnal disposition
which prompts to them. For the dative comp. Ephes. ii. 1, 5, where the
same expression occurs ; see Winer
Gramm. § xxxi. p. 270. On the other
hand in Rom. vi. 11 νεκροὺς μὲν τῇ
ἁμαρτίᾳ, ζῶντας δὲ τῷ Θεῷ, the dative
has a wholly different meaning, as the
context shows. The ἐν of the received
text, though highly supported, is doubtless an interpolation for the sake of
grammatical clearness.

τῇ ἀκροβυστίᾳ κ.τ.λ.] The external
fact is here mentioned, not for its own
sake but for its symbolical meaning.
The outward uncircumcision of the
Gentiles is a type of their unchastened
carnal mind. In other words, though
the literal meaning is not excluded,
the spiritual reference is most prominent, as appears from ver. 11 ἐν τῇ
ἀπεκδύσει τοῦ σώματος. Hence Theodore's comment, ἀκροβυστίαν (ἐκάλε
σεν) τὸ περικεῖσθαι ἔτι τὴν θνητότητα.
At the same time the choice of the
expression shows that the Colossian
converts addressed by St Paul were
mainly Gentiles.

συνεζωοποίησεν] It has been questioned whether the life here spoken of
should be understood in a spiritual
sense of the regeneration of the moral
being, or in a literal sense of the future life of immortality regarded as
conferred on the Christian potentially
now, though only to be realised hereafter. ·But is not such an issue altogether superfluous ? Is there any reason to think that St Paul would have
separated these two ideas of life ? To
him the future glorified life is only
the continuation of the present moral
and spiritual life. The two are the
same in essence, however the accidents

may differ. Moral and spiritual regeneration is salvation, is life.

ὑμᾶς] The pronoun is repeated for
the sake of emphasis. The omission
in some good copies is doubly explained ; (1) By the desire to simplify
the grammar ; (2) By the wish to relieve the awkwardness of the close
proximity between ὑμᾶς and ἡμῖν. This
latter consideration has led a few
good authorities to substitute ἡμᾶς for
ὑμᾶς, and others to substitute ὑμῖν for
ἡμῖν. For instances of these emphatic
repetitions in St Paul see the note on
i. 20 δι' αὐτοῦ.

σὺν αὐτῷ] 'with Christ,' as in Ephes.
ii. 5 συνεζωοποίησεν τῷ Χριστῷ. On
the inadmissibility of the reading αὐτῷ
see the note on εἰς αὐτὸν i. 20.

χαρισάμενος] '*having forgiven,*' as
in Luke vii. 42 sq., 2 Cor. ii. 7, 10,
xii. 13, Ephes. iv. 32; see also the note
on iii. 13 below. The idea of sin as a
debt incurred to God (Matt. vi. 12 τὰ
ὀφειλήματα ἡμῶν, comp. Luke xi. 4)
underlies this expression, as it does
also the commoner term for pardon,
ἄφεσις 'remission.' The image is
carried out in the cancelled bond,
ver. 14.

ἡμῖν] The person is changed; 'not
to you Gentiles only, but to us all
alike.' St Paul is eager to claim his
share in the transgression, that he
may claim it also in the forgiveness.
For other examples of the change
from the second to the first person,
see i. 10—13, iii. 3, 4, Ephes. ii. 2, 3,
13, 14, iv. 31, 32, v. 2 (the correct
reading), 1 Thess. v. 5, where the motive of the change is similar. See also
Gal. iii. 25, 26, iv. 5, 6, where there is
the converse transition.

14. ἐξαλείψας] '*having cancelled.*'
The word ἐξαλείφειν, like διαγράφειν,
signifying 'to blot out, to erase,' is
commonly opposed to ἐγγράφειν 'to
enter a name, etc.'; e.g. Arist. *Pax*

ὑμᾶς σὺν αὐτῷ, χαρισάμενος ἡμῖν πάντα τὰ παραπτώ-
ματα, ¹⁴ἐξαλείψας τὸ καθ᾽ ἡμῶν χειρόγραφον τοῖς

1181, Lysias c. Nicom. p. 183, Plato
Resp. vi. p. 501 B. More especially is
it so used in reference to an *item* in
an account, e.g. Demosth. c. *Aristog.*
i. p. 791 ἐγγράφονται πάντες οἱ ὀφλι-
σκάνοντες...ἐξαλήλιπται τὸ ὄφλημα.

τὸ καθ᾽ ἡμῶν κ.τ.λ.] '*the bond standing against us.*' The word χειρόγραφον, which means properly an autograph of any kind, is used almost exclusively for a note of hand, a bond or
obligation, as having the ' sign-manual '
of the debtor or contractor : e.g. Tobit
v. 3 (comp. ix. 5) ἔδωκεν αὐτῷ τὸ χειρόγραφον, Plut. *Mor.* p. 829 A τῶν χειρο-
γράφων καὶ συμβολαίων. It is more
common in Latin than in Greek, e.g.
Cic. *Fam.* vii. 18 ' Misi cautionem chi-
rographi mei,' Juv. *Sat.* xvi. 41 ' De-
bitor aut sumptos pergit non reddere
nummos, Vana supervacui dicens
chirographa ligni' (comp. xiii. 137).
Hence chirographum, chirographarius,
are frequent terms in the Roman law-
books; see Heumann-Hesse *Handlexicon zu den Quellen des römischen
Rechts* s.v. p. 74.

In the case before us the Jewish
people might be said to have signed
the contract when they bound themselves by a curse to observe all the
enactments of the law (Deut. xxvii.
14—26; comp. Exod. xxiv. 3); and
the primary reference would be to
them. But ἡμῖν, ἡμῶν, seem to include Gentiles as well as Jews, so that
a wider reference must be given to
the expression. The δόγματα therefore, though referring primarily to the
Mosaic ordinances, will include all
forms of positive decrees in which
moral or social principles are embodied or religious duties defined ; and
the ' bond ' is the moral assent of the
conscience, which (as it were) signs
and seals the obligation. The Gentiles, though ' not having a law, are a
law to themselves,' οἵτινες ἐνδείκνυνται

τὸ ἔργον τοῦ νόμου γραπτὸν ἐν ταῖς
καρδίαις αὐτῶν, συμμαρτυρούσης
αὐτῶν τῆς συνειδήσεως, Rom. ii. 14, 15.
See the notes on Gal. ii. 19, iv. 11.
Comp. Orig. *Hom. in Gen.* xiii. 4 (II.
p. 96).

τοῖς δόγμασιν] '*consisting in ordinances*': comp. Ephes. ii. 15 τὸν νόμον
τῶν ἐντολῶν ἐν δόγμασιν. The word
δόγμα is here used in its proper sense
of a ' decree,' ' ordinance,' corresponding to δογματίζεσθε below, ver. 20.
This is its only sense in the N. T.;
e.g. Luke ii. 1, Acts xvii. 7, of the
emperor's decrees ; Acts xvi. 4 of the
Apostolic ordinances. Here it refers
especially to the Mosaic law, as in
Joseph. *Ant.* xv. 5. 3 τὰ κάλλιστα τῶν
δογμάτων καὶ τὰ ὁσιώτατα τῶν ἐν τοῖς
νόμοις, Philo *Leg. All.* i. 16 (I. p. 54)
διατήρησις τῶν ἁγίων δογμάτων, 3 Macc.
i. 3 τῶν πατρίων δογμάτων. Comp.
Iren. *Fragm.* 38 (p. 855 Stieren) where,
immediately after a reference to our
text, τοῖς τῶν Ἰουδαίων δόγμασι προσ-
έρχεσθαι is opposed to πνευματικῶς
λειτουργεῖν. In the parallel passage,
Ephes. ii. 15, this is the exclusive
reference; but here (for reasons explained in the last note) it seems best
to give the term a secondary and
more extensive application.

The dative is perhaps best explained
as governed by the idea of γεγραμ-
μένον involved in χειρόγραφον (comp.
Plat. *Ep.* vii. p. 243 A τὰ γεγραμμένα
τύποις); as in 1 Tim. ii. 6 τὸ μαρτύριον
καιροῖς ἰδίοις, where καιροῖς depends
on an implied μεμαρτυρημένον. Otherwise it is taken as closely connected
with καθ᾽ ἡμῶν, ' the bond which was
in force against us by reason of the
ordinances': see Winer § xxxi. p. 273,
A. Buttmann p. 80. Possibly an ἐν
has dropped out of the text before
τοῖς δόγμασιν, owing to the similar
ending χειρογραφονεν (comp. Ephes.
ii. 15); but, if so, the omission must

δόγμασιν, ὃ ἦν ὑπεναντίον ἡμῖν· καὶ αὐτὸ ἦρκεν ἐκ

date from the earliest age, since no existing authorities exhibit any traces of such a reading; see the note on ver. 18 ἃ ἑόρακεν, and comp. Phil. ii. I εἴ τις σπλάγχνα.

A wholly different interpretation however prevails universally among Greek commentators both here and in Ephes. ii. 15. They take τοῖς δόγμασιν, ἐν δόγμασιν, to mean the 'doctrines or precepts of the Gospel,' and so to describe the instrument by which the abrogation of the law was effected. So Chrysostom, Severianus, Theodore of Mopsuestia, and Theodoret, followed by the later commentators Œcumenius and Theophylact. Strangely enough they do not allude to the correct interpretation; nor (with the exception of the passage ascribed to Irenæus which is quoted above) have I found any distinct traces of it in any Greek father. The grammatical difficulty would be taken to favour this interpretation, which moreover was characteristic of the age when the battle of creeds was fought. But it has been universally abandoned by modern interpreters, as plainly inappropriate to the context and also as severing the substantive δόγμα here from the verb δογματίζειν in ver. 20. The Latin fathers, who had either *decretis* or *sententiis* in their version, were saved from this false interpretation; e.g. Hilar. *de Trin.* i. 12 (II. p. 10), ix. 10 (II. p. 265 sq.), Ambros. *Apol. Dav.* 13 (I. p. 698), *de Fid.* iii. 2 (II. p. 499), August. *de Pecc. Mer.* i. 47 (x. p. 26): though they very commonly took τοῖς δόγμασιν, ἐν δόγμασιν, to refer to the decree of condemnation. Jerome however on Ephes. ii. 15 (VII. p. 581) follows the Greeks. The later Christian sense of δόγμα, meaning 'doctrine,' came from its secondary classical use, where it was applied to the authoritative and categorical 'sentences' of the philosophers: comp. Just. Mart. *Apol.* i. 7 (p. 56 D) οἱ ἐν

Ἕλλησι τὰ αὐτοῖς ἀρεστὰ δογματίσαντες ἐκ παντὸς τῷ ἑνὶ ὀνόματι φιλοσοφίας προσαγορεύονται, καίπερ τῶν δογμάτων ἐναντίων ὄντων, Cic. *Acad.* ii. 9 'de suis decretis quae philosophi vocant δόγματα,' Senec. *Epist.* xcv. 10 'Nulla ars contemplativa sine decretis suis est, quae Graeci vocant *dogmata*, nobis vel *decreta* licet adpellare vel *scita* vel *placita*.' See the indices to Plutarch, Epictetus, etc., for illustrations of the use of the term. There is an approach towards the ecclesiastical meaning in Ignat. *Magn.* 13 βεβαιωθῆναι ἐν τοῖς δόγμασιν τοῦ Κυρίου καὶ τῶν ἀποστόλων, Barnab. § 1 τρία οὖν δόγματά ἐστιν Κυρίου (comp. § 9, 10).

ὃ ἦν κ.τ.λ.] '*which was directly opposed to us*.' The former expression, τὸ καθ' ἡμῶν, referred to the *validity* of the bond; the present, ὃ ἦν ὑπεναντίον ἡμῖν, describes its *active hostility*. It is quite a mistake to suppose that the first preposition in ὑπεναντίος mitigates its force, as in ὑποδήλωσις, ὑπόλευκος, ὑπομαίνομαι, ὑποσημαίνειν, etc. Neither in classical writers nor in the LXX has the word any shade of this meaning. It is very commonly used, for instance, of things which are directly antagonistic and mutually exclusive: e. g. Aristot. *de Gen. et Corr.* i. 7 (p. 323) Δημόκριτος... φησὶ...τὸ αὐτὸ καὶ ὅμοιον εἶναι τό τε ποιοῦν καὶ τὸ πάσχον...ἐοίκασι δὲ οἱ τοῦτον τὸν τρόπον λέγοντες ὑπεναντία (i. e. self-contradictory) φαίνεσθαι λέγειν· αἴτιον δὲ τῆς ἐναντιολογίας κ.τ.λ., [Plato] *Alcib. Sec.* 138 c ΣΩ. Τὸ μαίνεσθαι ἆρα ὑπεναντίον σοι δοκεῖ τῷ φρονεῖν; ΑΛ. Πάνυ μὲν οὖν...139 B ΣΩ. Καὶ μὴν δύο γε ὑπεναντία ἑνὶ πράγματι πῶς ἂν εἴη; (i. e. how can one thing have two direct opposites?), where the whole argument depends on this sense of ὑπεναντίος. In compounds with ὑπὸ the force of the preposition will generally be determined by the meaning of the other element in the compound; and, as ἐναντίος (ἔναντι)

τοῦ μέσου, προσηλώσας αὐτὸ τῷ σταυρῷ· ¹⁵ ἀπεκδυ-

implies locality, a local sense is communicated to ὑπό. Thus ὑπεναντίος may be compared with ὑπαλλάσσειν, ὑπαντᾶν, ὑπαντιάζειν, ὑποτρέχειν (Xen. *Cyrop.* i. 2. 12 λῃστὰς ὑποδραμεῖν 'to hunt down'), ὑπελαύνειν (Xen. *Anab.* i. 8. 15 ὑπελάσας ὡς συναντῆσαι, 'riding up'), ὑφιστάναι (Polyb. i. 50 6 ὑπέστησε τὴν ἑαυτοῦ ναῦν ἀντίπρωρον τοῖς πολεμίοις,'he brought up' his own ship). With this meaning, 'over against,' 'close in upon,' the preposition does not weaken but enhance the force of ἐναντίος, so that the compound will denote ' direct,' ' close,' or ' persistent opposition.'

καὶ αὐτὸ ἦρκεν κ.τ.λ.] ' *and He*, i. e. Christ, *hath taken it away.*' There is a double change in this clause: (1) The participles (χαρισάμενος, ἐξαλεί-ψας) are replaced by a finite verb. (2) The aorists (συνεζωοποίησεν, χαρισάμενος, ἐξαλείψας) are replaced by a perfect. The substitution of ἦρεν for ἦρκεν in some copies betrays a consciousness on the part of the scribes of the dislocation produced by the new tense. As a new subject, ὁ Χριστός, must be introduced somewhere (see the note on ver. 13), the severance thus created suggests this as the best point of transition. The perfect ἦρκεν, 'He hath removed it,' is suggested by the feeling of relief and thanksgiving, which rises up in the Apostle's mind at this point. For the strong expression αἴρειν ἐκ [τοῦ] μέσου, 'to remove and put out of sight,' comp. LXX Is. lvii. 2, Epictet. iii. 3. 15, Plut. *Mor.* p. 519 D; so 2 Thess. ii. 7 ἐκ μέσου γένηται.

προσηλώσας κ.τ.λ.] ' The abrogation was even more emphatic. Not only was the writing erased, but the document itself was torn up and cast aside.' By προσηλώσας is meant that the law of ordinances was nailed to the cross, rent with Christ's body, and destroyed with His death: see the notes on Gal. vi. 14 δι' οὗ [τοῦ

σταυροῦ] ἐμοὶ κόσμος (the world, the sphere of material ordinances) ἐσταύρωται κἀγὼ κόσμῳ, where the idea is the same. It has been supposed that in some cities the abrogation of a decree was signified by running a nail through it and hanging it up in public. The image would thus gain force, but there is no distinct evidence of such a custom.

15. ἀπεκδυσάμενος κ.τ.λ.] This word appears not to occur at all before St Paul, and rarely if ever after his time, except in writers who may be supposed to have his language before them; e.g. Hippol. *Haer.* i. 24 ἀπεκδυσάμενον τὸ σῶμα ὃ περίκειται. In Joseph. *Ant.* vi. 14. 2 ἀπεκδὺς is only a variation for μετεκδὺς which seems to be the correct reading. The word also appears in some texts of Babrius *Fab.* xviii. 3, but it is merely a conjectural emendation. Thus the occurrence of ἀπεκδύεσθαι here and in iii. 9, and of ἀπέκδυσις above in ver. 11, is remarkable; and the choice of an unusual, if not a wholly new, word must have been prompted by the desire to emphasize the *completeness* of the action. The force of the double compound may be inferred from a passage of Lysias, where the two words ἀποδύεσθαι and ἐκδύεσθαι occur together; *c. Theomn.* i. 10 (p. 117) φάσκων θοἰμάτιον ἀποδεδύσθαι ἢ τὸν χιτωνίσκον ἐκδεδύσθαι. Here however the sense of ἀπεκδυσάμενος is difficult. The meaning generally assigned to it, 'having spoiled, stripped of their arms,' disregards the middle voice. St Jerome is chiefly responsible for this common error of interpretation: for in place of the Old Latin ' exuens se,' which was grammatically correct, he substituted ' exspolians ' in his revised version. In his interpretation however he was anticipated by the commentator Hilary, who read ' exuens ' for ' exuens se ' in his text. Discarding this sense, as inconsistent with

σάμενος τὰς ἀρχὰς καὶ   τὰς ἐξουσίας ἐδειγμάτι-

the voice, we have the choice of two interpretations.

(1) The common interpretation of the Latin fathers, '*putting off* the body,' thus separating ἀπεκδυσάμενος from τὰς ἀρχὰς κ.τ.λ. and understanding τὴν σάρκα or τὸ σῶμα with it; comp. 2 Cor. v. 3 ἐνδυσάμενοι. So Novat. *de Trin.* 16 'exutus carnem'; Ambros. *Expos. Luc.* v. § 107 (I. p. 1381) 'exuens se carnem,' comp. *de Fid.* iii. 2 (II. p. 499); Hilar. *de Trin.* i. 13 (II. p. 10) 'exutus carnem' (comp. ix. 10, p. 265), x. 48 (p. 355) 'spolians se carne' (comp. ix. 11, p. 266); Augustin. *Epist.* 149 (II. p. 513) 'exuens se carne,' etc. This appears to have been the sense adopted much earlier in a Docetic work quoted by Hippol. *Haer.* viii. 10 ψυχὴ ἐκείνη ἐν τῷ σώματι τραφεῖσα, ἀπεκδυσαμένη τὸ σῶμα καὶ προσηλώσασα πρὸς τὸ ξύλον καὶ θριαμβεύσασα κ.τ.λ. It is so paraphrased likewise in the Peshito Syriac and the Gothic. The reading ἀπεκδυσάμενος τὴν σάρκα καὶ τὰς ἐξουσίας (omitting τὰς ἀρχὰς καὶ), found in some ancient authorities, must be a corruption from an earlier text, which had inserted the gloss τὴν σάρκα after ἀπεκδυσάμενος, while retaining τὰς ἀρχὰς καὶ, and which seems to have been in the hands of some of the Latin fathers already quoted. This interpretation has been connected with a common metaphorical use of ἀποδύεσθαι, signifying 'to strip' and so 'to prepare for a contest'; e. g. Plut. *Mor.* 811 E πρὸς πᾶσαν ἀποδυόμενοι τὴν πολιτικὴν πρᾶξιν, Diod. Sic. ii. 29 ἐπὶ φιλοσοφίαν ἀποδύντες. The serious objection to this rendering is, that it introduces an isolated metaphor which is not explained or suggested by anything in the context.

(2) The common interpretation of the Greek fathers; '*having stripped off and put away the powers* of evil,' making ἀπεκδυσάμενος govern τὰς ἀρχὰς κ.τ.λ. So Chrysostom, Severianus,

Theodore of Mopsuestia, and Theodoret. This also appears to have been the interpretation of Origen, *in Matt.* xii. § 25 (III. p. 544), *ib.* § 40 (p. 560), *in Ioann.* vi. § 37 (IV. p. 155), *ib.* xx. § 29 (p. 356), though his language is not explicit, and though his translators, e. g. *in Libr. Ies. Hom.* vii. § 3 (II. p. 413), make him say otherwise. The meaning then will be as follows. Christ took upon Himself our human nature with all its temptations (Heb. iv. 15). The powers of evil gathered about Him. Again and again they assailed Him; but each fresh assault ended in a new defeat. In the wilderness He was tempted by Satan; but Satan retired for the time baffled and defeated (Luke iv. 13 ἀπέστη ἀπ' αὐτοῦ ἄχρι καιροῦ). Through the voice of His chief disciple the temptation was renewed, and He was entreated to decline His appointed sufferings and death. Satan was again driven off (Matt. xvi. 23 ὕπαγε ὀπίσω μου, Σατανᾶ, σκάνδαλον εἶ ἐμοῦ: comp. Matt. viii. 31). Then the last hour came. This was the great crisis of all, when 'the power of darkness' made itself felt (Luke xxii. 53 ἡ ἐξουσία τοῦ σκότους; see above i. 13), when the prince of the world asserted his tyranny (Joh. xii. 31 ὁ ἄρχων τοῦ κόσμου). The final act in the conflict began with the agony of Gethsemane; it ended with the cross of Calvary. The victory was complete. The enemy of man was defeated. The powers of evil, which had clung like a Nessus robe about His humanity, were torn off and cast aside for ever. And the victory of mankind is involved in the victory of Christ. In His cross we too are divested of the poisonous clinging garments of temptation and sin and death; τῷ ἀποθέσθαι τὴν θνητότητα, says Theodore, ἣν ὑπὲρ τῆς κοινῆς ἀφεῖλεν εὐεργεσίας, ἀπεδύσατο κἀκείνων (i. e. τῶν ἀντικειμένων δυνάμεων) τὴν αὐθεντείαν ἥπερ ἐκέχρηντο

σεν ἐν παρρησίᾳ, θριαμβεύσας αὐτοὺς ἐν αὐτῷ.

καθ' ἡμῶν. . For the image of the garments comp. Is. lxiv. 6, but especially Zech. iii. 1 sq., 'And he showed me Joshua the high-priest standing before the angel of the Lord and *Satan standing at his right hand to resist him.* And the Lord said unto Satan, The Lord rebuke thee, O Satan ... Now Joshua was clothed with filthy garments... And He answered and spake unto those that stood before Him, saying, *Take away the filthy garments* from him. And unto him He said, Behold, *I have caused thine iniquity to pass from thee.*' In this prophetic passage the image is used of His type and namesake, the Jesus of the Restoration, not in his own person, but as the high-priest and representative of a guilty but cleansed and forgiven people, with whom he is identified. For the metaphor of ἀπεκδυσάμενος more especially, see Philo *Quod det. pot. ins.* 13 (I. p. 199) ἐξαναστάντες δὲ καὶ διερεισάμενοι τὰς ἐντέχνους αὐτῶν περιπλοκὰς εὐμαρῶς ἐ κ δ υσ ό μ ε θ α, where the image in the context is that of a wrestling bout.

This interpretation is grammatical; it accords with St Paul's teaching; and it is commended by the parallel uses of the substantive in ver. 11 ἐν τῇ ἀπεκδύσει τοῦ σώματος τῆς σαρκός, and of the verb in iii. 9 ἀπεκδυσάμενοι τὸν παλαιὸν ἄνθρωπον κ.τ.λ. The ἀπέκδυσις accomplished in us when we are baptized into His death is a counterpart to the ἀπέκδυσις which He accomplished by His death. With Him indeed it was only the temptation, with us it is the sin as well as temptation; but otherwise the parallel is complete. In both cases it is a divestiture of the powers of evil, a liberation from the dominion of the flesh. On the other hand the common explanation ' spoiling' is not less a violation of St Paul's usage (iii. 9) than of grammatical rule.

τὰς ἀρχὰς κ.τ.λ.] What powers are especially meant here will appear from

Ephes. vi. 12 πρὸς τὰς ἀρχάς, πρὸς τὰς ἐξουσίας, πρὸς τοὺς κοσμοκράτορας τοῦ σκότους τούτου, πρὸς τὰ πνευματικὰ τῆς πονηρίας κ.τ.λ. See the note on i. 16.

ἐδειγμάτισεν] '*displayed,*' as a victor displays his captives or trophies in a triumphal procession: Hor. *Epist.* i. 17. 33 ' captos ostendere civibus hostes.' The word is extremely rare; Matt. i. 19 μὴ θέλων αὐτὴν δειγματίσαι (where it ought probably to be read for the more common word παραδειγματίσαι), *Act. Paul. et Petr.* 33 ἔλεγε πρὸς τὸν λαὸν ἵνα μὴ μόνον ἀπὸ τῆς τοῦ Σίμωνος ἀπάτης φύγωσιν ἀλλὰ καὶ δειγματίσουσιν αὐτόν. Nowhere does the word convey the idea of 'making an example' (παραδειγματίσαι) but signifies simply ' to display, publish, proclaim.' In the context of the last passage we have as the consequence, ὥστε πάντας τοὺς εὐλαβεῖς ἄνδρας βδελύττεσθαι Σίμωνα τὸν μάγον καὶ ἀνόσιον αὐτὸν κ α τ α γ γ έ λ λ ε ι ν, i.e. to *proclaim* his impieties. The substantive occurs on the Rosetta stone l. 30 (Boeckh *C. I.* 4697) τῶν συντετελεσμένων τὰ πρὸς τὸν δειγματισμὸν διάφορα.

ἐν παρρησίᾳ] '*boldly,*' not '*publicly.*' As παρρησία is 'unreservedness, plainness of speech' (παν-ρησία, its opposite being ἀρρησία ' silence'), so while applied still to language, it may be opposed either (1) to 'fear,' as John vii. 13, Acts iv. 29, or (2) to ' ambiguity, reserve,' Joh. xi. 14, xvi. 25, 29; but ' misgiving, apprehension' in some form or other seems to be always the correlative idea. Hence, when it is transferred from words to actions, it appears always to retain the idea of ' confidence, boldness'; e.g. 1 Macc. iv. 18 λήψετε τὰ σκῦλα μετὰ παρρησίας, *Test. xii Patr.* Rub. 4 οὐκ εἶχον παρρησίαν ἀτενίσαι εἰς πρόσωπον Ἰακώβ, Jos. *Ant.* ix. 10. 4 ὑπ' αἰσχύνης τε τοῦ συμβεβηκότος δεινοῦ καὶ τοῦ μηκέτ' αὐτῷ παρρησίαν εἶναι. The idea of publicity may sometimes be connected with the word as a secondary notion,

^{16}Μὴ οὖν τις ὑμᾶς κρινέτω ἐν βρώσει καὶ ἐν πόσει ἢ

16. ἢ ἐν πόσει.

e.g. in Joh. vii. 4, where ἐν παρρησίᾳ εἶναι 'to assume a bold attitude' is opposed to ἐν κρυπτῷ ποιεῖν (comp. xviii. 20); but it does not displace the primary sense.

θριαμβεύσας] '*leading them in triumph*,' the same metaphor as in 2 Cor. ii. 14 τῷ πάντοτε θριαμβεύοντι ἡμᾶς ἐν τῷ Χριστῷ κ.τ.λ., where it is wrongly translated in the A.V. 'causeth us to triumph.' Here however it is the defeated powers of evil, there the subjugated persons of men, who are led in public, chained to the triumphal car of Christ. This is the proper meaning and construction of θριαμβεύειν, as found elsewhere. This verb takes an accusative (1) of the person over whom the triumph is celebrated, e.g. Plut. *Vit. Arat.* 54 τοῦτον Αἰμίλιος ἐθριάμβευσε, *Thes. et Rom. Comp.* 4 βασιλεῖς ἐθριάμβευσε: (2) of the spoils exhibited in the triumph, e.g. Tatian *c. Graec.* 26 παύσασθε λόγους ἀλλοτρίους θριαμβεύοντες καί, ὥσπερ ὁ κυλοιός, οὐκ ἰδίοις ἐπικοσμούμενοι πτεροῖς: (3) more rarely of the substance of the triumph, e.g. *Vit. Camill.* 30 ὁ δὲ Κάμιλλος ἐθριάμβευσε...τὸν ἀπολωλυίας σωτῆρα πατρίδος γενόμενον, i. e. 'in the character of his country's saviour.' The passive θριαμβεύεσθαι is 'to be led in triumph,' 'to be triumphed over,' e.g. *Vit. C. Marc.* 35. So the Latins say 'triumphare aliquem' and 'triumphari.'

ἐν αὐτῷ] i. e. τῷ σταυρῷ: comp. Ephes. ii. 16 ἀποκαταλλάξῃ τοὺς ἀμφοτέρους...διὰ τοῦ σταυροῦ. The violence of the metaphor is its justification. The paradox of the crucifixion is thus placed in the strongest light—triumph in helplessness and glory in shame. The convict's gibbet is the victor's car.

16—19. 'Seeing then that the bond is cancelled, that the law of ordinances is repealed, beware of subjecting yourselves to its tyranny again. Suffer no

man to call you to account in the matter of eating or drinking, or again of the observance of a festival or a new moon or a sabbath. These are only shadows thrown in advance, only types of things to come. The substance, the reality, in every case belongs to the Gospel of Christ. The prize is now fairly within your reach. Do not suffer yourselves to be robbed of it by any stratagem of the false teachers. Their religion is an officious humility which displays itself in the worship of angels. They make a parade of their visions, but they are following an empty phantom. They profess humility, but they are puffed up with their vaunted wisdom, which is after all only the mind of the flesh. Meanwhile they have substituted inferior spiritual agencies for the One true Mediator, the Eternal Word. Clinging to these lower intelligences, they have lost their hold of the Head; they have severed their connexion with Him, on whom the whole body depends; from whom it derives its vitality, and to whom it owes its unity, being supplied with nourishment and knit together in one by means of the several joints and attachments, so that it grows with a growth which comes from God Himself.'

16 sq. The two main tendencies of the Colossian heresy are discernible in this warning (vv. 16—19), as they were in the previous statement (vv. 9 —15). Here however the order is reversed. The practical error, an excessive ritualism and ascetic rigour, is first dealt with (vv. 16, 17); the theological error, the interposition of angelic mediators, follows after (vv. 18, 19). The first is the substitution of a shadow for the substance; the second is the preference of an inferior member to the head. The reversal of order is owing to the connexion of the paragraphs; the opening subject in

ἐν μέρει ἑορτῆς ἢ νεομηνίας ἢ σαββάτων, ¹⁷ ἅ ἐστιν σκιὰ

17. ὅ ἐστιν σκιά.

the second paragraph being a continuation of the concluding subject in
the first, by the figure called chiasm:
comp. Gal. iv. 5.

κρινέτω] not 'condemn you,' but
'take you to task'; as e.g. Rom. xiv.
3 sq. The judgment may or may not
end in an acquittal; but in any case
it is wrong, since these matters ought
not to be taken as the basis of a judgment.

ἐν βρώσει κ.τ.λ.] 'in eating and
in drinking'; Rom. xiv. 17 οὐ γάρ
ἐστιν ἡ βασιλεία τοῦ Θεοῦ βρῶσις καὶ
πόσις, ἀλλὰ δικαιοσύνη κ.τ.λ., Heb. ix.
10 ἐπὶ βρώμασιν καὶ πόμασιν καὶ διαφόροις βαπτισμοῖς, δικαιώματα σαρκός,
comp. 1 Cor. viii. 8 βρῶμα δὲ ἡμᾶς οὐ
παραστήσει τῷ Θεῷ κ.τ.λ. The first
indication that the Mosaic distinctions
of things clean and unclean should be
abolished is given by our Lord Himself: Mark vii. 14 sq. (the correct reading in ver. 19 being καθαρίζων πάντα τὰ
βρώματα). They were afterwards formally annulled by the vision which appeared to St Peter: Acts x. 11 sq.
The ordinances of the Mosaic law
applied almost exclusively to meats.
It contained no prohibitions respecting drinks except in a very few cases;
e.g. of the priests ministering in the
tabernacle (Lev. x. 9), of liquids contained in unclean vessels etc. (Lev.
xi. 34, 36), and of Nazarite vows
(Num. vi. 3). These directions, taken
in connexion with the rigid observances which the later Jews had
grafted on them (Matt. xxiii. 24),
would be sufficient to explain the expression, when applied to the Mosaic
law by itself, as in Heb. l.c. The rigour
of the Colossian false teachers however, like that of their Jewish prototypes the Essenes, doubtless went far
beyond the injunctions of the law. It
is probable that they forbad wine and
animal food altogether: see the introduction pp. 86, 104 sq. For allusions

in St Paul to similar observances not
required by the law, see Rom. xiv. 2
ὁ δὲ ἀσθενῶν λάχανα ἐσθίει, ver. 21 καλὸν τὸ μὴ φαγεῖν κρέα μηδὲ πιεῖν οἶνον
κ.τ.λ., 1 Tim. iv. 2, 3 κωλυόντων...ἀπέ-
χεσθαι βρωμάτων ἃ ὁ Θεὸς ἔκτισεν κ.τ.λ.,
Tit. i. 14 μὴ προσέχοντες...ἐντολαῖς
ἀνθρώπων...πάντα καθαρὰ τοῖς καθαροῖς.
The correct reading seems to be καὶ
ἐν πόσει, thus connecting together the
words between which there is a natural affinity. Comp. Philo Vit. Moys.
i. § 33 (II. p. 110) δεσποίναις χαλεπαῖς
συνεζευγμένον βρώσει καὶ πόσει, Ign.
Trall. 2 οὐ γὰρ βρωμάτων καὶ ποτῶν
εἰσὶν διάκονοι.

ἐν μέρει] 'in the matter of,' etc.;
comp. 2 Cor. iii. 10, ix. 3 ἐν τῷ μέρει
τούτῳ. The expression seems originally to mean 'in the division or category,' and in classical writers most
commonly occurs in connexion with
such words as τιθέναι, ποιεῖσθαι, ἀριθ-
μεῖν, etc.: comp. Demosth. c. Aristocr.
§ 148 ὅσα...στρατιώτης ὢν ἐν σφενδο-
νήτου καὶ ψιλοῦ μέρει...ἐστράτευται, i.e.
'in the capacity of.' Hence it gets
to signify more widely, as here, 'with
respect to,' 'by reason of': comp.
Philo Quod det. pot. ins. § 2 (I. p. 192)
ἐν μέρει λόγου τοῦ προκόπτοντος κατὰ
τὸν πατέρα κοσμοῦνται, in Flacc. 20
(II. p. 542) ὅσα ἐν μέρει χάριτος καὶ δωρεᾶς ἔλαβον. But Ælian V. H. viii. 3
κρίνοντες ἕκαστον ἐν τῷ μέρει φόνου,
quoted by the commentators, is a false
parallel: for φόνου is there governed
by κρίνοντες and ἐν τῷ μέρει means 'in
his turn.'

ἑορτῆς κ.τ.λ.] The same three words
occur together, as an exhaustive enumeration of the sacred times among
the Jews, in 1 Chron. xxiii. 31, 2 Chron.
ii. 4, xxxi. 3, Ezek. xlv. 17, Hos. ii. 11,
Justin Dial. 8, p. 226; comp. Is. i. 13,
14. See also Gal. iv. 10 ἡμέρας παρα-
τηρεῖσθε καὶ μῆνας καὶ καιροὺς καὶ ἐνι-
αυτούς, where the first three words
correspond to the three words used

τῶν μελλόντων, τὸ δὲ σῶμα τοῦ Χριστοῦ. ¹⁸μηδεὶς

here, though the order is reversed. The ἑορτή here, like the καιροί there, refers chiefly to the *annual* festivals, the passover, pentecost, etc. The νεο-μηνία here describes more precisely the *monthly* festival, which is there designated more vaguely as μῆνες. The σάββατα here gives by name the *weekly* holy-day, which is there indicated more generally by ἡμέραι.

νεομηνίας] See Num. xxviii. 11 sq. The forms νεομηνία and νουμηνία seem to be used indifferently in the common dialect, though the latter is more common. In the Attic νουμηνία alone was held to be correct; see Lobeck *Phryn.* p. 148. On the whole the preference should perhaps be given to νεομηνίας here, as supported by some authorities which are generally trustworthy in matters of orthography, and as being the less usual form in itself.

σαββάτων] '*a sabbath-day*,' not, as the A. V., '*sabbath days*'; for the co-ordinated words ἑορτῆς, νεομηνίας, are in the singular. The word σάββατα is derived from the Aramaic (as distinguished from the Hebrew) form שַׁבְּתָא, and accordingly preserves the Aramaic termination in *a*. Hence it was naturally declined as a plural noun, σάββατα, σαββάτων. The general use of σάββατα, when a single sabbath-day was meant, will appear from such passages as Jos. *Ant.* i. 1. 1 ἄγο-μεν τὴν ἡμέραν, προσαγορεύοντες αὐτὴν σάββατα, *ib.* iii. 10. 1 ἑβδόμην ἡμέραν ἥτις σάββατα καλεῖται, Plut. *Mor.* 169 c Ἰουδαῖοι σαββάτων ὄντων ἐν ἀγνάμπτοις καθεζόμενοι, *ib.* 671 F οἶμαι δὲ καὶ τὴν τῶν σαββάτων ἑορτὴν μὴ παντά-πασιν ἀπροσδιόνυσον εἶναι, Hor. *Sat.* i. 9. 69 'hodie tricesima sabbata.' In the New Testament σάββατα is only once used distinctly of more than a single day, and there the plurality of meaning is brought out by the attached numeral; Acts xvii. 2 ἐπὶ σάβ-βατα τρία.

On the observance of days and seasons see again Gal. iv. 10, Rom. xiv. 5, 6. A strong anti-Judaic view on the subject is expressed in the *Epist. ad Diogn.* § 4. Origen *c. Cels.* viii. 21, 22, after referring to Thucyd. i. 70 μήτε ἑορτὴν ἄλλο τι ἡγεῖσθαι ἢ τὸ τὰ δέοντα πρᾶξαι, says ὁ τέλειος, ἀεὶ ἐν τοῖς λό-γοις ὢν καὶ τοῖς ἔργοις καὶ τοῖς διανοή-μασι τοῦ τῇ φύσει κυρίου λόγου Θεοῦ, ἀεί ἐστιν αὐτοῦ ἐν ταῖς ἡμέραις καὶ ἀεὶ ἄγει κυριακὰς ἡμέρας, and he then goes on to explain what is the παρασκευή, the πάσχα, the πεντηκοστή, of such a man. The observance of sacred times was an integral part of the old dispensation. Under the new they have ceased to have any value, except as a means to an end. The great principle that 'the sabbath was made for man and not man for the sabbath,' though underlying the Mosaic ordinances, was first distinctly pronounced by our Lord. The setting apart of special days for the service of God is a confession of our imperfect state, an avowal that we cannot or do not devote our whole time to Him. Sabbaths will then ultimately be superseded, when our life becomes one eternal sabbath. Meanwhile the Apostle's rebuke warns us against attributing to any holy days whatever a meaning and an importance which is alien to the spirit of the New Covenant. Bengel on the text writes, 'Sabbatum non laudatur, non imperatur; dominica memoratur, non praecipitur. Qui profundius in mundi negotiis haerent, his utilis et necessarius est dies definitus: qui semper sabbatizant, majori libertate gaudent.' Yes: but these last are just they who will most scrupulously restrict their liberty, so as ἀπρόσκοποι γίνεσθαι.

17. Two ideas are prominent in this image. (1) The contrast between the ordinances of the Law and the teaching of the Gospel, as the shadow and the substance respectively; Philo

ὑμᾶς καταβραβευέτω θέλων ἐν ταπεινοφροσύνῃ καὶ

de Conf. ling. 37 (I. p. 434) νομίσαντας τὰ μὲν ῥητὰ τῶν χρησμῶν σκιάς τινας ὡσανεὶ σωμάτων εἶναι, Joseph. *B. J.* ii. 2. 5 σκιὰν αἰτησόμενος βασιλείας ἧς ἥρπασεν ἑαυτῷ τὸ σῶμα; comp. Philo *in Flacc.* 19 (II. p. 541) σκιὰ πραγμάτων ἄρ᾽ ἦσαν, οὐ πράγματα. (2) The conception of the shadow as thrown before the substance (ἡ δὲ σκιὰ προτρέχει τοῦ σώματος, says a Greek commentator), so that the Law was a type and presage of the Gospel; Heb. x. 1 σκιὰν ἔχων ὁ νόμος τῶν μελλόντων ἀγαθῶν (comp. viii. 5). Thus it implies both the *unsubstantiality* and the *supersession* of the Mosaic ritual.

ἅ] '*which things,*' whether distinctions of meats or observances of times. If the other reading ὅ be taken, it will refer to the preceding sentence generally, as if the antecedent were 'the whole system of ordinances.'

τὸ δὲ σῶμα κ.τ.λ.] As the shadow belonged to Moses, so '*the substance belongs to Christ*'; i.e. the reality, the antitype, in each case is found in the Christian dispensation. Thus the passover typifies the atoning sacrifice; the unleavened bread, the purity and sincerity of the true believer; the pentecostal feast, the ingathering of the first fruits; the sabbath, the rest of God's people; etc.

18. The Christian's career is the contest of the stadium (δρόμος, Acts xx. 24, 2 Tim. iv. 7); Christ is the umpire, the dispenser of the rewards (2 Tim. iv. 8); life eternal is the bay wreath, the victor's prize (βραβεῖον, 1 Cor. ix. 24, Phil. iii. 14). The Colossians were in a fair way to win this prize; they had entered the lists duly; they were running bravely: but the false teachers, thrusting themselves in the way, attempted to trip them up or otherwise impede them in the race, and thus to rob them of their just reward. For the idea of καταβραβευέτω compare especially Gal. v. 7

ἐτρέχετε καλῶς· τίς ὑμᾶς ἐνέκοψεν κ.τ.λ.

καταβραβευέτω] '*rob of the prize,* the βραβεῖον'; comp. Demosth. *Mid.* p. 544 (one of the documents) ἐπιστάμεθα Στράτωνα ὑπὸ Μειδίου καταβραβευθέντα καὶ παρὰ πάντα τὰ δίκαια ἀτιμωθέντα, which presents a close parallel to the use of καταβραβεύειν here. See also Eustath. on *Il.* i. 403 sq. (p. 43) καταβραβεύει αὐτόν, ὥς φασιν οἱ παλαιοί, ib. *Opusc.* 277, etc. The false teachers at Colossæ are not regarded as umpires nor as successful rivals, but simply as persons frustrating those who otherwise would have won the prize. The word καταβραβεύειν is wide enough to include such. The two compounds καταβραβεύειν and παραβραβεύειν (Plut. *Mor.* p. 535 C οἱ παραβραβεύοντες ἐν τοῖς ἀγῶσι) only differ in this respect, that *deprivation* is the prominent idea in the former word and *trickery* in the latter. Jerome, *Epist.* cxxi *ad Algas.* (I. p. 879), sets down this word, which he wrongly interprets 'bravium accipiat adversum vos,' as one of St Paul's Cilicisms. The passages quoted (whether the document in the Midias be authentic or not) are sufficient to show that this statement is groundless.

θέλων ἐν] '*taking delight in,*' '*devoting himself to.*' The expression is common in the LXX, most frequently as a translation of "בְּ חָפֵץ, 1 Sam. xviii. 22, 2 Sam. xv. 26, 1 Kings x. 9, 2 Chron. ix. 8, Ps. cxi. 1, cxlvi. 10, but in one passage of "בְּ רָצָה, 1 Chron. xxviii. 4. So too *Test. xii Patr.* Asher 1 ἐὰν οὖν ἡ ψυχὴ θέλῃ ἐν καλῷ. Comp. also 1 Macc. iv. 42 θελητὰς νόμου, and see ἐθελοθρησκεία below. Against this construction no valid objection has been urged. Otherwise θέλων is taken absolutely, and various senses have been assigned to it, such as 'imperiously' or 'designedly' or 'wilfully' or 'gladly, readily'; but these are either unsupported by

θρησκεία τῶν ἀγγέλων, ἃ ἑόρακεν ἐμβατεύων, εἰκῇ φυ-

usage or inappropriate to the context.
Leclerc (*ad loc.*) and Bentley (*Crit.
Sacr.* p. 59) conjectured θέλγων; Toup
(*Emend. in Suid.* II. p. 63) more plau-
sibly ἐλθών; but the passages quoted
show that no correction is needed.

ταπεινοφροσύνη] Humility is a vice
with heathen moralists, but a virtue
with Christian Apostles; see the note
on Phil. ii. 3. In this passage, which
(with ver. 23) forms the sole exception
to the general language of the Apostles, the divergence is rather apparent than real. The disparagement is
in the accompaniments and not in the
word itself. Humility, when it becomes self-conscious, ceases to have
any value; and self-consciousness at
least, if not affectation, is implied by
θέλων ἐν. Moreover the character of
the ταπεινοφροσύνη in this case is further defined as θρησκεία τῶν ἀγγέλων,
which was altogether a perversion of
the truth.

θρησκείᾳ] This word is closely connected with the preceding by the vinculum of the same preposition. There
was an officious parade of humility in
selecting these lower beings as inter-
cessors, rather than appealing directly to the throne of grace. The
word refers properly to the external
rites of religion, and so gets to signify an over-scrupulous devotion to
external forms; as in Philo *Quod det.
pot. ins.* 7 (I. p. 195) θρησκείαν ἀντὶ
ὁσιότητος ἡγούμενος, Plut. *Vit. Alex.*
2 δοκεῖ καὶ τὸ θρησκεύειν ὄνομα ταῖς
κατακόροις γενέσθαι καὶ περιέργοις
ἱερουργίαις: comp. Acts xxvi. 5, and
see the well-known remarks of Cole-
ridge on James i. 26, 27, in *Aids to
Reflection* p. 14. In the LXX θρησκεύειν, θρησκεία, together occur four
times (Wisd. xi. 16, xiv. 16, 18, 27),
and in all these examples the reference is to idolatrous or false worship.
Indeed generally the usage of the
word exhibits a tendency to a bad
sense.

τῶν ἀγγέλων] For the angelology
and the angelolatry of these Colossian
false teachers, more especially in its
connexion with Essene teaching, see
the introduction, pp. 89 sq., 101 sq.,
110, 115 sq. For the prominence which
was given to angelology in the speculations of the Jews generally, see the
Preaching of Peter quoted in Clem.
Alex. *Strom.* vi. 5 (p. 760) μηδὲ κατὰ
Ἰουδαίους σέβεσθε, καὶ γὰρ ἐκεῖνοι...
οὐκ ἐπίστανται λατρεύοντες ἀγγέλοις
καὶ ἀρχαγγέλοις, Celsus in Orig. *c. Cels.*
v. 6 (I. p. 580) πρῶτον οὖν τῶν Ἰουδαίων
θαυμάζειν ἄξιον, εἰ τὸν μὲν οὐρανὸν καὶ
τοὺς ἐν τῷδε ἀγγέλους σέβουσι κ.τ.λ.,
comp. *ib.* i. 26 (p. 344). From Jews
it naturally spread to Judaizing
Christians; e.g. *Clem. Hom.* iii. 36
ἀγγέλων ὀνόματα γνωρίζειν, viii. 12 sq.,
Test. xii Patr. Levi 3 (quoted above
on l. 16). The interest however extended to more orthodox circles, as
appears from the passage in Ignat.
Trall. 5 μὴ οὐ δύναμαι τὰ ἐπουράνια
γράψαι ;...δύναμαι νοεῖν τὰ ἐπουράνια
καὶ τὰς τοποθεσίας τὰς ἀγγελικὰς καὶ
τὰς συστάσεις τὰς ἀρχοντικάς κ.τ.λ. (see
the note there). Of angelology among
Gnostic sects see Iren. ii. 30. 6, ii. 32.
5, Orig. *c. Cels.* vi. 30 sq. (I. p. 653),
Clem. Alex. *Exc. Theod.* p. 970 sq.,
Pistis Sophia pp. 2, 19, 23, etc.

ἃ ἑόρακεν κ.τ.λ.] literally '*invading
what he has seen*,' which is generally
explained to mean 'parading' or 'por-
ing over his visions.' For this sense of
ἐμβατεύειν, which takes either a genitive or a dative or an accusative, comp.
Philo *de Plant. Noe* ii. 19 (I. p. 341)
οἱ προσωτέρω χωροῦντες τῶν ἐπιστημῶν καὶ ἐπὶ πλέον ἐμβατεύοντες αὐταῖς,
2 Macc. ii. 30 τὸ μὲν ἐμβατεύοντες καὶ
περὶ πάντων ποιεῖσθαι λόγον καὶ πολυ-
πραγμονεῖν ἐν τοῖς κατὰ μέρος. At a
later date this sense becomes common, e.g. Nemesius *de Nat. Hom.*
p. 64 (ed. Matthæi) οὐρανὸν ἐμβατεύει
τῇ θεωρίᾳ. In Xen. *Symp.* iv. 27 ἐν
τῷ αὐτῷ βιβλίῳ ἀμφότεροι ἐμβατεύετέ

σιούμενος ὑπὸ τοῦ νοὸς τῆς σαρκὸς αὐτοῦ, ¹⁹καὶ οὐ

τι, the reading may be doubtful. But though ἃ ἑόρακεν singly might mean 'his visions,' and ἐμβατεύων 'busying himself with,' the combination 'invading what he has seen,' thus interpreted, is so harsh and incongruous as to be hardly possible; and there was perhaps some corruption in the text prior to all existing authorities (see the note on Phil. ii. 1 for a parallel case). Did the Apostle write ἑώρᾳ (or αἰώρᾳ) κενεμβατεύων? In this case the existing text ΑΕΩΡΑΚΕΝΕΜ ΒΑΤΕΥΩΝ might be explained partly by an attempt to correct the form ἑώρᾳ into αἰώρᾳ or conversely, and partly by the perplexity of transcribers when confronted with such unusual words. This reading had suggested itself to me independently without the knowledge that, so far as regards the latter word, it had been anticipated by others in the conjecture ἃ ἑώρᾳ (or ἃ ἑώρακεν) κενεμβατεύων. The word κενεμβατεῖν 'to walk on emptiness,' 'to tread the air' and so metaphorically (like ἀεροβατεῖν, αἰθεροβατεῖν, αἰθερεμβατεῖν, etc.) 'to indulge in vain speculations,' is not an uncommon word. For its metaphorical sense especially see Plut. *Mor.* p. 336 F οὕτως ἐρέμβετο κενεμβατοῦν καὶ σφαλλόμενον ὑπ' ἀναρχίας τὸ μέγεθος αὐτῆς, Basil. *Op.* I. p. 135 τὸν νοῦν...μυρία πλανηθέντα καὶ πολλὰ κενεμβατήσαντα κ.τ.λ., *ib.* I. p. 596 σοῦ δὲ μὴ κενεμβατείτω ὁ νοῦς, Synes. *de Insomn.* p. 156 οὔτε γὰρ κενεμβατοῦντας τοὺς λόγους ἐξήνεγκαν. Though the precise form κενεμβατεύειν does not occur, yet it is unobjectionable in itself. For the other word which I have ventured to suggest, ἑώρᾳ or αἰώρᾳ, see Philo *de Somn.* ii. 6 (I. p. 665) ὑποτυφούμενος ὑπ' αἰώρας φρενῶν καὶ κενοῦ φυσήματος, *ib.* § 9 (p. 667) τὴν ἐπ' αἰώρας φορουμένην κενὴν δόξαν, *Quod Deus immut.* § 36 (I. p. 298) ὥσπερ ἐπ' αἰώρας τινὸς ψευδοῦς καὶ ἀβεβαίου δόξης φορεῖσθαι κατὰ κενοῦ βαίνοντα. The

first and last passages more especially present striking parallels, and show how germane to St Paul's subject these ideas of 'suspension or balancing in the air' (ἑώρα or αἰώρα) and 'treading the void' (κενεμβατεύειν) would be, as expressing at once the spiritual pride and the emptiness of these speculative mystics; see also *de Somn.* ii. 2 (p. 661) ἐμφαίνεται καὶ τὸ τῆς κενῆς δόξης, ἐφ' ἣν, ὡς ἐφ' ἅρμα, διὰ τὸ κοῦφον ἀναβαίνει, φυσώμενος καὶ μετέωρον ἠωρηκὼς ἑαυτόν. The substantive, ἑώρα or αἰώρα, is used sometimes of the instrument for suspending, sometimes of the position of suspension. In this last sense it describes the poising of a bird, the floating of a boat on the waters, the balancing on a rope, and the like. Hence its expressiveness when used as a metaphor.

In the received text a negative is inserted, ἃ μὴ ἑώρακεν ἐμβατεύων. This gives a very adequate sense '*intruding into those things which he has not seen*'; οὐ γὰρ εἶδεν ἀγγέλους, says Chrysostom, ἀλλ' οὕτω διάκειται ὡς ἰδών: comp. Ezek. xiii. 3 οὐαὶ τοῖς προφητεύουσιν ἀπὸ καρδίας αὐτῶν καὶ τὸ καθόλου μὴ βλέπουσιν. But, though the difficulty is thus overcome, this cannot be regarded as the original reading of the text, the authorities showing that the negative was an after insertion. See the detached note on various readings.

For the form ἑόρακεν, which is better supported here than ἑώρακεν, see the note on ii. 1.

εἰκῆ φυσιούμενος] '*vainly puffed up.*' Their profession of humility was a cloke for excessive pride: for, as St Paul says elsewhere (1 Cor. viii. 1), ἡ γνῶσις φυσιοῖ. It may be questioned whether εἰκῆ should be connected with the preceding or the following words. Its usual position in St Paul, before the words which it qualifies (Rom. xiii. 4, 1 Cor. xv. 2,

κρατῶν τὴν κεφαλήν, ἐξ οὗ πᾶν τὸ σῶμα διὰ τῶν ἀφῶν

Gal. iv. 11; there is an exceptional reason for the exceptional position in Gal. iii. 4), points to the latter construction.

τοῦ νοὸς κ.τ.λ.] '*the mind of his flesh*,' i.e. unenlightened by the Spirit; comp. Rom. viii. 7 τὸ φρόνημα τῆς σαρκός. It would seem that the Apostle is here taking up some watchword of the false teachers. They doubtless boasted that they were directed ὑπὸ τοῦ νοός. Yes, he answers, but it is ὁ νοῦς τῆς σαρκὸς ὑμῶν. Compare Rev. ii. 24, where the favourite Gnostic boast γινώσκειν τὰ βαθέα is characterized by the addition of τοῦ Σατανᾶ (see *Galatians* p. 298, note 3). Comp. August. *Conf.* x. 67 'Quem invenirem qui me reconciliaret tibi? Ambiendum mihi fuit ad angelos? Qua prece? quibus sacramentis? Multi conantes ad te redire, neque per se ipsos valentes, sicut audio, tentaverunt haec et inciderunt in desiderium curiosarum visionum et digni habiti sunt illusionibus. Elati enim te quaerebant doctrinae fastu, etc.'

19. οὐ κρατῶν] '*not holding fast*.' This is the most common construction and meaning of κρατεῖν in the New Testament; e.g. Mark vii. 8 ἀφέντες τὴν ἐντολὴν τοῦ Θεοῦ κρατεῖτε τὴν παράδοσιν τῶν ἀνθρώπων; comp. Cant. iii. 4 εὗρον ὃν ἠγάπησεν ἡ ψυχή μου, ἐκράτησα αὐτὸν καὶ οὐκ ἀφῆκα αὐτόν.

τὴν κεφαλήν] '*the Head*' regarded as a title, so that a person is at once suggested, and the relative which follows is masculine, ἐξ οὗ; comp. the parallel passage, Ephes. iv. 16 ὅς ἐστιν ἡ κεφαλή, Χριστὸς ἐξ οὗ πᾶν τὸ σῶμα κ.τ.λ. The supplication and worship of angels is a substitution of inferior members for the Head, which is the only source of spiritual life and energy. See the introduction pp. 34, 78, 101 sq., 115 sq.

διὰ τῶν ἀφῶν κ.τ.λ.] '*through the junctures and ligaments*.' Galen, when describing the structure of the human

frame, more than once specifies the elements of union as twofold: the body owes its compactness partly to the *articulation*, partly to the *attachment*; e.g. *Op.* II. p. 734 (ed. Kühn) ἔστι δὲ ὁ τρόπος τῆς συνθέσεως αὐτῶν διττὸς κατὰ γένος, ὁ μὲν ἕτερος κατὰ ἄρθρον, ὁ δὲ ἕτερος κατὰ σύμφυσιν. Similarly, though with a more general reference, Aristotle speaks of two kinds of union, which he describes as ἀφή 'contact' and σύμφυσις 'cohesion' respectively; *Metaph.* iv. 4 (p. 1014) διαφέρει δὲ σύμφυσις ἀφῆς· ἔνθα μὲν γὰρ οὐδὲν παρὰ τὴν ἀφὴν ἕτερον ἀνάγκη εἶναι, ἐν δὲ τοῖς συμπεφυκόσιν ἐστί τι ἕν τὸ αὐτὸ ἐν ἀμφοῖν ὃ ποιεῖ ἀντὶ τοῦ ἅπτεσθαι συμπεφυκέναι καὶ εἶναι ἓν κ.τ.λ., *Phys. Ausc.* iv. 6 (p. 213) τούτοις ἀφή ἐστιν· σύμφυσις δέ, ὅταν ἄμφω ἐνεργείᾳ ἓν γένωνται (comp. *ib.* v. 3, p. 227), *Metaph.* x. 3 (p. 1071) ὅσα ἐστὶν ἀφῇ καὶ μὴ συμφύσει. The relation of contiguous surfaces and the connexion of different parts together effect structural unity. This same distinction appears in the Apostle's language here. Contact and attachment are the primary ideas in ἀφαί and σύνδεσμοι respectively.

Of the function of ἀφή, 'contact,' in physiology (περὶ ἀφῆς τῆς ἐν τοῖς φυσικοῖς) Aristotle speaks at some length in one passage, *de Gen. et Corr.* i. 6 (p. 322 sq.). It may be mentioned, as illustrating St Paul's image, that Aristotle in this passage lays great stress on the mutual sympathy and influence of the parts in contact, describing them as παθητικὰ καὶ ποιητικά and as κινητικὰ καὶ κινητὰ ὑπ' ἀλλήλων. Elsewhere, like St Paul here, he uses the plural αἱ ἀφαί; *de Caelo* i. 11 (p. 280) τὸ ἄνευ φθορᾶς ὁτὲ μὲν ὂν ὁτὲ δὲ μὴ ὄν, οἷον τὰς ἀφάς, ὅτι ἄνευ τοῦ φθείρεσθαι πρότερον οὖσαι ὕστερον οὐκ εἰσίν, *de Gen. et Corr.* i. 8 (p. 326) οὔτε γὰρ κατὰ τὰς ἀφὰς ἐνδέχεται διιέναι διὰ τῶν διαφανῶν οὔτε διὰ τῶν πόρων, *ib.* § 9 (p. 327) εἰ γὰρ διακρίνεσθαι δύναται

καὶ συνδέσμων ἐπιχορηγούμενον καὶ συνβιβαζόμενον

κατὰ τὰς ἀφάς, ὥσπερ φασί τινες, κἂν μήπω ᾖ διῃρημένον, ἔσται διῃρημένον· δυνατὸν γὰρ διαιρεθῆναι: comp. [Plat.] *Axioch.* p. 365 A συνειλεγμένον τὰς ἀφὰς καὶ τῷ σώματι ῥωμαλέον. It is quite clear from these passages of Aristotle, more especially from the distinction of ἀφαί and πόροι, that αἱ ἀφαί are the joinings, the junctures. When applied to the human body they would be 'joints,' provided that we use the word accurately of the relations between contiguous limbs, and not loosely (as it is often used) of the parts of the limbs themselves in the neighbourhood of the contact. Hippocrates indeed used ἀφαί as a physiological term in a different sense, employing it as a synonyme for ἅμματα i. e. the fasciculi of muscles (see Galen *Op.* XIX. p. 87), but this use was quite exceptional and can have no place here. Thus αἱ ἀφαί will be almost a synonyme for τὰ ἄρθρα, differing however (1) as being more wide and comprehensive, and (2) as not emphasizing so strongly the *adaptation* of the contiguous parts.

The considerations just urged seem decisive as to the meaning of the word. Some eminent modern critics however explain αἱ ἀφαί to be 'the senses,' following Theodoret on Ephes. iv. 16 ἀφὴν δὲ τὴν αἴσθησιν προσηγό-ρευσεν, ἐπειδὴ καὶ αὕτη μία τῶν πέντε αἰσθήσεων, καὶ ἀπὸ τοῦ μέρους τὸ πᾶν ὠνόμασε. St Chrysostom had led the way to this interpretation, though his language is less explicit than Theo-doret's. To such a meaning however there are fatal objections. (1) This sense of ἀφή is wholly unsupported. It is true that touch lies at the root of all sensations, and that this fact was recognised by ancient physiologists: e.g. Aristot. *de Anim.* i. 13 (p. 435) ἄνευ μὲν γὰρ ἀφῆς οὐδε-μίαν ἐνδέχεται ἄλλην αἴσθησιν ἔχειν. But here the connexion ends; and unless more cogent examples not hitherto ad-

duced are forthcoming, we are justified in saying that αἱ ἀφαί could no more be used for αἱ αἰσθήσεις, than in English ' the touches' could be taken as a synonyme for 'the senses.' (2) The image would be seriously marred by such a meaning. The ἀφαί and σύν-δεσμοι would no longer be an exhaustive description of the elements of union in the anatomical structure; the conjunction of things so incongruous under the vinculum of the same article and preposition, διὰ τῶν ἀφῶν καὶ συνδέσμων, would be unnatural; and the intrusion of the 'senses' would be out of place, where the result specified is the supply of nourishment (ἐπιχορηγούμενον) and the compacting of the parts (συνβιβαζό-μενον). (3) All the oldest versions, the Latin, the Syriac, and the Memphitic, explain it otherwise, so as to refer in some way to the connexion of the parts of the body; e.g. in the Old Latin it is rendered *nexus* here and *junctura* in Ephes. iv. 16.

συνδέσμων] '*bands,*' '*ligaments.*' The Greek σύνδεσμος, like the English 'ligament,' has a general and a special sense. In its general and comprehensive meaning it denotes any of the connecting bands which strap the body together, such as muscles or tendons or ligaments properly so called; in its special and restricted use it is a 'ligament' in the technical sense; comp. Galen *Op.* IV. p. 369 σύνδεσμος γάρ ἐστιν, ὁ γοῦν ἰδίως, οὐ κοινῶς ὀνομαζόμενος, σῶ-μα νευρῶδες ἐξ ὀστοῦ μὲν ὁρμώμενον πάντως διαπεφυκὸς δὲ ἢ εἰς ὀστοῦν ἢ εἰς μῦν. Of the σύνδεσμοι or ligaments properly so called Galen describes at length the several functions and uses, more especially as binding and holding together the διαρθρώσεις; *Op.* I. 236, II. 268, 739, III. 149, IV. 2, etc., comp. Tim. Locr. *de An. Mund.* p. 557 συν-δέσμοις ποττὰν κίνασιν τοῖς νεύροις συνάψε τὰ ἄρθρα (*Opusc. Mythol.* etc. ed. Gale). In our text indeed συν-

αὔξει τὴν αὔξησιν τοῦ Θεοῦ. ²⁰εἰ ἀπεθάνετε σὺν Χριστῷ

δεσμοί must be taken in its comprehensive sense; but the relation of the
ἀφαί to the σύνδεσμοι in St Paul still
remains the same as that of the διαρθρώσεις to the σύνδεσμοι in Galen.

ἐπιχορηγούμενον κ.τ.λ.] The two functions performed by the ἀφαί and σύνδεσμοι are *first* the supply of nutriment etc. (ἐπιχορηγούμενον), and *secondly* the compacting of the frame
(συνβιβαζόμενον). In other words
they are the communication of life
and energy, and the preservation of
unity and order. The *source* of all (ἐξ
οὗ) is Christ Himself the Head; but
the *channels* of communication (διὰ
τῶν κ.τ.λ.) are the different members
of His body, in their relation one to
another. For ἐπιχορηγούμενον 'bounti-
fully furnished' see the note on Gal.
iii. 5. Somewhat similarly Aristotle
speaks of σῶμα κάλλιστα πεφυκὸς καὶ
κεχορηγημένον, *Pol.* iv. 1 (p. 1288).
For examples of χορηγία applied to
functions of the bodily organs, see
Galen. *Op.* III. p. 617 ἐν ταῖς εἰσπνοαῖς
χορηγίᾳ ψυχρᾶς ποιότητος, Alex. *Probl.*
i. 81 τὸ πλεῖστον τῆς τροφῆς ἐξυδαρού-
μενον χορηγεῖται πρὸς γένεσιν τοῦ πά-
θους. For συνβιβαζόμενον, 'joined together, compacted,' see the note on
ii. 2. In the parallel passage, Ephes.
iv. 16, this part of the image is more
distinctly emphasized, συναρμολογούμενον καὶ συνβιβαζόμενον. The difference
corresponds to the different aims of
the two epistles. In the Colossian
letter the vital connexion with the
Head is the main theme; in the
Ephesian, the unity in diversity among
the members.

αὔξει τὴν αὔξησιν κ.τ.λ.] By the twofold means of contact and attachment nutriment has been diffused and
structural unity has been attained,
but these are not the ultimate result;
they are only intermediate processes;
the end is *growth*. Comp. Arist.
Metaph. iv.4(p.1014)αὔξησιν ἔχει δ'
ἑτέρου τῷ ἅπτεσθαι καὶ συμπεφυκέ-

ναι...διαφέρει δὲ σύμφυσις ἁφῆς,where
growth is attributed to the same two
physiological conditions as here.

τοῦ Θεοῦ] i.e. 'which partakes of
God, which belongs to God, which
has its abode in God.' Thus the finite
is truly united with the Infinite; the
end which the false teachers strove
in vain to compass is attained; the
Gospel vindicates itself as the true
theanthropism, after which the human
heart is yearning and the human intellect is feeling. See above, p. 117
sq. With this conclusion of the sentence contrast the parallel passage
Ephes. iv. 16 τὴν αὔξησιν τοῦ σώματος
ποιεῖται εἰς οἰκοδομὴν ἑαυτοῦ ἐν
ἀγάπῃ, where again the different
endings are determined by the different motives of the two epistles.

The discoveries of modern physiology have invested the Apostle's
language with far greater distinctness
and force than it can have worn to
his own contemporaries. Any exposition of the nervous system more
especially reads like a commentary on
his image of the relations between the
body and the head. At every turn
we meet with some fresh illustration
which kindles it with a flood of light.
The volition communicated from the
brain to the limbs, the sensations of
the extremities telegraphed back to
the brain, the absolute mutual sympathy between the head and the
members, the instantaneous paralysis
ensuing on the interruption of continuity, all these add to the completeness and life of the image. But
the following passages will show how
even ancient scientific speculation was
feeling after those physiological truths
which the image involves; Hippocr.
de Morb. Sacr. p. 309 (ed. Foese) κατὰ
ταῦτα νομίζω τὸν ἐγκέφαλον δύναμιν
πλείστην ἔχειν ἐν τῷ ἀνθρώπῳ...οἱ δὲ
ὀφθαλμοὶ καὶ τὰ οὔατα καὶ ἡ γλῶσσα
καὶ αἱ χεῖρες καὶ οἱ πόδες, οἷα ἂν ὁ ἐγκέφαλος γινώσκῃ, τοιαῦτα ὑπηρετοῦσι...

ἀπὸ τῶν στοιχείων τοῦ κόσμου, τί ὡς ζῶντες ἐν κόσμῳ

ἐς δὲ τὴν σύνεσιν ὁ ἐγκέφαλός ἐστιν ὁ
διαγγέλλων...διότι φημὶ τὸν ἐγκέφαλον
εἶναι τὸν ἑρμηνεύοντα τὴν σύνεσιν, αἱ δὲ
φρένες ἄλλως ὄνομα ἔχουσι τῇ τύχῃ
κεκτημένον...λέγουσι δέ τινες ὡς φρονέ-
ομεν τῇ καρδίῃ καὶ τὸ ἀνιώμενον τοῦτο
ἐστι καὶ τὸ φροντίζον· τὸ δὲ οὐχ οὕτως
ἔχει...τῆς...φρονήσιος οὐδετέρῳ μέτεσ-
τιν ἀλλὰ πάντων τουτέων ὁ ἐγκέφαλος
αἴτιός ἐστιν...πρῶτος αἰσθάνεται ὁ ἐγκέφαλος τῶν ἐν τῷ σώματι ἐνεόντων
(where the theory is mixed up with
some curious physiological speculations), Galen. *Op.* I. 235 αὐτὸς δὲ ὁ
ἐγκέφαλος ὅτι μὲν ἀρχὴ τοῖς νεύροις
ἅπασι τῆς δυνάμεώς ἐστιν, ἐναργῶς
ἐμάθομεν...πότερον δὲ ὡς αὐτὸς τοῖς
νεύροις, οὕτω ἐκείνῳ πάλιν ἕτερόν τι
μόριον ἐπιπέμπει, ἢ πηγή τις αὐτῶν
ἐστίν, ἔτ᾽ ἄδηλον, *ib.* IV. p. 11 ἀρχὴ μὲν
γὰρ αὐτῶν (i.e. τῶν νεύρων) ὁ ἐγκέφαλός
ἐστι, καὶ τὰ πάθη εἰς αὐτὸν φέρει, οἷον
εἰς ἄρουράν τινα τῆς λογιστικῆς ψυχῆς·
ἔκφυσις δ᾽ ἐντεῦθεν, οἷον πρέμνου τινὸς
εἰς δένδρον ἀνήκοντος μέγα, ὁ νωτιαῖός
ἐστι μυελός...σύμπαν δ᾽ οὕτω τὸ σῶμα
μεταλαμβάνει δι᾽ αὐτῶν πρώτης μὲν καὶ
μάλιστα κινήσεως, ἐπὶ ταύτῃ δ᾽ αἰσθή-
σεως, XIV. p. 313 αὕτη γὰρ (i.e. ἡ
κεφαλὴ) καθάπερ τις ἀκρόπολίς ἐστι τοῦ
σώματος καὶ τῶν τιμιωτάτων ‚καὶ ἀναγκαιοτάτων ἀνθρώποις αἰσθήσεων οἰκητή-
ριον. Plato had made the head the
central organ of the reason (*Tim.* 69
sq.: see Grote's *Plato* III. pp. 272,
287, *Aristotle* II. p. 179 sq.), if indeed the speculations of the Timæus
may be regarded as giving his serious
physiological views; but he had postulated other centres of the emotions
and the appetites, the heart and the
abdomen. Aristotle, while rightly re-
fusing to localise the mind as mind,
had taken a retrograde step physio-
logically, when he transferred the
centre of sensation from the brain to
the heart; e.g. *de Part. Anim.* ii. 10
(p. 656). Galen, criticizing his predecessors, says of Aristotle δῆλός ἐστι
κατεγνωκὼς μὲν αὐτοῦ (i.e. τοῦ ἐγκεφά-

λου) τελέαν ἀχρηστίαν, φανερῶς δ᾽ ὁμο-
λογεῖν αἰδούμενος (*Op.* III. p. 625). The
Stoics however (Ζήνων καὶ Χρύσιππος
ἅμα τῷ σφετέρῳ χορῷ παντί) were even
worse offenders; and in reply to them
more especially Galen elsewhere discusses the question πότερον ἐγκέφαλος
ἢ καρδία τὴν ἀρχὴν ἔχει, *Op.* V. p. 213
sq. Bearing in mind all this diversity
of opinion among ancient physiologists,
we cannot fail to be struck in the
text not only with the correctness of
the image but also with the propriety
of the terms; and we are forcibly
reminded that among the Apostle's
most intimate companions at this time
was one whom he calls 'the beloved
physician' (iv. 14).

20—23. 'You died with Christ to
your old life. All mundane relations
have ceased for you. Why then do
you—you who have attained your
spiritual manhood—submit still to
the rudimentary discipline of children?
Why do you—you who are citizens of
heaven—bow your necks afresh to
the tyranny of material ordinances, as
though you were still living in the
world? It is the same old story again;
the same round of hard, meaningless,
vexatious prohibitions, 'Handle not,'
'Taste not,' 'Touch not.' What folly!
When all these things—these meats
and drinks and the like—are earthly,
perishable, wholly trivial and unimportant! They are used, and there
is an end of them. What is this, but
to draw down upon yourselves the
denunciations uttered by the prophet
of old? What is this but to abandon
God's word for precepts which are
issued by human authority and inculcated by human teachers? All such
things have a show of wisdom, I grant.
There is an officious parade of religious devotion, an eager affectation
of humility; there is a stern ascetic
rigour, which ill-treats the body: but
there is nothing of any real value
to check indulgence of the flesh.'

δογματίζεσθε ;　²¹ Μὴ ἅψη μηδὲ γεύσῃ μηδὲ θίγῃς　²²(ἃ

20. From the theological tenets of the false teachers the Apostle turns to the ethical—from the objects of their worship to the principles of their conduct. The baptism into Christ, he argues, is death to the world. The Christian has passed away to another sphere of existence. Mundane ordinances have ceased to have any value for him, because his mundane life has ended. They belong to the category of the perishable; he has been translated to the region of the eternal. It is therefore a denial of his Christianity to subject himself again to their tyranny, to return once more to the dominion of the world. See again the note on iii. 1.

εἰ ἀπεθάνετε] '*if ye died*, when ye were baptized into Christ.' For this connexion between baptism and death see the notes on ii. 11, iii. 3. This death has many aspects in St Paul's teaching. It is not only a dying *with* Christ, 2 Tim. ii. 11 εἰ γὰρ συναπεθάνομεν ; but it is also a dying *to* or *from* something. This is sometimes represented as *sin*, Rom. vi. 2 οἵτινες ἀπεθάνομεν τῇ ἁμαρτίᾳ (comp. vv. 7, 8); sometimes as *self*, 2 Cor. v. 14, 15 ἄρα οἱ πάντες ἀπέθανον...ἵνα οἱ ζῶντες μηκέτι ἑαυτοῖς ζῶσιν ; sometimes as the *law*, Rom. vii. 6 κατηργήθημεν ἀπὸ τοῦ νόμου ἀποθανόντες, Gal. ii. 19 διὰ νόμου νόμῳ ἀπέθανον ; sometimes still more widely as the *world*, regarded as the sphere of all material rules and all mundane interests, so here and iii. 3 ἀπεθάνετε γάρ. In all cases St Paul uses the aorist ἀπέθανον, never the perfect τέθνηκα ; for he wishes to emphasize the one absolute *crisis*, which was marked by the change of changes. When the aorist is wanted, the compound verb ἀποθνήσκειν is used ; when the perfect, the simple verb θνήσκειν ; see Buttmann *Ausf. Gramm.* § 114. This rule holds universally in the Greek Testament.

ἀπὸ τῶν στοιχείων κ.τ.λ.] i.e. 'from

the rudimentary, disciplinary, ordinances, whose sphere is the mundane and sensuous': see the note on ver. 8. For the pregnant expression ἀποθανεῖν ἀπὸ comp. Gal. v. 4 κατηργήθητε ἀπὸ Χριστοῦ (so too Rom. vii. 2, 6), 2 Cor. xi. 3 φθαρῇ...ἀπὸ τῆς ἁπλότητος, and see A. Buttmann p. 277 note.

δογματίζεσθε] '*are ye overridden with precepts, ordinances.*' In the LXX the verb δογματίζειν is used several times, meaning 'to issue a decree,' Esth. iii. 9, 1 Esdr. vi. 33, 2 Macc. x. 8, xv. 36, 3 Macc. iv. 11. Elsewhere it is applied most commonly to the precepts of philosophers ; e.g. Justin *Apol.* i. 7 οἱ ἐν Ἕλλησι τὰ αὐτοῖς ἀρεστὰ δογματίσαντες ἐκ παντὸς τῷ ἑνὶ ὀνόματι φιλοσοφίας προσαγορεύονται (comp. § 4), Epict. iii. 7. 17 sq. εἰ θέλεις εἶναι φιλόσοφος...δογματίζων τὰ αἰσχρά. Here it would include alike the δόγματα of the Mosaic law (ver. 14) and the δόγματα of the 'philosophy' denounced above (ver. 8). Both are condemned; the one as superseded though once authoritative, the other as wholly vexatious and unwarrantable. Examples are given in the following verse, μὴ ἅψῃ κ.τ.λ. For the construction here, where the more remote object, which would stand in the dative with the active voice (2 Macc. x. 8 ἐδογμάτισαν...τῷ τῶν Ἰουδαίων ἔθνει), becomes the nominative of the passive, compare χρηματίζεσθαι Matt. ii. 12, 22, διακονεῖσθαι Mark x. 45, and see Winer § xxxix. p. 326, A. Buttmann p. 163, Kühner § 378, II. p. 109.

21. Μὴ ἅψῃ κ.τ.λ.] The Apostle disparagingly repeats the prohibitions of the false teachers in their own words, 'Handle not, neither taste, neither touch.' The rabbinical passages quoted in Schöttgen show how exactly St Paul's language reproduces, not only the spirit, but even the form, of these injunctions. The Latin commentators, Hilary and Pelagius, suppose

ἐστιν πάντα εἰς φθορὰν τῇ ἀποχρήσει), κατὰ τὰ

these prohibitions to be the Apostle's own, thus making a complete shipwreck of the sense. So too St Ambrose *de Noe et Arca* 25 (I. p. 267), *de Abr.* i. 6 (I. p. 300). We may infer from the language of St Augustine who argues against it, that this was the popular interpretation in his day: *Epist.* cxix (II. p. 512) 'tanquam praeceptum putatur apostoli, nescio quid tangere, gustare, attaminare, prohibentis.' The ascetic tendency of the age thus fastened upon a slight obscurity in the Greek and made the Apostle recommend the very practices which he disparaged. For a somewhat similar instance of a misinterpretation commonly received see the note on τοῖς δόγμασιν ver. 14. Jerome however (I. p. 878) had rightly interpreted the passage, illustrating it by the precepts of the Talmud. At a still earlier date Tertullian, *Adv. Marc.* v. 19, gives the correct interpretation.

These prohibitions relate to defilement contracted in divers ways by contact with impure objects. Some were doubtless reenactments of the Mosaic law; while others would be exaggerations or additions of a rigorous asceticism, such as we find among the Essene prototypes of these Colossian heretics, e.g. the avoidance of oil, of wine, or of flesh-meat, the shunning of contact with a stranger or a religious inferior, and the like; see pp. 85 sq. For the religious bearing of this asceticism, as springing from the *dualism* of these heretical teachers, see above, pp. 79, 104 sq.

ἅψῃ] The difference between ἅπτεσθαι and θιγγάνειν is not great, and in some passages where they occur together, it is hard to distinguish them: e.g. Exod. xix. 12 προσέχετε ἑαυτοῖς τοῦ ἀναβῆναι εἰς τὸ ὄρος καὶ θιγεῖν τι αὐτοῦ· πᾶς ὁ ἁψάμενος τοῦ ὄρους θανάτῳ τελευτήσει, Eur. *Bacch.* 617 οὔτ' ἔθιγεν οὔθ' ἥψαθ' ἡμῶν, Arist. *de Gen. et Corr.* i. 8 (p. 326) διὰ τί οὐ γίγνεται ἁψάμενα

ἕν, ὥσπερ ὕδωρ ὕδατος ὅταν θίγῃ; Dion Chrys. *Or.* xxxiv (II. p. 50) οἱ δ' ἐκ παρέργου προσίασιν ἁπτόμενοι μόνον τοῦ πράγματος, ὥσπερ οἱ σπονδῆς θιγγάνοντες, Themist. *Paraphr. Arist.* 95 τὴν δὲ ἀφὴν αὐτῶν ἅπτεσθαι τῶν αἰσθητῶν ἀναγκαῖον· καὶ γὰρ τοὔνομα αὐτῆς ἐκ τοῦ ἅπτεσθαι καὶ θιγγάνειν. But ἅπτεσθαι is the stronger word of the two. This arises from the fact that it frequently suggests, though it does not necessarily involve, the idea of a voluntary or conscious effort, 'to take hold of'—a suggestion which is entirely wanting in the colourless word θιγγάνειν; comp. Themist. *Paraphr. Arist.* 94 ἡ τῶν ζώων ἀφὴ κρίσις ἐστὶ καὶ ἀντίληψις τοῦ θιγγάνοντος. Hence in Xen. *Cyrop.* i. 3. 5 ὅτι σε, φάναι, ὁρῶ, ὅταν μὲν τοῦ ἄρτου ἅψῃ, εἰς οὐδὲν τὴν χεῖρα ἀποψώμενον, ὅταν δὲ τούτων τινὸς θίγῃς, εὐθὺς ἀποκαθαίρει τὴν χεῖρα εἰς τὰ χειρόμακτρα κ.τ.λ. Thus the words chosen in the Latin Versions, *tangere* for ἅπτεσθαι and *attaminare* or *contrectare* for θιγεῖν, are unfortunate, and ought to be transposed. Our English Version, probably influenced by the Latin, has erred in the same direction, translating ἅπτεσθαι by 'touch' and θιγεῖν by 'handle.' Here again they must be transposed. 'Handle' is too strong a word for either; though in default of a better it may stand for ἅπτεσθαι, which it more nearly represents. Thus the two words ἅψῃ and θίγῃς being separate in meaning, γεύσῃ may well interpose; and the three together will form a descending series, so that, as Beza (quoted in Trench *N. T. Syn.* § xvii. p. 57) well expresses it, 'decrescente semper oratione, intelligatur crescere superstitio.'

On the other hand ἅψῃ has been interpreted here as referring to the relation of husband and wife, as e.g. in 1 Cor. vii. 1 γυναικὸς μὴ ἅπτεσθαι; and the prohibition would then be illustrated by the teaching of the he-

ἐΝΤΆΛΜΑΤΑ ΚΑῚ ΔΙΔΑCΚΑΛΊΑC ΤῶΝ ἀΝΘΡῶΠΩΝ·

retics in 1 Tim. iv. 3 κωλυόντων γαμεῖν. But, whatever likelihood there may be that the Colossian false teachers also held this doctrine (see above, p. 85 sq.), it nowhere appears in the context, and we should not expect so important a topic to be dismissed thus cursorily. Moreover θιγγάνειν is used as commonly in this meaning as ἅπτεσθαι (see Gataker *Op. Crit.* p. 79, and examples might be multiplied); so that all ground for assigning it to ἅπτεσθαι especially is removed. Both ἅπτεσθαι and θιγγάνειν refer to defilement incurred through the sense of touch, though in different degrees; 'Handle not, nor yet taste, nor even touch.'

22. 'Only consider what is the real import of this scrupulous avoidance. Why, you are attributing an inherent value to things which are fleeting; you yourselves are citizens of eternity, and yet your thoughts are absorbed in the perishable.'

ἅ] '*which things,*' i.e. the meats and drinks and other material objects, regarded as impure to the touch. The antecedent to ἅ is implicitly involved in the prohibitions μὴ ἅψῃ κ.τ.λ.

ἐστιν εἰς φθοράν] '*are destined for corruption.*' For similar expressions see Acts viii. 20 εἴη εἰς ἀπώλειαν (comp. ver. 23 εἰς χολὴν πικρίας καὶ σύνδεσμον ἀδικίας...ὄντα), 2 Pet. ii. 12 γεγεννημένα......εἰς ἅλωσιν καὶ φθοράν. For the word φθορά, involving the idea of 'decomposition,' see the note on Gal. vi. 8. The expression here corresponds to εἰς ἀφεδρῶνα ἐκβάλλεται (ἐκπορεύεται), Matt. xv. 17, Mark vii. 19.

τῇ ἀποχρήσει] '*in the consuming.*' Comp. Senec. *de Vit. beat.* 7 'in ipso usu sui periturum.' While the verb ἀποχρῶμαι is common, the substantive ἀπόχρησις is extremely rare: Plut. *Mor.* p. 267 F χαίρειν ταῖς τοιαύταις ἀποχρήσεσι καὶ συστολαῖς τῶν περιττῶν (i.e. 'by such modes of consuming and abridging superfluities'), Dion. Hal.

A. R. i. 58 ἐν ἀποχρήσει γῆς μοίρας. The unusual word was chosen for its expressiveness: the χρῆσις here was an ἀπόχρησις; the things could not be used without rendering them unfit for further use. The subtlety of the expression in the original cannot be reproduced in any translation.

On the other hand the clause is sometimes interpreted as a continuation of the language of the ascetic teachers; 'Touch not things which all lead to ruin by their abuse.' This interpretation however has nothing to recommend it. It loses the point of the Apostle's argument; while it puts upon εἶναι εἰς φθοράν a meaning which is at least not natural.

κατὰ κ.τ.λ.] connected directly with vv. 20, 21, so that the words ἅ ἐστιν... τῇ ἀποχρήσει are a parenthetical comment.

τὰ ἐντάλματα κ.τ.λ.] The absence of both preposition and article before διδασκαλίας shows that the two words are closely connected. They are placed here in their proper order; for ἐντάλματα describes the source of authority and διδασκαλίας the medium of communication. The expression is taken ultimately from Isaiah xxix. 13, where the words run in the LXX, μάτην δὲ σέβονταί με, διδάσκοντες ἐντάλματα ἀνθρώπων καὶ διδασκαλίας. The Evangelists (Matt. xv. 9, Mark vii. 7), quoting the passage, substitute in the latter clause διδάσκοντες διδασκαλίας ἐντάλματα ἀνθρώπων.

The coincidences in St Paul's language here with our Lord's words as related in the Gospels (Matt. xv. 1—20, Mark vii. 1—23) are striking, and suggest that the Apostle had this discourse in his mind. (1) Both alike argue against these vexatious ordinances from the *perishableness* of meats. (2) Both insist upon the indifference of such things in themselves. In Mark vii. 19 the Evangelist emphasizes the importance of our Lord's

²³ ἅτινά ἐστιν λόγον μὲν ἔχοντα σοφίας ἐν ἐθελοθρη-

words on this occasion, as practically
abolishing the Mosaic distinction of
meats by declaring all alike to be
clean (καθαρίζων; see the note on ver.
16). (3) Both alike connect such ordinances with the practices condemned in the prophetic denunciation of
Isaiah.

23. 'All such teaching is worthless.
It may bear the semblance of wisdom;
but it wants the reality. It may make
an officious parade of religious service;
it may vaunt its humility; it may
treat the body with merciless rigour;
but it entirely fails in its chief aim.
It is powerless to check indulgence of
the flesh.'

ἅτινα] 'which sort of things.' Not
only these particular precepts, μὴ ἅψῃ
κ.τ.λ., but all precepts falling under
the same category are condemned.
For this force of ἅτινα as distinguished
from ἅ, see the notes on Gal. iv. 24,
v. 19, Phil. iv. 3. The antecedent
here is not ἐντάλματα καὶ διδασκαλίας κ.τ.λ., but the prohibitions given
in ver. 21.

λόγον μὲν κ.τ.λ.] 'having a reputation for wisdom,' but not the reality.
The corresponding member, which
should be introduced by δέ, is suppressed; the oppositive clause being
postponed and appearing later in a
new form, οὐκ ἐν τιμῇ τινι κ.τ.λ. Such
suppressions are common in classical
writers, more especially in Plato; see
Kühner § 531, II. p. 813 sq., Jelf § 766,
and comp. Winer § lxiii. p. 719 sq.
Jerome therefore is not warranted in
attributing St Paul's language here to
'imperitia artis grammaticae' (Epist.
cxxi, Op. II. p. 884). On the contrary
it is just the license which an adept
in a language would be more likely
to take than a novice.

In this sentence λόγον ἔχοντα σοφίας is best taken as a single predicate,
so that ἐστιν is disconnected from
ἔχοντα. Otherwise the construction
ἐστιν ἔχοντα (for ἔχει) would be

supported by many parallels in the
Greek Testament; see Winer § xlv.
p. 437.

The phrase λόγον ἔχειν τινός, so far
as I have observed, has four meanings.
(A) Two as applied to the thinking
subject. (i) 'To take account of, to hold
in account, to pay respect to': e.g.
Æsch. Prom. 231 βροτῶν δὲ τῶν τα-
λαιπώρων λόγον οὐκ ἔσχεν οὐδένα, Demosth. de Coron. § 199 εἴπερ ἢ δόξης
ἢ προγόνων ἢ τοῦ μέλλοντος αἰῶνος
εἶχε λόγον, Plut. Vit. Philop. 18 πῶς
ἄξιον ἐκείνου λόγον ἔχειν τοῦ ἀνδρὸς
κ.τ.λ. (ii) 'To possess the reason or
account or definition of,' 'to have a
scientific knowledge of'; Plato Gorg.
p. 465 A τέχνην δὲ αὐτὴν οὔ φημι εἶναι
ἀλλ' ἐμπειρίαν, ὅτι οὐκ ἔχει λόγον οὐδένα ὧν προσφέρει, ὁποῖα ἅττα τὴν φύσιν ἐστίν, and so frequently. These
two senses are recognised by Aristotle,
Eth. Nic. i. 13 (p. 1102), where he
distinguishes the meaning of the expressions ἔχειν λόγον τοῦ πατρὸς ἢ τῶν
φίλων and ἔχειν λόγον τῶν μαθητικῶν.
(B) Two as applied to the object of
thought. (iii) 'To have the credit or
reputation of,' as here. This sense of
ἔχειν λόγον, 'to be reputed,' is more
commonly found with an infinitive:
e.g. Plato Epin. 987 B αὐτὸς Ἀφροδί-
της εἶναι σχέδον ἔχει λόγον. (iv) 'To
fulfil the definition of, to possess the
characteristics, to have the nature of';
e.g. Philo Vit. Cont. 4 (II. p. 477) ἑκά-
τερον δὲ πηγῆς λόγον ἔχον, Plut. Mor.
p. 637 D τὸ δὲ ᾠὸν οὔτε ἀρχῆς ἔχει λόγον, οὐ γὰρ ὑφίσταται πρῶτον, οὔτε
ὅλου φύσιν, ἀτελὲς γάρ ἐστιν, ib. 640 F
δεῖ πρὸς τὸ ἐμφυτευόμενον χώρας λόγον
ἔχειν τὸ δεξόμενον. The senses of λόγον ἔχειν with other constructions, or
as used absolutely, are very various,
e.g. 'to be reasonable,' 'to hold discourse,' 'to bear a ratio,' etc., but do
not come under consideration here.
Nor again does such an expression as
Plut. Mor. p. 550 C μήτε τὸν λόγον
ἔχων τοῦ νομοθέτου, 'not being in pos-

σκεία καὶ ταπεινοφροσύνη [καὶ] ἀφειδείᾳ σώματος, οὐκ

session of, not knowing, the intention of the legislator'; for the definite article removes it from the category of the cases considered.

ἐν ἐθελοθρησκείᾳ] '*in volunteered*, self-imposed, officious, supererogatory *service*.' One or both of these two ideas, (i) 'excessive readiness, officious zeal,' (ii) 'affectation, unreality,' are involved in this and similar compounds; e.g. ἐθελοδουλεία, ἐθελοκάκησις, ἐθελοκίνδυνος, ἐθελοκωφεῖν, ἐθελορήτωρ, ἐθελοπρόξενος : these compounds being used most frequently, though not always (as this last word shows), in a bad sense. This mode of expression was naturalised in Latin, as appears from Augustine *Epist.* cxlix. 27 (II. p. 514) 'Sic enim et vulgo dicitur qui divitem affectat thelodives, et qui sapientem thelosapiens, et cetera hujusmodi.' Epiphanius, when writing of the Pharisees, not content with the word here supplied by St Paul, coins a double compound ἐθελοπερισσοθρησκεία, *Haer.* i. 16 (p. 34).

ταπεινοφροσύνη] The word is here disparaged by its connexion, as in ver. 18 (see the note there). The force of ἐθελο- may be regarded as carried on to it. Real genuine ταπεινοφροσύνη is commended below; iii. 12.

ἀφειδείᾳ σώματος] '*hard treatment of the body*.' The expression ἀφειδεῖν τοῦ σώματος is not uncommon, being used most frequently, not as here of ascetic discipline, but rather of courageous exposure to hardship and danger in war, e.g. Lysias *Or. Fun.* 25, Joseph. *B. J.* iii. 7. 18, Lucian *Anach.* 24, Plut. *Vit. Pericl.* 10; in Plut. *Mor.* p. 137 c however, of a student's toil, and *ib.* p. 135 E, more generally of the rigorous demands made by the soul on the body. The substantive ἀφείδεια or ἀφειδία does not often occur. On the forms in -εια and -ία derived from adjectives in -ης see Buttmann *Ausf. Gramm.* § 119, II. p. 416 sq. The great preponderance

of manuscript authority favours the form ἀφειδείᾳ here : but in such questions of orthography the fact carries less weight than in other matters. The καὶ before ἀφειδείᾳ should probably be omitted ; in which case ἀφειδείᾳ becomes an instrumental dative, explaining λόγον ἔχοντα σοφίας. While the insertion would naturally occur to scribes, the omission gives more point to the sentence. The ἐθελοθρησκεία καὶ ταπεινοφροσύνη as the religious elements are thus separated from the ἀφείδεια σώματος as the practical rule.

οὐκ ἐν τιμῇ κ.τ.λ.] 'yet *not* really *of any value to remedy indulgence of the flesh*.' So interpreted the words supply the oppositive clause to λόγον μὲν ἔχοντα σοφίας, as the presence of the negative οὐκ naturally suggests. If the sentence had been undisturbed, this oppositive clause would naturally have been introduced by δέ, but the interposition of ἐν ἐθελοθρησκείᾳ κ.τ.λ. has changed its form by a sort of attraction. For this sense of ἐν τιμῇ comp. Lucian *Merc. cond.* 17 τὰ καινὰ τῶν ὑποδημάτων ἐν τιμῇ τινὶ καὶ ἐπιμελείᾳ ἐστίν : similarly Hom. *Il.* ix. 319 ἐν δὲ ἰῇ τιμῇ κ.τ.λ. The preposition πρός, like our English '*for*,' when used after words denoting utility, value, sufficiency, etc., not uncommonly introduces the object to *check* or *prevent* or *cure* which the thing is to be employed. And even though utility may not be directly expressed in words, yet if the idea of a something to be *remedied* is present, this preposition is freely used notwithstanding. See Isocr. *Phil.* 16 (p. 85)πρὸς τοὺς βαρβάρους χρήσιμον, Arist. *H.A.* iii. 21 (p. 522) συμφέρει πρὸς τὰς διαρροίας ἡ τοιαύτη μάλιστα, *de Respir.* 8 (p. 474) ἀνάγκη γίνεσθαι κατάψυξιν, εἰ μέλλει τεύξεσθαι σωτηρίας· τοῦτο γὰρ βοηθεῖ πρὸς ταύτην τὴν φθοράν, Lucian *Pisc.* 27 χρήσιμον γοῦν καὶ πρὸς ἐκείνους τὸ τοιοῦτον, Galen *Op.* XII. p. 399 χρωμένῳ γε τίνι πρὸς τὸ πάθος ἀρκτείῳ στέ-

ἐν τιμῇ τινὶ πρὸς πλησμονὴν τῆς σαρκός.

ατι, p. 420 τοῦ δόντος αὐτὰ πρὸς ἀλω-
πεκίας φαλακρώσεις κ.τ.λ., p. 430 συνέ-
θηκαν...φάρμακα πρὸς ῥεούσας τρίχας,
p. 476 βραχυτάτην ἔχοντι δύναμιν ὡς
πρὸς τὸ προκείμενον σύμπτωμα, p. 482
τοῦτο δὲ καὶ τὰ ἐν ὅλῳ τῷ σώματι
ἐξανθήματα σφόδρα χρήσιμόν ἐστιν,p.514
χρηστέον δὲ πᾶσι τοῖς ἀναγεγραμμένοις
βοηθήμασι πρὸς τὰς γινομένας δι᾽ ἔγκαυ-
σιν κεφαλαλγίας, p. 601 κάλλιστον πρὸς
αὐτὴν φάρμακον ἐγχεόμενον νάρδινον
μύρον. These examples from Galen
are only a few out of probably some hun-
dreds, which might be collected from
the treatise in which they occur, the
de Compositione Medicamentorum.

The language, which the Colossian
false teachers would use, may be inferred from the account given by Philo
of a Judaic sect of mystic ascetics,
who may be regarded, not indeed as
their direct, but as their collateral
ancestors (see p. 86, note 2, p. 94), the
Therapeutes of Egypt; *de Vit. Cont.*
§ 4 (II. p. 476 sq.) τρυφῶσιν ὑπὸ σοφίας ἑστιώμενοι πλουσίως καὶ ἀφθόνως
τὰ δόγματα χορηγούσης, ὡς καὶ...μό-
λις δι᾽ ἓξ ἡμερῶν ἀπογεύεσθαι τροφῆς ἀναγκαίας...σιτοῦνται δὲ...ἄρτον εὐ-
τελῆ, καὶ ὄψον ἅλες...πότον ὕδωρ ναματιαῖον αὐτοῖς ἐστίν...πλησμονὴν ὡς
ἐχθρόν τε καὶ ἐπίβουλον ἐκτρεπόμενοι
ψυχῆς καὶ σώματος. St Paul apparently has before him some similar
exposition of the views of the Colossian heretics, either in writing or
(more probably) by report from Epaphras. In reply he altogether denies
the claims of this system to the title
of σοφία; he disputes the value of
these δόγματα; he allows that this
πλησμονή is the great evil to be check-
ed, the fatal disease to be cured; but
he will not admit that the remedies
prescribed have any substantial and
lasting efficacy.

The interpretation here offered is
not new, but it has been strangely
overlooked or despised. The passages adduced will I trust show the

groundlessness of objections which
have been brought against it owing to
the use of the preposition; and in all
other respects it seems to be far preferable to any rival explanation which
has been suggested. The favourite
interpretations in ancient or modern
times divide themselves into two
classes, according to the meaning assigned to πρὸς πλησμονὴν τῆς σαρκός.
(1) It is explained in a good sense:
' to satisfy the reasonable wants of the
body.' In this case οὐκ ἐν τιμῇ τινί is
generally interpreted, ' *not* holding it
(the body) *in any honour.*' So the
majority of the fathers, Greek and
Latin. This has the advantage of
preserving the continuity of the words
οὐκ ἐν τιμῇ τινὶ πρὸς πλησμονὴν κ.τ.λ.:
but it assigns an impossible sense to
πλησμονὴ τῆς σαρκός. For πλησμονή
always denotes ' repletion,' ' surfeit-
ing,' ' excessive indulgence,' and cannot be used of a reasonable attention
to the physical cravings of nature; as
Galen says, *Op.* XV. p. 113 πάντων εἰω-
θότων οὐ μόνον ἰατρῶν ἀλλὰ καὶ τῶν ἄλλων Ἑλλήνων τὸ τῆς πλησμονῆς ὄνομα
μᾶλλόν πως ἐπιφέρειν ταῖς ὑπερβο-
λαῖς τῆς συμμέτρου ποσότητος:
and certainly neither the Apostle nor
the Colossian ascetics were likely to
depart from this universal rule. To
the long list of passages quoted in
Wetstein may be added such references as Philo *Leg. ad Gai.* § 1 (II.
p. 546), *Clem. Hom.* viii. 15, Justin
Dial. 126, Dion. Alex. in Euseb. *H.E.*
vii. 25; but they might be increased
to any extent. (2) A bad sense is
attached to πλησμονή, as usage demands. And here two divergent interpretations have been put forward.
(i) The proper continuity of the sentence is preserved, and the words οὐκ
ἐν τιμῇ τινὶ πρὸς πλησμονὴν τῆς σαρκός
are regarded as an exposition of the
doctrine of the false teachers from
their own point of view. So Theodore of Mopsuestia, οὐ τίμιον νομίζον-

III.   ¹ Εἰ οὖν συνηγέρθητε τῷ Χριστῷ, τὰ ἄνω ζητεῖτε, οὗ ὁ Χριστός ἐστιν ἐν δεξιᾷ τοῦ Θεοῦ καθήμενος·

τας τὸ διὰ πάντων πληροῦν τὴν σάρκα,
ἀλλὰ γὰρ μᾶλλον αἱρουμένους ἀπέχεσθαι
τῶν πολλῶν διὰ τὴν τοῦ νόμου παράδοσιν. This able expositor however is
evidently dissatisfied, for he introduces his explanation with the words
ἀσαφὲς μέν ἐστι, βούλεται δὲ εἰπεῖν
κ.τ.λ.; and his explanation has not
been adopted by others. Either the
sentence, so interpreted, becomes flat
and unmeaning, though it is obviously
intended to clinch the whole matter;
or the Apostle is made to confirm the
value of the very doctrines which he
is combating. (ii) The sentence is
regarded as discontinuous; and it is
interpreted, 'not of any real value'
(or 'not consisting in anything commendable,' or 'not holding the body
in any honour') but 'tending to gratify the carnal desires' or 'mind.'
This in some form or other is almost
universally adopted by modern interpreters, and among the ancients is
found in the commentator Hilary.
The objections to it are serious. (a)
The dislocation of the sentence is inexplicable.   There is no indication
either in the grammar or in the vocabulary that a separate and oppositive
clause begins with πρὸς πλησμονὴν
κ.τ.λ., but on the contrary everything
points to an unbroken continuity. (β)
The sense which it attaches to πλησμονὴ τῆς σαρκός is either forced and
unnatural, or it makes the Apostle
say what he could not have said. If
πλησμονὴ τῆς σαρκός could have the
sense which Hilary assigns to it, 'sa-
gina carnalis sensus traditio humana
est,' or indeed if it could mean 'the
mind of the flesh' in any sense (as it
is generally taken by modern commentators), this is what St Paul might
well have said. But obviously πλησμονὴ τῆς σαρκός conveys a very different idea from such expressions as τὸ
φυσιοῦσθαι ὑπὸ τοῦ νοὸς τῆς σαρκός

(ver. 18) or τὸ φρόνημα τῆς σαρκός
(Rom. viii. 6, 7), which include pride,
self-sufficiency, strife, hatred, bigotry,
and generally everything that is earth-
bound and selfish. On the other hand,
if πλησμονὴ τῆς σαρκός be taken in its
natural meaning, as applying to coarse
sensual indulgences, then St Paul
could not have said without qualification, that this rigorous asceticism
conduced πρὸς πλησμονὴν τῆς σαρκός.
Such language would defeat its own
object by its extravagance.

III. 1—4. 'If this be so; if ye were
raised with Christ, if ye were translated into heaven, what follows? Why
you must realise the change. All your
aims must centre in heaven, where
reigns the Christ who has thus exalted you, enthroned on God's right
hand. All your thoughts must abide
in heaven, not on the earth. For, I
say it once again, you have nothing to
do with mundane things: you died,
died once for all to the world: you
are living another life. This life indeed is hidden now: it has no outward splendour as men count splendour; for it is a life with Christ, a life
in God. But the veil will not always
shroud it. Christ, our life, shall be
manifested hereafter; then ye also
shall be manifested with Him and the
world shall see your glory.'

1. Εἰ οὖν συνηγέρθητε κ.τ.λ.] 'If
then ye were raised,' not 'have been
raised.' The aorist συνηγέρθητε, like
ἀπεθάνετε (ii. 20), refers to their baptism; and the εἰ οὖν here is a resumption of the εἰ in ii. 20. The sacra-
ment of baptism, as administered in
the Apostolic age, involved a twofold
symbolism, a death or burial and
a resurrection : see the note on ii.
12.   In the rite itself these were represented by two distinct acts, the
disappearance beneath the water and
the emergence from the water: but

²τὰ ἄνω φρονεῖτε, μὴ τὰ ἐπὶ τῆς γῆς. ³ἀπεθάνετε γάρ, καὶ ἡ ζωὴ ὑμῶν κέκρυπται σὺν τῷ Χριστῷ ἐν τῷ Θεῷ·

in the change typified by the rite they are two aspects of the same thing, 'like the concave and convex in a circle,' to use an old simile. The negative side—the death and burial—implies the positive side—the resurrection. Hence the form of the Apostle's resumption, εἰ ἀπεθάνετε, εἰ οὖν συνηγέρθητε.

The change involved in baptism, if truly realised, must pervade a man's whole nature. It affects not only his practical conduct, but his intellectual conceptions also. It is nothing less than a removal into a new sphere of being. He is translated from earth to heaven; and with this translation his point of view is altered, his standard of judgment is wholly changed. Matter is to him no longer the great enemy; his position towards it is one of absolute neutrality. Ascetic rules, ritual ordinances, have ceased to have any absolute value, irrespective of their effects. All these things are of the earth, earthy. The material, the transitory, the mundane, has given place to the moral, the eternal, the heavenly.

τὰ ἄνω ζητεῖτε κ.τ.λ.] 'Cease to concentrate your energies, your thoughts on mundane ordinances, and realise your new and heavenly life, of which Christ is the pole-star.'

ἐν δεξιᾷ κ.τ.λ.] 'being seated on the right hand of God,' where καθήμενος must not be connected with ἐστιν; see the note on ἀπόκρυφοι, ii. 3. This participial clause is pertinent and emphatic, for the session of Christ implies the session of the believer also; Ephes. ii. 4—6 ὁ δὲ Θεός...ἡμᾶς... συνεζωοποίησεν......καὶ συνήγειρεν καὶ συνεκάθισεν ἐν τοῖς ἐπουρανίοις ἐν Χριστῷ Ἰησοῦ κ.τ.λ.; comp. Rev. iii. 21 ὁ νικῶν, δώσω αὐτῷ καθίσαι μετ' ἐμοῦ ἐν τῷ θρόνῳ μου, ὡς κἀγὼ ἐνίκησα καὶ ἐκάθισα μετὰ τοῦ πατρός μου ἐν τῷ

θρόνῳ αὐτοῦ, in the message addressed to the principal church of this district: see above, p. 42. Βαβαί, says Chrysostom, ποῦ τὸν νοῦν ἀπήγαγε τὸν ἡμέτερον; πῶς φρονήματος αὐτοὺς ἐπλήρωσε μεγάλου; οὐκ ἤρκει Τὰ ἄνω εἰπεῖν, οὐδέ, Οὗ ὁ Χριστός ἐστιν, ἀλλὰ τί; Ἐν δεξιᾷ τοῦ Θεοῦ καθήμενος· ἐκεῖθεν λοιπὸν τὴν γῆν ὁρᾶν παρεσκεύαζε.

2. τὰ ἄνω] The same expression repeated for emphasis; 'You must not only seek heaven; you must also think heaven.' For the opposition of τὰ ἄνω and τὰ ἐπὶ τῆς γῆς in connexion with φρονεῖν, comp. Phil. iii. 19, 20 οἱ τὰ ἐπίγεια φρονοῦντες, ἡμῶν γὰρ τὸ πολίτευμα ἐν οὐρανοῖς ὑπάρχει; see also Theoph. ad Autol. ii. 17. Extremes meet. Here the Apostle points the antithesis to controvert a Gnostic asceticism: in the Philippian letter he uses the same contrast to denounce an Epicurean sensualism. Both alike are guilty of the same fundamental error; both alike concentrate their thoughts on material, mundane things.

3. ἀπεθάνετε] 'ye died' in baptism. The aorist ἀπεθάνετε denotes the past act; the perfect κέκρυπται the permanent effects. For ἀπεθάνετε see the notes on ii. 12, 20.

κέκρυπται] 'is hidden, is buried out of sight, to the world.' The Apostle's argument is this: 'When you sank under the baptismal water, you disappeared for ever to the world. You rose again, it is true, but you rose only to God. The world henceforth knows nothing of your new life, and (as a consequence) your new life must know nothing of the world.' 'Neque Christum,' says Bengel, 'neque Christianos novit mundus; ac ne Christiani quidem plane seipsos'; comp. Joh. xiv. 17—19 τὸ πνεῦμα τῆς ἀληθείας ὃ ὁ κόσμος οὐ δύναται λαβεῖν, ὅτι οὐ θεωρεῖ αὐτὸ οὐδὲ γινώσκει

⁴ ὅταν ὁ Χριστὸς φανερωθῇ, ἡ ζωὴ ἡμῶν, τότε καὶ ὑμεῖς σὺν αὐτῷ φανερωθήσεσθε ἐν δόξῃ.

4. ἡ ζωὴ ὑμῶν.

αὐτὸ, ὑμεῖς [δὲ] γινώσκετε αὐτό...ὁ κόσμος με οὐκ ἔτι θεωρεῖ, ὑμεῖς δὲ θεωρεῖτέ με· ὅτι ἐγὼ ζῶ, καὶ ὑμεῖς ζήσετε.

4. ὁ Χριστός] A fourth occurrence of the name of Christ in this context; comp. ver. 2 τῷ Χριστῷ, ὁ Χριστός, ver. 3 σὺν τῷ Χριστῷ. A pronoun would have been more natural, but less emphatic.

ἡ ζωὴ ἡμῶν] This is an advance on the previous statement, ἡ ζωὴ ὑμῶν κέκρυπται σὺν τῷ Χριστῷ, in two respects : (1) It is not enough to have said that the life is shared *with* Christ. The Apostle declares that the life *is* Christ. Comp. 1 Joh. v. 12 ὁ ἔχων τὸν υἱὸν ἔχει τὴν ζωήν, Ign. *Ephes.* 7 ἐν θανάτῳ ζωὴ ἀληθινή (of Christ), *Smyrn.* 4 Ἰησοῦς Χριστὸς τὸ ἀληθινὸν ἡμῶν ζῆν, *Ephes.* 3 Ἰησοῦς Χριστὸς τὸ ἀδιάκριτον ἡμῶν ζῆν, *Magn.* 1 Ἰησοῦ Χριστοῦ τοῦ διαπαντὸς ἡμῶν ζῆν. (2) For ὑμῶν is substituted ἡμῶν. The Apostle hastens to include himself among the recipients of the bounty. For this characteristic transition from the second person to the first see the note on ii. 13. The reading ὑμῶν here has very high support, and on this account I have given it as an alternative; but it is most probably a transcriber's correction, for the sake of uniformity with the preceding.

τότε καὶ ὑμεῖς κ.τ.λ.] 'The veil which now shrouds your higher life from others, and even partly from yourselves, will then be withdrawn. The world which persecutes, despises, ignores now, will then be blinded with the dazzling glory of the revelation.' Comp. 1 Joh. iii. 1, 2 ὁ κόσμος οὐ γινώσκει ἡμᾶς, ὅτι οὐκ ἔγνω αὐτόν. ἀγαπητοί, νῦν τέκνα Θεοῦ ἐσμέν, καὶ οὔπω ἐφανερώθη τί ἐσόμεθα· οἴδαμεν ὅτι ἐὰν φανερωθῇ, ὅμοιοι αὐτῷ ἐσόμεθα κ.τ.λ., Clem. Rom. 50 οἱ φανερω-

θήσονται ἐν τῇ ἐπισκοπῇ τῆς βασιλείας τοῦ Χριστοῦ.

ἐν δόξῃ] Joh. xvii. 22 τὴν δόξαν ἣν δέδωκάς μοι, δέδωκα αὐτοῖς, Rom. viii. 17 ἵνα καὶ συνδοξασθῶμεν.

5—11. 'So then realise this death to the world; kill all your earthly members. Is it fornication, impurity of whatever kind, passion, evil desire ? Or again, is it that covetousness which makes a religion, an idolatry, of greed ? Do not deceive yourselves. For all these things God's wrath will surely come. In these sins ye, like other Gentiles, indulged in times past, when your life was spent amidst them. But now everything is changed. Now you also must put away not this or that desire, but all sins whatsoever. Anger, wrath, malice, slander, filthy abuse; banish it from your lips. Be not false one to another in word or deed; but cast off for ever the old man with his actions, and put on the new, who is renewed from day to day, growing unto perfect knowledge and refashioned after the image of his Creator. In this new life, in this regenerate man, there is not, there cannot be, any distinction of Greek or Jew, of circumcision or uncircumcision; there is no room for barbarian, for Scythian, for bond or free. Christ has displaced, has annihilated, all these; Christ is Himself all things and in all things.'

5. The false doctrine of the Gnostics had failed to check sensual indulgence (ii. 23). The true doctrine of the Apostle has power to kill the whole carnal man. The substitution of a comprehensive principle for special precepts—of the heavenly life in Christ for a code of minute ordinances—at length attains the end after which the Gnostic teachers have striven, and striven in vain.

⁵ Νεκρώσατε οὖν τὰ μέλη τὰ ἐπὶ τῆς γῆς· πορνείαν,
ἀκαθαρσίαν, πάθος, ἐπιθυμίαν κακήν, καὶ τὴν πλεον-

Νεκρώσατε οὖν] i.e. 'Carry out this
principle of *death* to the world (ii. 20
ἀπεθάνετε, iii. 3 ἀπεθάνετε), and kill
everything that is mundane and carnal in your being.'

τὰ μέλη κ.τ.λ.] Each person has a
twofold moral personality. There is
in him the 'old man,' and there is in
him also 'the new' (vv. 9, 10). The
old man with all his members must
be pitilessly slain. It is plain that τὰ
μέλη here is used, like ἄνθρωπος in
ver. 9, not physically, but morally.
Our actual limbs may be either τὰ ἐπὶ
τῆς γῆς or τὰ ἐν τοῖς οὐρανοῖς, according as they are made instruments for
the world or for Christ: just as we—
our whole being—may identify ourselves with the παλαιὸς ἄνθρωπος or
with the νέος ἄνθρωπος of our twofold
potentiality. For this use of the physical, as a symbol of the moral of
which it is the potential instrument,
compare Matt. v. 29 sq. εἰ δὲ ὁ ὀφθαλ-
μός σου ὁ δεξιὸς σκανδαλίζει σε, ἔξελε
αὐτόν κ.τ.λ.

I have ventured to punctuate
after τὰ ἐπὶ τῆς γῆς. Thus πορνείαν
κ.τ.λ. are prospective accusatives,
which should be governed directly by
some such word as ἀπόθεσθε. But
several dependent clauses interpose ;
the last of these incidentally suggests
a contrast between the past and the
present ; and this contrast, predomi-
nating in the Apostle's mind, leads to
an abrupt recasting of the sentence,
νυνὶ δὲ ἀπόθεσθε καὶ ὑμεῖς τὰ πάντα,
in disregard of the original construction. This opposition of ποτέ and νῦν
has a tendency to dislocate the construction in St Paul, as in i. 22 νυνὶ δὲ
ἀποκατηλλάγητε(or ἀποκατήλλαξεν),i. 26
νῦν δὲ ἐφανερώθη : see the note on this
latter passage. For the whole run of
the sentence (the parenthetic relative
clauses, the contrast of past and present, and the broken construction)

compare Ephes. ii. 1—5 καὶ ὑμᾶς...ἐν
αἷς ποτέ...ἐν οἷς καὶ...ποτε...ὁ δὲ Θεός...
καὶ ὄντας ἡμᾶς συνεζωοποίησεν.
With the common punctuation the
interpretation is equally awkward,
whether we treat τὰ μέλη and πορνείαν κ.τ.λ. as in direct apposition, or
as double accusatives, or in any other
way. The case is best put by Severianus, σάρκα καλεῖ τὴν ἁμαρτίαν, ἧς καὶ
τὰ μέλη καταριθμεῖ...ὁ παλαιὸς ἄνθρω-
πός ἐστιν τὸ φρόνημα τὸ τῆς ἁμαρτίας,
μέλη δὲ αὐτοῦ αἱ πράξεις τῶν ἁμαρτη-
μάτων; but this is an evasion of the
difficulty, which consists in the direct
apposition of the instruments and the
activities, from whatever point they
are viewed.

πορνείαν κ.τ.λ.] The general order
is from the less comprehensive to the
more comprehensive. Thus πορνεία is
a special kind of uncleanness, while
ἀκαθαρσία is uncleanness in any form,
Ephes. v. 3 πορνεία δὲ καὶ ἀκαθαρσία
πᾶσα ; comp. Gal. v. 19 πορνεία, ἀκαθαρσία, ἀσέλγεια, with the note there.
Thus again πάθος, though frequently
referring to this class of sins (Rom. i.
26, 1 Thess. iv. 5), would include other
base passions which do not fall under
the category of ἀκαθαρσία, as for instance gluttony and intemperance.

πάθος, ἐπιθυμίαν] The two words
occur together in 1 Thess. iv. 5 μὴ ἐν
πάθει ἐπιθυμίας. So in a passage closely
resembling the text, Gal. v. 24 οἱ δὲ
τοῦ Χριστοῦ Ἰησοῦ τὴν σάρκα ἐσταύρω-
σαν σὺν τοῖς παθήμασιν καὶ ταῖς ἐπιθυμίαις. The same vice may be viewed
as a πάθος from its passive and an ἐπιθυμία from its active side. The word
ἐπιθυμία is not used here in the restricted sense which it has e.g. in
Arist. *Eth. Nic.* ii. 4, where it ranges
with anger, fear, etc., being related
to πάθος as the species to the genus
(see Gal. l. c. note). In the Greek
Testament ἐπιθυμία has a much more

$$\epsilon\xi\iota\alpha\nu,\ \eta\tau\iota\varsigma\ \epsilon\sigma\tau\iota\nu\ \epsilon\iota\delta\omega\lambda o\lambda\alpha\tau\rho\epsilon\iota\alpha,\ ^{6}\delta\iota'\ \overset{\dot{}}{\alpha}\ \epsilon\rho\chi\epsilon\tau\alpha\iota\ \eta\ o\rho\gamma\eta$$

comprehensive sense; e.g. Joh. viii. 44 τὰς ἐπιθυμίας τοῦ πατρὸς ὑμῶν θέλετε ποιεῖν. Here, if anything, ἐπιθυμία is wider than πάθος. While πάθος includes all ungovernable affections, ἐπιθυμία κακή reaches to all evil longings. 'Ιδού, says Chrysostom, γενικῶς τὸ πᾶν εἶπε· πάντα γὰρ ἐπιθυμία κακή, βασκανία, ὀργή, λύπη. The epithet is added because ἐπιθυμία is capable of a good sense: comp. 1 Cor. x. 6 ἐπιθυμητὰς κακῶν.

καὶ τὴν πλεονεξίαν] '*and* especially *covetousness*.' Impurity and covetousness may be said to divide between them nearly the whole domain of human selfishness and vice; 'Si avaritia prostrata est, exsurgit libido' (Cypr. *de Mort.* 3). The one has been already dealt with; the other needs now to be specially denounced; comp. Ephes. v. 3 πορνεία δὲ καὶ ἀκαθαρσία πᾶσα ἢ πλεονεξία. ' Homo extra Deum,' says Bengel (on Rom. i. 29), 'quaerit pabulum in creatura materiali vel per voluptatem vel per avaritiam.' Comp. *Test. xii Patr.* Jud. 18 φυλάξασθε οὖν, τέκνα μου, ἀπὸ τῆς πορνείας καὶ τῆς φιλαργυρίας...ὅτι ταῦτα ἀφιστᾷ νόμου Θεοῦ. Similarly Lysis Pythag. 4 (*Epistol. Graec.* p. 602, ed. Hercher) ὀνομάξαιμι δ' ἂν αὐτῶν [i.e. the vices] πρᾶτον ἐπελθὼν τὰς ματέρας ἀκρασίαν τε καὶ πλεονεξίαν· ἄμφω δὲ πολύγονοι πεφύκαντι. It must be remembered that πλεονεξία is much wider than φιλαργυρία (see Trench *N. T. Syn.* § xxiv. p. 77 sq.), which itself is called ῥίζα πάντων τῶν κακῶν (1 Tim. vi. 10). The attempt to give πλεονεξία here and in other passages the sense of 'impurity' (see e.g. Hammond on Rom. i. 29) is founded on a misconception. The words πλεονεκτεῖν, πλεονεξία, will sometimes be used in relation to sins of uncleanness, because such may be acts of injustice also. Thus adultery is not only impurity, but it is robbery also: hence 1 Thess. iv. 6 τὸ μὴ ὑπερβαίνειν καὶ πλεονεκτεῖν ἐν τῷ πράγματι

τὸν ἀδελφὸν αὐτοῦ (see the note there). In other passages again there will be an accidental connexion; e.g. Ephes. iv. 19 εἰς ἐργασίαν ἀκαθαρσίας πάσης ἐν πλεονεξίᾳ, i.e. 'with greediness,' 'with entire disregard for the rights of others.' But nowhere do the words in themselves suggest this meaning. Here the particles καὶ τὴν show that a new type of sin is introduced with πλεονεξίαν: and in the parallel passage Ephes. v. 3 (quoted above) the same distinction is indicated by the change from the conjunctive particle καὶ to the disjunctive ἢ. It is an error to suppose that this sense of πλεονεξία is supported by Clem. Alex. *Strom.* iii. 12 (p. 551 sq.) ὡς γὰρ ἡ πλεονεξία πορνεία λέγεται, τῇ αὐταρκείᾳ ἐναντιουμένη. On the converse error of explaining ἀκαθαρσία to mean 'greediness,' 'covetousness,' see the note on 1 Thess. ii. 3.

ἥτις κ.τ.λ.] '*for it is idolatry*': comp. Ephes. v. 5 πλεονέκτης, ὅ (or ὅς) ἐστιν εἰδωλολάτρης, Polyc. *Phil.* 11 ' Si quis non abstinuerit ab avaritia, ab idolatria coinquinabitur' (see *Philippians* p. 63 on the misunderstanding of this passage). The covetous man sets up another object of worship besides God. There is a sort of religious purpose, a devotion of the soul, to greed, which makes the sin of the miser so hateful. The idea of avarice as a *religion* may have been suggested to St Paul by our Lord's words, Matt. vi. 24 οὐ δύνασθε Θεῷ δουλεύειν καὶ μαμωνᾷ, though it is a mistake to suppose that Mammon was the name of a Syrian deity. It appears however elsewhere in Jewish writers of this and later ages: e.g. Philo *de Mon.* i. 2 (II. p. 214 sq.) πανταχόθεν μὲν ἀργύριον καὶ χρυσίον ἐκπορίζουσι, τὸ δὲ πορισθὲν ὡς ἄγαλμα θεῖον ἐν ἀδύτοις θησαυροφυλακοῦσιν (with the whole context), and *Shemoth Rabba* fol. 121. 3 'Qui opes suas multiplicat per foenus, ille est idololatra' (with

τοῦ Θεοῦ· ⁷ἐν οἷς καὶ ὑμεῖς περιεπατήσατέ ποτε, ὅτε
ἐζῆτε ἐν τούτοις· ⁸νυνὶ δὲ ἀπόθεσθε καὶ ὑμεῖς τὰ πάντα,

other passages quoted by Wetstein
and Schöttgen on Ephes. v. 5). St
Chrysostom, *Hom. in Joann. lxv*
(VIII. p. 392 sq.), enlarges on the cult
of wealth—the consecration of it, the
worship paid to it, the sacrifices demanded by it: ἡ δὲ φιλαργυρία λέγει,
Θῦσόν μοι τὴν σαυτοῦ ψυχήν, καὶ πείθει·
ὁρᾷς οἵους ἔχει βωμούς, οἷα δέχεται θύ-
ματα (p. 393). The passage in *Test.
xii Patr.* Jud. 18 ἡ φιλαργυρία πρὸς
εἴδωλα ὁδηγεῖ is no real parallel to St
Paul's language, though at first sight
it seems to resemble it. For ἥτις,
'seeing that it,' see the note on Phil.
iv. 3.

6, 7. δι' ἃ κ.τ.λ.] The received
text requires correction in two points.
(1) It inserts the words ἐπὶ τοὺς υἱοὺς
τῆς ἀπειθείας after τοῦ Θεοῦ. Though
this insertion has preponderating support, yet the words are evidently interpolated from the parallel passage,
Ephes. v. 6 διὰ ταῦτα γὰρ ἔρχεται ἡ
ὀργὴ τοῦ Θεοῦ ἐπὶ τοὺς υἱοὺς τῆς ἀπειθείας. We are therefore justified in
rejecting them with other authorities,
few in number but excellent in character. See the detached note on various readings. When the sentence is
thus corrected, the parallelism of δι'
ἃ...ἐν οἷς καί...may be compared with
Ephes. i. 11 ἐν ᾧ καὶ ἐκληρώθημεν...ἐν ᾧ
καὶ ὑμεῖς...ἐν ᾧ καὶ πιστεύσαντες ἐσφρα-
γίσθητε, and ii. 21, 22 ἐν ᾧ πᾶσα [ἡ]
οἰκοδομὴ...ἐν ᾧ καὶ ὑμεῖς συνοικοδομεῖσθε. (2) The vast preponderance of authority obliges us to substitute τούτοις for αὐτοῖς.

6. ἔρχεται] This may refer either
to the present and continuous dispensation, or to the future and final judgment. The present ἔρχεσθαι is frequently used to denote the *certainty*
of a future event, e.g. Matt. xvii. 11,
Joh. iv. 21, xiv. 3, whence ὁ ἐρχόμενος
is a designation of the Messiah : see
Winer § xl. p. 332.

7. ἐν οἷς κ.τ.λ.] The clause ἐπὶ τοὺς
υἱοὺς τῆς ἀπειθείας having been struck
out, ἐν οἷς must necessarily be neuter
and refer to the same as δι' ἅ. Independently of the rejection of the
clause, this neuter seems more probable in itself than the masculine : for
(1) The expression περιπατεῖν ἐν is
most commonly used of things, not of
persons, especially in this and the
companion epistle : iv. 5, Ephes. ii. 2,
10, iv. 17, v. 2 ; (2) The Apostle would
hardly denounce it as a sin in his Colossian converts that they 'walked
among the sons of disobedience'; for
the Christian, though not of the world,
is necessarily in the world : comp. 1
Cor. v. 10. The apparent parallel,
Ephes. ii. 3 ἐν οἷς καὶ ἡμεῖς πάντες ἀνε-
στράφημέν ποτε ἐν ταῖς ἐπιθυμίαις τῆς
σαρκὸς ἡμῶν (where οἷς seems to be
masculine), does not hold, because the
addition ἐν ταῖς ἐπιθυμίαις κ.τ.λ. makes
all the difference. Thus the rejection
of the clause, which was decided by
textual considerations, is confirmed by
exegetical reasons.

καὶ ὑμεῖς] 'ye, like the other heathen'
(i. 6 καὶ ἐν ὑμῖν), but in the next
verse καὶ ὑμεῖς is rather 'ye yourselves,' 'ye notwithstanding your former lives.'

ὅτε ἐζῆτε κ.τ.λ.] 'When *ye* lived in
this atmosphere of sin, when ye had
not yet died to the world.'

ἐν τούτοις] '*in these things.*' We
should have expected αὐτοῖς, but
τούτοις is substituted as more emphatic and condemnatory : comp. Ephes.
v. 6 διὰ ταῦτα γὰρ ἔρχεται κ.τ.λ. The
two expressions ζῆν ἐν and περιπατεῖν
ἐν involve two distinct ideas, denoting
the condition of their life and the character of their practice respectively.
Their conduct was conformable to
their circumstances. Comp. Gal. v. 25
εἰ ζῶμεν πνεύματι, πνεύματι καὶ στοι-
χῶμεν.

ὀργήν, θυμόν, κακίαν, βλασφημίαν, αἰσχρολογίαν ἐκ
τοῦ στόματος ὑμῶν· ⁹ μὴ ψεύδεσθε εἰς ἀλλήλους· ἀπεκ-

8. The errors of the past suggest the obligations of the present. Thus the Apostle returns to the topic with which the sentence commenced. But the violence of the contrast has broken up the grammar of the sentence; see the note on ver. 5.

τὰ πάντα] 'not only those vices which have been specially named before (ver. 5), but *all* of whatever kind.' The Apostle accordingly goes on to specify sins of a wholly different type from those already mentioned, sins of uncharitableness, such as anger, detraction, malice, and the like.

ὀργήν, θυμόν] '*anger, wrath.*' The one denotes a more or less settled feeling of hatred, the other a tumultuous outburst of passion. This distinction of the two words was fixed chiefly by the definitions of the Stoics: Diog. Laert. vii. 114 ὁ δὲ θυμός ἐστιν ὀργὴ ἀρχομένη. So Ammonius θυμὸς μέν ἐστι πρόσκαιρος, ὀργὴ δὲ πολυχρόνιος μνησικακία, Greg. Naz. *Carm.* 34 (II. p. 612) θυμὸς μέν ἐστιν ἀθρόος ζέσις φρενός, ὀργὴ δὲ θυμὸς ἐμμένων. They may be represented in Latin by *ira* and *furor*; Senec. *de Ira* ii. 36 'Ajacem in mortem egit furor, in furorem ira,' and Jerome in Ephes. iv. 31 'Furor incipiens ira est': see Trench *N. T. Syn.* § xxxvii, p. 123 sq. On other synonymes connected with θυμός and ὀργή see the note on Ephes. iv. 31.

κακίαν] '*malice,*' or '*malignity,*' as it may be translated in default of a better word. It is not (at least in the New Testament) vice generally, but the vicious nature which is bent on *doing harm to others,* and is well defined by Calvin (on Ephes. iv. 31) 'animi pravitas, quae *humanitati et aequitati* est opposita.' This will be evident from the connexion in which it appears, e.g. Rom. i. 29, Eph. iv. 31, Tit. iii. 3. Thus κακία and πονηρία

(which frequently occur together, e.g. 1 Cor. v. 8) only differ in so far as the one denotes rather the vicious disposition, the other the active exercise of it. The word is carefully investigated in Trench *N. T. Syn.* § xi. p. 35 sq.

βλασφημίαν] '*evil speaking, railing, slandering,*' as frequently, e.g. Rom. iii. 8, xiv. 16, 1 Cor. iv. 13 (v.l.), x. 30, Ephes. iv. 31, Tit. iii. 2. The word has the same twofold sense, 'evil speaking' and 'blasphemy,' in classical writers, which it has in the New Testament.

αἰσχρολογίαν] '*foul-mouthed abuse.*' The word, as used elsewhere, has two meanings: (1) '*Filthy-talking,*' as defined in Clem. Alex. *Paed.* ii. 6 (p. 189 sq.), where it is denounced at length: comp. Arist.*Pol.* vii. 17, Epict. *Man.* 33, Plut. *Mor.* 9, and so commonly; (2) '*Abusive language,*' as e.g. Polyb. viii. 13. 8, xii. 13. 3, xxxi. 10. 4. If the two senses of the word had been quite distinct, we might have had some difficulty in choosing between them here. The former sense is suggested by the parallel passage Ephes. v. 4 αἰσχρότης καὶ μωρολογία ἢ εὐτραπελία; the second by the connexion with βλασφημία here. But the second sense is derived from the first. The word can only mean 'abuse,' when the abuse is 'foul-mouthed.' And thus we may suppose that both ideas, 'filthiness' and 'evil-speaking,' are included here.

9. ἀπεκδυσάμενοι κ.τ.λ.] '*putting off.*' Do these aorist participles describe an action coincident with or prior to the ψεύδεσθε? In other words are they part of the command, or do they assign the reason for the command? Must they be rendered 'putting off,' or ' seeing that ye did (at your baptism) put off'? The former seems the more probable interpretation; for (1) Though both ideas are

δυσάμενοι τὸν παλαιὸν ἄνθρωπον σὺν ταῖς πράξεσιν
αὐτοῦ, ¹⁰καὶ ἐνδυσάμενοι τὸν νέον, τὸν ἀνακαινούμενον
εἰς ἐπίγνωσιν κατ᾿ εἰκόνα τοῦ κτίσαντος αὐτόν· ¹¹ὅπου

found in St Paul, the imperative is the more usual; e.g. Rom. xiii. 12 sq. ἀποθώμεθα οὖν τὰ ἔργα τοῦ σκότους, ἐνδυσώμεθα δὲ τὰ ὅπλα τοῦ φωτός...ἐνδύσασθε τὸν Κύριον Ἰησοῦν Χριστόν, Ephes. vi. 11 ἐνδύσασθε τὴν πανοπλίαν with ver. 14 στῆτε οὖν...ἐνδυσάμενοι κ.τ.λ., 1 Thess. v. 8 νήφωμεν ἐνδυσάμενοι κ.τ.λ. The one exception is Gal. iii. 27 ὅσοι γὰρ εἰς Χριστὸν ἐβαπτίσθητε, Χριστὸν ἐνεδύσασθε. (2) The 'putting on' in the parallel passage, Ephes. iv. 24, is imperative, not affirmative, whether we read ἐνδύσασθαι or ἐνδύσασθε. (3) The participles here are followed immediately by an imperative in the context, ver. 12 ἐνδύσασθε οὖν, where the idea seems to be the same. For the synchronous aorist participle see Winer § xlv. p. 430. St Paul uses ἀπεκδυσάμενοι, ἐνδυσάμενοι (not ἀπεκδυόμενοι, ἐνδυόμενοι), for the same reason for which he uses ἐνδύσασθε (not ἐνδύεσθε), because it is a thing to be done *once for all*. For the double compound ἀπεκδύεσθαι see the notes on ii. 11, 15.

παλαιὸν ἄνθρωπον] as Rom. vi. 6, Ephes. iv. 22. With this expression compare ὁ ἔξω, ὁ ἔσω ἄνθρωπος, Rom. vii. 22, 2 Cor. iv. 16, Ephes. iii. 16; ὁ κρυπτὸς τῆς καρδίας ἄνθρωπος, 1 Pet. iii. 4; ὁ μικρός μου ἄνθρωπος, 'my insignificance,' Polycr. in Euseb. *H. E.* v. 24.

10. τὸν νέον κ.τ.λ.] In Ephes. iv. 24 it is ἐνδύσασθαι τὸν καινὸν ἄνθρωπον. Of the two words νέος and καινός, the former refers solely to time, the other denotes quality also; the one is new as being *young*, the other new as being *fresh*: the one is opposed to long duration, the other to effeteness; see Trench *N. T. Syn.* § lx. p. 206. Here the idea which is wanting to νέος, and which καινὸς gives

in the parallel passage, is more than supplied by the addition τὸν ἀνακαινούμενον κ.τ.λ.

The νέος or καινὸς ἄνθρωπος in these passages is not Christ Himself, as the parallel expression Χριστὸν ἐνδύσασθαι might suggest, and as it is actually used in Ign. *Ephes.* 20 εἰς τὸν καινὸν ἄνθρωπον Ἰησοῦν Χριστόν, but the regenerate man formed after Christ. The idea here is the same as in καινὴ κτίσις, 2 Cor. v. 17, Gal. vi. 15: comp. Rom. vi. 4 καινότης ζωῆς, Barnab. 16 ἐγενόμεθα καινοί, πάλιν ἐξ ἀρχῆς κτιζόμενοι.

τὸν ἀνακαινούμενον] '*which is* ever *being renewed*.' The force of the present tense is explained by 2 Cor. iv. 16 ὁ ἔσω ἡμῶν [ἄνθρωπος] ἀνακαινοῦται ἡμέρᾳ καὶ ἡμέρᾳ. Compare also the use of the tenses in the parallel passage, Ephes. iv. 22 sq. ἀποθέσθαι, ἀνανεοῦσθαι, ἐνδύσασθαι. For the opposite see Ephes. iv. 22 τὸν παλαιὸν ἄνθρωπον τὸν φθειρόμενον κ.τ.λ.

εἰς ἐπίγνωσιν] '*unto perfect knowledge*,' the true knowledge in Christ, as opposed to the false knowledge of the heretical teachers. For the implied contrast see above, pp. 44, 99 sq. (comp. the notes on i. 9, ii. 3), and for the word ἐπίγνωσις the note on i. 9. The words here are to be connected closely with ἀνακαινούμενον: comp. Heb. vi. 6 πάλιν ἀνακαινίζειν εἰς μετάνοιαν.

κατ᾿ εἰκόνα κ.τ.λ.] The reference is to Gen. i. 26 καὶ εἶπεν ὁ Θεός, Ποιήσωμεν ἄνθρωπον κατ᾿ εἰκόνα ἡμετέραν κ.τ.λ.; comp. ver. 28 κατ᾿ εἰκόνα Θεοῦ ἐποίησεν αὐτόν. See also Ephes. iv. 24 τὸν καινὸν ἄνθρωπον τὸν κατὰ Θεὸν κτισθέντα. This reference however does not imply an identity of the creation here mentioned with the creation of Genesis, but only an analogy between

οὐκ ἔνι ῞Ελλην καὶ ᾽Ιουδαῖος, περιτομὴ καὶ ἀκροβυστία,

the two. The spiritual man in each believer's heart, like the primal man in the beginning of the world, was created after God's image. The καινὴ κτίσις in this respect resembles the ἀρχαία κτίσις. The pronoun αὐτὸν cannot be referred to anything else but the νέος ἄνθρωπος, the regenerate man; and the aorist κτίσαντος (compare κτισθέντα in the parallel passage Ephes. iv. 24) refers to the time of this ἀναγέννησις in Christ. See Barnab. 6 ἀνακαινίσας ἡμᾶς ἐν τῇ ἀφέσει τῶν ἁμαρτιῶν ἐποίησεν ἡμᾶς ἄλλον τύπον...ὡσὰν δὴ ἀναπλάσσοντος αὐτοῦ ἡμᾶς, after which Gen. i. 26 is quoted. The new birth was a re-creation in God's image; the subsequent life must be a deepening of this image thus stamped upon the man.

The allusion to Genesis therefore requires us to understand τοῦ κτίσαντος of God, and not of Christ, as it is taken by St Chrysostom and others; and this seems to be demanded also by the common use of ὁ κτίσας. But if Christ is not ὁ κτίσας, may He not be intended by the εἰκὼν τοῦ κτίσαντος? In favour of this interpretation it may be urged (1) That Christ elsewhere is called the εἰκὼν of God, i. 15, 2 Cor. iv. 4; (2) That the Alexandrian school interpreted the term in Gen. i. 26 as denoting the Logos; thus Philo *de Mund. Op.* 6 (I. p. 5 M) τὸ ἀρχέτυπον παράδειγμα, ἰδέα τῶν ἰδεῶν ὁ Θεοῦ λόγος (comp. ib. §§ 7, 23, 24, 48), *Fragm.* II. p. 625 M θνητὸν γὰρ οὐδὲν ἀπεικονισθῆναι πρὸς τὸν ἀνωτάτω καὶ πατέρα τῶν ὅλων ἐδύνατο, ἀλλὰ πρὸς τὸν δεύτερον Θεὸν ὅς ἐστιν ἐκείνου λόγος κ.τ.λ. *Leg. Alleg.* i. 31, 32 (I. p. 106 sq.). Hence Philo speaks of the first man as εἰκὼν εἰκόνος (*de Mund. Op.* 6), and as παγκάλου παραδείγματος πάγκαλον μίμημα (ib. § 48). A pregnant meaning is thus given to κατά, and κατ᾽ εἰκόνα is rendered 'after the fashion (or pattern) of the Image.' But this interpretation seems very improbable in

St Paul; for (1) In the parallel passage Ephes. iv. 24 the expression is simply κατὰ Θεόν, which may be regarded as equivalent to κατ᾽ εἰκόνα τοῦ κτίσαντος here; (2) The Alexandrian explanation of Gen. i. 26 just quoted is very closely allied to the Platonic doctrine of ideas (for the εἰκών, so interpreted, is the archetype or ideal pattern of the sensible world), and thus it lies outside the range of those conceptions which specially recommended the Alexandrian terminology of the Logos to the Apostles, as a fit vehicle for communicating the truths of Christianity.

11. ὅπου] i.e. 'in this regenerate life, in this spiritual region into which the believer is transferred in Christ.'

οὐκ ἔνι] 'Not only does the distinction not exist, but it *cannot* exist.' It is a mundane distinction, and therefore it has disappeared. For the sense of ἔνι, negativing not merely the fact, but the possibility, see the note on Gal. iii. 28.

῞Ελληνκ.τ.λ.] Comparing the enumeration here with the parallel passage Gal. iii. 28, we mark this difference. In Galatians the abolition of all distinctions is stated in the broadest way by the selection of three typical instances; religious prerogative (᾽Ιουδαῖος, ῞Ελλην), social caste (δοῦλος, ἐλεύθερος), natural sex (ἄρσεν, θῆλυ). Here on the other hand the examples are chosen with special reference to the immediate circumstances of the Colossian Church. (1) The Judaism of the Colossian heretics is met by ῞Ελλην καὶ ᾽Ιουδαῖος, and as it manifested itself especially in enforcing circumcision, this is further emphasized by περιτομὴ καὶ ἀκροβυστία (see above, p. 73). (2) Their Gnosticism again is met by βάρβαρος, Σκύθης. They laid special stress on intelligence, penetration, gnosis. The Apostle offers the full privileges of the Gospel to barbarians and even barbarians of the low-

βάρβαρος, Σκύθης, δοῦλος, ἐλεύθερος, ἀλλὰ τὰ πάντα

est type (see p. 99 sq.). In Rom. i. 14 the division Ἕλλησίν τε καὶ βαρβάροις is almost synonymous with σοφοῖς τε καὶ ἀνοήτοις. (3) Special circumstances, connected with an eminent member of the Church of Colossæ, had directed his attention at this moment to the relation of masters and slaves. Hence he cannot leave the subject without adding δοῦλος, ἐλεύθερος, though this has no special bearing on the Colossian heresy. See above, p. 33, and the note on iii. 22, together with the introduction to the Epistle to Philemon.

περιτομὴ κ.τ.λ.] Enforcing and extending the lesson of the previous clause. This abolition of distinctions applies to religious privilege, not only as inherited by birth (Ἕλλην καὶ Ἰουδαῖος), but also as assumed by adoption (περιτομὴ καὶ ἀκροβυστία). If it is no advantage to be born a Jew, it is none to become as a Jew; comp. 1 Cor. vii. 19, Gal. v. 6, vi. 15.

βάρβαρος] To the Jew the whole world was divided into Ἰουδαῖοι and Ἕλληνες, the privileged and unprivileged portions of mankind, religious prerogative being taken as the line of demarcation (see notes Gal. ii. 3). To the Greek and Roman it was similarly divided into Ἕλληνες and βάρβαροι, again the privileged and unprivileged portion of the human race, civilisation and culture being now the criterion of distinction. Thus from the one point of view the Ἕλλην is contrasted disadvantageously with the Ἰουδαῖος, while from the other he is contrasted advantageously with the βάρβαρος. Both distinctions are equally antagonistic to the Spirit of the Gospel. The Apostle declares both alike null and void in Christ. The twofold character of the Colossian heresy enables him to strike at these two opposite forms of error with one blow.

The word βάρβαρος properly deno-

ted one who spoke an inarticulate, stammering, unintelligible language; see Max Müller Lectures on the Science of Language 1st ser. p. 81 sq., 114 sq., Farrar Families of Speech p. 21: comp. 1 Cor. xiv. 11. Hence it was adopted by Greek exclusiveness and pride to stigmatize the rest of mankind, a feeling embodied in the proverb πᾶς μὴ Ἕλλην βάρβαρος (Servius on Verg. Aen. ii. 504); comp. Plato Polit. 262 E τὸ μὲν Ἑλληνικὸν ὡς ἓν ἀπὸ πάντων ἀφαιροῦντες χωρίς, σύμπασι δὲ τοῖς ἄλλοις γένεσιν...βάρβαρον μιᾷ κλήσει προσείποντες αὐτὸ κ.τ.λ., Dionys. Hal. Rhet. xi. 5 διπλοῦν δὲ τὸ ἔθνος, Ἕλλην ἢ βάρβαρος κ.τ.λ. So Philo Vit. Moys. ii. 5 (II. p. 138) speaks of τὸ ἥμισυ τμῆμα τοῦ ἀνθρώπων γένους, τὸ βαρβαρικόν, as opposed to τὸ Ἑλληνικόν. It is not necessary to suppose that they adopted it from the Egyptians, who seem to have called non-Egyptian peoples berber (see Sir G. Wilkinson in Rawlinson's Herod. ii. 158); for the onomatopœia will explain its origin independently, Strabo xiv. 2. 28 (p. 662) οἶμαι δὲ τὸ βάρβαρον κατ' ἀρχὰς ἐκπεφωνῆσθαι οὕτως κατ' ὀνοματοποιίαν ἐπὶ τῶν δυσεκφόρως καὶ σκληρῶς καὶ τραχέως λαλούντων, ὡς τὸ βατταρίζειν κ.τ.λ. The Latins, adopting the Greek culture, adopted the Greek distinction also, e.g. Cic. de Fin. ii. 15 'Non solum Graecia et Italia, sed etiam omnis barbaria': and accordingly Dionysius, Ant. Rom. i. 69, classes the Romans with the Greeks as distinguished from the 'barbarians'—this twofold division of the human race being taken for granted as absolute and final. So too in v. 8, having mentioned the Romans, he goes on to speak of οἱ ἄλλοι Ἕλληνες. The older Roman poets however, writing from a Greek point of view, (more than half in irony) speak of themselves as barbari and of their country as barbaria; e.g. Plaut. Mil. Glor. ii. 2. 58 'poetae barbaro' (of Naevius), Asin. Prol. 11.

καὶ ἐν πᾶσιν Χριστός. ^{12}ἐνδύσασθε οὖν, ὡς ἐκλεκτοὶ

'Maccus vortit barbare,' *Poen.* iii. 2. 21 'in barbaria boves.'

In this classification the Jews necessarily ranked as 'barbarians'; Orig. *c. Cels.* i. 2. At times Philo seems tacitly to accept this designation (*Vit. Moys.* l. c.); but elsewhere he resents it, *Leg. ad Gai.* 31 (II. p. 578) ὑπὸ φρονήματος, ὡς μὲν ἔνιοι τῶν διαβαλλόντων εἴποιεν ἄν, βαρβαρικοῦ, ὡς δ᾽ ἔχει τὸ ἀληθές, ἐλευθερίου καὶ εὐγενοῦς. On the other hand the Christian Apologists with a true instinct glory in the 'barbarous' origin of their religion : Justin *Apol.* i. 5 (p. 56 A) ἀλλὰ καὶ ἐν βαρβάροις ὑπ᾽ αὐτοῦ τοῦ Λόγου μορφωθέντος καὶ ἀνθρώπου γενομένου, ib. § 46 (p. 83 D) ἐν βαρβάροις δὲ ᾽Αβραάμ κ.τ.λ., Tatian. *ad Graec.* 29 γραφαῖς τισὶν ἐντυχεῖν βαρβαρικαῖς, ib. 31 τὸν δὲ (Μωυσῆν) πάσης βαρβάρου σοφίας ἀρχηγόν, ib. 35 τῆς καθ᾽ ἡμᾶς βαρβάρου φιλοσοφίας. By glorying in the name they gave a practical comment on the Apostle's declaration that the distinction of Greek and barbarian was abolished in Christ. In a similar spirit Clem. Alex. *Strom.* i. 16 (p. 361) endeavours to prove that οὐ μόνον φιλοσοφίας ἀλλὰ καὶ πάσης σχεδὸν τέχνης εὑρεταὶ βάρβαροι.

'Not till that word *barbarian,*' writes Prof. Max Müller (l. c. p. 118), 'was struck out of the dictionary of mankind and replaced by *brother,* not till the right of all nations of the world to be classed as members of one genus or kind was recognised, can we look even for the first beginnings of our science. This change was effected by Christianity... *Humanity* is a word which you look for in vain in Plato or Aristotle; the idea of mankind as one family, as the children of one God, is an idea of Christian growth : and the science of mankind, and of the languages of mankind, is a science which, without Christianity, would never have sprung into life. When people had been taught to look upon all men as

brethren, then and then only, did the variety of human speech present itself as a problem that called for a solution in the eyes of thoughtful observers : and I therefore date the real beginning of the science of language from the first day of Pentecost... The common origin of mankind, the differences of race and language, the susceptibility of all nations of the highest mental culture, these become, in the new world in which we live, problems of scientific, because of more than scientific interest.' St Paul was the great exponent of the fundamental principle in the Christian Church which was symbolized on the day of Pentecost, when he declared, as here, that in Christ there is neither Ἕλλην nor βάρβαρος, or as in Rom. i. 14 that he himself was a debtor equally Ἕλλησίν τε καὶ βαρβάροις.

The only other passage in the New Testament (besides those quoted) in which βάρβαρος occurs is Acts xxviii. 2, 4, where it is used of the people of Melita. If this Melita be Malta, they would be of Phœnician descent.

Σκύθης] The lowest type of barbarian. There is the same collocation of words in Dionys. Halic. *Rhet.* xi. 5, 6 πατήρ, βάρβαρος, Σκύθης, νέος, Aesch. *c. Ctes.* 172 Σκύθης, βάρβαρος, ἑλληνίζων τῇ φωνῇ (of Demosthenes). The savageness of the Scythians was proverbial. The earlier Greek writers indeed, to whom *omne ignotum* was *pro magnifico,* had frequently spoken of them otherwise (see Strabo vii. 3. 7 sq., p. 300 sq.). Aeschylus for instance called them εὔνομοι Σκύθαι, *Fragm.* 189 (comp. *Eum.* 703). Like the other Hyperboreans, they were a simple, righteous people, living beyond the vices and the miseries of civilisation. But the common estimate was far different, and probably far more true: e.g. 3 Macc. vii. 5 νόμου Σκυθῶν ἀγριωτέραν...ὠμότητα (comp. 2 Macc. iv. 47), Joseph.

τοῦ Θεοῦ, ἅγιοι [καὶ] ἠγαπημένοι, σπλάγχνα οἰκτιρμοῦ,

c. Ap. ii. 37 Σκύθαι...βραχὺ τῶν θηρίων διαφέροντες, Philo Leg. ad Gai. 2 (ii. p. 547) Σαρματῶν γένη καὶ Σκυθῶν, ἅπερ οὐχ ἧττον ἐξηγρίωται τῶν Γερμανικῶν, Tertull. adv. Marc. i. 1 'Scytha tetrior,' Orig. c. Cels. i. 1 Σκυθῶν, καὶ εἴ τι Σκυθῶν ἀσεβέστερον. In Vit. Moys. ii. 4 (i. p. 137) Philo seems to place the Egyptians and the Scythians at the two extremes in the scale of barbarian nations. The passages given in Wetstein from classical writers are hardly less strong in the same direction. Anacharsis the Scythian is said to have retorted ἐμοὶ δὲ πάντες Ἕλληνες σκυθίζουσιν, Clem. Strom. i. 16 (p. 364).

The Jews had a special reason for their unfavourable estimate of the Scythians. In the reign of Josiah hordes of these northern barbarians had deluged Palestine and a great part of Western Asia (Herod. i. 103 —106). The incident indeed is passed over in silence in the historical books; but the terror inspired by these invaders has found expression in the prophets (Ezek. xxviii, xxxix, Jer. i. 13 sq., vi. 1 sq.), and they left behind them a memorial in the Greek name of Beth-shean, Σκυθῶν πόλις (Judith iii. 10, 2 Macc. xii. 29 : comp. Judges i. 27 LXX) or Σκυθόπολις, which seems to have been derived from a settlement on this occasion (Plin. N. H. v. 16; see Ewald Gesch. iii. p. 689 sq., Grove s. v. Scythopolis in Smith's Bibl. Dict.).

Hence Justin, Dial. § 28 (p. 246 A), describing the largeness of the new dispensation, says κἂν Σκύθης ᾖ τις ἢ Πέρσης, ἔχει δὲ τὴν τοῦ Θεοῦ γνῶσιν καὶ τοῦ Χριστοῦ αὐτοῦ καὶ φυλάσσει τὰ αἰώνια δίκαια...φίλος ἐστὶ τῷ Θεῷ, where he singles out two different but equally low types of barbarians, the Scythians being notorious for their ferocity, the Persians for their licentiousness (Clem. Alex. Paed. i. 7, p. 131, Strom. iii. 2, p. 515, and the Apologists generally). So too the Pseudo-Lucian, Philopatris 17, sati-

rising Christianity, KP. τόδε εἶπε, εἰ καὶ τὰ τῶν Σκυθῶν ἐν τῷ οὐρανῷ ἐγχαράτουσι. TP. πάντα, εἰ τύχοι γε χρηστὸς καὶ ἐν ἔθνεσι. From a misconception of this passage in the Colossians, heresiologers distinguished four main forms of heresy in the pre-Christian world, βαρβαρισμός, σκυθισμός, ἑλληνισμός, ἰουδαϊσμός; so Epiphan. Epist. ad Acac. 2 σαφῶς γὰρ περὶ τούτων τῶν τεσσάρων αἱρέσεων ὁ ἀπόστολος ἐπιτεμὼν ἔφη, Ἐν γὰρ Χριστῷ Ἰησοῦ οὐ βάρβαρος, οὐ Σκύθης, οὐχ Ἕλλην, οὐκ Ἰουδαῖος, ἀλλὰ καινὴ κτίσις: comp. Haer. i. 4, 7 sq., i. pp. 5, 8 sq., Anaceph. ii. pp. 127, 129 sq.

τὰ πάντα κ.τ.λ.] 'Christ is all things and in all things.' Christ has dispossessed and obliterated all distinctions of religious prerogative and intellectual preeminence and social caste; Christ has substituted Himself for all these; Christ occupies the whole sphere of human life and permeates all its developments : comp. Ephes. i. 23 τοῦ τὰ πάντα ἐν πᾶσιν πληρουμένου. For τὰ πάντα, which is stronger than οἱ πάντες, see Gal. iii. 22 συνέκλεισεν ἡ γραφὴ τὰ πάντα ὑπὸ ἁμαρτίαν with the note. In this passage ἐν πᾶσιν is probably neuter, as in 2 Cor. xi. 6, Phil. iv. 12, 1 Tim. iii. 11, 2 Tim. ii. 7, iv. 5, Ephes. iv. 6, vi. 16.

In the parallel passage Gal. iii. 28 the corresponding clause is πάντες ὑμεῖς εἷς ἐστε ἐν Χριστῷ Ἰησοῦ. The inversion here accords with a chief motive of the epistle, which is to assert the absolute and universal supremacy of Christ; comp. i. 17 sq., ii. 10 sq., 19. The two parts of the antithesis are combined in our Lord's saying, Joh. xiv. 20 ὑμεῖς ἐν ἐμοί, κἀγὼ ἐν ὑμῖν.

12—15. 'Therefore, as the elect of God, as a people consecrated to His service and specially endowed with His love, array yourselves in hearts of compassion, in kindliness and humi-

χρηστότητα, ταπεινοφρόσύνην, πραΰτητα, μακροθυ-

lity, in a gentle and yielding spirit.
Bear with one another, forgive freely
among yourselves. As your Master
forgave you His servants, so ought ye
to forgive your fellow-servants. And
over all these robe yourselves in love;
for this is the garment which binds
together all the graces of perfection.
And let the one supreme umpire in
your hearts, the one referee amidst
all your difficulties, be the peace of
Christ, which is the destined goal of
your Christian calling, in which is
realised the unity belonging to members of one body. Lastly of all; show
your gratitude by your thanksgiving.'

12. ἐνδύσασθε οὖν] '*Put on therefore,*' as men to whom Christ has become all in all. The incidental mention of Christ as superseding all other
relations gives occasion to this argumentative οὖν: comp. iii. 1, 5.

ὡς ἐκλεκτοὶ τοῦ Θεοῦ] '*as elect ones
of God.*' Comp. Rom. viii. 3, Tit. i. 1.
In the Gospels κλητοί and ἐκλεκτοί are
distinguished as an outer and an inner circle (Matt. xxii. 14 πολλοὶ γάρ
εἰσιν κλητοί, ὀλίγοι δὲ ἐκλεκτοί), κλητοί
being those summoned to the privileges of the Gospel and ἐκλεκτοί those
appointed to final salvation (Matt.
xxiv. 22, 24, 31, Mark xiii. 20, 22, 27,
Luke xviii. 7). But in St Paul no
such distinction can be traced. With
him the two terms seem to be coextensive, as two aspects of the same process, κλητοί having special reference to
the goal and ἐκλεκτοί to the starting-
point. The same persons are 'called'
to Christ, and 'chosen out' from the
world. Thus in 1 Thess. i. 4 εἰδότες
τὴν ἐκλογὴν ὑμῶν κ.τ.λ. the word clearly
denotes election to Church-membership. Thus also in 2 Tim. ii. 10, where
St Paul says that he endures all things
διὰ τοὺς ἐκλεκτούς, adding ἵνα καὶ αὐτοὶ
σωτηρίας τύχωσιν κ.τ.λ., the uncertainty
implied in these last words clearly
shows that election to final salvation
is not meant. In the same sense he

speaks of an individual Christian as
'elect,' Rom. xvi. 13. And again in
1 Cor. i. 26, 27 βλέπετε τὴν κλῆσιν
ὑμῶν...τὰ μῶρα τοῦ κόσμου ἐξελέξατο,
the words appear as synonymes. The
same is also the usage of St Peter.
Thus in an opening salutation he addresses whole Christian communities
as ἐκλεκτοί (1 Pet. i. 1; comp. v. 13 ἡ
συνεκλεκτὴ ἐν Βαβυλῶνι, i. e. probably
ἐκκλησία), as St Paul under similar
circumstances (Rom. i. 6, 7, 1 Cor.
i. 2) designates them κλητοί; and in
another passage (2 Pet. i. 10) he appeals to his readers to make their
κλῆσις and ἐκλογή sure. The use of
ἐκλεκτός in 2 Joh. 1, 13, is apparently
the same; and in Apoc. xvii. 14 οἱ
μετ' αὐτοῦ κλητοὶ καὶ ἐκλεκτοὶ καὶ πιστοί this is also the case, as we may
infer from the addition of πιστοί, which
points to those who have been *true* to
their 'calling and election.' Thus the
Gospels stand alone in this respect.
In fact ἐκλογή denotes election by
God not only to final salvation, but to
any special privilege or work, whether it be (1) Church-membership, as
in the passages cited from the epistles;
or (2) The work of preaching, as when
St Paul (Acts ix. 15) is called σκεῦος
ἐκλογῆς, the object of the 'election'
being defined in the words following,
τοῦ βαστάσαι τὸ ὄνομά μου ἐνώπιον
[τῶν] ἐθνῶν τε καὶ βασιλέων κ.τ.λ.; or
(3) The Messiahship, 1 Pet. ii. 4, 6; or
(4) The fatherhood of the chosen
people, as in the case of Isaac and Jacob, Rom. ix. 11; or (5) The faithful
remnant under the theocracy, Rom.
xi. 5, 7, 28. This last application presents the closest analogy to the idea
of final salvation: but even here St
Paul treats κλῆσις and ἐκλογή as coextensive, Rom. xi. 28, 29 κατὰ δὲ τὴν
ἐκλογὴν ἀγαπητοὶ διὰ τοὺς πατέρας·
ἀμεταμέλητα γὰρ τὰ χαρίσματα καὶ ἡ
κλῆσις τοῦ Θεοῦ.

ἅγιοι κ.τ.λ.] These are not to be
taken as vocatives, but as predicates

μίαν· ¹³ἀνεχόμενοι ἀλλήλων, καὶ χαριζόμενοι ἑαυτοῖς,

further defining the meaning of ἐκλεκτοί. All the three terms ἐκλεκτοί, ἅγιοι, ἠγαπημένοι, are transferred from the Old Covenant to the New, from the Israel after the flesh to the Israel after the Spirit. For the two former comp. 1 Pet. ii. 9 γένος ἐκλεκτόν ...ἔθνος ἅγιον; and for the sense of ἅγιοι, 'the consecrated people of God,' see the note on Phil. i. 1. For the third word, ἠγαπημένοι, see Is. v. 1 Ἄσω δὴ τῷ ἠγαπημένῳ κ.τ.λ., Hos. ii. 25 τὴν οὐκ ἠγαπημένην ἠγαπημένην (as quoted in Rom. ix. 25). In the New Testament it seems to be used always of the objects of God's love; e.g. 1 Thess. i. 4 εἰδότες, ἀδελφοὶ ἠγαπημένοι ὑπὸ Θεοῦ, τὴν ἐκλογὴν ὑμῶν, 2 Thess. ii. 13 ἀδελφοὶ ἠγαπημένοι ὑπὸ Κυρίου (comp. Jude 1); and so probably Rev. xx. 9 τὴν πόλιν τὴν ἠγαπημένην. For the connexion of God's election and God's love see Rom. xi. 28 (quoted above), 1 Thess. l. c. The καὶ is omitted in one or two excellent copies (though it has the great preponderance of authorities in its favour), and it is impossible not to feel how much the sentence gains in force by the omission, ἐκλεκτοὶ Θεοῦ, ἅγιοι, ἠγαπημένοι; comp. 1 Pet. ii. 6.

σπλάγχνα οἰκτιρμοῦ] 'a heart of pity.' For the meaning of σπλάγχνα see the note on Phil. i. 8, and for the whole expression comp. σπλάγχνα ἐλέους Luke i. 78, Test. xii Patr. Zab. 7, 8.

χρηστότητα κ.τ.λ.] The two words χρηστότης and ταπεινοφροσύνη, 'kindliness' and 'humility,' describe the Christian temper of mind generally, and this in two aspects, as it affects either (1) our relation to others (χρηστότης), or (2) our estimate of self (ταπεινοφροσύνη). For χρηστότης see the note on Gal. v. 22: for ταπεινοφροσύνη, the note on Phil. ii. 3.

πραΰτητα κ.τ.λ.] These next two words, πραΰτης and μακροθυμία, denote the exercise of the Christian temper in its outward bearing to-

wards others. They are best distinguished by their opposites. πραΰτης is opposed to 'rudeness, harshness,' ἀγριότης (Plato Symp. 197 D), χαλεπότης (Arist. H. A. ix. 1); μακροθυμία to 'resentment, revenge, wrath,' ὀργή (Prov. xvi. 32), ὀξυχολία (Herm. Mand. v. 1, 2). For the meaning of μακροθυμία see above, on i. 11; for the form of πραΰτης (πραότης), on Gal. v. 23. The words are discussed in Trench N. T. Syn. § xlii. p. 140 sq., § xliii. p. 145 sq., § liii. p. 184 sq. They appear in connexion Ephes. iv. 2, Ign. Polyc. 6 μακροθυμήσατε οὖν μετ' ἀλλήλων ἐν πραΰτητι.

13. ἀλλήλων, ἑαυτοῖς] The pronoun is varied, as in Ephes. iv. 32 γίνεσθε εἰς ἀλλήλους χρηστοί...χαριζόμενοι ἑαυτοῖς κ.τ.λ., 1 Pet. iv. 8—10 τὴν εἰς ἑαυτοὺς ἀγάπην ἐκτενῆ ἔχοντες ...φιλόξενοι εἰς ἀλλήλους...εἰς ἑαυτοὺς αὐτὸ [τὸ χάρισμα] διακονοῦντες. The reciprocal ἑαυτῶν differs from the reciprocal ἀλλήλων in emphasizing the idea of corporate unity: hence it is more appropriate here (comp. Ephes. iv. 2, 32) with χαριζόμενοι than with ἀνεχόμενοι: comp. Xen. Mem. iii. 5. 16 ἀντὶ μὲν τοῦ συνεργεῖν ἑαυτοῖς τὰ συμφέροντα, ἐπηρεάζουσιν ἀλλήλοις, καὶ φθονοῦσιν ἑαυτοῖς μᾶλλον ἢ τοῖς ἄλλοις ἀνθρώποις...καὶ προαιροῦνται μᾶλλον οὕτω κερδαίνειν ἀπ' ἀλλήλων ἢ συνωφελοῦντες αὑτούς, where the propriety of the two words in their respective places will be evident: and in. ii. 7. 12 ἀντὶ ὑφορωμένων ἑαυτὰς ἡδέως ἀλλήλας ἑώρων, where the variation is more subtle but not less appropriate. For instances of this use of ἑαυτῶν see Bleek Hebräerbrief iii. 13 (p. 453 sq.), Kühner Griech. Gramm. § 455 (II. p. 497 sq.).

χαριζόμενοι] i.e. 'forgiving'; see the note on ii. 13. An a fortiori argument lurks under the use of ἑαυτοῖς (rather than ἀλλήλοις): if Christ forgave them, much more should they forgive themselves.

ἐάν τις πρός τινα ἔχη μομφήν· καθὼς καὶ ὁ Κύριος
ἐχαρίσατο ὑμῖν, οὕτως καὶ ὑμεῖς· ¹⁴ἐπὶ πᾶσιν δὲ τούτοις

μομφήν] 'a complaint.' As μέμ-
φεσθαι is 'to find *fault* with,' referring
most commonly to errors of omission,
so μομφή here is regarded as a *debt*,
which needs to be remitted. The
rendering of the A. V. 'a quarrel'
(=querela) is only wrong as being an
archaism. The phrase μομφὴν ἔχειν
occurs several times in classical Greek,
but generally in poetry: e.g. Eur.
Orest. 1069, Arist. *Pax* 664.

καθὼς καὶ κ.τ.λ.] This must not be
connected with the preceding words,
but treated as an independent sentence, the καθὼς καί being answered
by the οὕτως καί. For the presence of
καί in both clauses of the comparison
see the note on i. 6. The phenomenon
is common in the best classical writers,
e.g. Xen. *Mem.* i. 6. 3 ὥσπερ καὶ τῶν
ἄλλων ἔργων οἱ διδάσκαλοι...οὕτω καὶ
σύ κ.τ.λ.; see the references in Hein-
dorf on Plato *Phaedo* 64 C, *Sophist.*
217 B, and Kühner *Griech. Gramm.*
§ 524 (II. p. 799).

ὁ Κύριος] This reading, which is
better supported than ὁ Χριστός, is
also more expressive. It recalls more
directly the lesson of the parable
which enforces the duty of fellow-
servant to fellow-servant; Matt. xviii.
27 σπλαγχνισθεὶς δὲ ὁ κύριος τοῦ
δούλου ἐκείνου ἀπέλυσεν αὐτὸν καὶ τὸ
δάνειον ἀφῆκεν αὐτῷ κ.τ.λ.: comp. below
iv. 1 εἰδότες ὅτι καὶ ὑμεῖς ἔχετε κύριον
ἐν οὐρανῷ. The reading Χριστὸς perhaps
comes from the parallel passage Ephes.
iv. 32 χαριζόμενοι ἑαυτοῖς, καθὼς καὶ ὁ
Θεὸς ἐν Χριστῷ ἐχαρίσατο ἡμῖν (or ὑμῖν).

οὕτως καὶ ὑμεῖς] sc. χαρίζεσθε ἑαυτοῖς.

14. ἐπὶ πᾶσιν] 'over and above all
these,' comp. Luke iii. 20 προσέθηκεν
καὶ τοῦτο ἐπὶ πᾶσιν. In Luke xvi. 26,
Ephes. vi. 16, the correct reading is
probably ἐν πᾶσιν. Love is the outer
garment which holds the others in
their places.

τὴν ἀγάπην] sc. ἐνδύσασθε, from ver.
12.

ὅ] 'which thing,' i.e. 'love'; comp.
Ephes. v. 5 πλεονέκτης, ὅ ἐστιν εἰδωλολάτρης, Ign. *Rom.* 7 ἄρτον Θεοῦ θέλω,
ὅ ἐστιν σὰρξ Χριστοῦ, *Magn.* 10 μετα-
βάλεσθε εἰς νέαν ζύμην ὅ ἐστιν Ἰησοῦς
Χριστός, *Trall.* 8 ἀνακτήσασθε ἑαυτοὺς
ἐν πίστει ὅ ἐστιν σὰρξ τοῦ Κυρίου.
Though there are various readings in
the passages of the Ignatian Epistles,
the ὅ seems to be generally right.
These instances will show that ὅ may
be referred to τὴν ἀγάπην alone. O-
therwise we might suppose the antecedent to be τὸ ἐνδύσασθαι τὴν ἀγάπην,
but this hardly suits the sense. The
common reading ἥτις is obviously a
scribe's correction.

σύνδεσμος κ.τ.λ.] 'the bond of perfection,' i. e. the power, which unites
and holds together all those graces
and virtues, which together make up
perfection. Πάντα ἐκεῖνα, says Chrysostom, αὕτη συσφίγγει· ὅπερ ἂν εἴπῃς
ἀγαθόν, ταύτης ἀπούσης οὐδέν ἐστιν
ἀλλὰ διαρρεῖ: comp. Clem. Rom. 49
τὸν δεσμὸν τῆς ἀγάπης τοῦ Θεοῦ τίς
δύναται ἐξηγήσασθαι; Thus the Pythagoreans (Simplic. *in Epictet.* p. 208 A)
περισσῶς τῶν ἄλλων ἀρετῶν τὴν φιλίαν
ἐτίμων καὶ σύνδεσμον αὐτὴν πασῶν τῶν
ἀρετῶν ἔλεγον. So too Themist. *Orat.*
i. (p. 5 C) βασιλικὴ (ἀρετὴ) παρὰ τὰς
ἄλλας εἰς ἣν ξυνδοῦνταί καὶ αἱ λοιπαί,
ὥσπερ εἰς μίαν κορυφὴν ἀνημμέναι.
The word will take a genitive either
of the object bound or of the binding
force: e.g. Plato *Polit.* 310 A τοῦτον
θειότερον εἶναι τὸν ξύνδεσμον ἀρετῆς
μερῶν φύσεως ἀνομοίων καὶ ἐπὶ τἀναντία
φερομένων, where the ἀρετὴ ξυνδεῖ and
the μέρη φύσεως ξυνδεῖται. We have
an instance of the one genitive (the
objective) here, of the other (the subjective) in Ephes. iv. 3 ἐν τῷ συνδέσμῳ
τῆς εἰρήνης (see the note there).

Another explanation makes σύνδεσ-

τὴν ἀγάπην, ὅ ἐστιν σύνδεσμος τῆς τελειότητος. ¹⁵καὶ
ἡ εἰρήνη τοῦ Χριστοῦ βραβευέτω ἐν ταῖς καρδίαις ὑμῶν,
εἰς ἣν καὶ ἐκλήθητε ἐν ἑνὶ σώματι. καὶ εὐχάριστοι

μος = σύνθεσις here, 'the bundle, the totality,' as e.g. Herodian. iv. 12 πάντα τὸν σύνδεσμον τῶν ἐπιστολῶν (comp. Ign. *Trall.* 3 σύνδεσμον ἀποστόλων); but this unusual metaphor is highly improbable and inappropriate here, not to mention that we should expect the definite article ὁ σύνδεσμος in this case. With either interpretation, the function assigned to ἀγάπη here is the same as when it is declared to be πλήρωμα νόμου, Rom. xiii. 10 (comp. Gal. v. 14). See also the all-embracing office which is assigned to it in 1 Cor. xiii.

15. ἡ εἰρήνη τοῦ Χριστοῦ] '*Christ's peace,*' which He left as a legacy to His disciples: Joh. xiv. 27 εἰρήνην ἀφίημι ὑμῖν, εἰρήνην τὴν ἐμὴν δίδωμι ὑμῖν; comp. Ephes. ii. 14 αὐτὸς γάρ ἐστιν ἡ εἰρήνη ἡμῶν with the context. The common reading ἡ εἰρήνη τοῦ Θεοῦ has a parallel in Phil. iv. 7.

βραβευέτω] '*be umpire,*' for the idea of a contest is only less prominent here, than in βραβεῖον 1 Cor. ix. 24, Phil. iii. 14 (see the note there). Στάδιον ἔνδον ἐποίησεν ἐν τοῖς λογισμοῖς, writes Chrysostom, καὶ ἀγῶνα καὶ ἄθλησιν καὶ βραβευτήν. Wherever there is a conflict of motives or impulses or reasons, the peace of Christ must step in and decide which is to prevail: Μὴ θυμὸς βραβευέτω, says Chrysostom again, μὴ φιλονεικία, μὴ ἀνθρωπίνη εἰρήνη· ἡ γὰρ ἀνθρωπίνη εἰρήνη ἐκ τοῦ ἀμύνεσθαι γίνεται, ἐκ τοῦ μηδὲν πάσχειν δεινόν.

For this metaphor of some one paramount consideration acting as umpire, where there is a conflict of internal motives, see Polyb. ii. 35. 3 ἅπαν τὸ γιγνόμενον ὑπὸ τῶν Γαλάτων θυμῷ μᾶλλον ἢ λογισμῷ βραβευέσθαι, Philo *de Migr. Abr.* 12 (I. p. 446) πορεύεται ὁ ἄφρων δι' ἀμφοτέρων θυμοῦ τε καὶ ἐπιθυμίας ἀεί...τὸν ἡνίοχον

καὶ βραβευτὴν λόγον ἀποβαλών (comp. *de Ebriet.* 19, I. p. 368), Jos. *B. J.* vi. 2. 6 ἐβράβευε τὰς τόλμας ὁ... φόβος. Somewhat similarly τύχη (Polyb. xxvii. 14. 4) or φύσις (Athen. xv. p. 670 A) are made βραβεύειν. In other passages, where ὁ Θεὸς or τὸ θεῖον is said βραβεύειν, this implies that, while man proposes, God disposes. In Philo ἀλήθεια βραβεύουσα (*Qui rer. div. her.* I. p. 486) is a rough synonyme for ἀλήθεια δικάζουσα (*de Abrah.* 14, II. p. 10, etc.): and in Josephus (*Ant.* vi. 3. 1) δικάζειν and βραβεύειν are used together of the same action. In all such cases it appears that the idea of a *decision* and an *award* is prominent in the word, and that it must not be taken to denote simply *rule* or *power*.

εἰς ἣν κ.τ.λ.] Comp. 1 Cor. vii. 15 ἐν δὲ εἰρήνῃ κέκληκεν ἡμᾶς ὁ Θεός.

ἐν ἑνὶ σώματι] 'As ye were called as members of one body, so let there be one spirit animating that body': Ephes. iv. 4 ἐν σῶμα καὶ ἐν πνεῦμα. This passage strikes the keynote of the companion Epistle to the Ephesians (see esp. ii. 16 sq., iv. 3 sq.).

εὐχάριστοι] 'And to crown all forget yourselves in thanksgiving towards God': see the notes on i. 12, ii. 7. The adjective εὐχάριστος, though not occurring elsewhere in the Greek Bible, is not uncommon in classical writers, and like the English 'grateful,' has two meanings; either (1) 'pleasurable' (e.g. Xen. *Cyr.* ii. 2. 1); or (2) 'thankful' (e.g. Boeckh *C. I.* no. 1625), as here.

16, 17. 'Let the inspiring word of Christ dwell in your hearts, enriching you with its boundless wealth and endowing you with all wisdom. Teach and admonish one another with psalms, with hymns of praise, with spiritual songs of all kinds. Only let them be

γίνεσθε. ¹⁶Ὁ λόγος τοῦ Χριστοῦ ἐνοικείτω ἐν ὑμῖν πλουσίως ἐν πάσῃ σοφίᾳ· διδάσκοντες καὶ νουθετοῦντες

pervaded with grace from heaven.
Sing to God in your hearts and not
with your lips only. And generally;
whatever ye do, whether in word or
in deed, let everything be done in the
name of Jesus Christ. And (again I
repeat it) pour out your thanksgiving
to God the Father through Him.'

16. Ὁ λόγος τοῦ Χριστοῦ] 'the word
of Christ,' τοῦ Χριστοῦ being the subjective genitive, so that Christ is the
speaker. Though ὁ λόγος τοῦ Θεοῦ
and ὁ λόγος τοῦ Κυρίου occur frequently, ὁ λόγος τοῦ Χριστοῦ is found
here only. There seems to be no direct reference in this expression to
any definite body of truths either
written or oral, but ὁ λόγος τοῦ Χριστοῦ denotes the presence of Christ in
the heart, as an inward monitor:
comp. 1 Joh. ii. 14 ὁ λόγος τοῦ Θεοῦ
ἐν ὑμῖν μένει, with ib. i. 10 ὁ λόγος αὐτοῦ οὐκ ἔστιν ἐν ἡμῖν, and so perhaps
Acts xviii. 5 συνείχετο τῷ λόγῳ (the
correct reading).

ἐν ὑμῖν] 'in your hearts,' not 'among
you' ; comp. Rom. viii. 9, 11 τὸ ἐνοικοῦν
αὐτοῦ πνεῦμα ἐν ὑμῖν, 2 Tim. i. 5, 14,
and Lev. xxvi. 12, as quoted in 2 Cor.
vi. 16, ἐνοικήσω ἐν αὐτοῖς.

πλουσίως] See above, p. 43 sq., and
the note on i. 27.

ἐν πάσῃ σοφίᾳ] 'in every kind of
wisdom.' It seems best to take these
words with the preceding clause,
though Clem. Alex. Paed. ii. 4 (p. 194)
attaches them to what follows. For
this position of ἐν πάσῃ σοφίᾳ, at the
end of the sentence to which it refers,
comp. i. 9, Ephes. i. 8. The connexion
here adopted is also favoured by the
parallel passage Ephes. v. 18, 19 (see
the note below). Another passage i.
28 νουθετοῦντες πάντα ἄνθρωπον καὶ
διδάσκοντες πάντα ἄνθρωπον ἐν πάσῃ
σοφίᾳ has a double bearing: while the
connexion favours our taking ἐν πάσῃ
σοφίᾳ here with the following words,

the order suggests their being attached to the preceding clause.

διδάσκοντες κ.τ.λ.] The participles
are here used for imperatives, as frequently in hortatory passages, e. g.
Rom. xii. 9 sq., 16 sq., Ephes. iv. 2, 3,
Hebr. xiii. 5, 1 Pet. ii. 12 [?], iii. 1,7,9,
15, 16. It is not, as some insist, that
the participle itself has any imperati-
val force; nor, as maintained by others,
that the construction should be explained by the hypothesis of a preceding parenthesis or of a verb substantive understood or by any other
expedient to obtain a regular grammatical structure (see Winer, § xlv.
p. 441 sq., § lxii. p. 707, § lxiii. p. 716,
§ lxiv. p. 732). But the absolute participle, being (so far as regards mood)
neutral in itself, takes its colour from
the general complexion of the sentence. Thus it is sometimes indicative (e.g. 2 Cor. vii. 5, and frequently),
sometimes imperative (as in the passages quoted), sometimes optative (as
above, ii. 2, 2 Cor. ix. 11, comp. Ephes.
iii. 17). On the distinction of διδάσκειν and νουθετεῖν see the note on i.
28; they describe respectively the positive and the negative side of instruction. On the reciprocal ἑαυτούς see
the note on iii. 13.

ψαλμοῖς κ.τ.λ.] To be connected with
the preceding sentence, as suggested
by Ephes. v. 18 sq. ἀλλὰ πληροῦσθε ἐν
πνεύματι, λαλοῦντες ἑαυτοῖς [ἐν] ψαλμοῖς καὶ ὕμνοις καὶ ᾠδαῖς [πνευματικαῖς],
ᾄδοντες καὶ ψάλλοντες τῇ καρδίᾳ ὑμῶν
τῷ Κυρίῳ. The datives describe the
instruments of the διδαχή and νουθεσία.

The three words ψαλμός, ὕμνος, ᾠδή,
are distinguished, so far as they are
distinguishable, in Trench N.T. Syn.
§ lxxviii. p. 279 sq. They are correctly defined by Gregory Nyssen in
Psalm. c. iii (1. p. 295) ψαλμὸς μέν
ἐστιν ἡ διὰ τοῦ ὀργάνου τοῦ μουσικοῦ

ἑαυτοὺς ψαλμοῖς ὕμνοις ᾠδαῖς πνευματικαῖς ἐν τῇ

μελῳδία, ᾠδὴ δὲ ἡ διὰ στόματος γενομένη τοῦ μέλους μετὰ ῥημάτων ἐπιφώ-
νησις...ὕμνος δὲ ἡ ἐπὶ τοῖς ὑπάρχουσιν
ἡμῖν ἀγαθοῖς ἀνατιθεμένη τῷ Θεῷ εὐφη-
μία; see also Hippol. p. 191 sq. (ed.
de Lagarde). In other words, while
the leading idea of ψαλμός is a musi-
cal accompaniment and that of ὕμνος
praise to God, ᾠδή is the general word
for a song, whether accompanied or
unaccompanied, whether of praise or
on any other subject. Thus it was
quite possible for the same song to
be at once ψαλμός, ὕμνος, and ᾠδή.
In the text the reference in ψαλμοῖς,
we may suppose, is specially, though
not exclusively (1 Cor. xiv. 26), to
the Psalms of David, which would
early form part of the religious worship of the Christian brotherhood.
On the other hand ὕμνοις would more
appropriately designate those hymns
of praise which were composed by the
Christians themselves on distinctly
Christian themes, being either set
forms of words or spontaneous effu-
sions of the moment. The third word
ᾠδαῖς gathers up the other two, and
extends the precept to all forms of
song, with the limitation however that
they must be πνευματικαί. St Chrysostom treats ὕμνοι here as an advance
upon ψαλμοί, which in one aspect they
are; οἱ ψαλμοί, he says, πάντα ἔχουσιν,
οἱ δὲ ὕμνοι πάλιν οὐδὲν ἀνθρώπινον·
ὅταν ἐν τοῖς ψαλμοῖς μάθῃ, τότε καὶ ὕμνους εἴσεται, ἅτε θειότερον πρᾶγμα.
Psalmody and hymnody were highly
developed in the religious services of
the Jews at this time: see Philo in
Flacc. 14 (II. p. 535) πάννυχοι δὲ δια-
τελέσαντες ἐν ὕμνοις καὶ ᾠδαῖς, de Vit.
Cont. § 3 (II. p. 476) ποιοῦσιν ᾄσματα
καὶ ὕμνους εἰς Θεὸν διὰ παντοίων μέτρων
καὶ μελῶν, ἃ ῥυθμοῖς σεμνοτέροις ἀναγκαίως χαράττουσι, § 10 (p. 484) ὁ ἀνα-
στὰς ὕμνον ᾄδει πεποιημένον εἰς τὸν
Θεόν, ἢ καινὸν αὐτὸς πεποιηκὼς ἢ ἀρ-
χαῖόν τινα τῶν πάλαι ποιητῶν· μέτρα
γὰρ καὶ μέλη καταλελοίπασι πολλὰ ἐπῶν

τριμέτρων, προσοδίων, ὕμνων, παρα-
σπονδείων, παραβωμίων, στασίμων, χο-
ρικῶν, στροφαῖς πολυστρόφοις εὖ διαμε-
μετρημένων κ.τ.λ., § 11 (p. 485) ᾄδουσι
πεποιημένους εἰς τὸν Θεὸν ὕμνους πολλοῖς μέτροις καὶ μέλεσι κ.τ.λ., with
the whole context. They would thus
find their way into the Christian
Church from the very beginning.
For instances of singing hymns or
psalms in the Apostolic age see Acts
iv. 24, xvi. 25, 1 Cor. xiv. 15, 26.
Hence even in St Paul's epistles, more
especially his later epistles, fragments
of such hymns appear to be quoted; e.g.
Ephes. v. 14 (see the note there). For
the use of hymnody in the early Church
of the succeeding generations see Plin.
Epist. x. 97 'Ante lucem convenire,
carmenque Christo quasi Deo dicere
secum invicem,' Anon. [Hippolytus] in
Euseb. *H. E.* v. 28 ψαλμοὶ δὲ ὅσοι καὶ
ᾠδαὶ ἀδελφῶν ἀπ' ἀρχῆς ὑπὸ πι-
στῶν γραφεῖσαι τὸν Λόγον τοῦ Θεοῦ τὸν
Χριστὸν ὑμνοῦσι θεολογοῦντες. The
reference in the text is not solely or
chiefly to public worship as such.
Clem. Alex. *Paed.* ii. 4 (p. 194) treats
it as applying to social gatherings;
and again Tertullian says of the agape,
Apol. 39 'Ut quisque de scripturis
sanctis vel de proprio ingenio potest,
provocatur in medium Deo canere,'
and of the society of husband and
wife, *Ad Uxor.* ii. 8 'Sonant inter
duos psalmi et hymni, et mutuo pro-
vocant quis melius Domino suo cantet.'
On the psalmody etc. of the early
Christians see Bingham *Antiq.* xiv.
c. 1, and especially Probst *Lehre und
Gebet* p. 256 sq.

ἐν τῇ χάριτι] 'in God's grace';
comp. 2 Cor. i. 12 οὐκ ἐν σοφίᾳ σαρκικῇ ἀλλ' ἐν χάριτι Θεοῦ. These
words are perhaps best connected with
the preceding clause, as by Chrysostom. Thus the parallelism with ἐν
πάσῃ σοφίᾳ is preserved. The correct reading is ἐν τῇ χάριτι, not ἐν
χάριτι. For ἡ χάρις, 'Divine grace'

χάριτι, ᾄδοντες ἐν ταῖς καρδίαις ὑμῶν τῷ Θεῷ· ¹⁷καὶ
πᾶν ὅ τι ἐὰν ποιῆτε ἐν λόγῳ ἢ ἐν ἔργῳ, πάντα ἐν
ὀνόματι Κυρίου Ἰησοῦ, εὐχαριστοῦντες τῷ Θεῷ πατρὶ
δι' αὐτοῦ.

¹⁸Αἱ γυναῖκες, ὑποτάσσεσθε τοῖς ἀνδράσιν, ὡς ἀνῆ-

see Phil. i. 7 συνκοινωνούς μου τῆς χάριτος with the note. The definite article seems to exclude all lower senses of χάρις here, such as 'accept-ableness,' 'sweetness' (see iv. 6). The interpretation 'with gratitude,' if otherwise tenable (comp. 1 Cor. x. 30), seems inappropriate here, because the idea of thanksgiving is introduced in the following verse.

ᾄδοντες κ.τ.λ.] This external mani-festation must be accompanied by the inward emotion. There must be the thanksgiving of the heart, as well as of the lips; comp. Ephes. v. 19 ᾄδοντες καὶ ψάλλοντες τῇ καρδίᾳ (probably the correct reading), where τῇ καρδίᾳ 'with the heart' brings out the sense more distinctly.

17. πᾶν ὅ τι κ.τ.λ.] This is proba-bly a nominative absolute, as Matt. x. 32 πᾶς οὖν ὅστις ὁμολογήσει... ὁμο-λογήσω κἀγὼ ἐν αὐτῷ (comp. Luke xii. 8), Luke xii. 10 πᾶς ὃς ἐρεῖ λόγον ...ἀφεθήσεται αὐτῷ, John xvii. 2 πᾶν ὃ δέδωκας αὐτῷ, δώσῃ αὐτοῖς κ.τ.λ.; comp. Matt. vii. 24 (v. l.).

πάντα] sc. ποιεῖτε, as the following εὐχαριστοῦντες suggests; comp. ver. 23.

ἐν ὀνόματι κ.τ.λ.] This is the great practical lesson which flows from the theological teaching of the epistle. Hence the reiteration of Κυρίῳ, ἐν Κυρίῳ, etc., vv. 18, 20, 22, 23, 24. See above p. 104.

εὐχαριστοῦντες] On this refrain see the notes on i. 12, ii. 7.

τῷ Θεῷ πατρί] This, which is quite the best authenticated reading, gives a very unusual, if not unique, colloca-tion of words, the usual form being either ὁ Θεὸς καὶ πατήρ or Θεὸς πατήρ. The καί before πατρί in the received

text is an obvious emendation. See the note on i. 3, and the appendix on various readings.

18—21. 'Ye wives, be subject to your husbands, for so it becomes you in Christ. Ye husbands, love and cherish your wives, and use no harsh-ness towards them. Ye children, be obedient to your parents in all things; for this is commendable and lovely in Christ. Ye parents, vex not your children, lest they lose heart and grow sullen.'

18 sq. These precepts, providing for the conduct of Christians in private households, should be compared with Ephes. v. 22—vi. 9, 1 Pet. ii. 18—iii. 7, Tit. ii. 1 sq.; see also Clem. Rom. 1, Polyc. Phil. 4 sq.

Αἱ γυναῖκες] 'Ye wives,' the nomina-tive with the definite article being used for a vocative, as frequently in the New Testament, e.g. Matt. xi. 26, Mark v. 41, Luke viii. 54; see Winer § xxix. p. 227 sq. The frequency of this use is doubtless due to the fact that it is a reproduction of the He-brew idiom. In the instances quoted from classical writers (see Bernhardy Syntax p. 67) the address is not so directly vocative, the nominative being used rather to define or select than to summon the person in ques-tion.

τοῖς ἀνδράσιν] The ἰδίοις of the received text may have been inserted (as it is inserted also in Ephes. v. 24) from Ephes. v. 22, Tit. ii. 5, 1 Pet. iii. 1, 5, in all which passages this same injunction occurs. The scribes how-ever show a general fondness for this adjective; e.g. Mark xv. 20, Luke ii. 3, Acts i. 19, Ephes. iv. 28, 1 Thess. ii. 15, iv. 11.

κεν ἐν Κυρίῳ. ¹⁹ Οἱ ἄνδρες, ἀγαπᾶτε τὰς γυναῖκας καὶ
μὴ πικραίνεσθε πρὸς αὐτάς. ²⁰ Τὰ τέκνα, ὑπακούετε
τοῖς γονεῦσιν κατὰ πάντα· τοῦτο γὰρ εὐάρεστόν ἐστιν
ἐν Κυρίῳ. ²¹ Οἱ πατέρες, μὴ ἐρεθίζετε τὰ τέκνα ὑμῶν,
ἵνα μὴ ἀθυμῶσιν. ²² Οἱ δοῦλοι, ὑπακούετε κατὰ πάντα

ἀνῆκεν] The imperfect, as Ephes. v. 4 ἃ οὐκ ἀνῆκεν (the correct reading); comp. *Clem. Hom.* Contest. 3 τοῦδε μὴ μεταδοῦναι χάριν, ὡς οὐ προσῆκεν, Xen. *de Re Equestr.* xii. 14 ἃ ἱππάρχῳ προσῆκεν εἰδέναι τε καὶ πράττειν; and see D'Orville on Charito viii. 2 (p. 699 sq.). The common uses of the imperfect ἔδει, ἔπρεπεν, etc., in classical writers do not present a very exact parallel; for they imply that the thing which ought to have been done has been left undone. And so we might interpret Acts xxii. 22 οὐ γὰρ καθῆκεν αὐτὸν ζῆν (the correct reading). Here however there can hardly be any such reference; and the best illustration is the English past tense 'ought' (='owed'), which is used in the same way. The past tense perhaps implies an essential *a priori* obligation. The use of χρῆν, ἔχρην, occasionally approximates to this; e.g. Eur. *Andr.* 423.

The idea of 'propriety' is the link which connects the primary meaning of such words as ἀνήκειν, προσήκειν, καθήκειν, 'aiming at or pertaining to,' with their ultimate meaning of moral obligation. The word ἀνήκειν occurs in the New Testament only here and in the contemporary epistles, Ephes. v. 4, Philem. 8.

ἐν Κυρίῳ] Probably to be connected with ὡς ἀνῆκεν, rather than with ὑποτάσσεσθε; comp. ver. 20 εὐάρεστόν ἐστιν ἐν Κυρίῳ.

19. μὴ πικραίνεσθε κ.τ.λ.] '*show no bitterness, behave not harshly*'; comp. Lynceus in Athen. vi. p. 242 c πικρανθείη πρός τινα τῶν συζώντων, Joseph. *Ant.* v. 7. 1 δεινῶς πρὸς τοὺς τοῦ δικαίου προϊσταμένους ἐκπικραινόμενος, Plut. *Mor.* p. 457 A πρὸς γύναια δια-

πικραίνονται. So also πικραίνεσθαι ἐπί τινα in the LXX, Jerem. xliv (xxxvii). 15, 3 Esdr. iv. 31. This verb πικραίνεσθαι and its compounds occur frequently in classical writers.

20. κατὰ πάντα] As in ver. 22. The rule is stated absolutely, because the exceptions are so few that they may be disregarded.

εὐάρεστόν ἐστιν] '*is well pleasing, commendable.*' The received text supplies this adjective with a dative of reference τῷ Κυρίῳ (from Ephes. v. 10), but ἐν Κυρίῳ is unquestionably the right reading. With the reading thus corrected εὐάρεστον, like ἀνῆκεν ver. 18, must be taken absolutely, as perhaps in Rom. xii. 2 τὸ θέλημα τοῦ Θεοῦ τὸ ἀγαθὸν καὶ εὐάρεστον καὶ τέλειον: comp. Phil. iv. 8 ὅσα σεμνά …ὅσα προσφιλῆ. The qualification ἐν Κυρίῳ implies 'as judged by a Christian standard,' 'as judged by those who are members of Christ's body.'

21. ἐρεθίζετε] '*provoke, irritate.*' The other reading παροργίζετε has higher support, but is doubtless taken from the parallel passage, Ephes. vi. 4. 'Irritation' is the first consequence of being too exacting with children, and irritation leads to moroseness (ἀθυμία). In 2 Cor. ix. 2 ἐρεθίζειν is used in a good sense and produces the opposite result, not despondency but energy.

ἀθυμῶσιν] '*lose heart, become spiritless,*' i. e. 'go about their task in a listless, moody, sullen frame of mind.' '*Fractus animus,*' says Bengel, 'pestis juventutis.' In Xen. *Cyr.* i. 6. 13 ἀθυμία is opposed to προθυμία, and in Thuc. ii. 88 and elsewhere ἀθυμεῖν is opposed to θαρσεῖν.

τοῖς κατὰ σάρκα κυρίοις, μὴ ἐν ὀφθαλμοδουλείᾳ ὡς
ἀνθρωπάρεσκοι, ἀλλ' ἐν ἁπλότητι καρδίας, φοβούμενοι
τὸν Κύριον. ²³ὃ ἐὰν ποιῆτε, ἐκ ψυχῆς ἐργάζεσθε ὡς

22. ἐν ὀφθαλμοδουλείαις.

22—iv. 1. 'Ye slaves, be obedient
in all things to the masters set over
you in the flesh, not rendering them
service only when their eyes are upon
you, as aiming merely to please men,
but serving in all sincerity of heart, as
living in the sight of your Heavenly
Master and standing in awe of Him.
And in everything that ye do, work
faithfully and with all your soul, as
labouring not for men, but for the
great Lord and Master Himself; knowing that ye have a Master, from whom
ye will receive the glorious inheritance
as your recompense, whether or not
ye may be defrauded of your due by
men. Yes, Christ is your Master and
ye are his slaves. He that does a
wrong shall be requited for his wrong-
doing. I say not this of slaves only,
but of masters also. There is no par-
tiality, no respect of persons, in God's
distribution of rewards and punish-
ments. Therefore, ye masters, do ye
also on your part deal justly and equi-
tably by your slaves, knowing that ye
too have a Master in heaven.'

22. Οἱ δοῦλοι] The relations of
masters and slaves, both here and in
the companion epistle (Ephes. vi.
5—9), are treated at greater length
than is usual with St Paul. Here
especially the expansion of this topic,
compared with the brief space assigned to the duties of wives and husbands
(vv. 18, 19), or of children and parents
(vv. 20, 21), deserves to be noticed.
The fact is explained by a contemporary incident in the Apostle's private
life. His intercourse with Onesimus
had turned his thoughts in this direction. See above, p.33, and the introduction to the Epistle to Philemon:
comp. also the note on ver. 11.

ὀφθαλμοδουλείᾳ] 'eye-service,' as
Ephes. vi. 6: comp. Apost. Const. iv.

12 μὴ ὡς ὀφθαλμόδουλος ἀλλ' ὡς φι-
λοδέσποτος. This happy expression
would seem to be the Apostle's own
coinage. At least there are no traces
of it earlier. Compare ἐθελοθρησκεία
ii. 23. The reading ὀφθαλμοδουλείᾳ
is better supported than ὀφθαλμοδουλείαις, though the plural is rendered
slightly more probable in itself by its
greater difficulty.

ἀνθρωπάρεσκοι] Again in Ephes. vi.
6. It is a LXX word, Ps. lii. 6, where
the Greek entirely departs from the
Hebrew: comp. also ἀνθρωπαρεσκεῖν
Ign. Rom. 2, ἀνθρωπαρέσκεια Justin
Apol. i. 2 (p. 53 E). So ὀχλοαρέσκης
or ὀχλοάρεσκος, Timo Phlias. in Diog.
Laert. iv. 42 (vv. ll.).

ἁπλότητι καρδίας] As in Ephes. vi. 5,
i. e. 'with undivided service'; a LXX
expression, I Chron. xxix. 17, Wisd. i. 1.

τὸν Κύριον] 'the one Lord and
Master,' as contrasted with τοῖς κατὰ
σάρκα κυρίοις: the idea being carried
out in the following verses. The received text, by substituting τὸν Θεόν,
blunts the edge of the contrast.

23. ἐργάζεσθε] i. e. 'do it dili-
gently,' an advance upon ποιῆτε.

οὐκ ἀνθρώποις] For the use of οὐ
rather than μὴ in antitheses, see Winer § lv. p. 601 sq. The negative
here is wholly unconnected with the
imperative, and refers solely to τῷ
Κυρίῳ.

24. ἀπὸ Κυρίου] 'However you may
be treated by your earthly masters,
you have still a Master who will recompense you.' The absence of the
definite article here (comp. iv. 1) is
the more remarkable, because it is
studiously inserted in the context, vv.
22—24, τὸν Κύριον, τῷ Κυρίῳ, τῷ Κυρίῳ. In the parallel passage Ephes.
vi. 8 it is παρὰ Κυρίου: for the difference between the two see Gal. i. 12.

τῷ Κυρίῳ, καὶ οὐκ ἀνθρώποις, ²⁴εἰδότες ὅτι ἀπὸ Κυρίου ἀπολήμψεσθε τὴν ἀνταπόδοσιν τῆς κληρονομίας· τῷ Κυρίῳ Χριστῷ δουλεύετε· ²⁵ὁ γὰρ ἀδικῶν κομίσεται ὁ

τὴν ἀνταπόδοσιν] 'the just recompense,' a common word both in the LXX and in classical writers, though not occurring elsewhere in the New Testament; comp. ἀνταπόδομα Luke xiv. 12, Rom. xi. 9. The double compound involves the idea of 'exact requital.'

τῆς κληρονομίας] 'which consists in the inheritance,' the genitive of apposition: see the note on τὴν μερίδα τοῦ κλήρου, i. 12. There is a paradox involved in this word: elsewhere the δοῦλος and the κληρονόμος are contrasted (Matt. xxi. 35—38, etc., Rom. viii. 15—17, Gal. iv. 1, 7), but here the δοῦλος is the κληρονόμος. This he is because, though δοῦλος ἀνθρώπων, he is ἀπελεύθερος Κυρίου (1 Cor. vii. 22) and thus κληρονόμος διὰ Θεοῦ (Gal. iv. 7); comp. Hermas Sim. v. 2 ἵνα συγκληρονόμος γένηται ὁ δοῦλος τῷ υἱῷ (with the context).

τῷ Κυρίῳ κ.τ.λ.] i. e. 'you serve as your master the great Master Christ.' This clause is added to explain how is meant by the preceding ἀπὸ Κυρίου. For this application of Κύριος compare (besides the parallel passage, Ephes. vi. 6—9) 1 Cor. vii. 22 ὁ γὰρ ἐν Κυρίῳ κληθεὶς δοῦλος ἀπελεύθερος Κυρίου ἐστίν κ.τ.λ. It seems best to take δουλεύετε here as an indicative, rather than as an imperative; for (1) The indicative is wanted to explain the previous ἀπὸ Κυρίου; (2) The imperative would seem to require ὡς τῷ Κυρίῳ, as in Ephes. vi. 7 (the correct text). On the other hand see Rom. xii. 11.

25. ὁ γὰρ ἀδικῶν κ.τ.λ.] Who is this unrighteous person? The slave who defrauds his master of his service, or the master who defrauds his slave of his reward? Some interpreters confine it exclusively to the former; others to the latter. It seems

best to suppose that both are included. The connexion of the sentence ὁ γὰρ ἀδικῶν (where γάρ, not δέ, is certainly the right reading) points to the slave. On the other hand the expression which follows, τὸ δίκαιον καὶ τὴν ἰσότητα κ.τ.λ., suggests the master. Thus there seems to be a twofold reference; the warning is suggested by the case of the slave, but it is extended to the case of the master; and this accords with the parallel passage, Ephes. vi. 8 ἕκαστος ὃ ἂν ποιήσῃ ἀγαθὸν τοῦτο κομίσεται παρὰ Κυρίου, εἴτε δοῦλος εἴτε ἐλεύθερος.

The recent fault of Onesimus would make the Apostle doubly anxious to emphasize the duties of the slave towards the master, lest in his love for the offender he should seem to condone the offence. This same word ἠδίκησεν is used by St Paul to describe the crime of Onesimus in Philem. 18. But on the other hand it is the Apostle's business to show that justice has a double edge. There must be a *reciprocity* between the master and the slave. The philosophers of Greece taught, and the laws of Rome assumed, that the slave was a chattel. But a chattel could have no rights. It would be absurd to talk of treating a chattel with justice. St Paul places the relations of the master and the slave in a wholly different light. Justice and equity are the expression of the Divine mind: and with God there is no προσωπολημψία. With Him the claims of the slave are as real as the claims of the master.

κομίσεται] For this sense of the middle, 'to recover,' 'to get back,' and so (with an accusative of the thing to be recompensed), 'to be requited for', see e.g. Lev. xx. 17 ἁμαρτίαν κομιοῦνται, 2 Cor. v. 10 κομίσηται ἕκαστος τὰ διὰ τοῦ σώματος; comp. Barnab.

ἠδίκησεν, καὶ οὐκ ἔστιν προσωποληνψία. IV. ¹Οἱ
κύριοι, τὸ δίκαιον καὶ τὴν ἰσότητα τοῖς δούλοις παρέ-
χεσθε, εἰδότες ὅτι καὶ ὑμεῖς ἔχετε Κύριον ἐν οὐρανῷ.

§ 4 ὁ Κύριος ἀπροσωπολήμπτως κρινεῖ
τὸν κόσμον· ἕκαστος, καθὼς ἐποίησεν,
κομιεῖται. In the parallel passage
Ephes. vi. 8, the form is certainly κομίσεται: here it is more doubtful, the
authorities being more equally divided
between κομιεῖται and κομίσεται. See
however the note on γνωρίσουσιν iv. 9.

προσωποληψία] On this word see
the note Gal. ii. 6. This προσωποληψ-
ψία, though generally found on the
side of rank and power, may also be
exercised in favour of the opposite ;
Lev. xix. 15 οὐ λήψῃ πρόσωπον πτω-
χοῦ οὐδὲ μὴ θαυμάσῃς πρόσωπον δυνά-
στου. There would be a tendency in
the mind of the slave to assume that,
because the προσωποληψία of man
was on the side of the master, there
must be a corresponding προσωποληψία of God on the side of the
slave. This assumption is corrected
by St Paul.

IV. 1. τὴν ἰσότητα] 'equity,' 'fair-
ness'; comp. Plut. Sol. et Popl. Comp. 3
νόμων ἰσότητα παρεχόντων. Somewhat
similarly Lysias Or. Fun. 77 (speaking of death) οὔτε γὰρ τοὺς πονηροὺς
ὑπερορᾷ οὔτε τοὺς ἀγαθοὺς θαυμάζει,
ἀλλ' ἴσον ἑαυτὸν παρέχει πᾶσιν.
It seems a mistake to suppose that
ἰσότης here has anything to do with
the treatment of slaves as equals
(comp. Philem. 16). When connected
with τὸ δίκαιον, the word naturally suggests an even-handed, impartial treatment, and is equivalent to the Latin
aequitas : comp. Arist. Top. vi. 5 (p.
143) ὁ τὴν δικαιοσύνην (λέγων) ἕξιν ἰσότητος ποιητικὴν ἢ διανεμητικὴν τοῦ ἴσου,
Philo de Creat. Princ. 14 (II. p. 373)
ἔστι γὰρ ἰσότης...μήτηρ δικαιοσύνης,
Clem. Alex. Strom. vi. 6 (p. 764) μετὰ
δικαιοσύνης καὶ ἰσότητος τῆς πρὸς τοὺς
ἐπιστρέφοντας. Thus in Arist. Eth.
Nic. v. 1 τὸ δίκαιον and τὸ ἴσον are
regarded as synonymes, and in Plut.

Mor. p. 719 the relation of ἰσότης to
δικαιότης is discussed. The word here
is used in the same sense in which the
adjective occurs in the common expressions ἴσος δικαστής, ἴσος ἀκροατής,
etc. Philo, describing the Essene
condemnation of slavery, says, Omn.
prob. lib. 12 (II. p. 457) καταγινώσκουσί
τε τῶν δεσποτῶν, οὐ μόνον ὡς ἀδίκων,
ἰσότητα λυμαινομένων, ἀλλὰ καὶ ὡς ἀσε-
βῶν κ.τ.λ., but he possibly does mean
'equality' rather than 'equity.'

παρέχεσθε] 'exhibit on your part.'
The middle παρέχεσθαι, 'to afford from
oneself,' will take different shades of
meaning according to the context, as
'to furnish one's quota' (e.g. Herod.
viii. 1, 2) or 'to put forward one's representative' (esp. of witnesses, e.g.
Plato Apol. 19 D). Here the idea is
'reciprocation,' the master's duty as
corresponding to the slave's.

ἔχετε Κύριον] As Ephes. vi. 9; comp.
1 Cor. vii. 22 ὁ ἐλεύθερος κληθεὶς δοῦλός ἐστιν Χριστοῦ.

2—6. 'Be earnest and unceasing
in prayer; keep your hearts and minds
awake while praying: remember also
(as I have so often told you) that
thanksgiving is the goal and crown of
prayer. Meanwhile in your petitions
forget not us—myself Paul—my fellow-
labourer Timothy — your evangelist
Epaphras — all the teachers of the
Gospel ; but pray that God may open
a door for the preaching of the word,
to the end that we may proclaim the
free offer of grace to the Gentiles—
that great mystery of Christ for which
I am now a prisoner in bonds. So
shall I declare it fearlessly, as I am
bound to proclaim it. Walk wisely
and discreetly in all your dealings with
unbelievers; allow no opportunity to
slip through your hands, but buy up
every passing moment. Let your language be always pervaded with grace

² Τῇ προσευχῇ προσκαρτερεῖτε, γρηγοροῦντες ἐν
αὐτῇ ἐν εὐχαριστίᾳ· ³προσευχόμενοι ἅμα καὶ περὶ ἡμῶν,
ἵνα ὁ Θεὸς ἀνοίξῃ ἡμῖν θύραν τοῦ λόγου, λαλῆσαι τὸ
μυστήριον τοῦ Χριστοῦ, δι' ὃ καὶ δέδεμαι· ⁴ἵνα φανε-

and seasoned with salt. So will you know how to give a fit answer to each man, as the occasion demands.'

2. προσκαρτερεῖτε] '*cling closely to*', '*remain constant to*' (comp. Mark iii. 9, Acts viii. 13, x. 7), and so 'continue stedfast in.' This word occurs again with τῇ προσευχῇ, ταῖς προσευχαῖς, Acts i. 14, ii. 42, vi. 4, Rom. xii. 12. The construction is with a simple dative both in the New Testament (ll. cc.) and in classical writers, except where it stands absolutely (Acts ii. 46, Rom. xiii. 6). The injunction here corresponds to the ἀδιαλείπτως προσεύχεσθε of 1 Thess. v. 17.

γρηγοροῦντες] Long continuance in prayer is apt to produce listlessness. Hence the additional charge that the heart must be *awake*, if the prayer is to have any value. The word is not to be taken literally here, but metaphorically. In Matt. xxvi. 41 etc., γρηγορεῖτε καὶ προσεύχεσθε, the idea is not quite the same.

ἐν εὐχαριστίᾳ] As the crown of all prayer; see the notes on i. 12, ii. 7.

3. ἡμῶν] '*us*,' 'the Apostles and preachers of the Gospel,' with reference more especially to Timothy (i. 1) and Epaphras (iv. 12, 13). Where the Apostle speaks of himself alone, he uses the singular (ver. 3, 4 δέδεμαι, φανερώσω). Indeed there is no reason to think that St Paul ever uses an 'epistolary' plural, referring to himself solely: see on 1 Thess. iii. 1.

ἵνα κ.τ.λ.] On the sense of ἵνα after προσεύχεσθαι etc., see the note on i. 9.

θύραν τοῦ λόγου] '*a door* of admission *for the word*,' i. e. 'an opportunity of preaching the Gospel,' as 1 Cor. xvi. 9 θύρα γάρ μοι ἀνέῳγεν μεγάλη καὶ ἐνεργής, 2 Cor. ii. 12 θύρας μοι ἀνεῳγμένης ἐν Κυρίῳ: comp.

Plut. *Mor.* p. 674 D ὥσπερ πύλης ἀνοιχθείσης, οὐκ ἀντέσχον…συνεισιοῦσι παντοδαποῖς ἀκροάμασιν. Similarly εἴσοδος is used in 1 Thess. i. 9, ii. 1. The converse application of the metaphor appears in Acts xiv. 27 ἤνοιξεν τοῖς ἔθνεσιν θύραν πίστεως, where the door is opened not to the teachers, but to the recipients of the Gospel. According to another interpretation (suggested by Ephes. vi. 19 ἵνα μοι δοθῇ λόγος ἐν ἀνοίξει τοῦ στόματός μου) it is explained 'the door of our speech,' i. e. 'our mouth': comp. Ps. cxli (cxl). 3, Mic. vii. 5, Ecclus. xxviii. 25. But the parallel passages do not favour this sense, nor will the words themselves admit it. In that case for ἡμῖν θύραν τοῦ λόγου we should require τὴν θύραν τῶν λόγων [ἡμῶν]. 'The word' here is 'the Gospel,' as frequently.

λαλῆσαι] '*so as to speak*,' the infinitive of the consequence, like εἰδέναι ver. 6; see Winer § xliv. p. 400.

τὸ μυστήριον κ.τ.λ.] i. e. the doctrine of the free admission of the Gentiles. For the leading idea which St Paul in these epistles attaches to 'the mystery' of the Gospel, see the note on i. 26.

δι' ὃ] St Paul might have been still at large, if he had been content to preach a Judaic Gospel. It was because he contended for Gentile liberty, and thus offended Jewish prejudices, that he found himself a prisoner. See Acts xxi. 28, xxii. 21, 22, xxiv. 5, 6, xxv. 6, 8. The other reading, δι' ὅν, destroys the point of the sentence.

καὶ δέδεμαι] 2 Tim. ii. 9 μέχρι δεσμῶν, Philem. 9 νυνὶ δὲ καὶ δέσμιος.

4. ἵνα φανερώσω κ.τ.λ.] This is best taken as dependent on the previous clause ἵνα ὁ Θεὸς…τοῦ Χριστοῦ. For instances of a double ἵνα, where

ρώσω αὐτό, ὡς δεῖ με λαλῆσαι. ⁵ἐν σοφίᾳ περιπατεῖτε
πρὸς τοὺς ἔξω, τὸν καιρὸν ἐξαγοραζόμενοι· ⁶ὁ λόγος

the second is not coordinated with, but subordinated to, the first, see the note on Gal. iii. 14. The immediate purport of the Colossians' prayers must be that the Apostle should have all opportunities of preaching the Gospel: the ulterior object, that he should use these opportunities boldly.

5. ἐν σοφίᾳ] Matt. x. 16 γίνεσθε οὖν φρόνιμοι ὡς οἱ ὄφεις.

τοὺς ἔξω] 'those without the pale' of the Church, the unbelievers; as in 1 Cor. v. 12, 13, 1 Thess. iv. 12. So οἱ ἔξωθεν, 1 Tim. iii. 7. The believers on the other hand are οἱ ἔσω, 1 Cor. v. 12. This mode of speaking was derived from the Jews, who called the heathen החיצונים (Schöttgen on 1 Cor. *l. c.*), translated οἱ ἐκτός Ecclus. Prol. and οἱ ἔξωθεν Joseph. *Ant.* xv. 9. 2.

ἐξαγοραζόμενοι κ.τ.λ.] '*buying up the opportunity for yourselves*,' letting no opportunity slip you, of saying and doing what may further the cause of God': comp. Ephes. v. 16. The expression occurs also in Dan. ii. 8 οἶδα ὅτι καιρὸν ὑμεῖς ἐξαγοράζετε, i. e. 'are eager to gain time.' Somewhat similar are the phrases τὸν χρόνον κερδαίνειν, τὸ παρὸν κερδαίνειν. So too Seneca *Ep.* i. 1 'Tempus...collige et serva.' In much the same sense Ignatius says, *Polyc.* 3 τοὺς καιροὺς καταμάνθανε. For this sense of ἐξαγοράζω 'coemo' (closely allied in meaning to συναγοράζω), see Polyb. iii. 42. 2 ἐξηγόρασε παρ' αὐτῶν τά τε μονόξυλα πλοῖα πάντα κ.τ.λ., Plut. *Vit. Crass.* 2. More commonly the word signifies 'to redeem' (see the note on Gal. iii. 13), and some would assign this sense to it here; but no appropriate meaning is thus obtained. In *Mart. Polyc.* 2 διὰ μιᾶς ὥρας τὴν αἰώνιον κόλασιν ἐξαγοραζόμενοι it means 'buying off,' a sense in which ἐξωνεῖσθαι occurs several times. The reason for the injunction is added in Ephes. v. 16, ὅτι αἱ ἡμέραι πονηραί εἰσιν: the

prevailing evil of the times makes the opportunities for good more precious.

6. ἐν χάριτι] '*with grace, favour*,' i. e. 'acceptableness,' 'pleasingness'; comp. Eccles. x. 12 λόγοι στόματος σοφοῦ χάρις, Ps. xliv (xlv). 3 ἐξεχύθη χάρις ἐν χείλεσί σου, Ecclus. xxi. 16 ἐπὶ χείλους συνετοῦ εὑρεθήσεται χάρις. In classical writers χάρις λόγων is a still more common connexion; e.g. Demosth. *c. Phil.* i. 38, Dionys. Hal. *de Lys.* §§ 10, 11, Plut. *Vit. Mar.* 44.

ἅλατι] Comp. Mark ix. 50 ἐὰν δὲ τὸ ἅλας ἄναλον γένηται, ἐν τίνι αὐτὸ ἀρτύσετε; ἔχετε ἐν ἑαυτοῖς ἅλα. The salt has a twofold purpose. (1) It gives a flavour to the discourse and recommends it to the palate: comp. Job vi. 6 εἰ βρωθήσεται ἄρτος ἄνευ ἁλός; εἰ δὲ καὶ ἔστι γεῦμα ἐν ῥήμασι κενοῖς; in which passage the first clause was rendered by Symmachus μήτι βρωθήσεται ἀνάρτυτον τῷ μὴ ἔχειν ἅλα; This is the primary idea of the metaphor here, as the word ἠρτυμένος seems to show. (2) It preserves from corruption and renders wholesome; Ign. *Magn.* 10 ἁλίσθητε ἐν αὐτῷ ἵνα μὴ διαφθαρῇ τις ἐν ὑμῖν, ἐπεὶ ἀπὸ τῆς ὀσμῆς ἐλεγχθήσεσθε. Hence the Pythagorean saying, Diog. Laert. viii. 1. 35 οἱ ἅλες πᾶν σώζουσιν ὅ τι καὶ παραλάβωσι. It may be inferred that this secondary application of the metaphor was present to the Apostle's mind here, because in the parallel epistle, Ephes. iv. 29, he says πᾶς λόγος σαπρὸς ἐκ τοῦ στόματος ὑμῶν μὴ ἐκπορευέσθω κ.τ.λ. In the first application the opposite to ἅλατι ἠρτυμένος would be μωρός '*insipid*' (Luke xiv. 34); in the second, σαπρός '*corrupt.*'

Heathen writers also insisted that discourse should be 'seasoned with salt'; e. g. Cic. *de Orat.* i. 34 'facetiarum quidam lepos quo, tanquam sale, perspergatur omnis oratio.' They

ὑμῶν πάντοτε ἐν χάριτι, ἅλατι ἠρτυμένος, εἰδέναι ὑμᾶς
πῶς δεῖ ἑνὶ ἑκάστῳ ἀποκρίνεσθαι.

⁷Τὰ κατ᾽ ἐμὲ πάντα γνωρίσει ὑμῖν Τύχικος ὁ ἀγα-

likewise dwelt on the connexion between χάρις and ἅλες; e. g. Plut. *Mor.* p. 514 F χάριν τινὰ παρασκευάζοντες ἀλλήλοις, ὥσπερ ἁλσὶ τοῖς λόγοις ἐφηδύνουσι τὴν διατριβήν, p. 697 D (comp. p. 685 A) οἱ πολλοὶ χάριτας καλοῦσιν [τὸν ἅλα], ὅτι ἐπὶ τὰ πλεῖστα μιγνύμενος εὐάρμοστα τῇ γεύσει καὶ προσφιλῆ ποιεῖ καὶ κεχαρισμένα, p. 669 A ἡ δὲ τῶν ἁλῶν δύναμις...χάριν αὐτῷ καὶ ἡδονὴν προστίθησι, Dion Chrys. *Or.* xviii. § 13. Their notion of 'salt' however was wit, and generally the kind of wit which degenerated into the εὐτραπελία denounced by St Paul in Ephes. v. 4 (see the note there).

The form ἅλας is common in the LXX and Greek Testament. Otherwise it is rare: see Buttmann *Gramm.* I. p. 220, and comp. Plut. *Mor.* 668 F.

εἰδέναι] '*so as to know*'; see the note on λαλῆσαι ver. 3.

ἑνὶ ἑκάστῳ] 'Not only must your conversation be opportune as regards the time; it must also be appropriate as regards the person.' The Apostle's precept was enforced by his own example, for he made it a rule to become τοῖς πᾶσιν πάντα, ἵνα πάντως τινὰς σώσῃ (1 Cor. ix. 22).

7—9. 'You will learn everything about me from Tychicus, the beloved brother who has ministered to me and served with me faithfully in the Lord. This indeed was my purpose in sending him to you: that you might be informed how matters stand with me, and that he might cheer your hearts and strengthen your resolves by the tidings. Onesimus will accompany him—a faithful and beloved brother, who is one of yourselves, a Colossian. These two will inform you of all that is going on here.'

7. Τὰ κατ᾽ ἐμὲ πάντα] '*all that relates to me*'; see the note on Phil. i. 12, and comp. Bion in Diog.

Laert. iv. 47. So Acts xxv. 14 τὰ κατὰ τὸν Παῦλον.

γνωρίσει] On this word see the note Phil. i. 22.

Τύχικος] Tychicus was charged by St Paul at this same time with a more extended mission. He was entrusted with copies of the circular letter, which he was enjoined to deliver in the principal churches of proconsular Asia (see above, p. 37, and the introduction to the Epistle to the Ephesians). This mission would bring him to Laodicea, which was one of these great centres of Christianity (see p. 8); and, as Colossæ was only a few miles distant, the Apostle would naturally engage him to pay a visit to the Colossians. At the same time the presence of an authorised delegate of St Paul, as Tychicus was known to be, would serve to recommend Onesimus, who owing to his former conduct stood in every need of such a recommendation. The two names Τύχικος and Ὀνήσιμος occur in proximity in Phrygian inscriptions found at Altentash (Bennisoa?) Boeckh 3857 r sq. appx.

Tychicus was a native of proconsular Asia (Acts xx. 4) and perhaps of Ephesus (2 Tim. iv. 12: see *Philippians* p. 11). He is found with St Paul at three different epochs in his life. (1) He accompanied him when on his way eastward at the close of the third missionary journey A.D. 58 (Acts xx. 4), and probably like Trophimus (Acts xxi. 29) went with him to Jerusalem (for the words ἄχρι τῆς Ἀσίας must be struck out in Acts xx. 4). It is probable indeed that Tychicus, together with others mentioned among St Paul's numerous retinue on this occasion, was a delegate appointed by his own church according to the Apostle's injunctions (1 Cor. xvi. 3, 4) to

πητὸς ἀδελφὸς καὶ πιστὸς διάκονος καὶ σύνδουλος ἐν
Κυρίῳ· ⁸ὃν ἔπεμψα πρὸς ὑμᾶς εἰς αὐτὸ τοῦτο, ἵνα

bear the contributions of his brethren
to the poor Christians of Judæa; and
if so, he may possibly be the person
commended as the brother οὗ ὁ ἔπαι-
νος ἐν τῷ εὐαγγελίῳ διὰ πασῶν τῶν ἐκκλησιῶν (2 Cor. viii. 18): but this will
depend on the interpretation of the
best supported reading in Acts xx. 5
οὗτοι δὲ προσελθόντες ἔμενον ἡμᾶς ἐν
Τρωάδι. (2) We find Tychicus again
in St Paul's company at the time with
which we are immediately concerned,
when this epistle was written, probably towards the end of the first Roman captivity, A.D. 62, 63 (see *Philippians* p. 31 sq.). (3) Once more, at the
close of St Paul's life (about A.D. 67),
he appears again to have associated
himself with the Apostle, when his
name is mentioned in connexion with
a mission to Crete (Tit. iii. 12) and
another to Ephesus (2 Tim. iv. 12).
For the legends respecting him, which
are slight and insignificant, see *Act.
Sanct. Boll.* April 29 (III. p. 619).

Tychicus is not so common a name
as some others which occur in the
New Testament, e. g. Onesimus, Trophimus; but it is found occasionally
in inscriptions belonging to Asia Minor, e.g. Boeckh *C. I.* 2918, 3665,
[3857 c], 3857 r, (comp. 3865 i, etc.);
and persons bearing it are commemorated on the coins of both Magnesia
ad Maeandrum (Mionnet III. p. 153 sq.,
Suppl. VI. p. 236) and Magnesia ad
Sipylum (*ib.* IV. p. 70). The name
occurs also in Roman inscriptions; e.g.
Muratori, pp. DCCCCXVII, MCCCXCIV,
MMLV. Along with several other
proper names similarly formed, this
word is commonly accentuated Τυχικός
(Chandler *Greek Accentuation* § 255),
and so it stands in all the critical
editions, though according to rule
(Winer § vi. p. 58) it should be Τύχικος.

καὶ πιστὸς κ.τ.λ.] The connexion of
the words is not quite obvious. It
seems best however to take ἐν Κυρίῳ

as referring to the whole clause πιστὸς
διάκονος καὶ σύνδουλος rather than to
σύνδουλος alone: for (1) The two substantives are thus bound together by
the preceding πιστός and the following
ἐν Κυρίῳ in a natural way: (2) The attachment of ἐν Κυρίῳ to πιστὸς διάκονος is suggested by the parallel passage Ephes. vi. 21 Τύχικος ὁ ἀγαπητὸς
ἀδελφὸς καὶ πιστὸς διάκονος ἐν Κυρίῳ.
The question of connecting ἐν Κυρίῳ
with ἀδελφός as well need not be entertained, since the idea of ἀδελφός,
'a Christian brother,' is complete in
itself: see the note on Phil. i. 14. The
adjective πιστός will here have its
passive sense, 'trustworthy, stedfast,'
as also in ver. 9: see *Galatians* p.
154 sq.

διάκονος] 'minister,' but to whom?
To the churches, or to St Paul himself? The following σύνδουλος suggests the latter as the prominent idea
here. So in Acts xix. 22 Timothy and
Erastus are described as δύο τῶν δια-
κονούντων αὐτῷ. Tychicus himself also
was one of several who ministered to
St Paul about that same time (Acts
xx. 4). It is not probable however,
that διάκονος has here its strict official
sense, 'a deacon,' as in Rom. xvi. 1,
Phil. i. 1, 1 Tim. iii. 8, 12.

σύνδουλος] The word does not occur elsewhere in St Paul, except in
i. 7, where it is said of Epaphras. It is
probably owing to the fact of St Paul's
applying the term in both these passages to persons whom he calls διάκονοι, that σύνδουλος seems to have been
adopted as a customary form of address in the early Church on the part
of a bishop, when speaking of a deacon.
In the Ignatian letters for instance,
the term is never used except of dea-
cons; *Ephes.* 2, *Magn.* 2, *Philad.* 4,
Smyrn. 12. Where the martyr has
occasion to speak of a bishop or a
presbyter some other designation is
used instead.

γνῶτε τὰ περὶ ἡμῶν καὶ παρακαλέσῃ τὰς καρδίας ὑμῶν,
⁹σὺν Ὀνησίμῳ τῷ πιστῷ καὶ ἀγαπητῷ ἀδελφῷ, ὅς
ἐστιν ἐξ ὑμῶν. πάντα ὑμῖν γνωρίσουσιν τὰ ὧδε.

8. ἔπεμψα] 'I send,' or 'I have sent,' ἔπεμψα being the epistolary aorist; see the note on ἔγραψα, Gal. vi. 11. Tychicus appears to have accompanied the letter itself. For similar instances of the epistolary ἔπεμψα, ἐπέστειλα, etc., see 2 Cor. viii. 18, 22, ix. 3, Ephes. vi. 22, Phil. ii. 25, 28, Philem. 11, Hebr. xiii. 22, Polyc. Phil. 13.

γνῶτε τὰ περὶ ἡμῶν] This must be preferred to the received reading, γνῷ τὰ περὶ ὑμῶν, for two independent reasons. (1) The preponderance of ancient authority is decidedly in its favour. (2) The emphatic εἰς αὐτὸ τοῦτο ἵνα seems imperatively to demand it. St Paul in the context twice states the object of Tychicus' visit to be that the Colossians might be informed about the Apostle's own doings, τὰ κατ' ἐμὲ πάντα γνωρίσει ὑμῖν (ver. 7), and πάντα ὑμῖν γνωρίσουσιν τὰ ὧδε. He could hardly therefore have described 'the very purpose' of his mission in the same breath as something quite different.

It is urged indeed, that this is a scribe's alteration to bring the passage into accordance with Ephes. vi. 21. But against this it may fairly be argued that, on any hypothesis as regards the authorship and relation of the two letters, this strange variation from γνῶτε τὰ περὶ ἡμῶν to γνῷ τὰ περὶ ὑμῶν in the author himself is improbable. On the other hand a transcriber was under a great temptation to substitute γνῷ for γνῶτε owing to the following παρακαλέσῃ, and this temptation would become almost irresistible, if by any chance περὶ ὑμῶν had been written for περὶ ἡμῶν in the copy before him, as we find to be the case in some MSS. See the detached note on various readings.

παρακαλέσῃ κ.τ.λ.] i.e. 'encourage you to persevere by his tidings and exhortations.' The phrase occurs again, Ephes. vi. 22, 2 Thess. ii. 17: see above ii. 2. The prominent idea in all these passages is not comfort or consolation but perseverance in the right way.

9. σὺν Ὀνησίμῳ] See above, p. 33, and the introduction to the Epistle to Philemon.

τῷ πιστῷ κ.τ.λ.] The man whom the Colossians had only known hitherto, if they knew him at all, as a worthless runaway slave, is thus commended to them as no more a slave but a brother, no more dishonest and faithless but trustworthy, no more an object of contempt but of love; comp. Philem. 11, 16.

γνωρίσουσιν] This form has rather better support from the MSS than γνωριοῦσιν: see also above iii. 25. On the Attic future from verbs in -ιζω in the Greek Testament generally see Winer § xiii. p. 88, A. Buttmann p. 32 sq. Is there any decisive instance of these Attic forms in St Paul, except in quotations from the LXX (e.g. Rom. x. 19, xv. 12)?

10—14. 'I send you greeting from Aristarchus who is a fellow-prisoner with me; from Marcus, Barnabas' cousin, concerning whom I have already sent you directions, that you welcome him heartily, if he pays you a visit; and from Jesus, surnamed Justus; all three Hebrew converts. They alone of their fellow-countrymen have worked loyally with me in spreading the kingdom of God; and their stedfastness has indeed been a comfort to me in the hour of trial. Greeting also from Epaphras, your fellow-townsman, a true servant of Christ, who is ever wrestling in his prayers on your behalf, that ye may stand firm in the faith, perfectly instructed and fully convinced in every will and pur-

¹⁰'Ασπάζεται ὑμᾶς 'Αρίσταρχος ὁ συναιχμάλωτός

pose of God. I bear testimony to the earnestness with which he labours for you and the brethren of Laodicea and those of Hierapolis. Greeting also from Luke the physician, my very dear friend, and from Demas.'

10. The salutations to Philemon are sent from the same persons as to the Colossians, except that in the former case the name of Jesus Justus is omitted.

'Αρίσταρχος] the Thessalonian. He had started with St Paul on his voyage from Jerusalem to Rome, but probably had parted from the Apostle at Myra (see *Philippians* p. 33 sq.). If so, he must have rejoined him at Rome at a later date. On this Aristarchus see *Philippians* p. 10, and the introduction to the Epistles to the Thessalonians. He would be well known in proconsular Asia, which he had visited from time to time; Acts xix. 29, xx. 4, xxvii. 2.

συναιχμάλωτός μου] In Philem. 23 this honourable title is withheld from Aristarchus and given to Epaphras. In Rom. xvi. 7 St Paul's kinsmen, Andronicus and Junias, are so called. On the possibility of its referring to a spiritual captivity or subjection see *Philippians* p. 11. In favour of this meaning it may be urged, that, though St Paul as a prisoner was truly a δέσ-μιος, he was not strictly an αἰχμάλωτος 'a prisoner of war'; nor could he have called himself so, except by a confusion of the actual and metaphorical. If on the other hand συναιχμάλωτός refers to a physical captivity, it cannot easily be explained by any known fact. The incident in Acts xix. 29 is hardly adequate. The most probable solution would be, that his relations with St Paul in Rome excited suspicion and led to a temporary confinement. Another possible hypothesis is that he voluntarily shared the Apostle's captivity by living with him.

Μάρκος] doubtless John Mark, who had been associated with St Paul in his earlier missionary work; Acts xii. 25, xv. 37 sq. This commendatory notice is especially interesting as being the first mention of him since the separation some twelve years before, Acts xv. 39. In the later years of the Apostle's life he entirely effaced the unfavourable impression left by his earlier desertion; 2 Tim. iv. 11 ἔστιν γάρ μοι εὔχρηστος εἰς διακονίαν.

This notice is likewise important in two other respects. (1) Mark appears here as commended to a church of proconsular *Asia*, and intending to visit those parts. To the churches of this same region he sends a salutation in 1 Pet. v. 13; and in this district apparently also he is found some few years later than the present time, 2 Tim. iv. 11. (2) Mark is now residing at *Rome*. His connexion with the metropolis appears also from 1 Pet. v. 13, if Βαβυλών there (as seems most probable) be rightly interpreted of Rome; and early tradition speaks of his Gospel as having been written for the Romans (Iren. iii. I. 1; comp. Papias in Euseb. *H. E.* iii. 39).

ὁ ἀνεψιός] '*the cousin.*' The term ἀνεψιοί is applied to cousins german, the children whether of two brothers or of two sisters or of a brother and sister, as it is carefully defined in Pollux iii. 28. This writer adds that αὐτανέψιοι means neither more nor less than ἀνεψιοί. As a synonyme we find ἐξάδελφος, which however is condemned as a vulgarism; Phryn. p. 306 (ed. Lobeck). Many instances of ἀνεψιοί are found in different authors of various ages (e.g. Herod. vii. 5, 82, ix. 10, Thucyd. i. 132, Plato *Charm.* 154 B, *Gorg.* 471 B, Andoc. *de Myst.* § 47, Isaeus *Hagn. Her.* § 8 sq., Demosth. *c. Macart.* § 24, 27, etc., Dion. Hal. *A. R.* i. 79, Plut. *Vit. Thes.* 7, *Vit. Caes.* 1, *Vit. Brut.* 13, Lucian *Dial. Mort.* xxix. 1, Hegesipp. in Euseb. *H. E.* iv. 22), where the rela-

μου, καὶ Μάρκος ὁ ἀνεψιὸς Βαρνάβα, περὶ οὗ ἐλάβετε

tionship is directly defined or already
known, and there is no wavering as to
the meaning. This sense also it has in
the LXX, Num. xxxvi. 11. In very late
writers however (e. g. Io. Malalas
Chron. xvii. p. 424, Io. Damasc. *adv.*
Const. Cab. 12, 11. p. 621; but in Theodt.
H. E. v. 39, which is also quoted by
E. A. Sophocles *Gr. Lex.* s. v. for
this meaning, the text is doubtful)
the word comes to be used for a
nephew, properly ἀδελφιδοῦς; and
to this later use the rendering of
our English versions must be traced.
The German translations also (Luther
and the Zürich) have 'Neffe.' The
earliest of the ancient versions (Latin,
Syriac, Egyptian) seem all to translate
it correctly; not so in every case apparently the later. There is no reason
to suppose that St Paul would or
could have used it in any other than
its proper sense. St Mark's relationship with Barnabas may have been
through his mother Mary, who is mentioned Acts xii. 12. The incidental
notice here explains why Barnabas
should have taken a more favourable
view of Mark's defection than St
Paul, Acts xv. 37—39. The notices in
this passage and in 2 Tim. iv. 11 show
that Mark had recovered the Apostle's good opinion. The studious recommendation of St Mark in both
passages indicates a desire to efface
the unfavourable impression of the
past.

The name of Mark occurs in five
different relations, as (1) The early
disciple, John Mark, Acts xii. 12, 25,
xv. 39; (2) The later companion of St
Paul, here and Philem. 24, 2 Tim. iv.
11; (3) The companion and 'son' of
St Peter, 1 Pet. v. 13; (4) The evangelist; (5) The bishop of Alexandria.
Out of these notices some writers get
three or even four distinct persons
(see the note of Cotelier on *Apost.*
Const. ii. 57). Even Tillemont (*Mem.*
Eccl. 11. p. 89 sq., 503 sq.) assumes two

Marks, supposing (1) (2) to refer to
one person, and (3) (4) (5) to another.
His main reason is that he cannot
reconcile the notices of the first with
the tradition (Euseb. *H. E.* ii. 15, 16)
that St Mark the evangelist accompanied St Peter to Rome in A.D. 43,
having first preached the Gospel in
Alexandria (p. 515). To most persons
however this early date of St Peter's
visit to Rome will appear quite irreconcilable with the notices in the
Apostolic writings, and therefore
with them Tillemont's argument will
carry no weight. But in fact Eusebius does not say, either that St Mark
went *with* St Peter to Rome, or that
he had preached in Alexandria *before*
this. The Scriptural notices suggest
that the same Mark is intended in all
the occurrences of the name, for they
are connected together by personal
links (Peter, Paul, Barnabas); and the
earliest forms of tradition likewise
identify them.

Βαρνάβα] On the affectionate tone
of St Paul's language, whenever he
mentions Barnabas after the colli-
sion at Antioch (Gal. ii. 11 sq.) and
the separation of missionary spheres
(Acts xv. 39), see the note on Gal. ii.
13. It has been inferred from the
reference here, that inasmuch as Mark
has rejoined St Paul, Barnabas must
have died before this epistle was
written (about A.D. 63); and this has
been used as an argument against
the genuineness of the letter bearing his name (Hefele *Sendschr. d.*
Apost. Barnab. p. 29 sq.); but this
argument is somewhat precarious.
From 1 Cor. ix. 6 we may infer that
he was still living, A.D. 57. The
notices bearing on the biography of
Barnabas are collected and discussed
by Hefele, p. 1 sq.

ἐλάβετε ἐντολάς] These injunctions
must have been communicated previously either by letter or by word of
mouth: for it cannot be a question

ἐντολάς, Ἐὰν ἔλθῃ πρὸς ὑμᾶς, δέξασθε αὐτόν, ¹¹καὶ
Ἰησοῦς ὁ λεγόμενος Ἰοῦστος, οἱ ὄντες ἐκ περιτομῆς·
οὗτοι μόνοι συνεργοὶ εἰς τὴν βασιλείαν τοῦ Θεοῦ, οἵτινες

here of an epistolary aorist. The
natural inference is, that they were
sent by St Paul himself, and not by
any one else, e.g. by St Peter or St
Barnabas, as some have suggested.
Thus the notice points to earlier communications between the Apostle and
Colossæ.

But what was their tenour? It
seems best to suppose that this is
given in the next clause ἐὰν ἔλθῃ
κ.τ.λ. By an abrupt change to the
oratio recta the injunction is repeated as it was delivered; comp. Ps.
cv (civ). 15 ἤλεγξεν ὑπὲρ αὐτῶν βα-
σιλεῖς· Μὴ ἅψησθε κ.τ.λ. After verbs
signifying 'to command, charge, etc.'
there is a tendency to pass from the
oblique to the direct; e.g. Luke v. 14,
Acts i. 4, xxiii. 22. The reading δέ-
ξασθαι gives the right sense, but can
hardly be correct. If this construction be not accepted, it is vain to
speculate what may have been the
tenour of the injunction.

11. καὶ Ἰησοῦς] He is not mentioned elsewhere. Even in the Epistle to Philemon his name is omitted.
Probably he was not a man of any
prominence in the Church, but his
personal devotion to the Apostle
prompted this honourable mention.
For the story which makes him bishop
of Eleutheropolis in Palestine, see Le
Quien *Oriens Christ.* III. p. 633.

Ἰοῦστος] A common name or surname of Jews and proselytes, denoting obedience and devotion to the
law. It is applied to two persons in
the New Testament, besides this Jesus; (1) Joseph Barsabbas, Acts i. 23;
(2) A proselyte at Corinth, Acts xviii.
7. It occurs twice in the list of early
Jewish Christian bishops of Jerusalem, in Euseb. *H. E.* iii. 35, iv. 5. It
was borne by a Jew of Tiberias who
wrote the history of the Jewish war

(Joseph. *Vit.* §§ 9, 65), and by a son
of the historian Josephus himself (*ib.*
§ 1). It occurs in the rabbinical writings (יוסטא or יוסטי, Schöttgen on
Acts i. 23, Zunz *Judennamen* p. 20),
and in monumental inscriptions from
Jewish cemeteries in various places
(Boeckh *C. I.* no. 9922, 9925; *Revue
Archéologique* 1860, II. p. 348; Garrucci *Dissertazioni Archeologiche* II.
p. 182). So also the corresponding
female name Justa (Garrucci *l. c.* p.
180). In *Clem. Hom.* ii. 19, iii. 73, iv.
1, xiii. 7, the Syrophœnician woman
of the Gospels is named Ἰοῦστα,
doubtless because she is represented
in this Judaizing romance as a prose-
lytess (προσήλυτος xiii. 7) who strictly
observes the Mosaic ordinances (τὴν
νόμιμον ἀναδεξαμένη πολιτείαν ii. 20),
and is contrasted with the heathen
'dogs' (τὰ ἔθνη ἐοικότα κυσίν ii. 19)
who disregard them. In some cases
Justus might be the only name of the
person, as a Latin rendering of the
Hebrew Zadok; while in others, as
here and in Acts i. 23, it is a surname.
Its Greek equivalent, ὁ δίκαιος, is the
recognised epithet of James the Lord's
brother: see *Galatians*, p. 348.

οἱ ὄντες κ.τ.λ.] i.e. 'converts from
Judaism' (see the note Gal. ii. 12),
or perhaps 'belonging to the Circumcision'; but in this latter case
περιτομῆς, though without the article,
must be used in a concrete sense,
like τῆς περιτομῆς, for 'the Jews.'
Of Mark and of Jesus the fact is
plain from their name or their connexions. Of Aristarchus we could not
have inferred a Jewish origin, independently of this direct statement.

μόνοι] i.e. of the Jewish Christians
in Rome. On this antagonism of the
converts from the Circumcision in the
metropolis, see *Philippians* p. 16 sq.
The words however must not be closely

ἐγενήθησάν μοι παρηγορία. ¹²ἀσπάζεται ὑμᾶς Ἐπαφρᾶς
ὁ ἐξ ὑμῶν, δοῦλος Χριστοῦ Ἰησοῦ, πάντοτε ἀγωνιζόμενος ὑπὲρ ὑμῶν ἐν ταῖς προσευχαῖς, ἵνα σταθῆτε τέ-

pressed, as if absolutely no Jewish
Christian besides had remained friendly; they will only imply that among
the more prominent members of
the body the Apostle can only name
these three as stedfast in their allegiance: comp. Phil. ii. 20 οὐδένα ἔχω
ἰσόψυχον ... πάντες γὰρ κ.τ.λ. (with
the note).

τὴν βασιλείαν κ.τ.λ.] See the note on
i. 13.

οἵτινες κ.τ.λ.] 'men whom I found
etc.'; comp. Acts xxviii. 15 οὓς ἰδὼν
ὁ Παῦλος εὐχαριστήσας τῷ Θεῷ ἔλαβεν
θάρσος, and see *Philippians* p. 17.
For οἵτινες, not specifying the individuals, but referring them to their
class characteristics, see the notes on
Gal. iv. 24, v. 19, Phil. iii. 7, iv. 3.

παρηγορία] 'encouragement,' 'comfort.' The range of meaning in this
word is even wider than in παραμυ-
θία or παράκλησις (see the note Phil.
ii. 1). The verb παρηγορεῖν denotes
either (1) 'to exhort, encourage' (Herod. v. 104, Apoll. Rhod. ii. 64);
(2) 'to dissuade' (Herod. ix. 54, 55);
(3) 'to appease,' 'quiet' (Plut. *Vit.
Pomp.* 13, *Mor.* p. 737 c); or (4) 'to
console, comfort' (Aesch. *Eum.* 507).
The word however, and its derivates
παρηγορία, παρηγόρημα, παρηγορικός,
παρηγορητικός, were used especially as
medical terms, in the sense of 'as-
suaging,' 'alleviating'; e.g. Hippocr.
pp. 392, 393, 394, Galen XIV. p. 335,
446, Plut. *Mor.* pp. 43 D, 142 D; and
perhaps owing to this usage, the idea
of consolation, comfort, is on the whole
predominant in the word; e. g. Plut.
Mor. p. 56 A τὰς ἐπὶ τοῖς ἀτυχήμασι
παρηγορίας, p. 118 A τοῖς ἀφαιρουμένοις
τὰς λύπας διὰ τῆς γενναίας καὶ σεμνῆς
παρηγορίας, *Vit. Cim.* 4 ἐπὶ παρηγορίᾳ
τοῦ πένθους. In Plut. *Mor.* p. 599 B
παρηγορία and συνηγορία are contrast-

ed, as the right and wrong method of dealing with the sorrows of
the exile; and the former is said to
be the part of men παρρησιαζομένων
καὶ διδασκόντων ὅτι τὸ λυπεῖσθαι καὶ
ταπεινοῦν ἑαυτὸν ἐπὶ παντὶ μὲν ἄχρη-
στόν ἐστι κ.τ.λ.

12. Ἐπαφρᾶς] His full name would
be Epaphroditus, but he is always
called by the shortened form Epaphras, and must not be confused with
the Philippian Epaphroditus (see *Philippians* p. 60), who also was with St
Paul at one period of his Roman
captivity. Of Epaphras, as the Evangelist of Colossæ, and perhaps of the
neighbouring towns, see above, pp. 29
sq., 34 sq.

ὁ ἐξ ὑμῶν] 'who belongs to you,'
'who is one of you,' i. e. a native, or
at least an inhabitant, of Colossæ, as
in the case of Onesimus ver. 9; comp.
Acts iv. 6, xxi. 8, Rom. xvi. 10, 11,
1 Cor. xii. 16, Phil. iv. 22, etc.

δοῦλος X. Ἰ.] This title, which the
Apostle uses several times of himself,
is not elsewhere conferred on any
other individual, except once on
Timothy (Phil. i. 1), and probably
points to exceptional services in the
cause of the Gospel on the part of
Epaphras.

ἀγωνιζόμενος] 'wrestling'; comp.
Rom. xv. 30 συναγωνίσασθαί μοι ἐν
ταῖς προσευχαῖς. See also the great
ἀγωνία of prayer in Luke xxii. 44.
Comp. Justin *Apol.* ii. 13 (p. 51 B)
καὶ εὐχόμενος καὶ παμμάχως ἀγωνιζόμενος. See also i. 29, ii. 1, with the
notes.

σταθῆτε] 'stand fast,' doubtless the
correct reading rather than στῆτε
which the received text has; comp.
Matt. ii. 9, xxvii. 11, where also the
received text substitutes the weaker
word.

λειοι καὶ πεπληροφορημένοι ἐν παντὶ θελήματι τοῦ
Θεοῦ. ¹³μαρτυρῶ γὰρ αὐτῷ ὅτι ἔχει πολὺν πόνον ὑπὲρ

πεπληροφορημένοι] '*fully persuaded*.' The verb πληροφορεῖν has several
senses. (1) 'To fulfil, accomplish'; 2
Tim. iv. 5 τὴν διακονίαν σου πληροφόρησον, *ib.* ver. 17 τὸ κήρυγμα πλη-
ροφορηθῇ, *Clem. Hom.* xix. 24 πεπληροφορημένων νῦν ἤδη τριῶν ἡμερῶν.
So perhaps Hermas *Sim.* 2 πληροφο-
ροῦσι τὸν πλοῦτον αὐτῶν... πληροφο-
ροῦσι τὰς ψυχὰς αὐτῶν, though it is a
little difficult to carry the same sense
into the latter clause, where the word
seems to signify rather 'to satisfy.'
(2) 'To persuade fully, to convince';
Rom. iv. 21 πληροφορηθεὶς ὅτι ὃ ἐπήγ-
γελται δυνατός ἐστιν καὶ ποιῆσαι, xiv.
5 ἐν τῷ ἰδίῳ νοῒ πληροφορείσθω, Clem.
Rom. 42 πληροφορηθέντες διὰ τῆς ἀναστάσεως κ.τ.λ., Ign. *Magn.* 8 εἰς τὸ
πληροφορηθῆναι τοὺς ἀπειθοῦντας, *ib.* 11
πεπληροφορῆσθαι ἐν τῇ γεννήσει κ.τ.λ.,
Philad. inscr. ἐν τῇ ἀναστάσει αὐτοῦ
πεπληροφορημένη ἐν παντὶ ἐλέει, *Smyrn.*
1 πεπληροφορημένους εἰς τὸν Κύριον
ἡμῶν, *Mart. Ign.* 7 πληροφορῆσαι τοὺς
ἀσθενεῖς ἡμᾶς ἐπὶ τοῖς προγεγονόσιν,
Clem. Hom. Ep. ad Iac. 10 πεπληροφο-
ρημένος ὅτι ἐκ Θεοῦ δικαίου, *ib.* xvii.
13, 14, xix. 24 συνετιθέμην ὡς πληρο-
φορούμενος. So too LXX Eccles. viii. 11
ἐπληροφορήθη καρδία τοῦ ποιῆσαι τὸ
πονηρόν. (3) 'To fill'; Rom. xv. 13 πληροφορῆσαι ὑμᾶς πάσης χαρᾶς (a doubtful
v.l.), Clem. Rom. 54 τίς πεπληροφορημέ-
νος ἀγάπης ; *Test. xii Patr.* Dan 2 τῇ
πλεονεξίᾳ ἐπληροφορήθην τῆς ἀναιρέσεως
αὐτοῦ, where it means 'I was filled
with,' i.e. 'I was fully bent on,' a
sense closely allied to the last.　From
this account it will be seen that there
is in the usage of the word no
justification for translating it 'most
surely believed' in Luke i. 1 τῶν
πεπληροφορημένων ἐν ἡμῖν πραγμάτων,
and it should therefore be rendered
'fulfilled, accomplished.'　The word
is almost exclusively biblical and ecclesiastical ; and it seems clear that
the passage from Ctesias in Photius

(*Bibl.* 72) πολλοῖς λόγοις καὶ ὅρκοις
πληροφορήσαντες Μεγάβυζον is not
quoted with verbal exactness.　In
Isocr. *Trapez.* § 8 the word is now
expunged from the text on the authority of the MSS.　For the substantive
πληροφορία see the note on ii. 2 above.
The reading of the received text here,
πεπληρωμένοι, must be rejected as of
inferior authority.

ἐν παντὶ κ.τ.λ.] '*in every thing
willed by God*'; comp. 1 Kings ix. 11.
So the plural τὰ θελήματα in Acts
xiii. 22, Ephes. ii. 3, and several times
in the LXX.　The words are best connected directly with πεπληροφορημένοι.
The passages quoted in the last note
amply illustrate this construction. The
preposition may denote (1) The abode
of the conviction, as Rom. xiv. 5 ἐν τῷ
ἰδίῳ νοῒ; or (2) The object of the
conviction, as Ign. *Magn.* 11 ἐν τῇ
γεννήσει, *Philad.* inscr. ἐν τῇ ἀναστάσει; or (3) The atmosphere, the
surroundings, of the conviction, as
Philad. inscr. ἐν παντὶ ἐλέει. This
last seems to be its sense here.　The
connexion σταθῆτε...ἐν, though legitimate in itself (Rom. v. 2, 1 Cor. xv.
1), is not favoured by the order of
the words here.

13.　πολὺν πόνον] '*much toil*,' both
inward and outward, though from the
connexion the former notion seems to
predominate, as in ἀγῶνα ii. 1 ; comp.
Plat. *Phaedr.* p. 247 B πόνος τε καὶ
ἀγὼν ἔσχατος ψυχῇ πρόκειται. Of the
two variations which transcribers
have substituted for the correct reading ζῆλον emphasizes the former idea
and κόπον the latter.　The true reading is more expressive than either.
The word πόνος however is very
rare in the New Testament (occurring only Rev. xvi. 10, 11, xxi. 4,
besides this passage), and was therefore liable to be changed.

καὶ τῶν κ.τ.λ.] The neighbouring
cities are taken in their geographical

ὑμῶν καὶ τῶν ἐν Λαοδικίᾳ καὶ τῶν ἐν Ἱεραπόλει.
¹⁴ ἀσπάζεται ὑμᾶς Λουκᾶς ὁ ἰατρὸς ὁ ἀγαπητός, καὶ
Δημᾶς.

order, commencing from Colossæ; see above, p. 2. Epaphras, though a Colossian, may have been the evangelist of the two larger cities also.

Λαοδικίᾳ] This form has not the same overwhelming preponderance of authority in its favour here and in vv. 15, 16, as in ii. 1, but is probably correct in all these places. It is quite possible however, that the same person would write Λαοδικια and Λαοδικεια indifferently. Even the form Λαοδικηα is found in Mionnet, Suppl. VII. p. 581. Another variation is the contraction of Λαοδ- into Λαδ-; e.g. Λαδικηνός, which occurs frequently in the edict of Diocletian.

14. Λουκᾶς] St Luke had travelled with St Paul on his last journey to Jerusalem (Acts xxi. 1 sq.). He had also accompanied him two years later from Jerusalem to Rome (Acts xxvii. 2 sq.). And now again, probably after another interval of two years (see *Philippians* p. 31 sq.), we find him in the Apostle's company. It is not probable that he remained with St Paul in the meanwhile (*Philippians*, p. 35), and this will account for his name not occurring in the Epistle to the Philippians. He was at the Apostle's side again in his second captivity (2 Tim. iv. 11).

Lucas is doubtless a contraction of Lucanus. Several Old Latin MSS write out the name *Lucanus* in the superscription and subscription to the Gospel, just as elsewhere Apollos is written in full Apollonius. On the frequent occurrence of this name Lucanus in inscriptions see *Ephem. Epigr.* II. p. 28 (1874). The shortened form Lucas however seems to be rare. He is here distinguished from οἱ ὄντες ἐκ περιτομῆς (ver. 11). This alone is fatal to his identification (mentioned as a tradition by Origen

ad loc.) with the Lucius, St Paul's 'kinsman' (i. e. a Jew; see *Philippians* pp. 17, 171, 173), who sends a salutation from Corinth to Rome (Rom. xvi. 21). It is equally fatal to the somewhat later tradition that he was one of the seventy (*Dial. c. Marc.* § 1 in Orig. *Op.* I. p. 806, ed. De la Rue; Epiphan. *Haer.* li. 11). The identification with Lucius of Cyrene (Acts xiii. 13) is possible but not probable. Though the example of Patrobius for Patrobas (Rom. xvi. 14) shows that such a contraction is not out of the question, yet probability and testimony alike point to Lucanus, as the longer form of the Evangelist's name.

ὁ ἰατρός] Indications of medical knowledge have been traced both in the third Gospel and in the Acts; see on this point Smith's *Voyage and Shipwreck of St Paul* p. 6 sq. (ed. 2). It has been observed also, that St Luke's first appearance in company with St Paul (Acts xvi. 10) nearly synchronizes with an attack of the Apostle's constitutional malady (Gal. iv. 13, 14); so that he may have joined him partly in a professional capacity. This conjecture is perhaps borne out by the personal feeling which breathes in the following ὁ ἀγαπητός. But whatever may be thought of these points, there is no ground for questioning the ancient belief (Iren. iii. 14. 1 sq.) that the physician is also the Evangelist. St Paul's motive in specifying him as the Physician may not have been to distinguish him from any other bearing the same name, but to emphasize his own obligations to his medical knowledge. The name in this form does not appear to have been common. The tradition that St Luke was a painter is quite late (Niceph. Call. ii. 43). It is worthy of notice that the two Evangelists are men-

¹⁵Ἀσπάσασθε τοὺς ἐν Λαοδικίᾳ ἀδελφοὺς καὶ Νυμ-
φᾶν καὶ τὴν κατ᾽ οἶκον αὐτῶν ἐκκλησίαν. ¹⁶Καὶ ὅταν

tioned together in this context, as also
in Philem. 24, 2 Tim. iv. 11.

ὁ ἀγαπητός] ' the beloved one,' not to
be closely connected with ὁ ἰατρός, for
ὁ ἀγαπητός is complete in itself ; comp.
Philem. 1, Rom. xvi. 12 (comp. vv. 5,
8, 9), 3 Joh. 1. For the form compare
the expression in the Gospels, Matt.
iii. 17, etc. ὁ υἱός μου, ὁ ἀγαπητός κ.τ.λ. ;
where a comparison of Is. xlii. 1, as
quoted in Matt. xii. 18, seems to show
that ὁ ἀγαπητός κ.τ.λ. forms a distinct
clause from ὁ υἱός μου.

Δημᾶς] On the probability that this
person was a Thessalonian (2 Tim. iv.
10) and that his name was Demetrius,
see the introduction to the Epistles to
the Thessalonians. He appears in
close connexion with St Luke in Philem.
24, as here. In 2 Tim. iv. 10 their
conduct is placed in direct contrast,
Δημᾶς με ἐγκατέλιπεν...Λοῦκας ἐστὶν μόνος μετ᾽ ἐμοῦ. There is perhaps a fore-
shadowing of this contrast in the language here. While Luke is described
with special tenderness as ὁ ἰατρός, ὁ
ἀγαπητός, Demas alone is dismissed
with a bare mention and without any
epithet of commendation.

15—17. ' Greet from me the brethren who are in Laodicea, especially
Nymphas, and the church which assembles in their house. And when
this letter has been read among you,
take care that it is read also in the
Church of the Laodiceans, and be sure
that ye also read the letter which I
have sent to Laodicea, and which ye
will get from them. Moreover give
this message from me to Archippus ;
Take heed to the ministry which thou
hast received from me in Christ, and
discharge it fully and faithfully.'

15. Νυμφᾶν] As the context shows,
an inhabitant of Laodicea. The name
in full would probably be Nymphodorus, as Artemas (Tit. iii. 12) for Arte-
midorus, Zenas (Tit. iii. 13) for Zeno-

dorus, Theudas (Acts v. 16) for Theodorus, Olympas (Rom. xvi. 15) for
Olympiodorus, and probably Hermas
(Rom. xvi. 14) for Hermodorus (see
Philippians, p. 174). Other names in
as occurring in the New Testament
and representing different terminations are Amplias (Ampliatus, a v. l.),
Antipas (Antipater), Demas (Demetrius ?), Epaphras (Epaphroditus), Lucas (Lucanus), Parmenas (Parme-
nides), Patrobas (Patrobius), Silas
(Sylvanus), Stephanas (Stephanepho-
rus), and perhaps Junias (Junianus,
Rom. xvi. 7). For a collection of
names with this contraction, found in
different places, see Chandler Greek
Accentuation § 34 ; comp. Lobeck Pa-
thol. p. 505 sq. Some remarkable
instances are found in the inscriptions ; e.g. Ἀσκλᾶς, Δημοσθᾶς, Διομᾶς,
Ἑρμογᾶς, Νικομᾶς, Ὀνησᾶς, Τροφᾶς,
etc.; see esp. Boeckh C. I. III. pp. 1072,
1097. The name Nymphodorus is
found not unfrequently ; e.g. Herod.
vii. 137, Thuc. ii. 29, Athen. i. p. 19 F,
vi. p. 265 C, Mionnet Suppl. VI. p. 88,
Boeckh C. I. no. 158, etc. The contracted form Νυμφᾶς however is very
rare, though it occurs in an Athenian
inscription, Boeckh C. I. 269 Νυνφᾶς,
and apparently also in a Spartan,
ib. 1240 Εὔτυχος Νυνφᾶ. In Murat.
MDXXXV. 6, is an inscription to one Nu.
Aquilius Nymphas, a freedman, where
the dative is Nymphadi. Other
names from which Nymphas might
be contracted are Nymphius, Nymphi-
cus, Nymphidius, Nymphodotus, the
first and last being the most common.

Those, who read αὐτῆς in the following clause, take it as a woman's
name (Νύμφαν, not Νυμφᾶν) ; and the
name Nymphe, Nympha, Nympa, etc.,
occurs from time to time in Latin
inscriptions ; e.g. C. I. L. II. 1099,
1783, 3763, III. 525, V. 607, etc. Murator. CMXXIV. 1, MCLIX. 8, MCCXCV. 9,

ἀναγνωσθῇ παρ᾽ ὑμῖν ἡ ἐπιστολή, ποιήσατε ἵνα καὶ

MDXCI. 3. But a Doric form of the Greek name here seems in the highest degree improbable.

τὴν κατ᾽ οἶκον κ.τ.λ.] The same expression is used of Prisca and Aquila both at Rome (Rom. xvi. 5) and at Ephesus (1 Cor. xvi. 19), and also of Philemon, whether at Colossæ or at Laodicea is somewhat uncertain (Philem. 2); comp. Acts xii. 12 τὴν οἰκίαν τῆς Μαρίας...οὗ ἦσαν ἱκανοὶ συνηθροισμένοι καὶ προσευχόμενοι, and see *Philippians* p. 56. Perhaps similar gatherings may be implied by the expressions in Rom. xvi. 14, 15 τοὺς σὺν αὐτοῖς ἀδελφούς, τοὺς σὺν αὐτοῖς πάντας ἁγίους (Probst *Kirchliche Disciplin* p. 182, 1873). See also *Act. Mart. Justin.* § 3 (II. p. 262 ed. Otto), *Clem. Recogn.* x. 71 'Theophilus... domus suae ingentem basilicam ecclesiae nomine consecraret' (where the word 'basilica' was probably introduced by the translator Ruffinus). Of the same kind must have been the 'collegium quod est in domo Sergiae Paulinae' (de Rossi *Roma Sotterranea* I. p. 209); for the Christians were first recognised by the Roman Government as 'collegia' or burial clubs, and protected by this recognition doubtless held their meetings for religious worship. There is no clear example of a separate building set apart for Christian worship within the limits of the Roman empire before the third century, though apartments in private houses might be specially devoted to this purpose. This, I think, appears as a negative result from the passages collected in Bingham viii. I. 13 and Probst p. 181 sq. with a different view. Hence the places of Christian assembly were not commonly called ναοί till quite late (Ignat. *Magn.* 7 is not really an exception), but οἶκοι Θεοῦ, οἶκοι ἐκκλησιῶν, οἶκοι εὐκτήριοι, and the like (Euseb. *H. E.* vii. 30, viii. 13, ix. 9, etc.).

αὐτῶν] The difficulty of this read-

ing has led to the two corrections, αὐτοῦ and αὐτῆς, of which the former appears in the received text, and the latter is supported by one or two very ancient authorities. Of these alternative readings however, αὐτοῦ is condemned by its simplicity, and αὐτῆς has arisen from the form Νυμφαν, which *prima facie* would look like a woman's name, and yet hardly can be so. We should require to know more of the circumstances to feel any confidence in explaining αὐτῶν. A simple explanation is that αὐτῶν denotes 'Nymphas and his friends,' by a transition which is common in classical writers; e.g. Xen. *Anab.* iii. 3. 7 προσ-ῄει μὲν (Μιθριδάτης)...πρὸς τοὺς Ἕλλη-νας· ἐπεὶ δ᾽ ἐγγὺς ἐγένοντο κ.τ.λ., iv. 5. 33 ἐπεὶ δ᾽ ἦλθον πρὸς Χειρίσοφον, κατελάμβανον καὶ ἐκείνους σκηνοῦν-τας: see also Kühner *Gramm.* § 371 (II. p. 77), Bernhardy *Syntax* p. 288. Or perhaps τοὺς ἐν Λαοδικίᾳ ἀδελφούς may refer not to the whole body of the Laodicean Church, but to a family of Colossian Christians established in Laodicea. Under any circumstances this ἐκκλησία is only a section of ἡ Λαοδικέων ἐκκλησία mentioned in ver. 16. On the authorities for the various readings see the detached note.

16. ἡ ἐπιστολή] '*the letter,*' which has just been concluded, for these salutations have the character of a postscript; comp. Rom. xvi. 22 Τέρ-τιος ὁ γράψας τὴν ἐπιστολήν, 2 Thess. iii. 14 διὰ τῆς ἐπιστολῆς, *Mart. Polyc.* 20 τὴν ἐπιστολὴν διαπέμψασθε. Such examples however do not countenance the explanation which refers ἔγραψα ὑμῖν ἐν τῇ ἐπιστολῇ in 1 Cor. v. 9 to the First Epistle itself, occurring (as it does) in the middle of the letter (comp. 2 Cor. vii. 8).

ποιήσατε ἵνα] '*cause that*'; so John xi. 37, Apoc. xiii. 15. In such cases the ἵνα is passing away from its earlier sense of *design* to its later sense of *result*. A corresponding classical

ἐν τῇ Λαοδικέων ἐκκλησίᾳ ἀναγνωσθῇ, καὶ τὴν ἐκ
Λαοδικίας ἵνα καὶ ὑμεῖς ἀναγνῶτε. ¹⁷Καὶ εἴπατε ᾿Αρ-
χίππῳ, Βλέπε τὴν διακονίαν ἣν παρέλαβες ἐν Κυρίῳ,
ἵνα αὐτὴν πληροῖς.

expression is ποιεῖν ὡς or ὅπως, e.g.
Xen. *Cyr.* vi. 3. 18.

A similar charge is given in 1 Thess.
v. 27. The precaution here is probably suggested by the distastefulness
of the Apostle's warnings, which might
lead to the suppression of the letter.

τὴν ἐκ Λαοδικίας] i.e. 'the letter left
at Laodicea, which you will procure
thence.' For this abridged expression compare Luke xi. 13 ὁ πατὴρ ὁ
ἐξ οὐρανοῦ δώσει πνεῦμα ἅγιον, xvi. 26
(v. l.) μηδὲ οἱ ἐκεῖθεν πρὸς ἡμᾶς
διαπερῶσιν, Susann. 26 ὡς δὲ ἤκουσαν
τὴν κραυγὴν ἐν τῷ παραδείσῳ οἱ ἐκ τῆς
οἰκίας, εἰσεπήδησαν κ.τ.λ. For instances
of this proleptic use of the preposition in classical writers, where it is extremely common, see Kühner *Gr.* §448
(II. p. 474), Jelf *Gr.* § 647, Matthiæ
Gr. § 596: e.g. Plat. *Apol.* 32 B τοὺς
οὐκ ἀνελομένους τοὺς ἐκ τῆς ναυμαχίας,
Xen. *Cyr.* vii. 2. 5 ἁρπασόμενοι τὰ ἐκ
τῶν οἰκιῶν, Isocr. *Paneg.* § 187 τὴν
εὐδαιμονίαν τὴν ἐκ τῆς ᾿Ασίας εἰς τὴν
Εὐρώπην διακομίσαιμεν. There are
good reasons for the belief that St
Paul here alludes to the so-called
Epistle to the Ephesians, which was
in fact a circular letter addressed to
the principal churches of proconsular
Asia (see above, p. 37, and the introduction to the Epistle to the Ephesians). Tychicus was obliged to pass
through Laodicea on his way to Colossæ, and would leave a copy there,
before the Colossian letter was delivered. For other opinions respecting
this 'letter from Laodicea' see the
detached note.

ἵνα καὶ ὑμεῖς κ.τ.λ.] 'see that ye also
read.' At first sight it might seem as
though this ἵνα also were governed by
ποιήσατε, like the former; but, inasmuch as ποιήσατε would be somewhat

awkward in this connexion, it is perhaps
better to treat the second clause as
independent and elliptical, (βλέπετε)
ἵνα κ.τ.λ. This is suggested also by
the position of τὴν ἐκ Λαοδικίας before ἵνα; comp. Gal. ii. 10 μόνον τῶν
πτωχῶν ἵνα μνημονεύωμεν (with the
note). Ellipses before ἵνα are frequent; e.g. John ix. 3, 2 Cor. viii. 13,
2 Thess. iii. 9, 1 Joh. ii. 19.

17. Καὶ εἴπατε] Why does not the
Apostle address himself directly to
Archippus? It might be answered that
he probably thought the warning
would come with greater emphasis,
when delivered by the voice of the
Church. Or the simpler explanation
perhaps is, that Archippus was not
resident at Colossæ but at Laodicea:
see the introduction to the Epistle
to Philemon. On this warning itself
see above, p. 42.

Βλέπε] 'Look to,' as 2 Joh. 8 βλέπετε
ἑαυτοὺς ἵνα μὴ κ.τ.λ. More commonly
it has the accusative of the thing to
be avoided; see Phil. iii. 2 (with the
note).

τὴν διακονίαν] From the stress which
is laid upon it, the διακονία here would
seem to refer, as in the case of Timothy cited below, to some higher function than the diaconate properly so
called. In Acts xii. 25 the same
phrase, πληροῦν τὴν διακονίαν, is used
of a temporary ministration, the collection and conveyance of the alms for
the poor of Jerusalem (Acts xi. 29);
but the solemnity of the warning here
points to a continuous office, rather
than an immediate service.

παρέλαβες] i.e. probably παρ᾿ ἐμοῦ.
The word suggests, though it does not
necessarily imply, a mediate rather
than a direct reception: see the note
Gal. i. 12. Archippus received the

¹⁸Ὁ ἀσπασμὸς τῇ ἐμῇ χειρὶ Παύλου. Μνημονεύετέ
μου τῶν δεσμῶν. Ἡ χάρις μεθ᾽ ὑμῶν.

charge immediately from St Paul, though ultimately from Christ. 'Non enim sequitur,' writes Bengel, '*a Domino* (1 Cor. xi. 23), sed *in Domino.*'

πληροῖς] '*fulfil*,' i. e. '*discharge fully*'; comp. 2 Tim. iv. 5 τὴν διακονίαν σου πληροφόρησον.

18. 'I add this salutation with my own hand, signing it with my name Paul. Be mindful of my bonds. God's grace be with you.'

Ὁ ἀσπασμὸς κ.τ.λ.] The letter was evidently written by an amanuensis (comp. Rom. xvi. 22). The final salutation alone, with the accompanying sentence μνημονεύετε κ.τ.λ., was in the Apostle's own handwriting. This seems to have been the Apostle's general practice, even where he does not call attention to his own signature. In 2 Thess. iii. 17 sq., 1 Cor. xvi. 21, as here, he directs his readers' notice to the fact, but in other epistles he is silent. In some cases however he writes much more than the final sentence. Thus the whole letter to Philemon is apparently in his own handwriting (see ver. 19), and in the Epistle to the Galatians he writes a long paragraph at the close (see the note on vi. 11).

τῇ ἐμῇ χειρὶ Παύλου] The same phrase occurs in 2 Thess. iii. 17, 1 Cor. xvi. 21. For the construction comp. e. g. Philo *Leg. ad Gai.* 8 (II. p. 554) ἐμόν ἐστι τοῦ Μάκρωνος ἔργον Γάιος, and see Kühner § 406 (II. p. 242), Jelf § 467.

τῶν δεσμῶν] His bonds establish an additional claim to hearing. He who is suffering for Christ has a right to speak on behalf of Christ. The

appeal is similar in Ephes. iii. 1 τούτου χάριν ἐγὼ Παῦλος ὁ δέσμιος τοῦ Χ. Ἰ., which is resumed again (after a long digression) in iv. 1 παρακαλῶ οὖν ὑμᾶς ἐγὼ ὁ δέσμιος ἐν Κυρίῳ ἀξίως περιπατῆσαι κ.τ.λ. (comp. vi. 20 ὑπὲρ οὗ πρεσβεύω ἐν ἁλύσει). So too Philem. 9 τοιοῦτος ὢν ὡς Παῦλος ... δέσμιος Χριστοῦ Ἰησοῦ. These passages seem to show that the appeal here is not for himself, but for his teaching—not for sympathy with his sufferings but for obedience to the Gospel. His bonds were not his own; they were τὰ δεσμὰ τοῦ εὐαγγελίου (Philem. 13). In Heb. x. 34 the right reading is not τοῖς δεσμοῖς μου, but τοῖς δεσμίοις συνεπαθήσατε (comp. xiii. 3). Somewhat similar is the appeal to his στίγματα in Gal. vi. 17, 'Henceforth let no man trouble me.' See the notes on Philem. 10, 13.

Ἡ χάρις κ.τ.λ.] This very short form of the final benediction appears only here and in 1 Tim. vi. 21, 2 Tim. iv. 22. In Tit. iii. 15 πάντων is inserted, and so in Heb. xiii. 25. In Ephes. vi. 24 the form so far agrees with the examples quoted, that ἡ χάρις is used absolutely, though the end is lengthened out. In all the earlier epistles ἡ χάρις is defined by the addition of τοῦ Κυρίου [ἡμῶν] Ἰησοῦ [Χριστοῦ]; 1 Thess. v. 28, 2 Thess. iii. 18, 1 Cor. xvi. 23, 2 Cor. xiii. 13, Gal. vi. 18, Rom. xvi. 20, [24], Phil. iv. 23. Thus the absolute ἡ χάρις in the final benediction may be taken as a chronological note. A similar phenomenon has been already observed (τῇ ἐκκλησίᾳ, ταῖς ἐκκλησίαις) in the opening addresses: see the note on i. 2.

On some Various Readings in the Epistle[1].

Harmonistic readings.

In one respect the letters to the Ephesians and Colossians hold a unique position among the Epistles of St Paul, as regards textual criticism. They alone have been exposed, or exposed in any considerable degree, to those harmonizing tendencies in transcribers, which have had so great an influence on the text of the Synoptic Gospels.

Preponderant evidence (1) for the correct reading;

In such cases there is sometimes no difficulty in ascertaining the correct reading. The harmonistic change is condemned by the majority of the oldest and best authorities; or there is at least a nearly even balance of external testimony, and the suspicious character of the reading is quite sufficient to turn the scale. Thus we cannot hesitate for a moment about such readings as i. 14 διὰ τοῦ αἵματος αὐτοῦ (from Ephes. i. 7), or iii. 16 ψαλμοῖς καὶ ὕμνοις καὶ ᾠδαῖς πνευματικαῖς, and τῷ Κυρίῳ (for τῷ Θεῷ) in the same verse (both from Ephes. v. 19).

(2) against the correct reading.

In other instances again there can hardly be any doubt about the text, even though the vast preponderance of authority is in favour of the harmonistic reading; and these are especially valuable because they enable us to test the worth of our authorities. Such examples are:

Examples.

iii. 6, words inserted.

iii. 6. The omission of the words ἐπὶ τοὺς υἱοὺς τῆς ἀπειθείας (taken from Ephes. v. 6). Apparently the only extant MS in favour of the omission is B. In D however they are written (though by the first hand) in smaller letters and extend beyond the line (in both Greek and Latin), whence we may infer that they were not found in a copy which was before the transcriber. They are wanting also in the Thebaic Version and in one form of the Ethiopic (Polyglott). They were also absent from copies used by Clement of Alexandria (*Paed.* iii, 11, p. 295, where however they are inserted in the printed texts; *Strom.* iii. 5, p. 531), by Cyprian (*Epist.* lv. 27, p. 645

---

[1] The references to the patristic quotations in the following pages have all been verified. I have also consulted the Egyptian and Syriac Versions in every case, and the Armenian and Latin in some instances, before giving the readings. As regards the MSS, I have contented myself with the collations as given in Tregelles and Tischendorf, not verifying them unless I had reason to suspect an error.

The readings of the Memphitic Version are very incorrectly given even by the principal editors, such as Tregelles and Tischendorf; the translation of Wilkins being commonly adopted, though full of errors, and no attention being paid to the various readings of Boetticher's text. Besides the errors corrected in the following pages, I have also observed these places where the text of this version is incorrectly reported; ii. 7 ἐν αὐτῇ not omitted; ii. 13 the second ὑμᾶς not omitted; ii. 17 the singular (ὅ), not the plural (ἅ); iii. 4 ὑμῶν, not ἡμῶν; iii. 16 τῷ Θεῷ, not τῷ Κυρίῳ; iii. 22 τὸν Κύριον, not τὸν Θεόν; iv. 3 doubtful whether δι' ὅ or δι' ὅν; and probably there are others.

ed. Hartel), by an unknown writer (*de Sing. Cler.* 39, in Cypr. *Op.* III. p. 215),
by the Ambrosian Hilary (*ad loc.*), and by Jerome (*Epist.* xiv. 5, I. p. 32)
though now found apparently in all the Latin MSS.

iii. 21. ἐρεθίζετε is only found in B K and in later hands of D (with its *iii. 21*
transcript E) among the uncial MSS. All the other uncials read παροργίζετε, *ἐρεθίζετε.*
which is taken from Ephes. vi. 4. In this case however the reading of B is
supported by the greater number of cursives, and it accordingly has a place
in the received text. The versions (so far as we can safely infer their readings) go almost entirely with the majority of uncials. The true readings of *Syriac*
the Syriac versions are just the reverse of those assigned to them even by *version misrepre-*
the chief critical editors, Tregelles and Tischendorf. Thus in the Peshito, *sented.*
the word used is the Aphel of ܓܙ, the same mood of the same verb being
employed to translate παροργίζειν, not only in Rom. x. 19, but even in
the parallel passage Ephes. vi. 4. The word in the text of the Harclean
is the same ܐܓܙܕ, but in the margin the alternative ܐܓܙܕ
is given. White interprets this as saying that the text is ἐρεθίζετε and the
margin παροργίζετε, and he is followed by Tregelles and Tischendorf. But
in this version, as in the Peshito, the former word translates παροργίζειν in
Rom. x. 19, Ephes. vi. 4; while in the Peshito the latter word is adopted
to render ἐρεθίζειν in 2 Cor. ix. 2 (the only other passage in the N. T.
where ἐρεθίζειν occurs). In the Harclean of 2 Cor. ix. 2 a different word
from either, ܕܘܕܠܘ, is used. It seems tolerably clear therefore that
παροργίζετε was read in the text of both Peshito and Harclean here, while
ἐρεθίζετε was given in the margin of the latter. The Latin versions seem *Latin*
also to have read παροργίζετε; for the Old Latin has *ad iram* (or *in iram* *versions.*
or *ad iracundiam*) *provocare*, and the Vulgate *ad indignationem provo-*
care here, while both have *ad iracundiam provocare* in Ephes. vi. 4.
The Memphitic too has the same rendering ϯⲭⲱⲛⲧ in both passages. Of
the earlier Greek fathers Clement, *Strom.* iv. 8 (p. 593), reads ἐρεθίζετε:
and it is found in Chrysostom and some later writers.

These examples show how singularly free B is from this passion for *Great*
harmonizing, and may even embolden us to place reliance on its authority *value of B.*
in extreme cases.

For instance, the parallel passages Ephes. v. 19 and Col. iii. 16 stand *Parallel*
thus in the received text: *passages.*

EPHESIANS.	COLOSSIANS.	*Col. iii. 16,*
λαλοῦντες ἑαυτοῖς ψαλμοῖς καὶ ὕμ-	διδάσκοντες καὶ νουθετοῦντες ἑαυ-	*Eph. v. 19.*
νοις καὶ ᾠδαῖς πνευματικαῖς ᾄδοντες	τοὺς ψαλμοῖς καὶ ὕμνοις καὶ ᾠδαῖς	
καὶ ψάλλοντες ἐν τῇ καρδίᾳ ὑμῶν	πνευματικαῖς ἐν χάριτι ᾄδοντες ἐν τῇ	
τῷ Κυρίῳ.	καρδίᾳ ὑμῶν τῷ Κυρίῳ.	

And A carries the harmonizing tendency still further by inserting ἐν
χάριτι before ᾄδοντες in Ephes. from the parallel passage.

In B they are read as follows:

λαλοῦντες ἑαυτοῖς ἐν ψαλμοῖς καὶ	διδάσκοντες καὶ νουθετοῦντες ἑαυ-
ὕμνοις καὶ ᾠδαῖς ᾄδοντες καὶ ψάλ-	τοὺς ψαλμοῖς ὕμνοις ᾠδαῖς πνευμα-
λοντες τῇ καρδίᾳ ὑμῶν τῷ Κυρίῳ.	τικαῖς ἐν τῇ χάριτι ᾄδοντες ἐν ταῖς
	καρδίαις ὑμῶν τῷ Θεῷ.

Altera-
tions for
the sake of
harmon-
izing.

Here are seven divergences from the received text. (1) The insertion of ἐν before ψαλμοῖς in Ephes.; (2) The omission of καί, καί, attaching ψαλμοῖς, ὕμνοις, ᾠδαῖς in Col.; (3) The omission of πνευματικαῖς in Ephes.; (4) The insertion of τῇ before χάριτι in Col.; (5) The omission of ἐν before τῇ καρδίᾳ in Ephes.; (6) The substitution of ταῖς καρδίαις for τῇ καρδίᾳ in Col.: (7) The substitution of τῷ Θεῷ for τῷ Κυρίῳ in Col.

Of these seven divergences the fourth alone does not affect the question: of the remaining six, the readings of B in (2), (6), (7) are supported by the great preponderance of the best authorities, and are unquestionably right. In (1), (3), (5) however the case stands thus:

ἐν ψαλμοῖς.

(1) ἐν ψαλμοῖς B, P, with the cursives 17, 67**, 73, 116, 118, and the Latin, d, e, vulg., with the Latin commentators Victorinus, Hilary, and Jerome. Of these however it is clear that the Latin authorities can have little weight in such a case, as the preposition might have been introduced by the translator. All the other Greek MSS with several Greek fathers omit ἐν.

πνευματι-
καῖς.

(3) πνευματικαῖς omitted in B, d, e. Of the Ambrosian Hilary Tischendorf says 'fluct. lectio'; but his comment 'In quo enim est spiritus, semper spiritualia meditatur' seems certainly to recognise the word. It appears to be found in every other authority.

τῇ καρδίᾳ.

(5) τῇ καρδίᾳ ℵ* B with Origen in Cramer's *Catena*, p. 201.

ἐν τῇ καρδίᾳ K L, and the vast majority of later MSS, the Armenian and Ethiopic Versions, Euthalius (Tischendorf's MS), Theodoret, and others. The Harclean Syriac (text) is quoted by Tischendorf and Tregelles in favour of ἐν τῇ καρδίᾳ, but it is impossible to say whether the translator had or had not the preposition.

ἐν ταῖς καρδίαις ℵ°A D F G P, 47, 8ᵖᵒ; the Old Latin, Vulgate, Memphitic, Peshito Syriac, and Gothic Versions, together with the margin of the Harclean Syriac; the fathers Basil (II. p. 464), Victorinus (probably), Theodore of Mopsuestia, the Ambrosian Hilary, Jerome, and others. Chrysostom (as read in the existing texts) wavers between ἐν τῇ καρδίᾳ and ἐν ταῖς καρδίαις. This form of the reading is an attempt to bring Ephes. into harmony with Col., just as (6) is an attempt to bring Col. into harmony with Ephes.

It will be seen how slenderly B is supported; and yet we can hardly resist the impression that it has the right reading in all three cases. In the omission of πνευματικαῖς more especially, where the support is weakest, this impression must, I think, be very strong.

Excellence
of B else-
where.

This highly favourable estimate of B is our starting-point; and on the whole it will be enhanced as we proceed. Thus for instance in i. 22 and ii. 2 we shall find this MS alone (with one important Latin father) retaining the correct text; in the latter case amidst a great complication of various readings. And when again, as in iv. 8, we find B for once on the side of a reading which might otherwise be suspected as a harmonistic change, this support alone will weigh heavily in its favour. Other cases in which B (with more or less support) preserves the correct reading against the mass of authorities are ii. 2 πᾶν πλοῦτος, ii. 7 τῇ πίστει, ii. 13 τοῖς παραπτώμασιν (omitting ἐν,

v. 12 σταθῆτε, together with several instances which will appear in the course of the following investigation. On the other hand its value must not be overestimated. Thus in iv. 3 τὸ μυστήριον τοῦ Χριστοῦ δι' ὃ καὶ δέδεμαι[1] there can be little doubt that the great majority of ancient autho- False rities correctly read δι' ὅ, though B F G have δι' ὅν: but the variation is readings in B. easily explained. A single stroke, whether accidental or deliberate, alone would be necessary to turn the neuter into a masculine and make the relative agree with the substantive nearest to it in position. Again in ii. 10 ὅς ἐστιν ἡ κεφαλή, the reading of B which substitutes ὅ for ὅς is plainly wrong, though supported in this instance by D F G 47*, by the Latin text d, and by Hilary in one passage (*de Trin.* ix. 8, 11. p. 263), though elsewhere (ib. i. 13, 1. p. 10) he reads ὅ. But here again we have only an instance of a very common interchange. Whether for grammatical reasons or from diplomatic confusion or from some other cause, five other instances of this interchange occur in this short epistle alone; i. 15 ὅ for ὅς F G; i. 18 ὅ for ὅς F G; i. 24 ὅς for ὅ C D* etc.; i. 27 ὅς for ὅ ℵ C D K L etc.; iii. 14 ὅς for ὅ ℵ* D. Such readings again as the omission of καὶ αἰτούμενοι i. 9 by B K, or of δι' αὐτοῦ in i. 20 by B D* F G etc., or of ἡ ἐπιστολή in iv. 16 by B alone, need not be considered, since the motive for the omission is obvious, and the authority of B will not carry as great weight as it would in other cases. Similarly the insertion of ἡ in i. 18, ἡ ἀρχή, by B, 47, 67**, bˢᶜʳ, and of καὶ in ii. 15, καὶ ἐδειγμάτισεν, by B alone, do not appear to deserve consideration, because in both instances these readings would suggest themselves as obvious improvements. In other cases, as in the omission of τῆς before γῆς (i. 20), and of ἑνί in ἐν ἑνὶ σώματι (iii. 15), the scribe of B has erred as any scribe might err.

The various readings in this epistle are more perplexing than perhaps in any portion of St Paul's Epistles of the same length. The following deserve special consideration.

i. 3 τῷ θεῷ πατρί.

On this very unusual collocation I have already remarked in the notes i. 3 τῷ θεῷ πατρί, (p. 133). The authorities stand as follows:

(1) τῷ θεῷ πατρί B C*.

(2) τῷ θεῷ τῷ πατρί D* F G Chrysostom.

One or other is also the reading of the Old Latin (d, e, g, harl.**), of the Memphitic, the two Syriac (Peshito and Harclean), the Ethiopic, and the Arabic (Erpenius, Bedwell, Leipzig) Versions; and of Augustine (*de Unit. Eccl.* 45, IX. p. 368) and Cassiodorus (II. p. 1351, Migne).

(3) τῷ θεῷ καὶ πατρί ℵ A C² Dᶜ K L P and apparently all the other MSS; the Vulgate and Armenian Versions; Euthalius (Tischendorf's MS), Theodore of Mopsuestia (transl.), Theodoret, the Ambrosian Hilary, and others.

A comparison of these authorities seems to show pretty clearly that τῷ θεῷ πατρί was the original reading. The other two were expedients

---

[1] In this passage B (with some few other authorities) has τοῦ Θεοῦ for τοῦ Χριστοῦ, thus substituting a commoner expression (ii. 2, 1 Cor. iv. 1, Rev. x. 7; comp. 1 Cor. ii. 1, v. l.) for a less common (Ephes. iii. 4).

for getting rid of a very unusual collocation of words. The scribes have
felt the same difficulty again in iii. 17 εὐχαριστοῦντες τῷ θεῷ πατρὶ δι᾿
αὐτοῦ, and there again we find καί inserted before πατρί. In this latter
instance however the great preponderance of ancient authority is in
favour of the unusual form τῷ θεῷ πατρί.

It is worth observing also that in i. 12, where τῷ πατρί has the highest
support, there is sufficient authority for τῷ θεῷ πατρί to create a suspicion
that there too it may be possibly the correct reading. Thus τῷ θεῷ πατρί
is read in ℵ 37, while θεῷ τῷ πατρί stands in F G. One or other must have
been the reading of some Old Latin and Vulgate texts (f, g, m, fuld.), of the
Peshito Syriac, of the Memphitic (in some texts, for others read τῷ πατρί
simply), of the Arabic (Bedwell), of the Armenian (Uscan), and of Origen
(II. p. 451, the Latin translator); while several other authorities, Greek
and Latin, read τῷ θεῷ καὶ πατρί.

There is no other instance of this collocation of words, ὁ Θεὸς πατήρ,
in the Greek Testament, so far as I remember; and it must be regarded
as peculiar to this epistle.

marginalia: compared with iii. 17, and i. 12. Unique collocation.

i. 4 ΤΗΝ ἈΓΆΠΗΝ [ἫΝ ἜΧΕΤΕ].

Here the various readings are;

(1) τὴν ἀγάπην B.
(2) τὴν ἀγάπην ἣν ἔχετε A ℵ C D* F G P 17, 37, 47; the Old
     Latin and Vulgate, Memphitic (apparently), and Harclean
     Syriac Versions; the Ambrosian Hilary, Theodore of
     Mopsuestia (transl.), and others.
(3) τὴν ἀγάπην τήν. Dᶜ K L; the Peshito Syriac (apparently)
     and Armenian (apparently) Versions; Chrysostom, Theo-
     doret and others.

If the question were to be decided by external authority alone, we
could not hesitate. It is important however to observe that (2) conforms
to the parallel passage Philem. 5 ἀκούων σου τὴν ἀγάπην καὶ τὴν πίστιν ἣν
ἔχεις, while (3) conforms to the other parallel passage Ephes. i. 15 καὶ [τὴν
ἀγάπην] τὴν εἰς πάντας τοὺς ἁγίους. Thus, though ἣν ἔχετε is so highly supported and though it helps out the sense, it is open to suspicion. Still the
omission in B may be an instance of that impatience of apparently superfluous words, which sometimes appears in this MS.

marginalia: i. 4 τὴν ἀγάπην [ἣν ἔχετε].

i. 7 ὙΠΈΡ ἩΜῶΝ ΔΙΆΚΟΝΟΣ.

Here there is a conflict between MSS and Versions.

(1) ἡμῶν A B ℵ* D* F G, 3, 13, 33, 43, 52, 80, 91, 109. This must
     also have been the reading of the Ambrosian Hilary
     though the editors make him write 'pro vobis'), for he ex-
     plains it 'qui eis ministravit gratiam Christi vice apostoli.'
(2) ὑμῶν ℵᶜ C Dᵇ K L P, 17, 37, 47, and many others; the Vul-
     gate, the Peshito and Harclean Syriac, the Memphitic,
     Gothic, and Armenian Versions; Chrysostom, Theodore
     of Mopsuestia (transl.), and Theodoret (in their respec-
     tive texts, for with the exception of Chrysostom there
     is nothing decisive in their comments), with others.

marginalia: i. 7 ὑπὲρ ἡμῶν.

The Old Latin is doubtful; d, e having *vobis* and g *nobis*.

Though the common confusion between these two words even in the best MSS is a caution against speaking with absolute certainty, yet such a combination of the highest authorities as we have here for ἡμῶν does not leave much room for doubt: and considerations of internal criticism point in the same direction. See the note on the passage.

i. 12 τῷ ἱκανώϲαντι.

Against this, which is the reading of all the other ancient authorities, we have

> (2) τῷ καλέσαντι D* F G, 17, 80, with the Latin authorities d, e, f, g, m, and the Gothic, Armenian, and Ethiopic Versions. It is so read also by the Ambrosian Hilary, by Didymus *de Trin.* iii. 4 (p. 346), and by Vigilius Thapsensis *c. Varim.* i. 50 (p. 409).
>
> (3) τῷ καλέσαντι καὶ ἱκανώσαντι, found in B alone.

Here the confusion between ΤΩΙΙΚΑΝΩϹΑΝΤΙ and ΤΩΙΚΑΛΕϹΑΝΤΙ would be easy, more especially at a period prior to the earliest existing MSS, when the iota adscript was still written; while at the same time καλέσαντι would suggest itself to scribes as the obvious word in such a connexion. It is a Western reading.

The text of B obviously presents a combination of both readings.

i. 12
ἱκανώσαντι.

i. 14 ἐν ᾧ ἔχομεν.

For ἔχομεν B, the Memphitic Version, and the Arabic (Bedwell, Leipzig), read ἔσχομεν. This is possibly the correct reading. In the parallel passage, Ephes. i. 7, several authorities (א* D*, the Memphitic and Ethiopic Versions, and the translator of Irenæus v. 14. 3) similarly read ἔσχομεν for ἔχομεν. It may be conjectured that ἔσχομεν in these authorities was a harmonistic change in Ephes. i. 7, to conform to the text which they or their predecessors had in Col. i. 14. Tischendorf on Ephes. l. c. says 'aut utroque loco εχομεν aut εσχομεν Paulum scripsisse puto'; but if any inference can be drawn from the phenomena of the MSS, they point rather to a different tense in the two passages.

i. 14
ἔχομεν or
ἔσχομεν?

i. 22 ἀποκατηλλάγητε.

This reading is perhaps the highest testimony of all to the great value of B.

The variations are;

> (1) ἀποκατηλλάγητε B. This also seems to be the reading of Hilary of Poitiers *In xci Psalm.* 9 (I. p. 270), who transfers the Apostle's language into the first person, 'cum aliquando essemus alienati et inimici sensus ejus in factis malis, nunc autem reconciliati sumus corpore carnis ejus.'
>
> (2) ἀποκατηλλάκηται 17.
>
> (3) ἀποκαταλλαγέντες D* F G, and the Latin authorities d, e, g,

i. 22
ἀποκατηλ-
λάγητε.

m, the Gothic Version, the translator of Irenæus (v. 14. 3), and others.

(4)　ἀποκατήλλαξεν, all the other authorities.

Of these (2) is obviously a corruption of (1) from similarity of sound; and (3) is an emendation, though a careless emendation, of (1) for the sake of the grammar. It should have been ἀποκαταλλαγέντας. The reading therefore must lie between ἀποκατηλλάγητε and ἀποκατήλλαξεν. This latter however is probably a grammatical correction to straighten the syntax. In the Memphitic a single letter ⲁⲧ for ⲁϥ would make the difference between ἀποκατηλλάγητε and ἀποκατήλλαξεν; but no variation from the latter is recorded.

ii. 2 ΤΟΥ ΘΕΟΥ, ΧΡΙΣΤΟΥ.

ii. 2
τοῦ Θεοῦ
Χριστοῦ.

The various readings here are very numerous and at first sight perplexing; but the result of an investigation into their several claims is far from unsatisfactory. The reading which explains all the rest may safely be adopted as the original.

Original reading.

(1)　ΤΟΥ ΘΕΟΥ ΧΡΙΣΤΟΥ.

This is the reading of B and of Hilary of Poitiers, *de Trin.* ix. 62 (1. p. 306), who quotes the passage *sacramenti Dei Christi in quo* etc., and wrongly explains it ' Deus Christus sacramentum est.'

Variations;

All the other variations are derived from this, either by explanation or by omission or by amplification.

By explanation we get ;

(a) by interpretation,

(2)　ΤΟΥ ΘΕΟΥ Ο ΕϹΤΙΝ ΧΡΙϹΤΟϹ,

the reading of D, with the Latin authorities d, e, which have *Dei quod est Christus.* So it is quoted by Vigilius Thapsensis *c. Varim.* i. 20 (p. 380), and in a slightly longer form by Augustine *de Trin.* xiii. 24 (VIII. p. 944) *mysterium Dei quod est Christus Jesus.*

(3)　ΤΟΥ ΘΕΟΥ ΕΝ ΧΡΙϹΤΩ.

So it is twice quoted by Clement of Alexandria *Strom.* v. 10 (p. 683), *ib.* 12 (p. 694); or

ΤΟΥ ΘΕΟΥ ΤΟΥ ΕΝ ΧΡΙϹΤΩ,

the reading of 17.

So the Ambrosian Hilary (both text and commentary) has *Dei in Christo.* And the Armenian has the same lengthened out, *Dei in Christo Jesu* (Zohrab) or *Dei patris in Christo Jesu* (Uscan).

(4)　*Domini quod de Christo*

is the Ethiopic rendering. Whether this represents another various reading in the Greek or whether the paraphrase is the translator's own, it is impossible to say.

The two following variations strive to overcome the difficulty by omission ;

(b) by omission,

(5)　ΤΟΥ ΘΕΟΥ,

the reading of D by a second hand, of P, 37, 67**, 71, 80, 116.

(6)　ΤΟΥ ΧΡΙϹΤΟΥ,

the reading of Euthalius in Tischendorf's MS; but Tischendorf adds the caution ' sed non satis apparet.'

All the remaining readings are attempts to remedy the text by ampli- *(c)* by fication. They fall into two classes; those which insert πατρός so as to amplifica-tion; make Χριστοῦ dependent on it, (7), (8), and those which separate Θεοῦ from Χριστοῦ by the interposition of a καί, (9), (10), (11).

(7) ΤΟΥ ΘΕΟΥ ΠΑΤΡΟC ΧΡΙCΤΟΥ,

the reading of א (by the first hand). Tischendorf also adds b^{scr} and (i) by in-serting o^{scr}; but I read Scrivener's collations differently (*Cod. Aug.* p. 506): or πατρός to govern ΤΟΥ ΘΕΟΥ ΠΑΤΡΟC ΤΟΥ ΧΡΙCΤΟΥ, Χριστοῦ; the reading of A C, 4.

One or other is the reading of the Thebaic Version (given by Gries-bach) and of the Arabic (Leipz.).

A lengthened form of the same, *Dei patris Christi Jesu*, appears in the oldest MSS of the Vulgate, am. fuld. f : and the same is also the reading of the Memphitic (Boetticher).

(8) ΤΟΥ ΘΕΟΥ ΚΑΙ ΠΑΤΡΟC ΤΟΥ ΧΡΙCΤΟΥ.

So א (the third hand) b^{scr}, o^{scr}, and a corrector in the Harclean Syriac.

(9) ΤΟΥ ΘΕΟΥ ΚΑΙ ΧΡΙCΤΟΥ, (ii) by the simplest form of the other class of emendations by amplification. separating Θεοῦ from It is found in Cyril. *Thes.* p. 287. Χριστοῦ by a con-(10) ΤΟΥ ΘΕΟΥ ΠΑΤΡΟC ΚΑΙ ΤΟΥ ΧΡΙCΤΟΥ. junction.

So 47, 73, the Peshito Syriac (ed. princeps and Schaaf). And so it stands in the commentators Chrysostom (but with various readings) and Theodore of Mopsuestia (*Spicil. Solesm.* I. p. 131 *Dei patris et Christi*, but in Rab. Maur. *Op.* VI. p. 521 *Dei patris Christi Jesu*).

Pelagius has *Dei patris et Christi Jesu*, and so the Memphitic (Wilkins).

(11) ΤΟΥ ΘΕΟΥ ΚΑΙ ΠΑΤΡΟC ΚΑΙ ΤΟΥ ΧΡΙCΤΟΥ. The com-This, which may be regarded as the latest development, is the reading mon text the latest of the received text. It is found in D (third hand) KL, and in the great develop-majority of cursives; in the text of the Harclean Syriac, and in Theodoret ment. and others.

Besides these readings some copies of the Vulgate exhibit other varia-tions; e. g. demid. *Dei patris et domini nostri Christi Jesu,* tolet. *Dei Christi Jesu patris et Domini.*

It is not necessary to add any remarks. The justification of τοῦ Θεοῦ Χριστοῦ as the original reading will have appeared in the variations to which it has given rise. The passage is altogether an instructive lesson in textual criticism.

ii. 16 ἐν βρώσει καὶ ἐν πόσει.

In this reading B stands alone among the MSS; but it is supported by ii. 16 the Peshito Syriac and Memphitic Versions, by Tertullian (*adv. Marc.* V. καὶ or ἤ? 19), and by Origen (*in Ioann.* X. § 11, IV. p. 174). The testimony of Ter-tullian however is invalidated by the fact that he uses *et* as the connecting particle throughout the passage; and the Peshito Syriac also has 'and' for ἤ in the two last clauses, though not in the second

The rest have ἐν βρώσει ἢ ἐν πόσει. This may be explained as a very obvious, though not very intelligent, alteration of scribes to conform to the disjunctive particles in the context, ἢ ἐν μέρει ἑορτῆς ἢ νεομηνίας ἢ σαββάτων.

In this same context it is probable that B retains the right form νεομηνίας (supported here by F G and others) as against the Attic νουμηνίας. In the same way in iii. 25 κομίσεται and iv. 9 γνωρίσουσιν B (with some others) has resisted the tendency to Attic forms.

ii. 18 ἃ ἑόρακεν.

ii. 18, the omission of the negative.

That this is the oldest reading which the existing texts exhibit, will appear from the following comparison of authorities.

(1) ἃ ἑώρακεν (ἑόρακεν) A B ℵ* D*, 17*, 28, 67**; the Old Latin authorities d, e, m; the Memphitic, Ethiopic, and Arabic (Leipz.) Versions; Tertull. *c. Marc.* v. 19 ('ex visionibus angelicis'; and apparently Marcion himself also); Origen (*c. Cels.* v. 8, I. p. 583, though the negative is here inserted by De la Rue, and *in Cant.* ii, III. p. 63, *in his quae videt*); Lucifer (*De non conv. c. haer.* p. 782 Migne); the Ambrosian Hilary (*ad loc.* explaining it 'Inflantur motum pervidentes stellarum, quas angelos vocat'). So too the unknown author of *Quaest. ex N. T.* ii. 62 in August. *Op.* III. Appx. p. 156. Jerome (*Epist. cxxi ad Alg.* § 10, I. p. 880) mentions both readings (with and without the negative) as found in the Greek text: and Augustine (*Epist.* 149, II. p. 514), while giving the preference to *quae non vidit*, says that some MSS have *quae vidit*.

(2) ἃ μὴ ἑώρακεν (ἑόρακεν) ℵᶜ C Dᵇᵒ K L P, and the great majority of cursives;

(3) ἃ οὐκ ἑώρακεν F G.

The negative is also read in g; in the Vulgate, the Gothic, both the Syriac and the Armenian Versions; in the translator of Origen *In Rom.* ix. § 42 (IV. p. 665), in Ambrose *in Psalm. cxviii Exp.* xx. (I. p. 1222), and in the commentators Pelagius, Chrysostom, Theodore of Mopsuestia (*Spic. Solesm.* I. p. 132 'quae nec sciunt'), Theodoret, and others.

From a review of these authorities we infer that the insertion of the negative was a later correction, and that ἃ ἑώρακεν (or ἑόρακεν) represents the prior reading. In my note I have expressed my suspicion that ἃ ἑώρακεν (or ἑόρακεν) is itself corrupt, and that the original reading is lost.

The form ἑόρακεν.

The unusual form ἑόρακεν is found in ℵ B* C D P, and is therefore to be preferred to ἑώρακεν.

ii. 23 [καὶ] ἀφειδίᾳ σώματος.

ii. 23. Is καί to be omitted?

Here καί is found in all the Greek copies except B, but is omitted in these Latin authorities, m, the translator of Origen (*In Rom.* ix. § 42, IV. p. 665), Hilary of Poitiers (*Tract. in xiv Ps.* § 7, p. 73), the Ambrosian Hilary, Ambrose (*de Noe* 25, p. 267), and Paulinus (*Epist.* 50, p. 292 sq.). We have more than once found B and Hilary alone in supporting the correct reading (i. 22, ii. 2); and this fact gives weight to their joint authority here. The omission also seems to explain the impossible reading of d, e, which have *in religione et humilitate sensus et vexationem corporis,* where for *et vexationem* we should perhaps read *ad vexationem,* as in the Ambrosian Hilary. There was every temptation for a scribe to insert the καί so as to make ἀφειδίᾳ range with the other datives: while on the other hand a finer appreciation of the bearing of the passage suggests that St Paul would have dissociated it, so as to give it a special prominence.

A similar instance occurs in iii. 12 ὡς ἐκλεκτοὶ τοῦ Θεοῦ, ἅγιοι καὶ ἠγαπημένοι, where B omits the καί with 17 and the Thebaic Version. In 219 καὶ ἅγιοι is read for ἅγιοι καί. The great gain in force leads to the suspicion that this omission may be correct, notwithstanding the enormous preponderance of authority on the other side.

iv. 8. ΓΝῶΤΕ Τὰ ΠΕΡῚ ἩΜῶΝ.

Of the various readings of this passage I have already spoken (p. 29 sq., note 1, p. 235).

The authorities are as follows:

iv. 8 γνῶτε τὰ περὶ ἡμῶν.

(1) γνῶτε τὰ περὶ ἡμῶν A B D*F G P, 10, 17, 33, 35, 37, 44, 47, 71, 111, 116, 137; d, e, g; the Armenian and Ethiopic Versions; Theodore of Mopsuestia[1], Theodoret[2], Jerome (on Ephes. vi. 21 sq., VII. p. 682), and Euthalius (Tischendorf's MS). This is also the reading of ℵ*, except that it has ὑμῶν for ἡμῶν.

(2) γνῷ τὰ περὶ ὑμῶν ℵᶜ C Dᵇᶜ K L and the majority of cursives; the Memphitic, Gothic, Vulgate, and both Syriac Versions; the Ambrosian Hilary, Jerome (on Philem. 1, VII. p. 748), Chrysostom (expressly), and others.

The internal evidence is considered in the note on the passage, and found to accord with the vast preponderance of external authority in favour of γνῶτε τὰ περὶ ἡμῶν. The reading of ℵ by the first hand exhibits a transitional stage. It would appear as though the transcriber intended it to be read γνῷ τε τὰ περὶ ὑμῶν. At all events this is the reading of 111 and of Io. Damasc. *Op.* II. p. 214. The variation γνῷ τὰ περὶ ὑμῶν is thus easily explained. (1) ἡμῶν would be accidentally substituted for ὑμῶν; (2) γνῶτε would then be read γνῷ τε; (3) the awkward and superfluous τε would be omitted. In illustration of the tendency to conform the persons of the two verbs γνῷ, παρακαλέσῃ (see p. 235), it may be mentioned that 17 reads γνῶτε, παρακαλέσητε, both here and in Ephes. vi. 22.

The various readings accounted for.

---

[1] It is true that in the text (*Spicil. Solesm.* I. p. 123, Rab. Maur. *Op.* VII. p. 539, Migne) he is credited with the later Latin reading *ut cognoscat quae circa vos sunt,* but his comment implies the other; 'Quoniam omnia vobis nota faciet Tychicus illa quae erga me sunt, propterea a me directus est cum Onesimo fratre qui a vobis venerat, ut nota vobis faciant quae erga nos sunt [=γνῶτε τὰ περὶ ἡμῶν]

et oblectent vos per suum adventum [=καὶ παρακαλέσῃ τὰς καρδίας ὑμῶν], omnia quae hic aguntur manifesta facientes vobis.' See *Spicil. Solesm.* l. c.; the comment is mutilated in Rab. Maur. *Op.* l. c.

[2] In the text; but in the commentary he is made to write ἵνα γνῷ γάρ, φησί, τὰ περὶ ἡμῶν, an impossible reading.

iv. 15. κατ᾽ οἶκον ἀγτῶν.

iv. 15
αὐτῶν.

The readings here are:

(1) αὐτῶν ℵ A C P, 5, 9, 17, 23, 34, 39, 47, 73; together with the Memphitic Version, the Arabic (Leipz.), and Euthalius (Tischendorf's ms). The Memphitic Version is commonly but wrongly quoted in favour of αὐτοῦ, owing to a mistranslation of Wilkins. But both Wilkins and Boetticher give without any various reading ⲡⲟⲩ̄ⲏⲓ, i.e. οἶκον αὐτῶν. This seems also to be the reading of Theodore of Mopsuestia (*Spic. Solesm.* i. p. 133) *quae in domo eorum est ecclesia;* though in Rab. Maur. *Op.* vi. p. 540 his text runs *quae in domo ejus est ecclesiam,* and he is made to say *Nympham cum omnibus suis qui in domo ejus sunt.*

(2) αὐτῆς B 67**.

(3) αὐτοῦ D F G K L and the great majority of cursives; and so the Gothic Version, Chrysostom, and Theodoret (the latter distinctly).

Nymphas or Nympha?

The singular, whether αὐτοῦ or αὐτῆς, is the reading of the old Latin and Vulgate, which have *ejus,* and of the Armenian. The pronoun is also singular in the Peshito and Harclean Syriac. In this language the same consonants express masculine and feminine alike, the difference lying in the pointing and vocalisation. And here the copies are inconsistent with themselves. In the Peshito (both the editio princeps and Schaaf) the proper name is vocalised as a feminine *Numphē* (=Νύμφη), and yet ܒܝܬܗ

The Syriac versions.

is treated as having a masculine affix, κατ᾽ οἶκον αὐτοῦ. In the text of the Harclean ܒܝܬܗ is pointed thus, as a feminine αὐτῆς; while the margin gives the alternative reading ܒܝܬܗ (without the point)=αὐτοῦ. The name itself is written Nympha, which according to the transliteration of this version might stand either for a masculine (as *Barnaba, Luka,* in the context, for Βαρνάβας, Λουκᾶς) or for a feminine (since *Demas, Epaphras,* are written with

The Latin authorities.

an *s*)[1]. The Latin *ejus* leaving the gender undetermined, the Latin commentators were free to take either Nymphas or Nympha; and, as Nympha was a common Latin form of Νύμφη, they would naturally adopt the female name. So the commentator Hilary distinctly.

It should be added that the word is accentuated as a masculine νυμφᾶν in Dᵒ L P, and as a feminine νύμφαν in Bᶜ and Euthalius (Tischendorf's ms).

---

[1] More probably the latter. In Rom. xvi the terminations -*a* and -*âs* for the feminine and masculine names respectively are carefully reproduced in the Harclean Version. In ver. 15 indeed we have *Julias,* but the translator doubtless considered the name to be a contraction for *Julianus.* The proper Syriac termination -*a* seems only to be employed for the Greek -*as* in very familiar names such as *Barnaba, Luka.*

On the meaning of πλήρωμα.

THE verb πληροῦν has two senses.   It signifies either (1) 'To fill', e. g. The mean-
Acts ii. 2 ἐπλήρωσεν ὅλον τὸν οἶκον; or (2) 'To fulfil, complete, perfect, ing of the
accomplish', e.g. Matt. xxvi. 56 ἵνα πληρωθῶσιν αἱ γραφαί, Rom. xiii. 8 verb
νόμον πεπλήρωκεν, Acts xii. 25 πληρώσαντες τὴν διακονίαν.   The latter sense
indeed is derived from the former, but practically it has become separate
from it.   The word occurs altogether about a hundred times in the New
Testament, and for every one instance of the former sense there are at
least four of the latter.

In the investigations which have hitherto been made into the significa- False issue
tion of the derived substantive πλήρωμα, as it occurs in the New Testa- raised
ment, an almost exclusive prominence has been given to the former mean- respecting
ing of the verb; and much confusion has arisen in consequence.   The πλήρωμα
question has been discussed whether πλήρωμα has an active or a passive
sense, whether it describes the filling substance or the filled receptacle:
and not unfrequently critics have arrived at the result that different
grammatical senses must be attached to it in different passages, even resulting
within the limits of the same epistle.   Thus it has been maintained that in theolo-
the word has a passive sense 'id quod impletur' in Ephes. i. 23 τῇ ἐκκλησίᾳ fusion
ἥτις ἐστὶν τὸ σῶμα αὐτοῦ, τὸ πλήρωμα τοῦ τὰ πάντα ἐν πᾶσιν πληρουμένου,
and an active sense 'id quod implet' in Ephes. iii. 19 ἵνα πληρωθῆτε εἰς πᾶν
τὸ πλήρωμα τοῦ Θεοῦ.   Indeed so long as we see in πληροῦν only the sense
'to fill', and refuse to contemplate the sense 'to complete', it seems impossible to escape from the difficulties which meet us at every turn, otherwise than by assigning to its derivative πλήρωμα both an active and a
passive sense; but the greatest violence is thus done to the connexion of
theological ideas.

Moreover the disregard of lexical rules is not less violent[1].   Substan- and disre-
tives in -μα, formed from the perfect passive, appear always to have a gard of
passive sense.   They may denote an abstract notion or a concrete thing; grammar.
they may signify the action itself regarded as complete, or the product of
the action; but in any case they give the *result* of the agency involved in Meaning
the corresponding verb.   Such for example are ἄγγελμα 'a message', ἄμμα tives in
'a knot', ἀργύρωμα 'a silver-made vessel', βούλευμα 'a plan', δικαίωμα 'a -μα.
righteous deed' or 'an ordinance', ζήτημα 'an investigation', κήρυγμα 'a
proclamation', κώλυμα 'a hindrance', ὁμοίωμα 'a likeness', ὅραμα 'a vision',

---

[1] The meaning of this word πλήρωμα
is the subject of a paper *De vocis* πλήρωμα *vario sensu in N. T.* in Storr's
Opusc. Acad. I. p. 144 sq., and of an elaborate note in Fritzsche's *Rom.* II. p.
469 sq.   Storr attempts to show that
it always has an active sense 'id quod
implet' in the New Testament.   Fritzsche rightly objects to assigning a
persistently active sense to a word
which has a directly passive termination: and he himself attributes to

it two main senses, 'id quod impletur' and 'id quo res impletur', the
latter being the more common.   He
apparently considers that he has sur-
mounted the difficulties involved in
Storr's view, for he speaks of this last
as a passive sense, though in fact it is
nothing more than 'id quod implet'
expressed in other words.   In Rom.
xiii. 10 πλήρωμα νόμου he concedes an
active sense 'legis completio', h. e.
'observatio'.

στρῶμα 'a carpet', σφαίρωμα 'a round thing', etc.   In many cases the same word will have two meanings, both however passive; it will denote both the completed action and the result or object of the action : e.g. ἅρπαγμα the 'robbery' or the 'booty', ἀντάλλαγμα the 'exchange' or the 'thing given or taken in exchange', θήρευμα the 'hunt' or the 'prey', πάτημα the 'tread' or the 'carpet', and the like.   But in all cases the word is strictly passive; it describes that which might have stood after the active verb, either as the direct object or as the cognate notion.   The

Apparent
excep-
tions. apparent exceptions are only apparent.   Sometimes this deceptive appearance is in the word itself.   Thus κάλυμμα 'a veil' seems to denote 'that which covers', but it is really derived from another sense and construction of καλύπτειν, not 'to hide', but 'to wrap round' (e.g. Hom. *Il.* v. 315 πρόσθε δέ οἱ πέπλοιο φαεινοῦ πτύγμ' ἐκάλυψεν, xxi. 321 τόσσην οἱ ἄσιν καθύπερθε καλύψω), and therefore is strictly passive.   Sometimes again we may be led astray by the apparent connexion with the following genitive.   Thus in Plut. *Mor.* 78 E δήλωμα τοῦ προκόπτειν the word does not mean, as might appear at first sight, 'a thing showing' but 'a thing shown', 'a demonstration given'; nor in 2 Thess. i. 5 ἔνδειγμα τῆς δικαίας κρίσεως must we explain ἔνδειγμα 'a thing proving', but 'a thing proved', 'a proof'.   And the same is probably the case also with such expressions as συμποσίων ἐρέθισμα (Critias in Athen. xiii. p. 600 D), τόξου ῥῦμα (Æsch. *Pers.* 147), and the like; where the substantives in -μα are no more deprived of their passive sense by the connexion, than they are in ὑπόδημα ποδῶν or στρῶμα κλίνης; though in such instances the license of poetical construction may often lead to a false inference.   Analogous to this last class of cases is Eur. *Troad.* 824 Ζηνὸς ἔχεις κυλίκων πλήρωμα, καλλίσταν λατρείαν, not 'the filling', but 'the fulness of the cups, the brimming cups, of Zeus.'

πλήρωμα
connected
with the
second
sense of
πληροῦν. Now if we confine ourselves to the second of the two senses above ascribed to πληροῦν, it seems possible to explain πλήρωμα in the same way, at all events in all the theological passages of St Paul and St John, without doing any violence to the grammatical form.   As πληροῦν is 'to complete', so πλήρωμα is 'that which is completed', i.e. the complement[1], the full tale, the entire number or quantity, the plenitude, the perfection.

Its uses in
classical
writers. This indeed is the primary sense to which its commonest usages in classical Greek can be most conveniently referred.   Thus it signifies (1)

(1) 'A
ship's
crew.' 'A ship's crew': e.g. Xen. *Hell.* i. 6. 16 διὰ το ἐκ πολλῶν πληρωμάτων ἐς ὀλίγας (ναῦς) ἐκλελέχθαι τοὺς ἀρίστους ἐρέτας.   In this sense, which is very frequent, it is generally explained as having an active force, 'that which fills the ships'; and this very obvious explanation is recommended by the fact that πληροῦν ναῦν is a recognised expression for 'manning a ship', e.g.

---

[1] The English word complement has two distinct senses.   It is either (i) the complete set, the entire quantity or number, which satisfies a given standard or cadre, as e.g. the complement of a regiment; or (ii) the number or quantity which, when added to a preexisting number or quantity, produces completeness; as e.g, the complement of an angle, i.e. the angle by which it falls short of being a complete right angle.   In other words, it is either the whole or the part.   As a theological term, πλήρωμα corresponds to the first of these two senses; and with this meaning alone the word 'complement' will be used in the following dissertation.

Xen. *Hell.* i. 6. 24. But πλήρωμα is used not only of the crew which mans a ship, but also of the ship which is manned with a crew; e.g. Polyb. i. 49. 4, 5, τὴν παρουσίαν τῶν πληρωμάτων...τὰ προσφάτως παραγεγονότα πληρώματα, Lucian *Ver. Hist.* ii. 37, 38, ἀπὸ δύο πληρωμάτων ἐμάχοντο...πέντε γὰρ εἶχον πληρώματα; and it is difficult to see how the word could be transferred from the crew to the ship as a whole, if the common explanation were correct. Fritzsche (*Rom.* II. p. 469 sq.), to whom I am chiefly indebted for the passages quoted in this paragraph, has boldly given the word two directly opposite senses in the two cases, explaining it in the one 'ea quibus naves complentur, *h. e.* vel socii navales vel milites classiarii vel utrique', and in the other 'id quod completur, *v. c.* navigium'; but this severance of meaning can hardly be maintained. On the other hand, if we suppose that the crew is so called as 'the complement', (i.e. 'not that which fills the ship', but 'that which is itself full or complete in respect of the ship'), we preserve the passive sense of the word, while at the same time the transference to the fully equipped and manned vessel itself becomes natural. In this sense 'a complement' we have the word used again of an army, Aristid. *Or.* I. p. 381 μήτε αὐτάρκεις ἔσεσθαι πλήρωμα ἑνὸς οἰκείου στρατεύματος παρασχέσθαι. (2) It sometimes signifies 'the population of a city', Arist. *Pol.* iii. 13 (p. 1284) μὴ μέντοι δυνατοὶ πλήρωμα παρασχέσθαι πόλεως (comp. iv. 4, p. 1291). Clearly the same idea of completeness underlies this meaning of the word, so that here again it signifies 'the complement': comp. Dion. Hal. *A. R.* vi. 51 τοῦ δ' ὀλίγου καὶ οὐκ ἀξιομάχου πληρώματος τὸ πλεῖόν ἐστι δημοτικόν κ.τ.λ., Eur. *Ion* 663 τῶν φίλων πλήρωμ' ἀθροίσας 'the whole body of his friends'. (3) 'The entire sum', Arist. *Vesp.* 660 τούτων πλήρωμα τάλαντ' ἐγγὺς δισχίλια γίγνεται ἡμῖν, 'From these sources a total of nearly two thousand talents accrues to us'. (4) 'The full term', Herod. iii. 22 ὀγδώκοντα δ' ἔτεα ζόης πλήρωμα ἀνδρὶ μακρότατον προκέεσθαι. (5) 'The perfect attainment', 'the full accomplishment', e.g. Philo *de Abr.* 46 (II. p. 39) πλήρωμα χρηστῶν ἐλπίδων. In short the fundamental meaning of the word generally, though perhaps not universally, is neither 'the filling material', nor 'the vessel filled'; but 'that which is complete in itself', or in other words 'plenitude, fulness, totality, abundance'.

(2) 'Population.'

(3) 'Total amount.'

(4) 'Entire term.'

(5) 'Fulfilment.'

In the Gospels the uses of the word present some difficulty. (1) In Matt. ix. 16 αἴρει γὰρ τὸ πλήρωμα αὐτοῦ ἀπὸ τοῦ ἱματίου καὶ χεῖρον σχίσμα γίνεται, it refers to the ἐπίβλημα ῥάκους ἀγνάφου which has gone before; but πλήρωμα need not therefore be equivalent to ἐπίβλημα so as to mean the patch itself, as is often assumed. The following pronoun αὐτοῦ is most naturally referred to ἐπίβλημα; and if so πλήρωμα describes 'the completeness', which results from the patch. The statement is thus thrown into the form of a direct paradox, the very completeness making the garment more imperfect than before. In the parallel passage Mark ii. 21 the variations are numerous, but the right reading seems certainly to be αἴρει τὸ πλήρωμα ἀπ' αὐτοῦ, τὸ καινὸν τοῦ παλαιοῦ κ.τ.λ. The received text omits the preposition before αὐτοῦ, but a glance at the authorities is convincing in favour of its insertion. In this case the construction will be αἴρει τὸ πλήρωμα (nom.) ἀπ' αὐτοῦ (i.e. τοῦ ἱματίου, which has been mentioned immediately before), τὸ καινὸν (πλήρωμα) τοῦ παλαιοῦ (ἱματίου); 'The completeness takes away from the garment, the new *completeness*

Use of πλήρωμα in the Gospels. Matt. ix. 16.

Mark ii. 21.

of the old *garment*', where the paradox is put still more emphatically.

Mark vi. 43. (2) In Mark vi. 43 the right reading is καὶ ἦραν κλασμάτων δώδεκα κοφίνους πληρώματα, i.e. 'full' or 'complete measures', where the apposition to κοφίνους obviates the temptation to explain πληρώματα as 'ea quae im-

Mark viii. 20. plent'. On the other hand in Mark viii. 20 πόσων σπυρίδων πληρώματα κλασμάτων ἤρατε; this would be the *prima facie* explanation; comp. Eccles. iv. 6 ἀγαθόν ἐστι πλήρωμα δρακὸς ἀναπαύσεως ὑπὲρ πληρώματα δύο δρακῶν μόχθου. But it is objectionable to give an active sense to πλήρωμα under any circumstances; and if in such passages the patch itself is meant, it must still be so called, not because it fills the hole, but because it is itself fulness or full measure as regards the defect which needs supplying.

Usage in St Paul's Epistles. 1 Cor. x. 26. From the Gospels we pass to the Epistles of St Paul, whose usage bears more directly on our subject. And here the evidence seems all to tend in the same direction. (1) In 1 Cor. x. 26 τοῦ Κυρίου γὰρ ἡ γῆ καὶ τὸ πλήρωμα αὐτῆς it occurs in a quotation from Ps. xxiv (xxiii). 1. The expressions τὸ πλήρωμα τῆς γῆς, τὸ πλήρωμα τῆς θαλάσσης, occur several times in the LXX (e.g. Ps. xcvi (xcv). 11, Jer. viii. 16), where τὸ πλήρωμα is a translation of מְלֹא, a word denoting primarily 'fulness', but having in its secondary uses a considerable latitude of meaning ranging between 'contents' and 'abundance'. This last sense seems to predominate in its Greek rendering πλήρωμα, and indeed the other is excluded altogether in

Rom. xiii. 10. some passages, e.g. Cant. v. 13 ἐπὶ πληρώματα ὑδάτων. (2) In Rom. xiii. 10 πλήρωμα νόμου ἡ ἀγάπη, the best comment on the meaning of the word is the context, ver. 8 ὁ ἀγαπῶν τὸν ἕτερον νόμον πεπλήρωκεν, so that πλήρωμα here means the 'completeness' and so 'fulfilment, accomplishment': see

Rom. xv. 29. the note on Gal. v. 14. (3) In Rom. xv. 29 ἐν πληρώματι εὐλογίας Χριστοῦ ἐλεύσομαι, it plainly has the sense of 'fulness, abundance'. (4) In Gal.

Gal. iv. 4. iv. 4 ὅτε δὲ ἦλθεν τὸ πλήρωμα τοῦ χρόνου and Ephes. i. 10 εἰς οἰκονομίαν τοῦ

Eph. i. 10. πληρώματος τῶν καιρῶν, its force is illustrated by such passages as Mark i. 15 πεπλήρωται ὁ καιρὸς καὶ ἤγγικεν ἡ βασιλεία κ.τ.λ., Luke xxi. 24 ἄχρι οὗ πληρωθῶσιν καιροὶ ἐθνῶν (comp. Acts ii. 1, vii. 23, 30, ix. 23, xxiv. 27), so that the expressions will mean 'the full measure of the time, the full tale

Rom. xi. 25. of the seasons'. (5) In Rom. xi. 25 πώρωσις ἀπὸ μέρους τῷ Ἰσραὴλ γέγονεν ἄχρις οὗ τὸ πλήρωμα τῶν ἐθνῶν εἰσέλθῃ, it seems to mean 'the full number', 'the whole body', (whether the whole absolutely, or the whole relatively to God's purpose), of whom only a part had hitherto been gathered

Rom. xi. 12. into the Church. (6) In an earlier passage in this chapter the same expression occurs of the Jews, xi. 12 εἰ δὲ τὸ παράπτωμα αὐτῶν πλοῦτος κόσμου καὶ τὸ ἥττημα αὐτῶν πλοῦτος ἐθνῶν, πόσῳ μᾶλλον τὸ πλήρωμα αὐτῶν. Here the antithesis between ἥττημα and πλήρωμα, 'failure' and 'fulness', is not sufficiently direct to fix the sense of πλήρωμα; and (in the absence of anything to guide us in the context) we may fairly assume that it is used in the same sense of the Jews here, as of the Gentiles in ver. 25.

General result. Thus, whatever hesitation may be felt about the exact force of the word as it occurs in the Gospels, yet substantially one meaning runs through all the passages hitherto quoted from St Paul. In these πλήρωμα has its proper passive force, as a derivative from πληροῦν 'to make complete'. It is 'the full complement, the entire measure, the plenitude, the fulness'. There is therefore a presumption in favour of this meaning in other passages where it occurs in this Apostle's writings.

We now come to those theological passages in the Epistles to the Colossians and Ephesians and in the Gospel of St John, for the sake of which this investigation has been undertaken. They are as follows; *Theologi-cal passages in*

Col. i. 19 ἐν αὐτῷ εὐδόκησεν πᾶν τὸ πλήρωμα κατοικῆσαι. *Colossians*

Col. ii. 9 ἐν αὐτῷ κατοικεῖ πᾶν τὸ πλήρωμα τῆς θεότητος σωματικῶς, καὶ ἐστὲ ἐν αὐτῷ πεπληρωμένοι. *and Ephe-sians.*

Ephes. i. 23 αὐτὸν ἔδωκεν κεφαλὴν ὑπὲρ πάντα τῇ ἐκκλησίᾳ, ἥτις ἐστὶν τὸ σῶμα αὐτοῦ, τὸ πλήρωμα τοῦ τὰ πάντα ἐν πᾶσιν πληρουμένου.

Ephes. iii. 19 ἵνα πληρωθῆτε εἰς πᾶν τὸ πλήρωμα τοῦ Θεοῦ.

Ephes. iv. 13 εἰς ἄνδρα τέλειον, εἰς μέτρον ἡλικίας τοῦ πληρώματος τοῦ Χριστοῦ.

John i. 14, 16, καὶ ὁ λόγος σὰρξ ἐγένετο καὶ ἐσκήνωσεν ἐν ἡμῖν (καὶ ἐθεα-σάμεθα τὴν δόξαν αὐτοῦ, δόξαν ὡς μονογενοῦς παρὰ πατρός) πλήρης χάριτος καὶ ἀληθείας...ἐκ τοῦ πληρώματος αὐτοῦ ἡμεῖς πάντες ἐλάβομεν καὶ χάριν ἀντὶ χάριτος. *St John.*

To these should be added two passages from the Ignatian Epistles[1], which as belonging to the confines of the Apostolic age afford valuable illustration of the Apostolic language. *Ignatius.*

Ephes. inscr. Ἰγνάτιος, ὁ καὶ Θεοφόρος, τῇ εὐλογημένῃ ἐν μεγέθει Θεοῦ πατρὸς πληρώματι[2]...τῇ ἐκκλησίᾳ τῇ ἀξιομακαρίστῳ τῇ οὔσῃ ἐν Ἐφέσῳ κ.τ.λ.

Trall. inscr. Ἰγνάτιος, ὁ καὶ Θεοφόρος...ἐκκλησίᾳ ἁγίᾳ τῇ οὔσῃ ἐν Τράλλε-σιν...ἣν καὶ ἀσπάζομαι ἐν τῷ πληρώματι, ἐν ἀποστολικῷ χαρακτῆρι.

It will be evident, I think, from the passages in St Paul, that the word πλήρωμα 'fulness, plenitude', must have had a more or less definite theo-logical value when he wrote. This inference, which is suggested by the frequency of the word, seems almost inevitable when we consider the form of the expression in the first passage quoted, Col. i. 19. The absolute use of the word, πᾶν τὸ πλήρωμα 'all *the* fulness', would otherwise be unintelli-gible, for it does not explain itself. In my notes I have taken ὁ Θεός to be the nominative to εὐδόκησεν, but if the subject of the verb were πᾶν τὸ πλήρωμα, as some suppose, the inference would be still more necessary. The word however, regarded as a theological term, does not appear to have been *The term has a re-cognised value*

---

[1] The first of the two passages is contained in the short Syriac recension, though loosely translated; the other is wanting there. I need not stop to en-quire whether the second was written by Ignatius himself or not. The seven epistles, even if not genuine (as I now believe them to be), can hardly date later than the middle of the second century and are therefore early enough to afford valuable illustrations of the Apostles' language.

[2] The common texts read καὶ πληρώ-ματι, but there can be little doubt (from a comparison of the authorities) that καὶ should be struck out. The

present Syriac text has *et perfectae* for πληρώματι; but there is no reason for supposing that the Syriac trans-lator had another reading before him. A slight change in the Syriac,

ܪܠܒܪܚܬ for ܪܠܒܪܚܘܐ,

would bring this version into entire accordance with the Greek; and the confusion was the more easy, because the latter word occurs in the imme-diate context. Or the translator may have indulged in a paraphrase ac-cording to his wont; just as in the longer Latin version πληρώματι here is translated *repletae*.

adopted, like so many other expressions in the Apostolic writers[1], from the
nomenclature of Alexandrian Judaism. At least no instance of its occurrence in this sense is produced from Philo. We may therefore conjecture
that it had a Palestinian origin, and that the Essene Judaizers of Colossæ,
whom St Paul is confronting, derived it from this source. In this case it
would represent the Hebrew מְלֹא, of which it is a translation in the LXX,
and the Aramaic ܡܠܐ or some other derivative of the same root,
such being its common rendering in the Peshito.

derived from Palestine and not Alexandria.

The sense in which St Paul employs this term was doubtless the sense
which he found already attached to it. He means, as he explicitly states in
the second Christological passage of the Colossian Epistle (ii. 9), the pleroma, the plenitude of 'the Godhead' or 'of Deity'. In the first passage
(i. 19), though the word stands without the addition τῆς θεότητος, the signification required by the context is the same. The true doctrine of the one
Christ, who is the absolute mediator in the creation and government of the
world, is opposed to the false doctrine of a plurality of mediators, 'thrones,
dominions, principalities, powers'. An absolute and unique position is
claimed for Him, because in Him resides 'all the pleroma', i.e. the full
complement, the aggregate of the Divine attributes, virtues, energies. This
is another way of expressing the fact that He is the Logos, for the Logos is
the synthesis of all the various δυνάμεις, in and by which God manifests
Himself whether in the kingdom of nature or in the kingdom of grace.

It denotes the totality of the Divine powers, etc. in the Colossian letter.

This application is in entire harmony with the fundamental meaning of
the word. The term has been transferred to the region of theology, but in
itself it conveys exactly the same idea as before. It implies that all the
several elements which are required to realise the conception specified are
present, and that each appears in its full proportions. Thus Philo, describing
the ideal state of prosperity which will result from absolute obedience
to God's law, mentions among other blessings the perfect development of
the family: 'Men shall be fathers and fathers too of goodly sons, and women
shall be mothers of goodly children, so that each household shall be the
pleroma of a numerous kindred, where no part or name is wanting of all
those which are used to designate relations, whether in the ascending line,
as parents, uncles, grandfathers, or again in the descending line in like
manner, as brothers, nephews, sons' sons, daughters' sons, cousins, cousins'
sons, kinsmen of all degrees[2].' So again Aristotle, criticizing the *Republic* of Plato, writes; 'Socrates says that a city (or state) is composed of
four classes, as its indispensable elements (τῶν ἀναγκαιοτάτων): by these he
means the weaver, the husbandman, the shoemaker, and the builder; and
again, because these are not sufficient by themselves, he adds the smith
and persons to look after the necessary cattle, and besides them the mer-
chant and the retail dealer: these together make up the *pleroma* of a
city in its simplest form (ταῦτα πάντα γίνεται πλήρωμα τῆς πρώτης πόλεως);

Analogy to its usage elsewhere: e.g.

in Philo, of the family,

and in Aristotle, of the state.

---

[1] See the notes on Col. i. 15 sq.

[2] *de Praem. et Poen.* 18 (II. p. 425).
The important words are ὡς ἕκαστον
οἶκον πλήρωμα εἶναι πολυανθρώπου συγ-
γενείας, μηδενὸς ἐλλειφθέντος ἢ μέρους

ἢ ὀνόματος τῶν ὅσα ἐπιφημίζεται κ.τ.λ.
The construction of the subsequent
part of the sentence is obscure; and
for ὁμοίους we should probably read
ὁμοίως.

thus he assumes that a city is formed to supply the bare necessities of life (τῶν ἀναγκαίων χάριν) etc.'[1]. From these passages it will be seen that the adequacy implied by the word, as so used, consists not less in the variety of the elements than in the fulness of the entire quantity or number.

So far the explanation seems clear. But when we turn from the Colossian letter to the Ephesian, it is necessary to bear in mind the different aims of the two epistles. While in the former the Apostle's main object is to assert the supremacy of the Person of Christ, in the latter his principal theme is the life and energy of the Church, as dependent on Christ[2]. So the pleroma residing in Christ is viewed from a different aspect, no longer in relation to God, so much as in relation to the Church. It is that plenitude of Divine graces and virtues which is communicated through Christ to the Church as His body. The Church, as *ideally* regarded, the bride 'without spot or wrinkle or any such thing', becomes in a manner identified with Him[3]. All the Divine graces which reside in Him are imparted to her; His 'fulness' is communicated to her: and thus she may be said to be His pleroma (i. 23). This is the ideal Church. The actual militant Church must be ever advancing, ever struggling towards the attainment of this ideal. Hence the Apostle describes the end of all offices and administrations in the Church to be that the collective body may attain its full and mature growth, or (in other words) may grow up to the complete stature of Christ's fulness[4]. But Christ's fulness is God's fulness. Hence in another passage he prays that the brethren may by the indwelling of Christ be fulfilled till they attain to the *pleroma* of God (iii. 19). It is another way of expressing the continuous aspiration and effort after holiness which is enjoined in our Lord's precept, 'Ye shall be perfect as your heavenly Father is perfect'[5].

The Gospel of St John, written in the first instance for the same churches to which the Epistle to the Ephesians was sent, has numerous and striking points of resemblance with St Paul's letter. This is the case here. As St Paul tells the Ephesians that the ideal Church is the pleroma of Christ and that the militant Church must strive to become the pleroma of Christ, so St John (i. 14 sq.) after describing our Lord as μονογενής, i.e. the unique and absolute representative of the Father, and as such 'full (πλήρης) of grace and of truth', says that they, the disciples, had 'received out of His pleroma' ever fresh accessions of grace. Each indi-

Marginal notes: Transition from Colossians to Ephesians. Corresponding application of πλήρωμα to the Church. Gospel of St John.

---

[1] Arist. *Pol.* iv. 4 (p. 1291).

[2] See the notes on Col. ii. 19 (p. 266).

[3] Ephes. v. 27 sq.

[4] The Apostle in this passage (Ephes. iv. 13) is evidently contemplating the collective body, and not the individual believers. He writes οἱ πάντες, not πάντες, and ἄνδρα τέλειον, not ἄνδρας τελείους. As he has said before ἑνὶ ἑκάστῳ ἡμῶν ἐδόθη [ἡ] χάρις κατὰ τὸ μέτρον τῆς δωρεᾶς τοῦ Χριστοῦ, so now he describes the result of

these various partial graces bestowed on *individuals* to be the unity and mature growth of the *whole*, 'the building up of the *body*', μέχρι καταντήσωμεν οἱ πάντες εἰς τὴν ἑνότητα... εἰς ἄνδρα τέλειον, εἰς μέτρον ἡλικίας τοῦ πληρώματος τοῦ Χριστοῦ. This corporate being must grow up into the one colossal Man, the standard of whose spiritual and moral stature is nothing less than the pleroma of Christ Himself.

[5] Matt. v. 48.

vidual believer in his degree receives a fraction of that pleroma which is
communicated whole to the ideal Church.

The use of the word is not very different in the Ignatian letters. St
Ignatius greets this same Ephesian Church, to which St Paul and St John
successively here addressed the language already quoted, as 'blessed in
greatness by the pleroma of God the Father', i. e. by graces imparted
from the pleroma. To the Trallians again he sends a greeting 'in the pleroma', where the word denotes the sphere of Divine gifts and operations, so
that ἐν τῷ πληρώματι is almost equivalent to ἐν τῷ Κυρίῳ or ἐν τῷ πνεύματι.

When we turn from Catholic Christianity to the Gnostic sects we find
this term used, though (with one important exception) not in great frequency. Probably however, if the writings of the earlier Gnostics had
been preserved, we should have found that it occupied a more important
place than at present appears. One class of early Gnostics separated the
spiritual being Christ from the man Jesus; they supposed that the Christ
entered Jesus at the time of His baptism and left him at the moment of
His crucifixion. Thus the Christ was neither born as a man nor suffered
as a man. In this way they obviated the difficulty, insuperable to the
Gnostic mind, of conceiving the connexion between the highest spiritual agency and gross corporeal matter, which was involved in the
Catholic doctrine of the Incarnation and Passion, and which Gnostics of
another type more effectually set aside by the theory of docetism, i.e. by
assuming that the human body of our Lord was only a phantom body and
not real flesh and blood. Irenæus represents the former class as teaching
that 'Jesus was the receptacle of the Christ', and that the Christ 'descended upon him from heaven in the form of a dove and after He had
declared (to mankind) the nameless Father, entered (again) into the pleroma imperceptibly and invisibly'[1]. Here no names are given. But in
another passage he ascribes precisely the same doctrine, without however
naming the pleroma, to Cerinthus[2]. And in a third passage, which links
together the other two, this same father, after mentioning this heresiarch,
again alludes to the doctrine which maintained that the Christ, having
descended on Jesus at his baptism, 'flew back again into His own pleroma'[3]. In this last passage indeed the opinions of Cerinthus are men-

[1] iii. 16. 1 'Quoniam autem sunt
qui dicunt Iesum quidem receptaculum
Christi fuisse, in quem desuper quasi
columbam descendisse, et quum indi-
casset innominabilem Patrem, incom-
prehensibiliter et invisibiliter *intrasse
in pleroma*'.

[2] i. 26. 1 'post baptismum descendisse in eum ab ea principalitate, quae
est super omnia, Christum figura co-
lumbae; et tunc annuntiasse incog-
nitum Patrem et virtutes perfecisse:
in fine autem *revolasse iterum* Christum
de Iesu et Iesum passum esse et
resurrexisse, etc.'

[3] iii. 11. 1 'iterum revolasse in suum
pleroma'. This expression is the connecting link between the other two
passages. This third passage is quoted
more at length above, p. 112. In this
passage however the reference of *illi*
in 'quemadmodum illi dicunt' is
doubtful. Several critics refer it to
the Valentinians, and certainly some
characteristic errors of the Valentinian
teaching are specified immediately
after. The probable explanation seems
to be that it is intended to include
the Gnostics generally, and that Irenæus mentions in illustration the
principal errors of Gnostic teaching,
irrespective of the schools to which

tioned in connexion with those of other Gnostics, more especially the Valentinians, so that we cannot with any certainty attribute this expression to Cerinthus himself. But in the first passage the unnamed heretics who maintained this return of the Christ 'into the pleroma' are expressly distinguished from the Valentinians; and presumably therefore the allusion is to the Cerinthians, to whom the doctrine, though not the expression, is ascribed in the second passage. Thus there seems to be sufficient reason for attributing the use of the term to Cerinthus[1]. This indeed is probable on other grounds. The term *pleroma*, we may presume, was common to St Paul and the Colossian heretics whom he controverts. To both alike it conveyed the same idea, the totality of the divine powers or attributes or agencies or manifestations. But after this the divergence begins. They maintained that a single divine power, a fraction of the pleroma, resided in our Lord: the Apostle urges on the contrary, that the whole pleroma has its abode in Him[2]. The doctrine of Cerinthus was a development of the Colossian heresy, as I have endeavoured to show above[3]. He would therefore inherit the term *pleroma* from it. At the same time he seems to have given a poetical colouring to his doctrine, and so doing to have treated the pleroma as a *locality*, a higher spiritual region, from which this divine power, typified by the dove-like form, issued forth as on wings, and to which, taking flight again, it reascended before the Passion. If so, his language would prepare the way for the still more elaborate poetic imagery of the Valentinians, in which the pleroma, conceived as a locality, a region, an *abode* of the divine powers, is conspicuous.

Connexion of this use with St Paul and with the Colossian heretics.

The pleroma localised.

The attitude of later Gnostics towards this term is widely divergent. The word is not, so far as I am aware, once mentioned in connexion with the system of Basilides. Indeed the nomenclature of this heresiarch belongs to a wholly different type; and, as he altogether repudiated the doctrine of emanations[4], it is not probable that he would have any fondness for a term which was almost inextricably entangled with this doctrine.

The term avoided by Basilides,

On the other hand with Valentinus and the Valentinians the doctrine of the *pleroma* was the very key-stone of their system; and, since at first sight it is somewhat difficult to connect their use of the term with St Paul's, a few words on this subject may not be out of place.

but prominent in Valentinianism.

Valentinus then dressed his system in a poetic imagery not unlike the

Poetic teaching

they belong. He goes on to say that St John in his Gospel desired to exclude 'omnia talia'.

[1] I have not been able however to verify the statement in Harvey's *Irenæus* I. p. lxxiii that 'The Valentinian notion of a spiritual marriage between the souls of the elect and the angels of the Pleroma originated with Cerinthus'.

[2] See p. 101 sq., and the notes on i. 19.

[3] p. 107 sq.

[4] Hippol. *R. H.* vii. 22 φεύγει γὰρ πάνυ καὶ δέδοικε τὰς κατὰ προβολὴν τῶν γεγονότων οὐσίας ὁ Βασιλείδης. Basilides asked why the absolute First Cause should be likened to a spider spinning threads from itself, or a smith or carpenter working up his materials. The later Basilideans, apparently influenced by Valentinianism, superadded to the teaching of their founder in this respect; but the strong language quoted by Hippolytus leaves no doubt about the mind of Basilides himself.

of Valen-
tinus.

*Topogra-
phical
conception
of the ple-
roma.*

Antithesis
of *pleroma*
and *keno-
ma.*

*Pleroma
the abode
of the
Æons.*

Different
forms of
Valenti-
nianism.

myths of his master Plato.   But a myth or story involves action, and action requires a scene of action.   Hence the mysteries of theology and cosmogony and redemption call for a *topographical* representation, and the pleroma appears not as an abstract idea, but as a locality.

The Valentinian system accordingly maps out the universe of things into two great regions, called respectively the *pleroma* and the *kenoma,* the 'fulness' and the 'void'.   From a Christian point of view these may be described as the kingdoms of light and of darkness respectively.   From the side of Platonism, they are the regions of real and of phenomenal existences—the world of eternal archetypes or ideas, and the world of material and sensible things.   The identification of these two antitheses was rendered easy for the Gnostic; because with him knowledge was one with morality and with salvation, and because also matter was absolutely bound up with evil.   It is difficult to say whether the Platonism or the Christianity predominates in the Valentinian theology; but the former at all events is especially prominent in their conception of the relations between the pleroma and the kenoma.

The pleroma is the abode of the Æons, who are thirty in number.   These Æons are successive emanations, of which the first pair sprang immediately from the preexistent Bythus or Depth.   This Bythus is deity in itself, the absolute first principle, as the name suggests; the profound, unfathomable, limitless, of whom or of which nothing can be predicated and nothing known.   Here again we have something like a *local* representation.   The Æons or emanations are plainly the attributes and energies of deity; they are, or they comprise, the eternal ideas or archetypes of the Platonic philosophy.   In short they are deity relative, deity under self-imposed limitations, deity derived and divided up, as it were, so as at length to be conceivable.

The topographical relation of Bythus to the derived Æons was differently given in different developments of the Valentinian teaching. According to one representation he was outside the pleroma; others placed his abode within it, but even in this case he was separated from the rest by Horus (Ὅρος), a personified Boundary or Fence, whom none, not even the Æons themselves, could pass[1].   The former mode of representa-

---

[1] For the various modes in which the relation of the absolute first principle to the pleroma was represented in different Valentinian schools, see Iren. i. 1. 1, i. 2. 4, i. 11. 1, 3, 5, i. 12. 1, etc.   The main distinction is that stated in the text; the first principle was represented in two ways; either (i) as a monad, outside the pleroma; or (ii) as a dyad, a syzygy, most commonly under the designation of Βυθός and Σιγή, included within the pleroma but fenced off from the other æons. The Valentinian doctrine as given by Hippolytus (vi. 29 sq.) represents the

former type.   There are good, though perhaps not absolutely decisive, reasons for supposing that this father gives the original teaching of Valentinus himself.   For (1) this very doctrine of the monad seems to point to an earlier date.   It is the link which connects the system of Valentinus not only with Pythagoreanism to which (as Hippolytus points out) he was so largely indebted, but also with the teaching of the earlier heresiarch Basilides, whose first principle likewise was a monad, the absolute nothing, the non-existent God.   The conception

tion might be thought to accord better with the imagery, at the same time that it is more accurate if regarded as the embodiment of a philosophical conception. Nevertheless the latter was the favourite mode of delineation; and it had at least this recommendation, that it combined in one all that is real, as opposed to all that is phenomenal. In this pleroma every existence which is suprasensual and therefore true has its abode.

Separated from this celestial region by Horus, another Horus or *Kenoma,* Boundary, which, or who, like the former is impassable, lies the 'kenoma' the region or 'void'—the kingdom of this world, the region of matter and material of phenomena. things, the land of shadow and darkness[1]. Here is the empire of the Demiurge or Creator, who is not a celestial Æon at all, but was born in this very void over which he reigns. Here reside all those phenomenal, deceptive, transitory things, of which the eternal counterparts are found only in the pleroma.

It is in this antithesis that the Platonism of the Valentinian theory Platonism reaches its climax. All things are set off one against another in these two of this antithesis. regions[2]: just as

> The swan on still St Mary's lake
> Floats double, swan and shadow.

Not only have the thirty Æons their terrestrial counterparts; but their subdivisions also are represented in this lower region. The kenoma too has its ogdoad, its decad, its dodecad, like the pleroma[3]. There is one Sophia in the supramundane region, and another in the mundane; there is one Christ who redeems the Æons in the spiritual world, and a second Christ who redeems mankind, or rather a portion of mankind, in the sensible world. There is an Æon Man and another Æon Ecclesia in the celestial kingdom, the ideal counterparts of the Human Race and the Christian Church in the terrestrial. Even individual men and women, as we shall see presently, have their archetypes in this higher sphere of intelligible being.

of the first principle as a dyad seems to have been a later, and not very happy, modification of the doctrine of the founder, being in fact an extension of the principle of syzygies which Valentinus with a truer philosophical conception had restricted to the derived essences. (2) The exposition of Hippolytus throughout exhibits a system at once more consistent and more simple, than the luxuriant developments of the later Valentinians, such as Ptolemæus and Marcus. (3) The sequence of his statement points to the same conclusion. He gives a consecutive account of some one system, turning aside from time to time to notice the variations of different Valentinian schools from this standard and again resuming the main thread

of his exposition. It seems most natural therefore that he should have taken the system of the founder as his basis. On the other hand Irenæus (i. 11. 1) states that Valentinus represented the first principle as a dyad (Ἄρρητος or Βυθός, and Σιγή): but there is no evidence that he had any direct or indirect knowledge of the writings of Valentinus himself, and his information was derived from the later disciples of the school, more especially from the Ptolemæans.

[1] Iren. i. 4. 1, 2, ii. 3. 1, ii. 4. 1, 3, ii. 5. 1, ii. 8. 1—3, ii. 14. 3, iii. 25. 6, 7, etc.

[2] Iren. i. 6. 3, i. 7. 1 sq., ii. 14. 3, ii. 15. 3 sq., ii. 20. 5, ii. 30. 3, etc.

[3] Iren. i. 5. 2, ii. 14. 3; comp. Hippol. vi. 34.

The locali-
sation of
the *plero-
ma* carried
out in de-
tail.

The topographical conception of the pleroma moreover is carried out in the details of the imagery. The second Sophia, called also Achamoth, is the desire, the offspring, of her elder namesake, separated from her mother, cast out of the pleroma, and left 'stranded' in the void beyond[1], being prevented from returning by the inexorable Horus who guards the frontier of the supramundane kingdom. The second Christ—a being compounded of elements contributed by all the Æons[2]—was sent down from the pleroma, first of all at the eve of creation to infuse something like order and to provide for a spiritual element in this lower world; and secondly, when He united Himself with the man Jesus for the sake of redeeming those who were capable of redemption[3]. At the end of all things Sophia Achamoth, and with her the spiritual portion of mankind, shall be redeemed and received up into the pleroma, while the psychical portion will be left outside to form another kingdom under the dominion of their father the Demiurge. This redemption and ascension of Achamoth (by a perversion of a scriptural image) was represented as her espousals with the Saviour, the second Christ; and the pleroma, the scene of this happy union, was called the bridal-chamber[4]. Indeed the localisation of the pleroma is as complete as language can make it. The constant repetition of the words 'within' and 'without', 'above' and 'beneath', in the development of this philosophical and religious myth still further impresses this local sense on the term[5].

The con-
nexion
with St
Paul's use
of the term
obscured,

owing
partly to
the false
antithesis
κένωμα

In this topographical representation the connexion of meaning in the word *pleroma* as employed by St Paul and by Valentinus respectively seems at first sight to be entirely lost. When we read of the contrast between the pleroma and the kenoma, the fulness and the void, we are naturally reminded of the *plenum* and the *vacuum* of physical speculations. The sense of pleroma, as expressing completeness and so denoting the aggregate or totality of the Divine powers, seems altogether to have disappeared. But in fact this antithesis of κένωμα was, so far as we can make out, a mere afterthought, and appears to have been borrowed, as Irenæus states, from the physical theories of Democritus and Epicurus[6]. It would naturally suggest itself both because the opposition of πλήρης and κενὸς was obvious, and because the word κένωμα materially assisted the imagery as a description of the kingdom of waste and shadow. But in

---

[1] Iren. i. 4. 1 λέγουσιν ἐν σκιαῖς [σκιᾶς] καὶ κενώματος τόποις ἐκβεβρά-σθαι κ.τ.λ. The Greek ms reads καὶ σκηνώματος, but the rendering of the early Latin translation 'in umbrae [et?] vacuitatis locis' leaves no doubt about the word in the original text. Tertullian says of this Achamoth (*adv. Valent.* 14) 'explosa est in loca luminis aliena...in vacuum atque inane illud Epicuri'. See note 6.

[2] Iren. i. 2. 6, Hippol. vi. 32.

[3] They quoted, as referring to this descent of the second Christ into the kenoma, the words of St Paul, Phil.

[ii]. 7 ἑαυτὸν ἐκένωσεν; Clem. Alex. *Exc. Theod.* 35 (p. 978).

[4] Iren. i. 7. 1 καὶ τοῦτο εἶναι νυμφίον καὶ νύμφην, νυμφῶνα δὲ τὸ πᾶν πλήρωμα: comp. Hippol. vi. 34 ὁ νυμφίος αὐτῆς.

[5] This language is so frequent that special references are needless. In Iren. ii. 5. 3 we have a still stronger expression, 'in ventre pleromatis'.

[6] Iren. ii. 14. 3 'Umbram autem et vacuum ipsorum a Democrito et Epicuro sumentes sibimetipsis *aptaverunt*, quum illi primum multum sermonem fecerint de vacuo et de atomis'.

itself it is a false antithesis. The true antithesis appears in another, and probably an earlier, term used to describe the mundane kingdom. In this earlier representation, which there is good reason for ascribing to Valentinus himself, it is called not κένωμα 'the void', but ὑστέρημα 'the deficiency, incompleteness'[1]. Moreover the common phraseology of the Valentinian schools shows that the idea suggested by this opposition to κένωμα was not the original idea of the term. They speak of τὸ πλήρωμα τῶν αἰώνων, τὸ πᾶν πλήρωμα τῶν αἰώνων, 'the whole aggregate of the Æons'[2]. And this (making allowance for the personification of the Æons) corresponds exactly to its use in St Paul.

borrowed from physical philosophers; but reappears in their common phraseology.

Again the teaching of the Valentinian schools supplies other uses which serve to illustrate its meaning. Not only does the supramundane kingdom as a whole bear this name, but each separate Æon, of which that kingdom is the aggregation, is likewise called a pleroma[3]. This designation is given to an Æon, because it is the fulness, the perfection, of which its mundane counterpart is only a shadowy and defective copy. Nor does the narrowing of the term stop here. There likewise dwells in this higher region a pleroma, or eternal archetype, not only of every comprehensive mundane power, but of each individual man; and to wed himself with this heavenly partner, this Divine ideal of himself, must be the study of his life. The profound moral significance which underlies the exaggerated Platonism and perverse exegesis of this conception will be at once apparent. But the manner in which the theory was carried out is curiously illustrated by the commentary of the Valentinian Heracleon on our Lord's discourse with the Samaritan woman[4]. This woman, such is his explana-

The original meaning shown by other uses.

Interpretation of John iv. 17, 18.

---

[1] Hippol. vi. 31 καλεῖται δὲ ὅρος μὲν οὗτος ὅτι ἀφορίζει ἀπὸ τοῦ πληρώματος ἔξω τὸ ὑστέρημα· μετοχεὺς δὲ ὅτι μετέχει καὶ τοῦ ὑστερήματος (i. e. as standing between the πλήρωμα and ὑστέρημα)· σταυρὸς δέ, ὅτι πέπηγεν ἀκλινῶς καὶ ἀμετανοήτως, ὡς μὴ δύνασθαι μηδὲν τοῦ ὑστερήματος καταγενέσθαι ἐγγὺς τῶν ἐντὸς πληρώματος αἰώνων. Irenæus represents the Marcosians as designating the Demiurge καρπὸς ὑστερήματος i. 17. 2, i. 19. 1, ii. praef. 1, ii. 1. 1 (comp. i. 14. 1). This was perhaps intended originally as an antithesis to the name of the Christ, who was καρπὸς πληρώματος. The Marcosians however apparently meant Sophia Achamoth by this ὑστέρημα. This transference from the whole to the part would be in strict accordance with their terminology: for as they called the supramundane æons πληρώματα (Iren. i. 14. 2, 5; quoted in Hippol. vi. 43, 46), so also by analogy they might designate the mundane powers ὑστερήματα (comp. Iren. i. 16. 3). The term, as it occurs in the docu-

ment used by Hippolytus, plainly denotes the *whole* mundane region. Hippolytus does not use the word κένωμα, though so common in Irenæus. This fact seems to point to the earlier date of the Valentinian document which he uses, and so to bear out the result arrived at in a previous note (p. 266) that we have here a work of Valentinus himself. The word ὑστέρημα appears also in *Exc. Theod.* 22 (p. 974).

[2] e.g. Hippol. vi. 34, Iren. i. 2. 6. See especially Iren. ii. 7. 3 'Quoniam enim pleroma ipsorum triginta Aeones sunt, ipsi testantur'.

[3] See the passages from Irenæus quoted above, note 1; comp. *Exc. Theod.* 32, 33 (p. 977). Similarly λόγοι is a synonym for the Æons, ὁμωνύμως τῷ Λόγῳ, *Exc. Theod.* 25 (p. 975).

[4] Heracleon in Orig. *in Ioann.* xiii, IV. p. 205 sq. The passages are collected in Stieren's Irenæus p. 947 sq. See especially p. 950 οἴεται [ὁ Ἡρακλέων] τῆς

tion, belongs to the spiritual portion of mankind. But she had had six[1] husbands, or in other words she had entangled herself with the material world, had defiled herself with sensuous things. The husband however, whom she now has, is not her husband; herein she has spoken rightly: the Saviour in fact means 'her partner from the pleroma'. Hence she is bidden to go and call him; that is, she must find 'her pleroma, that coming to the Saviour with him (or it), she may be able to obtain from Him the power and the union and the combination with her pleroma' (τὴν δύναμιν καὶ τὴν ἔνωσιν καὶ τὴν ἀνάκρασιν τὴν πρὸς τὸ πλήρωμα αὐτῆς). 'For', adds Heracleon, 'He did not speak of a mundane (κοσμικοῦ) husband when He told her to call him, since He was not ignorant that she had no lawful husband'.

Valentinians accept St Paul and St John,

Impossible as it seems to us to reconcile the Valentinian system with the teaching of the Apostles, the Valentinians themselves felt no such difficulty. They intended their philosophy not to supersede or contradict the Apostolic doctrine, but to supplement it and to explain it on philosophical principles. Hence the Canon of the Valentinians comprehended the Canon of Catholic Christianity in all its essential parts, though some Valentinian schools at all events supplemented it with Apocryphal writings. More particularly the Gospel of St John and the Epistles to the Colossians and Ephesians were regarded with especial favour; and those passages which speak of the pleroma are quoted more than once in their writings to illustrate their teaching. By isolating a few words from the context and interpreting them wholly without reference to their setting,

and quote them in support of their views.

they had no difficulty in finding a confirmation of their views, where we see only an incongruity or even a contradiction. For instance, their second Christ—the redeemer of the spiritual element in the mundane world—was, as we saw, compacted of gifts contributed by all the Æons of the pleroma. Hence he was called 'the common fruit of the pleroma', 'the fruit of all the pleroma'[2], 'the most perfect beauty and constellation of the pleroma'[3]; hence

---

Σαμαρείτιδος τὸν λεγόμενον ὑπὸ τοῦ σωτῆρος ἄνδρα τὸ πλήρωμα εἶναι αὐτῆς, ἵνα σὺν ἐκείνῳ γενομένη πρὸς τὸν σωτῆρα κομίσεσθαι παρ᾽ αὐτοῦ τὴν δύναμιν καὶ τὴν ἔνωσιν καὶ τὴν ἀνάκρασιν τὴν πρὸς τὸ πλήρωμα αὐτῆς δυνηθῇ· οὐ γὰρ περὶ ἀνδρός, φησί, κοσμικοῦ ἔλεγεν...... λέγων αὐτῇ τὸν σωτῆρα εἰρηκέναι, Φώνησόν σου τὸν ἄνδρα καὶ ἐλθὲ ἐνθάδε· δηλοῦντα τὸν ἀπὸ τοῦ πληρώματος σύζυγον. Lower down Heracleon says ἦν αὐτῆς ὁ ἀνὴρ ἐν τῷ Αἰῶνι. By this last expression I suppose he means that the great æon Man of the Ogdoad, the eternal archetype of mankind, comprises in itself archetypes corresponding to each individual man and woman, not indeed of the whole human race (for the Valentinian would exclude the psychical and carnal portion from any participation in this higher region) but of the spiritual portion thereof.

[1] Origen expressly states that Heracleon read ἕξ for πέντε. The number six was supposed to symbolize the material creature; see Heracleon on 'the forty and six years' of John ii. 20 (Stieren p. 947). There is no reason to think that Heracleon falsified the text here; he appears to have found this various reading already in his copy.

[2] The expression is ὁ κοινὸς τοῦ πληρώματος καρπὸς in Hippolytus vi. 32, 34, 36 (pp. 190, 191, 192, 193, 196). In Irenæus i. 8. 5 it is καρπὸς παντὸς τοῦ πληρώματος.

[3] Iren. i. 2. 6 τελειότατον κάλλος τε καὶ ἄστρον τοῦ πληρώματος.

a'.so he was designated 'All' (πᾶν) and 'All things' (πάντα)[1]. Accordingly, to this second Christ, not to the first, they applied these texts; Col. iii. 11 'And He is all things', Rom. xi. 36 'All things are unto Him and from Him are all things', Col. ii. 9 'In Him dwelleth all the fulness of the Godhead', Ephes. i. 10 'To gather together in one all things in Christ through God'[2]. So too they styled him Εὐδόκητος, with a reference to Col. i. 19, because 'all the pleroma was pleased through Him to glorify the Father'[3]. And inasmuch as this second Christ was according to the Valentinian theory instrumental in the creation of the mundane powers, they quoted, or rather misquoted, as referring to this participation in the work of the Demiurge, the passage Col. i. 16 'In Him were created all things, visible and invisible, thrones, deities, dominions'[4]. Indeed it seems clear that these adaptations were not always afterthoughts, but that in several instances at least their nomenclature was originally chosen for the sake of fitting the theory to isolated phrases and expressions in the Apostolic writings, however much it might conflict with the Apostolic doctrine in its main lines[5].

The heretics called Docetae by Hippolytus have no connexion with docetism, as it is generally understood, i.e. the tenet that Christ's body was not real flesh and blood, but merely a phantom body. Their views on this point, as represented by this father, are wholly different[6]. Of their system generally nothing need be said here, except that it is largely saturated with Valentinian ideas and phrases. From the Valentinians they evidently borrowed their conception of the pleroma, by which they understood the aggregate, or (as localised) the abode, of the Æons. With them, as with the Valentinians, the Saviour is the common product of all the Æons[7]; and in speaking of him they echo a common Valentinian phrase 'the pleroma of the entire Æons'[8]. *Use of the term by the Docetae,*

The Ophite heresy, Proteus-like, assumes so many various forms, that the skill of critics has been taxed to the utmost to bind it with cords and extract its story from it. It appears however from the notices of Hippolytus, that the term *pleroma* was used in a definite theological sense by at least two branches of the sect, whom he calls Naassenes and Peratae. *and by two Ophite sects.*

Of the Naassenes Hippolytus tells us that among other images borrowed from the Christian and Jewish Scriptures, as well as from heathen poetry, they described the region of true knowledge—their kingdom of *(i) Naassenes.*

---

[1] Iren. i. 2. 6, i. 3. 4.

[2] Iren. i. 3. 4. The passages are given in the text as they are quoted by Irenæus from the Valentinians. Three out of the four are incorrect.

[3] Iren. i. 12. 4; comp. *Exc. Theod.* 31 (p. 977) εἰ ὁ κατελθὼν εὐδοκία τοῦ ὅλου ἦν ἐν αὐτῷ γὰρ πᾶν τὸ πλήρωμα ἦν σωματικῶς.

[4] Iren. i. 4. 5 ὅπως ἐν αὐτῷ τὰ πάντα κτισθῇ, τὰ ὁρατὰ καὶ τὰ ἀόρατα, θρόνοι, θεότητες, κυριότητες, where the misquotation is remarkable. In *Exc. Theod.* 43 (p. 979) the words run πάντα γὰρ ἐν αὐτῷ ἐκτίσθη τὰ ὁρατὰ καὶ τὰ

ἀόρατα, θρόνοι, κυριότητες, βασιλεῖαι, θεότητες, λειτουργίαι· διὸ καὶ ὁ Θεὸς αὐτὸν ὑπερύψωσεν κ.τ.λ. (the last words being taken from Phil. ii. 9 sq.).

[5] Thus they interpreted Ephes. iii. 21 εἰς πάσας τὰς γενεὰς τοῦ αἰῶνος τῶν αἰώνων as referring to their generated æons: Iren. i. 3. 1. Similar is the use which they made of expressions in the opening chapter of St John, where they found their first Ogdoad described: *ib.* i. 8. 5.

[6] *R. H.* viii. 10 (p. 267).

[7] *ib.* viii. 9.

[8] *ib.* viii. 10 (p. 266).

heaven, which was entered by initiation into their mysteries—as the land flowing with milk and honey, 'which when the perfect (the true Gnostics, the fully initiated) have tasted, they are freed from subjection to kings (ἀβασιλεύτους) and partake of the pleroma.' Here is a plain allusion to Joh. i. 16. ' This', the anonymous Naassene writer goes on to say, 'is the pleroma, through which all created things coming into being are produced and fulfilled (πεπλήρωται) from the Uncreated'[1]. Here again, as in the Valentinian system, the conception of the pleroma is strongly tinged with Platonism. The pleroma is the region of ideas, of archetypes, which intervenes between the author of creation and the material world, and communicates their specific forms to the phenomenal existences of the latter.

(ii) Peratae.

Their theology

and corresponding application of πλήρωμα.

The theology of the second Ophite sect, the Peratae, as described by Hippolytus, is a strange phenomenon. They divided the universe into three regions, the uncreate, the self-create, and the created. Again the middle region may be said to correspond roughly to the Platonic kingdom of ideas. But their conception of deity is entirely their own. They postulate three of every being; three Gods, three Words, three Minds (i. e. as we may suppose, three Spirits), three Men. Thus there is a God for each region, just as there is a Man. In full accordance with this perverse and abnormal theology is their application of St Paul's language. Their Christ has three natures, belonging to these three kingdoms respectively; and this completeness of His being is implied by St Paul in Col. i. 19, ii. 9, which passages are combined in their loose quotation or paraphrase, 'All the pleroma was pleased to dwell in him bodily, and there is in him all the godhead', i. e. (as Hippolytus adds in explanation) 'of this their triple division (τῆς οὕτω διῃρημένης τριάδος)'[2]. This application is altogether arbitrary, having no relation whatever to the theological meaning of the term in St Paul. It is also an entire departure from the conception of the Cerinthians, Valentinians, and Naassenes, in which this meaning, however obscured, was not altogether lost. These three heresies took a horizontal section of the universe, so to speak, and applied the term as coextensive with the supramundane stratum. The Peratae on the other hand divided it vertically, and the pleroma, in their interpretation of the text, denoted the whole extent of this vertical section. There is nothing in common between the two applications beyond the fundamental meaning of the word, 'completeness, totality'.

Pistis Sophia.

Frequent use of the term.

The extant Gnostic work, called Pistis Sophia, was attributed at one time on insufficient grounds to Valentinus. It appears however to exhibit a late development of Ophitism[3], far more Christian and less heathen in its character than those already considered. In this work the word pleroma occurs with tolerable frequency; but its meaning is not easily fixed. Early in the treatise it is said that the disciples supposed a certain 'mystery', of which Jesus spoke, to be 'the end of all the ends' and 'the head (κεφαλήν) of the Universe' and 'the whole pleroma'[4]. Here we seem to have an allusion to the Platonic kingdom of ideas,

[1] *R. H.* v. 8.   [2] *R. H.* v. 12.   Tübingen 1854, p. 185.
[3] See Köstlin in *Theolog. Jahrb.*   [4] *Pistis Sophia* p. 3 sq.

i.e. of intelligible being, of absolute truth, as reproduced in the Valentinian pleroma. And the word is used sometimes in connexion with the completeness of revelation or the perfection of knowledge. Thus our Lord is represented as saying to His disciples, 'I will tell you the whole mystery and the whole pleroma, and I will conceal nothing from you from this hour; and in perfection will I perfect you in every pleroma and in every perfection and in every mystery, which things are the perfection of all the perfections and the pleroma of all the pleromas'[1]. Elsewhere however Mary, to whom Jesus is represented as making some of His chief revelations, is thus addressed by Him; 'Blessed art thou above (παρὰ) all women that are on the earth, for thou shalt be pleroma of all the pleromas and perfection of all the perfections'[2], where the word must be used in a more general sense.

One heresy still remains to be noticed in connexion with this word. *Monoimus the Arabian.* Hippolytus has preserved an account of the teaching of Monoimus the Arabian, of whom previously to the discovery of this father's treatise we knew little more than the name. In this strange form of heresy the absolute first principle is the uncreate, imperishable, eternal Man. I need not stop to enquire what this statement means. It is sufficient for the present purpose to add that this eternal Man is symbolized by the letter ι, the 'one iota', the 'one tittle' of the Gospel[3]; and this ι, as representing the number ten, includes in itself all the units from one to nine. 'This', added Monoimus, 'is (meant by) the saying (of scripture) *All the pleroma was pleased to dwell upon the Son of Man bodily*'[4]. Here the original idea of the word as denoting completeness, totality, is still preserved.

[1] *ib.* p. 15 sq.: comp. pp. 4, 60, 75, 187, 275.

[2] *ib.* p. 28 sq.: comp. p. 56. On p. 7 πλήρωμα is opposed to ἀρχή, apparently in the sense of 'completion'.

[3] Matt. v. 18.

[4] *R. H.* viii. 13.

The Epistle from Laodicea[1].

Different
theories
classified.
THE different opinions respecting the epistle thus designated by
St Paul, which have been held in ancient or modern times, will be seen
from the following table;

1. An *Epistle written by the Laodiceans;* to
    - (a) St Paul ;
    - (β) Epaphras ;
    - (γ) Colossæ.

2. An *Epistle written by St Paul from Laodicea.*
    - (a) 1 Timothy ;
    - (β) 1 Thessalonians ;
    - (γ) 2 Thessalonians ;
    - (δ) Galatians.

3. An *Epistle addressed to the Laodiceans* by
    - (a) St John (the First Epistle);
    - (b) Some companion of St Paul (Epaphras or Luke);
    - (c) St Paul himself;
        - (i) A lost Epistle.
        - (ii) One of the Canonical Epistles.
            - (a) Hebrews ;
            - (β) Philemon ;
            - (γ) Ephesians.
        - (iii) The Apocryphal Epistle.

In this maze of conflicting hypotheses we might perhaps be tempted to
despair of finding our way and give up the search as hopeless. Yet I venture to think that the true identification of the epistle in question is not,
or at least ought not to be, doubtful.

1. An
epistle
written by
the Laodi-
ceans.
Advocates
of this
theory.
1. The opinion that the epistle was addressed by the Laodiceans to
St Paul, and not conversely, found much support in the age of the Greek
commentators. It is mentioned by St Chrysostom as held by 'some persons', though he himself does not pronounce a definite opinion on the subject[2]. It is eagerly advocated by Theodore of Mopsuestia. He supposes
that the letter of the Laodiceans contained some reflexions on the Colossian Church, and that St Paul thought it good for the Colossians to hear

---

[1] The work of Anger, *Ueber den
Laodicenerbrief* (Leipzig 1843), is very
complete. He enumerates and discusses very thoroughly the opinions
of his predecessors, omitting hardly
anything relating to the literature of
the subject which was accessible at
the time when he wrote. His exposition of his own view, though not less
elaborate, is less satisfactory. A later
monograph by A. Sartori, *Ueber den
Laodicenserbrief* (Lubeck 1853), is much
slighter and contributes nothing new.

[2] *ad loc.* τινὲς λέγουσιν ὅτι οὐχὶ τὴν
Παύλου πρὸς αὐτοὺς ἀπεσταλμένην, ἀλλὰ
τὴν παρ᾽ αὐτῶν Παύλῳ· οὐ γὰρ εἶπε τὴν
πρὸς Λαοδικέας ἀλλὰ τὴν ἐκ Λαοδικείας.

what their neighbours said of them[1]. Theodoret, though not mentioning Theodore by name, follows in his footsteps[2]. The same opinion is also expressed in a note ascribed to Photius in the Œcumenian Catena. This view seems to have been very widely entertained in ancient times. It possibly underlies the Latin Version 'ea quæ Laodicensium est'[3]: it is distinctly expressed in the rendering of the Peshito, 'that which was written by the Laodiceans'[4]. At a more recent date too it found great favour. It was adopted on the one hand by Calvin[5] and Beza[6] and Davenant and Lightfoot[7], on the other by Baronius[8] and à Lapide and Estius, besides other very considerable names[9]. Latterly its popularity has declined, but it has secured the support of one or two commentators even in the present century.

The underlying motive of this interpretation was to withdraw the support which the apocryphal epistle seemed to derive from this reference, without being obliged at the same time to postulate a lost epistle of St Paul. The critical argument adduced in its support was the form of expression, τὴν ἐκ Λαοδικείας. The whole context however points to a different explanation. The Colossian and Laodicean Epistles are obviously regarded as in some sense companion epistles, of which the Apostle directs an interchange between the two churches. And again, if the letter in question had

Reasons for it.

Objections to it.

---

[1] Rab. Maur. *Op.* VI. p. 540 (Migne) 'Non quia ad Laodicenses scribit. Unde quidam falsam epistolam ad Laodicenses ex nomine beati Pauli confingendam esse existimaverunt; nec enim erat vera epistola. Æstimaverunt autem quidam illam esse, quæ in hoc loco est significata. Apostolus vero non [*ad*] *Laodicenses* dicit sed *ex Laodicea;* quam illi scripserunt ad apostolum, in quam aliqua reprehensionis digna inferebantur, quam etiam hac de causa jussit apud eos legi, ut ipsi reprehendant seipsos discentes quæ de ipsis erant dicta etc.' (see *Spic. Solesm.* I. p. 133).

[2] After repeating the argument based on the expression τὴν ἐκ Λαοδικείας, Theodoret says εἰκὸς δὲ αὐτοὺς ἢ τὰ ἐν Κολασσαῖς γενόμενα αἰτιάσασθαι ἢ τὰ αὐτὰ τούτοις νενοσηκέναι.

[3] This however may be questioned. On the other hand Beza (*ad loc.*), Whitaker (*Disputation on Scripture* pp. 108, 303, 468 sq., 526, 531, Parker Society's ed.), and others, who explain the passage in this way, urge that it is required by the Greek ἐκ Λαοδικείας, and complain that the other interpretation depends on the erroneous Latin rendering.

[4] Or, 'that which was written from Laodicea.' The difference depends on the vocalisation of ܠܕܝܩܝܐ which may be either (1) 'Laodicea,' as in vv. 13, 15, or (2) 'the Laodiceans,' as in the previous clause in this same ver. 16.

[5] Calvin is very positive; 'Bis hallucinati sunt qui Paulum arbitrati sunt ad Laodicenses scripsisse. Non dubito quin epistola fuerit ad Paulum missa ... Impostura autem nimis crassa fuit, quod nebulo nescio quis hoc prætextu epistolam supponere ausus est adeo insulsam, ut nihil a Pauli spiritu magis alienum fingi queat.' The last sentence reveals the motive which unconsciously led so many to adopt this unnatural interpretation of St Paul's language.

[6] *ad loc.* 'Multo fœdius errarunt qui ex hoc loco suspicati sunt quandam fuisse epistolam Pauli ad Laodicenses ...... quum potius significet Paulus epistolam aliquam ad se missam Laodicea, aut potius qua responsuri essent Laodicenses Colossensibus.'

[7] *Works* II. p. 326.

[8] *Ann. Eccl.* s. a. 60, § xiii.

[9] e.g. Tillemont *Mem. Eccl.* I. p. 576.

been written by the Laodiceans to St Paul, why should he enjoin the Colossians to get it from Laodicea? How could he assume that a copy had been kept by the Laodiceans; or, if kept, would be given up when required? Indeed the difficulties in this hypothesis are so great, that nothing but the most imperious requirements of the Greek language would justify its acceptance. But the expression in the original makes no such demand. It is equally competent for us to explain τὴν ἐκ Λαοδικείας either 'the letter written from Laodicea', or 'the letter to be procured from Laodicea', as the context may suggest. The latter accords at least as well with Greek usage as the former[1].

Views respecting the person addressed. The vast majority of those who interpret the expression in this way assume that the letter was written to (a) St Paul. The modifications of this view, which suppose it addressed to some one else, need hardly be considered. The theory for instance, which addresses it to (β) Epaphras[2], removes none of the objections brought against the simpler hypothesis. Another opinion, which takes (γ) the Colossians themselves to have been the recipients[3], does indeed dispose of one difficulty, the necessity of assuming a copy kept by the Laodiceans, but it is even more irreconcileable with the language of the context. Why then should St Paul so studiously charge them to see that they read it? Why above all should he say καὶ ὑμεῖς, 'ye also', when they were the only persons who would read it as a matter of course?

2. A letter written from Laodicea by St Paul. 2. A second class of identifications rests on the supposition that it was a letter written *from* Laodicea, though not by the Laodiceans themselves. The considerations which recommend this hypothesis for acceptance are the same as in the last case. It withdraws all support from the apocryphal Epistle to the Laodiceans, and it refrains from postulating a lost Apostolic epistle. It is not exposed to all the objections of the other theory, but it introduces new difficulties still more serious. Here a choice of several epistles is offered to us. (a) The *First Epistle to Timothy*.

1 Timothy. This view is distinctly maintained by John Damascene[4] and by Theophylact[5]; but it took its rise much earlier. It appears in the margin of the Philoxenian Syriac[6], and it seems to have suggested the subscriptions found in many authorities at the close of that epistle. The words ἐγράφη ἀπὸ Λαοδικείας are found in AKL 47 etc., and many of these define the place meant by the addition ἥτις ἐστὶ μητρόπολις Φρυγίας τῆς Πακατιανῆς. A similar note is found in some Latin MSS. It is quite possible that this subscription was prior to the theory respecting the interpretation of Col. iv. 16, and gave rise to it; but the converse is more probable, and in some

---

[1] See the note on iv. 16.

[2] e.g. Storr *Opusc.* II. p. 124 sq.

[3] So for instance Corn. à Lapide, as an alternative, 'vel certe ad ipsos Colossenses, ut vult Theodor.'; but I do not find anything of the kind in Theodoret. This view also commends itself to Beza.

[4] *Op.* II. p. 214 (ed. Lequien) τὴν πρὸς Τιμόθεον πρώτην λέγει. But he adds τινὲς φασὶν ὅτι οὐχὶ τὴν Παύλου

πρὸς αὐτοὺς ἐπεσταλμένην...ἀλλὰ τὴν παρ' αὐτῶν Παύλῳ ἐκ Λαοδικείας γραφεῖσαν.

[5] *ad loc.* τίς δὲ ἦν ἡ ἐκ Λαοδικείας; ἡ πρὸς Τιμόθεον πρώτη· αὕτη γὰρ ἐκ Λαοδικείας ἐγράφη. τινὲς δέ φασιν ὅτι ἦν οἱ Λαοδικεῖς Παύλῳ ἐπέστειλαν, ἀλλ' οὐκ οἶδα τί ἂν ἐκείνης ἔδει αὐτοῖς πρὸς βελτίωσιν.

[6] *ad loc.* 'Propter eam quæ est ad Timotheum dixit.'

MSS (a^ter 74) the bearing of this subscription on Col. iv. 16 is emphasized, ἰδοὺ δὴ καὶ ἡ ἐκ Λαοδικείας. This identification has not been altogether without support in later times[1]. (β) The *First Epistle to the Thessalo-* 1 Thessa-*nians.* A final colophon in the Philoxenian Syriac asserts that it was lonians. 'written from Laodicea': and the same is stated in a later hand of d, 'scribens a Laodicea.' Again an Ethiopic MS, though giving Athens as the place of writing, adds that it was 'sent with Timotheus, *Tychicus*, and *Onesimus*[2].' This identification was perhaps suggested by the fact that 1 Thessalonians follows next after Colossians in the common order of St Paul's Epistles. (γ) The *Second Epistle to the Thessalonians.* In the 2 Thessa-Peshito (as given by Schaaf[3]) there is a final colophon stating that this lonians. epistle 'was written from Laodicea of Pisidia and was sent by the hand of Tychicus[3].' Though the addition of Pisidia wrongly defines the place as *Laodicea Combusta*, instead of *Laodicea ad Lycum*, yet the mention of the messenger's name shows plainly that the identification with the missing epistle of Col. iv. 16 was contemplated. So too the Memphitic 'per Silva-num et *Tychicum*', and a Latin prologue 'per Titum et *Onesimum*.' Again, an Ethiopic MS points to the same identification, though strangely confused in its statements. In the superscription we are told that this epistle was written when the Apostle was at Laodicea, but in the sub-scription that it 'was written at Athens to Laodicea and sent by Tychicus'; while the prolegomena state that it was written and left at Laodicea, and that afterwards, when St Paul wrote his letter to the Colossians from Rome, he gave directions that it should be transmitted to the Thessalonians by the Colossians[4]. (δ) The *Epistle to the Galatians*[5]. This might have Galatians. been chosen, partly because it affords no internal data for deciding where it was written, partly because like the Colossian Epistle it is directed against a form of Judaism, and the advocates of this hypothesis might not be careful to distinguish the two types, though very distinct in themselves. I find no support for it in the subscriptions, except the notice 'per *Tychi-cum*' in some Slavonic MSS.

The special difficulties attending this class of solutions are manifold. Objections (1) It does not appear that St Paul had ever been at Laodicea when he to these wrote the letter to the Colossians. (2) All the epistles thus singled out solutions. are separated from the Colossian letter by an interval of some years at least. (3) In every case they can with a high degree of probability be shown to have been written elsewhere than at Laodicea. Indeed, as St Paul had been long a prisoner either at Cæsarea or at Rome, when he wrote to Colossæ, he could not have despatched a letter recently from Laodicea.

---

[1] It is adopted by Erasmus in his paraphrase; 'vicissim vos legatis e-pistolam quæ Timotheo scripta fuit ex Laodicensium urbe': but in his commentary he does not commit him-self to it. For other names see Anger p. 17, note k.

[2] *Catal. Bibl. Bodl. Cod. Æthiop.* p. 23.

[3] In the editio princeps (Vienna 1555) the latter part of this colophon, 'and was sent by the hand of Tychi-cus,' is wanting.

[4] *Catal. Bibl. Bodl. Cod. Æthiop.* p. 23.

[5] Bloch, quoted in Anger p. 17, note l.

3. A letter to the Lao-diceans written by (a) St John. (b) A companion of St Paul. (c) St Paul.

3. Thus we are thrown back on some form of the solution which makes it a letter written *to the Laodiceans*. And here we may at once reject the hypothesis that the writer was (a) St John[1]. The First Epistle of St John, which has been selected, was written (as is allowed on all hands) much later than this date. Nor again does St Paul's language favour the alternative, which others have maintained, that the letter in question was written by (b) one of St Paul's companions, e.g. Epaphras or Luke[2]. The writer must therefore have been (c) St Paul himself.

On this assumption three alternatives offer themselves.

(i) A lost letter.

(i) We may suppose that the epistle in question has been lost. It has been pointed out elsewhere that the Apostle must have written many letters which are not preserved in our Canon[3]. Thus there is no *a priori* objection to this solution; and, being easy and obvious in itself, it has found common support in recent times. If therefore we had no positive reasons for identifying the Laodicean letter with one of the extant epistles of our Canon, we might at once close with this account of the matter. But such reasons do exist. And moreover, as we are obliged to suppose that at least three letters—the Epistles to the Colossians, to the Ephesians, and to Philemon—were despatched by St Paul to Asia Minor at the same time, it is best not to postulate a fourth, unless we are obliged to do so.

(ii) A Canonical epistle. (a) Hebrews. Philastrius.

(ii) But, if it was not a lost letter, with which of the Canonical Epistles of St Paul can we identify it with most probability? Was it

(a) *The Epistle to the Hebrews?* The supporters of this hypothesis are able to produce ancient evidence of a certain kind, though not such as carries any real weight. Philastrius, writing about the close of the fourth century, says that some persons ascribed the authorship of the Epistle to the Hebrews to Luke the Evangelist, and adds that it was asserted (apparently by these same persons, though this is not quite clear) to have been written to the Laodiceans[4]. Again in the Græco-Latin MS G of St Paul's

---

[1] A conjecture of Lightfoot (*Works* II. pp. 326, 339, London 1684), but he does not lay much stress on it. He offers it 'rather then conceive that any epistle of Paul is lost.' See also Anger p. 17, note m.

[2] Baumgarten *Comm.* ad loc., quoted by Anger p. 25, note g.

[3] *Philippians* p. 136 sq.

[4] *Hær.* lxxxix 'Sunt alii quoque qui epistolam Pauli ad Hebræos non adserunt esse ipsius, sed dicunt aut Barnabæ esse apostoli aut Clementis de urbe Roma episcopi; alii autem Lucæ evangelistæ aiunt epistolam etiam ad Laodicenses scriptam. Et quia addiderunt in ea quædam non bene sentientes, inde non legitur in ecclesia; et si legitur a quibusdam, non tamen in ecclesia legitur populo, nisi tredecim epistolæ ipsius, et ad

Hebræos interdum. Et in ea quia rhetorice scripsit, sermone plausibili, inde non putant esse ejusdem apostoli; et quia factum Christum dicit in ea [Heb. iii. 2], inde non legitur; de pœnitentia autem [Heb. vi. 4, x. 26] propter Novatianos æque. Cum ergo factum dicit Christum, corpore, non divinitate, dicit factum, cum doceat ibidem quod divinæ sit et paternæ substantiæ filius, *Qui est splendor gloriæ*, inquit, *et imago substantiæ ejus* [Heb. i. 3]' etc. Oehler punctuates the sentence with which we are concerned thus: 'alii autem Lucæ evangelistæ. Aiunt epistolam etiam ad Laodicenses scriptam,' and in his note he adds 'videlicet Pauli esse apostoli.' Thus he supposes the clause to refer to the apocryphal Epistle to the Laodiceans: and Fa-

Epistles, the *Codex Boernerianus*, probably written in the ninth century, after the Epistle to Philemon, which breaks off abruptly at ver. 20, a vacant space is left, as if for the conclusion of this epistle: and then follows a fresh title

ad	laudicenses	incipit	epistola
ΠΡΟС	ΛΑΟΥΔΑΚΗСΑС	ΑΡΧΕΤΑΙ	ΕΠΙСΤΟΛΗ

This is evidently intended as the heading to another epistle. No other epistle however succeeds, but the leaf containing this title is followed by several leaves, which were originally left blank, but were filled at a later date with extraneous matter. What then was this Epistle to the Laodiceans, which was intended to follow, but which the scribe was prevented from transcribing? As the Epistle to the Hebrews is not found in this MS, and as in the common order of the Pauline Epistles it would follow the Epistle to Philemon, the title has frequently been supposed to refer to it. This opinion however does not appear at all probable. Anger[1] indeed argues in its favour on the ground that in the companion MS F, the *Codex Augiensis*, which (so far as regards the Greek text) must have been derived immediately from the same archetype[2], the Epistle to the Hebrews does really follow. But what are the facts? It is plain that the Greek texts of G and F came from the same original: but it is equally plain that the two scribes had different Latin texts before them—that of G being the Old Latin, and that of F Jerome's revised Vulgate. No argument therefore derived from the Latin text holds good for the Greek. But the phenomena of both MSS alike[3] show that the Greek text of their common archetype ended abruptly at Philem. 20 (probably owing to the loss of the final leaves of the volume). The two scribes therefore were left severally to the resources of their respective Latin MSS. The scribe of F, whose Greek and Latin texts are in parallel columns, concluded the Epistle to Philemon in Latin, though he could not match it with its proper Greek; and after this he added the Epistle to the Hebrews in Latin, no longer however leaving a blank column, as he had done for the last few verses of Philemon. On the other hand the Latin text in G is interlinear, the Latin

bricius explains the notice similarly. Such a reference however would be quite out of place here. The whole paragraph before and after is taken up with discussing the Epistle to the Hebrews; and the interposition of just six words, referring to a wholly different matter, is inconceivable. We must therefore punctuate either 'alii autem Lucæ evangelistæ aiunt epistolam, etiam ad Laodicenses scriptam', or 'alii autem Lucæ evangelistæ aiunt; epistolam etiam ad Laodicenses scriptam.' In either case it will mean that some persons supposed the Epistle to the Hebrews to have been written to the Laodiceans.

[1] *Laodicenerbrief* p. 29 sq.

[2] If indeed the Greek text of F was not copied immediately from G, as maintained by Dr Hort in the *Journal of Philology* III. p. 67. The divergent phenomena of the two Latin texts seem to me unfavourable to this hypothesis; but it ought not to be hastily rejected.

[3] Volkmar, the editor of Credner's *Geschichte des Neutestamentlichen Kanon* p. 299, with strange carelessness speaks of 'the appearance (das Vorkommen) of the Laodicean Epistle in both the *Codices Augiensis* and *Boernerianus* which in other respects are closely allied.' There is no mention of it in the Codex Augiensis.

words being written above the Greek to interpret them.   When therefore
the Greek text came to an end, the scribe's work was done, for he could no
longer interlineate.   But he left a blank space for the remainder of Philemon, hoping doubtless hereafter to find a Greek MS from which he could
fill it in; and he likewise gave the title of the epistle which he found next
in his Latin copy, in Greek as well as in Latin.   The Greek title however
he had to supply for himself.   This is clear from the form, which shows it
to have been translated from the Latin by a person who had the very
smallest knowledge of Greek.   No Greek in the most barbarous age would
have written ΛΑΟΥΔΑΚΗСΑС for ΛΑΟΔΙΚΕΑС or ΛΑΟΔΙΚΗΝΟΥС.   The ΔΟΥ is
a Latin corruption *au* for *ao*, and the termination ΑС is a Latin's notion of
the Greek accusative.   Thus the whole word is a reproduction of the Latin

'The spu-
rious Lao-
dicean
Epistle
intended.

'Laudicenses,' the *en* being represented as usual by the Greek η[1].   If so,
we have only to ask what writing would probably appear as *Epistola ad
Laudicenses* in a Latin copy; and to this question there can be only one
answer.   The apocryphal Epistle to the Laodiceans occurs frequently in
the Latin Bibles, being found at least two or three centuries before the
MS G was written.   Though it does not usually follow the Epistle to
Philemon, yet its place varies very considerably in different Latin copies,
and an instance will be given below[2] where it actually occurs in this
position.

This iden-
tification
unsatis-
factory.

Thus beyond the notice in Philastrius there is no ancient support for
the identification of the missing letter of Col. iv. 16 with the Epistle
to the Hebrews; and doubtless the persons to whom Philastrius alludes
had no more authority for their opinion than their modern successors.
Critical conjecture, not historical tradition, led them to this result.
The theory therefore must stand or fall by its own merits.   It has
been maintained by one or two modern writers[3], chiefly on the ground of
some partial coincidences between the Epistles to the Hebrews and the
Colossians; but the general character and purport of the two is wholly
dissimilar, and they obviously deal with antagonists of a very different
type.   The insuperable difficulty of supposing that two epistles so unlike
in style were written by the same person to the same neighbourhood at
or about the same time would still remain, even though the Pauline
authorship of the Epistle to the Hebrews should be for a moment granted.

(β) Phile-
mon.

(β) The *Epistle to Philemon* has been strongly advocated by Wieseler[4],

---

[1] It is curious that this MS, which
was written by an Irish scribe, should
give the same corrupt form, Laud*ac*-
for Laod*ac*-, which we find in the
Book of Armagh; see below, p. 282.

[2] See p. 286.   It occurs also in this
position in the list of Aelfric (see below
p. 362), where the order of the Pauline
Epistles is ... Col., Hebr., 1, 2 Tim.,
Tit., Philem., Laod.

[3] See especially Schneckenburger
Beiträge p. 153 sq.

[4] Some earlier writers who main-

tained this view are mentioned by
Anger, p. 25, note f.   It has since been
more fully developed and more vigor-
ously urged by Wieseler, first in a
programme *Commentat. de Epist. Lao-
dicena quam vulgo perditam putant*
1844, and afterwards in his well-known
work *Chronol. des Apostol. Zeit.* p.
405 sq.   It may therefore be identified with his name.   He speaks of it
with much confidence as 'scarcely
open to a doubt,' but he has not
succeeded in convincing others.

as the letter to which St Paul refers in this passage. For this identification it is necessary to establish two points; (1) that Philemon lived not at Colossae, but at Laodicea; and (2) that the letter is addressed not to a private individual, but to a whole church. For the first point there is something to be said. Though for reasons explained elsewhere the abode of Philemon himself appears to have been at Colossæ, wherever Archippus may have resided[1], still two opinions may very fairly be held on this point. But Wieseler's arguments entirely fail to establish his other position. The theme, the treatment, the whole tenour of the letter, mark it as private: and the mere fact that the Apostle's courtesy leads him to include in the opening salutation the Christians who met at Philemon's house is powerless to change its character. Why should a letter, containing such intimate confidences, be read publicly in the Church, not only at Laodicea but at Colossæ, by the express order of the Apostle? The tact and delicacy of the Apostle's pleading for Onesimus would be nullified at one stroke by the demand for publication. *This epistle does not answer the conditions.*

(γ) But may we not identify the letter in question with the *Epistle to the Ephesians*, which also is known to have been despatched at the same time with the Epistle to the Colossians? Unlike the Epistle to Philemon, it was addressed not to a private person but to a church or churches. If therefore it can be shown that the Laodiceans were the recipients, either alone or with others, we have found the object of our search. The arguments in favour of this solution are reserved for the introduction to that epistle. Meanwhile it is sufficient to say that educated opinion is tending, though slowly, in this direction, and to express the belief that ultimately this view will be generally received[2]. *(γ) Ephesians. This is the true solution.*

(iii) Another wholly different identification remains to be mentioned. It was neither a lost epistle nor a Canonical epistle, thought some, but the writing which is extant under the title of the 'Epistle to the Laodiceans,' though not generally received by the Church. Of the various opinions held respecting this apocryphal letter I shall have to speak presently. It is sufficient here to say that the advocates of its genuineness fall into two classes. Either they assign to it a place in the Canon with the other Epistles of St Paul, or they acquiesce in its exclusion, holding that the Church has authority to pronounce for or against the canonicity even of Apostolic writings. *(iii) The extant uncanonical Epistle to the Laodiceans.*

The apocryphal Epistle to the Laodiceans is a cento of Pauline phrases strung together without any definite connexion or any clear object. They are taken chiefly from the Epistle to the Philippians, but here and there one is borrowed elsewhere, e.g. from the Epistle to the Galatians. Of course it closes with an injunction to the Laodiceans to exchange epistles with the Colossians. The Apostle's injunction in Col. iv. 16 suggested the forgery, and such currency as it ever attained was due to the support which that passage was supposed to give to it. Unlike most forgeries, it had no ulterior aim. It was not framed to advance any *General character of the spurious epistle.*

---

[1] See the introduction to the Epistle to Philemon.
[2] See above p. 37.

particular opinions, whether heterodox or orthodox. It has no doctrinal peculiarities. Thus it is quite harmless, so far as falsity and stupidity combined can ever be regarded as harmless.

Among the more important MSS which contain this epistle are the following. The letters in brackets [ ] give the designations adopted in the apparatus of various readings which follows.

1. *Fuldensis* [F]. The famous MS of the Vulgate N. T. written for Victor Bishop of Capua, by whom it was read and corrected in the years 546, 547; edited by Ern. Ranke, *Marburgi et Lipsiae* 1868. The Laodicean Epistle occurs between Col. and 1 Tim. without any indication of doubtful authenticity, except that it has no argument or table of contents, like the other epistles. The scribe however has erroneously interpolated part of the argument belonging to 1 Tim. between the title and the epistle; see p. 291 sq. of Ranke's edition.

2. *Cavensis*. A MS of the whole Latin Bible, at the Monastery of La Cava near Salerno, ascribed to the 6th or 7th or 8th century. See Vercellone *Var. Lect. Vulg. Lat. Bibl.* I. p. lxxxviii. Unfortunately we have no account of the readings in the Laodicean Epistle (for which it would be the most important authority after the Codex Fuldensis), except the last sentence quoted by Mai *Nov. Patr. Bibl.* I. 2. p. 63, 'Et facite legi Colossensium vobis.' Laod. here occurs between Col. and 1 Thess. (Mai p. 62). Dr Westcott (Smith's *Dict. of the Bible* s. v. *Vulgate*, p. 1713) has remarked that the two oldest authorities for the interpolation of the three heavenly witnesses in 1 Joh. v. 7, this La Cava MS and the *Speculum* published by Mai, also support the Laodicean Epistle (see Mai l. c. pp. 7, 62 sq.). The two phenomena are combined in another very ancient MS, Brit. Mus. *Add.* 11,852, described below.

3. *Armachanus* [A]. A MS of the N. T., now belonging to Trinity College, Dublin, and known as the 'Book of Armagh.' It was written in the year 807, as ascertained by Bp. Graves; see the *Proceedings of the Royal Irish Academy* III. pp. 316, 356. The Laodicean Epistle follows Colossians on fol. 138, but with the warning that Jerome denies its genuineness. The text of the Laodicean Epistle in this MS is not so pure as might have been anticipated from its antiquity. I owe the collation of readings which is given below to the kindness of Dr Reeves, who is engaged in editing the MS.

4. *Darmstadiensis* [D]. A fol. MS of the whole Bible, defective from Apoc. xxii. 12 to the end, now in the Grand-ducal library at Darmstadt, but formerly belonging to the Cathedral Library at Cologne; presented by Hermann Pius, Archbishop of Cologne from A.D. 890—925. Laod. follows Col. A collation was made for Anger, from whom (p. 144) this account is taken.

5. *Bernensis* no. 334 [B]. A 4to MS of miscellaneous contents, ending with the Pauline Epistles, the last being the Epistle to the Laodiceans; written in the 9th cent. The Laodicean Epistle is a fragment, ending with 'Gaudete in Christo et praecavete sordibus in lucro' (ver. 13). This account is taken by Anger from Sinner *Catal. Cod. MSS. Bibl. Bern.* I. p. 28. In his Addenda (p. 179) Anger gives a collation of this MS.

6. *Toletanus* [T]. A MS of the Latin Bible belonging to the Cathedral Library at Toledo, and written ab   ʰe 8th century: see Westcott in Smith's

Dict. of the Bible, s. v. *Vulgate* p. 1710, Vercellone *Var. Lect.* I. p. lxxxiv. sq. The readings in the Laodicean Epistle are taken from the copy of Palomares given in Bianchini *Vind. Canon. Script. Vulg. Lat. Edit.* p. cxcv (Romae, 1740). In my first edition I had followed Joh. Mariana *Schol. in Vet. et Nov. Test.* p. 831 (Paris, 1620), where also this epistle is printed in full from the Toledo MS. The two differ widely, and the copy of Mariana is obviously very inaccurate. Anger (see p. 144) does not mention Bianchini's copy. In this MS Laod. follows Col.

7. *Parisiensis* Reg. Lat. 3 (formerly 3562)[1] [P₁]. A Latin Bible, in one volume fol., called after Anowarctha by whom it was given to the monastery of Glanfeuille (St Maur), and ascribed in the printed Catalogue to the 9th cent. Laod. follows Col. on fol. 379.

8. *Parisiensis* Reg. Lat. 6 [P₂]. A MS of the Latin Bible in 4 vols. fol., according to the Catalogue probably written in the 10th cent. [?]. It belonged formerly to the Duc de Noailles. Laod. follows Col. It contains numerous corrections in a later hand either between the lines or in the margin. The two hands are distinguished as P_2^*, P_2^{**}.

9. *Parisiensis* Reg. Lat. 250 (formerly 3572) [P₃]. A fol. MS of the N. T., described in the Catalogue as probably belonging to the end of the 9th cent. Laod. follows Col. It has a few corrections in a later hand. The two hands are distinguished as P_3^*, P_3^{**}.

These three Parisian MSS I collated myself, but I had not time to examine them as carefully as I could have wished.

10. *Brit. Mus.* Add. 11,852 [G]. An important MS of St Paul's Epistles written in the 9th cent. It formerly belonged to the monastery of St Gall, being one of the books with which the library there was enriched by Hartmot who was Abbot from A.D. 872 to 884 or 885. Laod. follows Heb. and has no capitula like the other epistles.

11. *Brit. Mus.* Add. 10,546 [C]. A fol. MS of the Vulgate, commonly known as 'Charlemagne's Bible,' but probably belonging to the age of Charles the Bald († 877). Laod. stands between Heb. and Apoc. It has no argument or capitula.

12. *Brit. Mus.* Reg. I. E. vii, viii [R]. An English MS of the Latin Bible from Christ Church, Canterbury, written about the middle of the 10th cent. Laod. follows Heb. This is the most ancient MS, so far as I am aware, in which the epistle has capitulations. It is here given in its fullest form, and thus presents the earliest example of what may be called the modern recension.

13. *Brit. Mus.* Harl. 2833, 2834 [H₁]. A MS of the 13th cent. written for the Cathedral of Angers. Laod. follows Apoc.

The readings of the four preceding MSS are taken from the collations in Westcott *Canon* Appx. E p. 572 sq. (ed. 4).

14. *Brit. Mus.* Harl. 3131 [H₂]. A smallish 4to of the 12th cent., said to be of German origin, with marginal and interlinear glosses in some parts. Laod. stands between Philem. and Heb. It has no heading but only a red initial letter P. At the end is 'Expl. Epla ad Laodicenses. Prologus ad Ebreos.'

---

[1] So at least I find the number given in my notes. But in *Bentl. Crit. Sacr.* p. xxxvii it is 3561.

15. *Brit. Mus.* Sloane 539 [S]. A small fol. of the 12th cent., said to be German. It contains St Paul's Epistles with glosses. The gloss on Col. iv. 16 'et ea quae est Laodicensium etc.' runs 'quam ego eis misi ut ipsi michi ut videatis hic esse responsum.' Laod. follows Heb., and has no glosses.

The two last MSS I collated myself.

16. *Bodl.* Laud. Lat. 13 (formerly 810) [L₁]. A 4to MS in double columns of the 13th cent. containing the Latin Bible. See *Catal. Bibl. Laud. Cod. Lat.* p. 10. Laod. follows Col. Notwithstanding the date of the MS, it gives a very ancient text of this epistle.

17. *Bodl.* Laud. Lat. 8 (formerly 757) [L₂]. A fol. MS of the Latin Bible, belonging to the end of the 12th cent. See *Catal. Bibl. Laud. Cod. Lat.* p. 9. This is the same MS, which Anger describes (p. 145) as 115 C (its original mark), and of which he gives a collation. Laod. stands between 2 Thess. and 1 Tim.

I am indebted for collations of these two Laudian MSS to the kindness of the Rev. J. Wordsworth, Fellow of Brasenose College.

18. *Vindob.* 287 [V]. The Pauline Epp., written by Marianus Scotus (i.e. the Irishman), A.D. 1079. See Alter *Nov. Test. ad Cod. Vindob. Graece Expressum* II. p. 1040 sq., Denis *Cod. MSS Lat. Bibl. Vindob.* I. no. lviii, Zeuss *Grammatica Celtica* p. xviii (ed. 2). The Epistle to the Laodiceans is transcribed from this MS by Alter l. c. p. 1067 sq. It follows Col.

19. *Trin. Coll. Cantabr.* B. 5. 1 [X]. A fol. MS of the Latin Bible, written probably in the 12th century. Laod. follows Col. I have given a collation of this MS, because (like Brit. Mus. Reg. I. E. viii) it is an early example of the completed form. The epistle is preceded by capitula, as follows.

INCIPIUNT CAPITULA EPISTOLE AD LAODICENSES.

1. Paulus apostolus pro Laodicensibus domino gratias refert et hortatur eos ne a seductoribus decipiantur.

2. De manifestis vinculis apostoli in quibus letatur et gaudet.

3. Monet Laodicenses apostolus ut sicut sui audierunt praesentia ita retineant et sine retractu faciant.

4. Hortatur apostolus Laodicenses ut fide sint firmi et quae integra et vera et deo placita sunt faciant. et salutatio fratrum. EXPLICIUNT CAPITULA. INCIPIT EPISTOLA BEATI PAULI APOSTOLI AD LAODICENSES.

These capitulations may be compared with those given by Dr Westcott from Reg. I. E. viii, with which they are nearly identical.

Besides these nineteen MSS, of which (with the exception of *Carensis*) collations are given below, it may be worth while recording the following, as containing this epistle.

Among the Lambeth MSS are (i) no. 4, large folio, 12th or 13th cent. Laod. stands between Col. and 1 Thess. (ii) no. 90, small folio, 13th or 14th cent. Laod. stands between Col. and 1 Thess. without title or heading of any kind. Apparently a good text. (iii) no. 348, 4to, 15th cent. Laod. stands between Col. and 1 Thess., without heading etc. (iv) no. 544, 8vo, 15th cent. Laod. stands between Col. and 1 Thess., without heading etc. (v) no. 1152, 4to, 13th or 14th cent. Laod. occupies the same position as in the four preceding MSS and has no heading or title. The first and last of these five MSS are collated by Dr Westcott (*Canon* p. 572 sq.). I inspected them all.

In the Bodleian Library at Oxford, belonging to the Canonici collection, are (i) Canon. Bibl. 82 (see *Catal.* p. 277), very small 4to, 13th cent., containing parts of the N. T. St Paul's Epp. are at the end of the volume, following Apoc. Laod. intervenes between Tit. and Philem., beginning 'Explicit epistola ad titum. Incipit ad laud.', and ending ' Explicit epistola ad laudicenses. Incipit ad phylemonem'. (ii) Canon. Bibl. 7 (see *Catal.* p. 251), small 4to, beginning of 14th cent., containing Evv., Acts, Cath. Epp., Apoc., Paul. Epp. Laod. is at the end. (iii) Canon. Bibl. 16 (*Catal.* p. 256), small 4to, containing the N. T., 15th cent., written by the hand 'Stephani de Tautaldis'. Laod. follows Col. (iv) Canon. Bibl. 25 (*Catal.* p. 258), very small 4to, mutilated, early part of the 15th cent. It contains a part of St Paul's Epp. (beginning in the middle of Gal.) and the Apocalypse. Laod. follows Col. For information respecting these MSS I am indebted to the Rev. J. Wordsworth.

In the University Library, Cambridge, I have observed the Epistle to the Laodiceans in the following MSS. (i) Dd. 5. 52 (see *Catal.* I. p. 273), 4to, double columns, 14th cent. Laod. is between Col. and 1 Thess. (ii) Ee. I. 9 (see *Catal.* II. p. 10), 4to, double columns, very small neat hand, 15th cent. It belonged to St Alban's. Laod. is between Col. and 1 Thess. (iii) Mm. 3. 2 (see *Catal.* IV. p. 174), fol., Latin Bible, double columns, 13th cent. Laod. is between Col. and 1 Thess., but the heading is ' Explicit epistola ad Colocenses, et hic incipit ad Thesalocenses', after which Laod. follows immediately. At the top of the page is 'Ad Laudonenses'. (iv) Ee. I. 16 (see *Catal.* II. p. 16), 4to, double columns, Latin Bible, 13th or 14th cent. The order of the N. T. is Evv., Acts, Cath. Epp., Paul. Epp., Apoc. Here Laod. is between Heb. and Rev.; it is treated like the other books, except that it has no prologue.

In the College Libraries at Cambridge I have accidentally noticed the following MSS as containing the epistle; for I have not undertaken any systematic search. (i) St Peter's, O. 4. 6, fol., 2 columns, 13th cent., Latin Bible. The order of the N. T. is Evv., Acts, Cath. Epp., Paul Epp., Apoc. The Epistle to the Laodiceans is between Heb. and Apoc. (ii) Sidney Δ. 5. 11, fol., 2 columns, Latin Bible, 13th cent. The order of the N. T. is Evv., Paul. Epp., Acts, Cath. Epp., Apoc.; and Laod. is between 2 Thess. and 1 Tim. (iii) Emman. 2. 1. 6, large fol., Latin Bible, early 14th cent. The order of the N. T. is different from the last, being Evv., Acts, Cath. Epp., Paul. Epp., Apoc.; but Laod. is in the same position, between 2 Thess. and 1 Tim.

Notice of a few other MSS, in which this epistle occurs, will be found in Hody *de Bibl. Text. Orig.* p. 664, and in Anger p. 145 sq.

This list, slight and partial as it is, will serve to show the wide circulation of the Laodicean Epistle. At the same time it will have been observed that its position varies very considerably in different copies.

(i) The most common position is immediately after Colossians, as the notice in Col. iv. 16 would suggest. This is its place in the most ancient authorities, e. g. the Fulda, La Cava, and Toledo MSS, and the Book of Armagh.

(ii) Another position is after 2 Thess. So Laud. Lat. 8, Sidn. Δ. 5. 11, Emman. 2. 1. 6: see also MSS in Hody *Bibl. Text. Orig.* p. 664. It must be remembered that in the Latin Bibles the Epistles to the Thessalonians sometimes precede and sometimes follow the Epistle to the Colossians. Hence we get three arrangements in different MSS; (1) 1, 2 Thess., Col. Laod.; (2) Col., Laod., 1, 2 Thess.; (3) Col., 1, 2 Thess., Laod.

(iii) It occurs at least in one instance between Titus and Philemon; Oxon. Bodl. Canon. 82. Mai also (*Nov. Patr. Bibl.* 1. 2. p. 63) mentions a 'very ancient MS', in which it stands between Titus and 1 John; but he does not say how Titus and 1 John appear in such close neighbourhood.

(iv) Again it follows Philemon in Brit. Mus. Harl. 3131. This also must have been its position in the Latin MS which the scribe of the Codex Boernerianus had before him: see above p. 280.

(v) Another and somewhat common position is after Hebrews; e.g. Brit. Mus. Add. 11,852, Add. 10,546, Reg. 1. E. viii, Sloane 539, Camb. Univ. Ee. 1. 16, Pet. O. 4. 6. See also Hody l. c.

(vi) It is frequently placed at the end of the New Testament, and so after the Apocalypse when the Apocalypse comes last, e.g. Harl. 2833. Sometimes the Pauline Epistles follow the Apocalypse, so that Laod. occurs at the end at once of the Pauline Epistles and of the N. T.; e.g. Bodl. Canon. Lat. 7.

Other exceptional positions, e.g. after Galatians or after 3 John, are found in versions and printed texts (see Anger p. 143); but no authority of Latin MSS is quoted for them.

The *Codex Fuldensis*, besides being the oldest MS, is also by far the most trustworthy. In some instances indeed a true reading may be preserved in later MSS, where it has a false one; but such cases are rare. The text however was already corrupt in several places at this time; and the variations in the later MSS are most frequently attempts of the scribes to render it intelligible by alteration or amplification. Such for instance is the case with the mutilated reading 'quod est' (ver. 13), which is amplified, even as early as the Book of Armagh, into 'quodcunque optimum est', though there can be little doubt that the expression represents τὸ λοιπόν of Phil. iii. 2, and the missing word therefore is 'reliquum'. The greatest contrast to F is presented by such MSS as RX, where the epistle has not only been filled out to the amplest proportions, but also supplied with a complete set of capitulations like the Canonical books. Though for this reason these two MSS have no great value, yet they are interesting as being among the oldest which give the amplified text, and I have therefore added a collation of them. On the other hand some much later MSS, especially L₁, preserve a very ancient text, which closely resembles that of F.[1]

[1] The epistle has been critically edited by Anger *Laodicenerbrief* p. 155 sq. and Westcott *Canon* App. E. p. 572. I have already expressed my obligations to both these writers for their collations of MSS.

In the apparatus of various readings, which is subjoined to the epistle, I have not attempted to give such minute differences of spelling as *e* and *ae*, or *c* and *t* (*Laodicia*, *Laoditia*), nor is the punctuation of the MSS noted.

AD LAODICENSES.

PAULUS Apostolus non ab hominibus neque per hominem sed per Text of the
Ihesum Christum, fratribus qui sunt Laodiciae. [2] Gratia vobis et pax epistle.
a Deo patre et Domino Ihesu Christo.

[3] Gratias ago Christo per omnem orationem meam, quod permanentes estis in eo et perseverantes in operibus eius, promissum expectantes in diem iudicii. [4] Neque destituant vos quorundam vanilo-
quia insinuantium, ut vos avertant a veritate evangelii quod a me
praedicatur. [5] Et nunc faciet Deus ut qui sunt ex me ad profectum
veritatis evangelii deservientes et facientes benignitatem operum quae
salutis vitae aeternae.

[6] Et nunc palam sunt vincula mea quae patior in Christo; quibus

Inc. ad laodicenses F; Incipit epistola ad laodicenses (laudicenses P$_2$R)
BDTP$_1$P$_2$P$_3$CRH$_2$SV; Epistola ad laodicenses M (*if this heading be not due to the
editor*); Incipit epistola pauli ad laodicenses GH$_1$; Incipit epistola beati pauli
ad laodicenses X; Incipit aepistola ad laudicenses sed hirunimus eam negat
esse pauli A: *no heading in* L$_1$L$_2$H$_2$.

apostolus] *om.* TM. hominibus] homine G. ihesum christum] christum
ihesum T. christum] *add.* 'et deum patrem omnipotentem qui suscitavit eum
a mortuis' RX. fratribus qui sunt] his qui sunt fratribus A. *For* fratribus
B *has* fratres. laodiciae] laudociae T; ladoicie L; laudaciae A; laudiciae R;
laodiceae B.

2. patre] et patre nostro L$_1$; patre nostro H$_1$H$_2$SM; nostro A. domino]
add. nostro P$_2$P$_3$RGL$_2$.

3. christo] deo meo DP$_1$P$_2$P$_3$CL$_1$; deo meo et christo ihesu RX. meam]
memoriam M. permanentes estis] estis permanentes AGR. in operibus
eius] in operibus bonis H$_1$H$_2$S; *om.* BDTP$_1$P$_2$P$_3$CM. promissum expectantes]
promissum spectantes T; et promissum expectantes M; promissionem expectantes V; sperantes promissionem AG; sperantes promissum RX. diem] die
BTDP$_1$P$_3$GCRH$_1$H$_2$SL$_1$VMX. iudicii] iudicationis GRX.

4. neque] *add.* enim R. destituant] distituant A; destituunt H$_1$;
destituat M, Spec.; destituit DTP$_1$P$_3$CM; distituit B; destitui P$_2$. vaniloquia]
vaniloquentia BDTP$_1$P$_2$P$_3$GCVM; vaneloquentia, Spec. insinuantium]
insinuantium se GM; insanientium H$_1$S. ut] sed ut BAT; sed peto ne R;
seductorem ne X. avertant] Spec.; evertant FTML$_2$; evertent B. evangelii]
aevanguelii A (*and so below*).

5. et nunc...veritatis evangelii] *om.* L. faciet deus] deus faciet AG.
ut] *add.* sint G. qui] que (*altered from* qui) P$_3$* (*or* P$_3$**). me] *add.* perveniant TM; *add.* proficiant V. ad profectum] imperfectum A; ad perfectum
R; in profectum G. veritatis evangelii] evangelii veritatis V. deservientes]
add. sint P$_2$**P$_3$**H$_1$H$_2$S. *For* deservientes RX *have* dei servientes. et faci-
entes] *repeated in* L$_1$. operum] eorum RX; operam T; opera L$_2$. quae]
om. M; *add.* sunt AP$_2$**GCRH$_1$H$_2$SVX. *It is impossible to say in many cases
whether a scribe intended* operum quae *or* operumque. *Ranke prints* operumque *in* F. salutis] *add.* L$_1$.

6. nunc] nō=non L$_2$. palam sunt] sunt palam G; sunt (*om.* palam) A.

Text of the   laetor et gaudeo.   [7] Et hoc mihi est ad salutem perpetuam ; quod
epistle.   ipsum factum orationibus vestris et administrante Spiritu sancto,
sive per vitam sive per mortem.   [8] Est enim mihi vivere in Christo
et mori gaudium.   [9] Et id ipsum in vobis faciet misericordia sua, ut
eandem dilectionem habeatis et sitis unianimes.

     [10] Ergo, dilectissimi, ut audistis praesentia mei, ita retinete et facite
in timore Dei, et erit vobis vita in aeternum : [11] Est enim Deus qui
operatur in vos.   [12] Et facite sine retractu quaecumque facitis.

     [13] Et quod est [reliquum], dilectissimi, gaudete in Christo ; et prae-
cavete sordidos in lucro.   [14] Omnes sint petitiones vestrae palam apud
Deum ; et estote firmi in sensu Christi.   [15] Et quae integra et vera et

Christo]   add. Ihesu (iesu) DP₁P₂P₃CVX.   quibus] in quibus TRMP₂.
et] ut C.

    7.   mihi] michi H₁S (*and so below*); enim (*for* mihi) M.   factum] fletum
TL₂M; factum est P₃**H₁S.   orationibus] operationibus B.   vestris] meis
DP₁.   et] est TM: *om.* GRL₁X.   administrante spiritu sancto] adminis-
trantem (*or* ad ministrantem) spiritum sanctum FBTL₂; amministrante
spiritum sanctum DCP₁P₂* (*but there is an erasure in* P₁). *For* administrante
L₁X *have* amministrante; *and for* spiritu sancto G *transposes and reads* sancto
spiritu.   per mortem] mortem (*om.* per) H₁.

    8.   mihi] *om.* M.   vivere] vivere vita DTP₁P₂P₃CVH₁H₂S; vere vita
FL₁RMX; vera vita B; vere (*altered into* vivere *prima manu*) vita L₂.   gaudium]
lucrum et gaudium A; gaudium ut lucrum H₂P₂**; gaudium vel lucrum H₁S.

    9.   et] qui V.   id ipsum] in ipsum FBL₂; in idipsum L₁V; ipsum TP₂GM;
ipse AH₁H₂SRX.   in vobis] vobis P₂; in nobis H₂.   misericordia sua]
misericordiam suam FBDAP₁P₂P₃CH₁H₂RSVL₁L₂X (*but written* misericordia
suā *in several cases*).   et] *om.* L₁; ut V.   unianimes] unanimes BDTP₁
P₂P₃GCH₁RL₁L₂VMSX.

    10.   ergo] ego H₂.   ut] et L₂.   praesentia mei] praesentiam ei DP ;
praesentiam mei T; praesentiam G**; in praesentia mei P₃**; praesentiam
mihi M; presenciam eius L₂; praesentiam dei A; præsentiam domini (dnī)
P₂**H₁H₂S.   ita] *om.* DP₁P₂**P₃CX.   retinete] retinere A.   in] cum TM;
om. B.   timore] timorem AB.   dei] domini H₁S.   vita] pax et vita RX.
in aeternum] in aeterno A; in aeterna G*; aeterna (eterna) G**PL₁.

    11.   enim] *om.* B.   vos] vobis GATH₁H₂SRVP₂** (*or* P₂*) P₃**MX.

    12.   retractu] retractatu BP₂RL₂; retractatione AGV; tractu T; reatu H₁S.
In P₂** ut peccato *is added; in* H₂ t peccato.   quaecumque] quodcumque
TM.

    13.   quod est reliquum] quod est FBTDP₁P₂*P₃*RCL₁L₂MX; quod est opti-
mum GH₁H₂SV; quodcunque optimum est A; quodcunque est obtimum
P₂**; quod bonum est P₃**: see p. 290.   dilectissimi] dilectissime B.   christo]
domino DP₁P₂P₃CX.   sordidos] add. omnes P₂**H₁H₂S; add. homines A.
in] ut L₁.   lucro] lucrum RX.

    14.   omnes] in omnibus G; homines (*attached to the preceding sentence*)
TM.   petitiones] petiones T.   sint] *omitted here and placed after* palam
H₁S.   apud] aput F; ante AG.   deum] dominum A.   estote] stote T.
firmi in sensu christi] sensu firmi in christo ihesu R.

    15.   quae] *add.* sunt R.   integra] intigra A.   vera] *add.* sunt DP₁P₂P₂

pudica et iusta et amabilia, facite. ^{16} Et quae audistis et accepistis in
corde retinete ; et erit vobis pax.

^{18} Salutant vos sancti.

^{19} Gratia Domini Ihesu cum spiritu vestro.

^{20} Et facite legi Colosensibus et Colosensium vobis.

CVX. pudica et iusta] iusta et pudica R. iusta] iusta et casta AGV;
casta et iusta P$_2$**H$_1$H$_2$S. amabilia] add. sunt TH$_1$H$_2$SM ; add. et sancta
RX.

16. audistis] add. et vidistis L$_2$. accepistis] accipistis A. pax] add.
ver. 17, salutate omnes fratres (sanctos for fratres GV) in osculo sancto AGP$_2$**
H$_1$H$_2$SRVX.

18. sancti] omnes sancti AGRH$_1$SVX; sancti omnes H$_2$; add. in christo
ihesu RX.

19. dcmini ihesu] domini nostri ihesu (iesu) christi DTAP$_1$P$_2$P$_3$GCH$_1$H$_2$S
VMRX.

20. et] add. hanc H$_1$H$_2$SP$_2$**. legi] add. epistolam L$_1$P$_3$**. colosensibus et] om. FTDP$_1$P$_2$*P$_3$CVL$_1$L$_2$. They are also omitted in the La Cava MS;
see above p. 282. colosensium] add. epistolam L$_2$. The words colosensibus,
colosensium, are commonly written with a single s, more especially in the oldest
MSS. In L$_1$ the form is cholosensium.

The last sentence et facite etc. is entirely omitted in M. In RX it is ex-
panded into et facite legi colosensibus hanc epistolam et colosensium (colosensibus R) vos legite. deus autem et pater domini nostri ihesu christi custodiat
vos immaculatos in christo ihesu cui est honor et gloria in secula seculorum.
amen.

Subscriptions. Explicit P$_2$P$_3$H$_1$; Exp. ad laodicenses F; Explicit epistola
ad laodicenses (laudicenses R) DP$_1$GCH$_2$SRVX; Finis T. There is no subscription in AL$_1$L$_2$, and none is given for M.

The following notes are added for the sake of elucidating one or two
points of difficulty in the text or interpretation of the epistle.

4 Neque] This is the passage quoted in the Speculum § 50 published by
Mai Nov. Patr. Bibl. I. 2. p. 62 sq., 'Item ad Laodicenses: Neque destituat
vos quorundam vaneloquentia (sic) insinuantium, ut vos avertant a veritate
evangelii quod a me praedicatur'. We ought possibly to adopt the reading
'destituat...vaniloquentia' of this and other old MSS in preference to the
'destituant...vaniloquia' of F. 'Vaniloquium' however is the rendering of
ματαιολογία 1 Tim. i. 6, and is supported by such analogies as inaniloquium,
maliloquium, multiloquium, stultiloquium, etc.; see Hagen Sprachl. Erörter.
zur Vulgata p. 74, Roensch Das Neue Testament Tertullians p. 710.

destituant] Properly 'leave in the lurch' and so 'cheat', 'beguile', e.g.
Cic. pro Rosc. Am. 40 'induxit, decepit, destituit, adversariis tradidit, omni
fraude et perfidia fefellit.' In Heb. ix. 26 εἰς ἀθέτησιν τῆς ἁμαρτίας is translated 'ad destitutionem peccati'. The original here may have been ἐξαπατήσωσιν or ἀθετήσωσιν. insinuantium] In late Latin this word means
little more than 'to communicate', 'to inculcate', 'to teach': see the references in Roensch Itala u. Vulgata p. 387, Heumann-Hesse Handlexicon
des römischen Rechts s. v., Ducange Glossarium s. v. So too 'insinuator'
Tertull. ad Nat. ii. 1, 'insinuatrix' August. Ep. 110 (II. p. 317). In Acts
xvii. 3 it is the rendering of παρατιθέμενος.

5 ut qui sunt etc.] The passage, as it stands, is obviously corrupt; and a comparison with Phil. i. 12 τὰ κατ᾽ ἐμὲ μᾶλλον εἰς προκοπὴν τοῦ εὐαγγελίου ἐλήλυθεν seems to reveal the nature of the corruption. (1) For 'qui' we should probably read 'quae', which indeed is found in some late MSS of no authority. (2) There is a lacuna somewhere in the sentence, probably after 'evangelii'. The original therefore would run in this form 'ut quae sunt ex me ad profectum veritatis [eveniant]...deservientes etc.', the participles belonging to a separate sentence of which the beginning is lost. The suppleménts 'perveniant', 'proficiant', found in some MSS give the right sense, though perhaps they are conjectural. The Vulgate of Phil. i. 12 is 'quae circa me sunt magis ad profectum venerunt evangelii'. In the latter part of the verse it is impossible in many cases to say whether a MS intends 'operum quae' or 'operumque'; but the former is probably correct, as representing ἔργων τῶν τῆς σωτηρίας: unless indeed this sentence also is corrupt or mutilated.

7 administrante etc.] Considering the diversity of readings here, we may perhaps venture on the emendation 'administratione spiritus sancti', as this more closely resembles the passage on which our text is founded, Phil. i. 19 διὰ τῆς ὑμῶν δεήσεως καὶ ἐπιχορηγίας τοῦ πνεύματος κ.τ.λ.

12 retractu] 'wavering', 'hesitation'. For this sense of 'retractare', 'to rehandle, discuss', and so 'to question, hesitate', and even 'to shirk', 'decline', see Oehler *Tertullian*, index p. cxciii, Roensch *N. T. Tertullians* p. 669, Ducange *Glossarium* s. v.: comp. e.g. Iren. v. 11. 1 'ne relinqueretur quaestio his qui infideliter retractant de eo'. So 'retractator' is equivalent to 'detractator' in Tert. *de Jejun.* 15 'retractatores hujus officii' (see Oehler's note); and in 1 Sam. xiv. 39 'absque retractatione morietur' is the rendering of 'dying he shall die', θανάτῳ ἀποθανεῖται. Here the expression probably represents χωρὶς...διαλογισμῶν of Phil. ii. 14, which in the Old Latin is 'sine...detractionibus'. All three forms occur, retractus (Tert. *Scorp.* 1), retractatus (Tert. *Apol.* 4, *adv. Marc.* i. 1, v. 3, *adv. Prax.* 2, and frequently), retractatio (Cic. *Tusc.* v. 29, 'sine retractatione' and so frequently; 1 Sam. l. c.). Here 'retractus' must be preferred, both as being the least common form and as having the highest MS authority. In Tert. *Scorp.* 1 however it is not used in this same sense.

13 quod est reliquum] I have already spoken of this passage, p. 286, and shall have to speak of it again, p. 291. The oldest and most trustworthy MSS have simply 'quod est'. The word 'reliquum' must be supplied, as Anger truly discerned (p. 163); for the passage is taken from Phil. iii. 1 τὸ λοιπόν, ἀδελφοί μου, χαίρετε ἐν Κυρίῳ. See the Vulgate translation of τὸ λοιπόν in 1 Cor. vii. 29. Later and less trustworthy authorities supply 'optimum' or 'bonum'.

14 in sensu Christi] *'in the mind of Christ'*: for in 1 Cor. ii. 16 νοῦν Χριστοῦ is rendered 'sensum Christi'.

20 facite legi etc.] Though the words 'Colosensibus et' are wanting in very many of the authorities which are elsewhere most trustworthy, yet I have felt justified in retaining them with other respectable copies, because (1) The homœoteleuton would account for their omission even in very ancient MSS; (2) The parallelism with Col. iv. 16 requires their insertion; (3) The insertion is not like the device of a Latin scribe, who would hardly

have manipulated the sentence into a form which savours so strongly of a Greek original.

It is the general, though not universal, opinion that this epistle was altogether a forgery of the Western Church[1]; and consequently that the Latin is not a translation from a lost Greek original, but preserves the earliest form of the epistle. Though the forgery doubtless attained its widest circulation in the West, there are, I venture to think, strong reasons for dissenting from this opinion. *Theory of a Greek original discussed.*

If we read the epistle in its most authentic form, divested of the additions contributed by the later MSS, we are struck with its cramped style. Altogether it has not the run of a Latin original. And, when we come to examine it in detail, we find that this constraint is due very largely to the fetters imposed by close adherence to Greek idiom. Thus for instance we have ver. 5 '*qui* [or *quae*] *sunt ex me*', οἱ [or τὰ] ἐξ ἐμοῦ; *operum quae salutis*, ἔργων τῶν τῆς σωτηρίας; ver. 6 *palam vincula mea quae patior*, φανεροὶ οἱ δεσμοί μου οὓς ὑπομένω; ver. 13 *sordidos in lucro*, αἰσχροκερδεῖς; ver. 20 *et facite legi Colosensibus et Colosensium vobis*, καὶ ποιήσατε ἵνα τοῖς Κολασσαεῦσιν ἀναγνωσθῇ καὶ ἡ Κολασσαέων ἵνα [καὶ] ὑμῖν. It is quite possible indeed that parallels for some of these anomalies may be found in Latin writers. Thus Tert. *c. Marc.* i. 23 'redundantia justitiae super *scribarum* et *Pharisaeorum*' is quoted to illustrate the genitive 'Colosensium' ver. 20[2]. The Greek cast however is not confined to one or two expressions but extends to the whole letter. *Frequent Grecisms in the epistle.*

But a yet stronger argument in favour of a Greek original remains. This epistle, as we saw, is a cento of passages from St Paul. If it had been written originally in Latin, we should expect to find that the passages were taken directly from the Latin versions. This however is not the case. Thus compare ver. 6 '*palam* sunt vincula mea' with Phil. i. 13 '*ut vincula mea manifesta* fierent': ver. 7 '*orationibus vestris et administrante* spiritu sancto' [*administratione* spiritus sancti'?] with Phil. i. 19 '*per vestram obsecrationem* (V. *orationem*) et *subministrationem* spiritus sancti'; ver. 9 'ut eandem *dilectionem* habeatis et sitis unianimes' with Phil. ii. 2 'eandem *caritatem* habentes, unanimes'; ver. 10 '*ergo*, dilectissimi, ut *audistis* praesentia mei...*facite in* timore' with Phil. ii. 12 '*Propter quod* (V. *Itaque*) dilectissimi mihi (V. *charissimi* mei) sicut semper *obaudistis* (V. *obedistis*)...praesentia (V. in praesentia) mei...*cum* timore (V. *metu*)...*operamini*'; ver. 11, 12 '*Est enim Deus* qui operatur in vos (v. l. vobis). Et facite sine *retractu* quaecumque facitis' with Phil. ii. 13, 14 *Deus enim est* qui operatur in vobis...Omnia autem facite sine...*detractionibus* (V. *haesitationibus*)'; ver. 13 '*quod est* [*reliquum*], dilectissimi, gaudete in Christo et *praecavete*' with Phil. iii. 1, 2 '*de caetero*, fratres mei, gaudete in Domino...*Videte*'; ib. '*sordidos in lucro*' with the Latin renderings of αἰσχροκερδεῖς 1 Tim. iii. 8 '*turpilucros*' (V. '*turpe lucrum sectantes*'), αἰσχροκερδῆ Tit. i. 7 *turpi-* *It differs widely from the Old Latin and Vulgate Versions.*

<hr>

[1] e.g. Anger *Laodicenerbrief* p. 142 sq., Westcott *Canon* p. 454 sq. (ed. 4). Erasmus asks boldly, 'Qui factum est ut haec epistola apud Latinos extet, cum nullus sit apud Graecos, ne vete- rum quidem, qui testetur eam a se lectam?' The accuracy of this statement will be tested presently.

[2] Anger p. 165.

lucrum (V. '*turpis lucri cupidum*'); ver. 14 '*sint petitiones* vestrae *palam* apud Deum' with Phil. iv. 6 '*postulationes* (V. petitiones) vestrae *innotescant* apud Deum'; ver. 20 'facite *legi* Colosensibus et *Colosensium vobis*' with Col. iv. 16 'facite *ut* et in Laodicensium ecclesia *legatur* et *eam quae Laodicensium* (MSS Laodiciam) *est ut* (om. V.) *vos legatis*'. These

Thus in-
ternal
evidence
favours
a Greek
original. examples tell their own tale. The occasional resemblances to the Latin Version are easily explained on the ground that reminiscences of this version would naturally occur to the translator of the epistle. The habitual divergences from it are only accounted for on the hypothesis that the original compiler was better acquainted with the New Testament in Greek than in Latin, and therefore presumably that he wrote in Greek.

External
testimony
to the
same ef-
fect.
[Murato-
rian Frag-
ment.] And, if we are led to this conclusion by an examination of the epistle itself, we shall find it confirmed by an appeal to external testimony. There is ample evidence that a spurious Epistle to the Laodiceans was known to Greek writers, as well as Latin, at a sufficiently early date. A mention of such an epistle occurs as early as the Muratorian Fragment on the Canon (about A.D. 170), where the writer speaks of two letters, one to the Laodiceans and another to the Alexandrians, as circulated under the name of Paul[1]. The bearing of the words however is uncertain. He may be referring to the Marcionite recension of the canonical Epistle to the Ephesians, which was entitled by that heretic an epistle to the Laodiceans[2]. Or, if this explanation of his words be not correct (as perhaps it is not), still we should not feel justified in assuming that he is referring to the extant apocryphal epistle. Indeed we should hardly expect that an epistle of this character would be written and circulated at so early a date. The reference in Col. iv. 16 offered a strong temptation to the forger, and proba-

---

[1] *Canon Murat.* p. 47 (ed. Tregelles). The passage stands in the MS, 'Fertur etiam ad Laudecenses alia ad Alexandrinos Pauli nomine fincte ad heresem Marcionis et alia plura quae in catholicam eclesiam recepi non potest.' There is obviously some corruption in the text. One very simple emendation is the repetition of 'alia', so that the words would run 'ad Laudicenses alia, alia ad Alexandrinos'. In this case fincte (=finctae) might refer to the two epistles first mentioned, and the Latin would construe intelligibly. The writing described as 'ad Laodicenses alia' might then be the Epistle to the Ephesians under its Marcionite title, the writer probably not having any personal knowledge of it, but supposing from its name that it was a different and a forged writing. But what can then be the meaning of 'alia ad Alexandrinos'? Is it, as some have thought, the Epistle to the Hebrews? But this could not under any circum-

stances be described as 'fincta ad haeresem Marcionis', even though we should strain the meaning of the preposition and interpret the words '*against* the heresy of Marcion'. And again our knowledge of Marcion's Canon is far too full to admit the hypothesis that it included a spurious Epistle to the Alexandrians, of which no notice is elsewhere preserved. We are therefore driven to the conclusion that there is a hiatus here, as in other places of this fragment, probably after 'Pauli nomine'; and 'finctae' will then refer not to the two epistles named before, but to the mutilated epistles of Marcion's Canon which he had 'tampered with to adapt them to his heresy'. In this case the letter 'ad Laudicenses' may refer to our apocryphal epistle or to some earlier forgery.

[2] See the Introduction to the Epistle to the Ephesians.

bly more than one unscrupulous person was induced by it to try his hand at falsification[1]. But, however this may be, it seems clear that before the close of the fourth century our epistle was largely circulated in the East and West alike. 'Certain persons', writes Jerome in his account of St Paul, 'read Jerome. also an Epistle to the Laodiceans, but it is rejected by all[2]'. No doubt is entertained that this father refers to our epistle. If then we find that Theodore. about the same time Theodore of Mopsuestia also mentions an Epistle to the Laodiceans, which he condemns as spurious[3], it is a reasonable inference that the same writing is meant. In this he is followed by Theodoret[4]; and Theodoret. indeed the interpretations of Col. iv. 16 given by the Greek Fathers of this age were largely influenced, as we have seen, by the presence of the spurious epistle which they were anxious to discredit[5]. Even two or three centuries later the epistle seems to have been read in the East. At the Second 2nd Coun-Council of Nicæa (A. D. 787) it was found necessary to warn people against cil of 'a forged Epistle to the Laodiceans' which was 'circulated, having a place Nicæa. in some copies of the Apostle[6].'

The Epistle to the Laodiceans then in the original Greek would run The Greek somewhat as follows[7]:   restored.

ΠΡΟΣ ΛΑΟΔΙΚΕΑΣ.

[a]ΠΑΥΛΟΣ ἀπόστολος οὐκ ἀπ᾽ ἀνθρώπων οὐδὲ δι᾽ ἀνθρώπου [a] Gal. i. 1. ἀλλὰ διὰ Ἰησοῦ Χριστοῦ, τοῖς ἀδελφοῖς τοῖς οὖσιν ἐν Λαοδικείᾳ. [b]Χάρις ὑμῖν καὶ εἰρήνη ἀπὸ Θεοῦ πατρὸς καὶ Κυρίου Ἰησοῦ [b] Gal. i. 3; Χριστοῦ.   Phil. i. 2.

---

[1] Timotheus, who became Patriarch of Constantinople in 511, while still a presbyter includes in a list of apocryphal works forged by the Manicheans ἡ πεντεκαιδεκάτη [i.e. τοῦ Παύλου] πρὸς Λαοδικεῖς ἐπιστολή, Meurse p. 117(quoted by Fabricius, *Cod. Apocr. N. T.* I. p. 139). Anger (p. 27) suggests that there is a confusion of the Marcionites and Manicheans here. I am disposed to think that Timotheus recklessly credits the Manicheans with several forgeries of which they were innocent, among others with our apocryphal Epistle to the Laodiceans. Still it is possible that there was another Laodicean Epistle forged by these heretics to support their peculiar tenets.

[2] *Vir. Ill.* 5 (II. p. 840) 'Legunt quidam et ad Laodicenses, sed ab omnibus exploditur'.

[3] The passage is quoted above, p. 275, note 1.

[4] τινὲς ὑπέλαβον καὶ πρὸς Λαοδικέας αὐτὸν γεγραφέναι· αὐτίκα τοίνυν καὶ προσφέρουσι πεπλασμένην ἐπιστολήν.

[5] Anger (p. 143) argues against a Greek original on the ground that the Eastern Church, unlike the Latin, did not generally interpret Col. iv. 16 as meaning an epistle written *to* the Laodiceans. The fact is true, but the inference is wrong, as the language of the Greek commentators themselves shows.

[6] Act. vi. Tom. V (Labbe VIII. p. 1125 ed. Colet.) καὶ γὰρ τοῦ θείου ἀποστόλου πρὸς Λαοδικεῖς φέρεται πλαστὴ ἐπιστολὴ ἔν τισι βίβλοις τοῦ ἀποστόλου ἐγκειμένη, ἣν οἱ πατέρες ἡμῶν ἀπεδοκίμασαν ὡς αὐτοῦ ἀλλοτρίαν.

[7] A Greek version is given in Elias Hutter's Polyglott New Testament (Noreb. 1599): see Anger p. 147, note g. But I have retranslated the epistle anew, introducing the Pauline passages, of which it is almost entirely made up, as they stand in the Greek Testament. The references are given in the margin.

c Phil. i. 3.
d Gal. v. 5.
e 2 Pet. ii. 9;
iii. 7; cf.
Phil. ii. 16.
f 1 Tim. i. 6.
g 2 Tim. iv. 4.
h Col. i. 5;
Gal. ii. 5, 14.
i Gal. i. 11
(cf. i. 8).
k Phil. i. 12.

l Phil. i. 13.
m Matt. v. 12;
cf. Phil. i. 18.
n Phil. i. 19.

o Phil. i. 20.
p Phil. i. 21.

q Phil. ii. 2.

r Phil. ii. 12.

s 2 Thess. ii. 5
(see vulg.).
t Phil. ii. 13.
u Phil. ii. 14.
x Col. iii.17,23.
y Phil. iii. 1.
z 1 Tim. iii. 8;
Tit. i. 7.
a Phil. iv. 6.
b 1 Cor. xv. 58.
c 1 Cor. ii. 16.
d Phil. iv. 8, 9.

e Phil. iv. 22.

f Phil. iv. 23.

g Col. iv. 16.

³ᶜΕὐχαριστῶ τῷ Χριστῷ ἐν πάσῃ δεήσει μου, ὅτι ἐστὲ ἐν αὐτῷ μένοντες καὶ προσκαρτεροῦντες τοῖς ἔργοις αὐτοῦ, ᵈἀπεκδεχόμενοι τὴν ἐπαγγελίαν ᵉεἰς ἡμέραν κρίσεως.

⁴Μηδὲ ὑμᾶς ἐξαπατήσωσιν ᶠματαιολογίαι τινῶν διδασκόντων ἵνα ᵍἀποστρέψωσιν ὑμᾶς ἀπὸ ʰτῆς ἀληθείας ⁱτοῦ εὐαγγελίου τοῦ εὐαγγελισθέντος ὑπ' ἐμοῦ. ⁵καὶ νῦν ποιήσει ὁ Θεὸς ἵνα ᵏτὰ ἐξ ἐμοῦ εἰς προκοπὴν τῆς ἀληθείας τοῦ εὐαγγελίου * * * λατρεύοντες καὶ ποιοῦντες χρηστότητα ἔργων τῶν τῆς σωτηρίας [καὶ] τῆς αἰωνίου ζωῆς. ⁶καὶ νῦν ˡφανεροὶ οἱ δεσμοί μου, οὓς ὑπομένω ἐν Χριστῷ, ἐν οἷς ᵐχαίρω καὶ ἀγαλλιῶμαι. ⁷καὶ ⁿτοῦτό ἐστίν μοι εἰς σωτηρίαν δίδιον, ὃ καὶ ἀπέβη διὰ τῆς ὑμῶν δεήσεως καὶ ἐπιχορηγίας πνεύματος ἁγίου, ᵒεἴτε διὰ ζωῆς εἴτε διὰ θανάτου. ⁸ᵖἐμοὶ γὰρ τὸ ζῆν ἐν Χριστῷ καὶ τὸ ἀποθανεῖν χαρά. ⁹καὶ τὸ αὐτὸ ποιήσει [καὶ] ἐν ὑμῖν διὰ τοῦ ἐλέους αὐτοῦ, ἵνα ᵠτὴν αὐτὴν ἀγάπην ἔχητε, σύμψυχοι ὄντες. ¹⁰ʳὥστε, ἀγαπητοί, καθὼς ὑπηκούσατε ἐν τῇ παρουσίᾳ μου, οὕτως ˢμνημονεύοντες μετὰ φόβου Κυρίου ἐργάζεσθε, καὶ ἔσται ὑμῖν ζωὴ εἰς τὸν αἰῶνα· ¹¹ᵗΘεὸς γάρ ἐστιν ὁ ἐνεργῶν ἐν ὑμῖν. ¹²καὶ ᵘποιεῖτε χωρὶς διαλογισμῶν ˣὅ τι ἐὰν ποιῆτε.

¹³Καὶ ʸτὸ λοιπόν, ἀγαπητοί, χαίρετε ἐν Χριστῷ. βλέπετε δὲ τοὺς ᶻαἰσχροκερδεῖς. ¹⁴ᵃπάντα τὰ αἰτήματα ὑμῶν γνωριζέσθω πρὸς τὸν Θεόν. καὶ ᵇἑδραῖοι γίνεσθε ἐν ᶜτῷ νοΐ τοῦ Χριστοῦ. ¹⁵ᵈὅσα τε ὁλόκληρα καὶ ἀληθῆ καὶ σεμνὰ καὶ δίκαια καὶ προσφιλῆ, ταῦτα πράσσετε. ¹⁶ἃ καὶ ἠκούσατε καὶ παρελάβετε, ἐν τῇ καρδίᾳ κρατεῖτε, καὶ ἡ εἰρήνη ἔσται μεθ' ὑμῶν.

¹⁸ᵉἈσπάζονται ὑμᾶς οἱ ἅγιοι.

¹⁹ᶠἩ χάρις τοῦ Κυρίου Ἰησοῦ Χριστοῦ μετὰ τοῦ πνεύματος ὑμῶν.

²⁰ᵍκαὶ ποιήσατε ἵνα τοῖς Κολασσαεῦσιν ἀναγνωσθῇ, καὶ ἡ τῶν Κολασσαέων ἵνα καὶ ὑμῖν.

Scanty circulation in the East, But, though written originally in Greek, it was not among Greek Christians that this epistle attained its widest circulation. In the latter part of the 8th century indeed, when the Second Council of Nicæa met, it had found its way into some copies of St Paul's Epistles[1]. But the denunciation of this Council seems to have been effective in securing its ultimate exclusion. We discover no traces of it in any extant Greek MS, with the very doubtful **but wide diffusion in the West.** exception which has already been considered[2]. But in the Latin Church the case was different. St Jerome, as we saw, had pronounced very decidedly against it. Yet even his authority was not sufficient to stamp it

---

[1] Quoted above, p. 293, note 6.　　　　[2] See above, p. 279 sq.

out. At least as early as the sixth century it found a place in some copies of the Latin Bibles: and before the close of that century its genuineness was affirmed by perhaps the most influential theologian whom the Latin Church produced during the eleven centuries which elapsed between the age of Jerome and Augustine and the era of the Reformation. Gregory the Great Gregory did not indeed affirm its canonicity. He pronounced that the Church had the Great. restricted the canonical Epistles of St Paul to fourteen, and he found a mystical explanation of this limitation in the number itself, which was attained by adding the number of the Commandments to the number of the Gospels and thus fitly represented the teaching of the Apostle which combines the two[1]. But at the same time he states that the Apostle wrote fifteen; and, though he does not mention the Epistle to the Laodiceans by name, there can be little doubt that he intended to include this as his fifteenth epistle, and that his words were rightly understood by subsequent writers as affirming its Pauline authorship. The influence of this great name is perceptible in the statements of later writers. Haymo of Halber- Haymo of stadt, who died A.D. 853, commenting on Col. iv. 16, says, The Apostle 'en- Halber-joins the Laodicean Epistle to be read to the Colossians, because though it stadt. is very short and is not reckoned in the Canon, yet still it has some use[2]'. And between two or three centuries later Hervey of Dole (c. A.D. 1130), if it Hervey of be not Anselm of Laon[3], commenting on this same passage, says: 'Although Dole. the Apostle wrote this epistle also as his fifteenth or sixteenth[4], and it is established by Apostolic authority like the rest, yet holy Church does not reckon more than fourteen', and he proceeds to justify this limitation of the Canon with the arguments and in the language of Gregory[5]. Others

---

[1] Greg. Magn. *Mor. in Iob.* xxxv. § 25 (III. p. 433, ed. Gallicc.) 'Recte vita ecclesiae multiplicata per decem et quattuor computatur; quia utrumque testamentum custodiens, et tam secundum Legis decalogum quam secundum quattuor Evangelii libros vivens, usque ad perfectionis culmen extenditur. Unde et Paulus apostolus quamvis epistolas quindecim scripserit, sancta tamen ecclesia non amplius quam quatuordecim tenet, ut ex ipso epistolarum numero ostenderet quod doctor egregius Legis et Evangelii secreta rimasset'.

[2] *Patrol. Lat.* cxvii. p. 765 (ed. Migne) 'Et eam quae erat Laodicensium ideo praecipit Colossensibus legi, quia, licet perparva sit et in Canone non habeatur, aliquid tamen utilitatis habet'. He uses the expression 'eam quae erat Laodicensium', because τὴν ἐκ Λαοδικείας was translated in the Latin Bible 'eam quae Laodicensium est'.

[3] See *Galatians* p. 232 on the authorship of this commentary.

[4] A third Epistle to the Corinthians being perhaps reckoned as the 15th; see Fabric. *Cod. Apocr. Nov. Test.* II. p. 866.

[5] *Patrol. Lat.* CLXXXI. p. 1355 sq. (ed. Migne) '*et ea* similiter epistola, *quae Laodicensium* est, i.e. quam ego Laodicensibus misi, legatur vobis. Quamvis et hanc epistolam quintamdecimam vel sextamdecimam apostolus scripserit, et auctoritas eam apostolica sicut caetera firmavit, sancta tamen ecclesia non amplius quam quatuordecim tenet, ut ex ipso epistolarum numero ostenderet etc.' At the end of the notes to the Colossians he adds, 'Hucusque protenditur epistola quae missa est ad Colossenses. Congruum autem videtur ut propter notitiam legentium subjiciamus eam quae est ad Laodicenses directa; quam, ut diximus, in usu non habet ecclesia. Est ergo talis.' Then follows the text of the Laodicean Epistle, but it is not annotated.

however did not confine themselves to the qualified recognition given to the epistle by the great Bishop of Rome. Gregory had carefully distinguished between genuineness and canonicity; but this important distinction was not **English** seldom disregarded by later writers. In the English Church more especi-**Church.** ally it was forgotten. Thus Aelfric abbot of Cerne, who wrote during the **Aelfric.** closing years of the tenth century, speaks as follows of St Paul: 'Fifteen epistles wrote this one Apostle to the nations by him converted unto the faith : which are large books in the Bible and make much for our amendment, if we follow his doctrine that was teacher of the Gentiles'. He then gives a list of the Apostle's writings, which closes with 'one to Philemon and one to the Laodiceans; fifteen in all as loud as thunder to faithful **John of** people[1]'. Again, nearly two centuries later John of Salisbury, likewise **Salisbury.** writing on the Canon, reckons 'Fifteen epistles of Paul included in one volume, though it be the wide-spread and common opinion of nearly all that there are only fourteen; ten to churches and four to individuals: supposing that the one addressed to the Hebrews is to be reckoned among the Epistles of Paul, as Jerome the doctor of doctors seems to lay down in his preface, where he refuteth the cavils of those who contended that it was not Paul's. But the fifteenth is that which is addressed to the Church of the Laodiceans; and though, as Jerome saith, it be rejected by all, nevertheless was it written by the Apostle. Nor is this opinion assumed on the conjecture of others, but it is confirmed by the testimony of the Apostle himself: for he maketh mention of it in the Epistle to the Colossians in these words, *When this epistle shall have been read among you*, etc. (Col. iv. 16)[2]'. Aelfric and John are the typical theologians of the Church in this country in their respective ages. The Conquest effected a revolution in ecclesiastical and theological matters. The Old English Church was separated from the Anglo-Norman Church in not a few points both of doctrine and of discipline. Yet here we find the representative men of learning in both agreed on this one point—the authorship and canonicity of the Epistle to the Laodiceans. From the language of John of Salisbury however it appears that such was not the common verdict at least in his age, and that on this point the instinct of the many was more sound than the learning of the few. Nor indeed was it the undisputed opinion even of the learned in this coun-**The epis-** try during this interval. The first Norman Archbishop, Lanfranc, an Italian **tle repu-** by birth and education, explains the passage in the Colossian Epistle as **diated by** referring to a letter written by the Laodiceans to the Apostle, and adds that **Lanfranc.**

---

[1] *A Saxon Treatise concerning the Old and New Testament* by Ælfricus Abbas, p. 28 (ed. W. L'Isle, London 1623).

[2] Ioann. Sarisb. *Epist.* 143 (I. p. 210 ed. Giles) 'Epistolae Pauli quindecim uno volumine comprehensae, licet sit vulgata et fere omnium communis opinio non esse nisi quatuordecim, decem ad ecclesias, quatuor ad personas; si tamen illa quae ad Hebraeos est connumeranda est epistolis Pauli, quod in praefatione ejus astruere videtur doctorum doctor Hieronymus, illo-rum dissolvens argutias qui eam Pauli non esse contendebant. Caeterum quintadecima est illa quae ecclesiae Laodicensium scribitur; et licet, ut ait Hieronymus, ab omnibus explodatur, tamen ab apostolo scripta est: neque sententia haec de aliorum praesumitur opinione sed ipsius apostoli testimonio roboratur. Meminit enim ipsius in epistola ad Colossenses his verbis, *Quum lecta fuerit apud vos haec epistola, etc.*'

otherwise 'there would be more than thirteen Epistles of Paul[1]'. Thus he tacitly ignores the Epistle to the Laodiceans, with which he can hardly have been unacquainted.

Indeed the safest criterion of the extent to which this opinion prevailed, is to be found in the manuscripts. At all ages from the sixth to the fifteenth century we have examples of its occurrence among the Pauline Epistles and most frequently without any marks which imply doubt respecting its canonicity. These instances are more common in proportion to the number of extant MSS in the earlier epoch than in the later[2]. In one of the three or four extant authorities for the Old Latin Version of the Pauline Epistles it has a place[3]. In one of the two most ancient copies of Jerome's revised Vulgate it is found[4]. Among the first class MSS of this latter version its insertion is almost as common as its omission. This phenomenon moreover is not confined to any one country. Italy, Spain, France, Ireland, England, Germany, Switzerland—all the great nations of Latin Christendom—contribute examples of early manuscripts in which this epistle has a place[5]. *{Occurrence in MSS of all ages and countries.}*

And, when the Scriptures came to be translated into the vernacular languages of modern Europe, this epistle was not uncommonly included. Thus we meet with an Albigensian version, which is said to belong to the thirteenth century[6]. Thus too it is found in the Bohemian language, both in manuscript and in the early printed Bibles, in various recensions[7]. And again an old German translation is extant, which, judging from linguistic peculiarities, cannot be assigned to a later date than about the fourteenth century, and was printed in not less than fourteen editions of the German Bible at the close of the fifteenth and the beginning of the sixteenth centuries, before Luther's version appeared[8]. In the early English Bibles too it has a place. Though it was excluded by both Wycliffe and Purvey, yet it did not long remain untranslated and appears in two different and quite independent versions, in MSS written before the middle of the fifteenth century[9]. The prologue prefixed to the commoner of the two forms runs as follows : *{Versions. Albigensian. Bohemian. German. English.}*

---

[1] *Patrol. Lat.* CL. p. 331 (ed. Migne) on Col. iv. 16 'Haec si esset apostoli, *ad Laodicenses* diceret, non *Laodicensium*; et plusquam tredecim essent epistolae Pauli'. We should perhaps read xiiii for xiii, 'quatuordecim' for 'tredecim', as Lanfranc is not likely to have questioned the Pauline authorship of the Epistle to the Hebrews.

[2] The proportion however is very different in different collections. In the Cambridge University Library I found the epistle in four only out of some thirty MSS which I inspected; whereas in the Lambeth Library the proportion was far greater.

[3] The *Speculum* of Mai, see above, p. 282.

[4] The Codex Fuldensis, which was written within a few years of the Codex Amiatinus.

[5] The list of MSS given above, p. 282 sq., will substantiate this statement.

[6] An account of this MS, which is at Lyons, is given by Reuss in the *Revue de Théologie* v. p. 334 (Strassb. 1852). He ascribes the translation of the New Testament to the 13th century, and dates the MS a little later.

[7] This version is printed by Anger, p. 170 sq.

[8] See Anger, p. 149 sq., p. 166 sq.

[9] These two versions are printed in Lewis's *New Testament translated by J. Wiclif* (1731) p. 99 sq., and in Forshall and Madden's *Wycliffite Versions of the Holy Bible* (1850) IV. p. 438 sq. They are also given by Anger p. 168 sq.

English prologue.

'Laodicensis ben also Colocenses, as tweye townes and oo peple in maners. These ben of Asie, and among hem hadden be false apostlis, and disceyuede manye. Therfore the postle bringith hem to mynde of his conuersacion and trewe preching of the gospel, and excitith hem to be stidfast in the trewe witt and loue of Crist, and to be of oo wil. But this pistil is not in comyn Latyn bookis, and therfor it was but late translatid into Englisch tunge[1].'

Two Versions of the epistle.

The two forms of the epistle in its English dress are as follows[2]. The version on the left hand is extant only in a single MS ; the other, which occupies the right column, is comparatively common.

'Poul, apostle, not of men, ne bi man, but bi Jhesu Crist, to the britheren that ben of Laodice, grace to ȝou, and pees of God the fadir, and of the Lord Jhesu Crist. Gracis I do to Crist bi al myn orisoun, that ȝe be dwellinge in him and lastinge, bi the biheest abidinge in the dai of doom. Ne he vnordeynede vs of sum veyn speche feynynge, that vs ouerturne fro the sothfastnesse of the gospel that of me is prechid. Also now schal God do hem leuynge, and doynge of blessdnesse of werkis, which heelthe of lyf is. And now openli ben my boondis, whiche I suffre in Crist Jhesu, in whiche I glad and ioie. And that is to me heelthe euerlastynge, that that I dide with oure preieris, and mynystringe the Holy Spirit, bi lijf

'Poul, apostle, not of men, ne by man, but bi Jhesu Crist, to the britheren that ben at Laodice, grace to ȝou, and pees of God the fadir, and of the Lord Jhesu Crist. I do thankyngis to my God bi al my preier, that ȝe be dwelling and lastyng in him, abiding the biheest in the day of doom. For neithir the veyn spekyng of summe vnwise men hath lettide ȝou, the whiche wolden turne ȝou fro the treuthe of the gospel, that is prechid of me. And now hem that ben of me, to the profiȝt of truthe of the gospel, God schal make disseruyng, and doyng benygnyte of werkis, and helthe of euerlasting lijf. And now my boondis ben open, which Y suffre in Crist Jhesu, in whiche Y glade and ioie. And that is to me to euerlastyng helthe, that this same thing be doon by ȝoure preiers, and mynystryng of the Holi Goost, either bi

(1843), who takes the rarer form from Lewis and the other from a Dresden MS. Dr Westcott also has printed the commoner version in his *Canon*, p. 457 (ed. 4), from Forshall and Madden.

Of one of these two versions Forshall and Madden give a collation of several MSS ; the other is taken from a single MS (I. p. xxxii). Lewis does not state whence he derived the rarer of these two versions, but there can be little doubt that it came from the same MS *Pepys*. 2073 (belonging to Magd. Coll. Cambridge) from which it was taken by Forshall and Madden (I. p. lvii); since he elsewhere mentions using this MS (p. 104). The version is not known to

exist in any other. Forshall and Madden given the date of the MS as about 1440.

[1] From Forshall and Madden, IV. p. 438. The earliest MSS which contain the common version of the Laodicean Epistle (to which this prologue is prefixed) date about A.D. 1430.

[2] Printed from Forshall and Madden l.c. I am assured by those who are thoroughly conversant with old English, that they can discern no difference of date in these two versions, and that they both belong probably to the early years of the 15th century. The rarer version is taken from a better Latin text than the other.

or bi deeth. It is forsothe to me lijf into Crist, and to die ioie withouten eende. In vs he schal do his merci, that ȝe haue the same louynge, and that ȝe be of o wil. Therfore, derlyngis, as ȝe han herd in presence of me, hold ȝe, and do ȝe in drede of God; and it schal be to ȝou lijf withouten eend. It is forsothe God that worchith in vs. And do ȝe withouten ony withdrawinge, what soeuere ȝe doon. And that it is, derlyngis, ioie ȝe in Crist, and flee ȝe maad foul in clay. Alle ȝoure axingis ben open anentis God, and be ȝe fastned in the witt of Crist. And whiche been hool, and sooth, and chast, and rightwijs, and louable, do ȝe; and whiche herden and take in herte, hold ȝe; and it schal be to ȝou pees. Holi men greeten ȝou weel, in the grace of oure Lord Jhesu Crist, with the Holi Goost. And do ȝe that pistil of Colosensis to be red to ȝou. Amen.

lijf, either bi deeth. Forsothe to me it is lijf to lyue in Crist, and to die ioie. And his mercy schal do in ȝou the same thing, that ȝe moun haue the same loue, and that ȝe be of oo will. Therfore, ȝe weel biloued britheren, holde ȝe, and do ȝe in the dreede of God, as ȝe han herde the presence of me; and lijf schal be to ȝou withouten eende. Sotheli it is God that worchith in ȝou. And, my weel biloued britheren, do ȝe without eny withdrawyng what euer thingis ȝe don. Joie ȝe in Crist, and eschewe ȝe men defoulid in lucre, *either foul wynnyng*. Be alle ȝoure askyngis open anentis God, and be ȝe stidefast in the witt of Crist. And do ȝe tho thingis that ben hool, and trewe, and chaast, and iust, and able to be loued; and kepe ȝe in herte tho thingis that ȝe haue herd and take; and pees schal be to ȝou. Alle holi men greten ȝou weel. The grace of oure Lord Jhesu Crist be with ȝoure spirit. And do ȝe that pistil of Colocensis to be red to ȝou.

Thus for more than nine centuries this forged epistle hovered about the doors of the sacred Canon, without either finding admission or being peremptorily excluded. At length the revival of learning dealt its death-blow to this as to so many other spurious pretensions. As a rule, Roman Catholics and Reformers were equally strong in their condemnation of its worthlessness. The language of Erasmus more especially is worth quoting for its own sake, and must not be diluted by translation : *Revival of learning and condemnation of the epistle.*

'Nihil habet Pauli praeter voculas aliquot ex caeteris ejus epistolis mendicatas......Non est cujusvis hominis Paulinum pectus effingere. Tonat, fulgurat, meras flammas loquitur Paulus. At haec, praeterquam quod brevissima est, quam friget, quam jacet!...Quanquam quid attinet argumentari ? Legat, qui volet, epistolam......Nullum argumentum efficacius persuaserit eam non esse Pauli quam ipsa epistola. Et si quid mihi naris est, ejusdem est opificis qui naeniis suis omnium veterum theologorum omnia scripta contaminavit, conspurcavit, perdidit, ac praecipue ejus qui prae caeteris indignus erat ea contumelia, nempe D. Hieronymi[1].' *Strictures of Erasmus.*

[1] On Col. iv. 16. Erasmus is too hard upon the writer of this letter, when he charges him with such a mass of forgeries. He does not explain how this hypothesis is consistent with the condemnation of the Epistle to the Laodiceans in Hieron. *Vir. Ill.* 5 (quoted above p. 293).

Excep-
tions.

But some eccentric spirits on both sides were still found to maintain its genuineness. Thus on the one hand the Lutheran Steph. Prætorius prefaces his edition of this epistle (A.D. 1595) with the statement that he 'restores

Prætorius. it to the Christian Church'; he gives his opinion that it was written 'either by the Apostle himself or by some other Apostolic man': he declares that to himself it is 'redolent of the spirit and grace of the most divine Paul'; and he recommends younger teachers of the Gospel to 'try their strength in explaining it', that thus 'accustoming themselves gradually to the Apostolic doctrine they may extract thence a flavour sweeter than

Stapleton. ambrosia and nectar[1].' On the other hand the Jesuit Stapleton was not less eager in his advocacy of this miserable cento. To him its genuineness had a controversial value. Along with several other apocryphal writings which he accepted in like manner, it was important in his eyes as showing that the Church had authority to exclude even Apostolic writings from the Canon, if she judged fit[2]. But such phenomena were quite abnormal. The dawn of the Reformation epoch had effectually scared away this ghost of a Pauline epistle, which (we may confidently hope) has been laid for ever and will not again be suffered to haunt the mind of the Church.

---

[1] *Pauli Apostoli ad Laodicenses Epistola, Latine et Germanice*, Hamburg. 1595, of which the preface is given in Fabricius *Cod. Apocr. Nov. Test.* II. p. 867. It is curious that the only two arguments against its genuineness which he thinks worthy of notice are (1) Its brevity; which he answers by appealing to the Epistle to Philemon; and (2) Its recommendation of works ('quod scripsit opera esse facienda quae sunt salutis aeternae'); which he explains to refer to works that proceed of faith.

[2] See Bp. Davenant on Col. iv. 16: 'Detestanda Stapletonis opinio, qui ipsius Pauli epistolam esse statuit, quam omnes patres ut adulterinam et insulsam repudiarunt; nec sanior conclusio, quam inde deducere voluit, posse nimirum ecclesiam germanam et veram apostoli Pauli epistolam pro sua authoritate e Canone excludere'. So also Whitaker *Disputation on Scripture* passim (see the references given above, p. 275, note 3).

EPISTLE TO PHILEMON.

INTRODUCTION TO THE EPISTLE.

THE Epistle to Philemon holds a unique place among the Unique character of the epistle. Apostle's writings. It is the only strictly private letter which has been preserved. The Pastoral Epistles indeed are addressed to individuals, but they discuss important matters of Church discipline and government. Evidently they were intended to be read by others besides those to whom they are immediately addressed. On the other hand the letter before us does not once touch upon any question of public interest. It is addressed apparently to a layman. It is wholly occupied with an incident of domestic life. The occasion which called it forth was altogether common-place. It is only one sample of numberless letters which must have been written to his many friends and disciples by one of St Paul's eager temperament and warm affections, in the course of a long and chequered life. Yet to ourselves this fragment, which has been rescued, we know not how, from the wreck of a large Its value. and varied correspondence, is infinitely precious. Nowhere is the social influence of the Gospel more strikingly exerted; nowhere does the nobility of the Apostle's character receive a more vivid illustration than in this accidental pleading on behalf of a runaway slave.

The letter introduces us to an ordinary household in a The persons addressed. small town in Phrygia. Four members of it are mentioned by name, the father, the mother, the son, and the slave.

1. The head of the family bears a name which, for good or 1. Phile-mon. for evil, was not unknown in connexion with Phrygian story.

Occur-
rence of
the name
in Phry-
gia.

The legend of Philemon and Baucis, the aged peasants who
entertained not angels but gods unawares, and were rewarded
by their divine guests for their homely hospitality and their
conjugal love[1], is one of the most attractive in Greek mythology, and contrasts favourably with many a revolting tale in
which the powers of Olympus are represented as visiting this
lower earth. It has a special interest too for the Apostolic
history, because it suggests an explanation of the scene at
Lystra, when the barbarians would have sacrificed to the
Apostles, imagining that the same two gods, Zeus and Hermes,
had once again deigned to visit, in the likeness of men, those
regions which they had graced of old by their presence[2]. Again,
in historical times we read of one Philemon who obtained an
unenviable notoriety at Athens by assuming the rights of
Athenian citizenship, though a Phrygian and apparently a
slave[3]. Otherwise the name is not distinctively Phrygian. It
does not occur with any special frequency in the inscriptions
belonging to this country; and though several persons bearing
this name rose to eminence in literary history, not one, so far
as we know, was a Phrygian.

This Phi-
lemon a
Colossian

The Philemon with whom we are concerned was a native,
or at least an inhabitant, of Colossæ. This appears from the
fact that his slave is mentioned as belonging to that place. It
may be added also, in confirmation of this view, that in one of
two epistles written and despatched at the same time St Paul

---

[1] Ovid. *Met.* vii. 626 sq. 'Jupiter
huc, *specie mortali*, cumque parente
Venit Atlantiades positis caducifer alis'
etc.

[2] Acts xiv. 11 οἱ θεοὶ ὁμοιωθέντες
ἀνθρώποις κατέβησαν πρὸς ἡμᾶς κ.τ.λ.
There are two points worth observing
in the Phrygian legend, as illustrating
the Apostolic history. (1) It is a
miracle, which opens the eyes of the
peasant couple to the divinity of their
guests thus disguised; (2) The immediate effect of this miracle is their
attempt to sacrifice to their divine
visitors, 'dis hospitibus mactare para-

bant'. The familiarity with this
beautiful story may have suggested to
the barbarians of Lystra, whose 'Lycaonian speech' was not improbably
a dialect of Phrygian, that the same
two gods, Zeus and Hermes, had again
visited this region on an errand at
once of beneficence and of vengeance,
while at the same time it would prompt
them to conciliate the deities by a
similar mode of propitiation, ἤθελον
θύειν.

[3] Aristoph. *Av.* 762 εἰ δὲ τυγχάνει
τις ὢν Φρὺξ...φρυγίλος ὄρνις ἐνθάδ᾽ ἔσται,
τοῦ Φιλήμονος γένους.

announces the restoration of Onesimus to his master, while in the other he speaks of this same person as revisiting Colossæ[1]. On the other hand it would not be safe to lay any stress on the statement of Theodoret that Philemon's house was still standing at Colossæ when he wrote[2], for traditions of this kind have seldom any historical worth.

Philemon had been converted by St Paul himself[3]. At what time or under what circumstances he received his first lessons in the Gospel, we do not know: but the Apostle's long residence at Ephesus naturally suggests itself as the period when he was most likely to have become acquainted with a citizen of Colossæ[4]. *converted by St Paul.*

Philemon proved not unworthy of his spiritual parentage. Though to Epaphras belongs the chief glory of preaching the Gospel at Colossæ[5], his labours were well seconded by Philemon. The title of 'fellow-labourer,' conferred upon him by the Apostle[6], is a noble testimony to his evangelical zeal. Like Nymphas in the neighbouring Church of Laodicea[7], Philemon had placed his house at the disposal of the Christians at Colossæ for their religious and social gatherings[8]. Like Gaius[9], to whom the only other private letter in the Apostolic Canon is addressed[10], he was generous in his hospitalities. All those with whom he came in contact spoke with gratitude of his *His evangelical zeal, and wide hospitality.*

---

[1] Compare Col. iv. 9 with Philem. 11 sq.

[2] Theodoret in his preface to the epistle says πόλιν δὲ εἶχε [ὁ Φιλήμων] τὰς Κολάσσας· καὶ ἡ οἰκία δὲ αὐτοῦ μέχρι τοῦ παρόντος μεμένηκε. This is generally taken to mean that Philemon's house was still standing, when Theodoret wrote. This may be the correct interpretation, but the language is not quite explicit.

[3] ver. 19.

[4] See above, p. 30 sq.

[5] See above, p. 31 sq.

[6] ver. 1 συνεργῷ ἡμῶν.

[7] Col. iv. 15.

[8] ver. 2 τῇ κατ' οἶκόν σου ἐκκλησίᾳ. The Greek commentators, Chrysostom and Theodoret, suppose that St Paul

designates Philemon's own family (including his slaves) by this honourable title of ἐκκλησία, in order to interest them in his petition. This is plainly wrong. See the note on Col. iv. 15.

[9] 3 Joh. 5 sq.

[10] I take the view that the κυρία addressed in the Second Epistle of St John is some church personified, as indeed the whole tenour of the epistle seems to imply: see esp. vv. 4, 7 sq. The salutation to the 'elect lady' (ver. 1) from her 'elect sister' (ver. 15) will then be a greeting sent to one church from another; just as in 1 Peter the letter is addressed at the outset ἐκλεκτοῖς Πόντου κ.τ.λ. (i. 1) and contains at the close a salutation from ἡ ἐν Βαβυλῶνι συνεκλεκτή (v. 13).

Legendary martyr-dom. kindly attentions[1]. Of his subsequent career we have no certain knowledge. Legendary story indeed promotes him to the bishopric of Colossæ[2], and records how he was martyred in his native city under Nero[3]. But this tradition or fiction is not entitled to any credit. All that we really know of Philemon is contained within this epistle itself.

2. Apphia his wife.   2. It is a safe inference from the connexion of the names that Apphia was the wife of Philemon[4]. The commentators assume without misgiving that we have here the familiar Roman name Appia, though they do not explain the intrusion **A strictly Phrygian name.** of the aspirate[5]. This seems to be a mistake. The word occurs very frequently on Phrygian inscriptions as a proper name, and is doubtless of native origin. At Aphrodisias and Philadelphia, at Eumenia and Apamea Cibotus, at Stratonicea, at Philomelium, at Æzani and Cotiæum and Dorylæum, at almost all the towns far and near, which were either Phrygian or subject to Phrygian influences, and in which any fair number of inscriptions has been preserved, the name is found. If no example has been discovered at Colossæ itself, we must remember that not a single proper name has been preserved on any monumental inscription at this place. It is generally written either Apphia or Aphphia[6]; more rarely Aphia, which is perhaps

---

[1] vv. 5, 7.

[2] *Apost. Const.* vii. 46 τῆς δὲ ἐν Φρυγίᾳ Λαοδικείας [ἐπίσκοπος] Ἄρχιππος, Κολασσαέων δὲ Φιλήμων, Βεροίας δὲ τῆς κατὰ Μακεδονίαν Ὀνήσιμος ὁ Φιλήμονος. The Greek *Menaea* however make Philemon bishop of Gaza; see Tillemont I. p. 574, note lxvi.

[3] See Tillemont I. pp. 290, 574, for the references.

[4] Boeckh *Corp. Inscr.* 3814 Νείκανδρος καὶ Ἀφφία γυνὴ αὐτοῦ. In the following inscriptions also a wife bearing the name Apphia (Aphphia, Aphia) or Apphion (Aphphion, Aphion) is mentioned in connexion with her husband; 2720, 2782, 2836, 3446, 2775 b, c, d, 2837 b, 3849, 3902 m, 3962, 4141, 4277, 4321 f, 3846 z¹⁷, etc.

M. Renan (*Saint Paul* p. 360) says 'Appia, diaconesse de cette ville.'

Like other direct statements of this same writer, as for instance that the Colossians sent a deputation to St Paul (*L'Antéchrist* p. 90), this assertion rests on no authority.

[5] They speak of Ἀπφία as a softened form of the Latin *Appia*, and quote Acts xxviii. 15, where however the form is Ἀππίου. Even Ewald writes the word Appia.

[6] Ἀπφία, no. 2782, 2835, 2950, 3432, 3446, 2775 b, c, d, 2837 b, 3902 m, 3962, 4124, 4145: Ἀφφία, no. 3814, 4141, 4277, 4321 f, 3827 l, 3846 z, 3846 z¹⁷. So far as I could trace any law, the form Ἀφφία is preferred in the northern and more distant towns like Æzani and Cotiæum, while Ἀπφία prevails in the southern towns in the more immediate neighbourhood of Colossæ, such as Aphrodisias. This

due merely to the carelessness of the stonecutters [1]. But, so far as I have observed, it always preserves the aspirate. Its diminutive is Apphion or Aphphion or Aphion [2]. The allied form Aphphias or Aphias, also a woman's name, is found, though less commonly [3]; and we likewise frequently meet with the shorter form Apphe or Aphphe [4]. The man's name corresponding to Apphia is Apphianos, but this is rare [5]. The root would appear to be some Phrygian term of endearment or relationship [6]. It occurs commonly in connexion with other Phrygian names of a like stamp, more especially Ammia, which undergoes the same modifications of form, Amia, Ammias, Ammion or Amion, Ammiane or Ammiana, with the corresponding masculine Ammianos [7]. With these we may also compare

accords with the evidence of our MSS, in which 'Απφία is the best supported form, though 'Αφφία is found in some. In Theod. Mops. (Cramer's *Cat.* p. 105) it becomes 'Αμφία by a common corruption; and Old Latin copies write the dative *Apphiadi* from the allied form *Apphias*.

The most interesting of these inscriptions mentioning the name is no. 2782 at Aphrodisias, where there is a notice of Φλ. 'Απφίας ἀρχιερείας 'Ασίας, μητρὸς καὶ ἀδελφῆς καὶ μάμμης συνκλητικῶν, φιλοπάτριδος κ.τ.λ.

[1] no. 2720, 3827.

[2] "Απφιον or "Αφφιον 2733, 2836, 3295, 3849, 3902 m, 4207; "Αφιον, 3846 z[34] and "Αφειον 3846 z[31]; and even "Απφειν and "Αφφειν, 3167, 3278. In 3902 m the mother's name is 'Απφία and the daughter's "Απφιον.

[3] 'Αφφίας 3697, 3983; 'Αφίας 3879.

[4] "Αφφη 3816, 3390, 4143; "Απφη 3796, 4122.

[5] It is met with at the neighbouring town of Hierapolis, in the form 'Απφίανος no. 3911. It also occurs on coins of not very distant parts of Asia Minor, being written either 'Απφίανος or 'Αφφίανος; Mionnet III. p. 179, 184, IV. p. 65, 67, *Suppl.* VI. p. 293, VII. p. 365.

[6] Suidas "Απφα· ἀδελφῆς καὶ ἀδελφοῦ ὑποκόρισμα, and so Bekk. *Anecd.* p. 441. Eustath. *Il.* p. 565 says ἀπφαν

τὴν ἀδελφὴν 'Αττικῶς μόνη ἡ ἀδελφὴ εἴποι ἄν, καὶ πάππαν τὸν πατέρα μόνος ὁ παῖς κ.τ.λ., and he adds ἰστέον δὲ ὅτι ἐκ τοῦ ὡς ἐρρέθη ἄπφα γίνεται καὶ τὸ ἄπφιον, ὑποκόρισμα ὃν ἐρωμένης· τινὲς δὲ καὶ τὸ ἄπφα ὑποκόρισμά φασιν 'Αττικόν. These words were found in writers of Attic comedy (Pollux iii. 74 ἡ παρὰ τοῖς νέοις κωμῳδοῖς ἀπφία καὶ ἀπφίον καὶ ἀπφάριον; comp. Xenarchus τοὺς μὲν γέροντας ὄντας ἐπικαλούμεναι πατρίδια, τοὺς δ' ἀπφάρια, τοὺς νεωτέρους, Meineke *Fragm. Com.* III. p. 617): and doubtless they were heard commonly in Attic homes. But were they not learnt in the nursery from Phrygian slaves? 'Απφάριον appears in two inscriptions almost as a proper name, 2637 Κλαυδία ἀπφάριον, 3277 ἀπφάριον Λολλιανή. In no. 4207 (at Telmissus) we have 'Ελένη ἡ καὶ "Αφφιον, so that it seems sometimes to have been employed side by side with a Greek name; comp. no. 3912a Παπίας...ὁ καλούμενος Διογένης, quoted above, p. 48. This will account for the frequency of the names, Apphia, Apphion, etc. In Theocr. XV. 13 we have ἀπφῦς, and in Callim. *Hym. Dian.* 6 ἄππα, as a term of endearment applied to a father.

[7] This appears from the fact that Ammias and Ammianos appear sometimes as the names of mother and son respectively in the same inscriptions; e. g. 3846 z[82], 3847 k, 3882 i.

Tatia, Tatias, Tation, Tatiane or Tatiana, Tatianos.   Similar
too is the name Papias or Pappias, with the lengthened form
Papianos, to which corresponds the feminine Papiane[1].   So
again we have Nannas or Nanas, Nanna or Nana, with their

Not to be confused with the Latin Appia.

derivatives, in these Phrygian inscriptions[2].   There is a tendency in some of the allied forms of Apphia or Aphphia to drop
the aspirate so that they are written with a *pp*, more especially
in Appe[3], but not in the word itself; nor have I observed conversely any disposition to write the Roman name Appia with an
aspirate, Apphia or Aphphia[4].   Even if such a disposition could
be proved, the main point for which I am contending can
hardly be questioned.   With the overwhelming evidence of the
inscriptions before us, it is impossible to doubt that Apphia is
a native Phrygian name[5].

Her share in the letter.

Of this Phrygian matron we know nothing more than can
be learnt from this epistle.   The tradition or fiction which
represents her as martyred together with her husband may be
safely disregarded.   St Paul addresses her as a Christian[6].
Equally with her husband she had been aggrieved by the mis-
conduct of their slave Onesimus, and equally with him she
might interest herself in the penitent's future well-being.

3. Archippus, the son.

3.   With less confidence, but still with a reasonable degree
of probability, we may infer that Archippus, who is likewise
mentioned in the opening salutation, was a son[7] of Philemon

---

[1] On the name Papias or Pappias see above, p. 48.

[2] See Boeckh *Corp. Inscr.* III. p. 1085 for the names Νάνας, etc.

[3] We have not only the form Ἄππη several times (e.g. 3827 x, 3846 p, 3846 x, 3846 z[46], etc.); but also Ἄππης 3827 g, 3846 n, 3846 z[77], still as a woman's name.   These all occur in the same neighbourhood, at Cotiæum and Æzani.   I have not noticed any instance of this phenomenon in the names Apphia, Apphion; though pro-bably, where Roman influences were especially strong, there would be a tendency to transform a Phrygian name into a Roman, e. g. Apphia into Appia, and Apphianus into Appianus.

[4] In the Greek historians of Rome for instance the personal name is al-ways Ἄππιος and the road Ἀππία; so too in Acts xxviii. 15 it is Ἀππίου Φόρον.

[5] The point to be observed is that examples of these names are thickest in the heart of Phrygia, that they di-minish in frequency as Phrygian in-fluence becomes weaker, and that they almost, though not entirely, disappear in other parts of the Greek and Roman world.

[6] ver. 2 τῇ ἀδελφῇ.   See the note.

[7] So Theodore of Mopsuestia.   But Chrysostom ἕτερόν τινα ἴσως φίλον, and Theodoret ὁ δὲ Ἄρχιππος τὴν διδασκα-λίαν αὐτῶν ἐπεπίστευτο.

and Apphia. The inscriptions do not exhibit the name in
any such frequency, either in Phrygia or in the surrounding districts, as to suggest that it was characteristic of these parts[1].
Our Archippus held some important office in the Church[2]; His office
but what this was, we are not told. St Paul speaks of it as
a 'ministry' (διακονία). Some have interpreted the term tech-
nically as signifying the diaconate; but St Paul's emphatic
message seems to imply a more important position than this.
Others again suppose that he succeeded Epaphras as bishop of
Colossæ, when Epaphras left his native city to join the Apostle
at Rome[3]; but the assumption of a regular and continuous
episcopate in such a place as Colossæ at this date seems to
involve an anachronism. More probable than either is the
hypothesis which makes him a presbyter. Or perhaps he held
a missionary charge, and belonged to the order of 'evangelists[4].'
Another question too arises respecting Archippus. Where
was he exercising this ministry, whatever it may have been?
At Colossæ, or at Laodicea? His connexion with Philemon and abode,
would suggest the former place. But in the Epistle to the
Colossians his name is mentioned immediately after the salutation to the Laodiceans and the directions affecting that
Church; and this fact seems to connect him with Laodicea. Laodicea,
On the whole this appears to be the more probable solution[5]. rather than
Laodicea was within walking distance of Colossæ[6]. Archippus Colossæ.
must have been in constant communication with his parents,
who lived there; and it was therefore quite natural that,
writing to the father and mother, St Paul should mention the
son's name also in the opening address, though he was not on
the spot. An early tradition, if it be not a critical inference

[1] It occurs in two Smyrnæan inscriptions, no. 3143, 3224.

[2] Col. iv. 27 βλέπε τὴν διακονίαν ἣν
παρέλαβες ἐν Κυρίῳ, ἵνα αὐτὴν πληροῖς.

[3] So the Ambrosian Hilary on Col.
iv. 17.

[4] Ephes. iv. 11 bears testimony to
the existence of the office of evangelist
at this date.

[5] It is adopted by Theodore of

Mopsuestia. On the other hand Theodoret argues against this view on
critical grounds; τινὲς ἔφασαν τοῦτον
Λαοδικείας γεγενῆσθαι διδάσκαλον, ἀλλ'
ἡ πρὸς Φιλήμονα ἐπιστολὴ διδάσκει ὡς
ἐν Κολασσαῖς οὗτος ᾤκει· τῷ γὰρ Φιλήμονι καὶ τοῦτον συντάττει: but he
does not allege any traditional support
for his own opinion.

[6] See above, pp. 2, 15.

from the allusion in the Colossian letter, makes him bishop not of Colossæ, but of Laodicea[1].

His career. Of the apprehensions which the Apostle seems to have entertained respecting Archippus, I have already spoken[2]. It is not improbable that they were suggested by his youth and inexperience. St Paul here addresses him as his 'fellow-soldier[3],' but we are not informed on what spiritual campaigns they had served in company. Of his subsequent career we have no trustworthy evidence. Tradition represents him as having suffered martyrdom at Colossæ with his father and mother.

4. Onesimus. 4. But far more important to the history of Christianity than the parents or the son of the family, is the servant. The name Onesimus was very commonly borne by slaves. Like other words signifying utility, worth, and so forth, it naturally lent itself to this purpose[4]. Accordingly the inscriptions offer a very large number of examples in which it appears as the name of some slave or freedman[5]; and even where this is **A servile name.** not the case, the accompaniments frequently show that the person was of servile descent, though he might never himself have been a slave[6]. Indeed it occurs more than once as a fictitious name for a slave[7], a fact which points significantly to

---

[1] *Apost. Const.* vii. 46 quoted above, p. 306, note 1.

[2] See p. 42.

[3] ver. 2 τῷ συνστρατιώτῃ ἡμῶν. See the note.

[4] e. g. Chresimus, Chrestus, Onesiphorus, Symphorus, Carpus, etc. So too the corresponding female names Onesime, Chreste, Sympherusa, etc.: but more commonly the women's names are of a different cast of meaning, Arescusa, Prepusa, Terpusa, Thallusa, Tryphosa, etc.

[5] e.g. in the *Corp. Inscr. Lat.* III. p. 223, no. 2146, p. 359, no. 2723, p. 986, no. 6107 (where it is spelled Honesimus); and in Muratori, cc. 6, DXXIX. 5, CMLXVIII. 4, MIII. 2, MDXVIII. 2, MDXXIII. 4, MDLI. 9, MDLXXI. 5, MDLXXV. I, MDXCII. 8, MDXCVI. 7, MDCVI. 2, MDCX. 19, MDCXIV. 17, 39; and the corre-

sponding female name Onesime in MCCXXXIX. 12, MDXLVI. 6, MDCXII. 9. A more diligent search than I have made would probably increase the number of examples very largely.

[6] e.g. *Corp. Inscr. Lat.* III. p. 238, no. 1467, D. M. M. AVR . ONESIMO . CARPION . AVG . LIB . TABVL . FILIO. In the next generation any direct notice of servile origin would disappear; but the names very often indicate it. It need not however necessarily denote low extraction: see e.g. Liv. xliv. 16.

[7] Menander *Inc.* 312 (Meineke *Fragm. Com.* IV. p. 300), where the Ὀνήσιμος addressed is a slave, as appears from the mention of his τρόφιμος, i. e. master; Galen *de Opt. Doctr.* 1 (1. p. 41) ed. Kühn), where there is a reference to a work of Phavorinus in which was introduced one Onesimus ὁ Πλουτάρχου

the social condition naturally suggested by it. In the inscriptions of proconsular Asia it is found[1]; but no stress can be laid on this coincidence, for its occurrence as a proper name was doubtless coextensive with the use of the Greek language. More important is the fact that in the early history of Christianity it attains some eminence in this region. One Onesimus is bishop of Ephesus in the first years of the second century, when Ignatius passes through Asia Minor on his way to martyrdom, and is mentioned by the saint in terms of warm affection and respect[2]. Another, apparently an influential layman, about half a century later urges Melito bishop of Sardis to compile a volume of extracts from the Scriptures; and to him this father dedicates the work when completed[3]. Thus it would appear that the memory of the Colossian slave had invested the name with a special popularity among Christians in this district.

Its prominence among the Christians of proconsular Asia.

Onesimus represented the least respectable type of the least respectable class in the social scale. He was regarded by philosophers as a 'live chattel,' a 'live implement[4]'; and he had taken philosophy at her word. He had done what a chattel or an implement might be expected to do, if endued with life and intelligence. He was treated by the law as having no rights[5]; and he had carried the principles of the law to their logical consequences. He had declined to entertain any responsibilities.

Position and conduct of Onesimus.

δοῦλος ʼΕπικτήτῳ διαλεγόμενος; Anthol. Graec. II. p. 161, where the context shows that the person addressed as Onesimus is a slave; ib. II. p. 482, where the master, leaving legacies to his servants, says ʼΟνήσιμος εἴκοσι πέντε | μνᾶς ἐχέτω Δάος δʼ εἴκοσι μνᾶς ἐχέτω· | πεντήκοντα Σύρος· Συνέτη δέκα, κ.τ.λ. See also the use of the name in the Latin play quoted Suet. Galb. 13 (according to one reading).

[1] It occurs as near to Colossæ as Aphrodisias; Boeckh C. I. no. 2743.

[2] Ign. Ephes. 1 ἐν ʼΟνησίμῳ τῷ ἐν ἀγάπῃ ἀδιηγήτῳ ὑμῶν δὲ ἐν σαρκὶ ἐπισκόπῳ...εὐλόγητος ὁ χαρισάμενος ὑμῖν ἀξίοις οὖσιν τοιοῦτον ἐπίσκοπον κεκτῆ-

σθαι; see also §§ 2, 5, 6.

[3] Melito in Euseb. H. E. iv. 26 Μελίτων ʼΟνησίμῳ τῷ ἀδελφῷ χαίρειν. ʼΕπειδὴ πολλάκις ἠξίωσας κ.τ.λ.

[4] Aristot. Pol. i. 4 (p. 1253) ὁ δοῦλος κτῆμά τι ἔμψυχον, Eth. Nic. viii. 13 (p. 1161) ὁ γὰρ δοῦλος ἔμψυχον ὄργανον, τὸ δʼ ὄργανον ἄψυχος δοῦλος. See also the classification of 'implements' in Varro, de Re rust. I. 17. 1 'Instrumenti genus vocale et semivocale et mutum: vocale, in quo sunt servi; semivocale, in quo boves; mutum, in quo plaustra.'

[5] Dig. iv. 5 'Servile caput nullum jus habet' (Paulus); ib. l. 17 'In personam servilem nulla cadit obligatio' (Ulpianus).

There was absolutely nothing to recommend him. He was
a slave, and what was worse, a Phrygian slave; and he had
confirmed the popular estimate of his class[1] and nation[2] by
his own conduct. He was a thief and a runaway. His offence
did not differ in any way, so far as we know, from the vulgar
type of slavish offences. He seems to have done just what
the representative slave in the Roman comedy threatens to do,
when he gets into trouble. He had 'packed up some goods
and taken to his heels[3].' Rome was the natural cesspool for
these offscourings of humanity[4]. In the thronging crowds of
the metropolis was his best hope of secresy. In the dregs of
the city rabble he would find the society of congenial spirits.

His en-
counter
with St
Paul in
Rome

But at Rome the Apostle spread his net for him, and he
was caught in its meshes. How he first came in contact with
the imprisoned missionary we can only conjecture. Was it an
accidental encounter with his fellow-townsman Epaphras in the
streets of Rome which led to the interview? Was it the
pressure of want which induced him to seek alms from one
whose large-hearted charity must have been a household word
in his master's family? Or did the memory of solemn words,
which he had chanced to overhear at those weekly gatherings in the upper chamber at Colossæ, haunt him in his
loneliness, till, yielding to the fascination, he was constrained
to unburden himself to the one man who could soothe his

---

[1] Plaut. *Pseud.* I. 2, 6 'Ubi data
occasiost, rape, clepe, tene, harpaga,
bibe, es, fuge; hoc eorum opust'; Ovid
Amor. i. 15. 17 'Dum fallax servus.'

[2] Cicero speaks thus of Phrygia and
the neighbouring districts; *pro Flacc.* 27
'Utrum igitur nostrum est an vestrum
hoc proverbium *Phrygem plagis fieri
solere meliorem?* Quid de tota Caria?
Nonne hoc vestra voce vulgatum est;
si quid cum periculo experiri velis, *in
Care* id potissimum esse faciendum?
Quid porro in Graeco sermone tam
tritum est, quam si quis despicatui
ducitur, ut *Mysorum ultimus* esse di-
catur? Nam quid ego dicam de Lydia?
Quis unquam Graecus comoediam scripsit in qua servus primarum partium

non Lydus esset': comp. Alciphr.
Epist. iii. 38 Φρύγα οἰκέτην ἔχω πονηρόν κ.τ.λ.: Apollod. Com. (Meineke,
IV. p. 451) οὐ πανταχοῦ Φρύξ εἰμι
κ.τ.λ. This last passage refers to the
cowardice with which, besides all their
other bad qualities, the Phrygians were
credited: comp. Anon. Com. (*ib.* IV.
p. 652) δειλότερον λαγὼ Φρυγός, Tertull.
de Anim. 20 'Comici Phrygas timidos
illudunt': see Ribbeck *Com. Lat.* p.
106.

[3] Ter. *Phorm.* i. 4. 13 'aliquid con-
vasassem, atque hinc me protinam
conjicerem in pedes.'

[4] Sall. *Cat.* xxxvii. 5 'Romam sicuti
in sentinam confluxerant': comp. Tac.
Ann xv. 44.

terrors and satisfy his yearnings? Whatever motive may have drawn him to the Apostle's side—whether the pangs of hunger or the gnawings of conscience—when he was once within the range of attraction, he could not escape. He listened, was impressed, was convinced, was baptized. The slave of Philemon became the freedman of Christ[1]. St Paul found not only a sincere convert, but a devoted friend, in his latest son in the faith. Aristotle had said that there ought not to be, and could not be, any friendship with a slave *qua* slave, though there might be *qua* man[2]; and others had held still stronger language to the same effect. The Apostle did not recognise the philosopher's subtle distinction. For him the conventional barrier between slave and free had altogether vanished before the dissolving presence of an eternal verity[3]. He found in Onesimus something more than a slave, a beloved brother, both as a slave and as a man, 'both in the flesh and in the Lord[4].' The great capacity for good which appears in the typical slave of Greek and Roman fiction, notwithstanding all the fraud and profligacy overlying it, was evoked and developed here by the inspiration of a new faith and the incentive of a new hope. The genial, affectionate, winning disposition, purified and elevated by a higher knowledge, had found its proper scope. Altogether this new friendship was a solace and a strength to the Apostle in his weary captivity, which he could ill afford to forego. To take away Onesimus was to tear out Paul's heart[5].

But there was an imperious demand for the sacrifice. Onesimus had repented, but he had not made restitution. He could only do this by submitting again to the servitude from

Marginal notes: He and conversion. — St Paul's affection for him. — Necessity for his return

---

[1] 1 Cor. vii. 22.

[2] *Eth. Nic.* viii. 13 (p. 1161) φιλία δ' οὐκ ἔστι πρὸς τὰ ἄψυχα οὐδὲ δίκαιον· ἀλλ' οὐδὲ πρὸς ἵππον ἢ βοῦν, οὐδὲ πρὸς δοῦλον ᾗ δοῦλος· οὐδὲν γὰρ κοινόν ἐστιν· ὁ γὰρ δοῦλος ἔμψυχον ὄργανον, τὸ δ' ὄργανον ἄψυχος δοῦλος· ᾗ μὲν οὖν δοῦλος, οὐκ ἔστι φιλία πρὸς αὐτόν, ᾗ δ' ἄνθρωπος κ.τ.λ. On the views of Aristotle respecting slavery see Becker's *Charikles*

III. p. 2 sq. (ed. 2, 1854) with the editor K. F. Hermann's references to the literature of the subject, p. 5.

[3] 1 Cor. vii. 21 sq., Gal. iii. 28, Col. iii. 11. With this contrast the expression attributed to a speaker in Macrob. *Sat.* i. 11 'quasi vero curent divina de servis.'

[4] Philem. 16.

[5] ver. 12.

which he had escaped. Philemon must be made to feel that
when Onesimus was gained for Christ, he was regained for his
old master also. But if the claim of duty demanded a great
sacrifice from Paul, it demanded a greater still from Onesimus.

notwith-standing the risk. By returning he would place himself entirely at the mercy of the
master whom he had wronged. Roman law, more cruel than
Athenian, practically imposed no limits to the power of the
master over his slave[1]. The alternative of life or death rested
solely with Philemon, and slaves were constantly crucified for
far lighter offences than his[2]. A thief and a runaway, he had
no claim to forgiveness.

Mediation of Tychicus A favourable opportunity occurred for restoring Onesimus
to his master. Tychicus, as the bearer of letters from the
Apostle to Laodicea and Colossæ, had occasion to visit those
parts. He might undertake the office of mediator, and plead
the cause of the penitent slave with the offended master.
Under his shelter Onesimus would be safer than if he en-

supple-mented by the Apostle's letter. countered Philemon alone. But St Paul is not satisfied with
this precaution. He will with his own hand write a few words
of eager affectionate entreaty, identifying himself with the
cause of Onesimus. So he takes up his pen.

Analysis of the letter. After the opening salutation to Philemon and the members
of his family, he expresses his thankfulness for the report which
has reached his ears of his friend's charitable deeds. It is a
great joy and encouragement to the Apostle that so many
brethren have had cause to bless his name. This wide-spread
reputation for kindliness emboldens him to reveal his object in
writing. Though he has a right to command, he prefers rather
to entreat. He has a petition to prefer on behalf of a child of

---

[1] *Dig.* i. 6 'In potestate sunt servi
dominorum; quae quidem potestas
juris gentium est: nam apud omnes
peraeque gentes animadvertere possu-
mus dominis in servos vitae necisque
potestatem fuisse.' Comp. Senec. *de
Clem.* i. 18 'Cum in servum omnia
liceant.'

[2] So the mistress in Juv. *Sat.* vi.
219 sq. 'Pone crucem servo. Meruit

quo crimine servus supplicium? quis
testis adest? quis detulit?... O demens,
ita servus homo est? nil fecerit, esto.
Hoc volo, sic jubeo, etc.' Compare
the words of the slave in Plautus *Mil.
Glor.* ii. 4. 19 'Noli minitari: scio
crucem futuram mihi sepulcrum: Ibi
mei sunt majores siti, pater, avos,
proavos, abavos.'

his own. This is none other than Onesimus, whom Philemon will remember only as a worthless creature, altogether untrue to his name, but who now is a reformed man. He would have wished to detain Onesimus, for he can ill afford to dispense with his loving services. Indeed Philemon would doubtless have been glad thus to minister vicariously to the Apostle's wants. But a benefit which wears the appearance of being forced, whether truly so or not, loses all its value, and therefore he sends him back. Nay, there may have been in this desertion a Divine providence which it would ill become him Paul to thwart, Onesimus may have been withheld from Philemon for a time, that he might be restored to him for ever. He may have left as a slave, that he might return more than a slave. To others— to the Apostle himself especially—he is now a dearly beloved brother. Must he not be this and more than this to Philemon, whether in earthly things or in heavenly things? He therefore begs Philemon to receive Onesimus as he would receive himself. As for any injury that he may have done, as for any money that he may owe, the Apostle makes himself responsible for this. The present letter may be accepted as a bond, a security for repayment. Yet at the same time he cannot refrain from reminding Philemon that he might fairly claim the remission of so small an amount. Does not his friend owe to him his own soul besides? Yes, he has a right to look for some filial grati- tude and duty from one to whom he stands in the relation of a spiritual father. Philemon will surely not refuse him this com- fort in his many trials. He writes in the full confidence that he will be obeyed; he is quite sure that his friend will do more than is asked of him. At the same time he trusts to see him before very long, and to talk over this and other matters. Philemon may provide him a lodging: for he hopes through their prayers that he may be liberated, and given back to them. Then follow the salutations, and the letter ends with the Apostle's benediction.

Of the result of this appeal we have no certain knowledge. It is reasonable to suppose however that Philemon would not

belie the Apostle's hopes; that he would receive the slave as a
brother; that he would even go beyond the express terms of
the Apostle's petition, and emancipate the penitent.   But all
this is a mere conjecture.   One tradition makes Onesimus bishop
of Ephesus [1].   But this obviously arises from a confusion with
Legendary his namesake, who lived about half a century later [2].   Another
history.
story points to Berœa in Macedonia as his see [3].   This is at least
free from the suspicion of having been suggested by any notice
in the Apostolic writings: but the authority on which it rests
does not entitle it to much credit.   The legend of his missionary
labours in Spain and of his martyrdom at Rome may have been
built on the hypothesis of his continuing in the Apostle's
company, following in the Apostle's footsteps, and sharing the
Apostle's fate.   Another story, which gives a circumstantial
account of his martyrdom at Puteoli, seems to confuse him with
a namesake who suffered, or was related to have suffered, in the
Decian persecution [4].

Deprecia-   The estimate formed of this epistle at various epochs has
tion of the
epistle   differed widely.   In the fourth century there was a strong bias
in early   against it.   The 'spirit of the age' had no sympathy with either
times.
the subject or the handling.   Like the spirit of more than one
later age, it was enamoured of its own narrowness, which it
mistook for largeness of view, and it could not condescend to
such trivialities as were here offered to it.   Its maxim seemed
to be *De minimis non curat evangelium*.   Of what account was
the fate of a single insignificant slave, long since dead and gone,
to those before whose eyes the battle of the creeds was still
raging?   This letter taught them nothing about questions of
theological interest, nothing about matters of ecclesiastical disci-

---

[1] See *Acta Sanct. Boll.* xvi Febr.
(II. p. 857 sq. ed. nov.) for the authorities, if they deserve the name.

[2] If we take the earlier date of the
Epistles of St Ignatius, A.D. 107, we
get an interval of 44 years between the
Onesimus of St Paul and the Onesimus
of Ignatius.   It is not altogether impossible therefore that the same person

may be intended.   But on the other
hand the language of Ignatius (*Ephes.*
I sq.) leaves the impression that he is
speaking of a person comparatively
young and untried in office.

[3] *Apost. Const.* vii. 46, quoted above,
p. 306, note I.

[4] For the legend compare *Act.*
Sanct. l. c. p. 858 sq.   See also the

pline; and therefore they would have none of it. They denied that it had been written by St Paul. It mattered nothing to them that the Church from the earliest ages had accepted it as genuine, that even the remorseless 'higher criticism' of a Marcion had not ventured to lay hands on it[1]. It was wholly unworthy of the Apostle. If written by him, they contended, it must have been written when he was not under the influence of the Spirit: its contents were altogether so unedifying. We may infer from the replies of Jerome[2], of Chrysostom[3], and of Theodore of Mopsuestia[4], that they felt themselves to be stemming a fierce current of prejudice which had set in this direction. But they were strong in the excellence of their cause, and they nobly vindicated this epistle against its assailants. *Reply of the fathers.*

In modern times there has been no disposition to under-rate its value. Even Luther and Calvin, whose bias tended to the depreciation of the ethical as compared with the doctrinal portions of the scriptures, show a true appreciation of its beauty and significance. 'This epistle', writes Luther, 'showeth a right noble lovely example of Christian love. Here we see how *High estimate of modern writers.* *Luther.*

---

note on the Ignatian *Mart. Rom.* 10.

[1] Hieron. *Comm. in Philem.* praef. vii. p. 743 'Pauli esse epistolam ad Philemonem saltem Marcione auctore doceantur: qui, quum caeteras epistolas ejusdem vel non susceperit vel quaedam in his mutaverit atque corroserit, in hanc solam manus non est ausus mittere, quia sua illam brevitas defendebat.' St Jerome has in his mind Tertullian *adv. Marc.* v. 21 'Soli huic epistolae brevitas sua profuit, ut falsarias manus Marcionis evaderet.'

[2] *ib.* p. 742 sq. 'Qui nolunt inter epistolas Pauli eam recipere quae ad Philemonem scribitur, aiunt non semper apostolum nec omnia Christo in se loquente dixisse, quia nec humana imbecillitas unum tenorem Sancti Spiritus ferre potuisset etc...His et caeteris istius modi volunt aut epistolam non esse Pauli quae ad Philemonem scribitur aut, etiamsi Pauli sit, nihil ha-

bere quod aedificare nos possit etc.... sed mihi videntur, dum epistolam simplicitatis arguunt, suam imperitiam prodere, non intelligentes quid in singulis sermonibus virtutis et sapientiae lateat.'

[3] *Argum. in Philem.* ἀλλ' ἐπειδὴ τινές φασι περιττὸν εἶναι τὸ καὶ ταύτην προσκεῖσθαι τὴν ἐπιστολήν, εἴγε ὑπὲρ πράγματος μικροῦ ἠξίωσεν, ὑπὲρ ἑνὸς ἀνδρός, μαθέτωσαν ὅσοι ταῦτα ἐγκαλοῦσιν ὅτι μυρίων εἰσὶν ἐγκλημάτων ἄξιοι κ.τ.λ., and he goes on to discuss the value of the epistle at some length.

[4] *Spicil. Solesm.* I. p. 149 'Quid vero ex ea lucri possit acquiri, convenit manifestius explicare, quia nec omnibus id existimo posse esse cognitum; quod maxime heri jam ipse a nobis disseri postulasti'; *ib.* p. 152 'De his et nunc superius dixi, quod non omnes similiter arbitror potius se (potuisse?) prospicere.'

St Paul layeth himself out for poor Onesimus, and with all his means pleadeth his cause with his master: and so setteth himself as if he were Onesimus, and had himself done wrong to Philemon. Even as Christ did for us with God the Father, thus also doth St Paul for Onesimus with Philemon...We are all his Onesimi, to my thinking.' 'Though he handleth a subject,' says Calvin, 'which otherwise were low and mean, yet after his manner he is borne up aloft unto God. With such modest entreaty doth he humble himself on behalf of the lowest of men, that scarce anywhere else is the gentleness of his spirit portrayed more truly to the life.' And the chorus of admiration has been swelled by later voices from the most opposite quarters. 'The single Epistle to Philemon,' says one quoted by Bengel, 'very far surpasses all the wisdom of the world[1].' 'Nowhere,' writes Ewald, 'can the sensibility and warmth of a tender friendship blend more beautifully with the loftier feeling of a commanding spirit, a teacher and an Apostle, than in this letter, at once so brief, and yet so surpassingly full and significant[2].' 'A true little chef d'œuvre of the art of letter-writing,' exclaims M. Renan characteristically[3]. 'We have here,' writes Sabatier, 'only a few familiar lines, but so full of grace, of salt, of serious and trustful affection, that this short epistle gleams like a pearl of the most exquisite purity in the rich treasure of the New Testament[4].' Even Baur, while laying violent hands upon it, is constrained to speak of this 'little letter' as 'making such an agreeable impression by its attractive form' and as penetrated 'with the noblest Christian spirit[5].'

Calvin.

Later writers.

The epistle compared with a letter of Pliny,

The Epistle to Philemon has more than once been compared with the following letter addressed to a friend by the younger Pliny on a somewhat similar occasion[6]:

Your freedman, with whom you had told me you were vexed, came to me, and throwing himself down before me clung to my feet,

[1] Franke *Praef. N. T. Graec.* p. 26, 27, quoted by Bengel on Philem. 1.
[2] *Die Sendschreiben* etc. p. 458.
[3] *L'Antéchrist* p. 96.
[4] *L'Apôtre Paul* p. 194. He goes on to say; 'Never has the precept which

Paul himself gave at the end of his letter to the Colossians been better realised, ὁ λόγος ὑμῶν πάντοτε ἐν χάριτι, ἅλατι ἠρτυμένος κ.τ.λ. (Col. iv. 6).'
[5] *Paulus* p. 476.
[6] Plin. *Ep.* ix. 21.

as if they had been yours. He was profuse in his tears and his entreaties; he was profuse also in his silence. In short, he convinced me of his penitence. I believe that he is indeed a reformed character, because he feels that he has done wrong. You are angry, I know; and you have reason to be angry, this also I know: but mercy wins the highest praise just when there is the most righteous cause for anger. You loved the man, and, I hope, will continue to love him: meanwhile it is enough, that you should allow yourself to yield to his prayers. You may be angry again, if he deserves it; and in this you will be the more readily pardoned if you yield now. Concede something to his youth, something to his tears, something to your own indulgent disposition. Do not torture him, lest you torture yourself at the same time. For it *is* torture to you, when one of your gentle temper is angry. I am afraid lest I should appear not to ask but to compel, if I should add my prayers to his. Yet I will add them the more fully and unreservedly, because I scolded the man himself with sharpness and severity; for I threatened him straitly that I would never ask you again. This I said to him, for it was necessary to alarm him; but I do not use the same language to you. For perchance I shall ask again, and shall be successful again; only let my request be such, as it becomes me to prefer and you to grant. Farewell.

The younger Pliny is the noblest type of a true Roman gentleman, and this touching letter needs no words of praise. Yet, if purity of diction be excepted, there will hardly be any difference of opinion in awarding the palm to the Christian Apostle. As an expression of simple dignity, of refined courtesy, of large sympathy, and of warm personal affection, the Epistle to Philemon stands unrivalled. And its pre-eminence is the more remarkable because in style it is exceptionally loose. It owes nothing to the graces of rhetoric; its effect is due solely to the spirit of the writer. *as an expression of character.*

But the interest which attaches to this short epistle as an expression of individual character is far less important than its significance as exhibiting the attitude of Christianity to a widely spread and characteristic social institution of the ancient world. *Its higher interest.*

Slavery was practised by the Hebrews under the sanction of the Mosaic law, not less than by the Greeks and Romans.

Slavery among the Hebrews. But though the same in name, it was in its actual working something wholly different. The Hebrew was not suffered either by law-giver er by prophet to forget that he himself had been a bondman in the land of Egypt; and all his relations to his dependents were moulded by the sympathy of this recollection. His slaves were members of his family; they were members also of the Holy Congregation. They had their religious, as well as their social, rights. If Hebrews, their liberty was secured to them after six years' service at the outside. If foreigners, they were protected by the laws from the tyranny and violence of their masters. Considering the conditions of ancient society, and more especially of ancient warfare, slavery as practised among the Hebrews was probably an escape from alternatives which would have involved a far greater amount of human misery. Still even in this form it was only a temporary concession, till the fulness of time came, and the world was taught that 'in Christ is neither bond nor free[1].'

Among the Jews the slaves formed only a small fraction of the whole population[2]. They occupy a very insignificant place in the pictures of Hebrew life and history which have been handed down to us. But in Greece and Rome the case was far different. In our enthusiastic eulogies of free, enlightened, democratic Athens, we are apt to forget that the interests of the many were ruthlessly sacrificed to the selfishness of the few. The slaves of Attica on the most probable computation were about four times as numerous as the citizens, and about three times as numerous as the whole free population of the state, including the resident aliens[3]. They were consigned for the most part to labour in gangs in the fields or the mines

Large number of slaves in Greece and Rome.

---

[1] On slavery among the Hebrews see the admirable work of Prof. Goldwin Smith *Does the Bible sanction American slavery?* p. 1 sq.

[2] In Ezra ii. 65 the number of slaves compared with the number of free is a little more than one to six.

[3] Boeckh *Public Economy of Athens* p. 35 sq. According to a census taken by Demetrius Phalereus there were in the year 309 B.C. 21,000 citizens, 10,000 residents, and 400,000 slaves (Ctesicles in Athen. vi. p. 272 B). This would make the proportion of slaves to citizens nearly twenty to one. It is supposed however that the number of citizens here includes only adult males, whereas the number of slaves may comprise both sexes and all ages. Hence Boeckh's estimate

or the factories, without any hope of bettering their condition. In the light of these facts we see what was really meant by popular government and equal rights at Athens. The proportions of the slave population elsewhere were even greater. In the small island of Ægina, scarcely exceeding forty English square miles in extent, there were 470,000 slaves; in the contracted territory of Corinth there were not less than 460,000[1]. The statistics of slave-holding in Italy are quite as startling. We are told that wealthy Roman landowners sometimes possessed as many as ten or twenty thousand slaves, or even more[2]. We may indeed not unreasonably view these vague and general statements with suspicion: but it is a fact that, a few years before the Christian era, one Claudius Isidorus left by will more than four thousand slaves, though he had incurred serious losses by the civil war[3].

And these vast masses of human beings had no protection from Roman law[4]. The slave had no relationships, no conjugal rights. Cohabitation was allowed to him at his owner's pleasure, but not marriage. His companion was sometimes assigned to him by lot[5]. The slave was absolutely at his master's disposal; for the smallest offence he might be scourged, mutilated, crucified, thrown to the wild beasts[6]. Only two or

Cruelty of Roman law towards slaves.

which is adopted in the text. For other calculations see Wallon *Histoire de l'Esclavage* I. p. 221 sq.

[1] Athen. *l. c.* p. 272 B, D. The statement respecting Ægina is given on the authority of Aristotle; that respecting Corinth on the authority of Epitimæus.

[2] Athen. *l. c.* Ῥωμαίων ἕκαστος ... πλείστους ὅσους κεκτημένος οἰκέτας· καὶ γὰρ μυρίους καὶ δισμυρίους καὶ ἔτι πλείους δὲ πάμπολλοι κέκτηνται. See Becker *Gallus* II. p. 113 (ed. 3).

[3] Plin. *N. H.* xxxiii. 47.

[4] On the condition of Greek and Roman slaves the able and exhaustive work of Wallon *Histoire de l'Esclavage dans l'Antiquité* (Paris 1847) is the chief authority. See also Becker and Marquardt *Röm. Alterth.* v. I. p. 139 sq.; Becker *Charikles* II. p. 1 sq., *Gallus* II. p. 99 sq. The practical

working of slavery among the Romans is placed in its most favourable light in Gaston Bossier *La Religion Romaine* II. p. 343 sq. (Paris 1874), and in Overbeck *Studien zur Gesch. d. Alten Kirche* I. p. 158 sq.

[5] *Röm. Alterth.* l. c. p. 184 sq.; *Gallus* II. p. 144 sq. In this, as in other respects, the cruelty of the legislature was mitigated by the humanity of individual masters; and the inscriptions show that male and female slaves in many cases were allowed to live together through life as man and wife, though the law did not recognise or secure their union. It was reserved for Constantine to take the initiative in protecting the conjugal and family rights of slaves by legislature; *Cod. Theod.* ii. 25. 1.

[6] Wallon II. p. 177 sq.; *Röm. Alterth.* l. c.; *Gallus* II. p. 145 sq.; Rein *Privat-*

three years before the letter to Philemon was written, and probably during St Paul's residence in Rome, a terrible tragedy had been enacted under the sanction of the law [1]. Pedanius Secundus, a senator, had been slain by one of his slaves in a fit of anger or jealousy. The law demanded that in such cases all the slaves under the same roof at the time should be put to death. On the present occasion four hundred persons were condemned to suffer by this inhuman enactment. The populace however interposed to rescue them, and a tumult ensued. The Senate accordingly took the matter into deliberation. Among the speakers C. Cassius strongly advocated the enforcement of the law. 'The dispositions of slaves,' he argued, 'were regarded with suspicion by our ancestors, even when they were born on the same estates or in the same houses and learnt to feel an affection for their masters from the first. Now however, when we have several nations among our slaves, with various rites, with foreign religions or none at all, it is not possible to keep down such a rabble except by fear.' These sentiments prevailed, and the law was put in force. But the roads were lined by a military guard, as the prisoners were led to execution, to prevent a popular outbreak. This incident illustrates not only the heartless cruelty of the law, but also the social dangers arising out of slavery. Indeed the universal distrust had already found expression in a common proverb, 'As many enemies as slaves [2].' But this was not the only way in which slavery avenged itself on the Romans. The spread of luxury and idleness was a direct consequence of this state of things. Work came to be regarded as a low and degrading, because a servile occupation. Meanwhile sensuality in its vilest

recht der Römer p. 552 sq. Hadrian first took away from masters the power of life and death over their slaves; Spart. *Vit. Hadr.* 18 'Servos a dominis occidi vetuit eosque jussit damnari per judices, si digni essent'. For earlier legislative enactments which had afforded a very feeble protection to slaves, see below p. 327.

[1] Tac. *Ann.* xiv. 42. This incident

took place A.D. 61. The law in question was the *Senatusconsultum Silonianum*, passed under Augustus A. D. 10.

[2] Senec. *Ep. Mor.* 47 'Deinde ejusdem arrogantiae proverbium jactatur *totidem hostes esse quot servos*'; comp. Macrob. i. 11. 13. See also Festus p. 261 (Ed. Mueller) '*Quot servi tot hostes* in proverbio est'.

forms was fostered by the tremendous power which placed the slave at the mercy of the master's worst passions[1].

With this wide-spread institution Christianity found itself in conflict. How was the evil to be met? Slavery was inwoven into the texture of society; and to prohibit slavery was to tear society into shreds. Nothing less than a servile war with its certain horrors and its doubtful issues must have been the consequence. Such a mode of operation was altogether alien to the spirit of the Gospel. 'The New Testament', it has been truly said, 'is not concerned with any political or social institutions; for political and social institutions belong to particular nations and particular phases of society.' 'Nothing marks the divine character of the Gospel more than its perfect freedom from any appeal to the spirit of political revolution[2].' It belongs to all time: and therefore, instead of attacking special abuses, it lays down universal principles which shall undermine the evil. *Christianity not revolutionary.*

Hence the Gospel never directly attacks slavery as an institution: the Apostles never command the liberation of slaves as an absolute duty. It is a remarkable fact that St Paul in this epistle stops short of any positive injunction. The word 'emancipation' seems to be trembling on his lips, and yet he does not once utter it. He charges Philemon to take the runaway slave Onesimus into his confidence again; to receive him *St Paul's treatment of the case of Onesimus.*

---

[1] See the saying of Haterius in the elder Seneca *Controv.* iv. Praef., 'Impudicitia in ingenuo crimen est, *in servo necessitas*, in liberto officium', with its context. Wallon (I. p. 332) sums up the condition of the slave thus: 'L'esclave appartenait au maître: par lui même, il n'était rien, il n'avait rien. Voilà le principe; et tout ce qu'on en peut tirer par voie de conséquence formait aussi, en fait, l'état commun des esclaves dans la plupart des pays. A toutes les époques, dans toutes les situations de la vie, cette autorité souveraine plane sur eux et modifie leur destinée par ses rigueurs comme par son indif-

ference. Dans l'âge de la force et dans la plénitude de leurs facultés, elle les vouait, à son choix, soit au travail, soit au vice; au travail les natures grossières; au vice, les natures plus délicates, nourries pour le plaisir du maître, et qui lorsqu'il en était las, étaient reléguées dans la prostitution a son profit. Avant et après l'âge du travail, abandonnés a leur faiblesse ou a leurs infirmités; enfants, ils grand-issaient dans le désordre; viellards, ils mouraient souvent dans la misère; morts, ils étaient quelquefois délaissés sur la voie publique...'

[2] G. Smith *Does the Bible etc.?* pp. 95, 96.

with all affection; to regard him no more as a slave but as
a brother; to treat him with the same consideration, the same
love, which he entertains for the Apostle himself to whom he
owes everything. In fact he tells him to do very much more
than emancipate his slave, but this one thing he does not
directly enjoin. St Paul's treatment of this individual case
is an apt illustration of the attitude of Christianity towards
slavery in general.

His lan-
guage re-
specting
slavery
elsewhere.

Similar also is his language elsewhere. Writing to the
Corinthians, he declares the absolute equality of the freeman
and the slave in the sight of God[1]. It follows therefore that
the slave may cheerfully acquiesce in his lot, knowing that all
earthly distinctions vanish in the light of this eternal truth.
If his freedom should be offered to him, he will do well to
accept it, for it puts him in a more advantageous position[2]:
but meanwhile he need not give himself any concern about
his lot in life. So again, when he addresses the Ephesians and
Colossians on the mutual obligations of masters and slaves,
he is content to insist on the broad fact that both alike are
slaves of a heavenly Master, and to enforce the duties which

---

[1] 1 Cor. vii. 21 sq.

[2] The clause, ἀλλ' εἰ καὶ δύνασαι
ἐλεύθερος γενέσθαι, μᾶλλον χρῆσαι, has
been differently interpreted from early
times, either as recommending the
slave to avail himself of any opportunity of emancipation, or as advising
him to refuse the offer of freedom and
to remain in servitude. The earliest
commentator whose opinion I have
observed, Origen (in Cram. *Cat.* p.
140), interprets it as favourable to
liberty, but he confuses the meaning by giving a metaphorical sense to
slavery, δοῦλον ὠνόμασεν ἀναγκαίως τὸν
γεγαμηκότα. Again, Severianus (ib. p.
141) distinctly explains it as recommending a state of liberty. On the
other hand Chrysostom, while mentioning that 'certain persons' interpret
it εἰ δύνασαι ἐλευθερωθῆναι, ἐλευθερώθητι,
himself supposes St Paul to advise the
slave's remaining in slavery. And so
Theodoret and others. The balance

of argument seems to be decidedly in
favour of the former view.

(1) The actual language must be
considered first. And here (i) the
particles εἰ καὶ will suit either interpretation. If they are translated ' even
though', the clause recommends the
continuance in slavery. But καὶ may
be equally well taken with δύνασαι, and
the words will then mean 'if it *should*
be in your power to obtain your freedom'. So above ver. 11 ἐὰν δὲ καὶ
χωρισθῇ: comp. Luke xi. 18 εἰ δὲ καὶ
ὁ Σατανᾶς ἐφ' ἑαυτὸν διεμερίσθη, 1 Pet.
iii. 14 ἀλλ' εἰ καὶ πάσχοιτε διὰ δικαιοσύνην. (ii) The expression μᾶλλον χρῆσαι
seems to direct the slave to avail himself of some *new*-opportunity offered,
and therefore to recommend liberty;
comp. ix. 12, 15.

(2) The immediate context will
admit either interpretation. If slavery
be preferred, the sentence is continuous. If liberty, the clause ἀλλ' εἰ

flow from its recognition[1]. He has no word of reproach for the masters on the injustice of their position; he breathes no hint to the slaves of a social grievance needing redress.

But meanwhile a principle is boldly enunciated, which must in the end prove fatal to slavery. When the Gospel taught that God had made all men and women upon earth of one family; that all alike were His sons and His daughters; that, whatever conventional distinctions human society might set up, the supreme King of Heaven refused to acknowledge any; that the slave notwithstanding his slavery was Christ's freedman, and the free notwithstanding his liberty was Christ's slave; when the Church carried out this principle by admitting the slave to her highest privileges, inviting him to kneel side by side with his master at the same holy table; when in short the Apostolic precept that 'in Christ Jesus is neither bond nor free' was not only recognised but acted upon, then slavery was doomed. Henceforward it was only a question of time. Here was the idea which must act as a solvent, must disintegrate this venerable institution, however deeply rooted and however widely spread. 'The brotherhood of man, in short, is the idea

The Christian idea fatal to slavery.

καὶ...μᾶλλον χρῆσαι is parenthetical. In this latter case its motive is to correct misapprehension, as if the Apostle would say, 'When I declare the absolute indifference of the two states in the sight of God, I do not mean to say that you should not avail yourselves of freedom, if it comes in your way; it puts you in a more advantageous position, and you will do well to prefer it'. Such a corrective parenthesis is altogether after St Paul's manner, and indeed instances occur in this very context: e.g. ver. 11 ἐὰν δὲ καὶ χωρισθῇ κ.τ.λ., ver. 15 εἰ δὲ ὁ ἄπιστος χωρίζεται κ.τ.λ. This last passage is an exact parallel, for the γὰρ of ver. 16 is connected immediately with ver. 14, the parenthesis being disregarded as here.

(3) The argument which seems decisive is the extreme improbability that St Paul should have recommended slavery in preference to freedom. For

(i) Such a recommendation would be alien to the spirit of a man whose sense of political right was so strong, and who asserted his citizenship so stanchly on more than one occasion (Acts xvi. 37, xxii. 28). (ii) The independent position of the freeman would give him an obvious advantage in doing the work of Christ, which it is difficult to imagine St Paul enjoining him deliberately to forego. (iii) Throughout the passage the Apostle, while maintaining the indifference of these earthly relations in the sight of God, yet always gives the preference to a position of *independence*, whenever it comes to a Christian naturally and without any undue impatience on his part. The spirit which animates St Paul's injunctions here may be seen from vv. 8, 11, 15, 26, 27 etc.

[1] Ephes. vi. 5—9, Col. iii. 22—iv. 1.

Its general which Christianity in its social phase has been always striving
tendency. to realise, and the progress of which constitutes the social
history of Christendom. With what difficulties this idea has
struggled; how it has been marred by revolutionary violence, as
well as impeded by reactionary selfishness; to what chimerical
hopes, to what wild schemes, to what calamitous disappoint-
ments, to what desperate conflicts, it has given birth; how
often being misunderstood and misapplied, it has brought not
peace on earth but a sword—it is needless here to rehearse.
Still, as we look back over the range of past history, we can
see beyond doubt that it is towards this goal that Christianity
as a social principle has been always tending and still tends[1].'

Its effects   And this beneficent tendency of the Gospel was felt at
on slavery. once in its effects on slavery. The Church indeed, even in
the ardour of her earliest love, did not prohibit her sons from
retaining slaves in their households. It is quite plain from
extant notices, that in the earlier centuries, as in the later,
Christians owned slaves[2] like their heathen neighbours, without forfeiting consideration among their fellow-believers. But
nevertheless the Christian idea was not a dead-letter. The
Protection chivalry of the Gospel which regarded the weak and helpless
and manu-
mission of from whatever cause, as its special charge, which extended its
slaves.   protection to the widow, the orphan, the sick, the aged, and the
prisoner, was not likely to neglect the slave. Accordingly we
find that one of the earliest forms which Christian benevolence
took was the contribution of funds for the liberation of slaves[2].
Honours   But even more important than overt acts like these was the
paid to
slave mar- moral and social importance with which the slave was now
tyrs.   invested. Among the heroes and heroines of the Church were
found not a few members of this class. When slave girls like

---

[1] G. Smith *Does the Bible etc.?* p.
121.

[2] Athenag. *Suppl.* 35 δοῦλοί εἰσιν
ἡμῖν, τοῖς μὲν καὶ πλείους τοῖς δ᾽ ἐλάττους.
It would even appear that the domestic servant who betrayed Polycarp
(*Mart. Polyc.* 6) was a slave, for he
was put to the torture. Comp. Justin.
Apol. ii. 12. See also passages from

Christian writers collected in Babington *Abolition of Slavery* p. 20 sq.

[3] Ignat. *Polyc.* 4 μὴ ἐράτωσαν ἀπὸ
τοῦ κοινοῦ ἐλευθεροῦσθαι, *Apost. Const.*
iv. 9 τὰ ἐξ αὐτῶν, ὡς προειρήκαμεν,
ἀθροιζόμενα χρήματα διατάσσετε διακονοῦντες εἰς ἀγορασμοὺς τῶν ἁγίων, ῥυό-
μενοι δούλους καὶ αἰχμαλώτους, δε-
σμίους, κ.τ.λ.

Blandina in Gaul or Felicitas in Africa, having won for themselves the crown of martyrdom, were celebrated in the festivals of the Church with honours denied to the most powerful and noblest born of mankind, social prejudice had received a wound which could never be healed.

While the Church was still kept in subjection, moral influence and private enterprise were her only weapons. But Christianity was no sooner seated on the throne of the Cæsars than its influence began to be felt in the imperial policy[1]. The legislation of Constantine, despite its startling inequalities, forms a unique chapter in the statute-book of Rome. In its mixed character indeed it reflects the transitional position of its author. But after all allowance made for its very patent defects, its general advance in the direction of humanity and purity is far greater than can be traced in the legislation even of the most humane and virtuous of his heathen predecessors. More especially in the extension of legal protection to slaves, and in the encouragement given to emancipation, we have an earnest of the future work which Christianity was destined to do for this oppressed class of mankind, though the relief which it gave was after all very partial and tentative[2].

Christianity predominant.

Legislation of Constantine.

[1] It must not however be forgotten that, even before Christianity became the predominant religion, a more humane spirit had entered into Roman legislation. The important enactment of Hadrian has been already mentioned, p. 321, note 6. Even earlier the *lex Petronia* (of which the date is uncertain) had prohibited masters from making their slaves fight with wild beasts in mere caprice and without an order from a judge (*Dig.* xlviii. 8. 11); and Claudius (A.D. 47), finding that the practice of turning out sick slaves into the streets to die was on the increase, ordered that those who survived this treatment should have their freedom (Dion Cass. lx. 29, Suet. *Claud.* 25). For these and similar enactments of the heathen emperors see Wallon III. p. 60 sq., *Röm. Alterth.* v. I. 197, Rein *Privatrecht d. Römer*

p. 560 sq. The character of this exceptional legislation is the strongest impeachment of the general cruelty of the law; while at the same time subsequent notices show how very far from effective it was even within its own narrow limits. See for instance the passage in Galen, v. p. 17 (ed. Kühn) λακτίζουσι καὶ τοὺς ὀφθαλμοὺς ἐξορύττουσι καὶ γραφείῳ κεντοῦσιν κ.τ.λ. (comp. *ib.* p. 584), or Seneca *de Ira* iii. 3. 6 'eculei et fidiculae et ergastula et cruces et circumdati defossis corporibus ignes et cadavera quoque trahens uncus, varia vinculorum genera, varia poenarum, lacerationes membrorum, inscriptiones frontis et bestiarum immanium caveae.'
On the causes of these ameliorations in the law see *Röm. Alterth.* v. I. p. 199.
[2] On the legislation of Constantine affecting slavery see De Broglie

And on the whole this part has been faithfully and courageously performed by the Church. There have been shameful exceptions now and then: there has been occasional timidity and excess of caution. The commentaries of the fathers on this epistle are an illustration of this latter fault[1]. Much may be pardoned to men who shrink from seeming to countenance a violent social revolution. But notwithstanding, it is a broad and patent fact that throughout the early and middle ages the influence of the Church was exerted strongly on the side of humanity in this matter[2]. The emancipation of slaves was regarded as the principal aim of the higher Christian life[3]; the amelioration of serfdom was a matter of constant solicitude with the rulers of the Church.

The conquests and
hopes of
the present time.
And at length we seem to see the beginning of the end. The rapid strides towards emancipation during the present generation are without a parallel in the history of the world. The abolition of slavery throughout the British Empire at an enormous material sacrifice is one of the greatest moral

---

L'Eglise et L'Empire Romain i. p. 304 sq. (ed. 5), Chawner *Influence of Christianity upon the Legislation of Constantine the Great* p. 73 sq., Wallon iii. p. 414 sq. The legislation of Justinian is still more honourably distinguished for its alleviation of the evils of slavery.

[1] *E.g.* Chrysostom and Theodore of Mopsuestia (*Spic. Solesm.* i. p. 152). Yet St Chrysostom himself pleads the cause of slaves earnestly elsewhere. In *Hom. xl ad* i *Cor.*, x. p. 385 he says of slavery, 'It is the penalty of sin and the punishment of disobedience. But when Christ came, he annulled even this, *For in Christ Jesus there is no slave nor free.* Therefore it is not necessary to have a slave; but, if it should be necessary, then one only or at most a second'. And he then tells his audience that if they really care for the welfare of slaves, they must 'buy them, and having taught them some art that they may maintain themselves, set them free.' 'I know,' he adds, 'that I am annoying my hearers; but

what can I do? For this purpose I am appointed, and I will not cease speaking so.' On the attitude of this father towards slavery see Möhler p. 89 sq.

[2] On the influence of Christianity in this respect see Wallon iii. p. 314 sq., Biot *De l'Abolition de l'Esclavage Ancien en Occident* (1840), Ch. Babington *Influence of Christianity in promoting the Abolition of Slavery* etc. (1846), Schmidt *Essai historique sur la Société Civile dans le Monde Romain* etc. p. 228 sq. (1853), Möhler *Gesammelte Schriften* ii. p. 54 sq., G. Smith *Does the Bible etc.?* p. 95 sq., E. S. Talbot *Slavery as affected by Christianity* (1869), Lecky *Rationalism in Europe* ii. p. 255 sq., *European Morals* ii. p. 65 sq., Overbeck *Studien etc.* i. p. 172 sq., Allard *Les Esclaves Chrétiens* (1876). The last-mentioned work, which appeared after this introduction was first published (1875), treats the question very fully.

[3] Möhler p. 99 sq., Schmidt p. 246 sq., Lecky *E. M.* ii. p. 73 sq.

conquests which England has ever achieved. The liberation of twenty millions of serfs throughout the Russian dominions has thrown a halo of glory round the name of Alexander II., which no time can dim. The emancipation of the negro in the vast republic of the New World was a victory not less important than either to the well-being of the human race. Thus within the short period of little more than a quarter of a century this reproach of civilisation and humanity has been wiped out in the three greatest empires of the world. It is a fit sequel to these achievements, that at length a well-directed attack should have been made on the central fortress of slavery and the slave-trade, the interior of Africa. May we not venture to predict that in future ages, when distance of view shall have adjusted the true relations of events, when the brilliancy of empires and the fame of wars shall have sunk to their proper level of significance, this epoch will stand out in the history of mankind as the era of liberation? If so, the Epistle to Philemon, as the earliest prelude to these magnificent social victories, must be invested with more than common interest for our generation.

ΠΡΟΣ ΦΙΛΗΜΟΝΑ.

WHERE THE SPIRIT OF THE LORD IS, THERE
IS LIBERTY.

WHO IS WEAK, AND I AM NOT WEAK?
WHO IS OFFENDED, AND I BURN NOT?

———————

Such ever was love's way: to rise, it stoops.

ΠΡΟΣ ΦΙΛΗΜΟΝΑ.

¹ ΠΑΥΛΟΣ, δέσμιος Χριστοῦ Ἰησοῦ καὶ Τιμόθεος ὁ
ἀδελφός, Φιλήμονι τῷ ἀγαπητῷ καὶ συνεργῷ ἡμῶν
² καὶ Ἀπφίᾳ τῇ ἀδελφῇ καὶ Ἀρχίππῳ τῷ συνστρατιώτῃ
ἡμῶν καὶ τῇ κατ᾽ οἶκόν σου ἐκκλησίᾳ· ³ χάρις ὑμῖν

1—3. 'PAUL, now a prisoner of Christ Jesus, and TIMOTHY a brother in the faith, unto PHILEMON our dearly-beloved and fellow-labourer in the Gospel, and unto APPHIA our sister, and unto ARCHIPPUS our fellow-soldier in Christ, and to the Church which assembles in thy house. Grace and peace to you all from God our Father and the Lord Jesus Christ.'

1. δέσμιος] The authoritative title of 'Apostle' is dropped, because throughout this letter St Paul desires to entreat rather than to command (ver. 8, 9); see the note on Phil. i. 1. In its place is substituted a designation which would touch his friend's heart. How could Philemon resist an appeal which was penned within prison walls and by a manacled hand? For this characteristic reference to his 'bonds' see the note on ver. 13.

Τιμόθεος] Timothy seems to have been with St Paul during a great part of his three years' sojourn in Ephesus (Acts xix. 22), and could hardly have failed to make the acquaintance of Philemon. For the designation ὁ ἀδελφός applied to Timothy see the note on Col. i. 1.

Φιλήμονι κ.τ.λ.] On the persons here addressed, and the language in which they are described, see the introduction p. 303 sq.

συνεργῷ] It would probably be during St Paul's long sojourn at Ephe-

sus that Philemon had laboured with him: see above p. 31 sq.

ἡμῶν] should probably be attached to ἀγαπητῷ as well as to συνεργῷ; comp. Rom. xvi. 5, 8, 9, 1 Cor. x. 14, Phil. ii. 12.

2. τῇ ἀδελφῇ] For this the received text has τῇ ἀγαπητῇ. Internal probabilities can be urged in favour of both readings. On the one hand ἀγαπητῇ might have been introduced for the sake of conformity to the preceding ἀγαπητῷ; on the other ἀδελφῇ might have been substituted for ἀγαπητῇ on grounds of false delicacy. Theodore of Mopsuestia (Spicil. Solesm. I. p. 154), who had the reading ἀγαπητῇ, feels an apology necessary: 'Istius temporis (i. e. of the present time) homines propemodum omnes in crimine vocandos esse existimant, modo si audierint nomen charitatis. Apostolus vero non sic sentiebat; sed contrario etc.' I have preferred τῇ ἀδελφῇ, because the preponderance of ancient authority is very decidedly in its favour.

συνστρατιώτῃ] These spiritual campaigns, in which Archippus was his comrade, probably took place while St Paul was at Ephesus (A.D. 24—57). For the word συνστρατιώτης see Phil. ii. 25. The metaphor of στρατεία, στρατεύεσθαι, is common in St Paul.

τῇ κατ᾽ οἶκον κ.τ.λ.] probably at Colossæ; see above p. 304 sq. For the

καὶ εἰρήνη ἀπὸ Θεοῦ πατρὸς ἡμῶν καὶ Κυρίου Ἰησοῦ
Χριστοῦ.

⁴Εὐχαριστῶ τῷ Θεῷ μου πάντοτε, μνείαν σου ποιούμενος ἐπὶ τῶν προσευχῶν μου, ⁵ἀκούων σου τὴν ἀγάπην

meaning of the expression see the
note on Col. iv. 15.

4—7. 'I never cease to give thanks
to my God for thy well-doing, and thou
art ever mentioned in my prayers.
For they tell me of thy love and faith
—thy faith which thou hast in the
Lord Jesus, and thy love which thou
showest towards all the saints; and it
is my prayer that this active sympathy
and charity, thus springing from thy
faith, may abound more and more, as
thou attainest to the perfect knowledge of every good thing bestowed
upon us by God, looking unto and
striving after Christ. For indeed it
gave me great joy and comfort to hear
of thy loving-kindness, and to learn
how the hearts of God's people had
been cheered and refreshed by thy
help, my dear brother'.

The Apostle's thanksgiving and in-
tercessory prayer (ver. 4)—the cause
of his thanksgiving (ver. 5)—the purport of his prayer (ver. 6)—the joy
and comfort which he has in Philemon's good deeds (ver. 7)—this is the
very simple order of topics in these
verses. But meanwhile all established
principles of arrangement are defied
in the anxiety to give expression to
the thought which is uppermost for
the moment. The clause ἀκούων κ.τ.λ.
is separated from εὐχαριστῶ κ.τ.λ., on
which it depends, by the intervening
clause μνείαν σου κ.τ.λ. which introduces another thought. It itself interposes between two clauses, μνείαν
σου κ.τ.λ. and ὅπως ἡ κοινωνία κ.τ.λ.,
which stand in the closest logical and
grammatical connexion with each
other. Its own component elements
are dislocated and inverted in the
struggle of the several ideas for immediate utterance. And lastly, in χα-

ρὰν γὰρ κ.τ.λ. there is again a recurrence to a topic which has occurred
in an earlier part of the sentence (τὴν
ἀγάπην...εἰς πάντας τοὺς ἁγίους) but
which has been dropped, before it was
exhausted, owing to the pressure of
another more importunate thought.

4. Εὐχαριστῶ] See the note on
1 Thess. i. 2.

πάντοτε] should probably be taken
with εὐχαριστῶ (rather than with
μνείαν κ.τ.λ.), according to St Paul's
usual collocation in these opening
thanksgivings: see the notes on Col.
i. 3, Phil. i. 3.

μνείαν σου κ.τ.λ.] 'making mention
of thee.' For μνείαν ποιεῖσθαι see the
note on 1 Thess. i. 2. Here the 'mention' involves the idea of intercession
on behalf of Philemon, and so introduces the ὅπως κ.τ.λ. of ver. 6. See
the note there.

5. ἀκούων] This information would
probably come from Epaphras (Col. i.
7, 8, iv. 12) rather than from Onesimus. The participle is connected
more directly with εὐχαριστῶ than
with the intervening words, and explains the grounds of the Apostle's
thanksgiving.

τὴν ἀγάπην κ.τ.λ.] i. e. 'the faith
which thou hast towards the Lord Jesus Christ and the love which thou
showest to all the saints. The logical
order is violated, and the clauses are
inverted in the second part of the sentence, thus producing an example of
the figure called chiasm; see Gal. iv.
4, 5. This results here from the Apostle's setting down the thoughts in
the sequence in which they occur to
him, without paying regard to sym-
metrical arrangement. The first and
prominent thought is Philemon's love.
This suggests the mention of his faith,

καὶ τὴν πίστιν ἣν ἔχεις πρὸς τὸν Κύριον Ἰησοῦν καὶ εἰς
πάντας τοὺς ἁγίους, ⁶ὅπως ἡ κοινωνία τῆς πίστεώς σου
ἐνεργὴς γένηται ἐν ἐπιγνώσει παντὸς ἀγαθοῦ τοῦ ἐν

as the source from which it springs.
This again requires a reference to the
object of faith. And then at length
comes the deferred sequel to the first
thought—the range and comprehen-
siveness of his love. The transition
from the object of faith to the object
of love is more easy, because the love
is represented as springing from the
faith. Some copies transpose the
order, reading τὴν πίστιν καὶ τὴν ἀγάπην—an obvious emendation. Others
would obviate the difficulty by giving
to πίστιν the meaning 'fidelity, stedfastness'; Winer § 1. p. 511 sq. Thus
they are enabled to refer both words,
πίστιν καὶ ἀγάπην, equally to both
the clauses which follow. But though
this is a legitimate sense of πίστις
in St Paul (see *Galatians* p. 155),
yet in immediate connexion with ἣν
ἔχεις πρὸς τὸν Κύριον Ἰησοῦν, it is
hardly possible that the word can
have any other than its proper theological meaning. See the opening of
the contemporary epistle, Col. i. 4.

πρὸς κ.τ.λ.] The change of prepositions, πρὸς τὸν Κύριον '*towards* the
Lord' and εἰς τοὺς ἁγίους '*unto* the
saints', deserves attention. It seems
to arise from the instinctive desire to
separate the two clauses, as they refer
to different words in the preceding
part of the sentence. Of the two prepositions the former (προ-s) signifies
direction 'forward to', 'towards'; the
latter (ἐν-s) *arrival* and so *contact*,
' in-to', 'unto.' Consequently either
might be used in either connexion;
and as a matter of fact εἰς is much
more common with πίστις (πιστεύειν), as
it is also with ἀγάπη, πρός being quite
exceptional (1 Thess. i. 8 ἡ πίστις ὑμῶν
ἡ πρὸς τὸν Θεόν; comp. 2 Cor. iii. 4).
But where a distinction is necessary,
there is a propriety in using πρός of
the faith which aspires *towards* Christ,

and εἰς of the love which is exerted
upon men. Some good copies read
εἰς here in both clauses.

6. ὅπως κ.τ.λ.] to be taken with
μνείαν σου ποιούμενος κ.τ.λ., as giving
the aim and purport of St Paul's
prayer. Others connect it with ἣν
ἔχεις, as if it described the tendency
of Philemon's faith, 'ita ut'; but, even
if ὅπως could bear this meaning, such
a connexion is altogether harsh and
improbable.

ἡ κοινωνία κ.τ.λ.] Of many interpretations which have been, or might be,
given of these words, two seem to deserve consideration. (1)'Your friendly
offices and sympathies, your kindly
deeds of charity, which spring from
your faith': comp. Phil. i. 5 ἐπὶ τῇ
κοινωνίᾳ ὑμῶν εἰς τὸ εὐαγγέλιον, Heb.
xiii. 16 τῆς εὐποιΐας καὶ κοινωνίας,
whence κοινωνία is used especially
of 'contributions, almsgiving', Rom.
xv. 26, 2 Cor. viii. 4, ix. 13.   (2)
'Your communion with God through
faith': comp. 1 Cor. i. 9, and see also
2 Cor. xiii. 13, 1 Joh. i. 3, 6, 7. The
parallel passages strongly support
the former sense. Other interpretations proposed are, 'The participation of others in your faith, through
your example', or 'your communion
with me, springing out of your faith'.
This last, which is widely received, is
suggested by ver. 17; εἰ κοινωνὸς εἶ,
φησί, κατὰ τὴν πίστιν, writes Chrysostom, καὶ κατὰ τὰ ἄλλα ὀφείλεις κοινω-
νεῖν (comp. Tit. i. 3 κατὰ κοινὴν πίστιν):
but it is out of place in this context.

ἐνεργής] '*effective*'.   The Latin
translators must have read ἐναργής,
for they render the word *evidens* or
manifesta. Jerome (*ad. loc.*) speaks
of *evidens* as the reading of the Latin,
and *efficax* of the Greek text. The
converse error appears in the MSS of
Clem. Hom. xvii. 5, ἐνέργεια for ἐνάρ-

ἡμῖν εἰς Χριστόν. ⁷χαρὰν γὰρ πολλὴν ἔσχον καὶ παρά-
κλησιν ἐπὶ τῇ ἀγάπῃ σου, ὅτι τὰ σπλάγχνα τῶν ἁγίων
ἀναπέπαυνται διὰ σοῦ, ἀδελφέ.

6. ἐν ὑμῖν εἰς Χριστόν.

γεια. See also similar vv. ll. in Orig.
c. Cels. i. 25, ii. 52, iv. 89.

ἐν ἐπιγνώσει κ.τ.λ.] 'in the perfect
knowledge of every good thing'. This
ἐπίγνωσις, involving as it does the
complete appropriation of all truth
and the unreserved identification with
God's will, is the goal and crown of
the believer's course. The Apostle
does not say 'in the possession' or 'in
the performance' but 'in the knowledge of every good thing'; for, in this
higher sense of knowledge, to know is
both to possess and to perform. In
all the epistles of the Roman captivity St Paul's prayer for his correspondents culminates in this word
ἐπίγνωσις: see the note on Col. i. 9.
This ἐπίγνωσις is the result and the
reward of faith manifesting itself in
deeds of love, ὅπως ἡ κοινωνία τῆς πίστεως κ.τ.λ. For the sequence comp.
Ephes. iv. 13 εἰς τὴν ἑνότητα τῆς πίστεως καὶ τῆς ἐπιγνώσεως κ.τ.λ., Tit.
i. 1 κατὰ πίστιν ἐκλεκτῶν Θεοῦ καὶ ἐπίγνωσιν ἀληθείας τῆς κατ᾽ εὐσέβειαν.
The ἐπίγνωσις therefore which the
Apostle contemplates is Philemon's
own. There is no reference to the
force of his example on others, as it
is sometimes interpreted, 'in their recognition of every good thing which
is wrought in you'.

τοῦ ἐν ἡμῖν] 'which is in us Christians', 'which is placed within our
reach by the Gospel'; i.e. the whole
range of spiritual blessings, the complete cycle of Christian truth. If the
reading τοῦ ἐν ὑμῖν be adopted, the
reference will be restricted to the
brotherhood at Colossæ, but the
meaning must be substantially the
same. Though ὑμῖν has somewhat
better support, we seem to be justified in preferring ἡμῖν as being much
more expressive. In such cases the

MSS are of no great authority; and in
the present instance scribes would be
strongly tempted to alter ἡμῖν into
ὑμῖν from a misapprehension of the
sense, and a wish to apply the words
to Philemon and his household. A
similar misapprehension doubtless led
in some copies to the omission of τοῦ,
which seemed to be superfluous but
is really required for the sense.

εἰς Χριστόν] 'unto Christ', i.e. leading to Him as the goal. The words
should be connected not with τοῦ ἐν
ἡμῖν, but with the main statement of
the sentence ἐνεργὴς γένηται κ.τ.λ.

7. χαρὰν γάρ] This sentence again
must not be connected with the words
immediately preceding. It gives the
motive of the Apostle's thanksgiving
mentioned in ver. 4. This thanksgiving was the outpouring of gratitude
for the joy and comfort that he had
received in his bonds from the report
of Philemon's generous charity. The
connexion therefore is εὐχαριστῶ τῷ
Θεῷ μου......ἀκούων σου τὴν ἀγάπην
...χαρὰν γὰρ πολλὴν ἔσχον κ.τ.λ. For
χαράν the received text (Steph. but not
Elz.) reads χάριν, which is taken to
mean 'thankfulness' (1 Tim. i. 12,
2 Tim. i. 3); but this reading is absolutely condemned by the paucity of
ancient authority.

τὰ σπλάγχνα] 'the heart, the spirits'. On τὰ σπλάγχνα, the nobler vis-
cera, regarded as the seat of the emotions, see the note on Phil. i. 8. Here
the prominent idea is that of terror,
grief, despondency, etc.

ἀναπέπαυνται] 'have been relieved,
refreshed', comp. ver. 20. The compound ἀναπαύεσθαι expresses a temporary relief, as the simple παύεσθαι
expresses a final cessation: Plut. Vit.
Lucull. 5 πολλῶν αὖθις ἀνακινούντων
τὸν Μιθριδατικὸν πόλεμον ἔφη Μάρκος

⁸Διὸ πολλὴν ἐν Χριστῷ παρρησίαν ἔχων ἐπιτάσσειν
σοι τὸ ἀνῆκον, ⁹διὰ τὴν ἀγάπην μᾶλλον παρακαλῶ,
τοιοῦτος ὢν ὡς Παῦλος πρεσβύτης νυνὶ δὲ καὶ δέσμιος

9.   νῦν δὲ καὶ δέσμιος.

αὐτὸν οὐ πεπαῦσθαι ἀλλ᾽ ἀναπε-
παῦσθαι. Thus it implies 'relaxation,
refreshment', as a preparation for the
renewal of labour or suffering. It is
an Ignatian as well as a Pauline word;
Ephes. 2, *Smyrn.* 9, 10, 12, *Trall.* 12,
Magn. 15, *Rom.* 10.

ἀδελφέ] For the appeal suggested
by the emphatic position of the word,
comp. Gal. vi. 18. See also the note
on ver. 20 below.

8—17. 'Encouraged by these tidings of thy loving spirit, I prefer to
entreat, where I might command. My
office gives me authority to dictate
thy duty in plain language, but love
bids me plead as a suitor. Have I not
indeed a right to command—I Paul
whom Christ Jesus long ago commis-
sioned as His ambassador, and whom
now He has exalted to the rank of His
prisoner? But I entreat thee. I have
a favour to ask for a son of my own—
one doubly dear to me, because I became his father amidst the sorrows of
my bonds. I speak of Onesimus, who
in times past was found wholly untrue
to his name, who was then far from
useful to thee, but now is useful to
thee—yea, and to myself also. Him I
send back to thee, and I entreat thee
to take him into thy favour, for in
giving him I am giving my own heart.
Indeed I would gladly have detained
him with me, that he might minister
to me on thy behalf, in these bonds
with which the Gospel has invested
me. But I had scruples. I did not
wish to do anything without thy direct
consent; for then it might have seemed (though it were only seeming) as if
thy kindly offices had been rendered
by compulsion and not of free will.
So I have sent him back. Indeed it
may have been God's providential design, that he was parted from thee for

a season, only that thou mightest re-
gain him for ever; that he left thee as
a slave, only that he might return to
thee a beloved brother. This indeed
he is to me most of all; and, if to me,
must he not be so much more to thee,
both in worldly things and in spiritual?
If therefore thou regardest me as a
friend and companion, take him to
thee, as if he were myself.'

8. Διό] i.e. 'Seeing that I have
these proofs of thy love, I prefer to
entreat, where I might command.'

παρρησίαν] 'confidence', literally
'freedom' or 'privilege of speech';
see the notes on Col. ii. 15, Ephes. iii.
12. It was his Apostolic authority
which gave him this right to command
in plain language. Hence the addition ἐν Χριστῷ.

τὸ ἀνῆκον] 'what is fitting': see
the note on Col. iii. 18.

9. διὰ τὴν ἀγάπην] 'for love's sake',
i.e. 'having respect to the claims of
love'. It is not Philemon's love (vv.
5, 7), nor St Paul's own love, but love
absolutely, love regarded as a principle
which demands a deferential respect.

τοιοῦτος ὢν κ.τ.λ.] 'being such an
one as Paul an ambassador, and now
also a prisoner, of Christ Jesus'.
Several questions of more or less difficulty arise on these words. (1) Is
τοιοῦτος ὢν to be connected with or
separated from ὡς Παῦλος κ.τ.λ.? If separated, τοιοῦτος ὢν will mean 'though
as an Apostle I am armed with such
authority', and ὡς Παῦλος κ.τ.λ. will
describe his condescension to entreaty,
'yet as simply Paul, etc.' But the
other construction is much more probable for the following reasons. (a)
τοιοῦτος ὢν so used, implying, as it
would, something of a *personal* boast,
seems unlike St Paul's usual mode
of speaking. Several interpreters in-

Χριστοῦ Ἰησοῦ.　¹⁰παρακαλῶ σε περὶ τοῦ ἐμοῦ τέκνου,

deed, taking τοιοῦτος ὤν separately, refer it to ver. 8, 'seeing that this is my disposition', i.e. 'seeing that I desire to entreat'; but τοιοῦτος suggests more than an accidental impulse. (b) As τοιοῦτος and ὡς are correlative words, it is more natural to connect them together; comp. Plato *Symp.* 181 E προσαναγκάζειν τὸ τοιοῦτον ὥσπερ καὶ κ.τ.λ., Alexis (Meineke *Fragm. Com.* III. p. 399) τοιοῦτο τὸ ζῆν ἐστιν ὥσπερ οἱ κύβοι. Such passages are an answer to the objection that τοιοῦτος would require some stronger word than ὡς, such as οἷος, ὅς, or ὥστε. Even after such expressions as ὁ αὐτός, τὸ αὐτό, instances occur of ὡς (ὥσπερ): see Lobeck *Phryn.* p. 427, Stallbaum on Plat. *Phæd.* 86 A. Indeed it may be questioned whether any word but ὡς would give exactly St Paul's meaning here. (c) All the Greek commentators without a single exception connect the words τοιοῦτος ὤν ὡς Παῦλος together. (2) Assuming that the words τοιοῦτος ὤν ὡς κ.τ.λ. are taken together, should they be connected with the preceding or the following sentence? On the whole the passage is more forcible, if they are linked to the preceding words. In this case the resumptive παρακαλῶ (ver. 10) begins a new sentence, which introduces a fresh subject. The Apostle has before described the character of his appeal; he now speaks of its object. (3) In either connexion, what is the point of the words τοιοῦτος ὤν ὡς Παῦλος κ.τ.λ.? Do they lay down the grounds of his *entreaty*, or do they enforce his right to *command?* If the view of πρεσβύτης adopted below be correct, the latter must be the true interpretation; but even though πρεσβύτης be taken in its ordinary sense, this will still remain the more probable alternative; for, while πρεσβύτης and δέσμιος would suit either entreaty or command, the addition Χριστοῦ Ἰησοῦ suggests an appeal to authority.

ὡς Παῦλος] The mention of his personal name involves an assertion of authority, as in Ephes. iii. 1; comp. Gal. v. 2, with the note there. Theodoret writes, ὁ Παῦλον ἀκούσας τῆς οἰκουμένης ἀκούει τὸν κήρυκα, γῆς καὶ θαλάττης τὸν γεωργόν, τῆς ἐκλογῆς τὸ σκεῦος, κ.τ.λ.

πρεσβύτης] Comparing a passage in the contemporary epistle, Ephes. vi. 20 ὑπὲρ οὗ πρεσβεύω ἐν ἁλύσει, it had occurred to me that we should read πρεσβευτής here, before I was aware that this conjecture had been anticipated by others, e.g. by Bentley (*Crit. Sacr.* p. 93) and by Benson (*Paraphrase etc. on Six Epistles of St Paul*, p. 357). It has since been suggested independently in Linwood's *Observ. quæd. in nonnulla N. T. loca* 1865, and probably others have entertained the same thought. Still believing that St Paul here speaks of himself as an 'ambassador', I now question whether any change is necessary. There is reason for thinking that in the common dialect πρεσβύτης may have been written indifferently for πρεσβευτής in St Paul's time; and if so, the form here may be due, not to some comparatively late scribe, but to the original autograph itself or to an immediate transcript. In 1 Macc. xiv. 21 the Sinaitic MS has οἱ πρεσβυτεροι (a corruption of οἱ πρεσβυται οἱ, for the common reading is οἱ πρεσβευταὶ οἱ); in xiv. 22 it reads πρεσβυται Ιουδαιων; but in xiii. 21 πρεσβευτας: though in all passages alike the meaning is 'ambassadors'. Again the Alexandrian MS has πρεσβυτας in xiii. 21, but πρεσβευται in xiv. 22, and οι πρεσβευτε οι (i.e. οἱ πρεσβευταὶ οἱ) in xiv. 21. In 2 Macc. xi. 34 this same MS has πρεσβυτε, and the reading of the common texts of the LXX (even Tischendorf and Fritzsche) here is πρεσβῦται. Grimm treats it as meaning 'ambassadors', without even noticing the form. Other MSS are also mentioned in Holmes and Parsons which have the form πρεσβυτης in 1 Macc. xiii. 21. In 2 Chron. xxxii. 31 again the word for 'ambassador'

ὃν [ἐγὼ] ἐγέννησα ἐν τοῖς δεσμοῖς, Ὀνήσιμον, ¹¹τόν ποτέ

is written thus in the *Vatican* MS,
though the ε is added above the line;
and here too several MSS in Holmes
and Parsons agree in reading πρεσ-
βύταις. Thus it is plain that, in
the age of our earliest extant MSS
at all events, the scribes used both
forms indifferently in this sense. So
also Eusebius on Isaiah xviii. 2 writes
ὁ δὲ Ἀκύλας πρεσβύτας ἐξέδωκεν
εἰπών, Ὁ ἀποστέλλων ἐν θαλάσσῃ πρεσβύτας. Again in Ignat. *Smyrn.* 11
θεοπρεσβύτης is the form in all the
MSS of either recension, though the
meaning is plainly 'an ambassador
of God.' So too in *Clem. Hom.* Ep.
Clem. 6 the MSS read ὁ τῆς ἀληθείας
πρεσβύτης, which even Schwegler and
Dressel tacitly retain. See also Appian *Samn.* 7, where πρεσβευτοῦ is due
to the later editors, and *Acta Thomae*
§ 10, where there is a v. l. πρεσβύτης
in at least one MS. And probably examples of this substitution might be
largely multiplied.

The main reason for adopting this
rendering is the parallel passage, which
suggests it very strongly. The difficulty which many find in St Paul's
describing himself as an old man is
not serious. On any showing he must
have been verging on sixty at this
time and may have been some years
older. A life of unintermittent toil
and suffering, such as he had lived,
would bring a premature decay; and
looking back on a long eventful life,
he would naturally so think and speak
of himself. Thus Roger Bacon (*Opus
Majus* I. 10, p. 15, ed. Jebb; *Opus Ter-
tium* p. 63, ed. Brewer) writes 'me
senem', 'nos senes', in 1267, though
he appears to have been not more
than fifty-two or fifty-three at the
time and lived at least a quarter of a
century after (see E. Charles *Roger
Bacon, Sa Vie etc.* pp. 4 sq., 40). So
too Scott in his fifty-fifth year speaks
of himself as 'an old grey man'
and 'aged' (Lockhart's *Life* VIII. pp.
327, 357). It is more difficult to

understand how St Paul should make
his age a ground of appeal to Philemon who, if Archippus was his
son, cannot have been much younger
than himself. The commentator Hilary says that the Apostle appeals
to his friend 'quasi coaevum aeta-
tis', but this idea is foreign to the
context. The comment of Theophylact is, τοιοῦτος ὤν, φησι, πρεσβευτής, καὶ οὕτως ἄξιος ἀκούεσθαι, ὡς
εἰκὸς Παῦλον πρεσβύτην, τουτέστι καὶ
ἀπὸ τοῦ διδασκαλικοῦ ἀξιώματος καὶ
τοῦ χρόνου τὸ αἰδέσιμον ἔχοντα κ.τ.λ.
Does he mean to include both meanings in πρεσβύτης? Or is he accidentally borrowing the term 'ambassador'
from some earlier commentator without seeing its bearing?

καὶ δέσμιος] Another title to respect.
The mention of his bonds might suggest either an appeal for commisera-
tion or a claim of authority: see the
note on ver. 13. Here the addition of
Χριστοῦ Ἰησοῦ invests it with the character of an official title, and so gives
prominence to the latter idea. To his
old office of 'ambassador' Christ has
added the new title of 'prisoner.' The
genitive Χριστοῦ Ἰησοῦ belongs to
πρεσβύτης as well as to δέσμιος, and
in both cases describes the person who
confers the office or rank.

10. παρακαλῶ σε κ.τ.λ.] St Chrysostom remarks on the Apostle's with-
holding the name, until he has favourably disposed Philemon both to the
request and to the object of it; τοσού-
τοις δὲ προλεάνας αὐτοῦ τὴν ψυχήν,
οὐδὲ εὐθέως ἐνέβαλε τὸ ὄνομα, ἀλλὰ
τοσαύτην ποιησάμενος αἴτησιν ἀναβάλ-
λεται κ.τ.λ. The whole passage deserves to be read.

ὃν ἐγέννησα κ.τ.λ.] So too 1 Cor. iv.
15. In Gal. iv. 19 he speaks of himself as suffering a mother's pangs for
his children in the faith. Comp. Phil.
Leg. ad Cai. 8 (II. p. 554) ἐμόν ἐστι
τοῦ Μάκρωνος ἔργον Γάιος· μᾶλλον αὐτὸν
ἢ οὐχ ἧττον τῶν γονέων γεγέννηκα.

ἐν τοῖς δεσμοῖς] He was doubly

σοι ἄχρηστον, νυνὶ δὲ [καὶ] σοὶ καὶ ἐμοὶ εὔχρηστον· ὃν
ἀνέπεμψά σοι. ¹²αὐτόν, τουτέστιν τὰ ἐμὰ σπλάγχνα,

dear to the Apostle, as being the child
of his sorrows.

'Ονήσιμον] for 'Ονησίμου by attraction, as e.g. Mark vi. 16 ὃν ἐγὼ ἀπεκε-
φάλισα Ἰωάννην, οὗτός ἐστιν. Henceforward he will be true to his name,
no longer ἀνόνητος, but ὀνήσιμος: comp.
Ruth i. 20 'Call me not Naomi (pleasant) but call me Mara (bitter) etc.'
The word ἄχρηστος is a synonyme for
ἀνόνητος, Demosth. Phil. iii. § 40 (p.
121) ἅπαντα ταῦτα ἄχρηστα ἄπρακτα
ἀνόνητα κ.τ.λ.: comp. Pseudophocyl.
37 (34) χρηστὸς ὀνήσιμός ἐστι, φίλος
δ' ἀδικῶν ἀνόνητος. The significance
of names was a matter of special importance among the ancients. Hence
they were careful in the inauguration
of any great work that only those who
had bona nomina, prospera nomina,
fausta nomina, should take part: Cic.
de Div. i. 45, Plin. N. H. xxviii. 2. 5,
Tac. Hist. iv. 53. On the value attached to names by the ancients, and
more especially by the Hebrews, see
Farrar Chapters on Language p. 267
sq., where a large number of instances
are collected. Here however there is
nothing more than an affectionate
play on a name, such as might occur
to any one at any time: comp. Euseb.
H. E. v. 24 ὁ Εἰρηναῖος φερώνυμός τις
ὢν τῇ προσηγορίᾳ, αὐτῷ τε τῷ τρόπῳ εἰρηνοποιός.

11. ἄχρηστον, εὔχρηστον] Comp. Plat.
Resp. iii. p. 411 A χρήσιμον ἐξ ἀχρή-
στου...ἐποίησεν. Of these words, ἄχρηστος is found only here, εὔχρηστος
occurs also 2 Tim. ii. 21, iv. 11, in the
New Testament. Both appear in the
LXX. In Matt. xxv. 30 a slave is described as ἀχρεῖος. For the mode of
expression comp. Ephes. v. 15 μὴ ὡς
ἄσοφοι ἀλλ' ὡς σόφοι. Some have discovered in these words a reference to
χριστός, as commonly pronounced χρη-
στός; comp. Theoph. ad Autol. i. 12
τὸ χριστὸν ἡδὺ καὶ εὔχρηστον κ.τ.λ.
and see Philippians p. 16 note. Any

such allusion however, even if it should
not involve an anachronism, is far too
recondite to be probable here. The
play on words is exhausted in the
reference to 'Ονήσιμος.

καὶ ἐμοί] An after-thought; comp.
Phil. ii. 27 ἠλέησεν αὐτόν, οὐκ αὐτὸν
δὲ μόνον ἀλλὰ καὶ ἐμέ. This accounts
for the exceptional order, where according to common Greek usage the
first person would naturally precede
the second.

ἀνέπεμψα] 'I send back', the epistolary aorist used for the present: see
the notes on Phil. ii. 25,28. So too ἔγραψα, ver. 19, 21 (see the note). It is
clear both from the context here, and
from Col. iv. 7—9, that Onesimus accompanied the letter.

12. αὐτὸν κ.τ.λ.] The reading of
the received text is σὺ δὲ αὐτόν, τουτέστι τὰ ἐμὰ σπλάγχνα, προσλαβοῦ.
The words thus supplied doubtless
give the right construction, but must
be rejected as deficient in authority.
The accusative is suspended; the sentence changes its form and loses itself
in a number of dependent clauses;
and the main point is not resumed till
ver. 17 προσλαβοῦ αὐτὸν ὡς ἐμέ, the
grammar having been meanwhile dislocated. For the emphatic position
of αὐτόν comp. John ix. 21, 23, Ephes.
i. 22.

τὰ ἐμὰ σπλάγχνα] 'my very heart',
a mode of speech common in all languages. For the meaning of σπλάγχνα
see the note on Phil. i. 8. Comp.
Test. Patr. Zab. 8, Neph. 4, in both
which passages Christ is called τὸ
σπλάγχνον of God, and in the first it
is said ἔχετε εὐσπλαγχνίαν...ἵνα καὶ ὁ
Κύριος εἰς ὑμᾶς σπλαγχνισθεὶς ἐλεήσῃ
ὑμᾶς· ὅτι καίγε ἐπ' ἐσχάτων ἡμερῶν
ὁ Θεὸς ἀποστέλλει τὸ σπλάγχνον αὐτοῦ ἐπὶ τῆς γῆς κ.τ.λ. Otherwise
τὰ ἐμὰ σπλάγχνα has been interpreted
'my son' (comp. ver. 10 ὃν ἐγέννησα
κ.τ.λ.), and it is so rendered here in

¹³ὃν ἐγὼ ἐβουλόμην πρὸς ἐμαυτὸν κατέχειν, ἵνα ὑπὲρ
σοῦ μοι διακονῇ ἐν τοῖς δεσμοῖς τοῦ εὐαγγελίου· ¹⁴χωρὶς

the Peshito. For this sense of σπλάγχνα comp. Artemid. *Oneir.* i. 44 οἱ
παῖδες σπλάγχνα λέγονται, *ib.* v. 57
τὰ δὲ σπλάγχνα [ἐσήμαινε] τὸν παῖδα,
οὕτω γὰρ καὶ τὸν παῖδα καλεῖν ἔθος ἐστί.
With this meaning it is used not less
of the father than of the mother;
e.g. Philo *de Joseph.* 5 (II. p. 45) θηρ-
σὶν εὐωχία καὶ θοίνη γέγονας γευσαμέ-
νοις...τῶν ἐμῶν σπλάγχνων, Basil. *Op.*
III. p. 501 ὁ μὲν προτείνεται τὰ σπλάγχνα τιμὴν τῶν τροφῶν. The Latin *vis-
cera* occurs still more frequently in
this sense, as the passages quoted in
Wetstein and Suicer show. For this
latter interpretation there is much to
be said. But it adds nothing to the
previous ὃν ἐγέννησα κ.τ.λ., and (what
is a more serious objection) it is
wholly unsupported by St Paul's
usage elsewhere, which connects
σπλάγχνα with a different class of
ideas: see e.g. vv. 7, 20.

13. ἐβουλόμην] '*I was of a mind*',
distinguished from ἠθέλησα, which
follows, in two respects; (1) While
βούλεσθαι involves the idea of 'purpose, deliberation, desire, mind', θέλειν denotes simply 'will'; Epictet. i.
12. 13 βούλομαι γράφειν, ὡς θέλω, τὸ
Δίωνος ὄνομα; οὔ· ἀλλὰ διδάσκομαι θέλειν ὡς δεῖ γράφεσθαι, iii. 24. 54 τοῦτον θέλε ὁρᾷν, καὶ ὃν βούλει ὄψει. (2)
The change of tenses is significant.
The imperfect implies a tentative, inchoate process; while the aorist describes a definite and complete act.
The will stepped in and put an end
to the inclinations of the mind. Indeed the imperfect of this and similar
verbs are not infrequently used where
the wish is stopped at the outset by
some antecedent consideration which
renders it impossible, and thus practically it is not entertained at all: e.g.
Arist. *Ran.* 866 ἐβουλόμην μὲν οὐκ
ἐρίζειν ἐνθάδε, Antiph. *de Herod. caed.*
I (p. 129) ἐβουλόμην μὲν...νῦν δὲ κ.τ.λ.;
Isaeus *de Arist. haer.* I. (p. 79) ἐβουλό-

μην μὲν...νῦν δὲ οὐκ ἐξ ἴσου κ.τ.λ.,
Æsch. *c. Ctes.* 2 (p. 53) ἐβουλόμην
μὲν οὖν, ὦ 'Αθηναῖοι...ἐπειδὴ δὲ πάντα
κ.τ.λ., Lucian *Abd.* 1 ἐβουλόμην μὲν
οὖν τὴν ἰατρικὴν κ.τ.λ....νυνὶ δὲ κ.τ.λ.;
see Kühner § 392 *b* (II. p. 177). So
Acts xxv. 22 ἐβουλόμην καὶ αὐτὸς
τοῦ ἀνθρώπου ἀκοῦσαι, not 'I should
wish' (as Winer § xli. p. 353) but 'I
could have wished', i.e. 'if it had not
been too much to ask'. Similarly
ἤθελον Gal. iv. 20, ηὐχόμην Rom. ix. 3.
See *Revision of the English New
Testament* p. 96. So here a not improbable meaning would be not 'I
was desirous', but 'I could have desired'.

κατέχειν] '*to detain*' or '*retain*',
opposed to the following ἀπέχῃς, ver.
15.

ὑπὲρ σοῦ κ.τ.λ.] Comp. Phil. ii. 30
ἵνα ἀναπληρώσῃ τὸ ὑμῶν ὑστέρημα τῆς
πρός με λειτουργίας, 1 Cor. xvi. 17 τὸ
ὑμέτερον ὑστέρημα αὐτοὶ ἀνεπλήρωσαν.
See the note on Col. i. 7. With a de-
licate tact the Apostle assumes that
Philemon would have wished to perform these friendly offices in person,
if it had been possible.

ἐν τοῖς δεσμοῖς] An indirect appeal
to his compassion: see vv. 1, 9, 10.
In this instance however (as in ver. 9)
the appeal assumes a tone of authority, by reference to the occasion of his
bonds. For the genitive τοῦ εὐαγγελίου, describing the origin, comp. Col.
i. 23 τῆς ἐλπίδος τοῦ εὐαγγελίου. They
were not shackles which self had
riveted, but a chain with which
Christ had invested him. Thus they
were as a badge of office or a decora-
tion of honour. In this respect, as in
others, the language of St Paul is
echoed in the epistles of St Ignatius.
Here too entreaty and triumph alter-
nate; the saint's bonds are at once
a ground for appeal and a theme of
thanksgiving: *Trall.* 12 παρακαλεῖ
ὑμᾶς τὰ δεσμά μου, *Philad.* 7 μάρτυς

δὲ τῆς σῆς γνώμης οὐδὲν ἠθέλησα ποιῆσαι, ἵνα μὴ ὡς
κατὰ ἀνάγκην τὸ ἀγαθόν σου ᾖ, ἀλλὰ κατὰ ἑκούσιον·
¹⁵τάχα γὰρ διὰ τοῦτο ἐχωρίσθη πρὸς ὥραν, ἵνα αἰώνιον
αὐτὸν ἀπέχῃς, ¹⁶οὐκέτι ὡς δοῦλον, ἀλλὰ ὑπὲρ δοῦλον,

δέ μοι ἐν ᾧ δέδεμαι, *Ephes.* 11 ἐν ᾧ ᾧ (i.e.
Χριστῷ Ἰησοῦ) τὰ δεσμὰ περιφέρω,
τοὺς πνευματικοὺς μαργαρίτας, *Smyrn.*
10 ἀντίψυχον ὑμῶν τὸ πνεῦμά μου καὶ
τὰ δεσμά μου, *Magn.* 1 ἐν οἷς περιφέρω
δεσμοῖς ᾄδω τὰς ἐκκλησίας; see also
Ephes. 1, 3, 21, *Magn.* 12, *Trall.* 1, 5,
10, *Smyrn.* 4, 11, *Polyc.* 2, *Rom.* 1, 4,
5, *Philad.* 5.

14. χωρὶς κ.τ.λ.] ‘*without thy approval, consent*’; Polyb. ii. 21. 1, 3,
χωρὶς τῆς σφετέρας γνώμης, χωρὶς τῆς
αὑτοῦ γνώμης: similarly ἄνευ [τῆς]
γνώμης, e.g. Polyb. xxi. 8. 7, Ign.
Polyc. 4.

ὡς κατὰ ἀνάγκην] St Paul does not
say κατὰ ἀνάγκην but ὡς κατὰ ἀνάγκην.
He will not suppose that it would
really be by constraint; but it must
not even wear *the appearance* (ὡς) of
being so; comp. 2 Cor. xi. 17 ὡς ἐν
ἀφροσύνῃ. See Plin. *Ep.* ix. 21 ‘Vereor
ne videar non rogare sed cogere’;
where, as here, the writer is asking
his correspondent to forgive a domestic who has offended.

τὸ ἀγαθόν σου] ‘*the benefit* arising
from thee’, i.e. ‘the good which I
should get from the continued presence of Onesimus, and which would
be owing to thee’.

κατὰ ἑκούσιον] as in Num. xv. 3. The
form καθ᾽ ἑκουσίαν is perhaps more
classical: Thuc. viii. 27 καθ᾽ ἑκουσίαν
ἢ πάνυ γε ἀνάγκῃ. The word understood in the one case appears to be
τρόπον (Porphyr. *de Abst.* i. 9 καθ᾽
ἑκούσιον τρόπον, comp. Eur. *Med.* 751
ἑκουσίῳ τρόπῳ); in the other, γνώμην
(so ἑκουσίᾳ, ἐξ ἑκουσίας, etc.): comp.
Lobeck *Phryn.* p. 4.

15. τάχα γὰρ κ.τ.λ.] The γὰρ explains an additional motive which
guided the Apostle's decision: ‘I did
not dare to detain him, however

much I desired it. I might have defeated the purpose for which God in
His good providence allowed him to
leave thee’.

ἐχωρίσθη] ‘He does not say’, writes
Chrysostom, ‘*For this cause he fled*,
but *For this cause he was parted*:
for he would appease Philemon by a
more euphemistic phrase. And again
he does not say *he parted himself*,
but *he was parted*: since the design
was not Onesimus' own to depart for
this or that reason: just as Joseph
also, when excusing his brethren,
says (Gen. xlv. 5) *God did send me
hither*.’

πρὸς ὥραν] ‘*for an hour*,’ ‘*for a
short season*’: 2 Cor. vii. 8, Gal. ii. 5.
‘It was only a brief moment after all’,
the Apostle would say, ‘compared
with the magnitude of the work
wrought in it. He departed a repro-
bate; he returns a saved man. He
departed for a few months; he returns
to be with you for all time and for
eternity’. This sense of αἰώνιον must
not be arbitrarily limited. Since he
left, Onesimus had obtained eternal
life, and eternal life involves eternal
interchange of friendship. His services to his old master were no longer
barred by the gates of death.

ἀπέχῃς] In this connexion ἀπέχειν
may bear either of two senses: (1) ‘*to
have back, to have in return*’: or (2)
‘*to have to the full, to have wholly*’,
as in Phil. iv. 18 ἀπέχω πάντα (see the
note). In other words the prominent
idea in the word may be either *restitution*, or *completeness*. The former
is the more probable sense here, as
suggested by κατέχειν in verse 13 and
by ἐχωρίσθη in this verse.

16. ὡς δοῦλον] St Paul does not
say δοῦλον but ὡς δοῦλον. It was a

ἀδελφὸν ἀγαπητόν, μάλιστα ἐμοί, πόσῳ δὲ μᾶλλον
σοὶ καὶ ἐν σαρκὶ καὶ ἐν Κυρίῳ. ¹⁷εἰ οὖν με ἔχεις κοι-
νωνόν, προσλαβοῦ αὐτὸν ὡς ἐμέ· ¹⁸εἰ δέ τι ἠδίκησέν σε
ἢ ὀφείλει, τοῦτο ἐμοὶ ἐλλόγα. ¹⁹ἐγὼ Παῦλος ἔγραψα

matter of indifference whether he
were outwardly δοῦλος or outwardly
ἐλεύθερος, since both are one in Christ
(Col. iii. 11). But though he might
still remain a slave, he could no longer
be *as* a slave. A change had been
wrought in him, independently of his
possible manumission : in Christ he
had become a brother. It should be
noticed also that the negative is not
μηκέτι, but οὐκέτι. The negation is
thus wholly independent of ἵνα...ἀπέ-
χῃς. It describes not the possible
view of Philemon, but the actual state
of Onesimus. The 'no more as a slave'
is an absolute fact, whether Philemon
chooses to recognise it or not.

ἀδελφὸν ἀγαπητόν] καὶ τῷ χρόνῳ κε-
κέρδακας καὶ τῇ ποιότητι, writes Chrysostom, apostrophizing Philemon.

πόσῳ δὲ μᾶλλον κ.τ.λ.] Having first
said 'most of all to me', he goes a
step further, 'more than most of all
to thee'.

καὶ ἐν σαρκὶ κ.τ.λ.] 'In both spheres
alike, in the affairs of this world and
in the affairs of the higher life.' In
the former, as Meyer pointedly says,
Philemon had the brother for a slave;
in the latter he had the slave for a
brother: comp. Ign. *Trall.* 12 κατὰ
πάντα με ἀνέπαυσαν σαρκί τε καὶ πνεύματι.

17. ἔχεις κοινωνόν] '*thou holdest
me to be a comrade, an intimate
friend.*' For this use of ἔχειν comp.
Luke xiv. 18 ἔχε με παρητημένον, Phil.
ii. 29 τοὺς τοιούτους ἐντίμους ἔχετε.
Those are κοινωνοί, who have common
interests, common feelings, common
work.

18—22. 'But if he has done thee
any injury, or if he stands in thy debt,
set it down to my account. Here is my
signature—*Paul*—in my own hand-

writing. Accept this as my bond. I
will repay thee. For I will not insist, as I might, that thou art indebted
to me for much more than this ; that
thou owest to me thine own self. Yes,
dear brother, let me receive from my
son in the faith such a return as a
father has a right to expect. Cheer
and refresh my spirits in Christ. I
have full confidence in thy compli-
ance, as I write this ; for I know that
thou wilt do even more than I ask.
At the same time also prepare to
receive me on a visit; for I hope that
through your prayers I shall be set
free and given to you once more.'

18. εἰ δέ τι] The case is stated
hypothetically but the words doubtless describe the actual offence of
Onesimus. He had done his master
some injury, probably had robbed
him; and he had fled to escape punishment. See the introduction.

ἢ ὀφείλει] defining the offence which
has been indicated in ἠδίκησεν. But
still the Apostle refrains from using
the plain word ἔκλεψεν. He would
spare the penitent slave, and avoid
irritating the injured master.

ἐλλόγα] '*reckon it in*', '*set it down*'.
This form must be adopted instead of
ἐλλόγει which stands in the received
text, as the great preponderance of
authority shows. On the other hand
we have ἐλλογεῖται Rom. v. 13 (though
with a v. l. ἐλλογᾶται), ἐλλογουμένων
Boeckh *C. I.* no. 1732 A, and ἐνλογεῖ-
σθαι *Edict. Diocl.* in *Corp. Inscr. Lat.*
III. p. 836. But the word is so rare
in any form, that these occurrences of
ἐλλογεῖν afford no ground for excluding ἐλλογᾶν as impossible. The two
forms might be employed side by side,
just as we find ἐλεᾶν and ἐλεεῖν, ξυρᾶν
and ξυρεῖν, ἐρωτᾶν and ἐρωτεῖν (Matt.

τῇ ἐμῇ χειρί, ἐγὼ ἀποτίσω· ἵνα μὴ λέγω σοι, ὅτι καὶ
σεαυτόν μοι προσοφείλεις. ²⁰ναί, ἀδελφέ, ἐγώ σου ὀναίμην ἐν Κυρίῳ· ἀνάπαυσόν μου τὰ σπλάγχνα ἐν Χριστῷ.

xv. 23), and the like; see Buttmann *A usf. Gramm.* § 112 (II. p. 53). The word λογᾶν, as used by Lucian *Lexiph.* 15 (where it is a desiderative 'to be eager to speak', like φονᾶν, θανατᾶν, φαρμακᾶν, etc.), has nothing to do with the use of ἐλλογᾶν here.

19. ἐγὼ Παῦλος] The introduction of his own name gives it the character of a formal and binding signature: comp. 1 Cor. xvi. 21, Col. iv. 18, 2 Thess. iii. 17. A signature to a deed in ancient or mediæval times would commonly take this form, ἐγὼ ὁ δεῖνα,—'*I* so and so'; where we should omit the marks of the first person.

ἔγραψα] An epistolary or documentary aorist, as in ver. 21; so too ἀνέπεμψα ver. 11. See the note on ἔγραψα Gal. vi. 11. The aorist is the tense commonly used in signatures; e.g. ὑπέγραψα to the conciliar decrees.

This incidental mention of his autograph, occurring where it does, shows that he wrote the whole letter with his own hand. This procedure is quite exceptional, just as the purport of the letter is exceptional. In all other cases he appears to have employed an amanuensis, only adding a few words in his own handwriting at the close: see the note on Gal. *l. c.*

ἵνα μὴ λέγω] '*not to say*', as 2 Cor. ix. 4. There is a suppressed thought, 'though indeed you cannot fairly claim repayment', 'though indeed you owe me (ὀφείλεις) as much as this', on which the ἵνα μὴ κ.τ.λ. is dependent. Hence προσοφείλεις '*owest besides*'; for this is the common meaning of the word.

σεαυτόν] St Paul was his spiritual father, who had begotten him in the faith, and to whom therefore he owed his being; comp. Plato *Legg.* iv. p. 717 B ὡς θέμις ὀφείλοντα ἀποτίνειν

τὰ πρῶτά τε καὶ μέγιστα ὀφειλήματα... νομίζειν δὲ, ἃ κέκτηται καὶ ἔχει, πάντα εἶναι τῶν γεννησάντων...ἀρχόμενον ἀπὸ τῆς οὐσίας, δεύτερα τὰ τοῦ σώματος, τρίτα τὰ τῆς ψυχῆς, ἀποτίνοντα δανείσματα κ.τ.λ.

20. ναί] introducing an affectionate appeal as in Phil. iv. 3 ναὶ ἐρωτῶ καὶ σέ.

ἀδελφέ] It is the entreaty of a brother to a brother on behalf of a brother (ver. 16). For the pathetic appeal involved in the word see the notes on Gal. iii. 15, vi. 1, 18; and comp. ver. 7.

ἐγώ] 'I seem to be entreating for Onesimus; but I am pleading for *myself*: the favour will be done to me'; comp. ver. 17 προσλαβοῦ αὐτὸν ὡς ἐμέ. The emphatic ἐγώ identifies the cause of Onesimus with his own.

σου ὀναίμην] '*may I have satisfaction, find comfort in thee*', i.e. 'may I receive such a return from thee, as a father has a right to expect from his child.' The common use of the word ὀναίμην would suggest the thought of filial offices; e.g. Arist. *Thesm.* 469 οὕτως ὀναίμην τῶν τέκνων, Lucian *Philops.* 27 πρὸς τὴν ὄψιν τῶν υἱέων, οὕτως ὀναίμην, ἔφη, τούτων, Ps-Ignat. *Hero* 6 ὀναίμην σου, παιδίον ποθεινόν, Synes. *Ep.* 44 οὕτω τῆς ἱερᾶς φιλοσοφίας ὀναίμην καὶ προσέτι τῶν παιδίων τῶν ἐμαυτοῦ, with other passages quoted in Wetstein. So too for ὄνασθαι, ὄνησις, compare Eur. *Med.* 1025 sq. πρὶν σφῶν ὄνασθαι... ἄλλως ἄρ' ὑμᾶς, ὦ τέκν', ἐξεθρεψάμην, *Alc.* 333 ἅλις δὲ παιδῶν· τῶνδ' ὄνησιν εὔχομαι θεοῖς γενέσθαι, Philem. *Inc.* 64 (IV. p. 55 Meineke) ἔτεκές με, μῆτερ, καὶ γένοιτό σοι τέκνων ὄνησις, ὥσπερ καὶ δίκαιόν ἐστι σοι, Ecclus. xxx. 2 ὁ παιδεύων τὸν υἱὸν αὐτοῦ ὀνήσεται ἐπ' αὐτῷ (the

²¹Πεποιθὼς τῇ ὑπακοῇ σου ἔγραψά σοι, εἰδὼς ὅτι καὶ
ὑπὲρ ἃ λέγω ποιήσεις. ²²ἅμα δὲ καὶ ἑτοίμαζέ μοι
ξενίαν· ἐλπίζω γὰρ ὅτι διὰ τῶν προσευχῶν ὑμῶν χα-
ρισθήσομαι ὑμῖν.

only passage in the LXX where the
word occurs). The prayer ὀναίμην σου,
ὀναίμην ὑμῶν, etc., occurs several times
in Ignatius; *Polyc.* 1, 6, *Magn.* 2, 12,
Ephes. 2. It is not unlikely that ὀναίμην here involves a reference to the
name Onesimus; see the note on ver.
11. The Hebrew fondness for playing
on names makes such an allusion at
least possible.

ἐν Κυρίῳ] As he had begotten Philemon ἐν Κυρίῳ (comp. 1 Cor. iv. 15, 17),
so it was ἐν Κυρίῳ that he looked for
the recompense of filial offices.

ἀνάπαυσόν κ.τ.λ.] See the note ver. 7.

21. ἔγραψα] '*I write*': see the note
on ver. 19.

ὑπὲρ ἃ λέγω κ.τ.λ.] What was the
thought upmost in the Apostle's mind
when he penned these words? Did
he contemplate the manumission of
Onesimus? If so, the restraint which
he imposes upon himself is significant. Indeed throughout this epistle
the idea would seem to be present to
his thoughts, though the word never
passes his lips. This reserve is eminently characteristic of the Gospel.
Slavery is never directly attacked as
such, but principles are inculcated
which must prove fatal to it.

22. ἅμα δὲ κ.τ.λ.] When St Paul
first contemplated visiting Rome, he
had intended, after leaving the metropolis, to pass westward into Spain;
Rom. xv. 24, 28. But by this time he
appears to have altered his plans, pur-
posing first to revisit Greece and Asia
Minor. Thus in Phil. ii. 24 he looks
forward to seeing the Philippians
shortly; while here he contemplates a
visit to the Churches of the Lycus
valley.

There is a gentle compulsion in this
mention of a personal visit to Colossæ.
The Apostle would thus be able to

see for himself that Philemon had not
disappointed his expectations. Similarly Serapion in Eus. *H. E.* vi. 12
προσδοκᾶτέ με ἐν τάχει.

ξενίαν] '*a lodging*'; comp. *Clem.
Rom.* xii. 2 προάξωσιν τὰς ξενίας ἑτοι-
μάζοντες. So the Latin *parare hospitium* Cic. *ad Att.* xiv. 2, Mart. *Ep.*
ix. 1. This latter passage, 'Vale et
para hospitium', closely resembles St
Paul's language here. In the expression before us ξενία is probably the
place of entertainment: but in such
phrases as καλεῖν ἐπὶ ξενίᾳ, παρακαλεῖν
ἐπὶ ξενίαν, φροντίζειν ξενίας, and the
like, it denotes the offices of hospitality. The Latin *hospitium* also includes both senses. The ξενία, as a
lodging, may denote either quarters
in an inn or a room in a private house:
see *Philippians* p. 9. For the latter
comp. Plato *Tim.* 20 c παρὰ Κριτίαν
πρὸς τὸν ξενῶνα, οὗ καὶ καταλύομεν,
ἀφικόμεθα. In this case the response
would doubtless be a hospitable reception in Philemon's home; but the
request does not assume so much as
this.

χαρισθήσομαι] '*I shall be granted
to you*'. The grant (χαρίζεσθαι) of
one person to another, may be for
purposes either (1) of destruction, as
Acts xxv. 11 οὐδείς με δύναται αὐτοῖς
χαρίσασθαι (comp. ver. 16), or (2) of
preservation, as Acts iii. 14 ᾐτήσασθε
ἄνδρα φονέα χαρισθῆναι ὑμῖν, and
here.

23—25. 'Epaphras my fellow-cap-
tive in Christ Jesus salutes you. As
do also Mark, Aristarchus, Demas,
and Luke, my fellow-labourers. The
grace of our Lord Jesus Christ be with
thee and thy household, and sanctify
the spirit of you all.'

23 sq. For these salutations see
the notes on Col. iv. 10 sq. Epaphras

²³Ἀσπάζεταί σε Ἐπαφρᾶς ὁ συναιχμάλωτός μου ἐν
Χριστῷ Ἰησοῦ, ²⁴Μάρκος, Ἀρίσταρχος, Δημᾶς, Λουκᾶς,
οἱ συνεργοί μου.

²⁵Ἡ χάρις τοῦ Κυρίου [ἡμῶν] Ἰησοῦ Χριστοῦ μετὰ
τοῦ πνεύματος ὑμῶν.

is mentioned first because he was a
Colossian (Col. iv. 12) and, as the evangelist of Colossæ (see p. 29 sq.), doubtless well known to Philemon. Of the
four others Aristarchus and Mark belonged to the Circumcision (Col. iv. 11)
while Demas and Luke were Gentile
Christians. All these were of Greek
or Asiatic origin and would probably
be well known to Philemon, at least
by name. On the other hand Jesus
Justus, who is honourably mentioned
in the Colossian letter (iv. 11), but
passed over here, may have been a
Roman Christian.

ὁ συναιχμάλωτος] On the possible
meanings of this title see Col. iv. 10,
where it is given not to Epaphras but
to Aristarchus.

25. Ἡ χάρις κ.τ.λ.] The same form
of farewell as in Gal. vi. 18; comp.
2 Tim. iv. 22.

ὑμῶν] The persons whose names
are mentioned in the opening salutation.

DISSERTATIONS.

On some points connected with the Essenes.

I.
THE NAME ESSENE.

II.
ORIGIN AND AFFINITY OF THE ESSENES.

III.
ESSENISM AND CHRISTIANITY.

I.

THE NAME ESSENE.

The name is variously written in Greek: Various forms of the name in Greek.

1. Ἐσσηνός: Joseph. *Ant.* xiii. 5. 9, xiii. 10. 6, xv. 10. 5, xviii. 1. **2**, **5**, *B. J.* ii. 8. 2, 13, *Vit.* 2; Plin. *N. H.* v. 15. 17 (Essenus); Dion Chrys. in Synes. *Dion* 3; Hippol. *Haer.* ix. 18, 28 (MS ἐσηνός); Epiphan. *Haer.* p. 28 sq., 127 (ed. Pet.).

2. Ἐσσαῖος: Philo II. pp. 457, 471, 632 (ed. Mang.); Hegesippus in Euseb. *H. E.* iv. 22; Porphyr. *de Abstin.* iv. 11. So too Joseph. *B. J.* ii. 7. 3, ii. 20. 4, iii. 2. 1; *Ant.* xv. 10. 4; though in the immediate context of this last passage he writes Ἐσσηνός, if the common texts may be trusted.

3. Ὀσσαῖος: Epiphan. *Haer.* pp. 40 sq., 125, 462. The common texts very frequently make him write Ὀσσηνός, but see Dindorf's notes, Epiphan. *Op.* I. pp. 380, 425. With Epiphanius the Essenes are a Samaritan, the Ossæans a Judaic sect. He has evidently got his information from two distinct sources, and does not see that the same persons are intended.

4. Ἰεσσαῖος, Epiphan. *Haer.* p. 117. From the connexion the same sect again seems to be meant: but owing to the form Epiphanius conjectures (οἶμαι) that the name is derived from Jesse, the father of David.

If any certain example could be produced where the name occurs in any early Hebrew or Aramaic writing, the question of its derivation would probably be settled; but in the absence of a single decisive instance a wide field is opened for conjecture, and critics have not All etymologies to be rejected which derive the name

been backward in availing themselves of the license. In discussing the claims of the different etymologies proposed we may reject:

(i) From the Greek;   *First*: derivations from the Greek. Thus Philo connects the word with ὅσιος 'holy': *Quod omn. prob.* 12, p. 457 Ἐσσαῖοι...διαλέκτου ἑλληνικῆς παρώνυμοι ὁσιότητος, § 13, p. 459 τῶν Ἐσσαίων ἢ ὁσίων, *Fragm.* p. 632 καλοῦνται μὲν Ἐσσαῖοι, παρὰ τὴν ὁσιότητα, μοὶ δοκῶ [δοκεῖ ?], τῆς προσηγορίας ἀξιωθέντες. It is not quite clear whether Philo is here playing with words after the manner of his master Plato, or whether he holds a pre-established harmony to exist among different languages by which similar sounds represent similar things, or whether lastly he seriously means that the name was directly derived from the Greek word ὅσιος. The last supposition is the least probable; but he certainly does not reject this derivation 'as incorrect' (Ginsburg *Essenes* p. 27), nor can παρώνυμοι ὁσιότητος be rendered 'from an incorrect derivation from the Greek homonym *hosiotes*' (ib. p. 32), since the word παρώνυμος never involves the notion of *false* etymology. The amount of truth which probably underlies Philo's statement will be considered hereafter. Another Greek derivation is ἴσος, 'companion, associate,' suggested by Rapoport, *Erech Millin* p. 41. Several others again are suggested by Löwy, s. v. Essäer, e.g. ἔσω from their esoteric doctrine, or αἶσα from their fatalism. All such may be rejected as instances of ingenious trifling, if indeed they deserve to be called ingenious.

(ii) From names of persons or places;   *Secondly*: derivations from proper names whether of persons or of places. Thus the word has been derived from *Jesse* the father of David (Epiphan. l. c.), or from one יסי *Isai*, the disciple of R. Joshua ben Perachia who migrated to Egypt in the time of Alexander Jannæus (Löw in *Ben Chananja* I. p. 352). Again it has been referred to the town *Essa* (a doubtful reading in Joseph. *Ant.* xiii. 15. 3) beyond the Jordan. And other similar derivations have been suggested.

(iii) From Hebrew roots not supplying the right consonants,   *Thirdly*: etymologies from the Hebrew or Aramaic, which do not supply the right consonants, or do not supply them in the right order. Under this head several must be rejected;

אסר *āsar* 'to bind,' Adler *Volkslehrer* VI. p. 50, referred to by Ginsburg *Essenes* p. 29.

חסיד *chāsīd* 'pious,' which is represented by Ἀσιδαῖος (1 Macc. ii. 42 (v. l.), vii. 13, 2 Macc. xiv. 6), and could not possibly assume the form Ἐσσαῖος or Ἐσσηνός. Yet this derivation appears in Josippon ben Gorion (iv. 6, 7, v. 24, pp. 274, 278, 451), who substitutes *Chasidim* in narratives where the Essenes are mentioned in the original of Josephus; and it has been adopted by many more recent writers.

סְחָא *s'chā* 'to bathe,' from which with an *Aleph* prefixed we might get אַסְחַאי *as'chai* 'bathers' (a word however which does not occur): Grätz *Gesch. der Juden* III. pp. 82, 468.

צָנוּעַ *tsanūaɛ* 'retired, modest,' adopted by Frankel (*Zeitschrift* 1846, p. 449, *Monatsschrift* II. p. 32) after a suggestion by Löw.

To this category must be assigned those etymologies which contain a נ as the third consonant of the root; since the comparison of the parallel forms Ἐσσαῖος and Ἐσσηνός shows that in the latter word the ν is only formative. On this ground we must reject: *such as those which make n part of the root.*

חֲסִין *chāsīn*; see below under עָשׁין.

חֹצֶן *chōtsen* 'a fold' of a garment, and so supposed to signify the περίζωμα or 'apron', which was given to every neophyte among the Essenes (Joseph. *B. J.* ii. 8. 5, 7): suggested by Jellinek *Ben Chananja* IV. p. 374.

עָשִׁין *ɛāshīn* 'strong': see Cohn in Frankel's *Monatsschrift* VII. p. 271. This etymology is suggested to explain Epiphanius *Haer.* p. 40 τοῦτο δὲ τὸ γένος τῶν Ὀσσηνῶν ἑρμηνεύεται διὰ τῆς ἐκδόσεως τοῦ ὀνόματος στιβαρὸν γένος ('a sturdy race'). The name 'Essene' is so interpreted also in Makrisi (de Sacy, *Chrestom. Arab.* I. p. 114, 306); but, as he himself writes it with *Elif* and not *Ain*, it is plain that he got this interpretation from some one else, probably from Epiphanius. The correct reading however in Epiphanius is Ὀσσαίων, not Ὀσσηνῶν; and it would therefore appear that this father or his informant derived the word from the Hebrew root עָזַז rather than from the Aramaic עְשַׁן. The Ὀσσαῖοι would then be the עַזִּים, and this is so far a possible derivation, that the *n* does not enter into the root. Another word suggested to explain the etymology of Epiphanius is the Hebrew and Aramaic חָסִין *chasīn* 'powerful, strong' (from חָסַן); but this is open to the same objections as עָשׁין.

When all such derivations are eliminated as untenable or improbable, considerable uncertainty still remains. The 1st and 3rd radicals might be any of the gutturals א, ה, ח, ע; and the Greek σ, as the 2nd radical, might represent any one of several Shemitic sibilants. *Other derivations considered:*

Thus we have the choice of the following etymologies, which have found more or less favour.

(1) אסיא 'a physician';   (1) אסא *āsā* 'to heal,' whence אסיא *asyā*, 'a physician.' The Essenes are supposed to be so called because Josephus states (*B. J.* ii. 8. 6) that they paid great attention to the qualities of herbs and minerals with a view to the healing of diseases (πρὸς θεραπείαν παθῶν). This etymology is supported likewise by an appeal to the name θεραπευταί, which Philo gives to an allied sect in Egypt (*de Vit. Cont.* § 1, II. p. 471). It seems highly improbable however, that the ordinary name of the Essenes should have been derived from a pursuit which was merely secondary and incidental; while the supposed analogy of the Therapeutæ rests on a wrong interpretation of the word. Philo indeed (l. c.), bent upon extracting from it as much moral significance as possible, says, θεραπευταὶ καὶ θεραπευτρίδες καλοῦνται, ἤτοι παρ' ὅσον ἰατρικὴν ἐπαγγέλλονται κρείσσονα τῆς κατὰ πόλεις (ἡ μὲν γὰρ σώματα θεραπεύει μόνον, ἐκείνη δὲ καὶ ψυχὰς κ.τ.λ.) ἢ παρ' ὅσον ἐκ φύσεως καὶ τῶν ἱερῶν νόμων ἐπαιδεύθησαν θεραπεύειν τὸ ὂν κ.τ.λ. : but the latter meaning alone accords with the usage of the word; for θεραπευτής, used absolutely, signifies 'a worshipper, devotee,' not 'a physician, healer.' This etymology of Ἐσσαῖος is ascribed, though wrongly, to Philo by Asaria de' Rossi (*Meor Enayim* 3, fol. 33 *a*) and has been very widely received. Among more recent writers, who have adopted or favoured it, are Bellermann (*Ueber Essäer u. Therapeuten* p. 7), Gfrörer (*Philo* II. p. 341), Dähne (*Ersch u. Gruber*, s. v.), Baur (*Christl. Kirche der drei erst. Jahrh.* p. 20), Herzfeld (*Gesch. des Judenthums* II. p. 371, 395, 397 sq.), Geiger (*Urschrift* p. 126), Derenbourg (*L'Histoire et la Géographie de la Palestine* pp. 170, 175, notes), Keim (*Jesus von Nazara* I. p. 284 sq.), and Hamburger (*Real-Encyclopädie für Bibel u. Talmud*, s. v.). Several of these writers identify the Essenes with the Baithusians (ביתוסין) of the Talmud, though in the Talmud the Baithusians are connected with the Sadducees. This identification was suggested by Asaria de' Rossi (l. c. fol. 33 *b*), who interprets 'Baithusians' as 'the school of the Essenes' (בית איסיא) : while subsequent writers, going a step further, have explained it 'the school of the physicians' (בית אסיא).

(2) חויא 'a seer';   (2) חזא *chăzā* 'to see', whence חזיא *chazyā* 'a seer', in reference to the prophetic powers which the Essenes claimed, as the result of ascetic contemplation: Joseph. *B. J.* ii. 8. 12 εἰσὶ δὲ ἐν αὐτοῖς

οἳ καὶ τὰ μέλλοντα προγινώσκειν ὑπισχνοῦνται κ.τ.λ. For instances of such Essene prophets see *Ant.* xiii. 11. 2, xv. 10. 5, *B. J.* i. 3. 5, ii. 7. 3. Suidas, s. v. Ἐσσαῖοι, says : θεωρίᾳ τὰ πολλὰ παραμένουσιν, ἔνθεν καὶ Ἐσσαῖοι καλοῦνται, τοῦτο δηλοῦντος τοῦ ὀνόματος, τουτέστι, θεωρητικοί. For this derivation, which was suggested by Baumgarten (see Bellermann p. 10) and is adopted by Hilgenfeld (*Jüd. Apocal.* p. 278), there is something to be said : but הזא is rather ὁρᾶν than θεωρεῖν; and thus it must denote the result rather than the process, the *vision* which was the privilege of the few rather than the *contemplation* which was the duty of all. Indeed in a later paper (*Zeitschr.* XI. p. 346, 1868) Hilgenfeld expresses himself doubtfully about this derivation, feeling the difficulty of explaining the σσ from the ז. This is a real objection. In the transliteration of the LXX the ז is persistently represented by ζ, and the צ by σ. The exceptions to this rule, where the manuscript authority is beyond question, are very few, and in every case they seem capable of explanation by peculiar circumstances.

(3) עָשָׂה *ᶜāsāh* 'to do,' so that Ἐσσαῖοι would signify 'the doers, the observers of the law,' thus referring to the strictness of Essene practices : see Oppenheim in Frankel's *Monatsschrift* VII. p. 272 sq. It has been suggested also that, as the Pharisees were especially designated the teachers, the Essenes were called the 'doers' by a sort of antithesis : see an article in Jost's *Annalen* 1839, p. 145. Thus the Talmudic phrase אנשי מעשה, interpreted 'men of practice, of good deeds,' is supposed to refer to the Essenes (see Frankel's *Zeitschrift* III. p. 458, *Monatsschrift* II. p. 70). In some passages indeed (see Surenhuis *Mishna* III. p. 313) it may possibly mean 'workers of miracles' (as ἔργον Joh. v. 20, vii. 21, x. 25, etc.); but in this sense also it might be explained of the thaumaturgic powers claimed by the Essenes. (See below, p. 362.) On the use which has been made of a passage in the *Aboth* of R. Nathan c. 37, as supporting this derivation, I shall have to speak hereafter. Altogether this etymology has little or nothing to recommend it.

I have reserved to the last the two derivations which seem to deserve most consideration.

(4) ܚܣܐ *chasi* (ܚ'ܣܐ *ch'sē*) or ܚܣܝܐ *chasyo*, 'pious,' in Syriac. This derivation, which is also given by de Sacy (*Chrestom. Arab.* I. p. 347), is adopted by Ewald (*Gesch. des V. Isr.* IV. p. 484,

(3) עשה 'to do';

(4) chasyo 'pious';

ed. 3, 1864, VII. pp. 154, 477, ed. 2, 1859), who abandons in its favour another etymology (חזן *chazzan* 'watcher, worshipper' = θερα
πευτής) which he had suggested in an earlier edition of his fourth
volume (p. 420). It is recommended by the fact that it resembles
not only in sound, but in meaning, the Greek ὅσιος, of which it is a
common rendering in the Peshito (Acts ii. 27, xiii. 35, Tit. i. 8).
Thus it explains the derivation given by Philo (see above, p. 350),
and it also accounts for the tendency to write 'Οσσαῖος for 'Εσσαῖος
in Greek. Ewald moreover points out how an Essenizing Sibylline
poem (*Orac. Sib.* iv ; see above, p. 96) dwells on the Greek equivalents, εὐσεβής, εὐσεβίη, etc. (vv. 26, 35, 42 sq., 148 sq., 162, 165 sq.,
178 sq., ed. Alexandre), as if they had a special value for the
writer : see *Gesch.* VII. p. 154, *Sibyll. Bücher* p. 46. Lipsius (Schenkel's
Bibel-Lexicon, s. v.) also considers this the most probable etymology.

(5) חשאים
'silent
ones.'

(5) **חשׁא** *chāshā* (also חשה) Heb. 'to be silent'; whence חשאים
chashshāīm 'the silent ones,' who meditate on mysteries. Jost (*Gesch.
d. Judenth.* I. p. 207) believes that this was the derivation accepted
by Josephus, since he elsewhere (*Ant.* iii. 7. 5, iii. 8. 9) writes out חשן,
chōshen 'the high-priest's breast-plate' (Exod. xxviii. 15 sq.), ἐσσήν or
ἐσσήνης in Greek, and explains it σημαίνει τοῦτο κατὰ τὴν Ἑλλήνων
γλῶτταν λογεῖον (i. e. the 'place of oracles' or 'of reason': comp. Philo
de Mon. ii. § 5, II. p. 226, καλεῖται λογεῖον ἐτύμως, ἐπειδὴ τὰ ἐν οὐρανῷ
πάντα λόγοις καὶ ἀναλογίαις δεδημιούργηται κ.τ.λ.), as it is translated
in the LXX. Even though modern critics should be right in connecting חשן with the Arab. ḥasuna 'pulcher fuit, ornavit' (see Gesen. *Thes.*
p. 535, s. v.), the other derivation may have prevailed in Josephus'
time. We may illustrate this derivation by Josephus' description of
the Essenes, *B. J.* ii. 8. 5 τοῖς ἔξωθεν ὡς μυστήριόν τι φρικτὸν ἡ τῶν
ἔνδον σιωπὴ καταφαίνεται ; and perhaps this will also explain the Greek
equivalent θεωρητικοί, which Suidas gives for 'Εσσαῖοι. The use of
the Hebrew word חשאים in Mishna *Shekalim* v. 6, though we need
not suppose that the Essenes are there meant, will serve to show how
it might be adopted as the name of the sect. On this word see Levy
Chaldäisches Wörterbuch p. 287. On the whole this seems the most
probable etymology of any, though it has not found so much favour
as the last. At all events the rules of transliteration are entirely
satisfied, and this can hardly be said of the other derivations which
come into competition with it.

ORIGIN AND AFFINITIES OF THE ESSENES.

THE ruling principle of the Restoration under Ezra was the isola- The prin-
tion of the Jewish people from all influences of the surrounding ciple of
the resto-
nations. Only by the rigorous application of this principle was it ration.
possible to guard the nationality of the Hebrews, and thus to preserve
the sacred deposit of religious truth of which this nationality was the
husk. Hence the strictest attention was paid to the Levitical ordinances, and more especially to those which aimed at ceremonial
purity. The principle, which was thus distinctly asserted at the
period of the national revival, gained force and concentration at a
later date from the active antagonism to which the patriotic Jews
were driven by the religious and political aggressions of the Syrian
kings. During the Maccabæan wars we read of a party or sect Rise of
the Asi-
called the *Chasidim* or *Asidæans* (Ἀσιδαῖοι), the 'pious' or 'devout,' dæans.
who zealous in their observance of the ceremonial law stoutly resisted any concession to the practices of Hellenism, and took their
place in the van of the struggle with their national enemies, the
Antiochene monarchs (1 Macc. ii. 42, vii. 13, 2 Macc. xiv. 6). But,
though their names appear now for the first time, they are not mentioned as a newly formed party; and it is probable that they had their
origin at a much earlier date.

The subsequent history of this tendency to exclusiveness and
isolation is wrapt in the same obscurity. At a somewhat later date Pharisaism and
it is exhibited in the *Pharisees* and the *Essenes;* but whether these Essenism
were historically connected with the Chasidim as divergent offshoots traced to
the same
of the original sect, or whether they represent independent develop- principle.
ments of the same principle, we are without the proper data for
deciding. The principle itself appears in the name of the Pharisees,

which, as denoting 'separation,' points to the avoidance of all foreign
and contaminating influences.   On the other hand the meaning of
the name *Essene* is uncertain, for the attempt to derive it directly
from *Chasidim* must be abandoned; but the tendency of the sect is
unmistakeable.   If with the Pharisees ceremonial purity was a
principal aim, with the Essenes it was an absorbing passion.   It was
enforced and guarded moreover by a special organization.   While the
Pharisees were a sect, the Essenes were an order.   Like the Pythagoreans in Magna Græcia and the Buddhists in India before them,
like the Christian monks of the Egyptian and Syrian deserts after
them, they were formed into a religious brotherhood, fenced about by
minute and rigid rules, and carefully guarded from any contamination
with the outer world.

Foreign
elements
in Esse-
nism.

Thus the sect may have arisen in the heart of Judaism.   The
idea of ceremonial purity was essentially Judaic.   But still, when we
turn to the representations of Philo and Josephus, it is impossible to
overlook other traits which betoken foreign affinities.   Whatever the
Essenes may have been in their origin, at the Christian era at least
and in the Apostolic age they no longer represented the current type
of religious thought and practice among the Jews.   This foreign
element has been derived by some from the Pythagoreans, by others
from the Syrians or Persians or even from the farther East; but,
whether Greek or Oriental, its existence has until lately been almost
universally allowed.

Frankel's
theory
well re-
ceived,

The investigations of Frankel, published first in 1846 in his
Zeitschrift, and continued in 1853 in his *Monatsschrift*, have given
a different direction to current opinion.   Frankel maintains that
Essenism was a purely indigenous growth, that it is only Pharisaism
in an exaggerated form, and that it has nothing distinctive and owes
nothing, or next to nothing, to foreign influences.   To establish this
point, he disparages the representations of Philo and Josephus as
coloured to suit the tastes of their heathen readers, while in their
place he brings forward as authorities a number of passages from talmudical and rabbinical writings, in which he discovers references to
this sect.   In this view he is followed implicitly by some later
writers, and has largely influenced the opinions of others; while
nearly all speak of his investigations as throwing great light on
the subject.

It is perhaps dangerous to dissent from a view which has found but
so much favour; but nevertheless I am obliged to confess my belief ground-less and
that, whatever value Frankel's investigations may have as contribu-misleading.
tions to our knowledge of Jewish religious thought and practice, they
throw little or no light on the Essenes specially; and that the blind
acceptance of his results by later writers has greatly obscured the
distinctive features of this sect. I cannot but think that any one,
who will investigate Frankel's references and test his results step by
step, will arrive at the conclusion to which I myself have been led,
that his talmudical researches have left our knowledge of this sect
where it was before, and that we must still refer to Josephus and
Philo for any precise information respecting them.

Frankel starts from the etymology of the name. He supposes His double
that 'Εσσαῖος, 'Εσσηνός, represent two different Hebrew words, the derivation of the
former חסיד chāsīd, the latter צנוע tsanūaʒ, both clothed in suit-name.
able Greek dresses[1]. Wherever therefore either of these words
occurs, there is, or there may be, a direct reference to the
Essenes.

It is not too much to say that these etymologies are impossible; Fatal ob-
and this for several reasons. (1) The two words 'Εσσαῖος, 'Εσση-jections to it.
νός, are plainly duplicate forms of the same Hebrew or Aramaic
original, like Σαμψαῖος and Σαμψηνός (Epiphan. Haer. pp. 40, 47,
127, and even Σαμψίτης p. 46), Ναζωραῖος and Ναζαρηνός, Γιτταῖος
and Γιττηνός (Steph. Byz. s. v., Hippol. Hær. vi. 7), with which we
may compare Βοστραῖος and Βοστρηνός, Μελιταῖος and Μελιτηνός, and
numberless other examples. (2) Again; when we consider either
word singly, the derivation offered is attended with the most serious
difficulties. There is no reason why in 'Εσσαῖος the d should have
disappeared from chasid, while it is hardly possible to conceive that
tsanuaʒ should have taken such an incongruous form as 'Εσσηνός.
(3) And lastly; the more important of the two words, chasid, had
already a recognised Greek equivalent in 'Ασιδαῖος; and it seems
highly improbable that a form so divergent as 'Εσσαῖος should have
taken its place.

Indeed Frankel's derivations are generally, if not universally, Depend-
abandoned by later writers; and yet these same writers repeat his ence of the theory

---

[1] *Zeitschrift* p. 449 'Für *Essäer* liegt,
wie schon von anderen Seiten bemerkt
wurde, das Hebr. חסיד, für *Essener*,
nach einer Bemerkung des Herrn L.
Löw im *Orient*, das Hebr. צנוע nahe';
see also pp. 454, 455; *Monatsschrift* p. 32.

quotations and accept his results, as if the references were equally valid, though the name of the sect has disappeared. They seem to be satisfied with the stability of the edifice, even when the foundation is undermined. Thus for instance Grätz not only maintains after Frankel that the Essenes 'were properly nothing more than stationary or, more strictly speaking, logically consistent (consequente) *Chasidim*,' and 'that therefore they were not so far removed from the Pharisees that they can be regarded as a separate sect,' and 'accepts entirely these results' which, as he says, 'rest on critical investigation' (III. p. 463), but even boldly translates *chasiduth* 'the Essene mode of life' (ib. 84), though he himself gives a wholly different derivation of the word 'Essene,' making it signify 'washers' or 'baptists' (see above, p. 351). And even those who do not go to this length of inconsistency, yet avail themselves freely of the passages where *chasid* occurs, and interpret it of the Essenes, while distinctly repudiating the etymology[1].

The term
chasid
not ap-
plied
specially
to the
Essenes.

But, although Ἐσσαῖος or Ἐσσηνός is not a Greek form of *chasid*, it might still happen that this word was applied to them as an epithet, though not as a proper name. Only in this case the reference ought to be unmistakeable, before any conclusions are based upon it. But in fact, after going through all the passages, which Frankel gives, it is impossible to feel satisfied that in a single instance there is a direct allusion to the Essenes. Sometimes the word seems to refer to the old sect of the *Chasidim* or *Asidæans*, as for instance when Jose ben Joezer, who lived during the Maccabæan war, is called a *chasid*[2]. At all events this R. Jose is known to have been a married man, for he is stated to have disinherited his children (*Baba Bathra* 133 b); and therefore he cannot have belonged to the stricter order of Essenes. Sometimes it is employed quite generally to denote pious observers of the ceremonial law, as for instance when it is said that with the death of certain famous teachers the Chasidim ceased[3]. In this latter sense the expression חסידים הראשונים, 'the ancient or primitive Chasidim' (*Monatsschr.* pp. 31, 62), is perhaps used; for these primitive Chasidim again are mentioned as having

---

[1] e.g. Keim (p. 286) and Derenbourg (p. 166, 461 sq.), who both derive Essene from אסיא 'a physician.'

[2] Mishna *Chagigah* ii. 7; *Zeitschr.* p. 454, *Monatsschr.* pp. 33, 62. See

Frankel's own account of this R. Jose in an earlier volume, *Monatsschr.* I. p. 405 sq.

[3] *Zeitschr.* p. 457, *Monatsschr.* p. 69 sq.; see below, p. 362.

wives and children[1], and it appears also that they were scrupulously
exact in bringing their sacrificial offerings[2]. Thus it is impossible to
identify them with the Essenes, as described by Josephus and Philo.
Even in those passages of which most has been made, the reference
is more than doubtful. Thus great stress is laid on the saying of R.
Joshua ben Chananiah in Mishna *Sotah* iii. 4, 'The foolish *chasid* and
the clever villain (חסיד שוטה ורשע ערום), etc., are the ruin of the world.'
But the connexion points to a much more general meaning of *chasid*,
and the rendering in Surenhuis, ' Homo pius qui insipiens, improbus
qui astutus,' gives the correct antithesis. So we might say that
there is no one more mischievous than the wrong-headed conscientious
man. It is true that the Gemaras illustrate the expression by examples of those who allow an over-punctilious regard for external
forms to stand in the way of deeds of mercy. And perhaps rightly.
But there is no reference to any distinctive Essene practices in the
illustrations given. Again; the saying in Mishna *Pirke Aboth* v.
10, 'He who says Mine is thine and thine is thine is [a] *chasid*
(שלי שלך ושלך שלך חסיד), is quoted by several writers as though it
referred to the Essene community of goods[3]. But in the first place
the idea of community of goods would require, ' Mine is thine and
thine is mine': and in the second place, the whole context, and
especially the clause which immediately follows (and which these
writers do not give), 'He who says Thine is mine and mine is
mine is wicked (רשע),' show plainly that חסיד must be taken in its
general sense 'pious,' and the whole expression implies not reciprocal interchange but individual self-denial.

---

[1] *Niddah* 38 *a*; see Löwy s. v. Essäer.

[2] Mishna *Kerithuth* vi. 3, *Nedarim*
10 *a*; see *Monatsschr.* p. 65.

[3] Thus Grätz (III p. 81) speaking of
the community of goods among the
Essenes writes, 'From this view springs
the proverb; Every Chassid says; *Mine
and thine belong to thee* (not *me*)' thus
giving a turn to the expression which
in its original connexion it does not
at all justify. Of the existence of such
a proverb I have found no traces. It
certainly is not suggested in the passage of *Pirke Aboth*. Later in the volume (p. 467) Grätz tacitly alters the
words to make them express, as he

supposes, reciprocation or community
of goods, substituting 'Thine is mine'
for 'Thine is thine' in the second
clause; 'The Chassid must have no
property of his own, but must treat
it as belonging to the Society (שלי
שלך שלך שלי חסיד).' At least, as he
gives no reference, I suppose that he
refers to the same passage. This very
expression 'mine is thine and thine is
mine' does indeed occur previously
in the same section, but it is applied
as a formula of disparagement to the
ξam haarets (see below p. 366), who
expect to receive again as much as they
give. In this loose way Grätz treats
the whole subject. Keim (p. 294)

It might indeed be urged, though this is not Frankel's plea, that supposing the true etymology of the word Ἐσσαῖος, Ἐσσηνός, to be the Syriac ܚܣܶܐ, ܚܰܣܝܳܐ, *ch'sē*, *chasyo* (a possible derivation), *chasid* might have been its Hebrew equivalent as being similar in sound and meaning, and perhaps ultimately connected in derivation, the exactly corresponding triliteral root חסא (comp. חום) not being in use in Hebrew[1]. But before we accept this explanation we have a right to demand some evidence which, if not demonstrative, is at least circumstantial, that *chasid* is used of the Essenes: and this we have seen is not forthcoming. Moreover, if the Essenes had thus inherited the name of the *Chasidim*, we should have expected that its old Greek equivalent Ἀσιδαῖοι, which is still used later than the Maccabæan era, would also have gone with it; rather than that a new Greek word Ἐσσαῖος (or Ἐσσηνός) should have been invented to take its place. But indeed the Syriac Version of the Old Testament furnishes an argument against this convertibility of the Hebrew *chasid* and the Syriac *chasyo*, which must be regarded as

almost decisive. The numerous passages in the Psalms, where the expressions 'My *chasidim*,' 'His *chasidim*,' occur (xxx. 5, xxxi. 24, xxxvii. 28, lii. 11, lxxix. 2, lxxxv. 9, xcvii. 10, cxvi. 15, cxxxii. 9, cxlix. 9: comp. xxxii. 6, cxlix. 1, 5), seem to have suggested the assumption of the name to the original Asidæans. But in such passages חסיד is commonly, if not universally, rendered in the Peshito not by ܚܣܶܐ, ܚܰܣܝܳܐ, but by a wholly different word ܙܰܕܝܩ *zadīk*. And again, in the Books of Maccabees the Syriac rendering for the name Ἀσιδαῖοι, *Chasidim*, is a word derived from another quite distinct root. These facts show that the Hebrew *chasid* and the Syriac *chasyo* were not practically equivalents, so that the one would suggest the other; and thus all presumption in favour of a connexion between Ἀσιδαῖος and Ἐσσαῖος is removed.

Frankel's
second
derivation
tsanua
consider-
ed.

Frankel's other derivation צנוע, *tsanūa*, suggested as an equivalent to Ἐσσηνός, has found no favour with later writers, and indeed is too far removed from the Greek form to be tenable. Nor do the passages quoted by him[2] require or suggest any allusion

---

quotes the passage correctly, but refers it nevertheless to Essene communism.

[1] This is Hitzig's view (*Geschichte des Volkes Israel* p. 427). He maintains that "they were called '*Hasidim*'

by the later Jews because the Syrian *Essenes* means exactly the same as '*Hasidim*.'"

[2] *Zeitschr.* pp. 455, 457; *Monatsschr.* p. 32.

to this sect. Thus in Mishna *Demai*, vi. 6, we are told that the
school of Hillel permits a certain license in a particular matter, but
it is added, 'The צנוע of the school of Hillel followed the precept of the school of Shammai.' Here, as Frankel himself confesses,
the Jerusalem Talmud knows nothing about Essenes, but explains
the word by כשרי, i. e. 'upright, worthy[1]; while elsewhere, as he
allows[2], it must have this general sense. Indeed the mention of the
'school of Hillel' here seems to exclude the Essenes. In its comprehensive meaning it will most naturally be taken also in the other
passage quoted by Frankel, *Kiddushin* 71 *a*, where it is stated that
the pronunciation of the sacred name, which formerly was known to
all, is now only to be divulged to the צנועים, i. e. the discreet, among
the priests; and in fact it occurs in reference to the communication
of the same mystery in the immediate context also, where it could
not possibly be treated as a proper name; שצנוע ועניו ועומד בחצי ימיו,
'who is *discreet* and meek and has reached middle age,' etc.

Of other etymologies, which have been suggested, and through
which it might be supposed the Essenes are mentioned by name in
the Talmud, אסיא, *asya*, 'a physician,' is the one which has found
most favour. For the reasons given above (p. 352) this derivation
seems highly improbable, and the passages quoted are quite insufficient to overcome the objections. Of these the strongest is in the
Talm. Jerus. *Yoma* iii. 7, where we are told that a certain physician
(אסי) offered to communicate the sacred name to R. Pinchas the
son of Chama, and the latter refused on the ground that he ate of
the tithes—this being regarded as a disqualification, apparently
because it was inconsistent with the highest degree of ceremonial
purity[3]. The same story is told with some modifications in Midrash
Qoheleth iii. 11[4]. Here Frankel, though himself (as we have seen)
adopting a different derivation of the word 'Essene,' yet supposes
that this particular physician belonged to the sect, on the sole ground
that ceremonial purity is represented as a qualification for the
initiation into the mystery of the Sacred Name. Löwy (l. c.) denies
that the allusion to the tithes is rightly interpreted: but even supposing it to be correct, the passage is quite an inadequate basis either

[Marginal notes:] Other sup-posed ety-mologics in the Talmud. (1) *Asya* 'a physi-cian,' not sup-ported by the pas-sages quoted in its behalf.

---

[1] *Monatsschr.* p. 32.
[2] *Zeitschr.* p. 455.
[3] Frankel *Monatsschr.* p. 71: comp.

Derenbourg p. 170 sq.
[4] See Löwy *Krit.-Talm. Lex.* s. v.
Essäer.

for Frankel's conclusion that this particular physician was an Essene, or for the derivation of the word Essene which others maintain. Again, in the statement of Talm. Jerus. *Kethuboth* ii. 3, that correct manuscripts were called books of אסי[1], the word *Asi* is generally taken as a proper name. But even if this interpretation be false, there is absolutely nothing in the context which suggests any allusion to the Essenes[2]. In like manner the passage from *Sanhedrin* 99 b, where a physician is mentioned[3], supports no such inference. Indeed, as this last passage relates to the family of the *Asi*, he obviously can have had no connexion with the celibate Essenes.

(2) *ḡasah* 'to do.'   Hitherto our search for the name in the Talmud has been unsuccessful. One possibility however still remains. The talmudical writers speak of certain אנשי מעשה 'men of deeds'; and if (as some suppose) the name Essene is derived from עשה have we not here the mention which we are seeking? Frankel rejects the etymology, but presses the identification[4]. The expression, he urges, is often used in connexion with *chasidim*. It signifies 'miracle workers,' and therefore aptly describes the supernatural powers supposed to be exercised by the Essenes[5]. Thus we are informed in Mishna *Sotah* ix. 15, that 'When R. Chaninah ben Dosa died, the men of deeds ceased; when R. Jose Ketinta died, the chasidim ceased.' In the Jerusalem Talmud however this mishna is read, 'With the death of R. Chaninah ben Dosa and R. Jose Ketinta the chasidim ceased'; while the Gemara there explains R. Chaninah to have been one of the אנשי מעשה. Thus, Frankel concludes, 'the identity of these with חסידים becomes still more plain.' Now it seems clear that this expression אנשי מעשה in some places cannot refer to miraculous powers, but must mean 'men of practical goodness,' as for instance in *Succah* 51 a, 53 a; and being a general term expressive of moral excellence, it is naturally connected with *chasidim*, which is likewise a general

---

[1] Urged in favour of this derivation by Herzfeld II. p. 398.

[2] The oath taken by the Essenes (Joseph. *B. J.* ii. 8. 7) συντηρήσειν... τὰ τῆς αἱρέσεως αὐτῶν βιβλία can have nothing to do with accuracy in transcribing copies, as Herzfeld (II. pp. 398, 407) seems to think. The natural meaning of συντηρεῖν, 'to keep safe or close' and so 'not to divulge' (e.g. Polyb.

xxxi. 6. 5 οὐκ ἐξέφαινε τὴν ἑαυτῆς γνώμην ἀλλὰ συνετήρει παρ' ἑαυτῇ), is also the meaning suggested here by the context.

[3] The passage is adduced in support of this derivation by Derenbourg p. 175.

[4] See *Zeitschr.* p. 438, *Monatsschr.* pp. 68—70.

[5] See above, p. 353.

term expressive of piety and goodness. Nor is there any reason why
it should not always be taken in this sense. It is true that stories
are told elsewhere of this R. Chaninah, which ascribe miraculous
powers to him[1], and hence there is a temptation to translate it ' won-
der-worker,' as applied to him. But the reason is quite insufficient.
Moreover it must be observed that R. Chaninah's wife is a prominent person in the legends of his miracles reported in *Taanith* 24 *b*;
and thus we need hardly stop to discuss the possible meanings of
אנשי מעשה, since his claims to being considered an Essene are barred
at the outset by this fact[2].

It has been asserted indeed by a recent author, that one very
ancient Jewish writer distinctly adopts this derivation, and as distinctly states that the Essenes were a class of Pharisees[3]. If this
were the case, Frankel's theory, though not his etymology, would
receive a striking confirmation : and it is therefore important to
enquire on what foundation the assertion rests.

Dr Ginsburg's authority for this statement is a passage from
the *Aboth* of Rabbi Nathan, c. 37, which, as he gives it, appears
conclusive ; ' There are eight kinds of Pharisees...and those Pharisees who live in celibacy are Essenes.' But what are the facts
of the case ?   *First ;* This book was certainly not written by its
reputed author, the R. Nathan who was vice-president under the
younger Gamaliel about A.D. 140.   It may possibly have been
founded on an earlier treatise by that famous teacher, though even
this is very doubtful : but in its present form it is a comparatively
modern work.   On this point all or almost all recent writers
on Hebrew literature are agreed[4].   *Secondly ;* Dr Ginsburg has taken
the reading מחופתו עשאני, without even mentioning any alternative.
Whether the words so read are capable of the meaning which he
has assigned to them, may be highly questionable ; but at all events
this cannot have been the original reading, as the parallel passages,

The au-
thority
for this
derivation
traced to
an error.

---

[1] *Taanith* 24 *b*, *Yoma* 53 *b*; see Surenhuis *Mishna* III. p. 313.

[2] In this and similar cases it is un-
necessary to consider whether the persons mentioned might have belonged
to those looser disciples of Essenism,
who married (see above, p. 85): because the identification is meaningless
unless the strict order were intended.

[3] Ginsburg in Kitto's *Cyclopaedia*
s. v., I. p. 829: comp. *Essenes* pp. 22,
28.

[4] e.g. Geiger *Zeitschrift f. Jüdische
Theologie* VI. p. 20 sq.; Zunz *Gottes-
dienstliche Vorträge* p. 108 sq.: comp.
Steinschneider *Catal. Heb. Bibl. Bodl.*
col. 2032 sq. These two last references
are given by Dr Ginsburg himself.

Babl. *Sotah* fol. 22 *b*, Jerus. *Sotah* v. 5, Jerus. *Berakhoth* ix. 5, (quoted by Buxtorf and Levy, s.v. פריש), distinctly prove. In Babl. *Sotah* l.c., the corresponding expression is מה חובתי ואעשנה 'What is my duty, and I will do it,' and the passage in Jerus. *Berakhoth* l.c. is to the same effect. These parallels show that the reading מה חובתי ואעשנה must be taken also in *Aboth* c. 37, so that the passage will be rendered, 'The Pharisee *who says*, What is my duty, and I will do it.' Thus the Essenes and celibacy disappear together. *Lastly;* Inasmuch as Dr Ginsburg himself takes a wholly different view of the name Essene, connecting it either with חצן 'an apron,' or with חסיא 'pious[1],' it is difficult to see how he could translate עשאני 'Essene' (from עשא 'to do') in this passage, except on the supposition that R. Nathan was entirely ignorant of the orthography and derivation of the word Essene. Yet, if such ignorance were conceivable in so ancient a writer, his authority on this question would be absolutely worthless. But indeed Dr Ginsburg would appear to have adopted this reference to R. Nathan, with the reading of the passage and the interpretation of the name, from some other writer[2]. At all events it is quite inconsistent with his own opinion as expressed previously.

Are the Essenes alluded to, though not named, in the Talmud?

But, though we have not succeeded in finding any direct mention of this sect by name in the Talmud, and all the identifications of the word Essene with diverse expressions occurring there have failed us on examination, it might still happen that allusions to them were so frequent as to leave no doubt about the persons meant. Their organisation or their practices or their tenets might be precisely described, though their name was suppressed. Such allusions Frankel finds scattered up and down the Talmud in great profusion.

(1) The *chaber* or Associate.

(1) He sees a reference to the Essenes in the חבורא *chăbūra* or 'Society,' which is mentioned several times in talmudical writers[3]. The *chăber* (חבר) or 'Associate' is, he supposes, a member of this brotherhood. He is obliged to confess that the word cannot always have this sense, but still he considers this to be a common desig-

---

[1] *Essenes* p. 30; comp. *Kitto's Cyclopaedia*, s.v. Essenes.

[2] It is given by Landsberg in the *Allgemeine Zeitung des Judenthums*

1862, no. 33, p. 459, a reference pointed out to me by a friend.

[3] *Zeitschr.* p. 450 sq., *Monatsschr.* pp. 31, 70.

nation of the Essenes. The chaber was bound to observe certain rules of ceremonial purity, and a period of probation was imposed upon him before he was admitted. With this fact Frankel connects the passage in Mishna *Chagigah* ii. 5, 6, where several degrees of ceremonial purity are specified. Having done this, he considers that he has the explanation of the statement in Josephus (*B. J.* ii. 8. 7, 10), that the Essenes were divided into four different grades or orders according to the time of their continuance in the ascetic practices demanded by the sect.

But in the first place there is no reference direct or indirect to the chaber, or indeed to any organisation of any kind, in the passage of *Chagigah*. It simply contemplates different degrees of purification as qualifying for the performance of certain Levitical rites in an ascending scale. There is no indication that these lustrations are more than temporary and immediate in their application; and not the faintest hint is given of distinct orders of men, each separated from the other by formal barriers and each demanding a period of probation before admission from the order below, as was the case with the grades of the Essene brotherhood described by Josephus. Moreover the orders in Josephus are four in number[1],

A passage in Cha-gigah con-sidered.

---

[1] As the notices in Josephus (*B. J.* ii. 8) relating to this point have been frequently misunderstood, it may be well once for all to explain his meaning. The grades of the Essene order are mentioned in two separate notices, apparently, though not really, discordant. (1) In § 10 he says that they are 'divided into four sections according to the duration of their discipline' (διῄρηνται κατὰ χρόνον τῆς ἀσκήσεως εἰς μοίρας τέσσαρας), adding that the older members are considered to be defiled by contact with the younger, i. e. each superior grade by contact with the inferior. So far his meaning is clear. (2) In § 8 he states that one who is anxious to become a member of the sect undergoes a year's probation, submitting to discipline but 'remaining outside.' Then, 'after he has given evidence of his perseverance (μετὰ τὴν τῆς καρτερίας ἐπίδειξιν), his character is tested for two years more; and, if found worthy, he is accordingly ad-

mitted into the society.' A comparison with the other passage shows that these two years comprise the period spent in the second and third grades, each extending over a year. After passing through these three stages in three successive years, he enters upon the fourth and highest grade, thus becoming a perfect member.

It is stated by Dr Ginsburg (*Essenes* p. 12 sq., comp. Kitto's *Cyclopaedia* s. v. p. 828) that the Essenes passed through eight stages 'from the beginning of the noviciate to the achievement of the highest spiritual state,' this last stage qualifying them, like Elias, to be forerunners of the Messiah. But it is a pure hypothesis that the Talmudical notices thus combined have anything to do with the Essenes; and, as I shall have occasion to point out afterwards, there is no ground for ascribing to this sect any Messianic expectations whatever.

while the degrees of ceremonial purity in *Chagigah* are five. Frankel indeed is inclined to maintain that only four degrees are intended in *Chagigah*, though this interpretation is opposed to the plain sense of the passage. But, even if he should be obliged to grant that the number of degrees is five[1], he will not surrender the allusion to the Essenes, but meets the difficulty by supposing (it is a pure hypothesis) that there was a fifth and highest degree of purity among the Essenes, to which very few attained, and which, as I understand him, is not mentioned by Josephus on this account. But enough has already been said to show, that this passage in *Chagigah* can have no connexion with the Essenes and gives no countenance to Frankel's views.

Difference between the chaber and the Essene. As this artificial combination has failed, we are compelled to fall back on the notices relating to the chaber, and to ask whether these suggest any connexion with the account of the Essenes in Josephus. And the facts oblige us to answer this question in the negative. Not only do they not suggest such a connexion, but they are wholly irreconcilable with the account in the Jewish historian. This association or confraternity (if indeed the term is applicable to an organisation so loose and so comprehensive) was maintained for the sake of securing a more accurate study and a better observance of the ceremonial law. Two grades of purity are mentioned in connexion with it, designated by different names and presenting some difficulties[2], into which it is not necessary to enter here. A chaber, it would appear, was one who had entered upon the second or higher stage. For this a period of a year's probation was necessary. The chaber enrolled himself in the presence of three others who were already members of the association. This apparently was all the formality necessary : and in the case of a teacher even this was dispensed with, for being presumably acquainted with the law of things clean and unclean he was regarded as *ex officio* a chaber. The chaber was bound to keep himself from ceremonial defilements, and was thus distinguished from the *ʿam haarets* or common people[3]; but he was under no external surveillance and

---

[1] *Zeitschr.* p. 452, note.

[2] The entrance into the lower grade was described as 'taking כנפים' or 'wings.' The meaning of this expression has been the subject of much discus-

sion; see e.g. Herzfeld II. p. 390 sq., Frankel *Monatsschr.* p. 33 sq.

[3] The contempt with which a chaber would look down upon the vulgar herd, the *ʿam haarets*, finds expression in

decided for himself as to his own purity. Moreover he was, or might be a married man : for the doctors disputed whether the wives and children of an associate were not themselves to be regarded as associates[1]. In one passage, *Sanhedrin* 41 *a*, it is even assumed, as a matter of course, that a woman may be an associate (חברה). In another (*Niddah* 33 *b*)[2] there is mention of a Sadducee and even of a Samaritan as a chaber. An organisation so flexible as this has obviously only the most superficial resemblances with the rigid rules of the Essene order; and in many points it presents a direct contrast to the characteristic tenets of that sect.

(2) Having discussed Frankel's hypothesis respecting the chaber, I need hardly follow his speculations on the *Bĕnē-hakkĕneseth,* בני הכנסת, 'sons of the congregation' (*Zabim* iii. 2), in which expression probably few would discover the reference, which he finds, to the lowest of the Essene orders[3].

(2) The *Bene hak-keneseth.*

(3) But mention is also made of a 'holy congregation' or 'assembly' (קהלא קדישא, עדה קדישה) 'in Jerusalem'; and, following Rapoport, Frankel sees in this expression also an allusion to the Essenes[4]. The grounds for this identification are, that in one passage (*Berakhoth* 9 *b*) they are mentioned in connexion with prayer at daybreak, and in another (Midrash *Qoheleth* ix. 9) two persons are stated to belong to this 'holy congregation,' because they divided their day into three parts, devoting one-third to learning, another to prayer, and another to work. The first notice would suit the Essenes very well, though the practice mentioned was not so distinctively Essene as to afford any safe ground for this hypothesis. Of the second it should be observed, that no such division of the day is recorded of the Essenes, and indeed both Josephus (*B. J.* ii. 8. 5) and Philo (*Fragm.* p. 633) describe them as working from morning till night with the single interruption of their mid-day meal[5]. But

(3) The 'holy congregation at Jerusalem'

---

the language of the Pharisees, Joh. vii. 49 ὁ ὄχλος οὗτος ὁ μὴ γινώσκων τὸν νόμον ἐπάρατοί εἰσιν. Again in Acts iv. 13, where the Apostles are described as ἰδιῶται, the expression is equivalent to *ẹam haarets*. See the passages quoted in Buxtorf, *Lex.* p. 1626.

[1] All these particulars and others may be gathered from *Bekhoroth* 30 *b*, Mishna *Demai* ii. 2. 3, Jerus. *Demai*

ii. 3, v. 1, Tosifta *Demai* 2, *Aboth R. Nathan* c. 41.

[2] See Herzfeld II. p. 386.

[3] *Monatsschr.* p. 35.

[4] *Zeitschr.* pp. 458, 461, *Monatsschr.* pp. 32, 34.

[5] It is added however in Midrash *Qoheleth* ix. 9 'Some say that they (the holy congregation) devoted the whole of the winter to studying the Scriptures and the summer to work.'

in fact the identification is beset with other and more serious difficulties. For this 'holy congregation' at Jerusalem is mentioned long

not an Essene commu- nity. after the second destruction of the city under Hadrian[1], when on
Frankel's own showing[2] the Essene society had in all probability
ceased to exist. And again certain members of it, e. g. Jose ben
Meshullam (Mishna *Bekhoroth* iii. 3, vi. 1), are represented as uttering
precepts respecting animals fit for sacrifice, though we have it on
the authority of Josephus and Philo that the Essenes avoided the
temple sacrifices altogether. The probability therefore seems to be
that this 'holy congregation' was an assemblage of devout Jews
who were drawn to the neighbourhood of the sanctuary after the
destruction of the nation, and whose practices were regarded with
peculiar reverence by the later Jews[3].

(4) The Vathikin. (4) Neither can we with Frankel[4] discern any reference to the
Essenes in those וחיקין *Vathikin*, 'pious' or 'learned' men (whatever
may be the exact sense of the word), who are mentioned in *Berakhoth*
9 *b* as praying before sunrise; because the word itself seems quite
general, and the practice, though enforced among the Essenes, as
we know from Josephus (*B. J.* ii. 8. 5), would be common to all
devout and earnest Jews. If we are not justified in saying that
these וחיקין were not Essenes, we have no sufficient grounds for
maintaining that they were.

(5) The 'primitive elders.' (5) Nor again can we find any such reference in the זקנים
הראשונים or 'primitive elders[5].' It may readily be granted that this
term is used synonymously, or nearly so, with חסידים הראשונים
'the primitive chasidim'; but, as we failed to see anything more
than a general expression in the one, so we are naturally led to
take the other in the same sense. The passages where the expression
occurs (e.g. *Shabbath* 64 *b*) simply refer to the stricter observances
of early times, and do not indicate any reference to a particular
society or body of men.

(6) The 'morning bathers.' (6) Again Frankel finds another reference to this sect in the
טבלי שחרית *Tōblē-shachărīth*, or 'morning-bathers,' mentioned in
Tosifta *Yadayim* c. 2[6]. The identity of these with the ἡμεροβα-
πτισταί of Greek writers seems highly probable. The latter however, though they may have had some affinities with Essene practices

---

[1] *Monatsschr.* p. 32.   [4] *Monatsschr.* p. 32.
[2] *Ib.* p. 70.   [5] *Monatsschr.* pp. 32, 68.
[3] See Derenbourg p. 175.   [6] *Ib.* p. 67.

and tenets, are nevertheless distinguished from this sect wherever they are mentioned[1]. But the point to be observed is that, even though we should identify these Toble-shacharith with the Essenes, the passage in Tosifta *Yadayim*, so far from favouring, is distinctly adverse to Frankel's view which regards the Essenes as only a branch of Pharisees: for the two are here represented as in direct antagonism. The Toble-shacharith say, 'We grieve over you, Pharisees, because you pronounce the (sacred) Name in the morning without having bathed.' The Pharisees retort, 'We grieve over you, Toble-shacharith, because you pronounce the Name from this body in which is impurity.'

(7) In connexion with the Toble-shacharith we may consider another name, *Banāīm* (בנאים), in which also Frankel discovers an allusion to the Essenes[2]. In Mishna *Mikvaoth* ix. 6 the word is opposed to בור *bōr*, 'an ignorant or stupid person'; and this points to its proper meaning 'the builders,' i.e. the edifiers or teachers, according to the common metaphor in Biblical language. The word is discussed in *Shabbath* 114 and explained to mean 'learned.' But, because in *Mikvaoth* it is mentioned in connexion with ceremonial purity, and because in Josephus the Essenes are stated to have carried an 'axe and shovel' (*B. J.* ii. 8. 7, 9), and because moreover the Jewish historian in another place (*Vit.* 2) mentions having spent some time with one Banus a dweller in the wilderness, who lived on vegetables and fruits and bathed often day and night for the sake of purity, and who is generally considered to have been an Essene; therefore Frankel holds these Banaim to have been Essenes. This is a specimen of the misplaced ingenuity which distinguishes Frankel's learned speculations on the Essenes. Josephus does not mention an 'axe *and* shovel,' but an axe only (§ 7 ἀξινάριον), which he afterwards defines more accurately as a spade (§ 9 τῇ σκαλίδι, τοιοῦτον γάρ ἐστι τὸ διδόμενον ὑπ' αὐτῶν ἀξινίδιον τοῖς νεοσυστάτοις) and which, as he distinctly states, was given them for the purpose of burying impurities out of sight (comp. Deut. xxiii. 12—14). Thus it has no connexion whatever with any 'building' implement. And again, it is true that Banus has frequently been regarded as an Essene, but there is absolutely no ground for this supposition. On the contrary the narrative of Josephus in his *Life* seems to

Margin: (7) The *Banaim*.

Margin: Josephus misinterpreted.

---

[1] See below, p. 406.　　　[2] *Zeitschr.* p. 455.

Another
derivation
of Bana-
im.
exclude it, as I shall have occasion to show hereafter[1]. I should add
that Sachs interprets Banaim 'the bathers,' regarding the explanation
in *Shabbath* l. c. as a 'later accommodation[2].' This seems to me very
improbable ; but, if it were conceded, the Banaim would then apparently be connected not with the Essenes, but with the Hemerobaptists.

Results of
this inves-
tigation.
From the preceding investigation it will have appeared how
little Frankel has succeeded in establishing his thesis that 'the
'talmudical sources are acquainted with the Essenes and make
mention of them constantly[3].' We have seen not only that no
instance of the name Essene has been produced, but that all those
passages which are supposed to refer to them under other designations, or to describe their practices or tenets, fail us on closer examination. In no case can we feel sure that there is any direct
reference to this sect, while in most cases such reference seems to be
excluded by the language or the attendant circumstances[4]. Thus we are
Philo and
Josephus
our main
authori-
ties.
obliged to fall back upon the representations of Philo and Josephus.
Their accounts are penned by eye-witnesses. They are direct and
explicit, if not so precise or so full as we could have wished. The
writers obviously consider that they are describing a distinct and
exceptional phenomenon. And it would be a reversal of all established rules of historical criticism to desert the solid standing-
ground of contemporary history for the artificial combinations and
shadowy hypotheses which Frankel would substitute in its place.

Frankel's
deprecia-
tion of
them is
unreason-
able, and
explains
nothing.
But here we are confronted with Frankel's depreciation of these
ancient writers, which has been echoed by several later critics. They
were interested, it is argued, in making their accounts attractive
to their heathen contemporaries, and they coloured them highly
for this purpose[5]. We may readily allow that they would not be
uninfluenced by such a motive, but the concession does not touch the
main points at issue. This aim might have led Josephus, for example,
to throw into bold relief the coincidences between the Essenes and
Pythagoreans; it might even have induced him to give a semi-pagan

---

[1] See below, p. 401.
[2] *Beiträge* II. p. 199. In this derivation he is followed by Graetz (III.
p. 82, 468) and Derenbourg (p. 166).
[3] *Monatsschr.* p. 31.
[4] 'The attempt to point out the Es-

senes in our patristic (i. e. rabbinical)
literature,' says Herzfeld truly (II.
p. 397), 'has led to a splendid hypo-
thesis-hunt (*einer stattlichen Hypo-
thesenjagd*).'
[5] *Monatsschr.* p. 31.

tinge to the Essene doctrine of the future state of the blessed (*B. J.* ii. 8. 11). But it entirely fails to explain those peculiarities of the sect which marked them off by a sharp line from orthodox Judaism, and which fully justify the term 'separatists' as applied to them by a recent writer. In three main features especially the portrait of the Essenes retains its distinctive character unaffected by this consideration.

(i) How, for instance, could this principle of accommodation have led both Philo and Josephus to lay so much stress on their divergence from Judaic orthodoxy in the matter of sacrifices? Yet this is perhaps the most crucial note of heresy which is recorded of the Essenes. What was the law to the orthodox Pharisee without the sacrifices, the temple-worship, the hierarchy? Yet the Essene declined to take any part in the sacrifices; he had priests of his own independently of the Levitical priesthood. On Frankel's hypothesis that Essenism is merely an exaggeration of pure Pharisaism, no explanation of this abnormal phenomenon can be given. Frankel does indeed attempt to meet the case by some speculations respecting the red heifer[1], which are so obviously inadequate that they have not been repeated by later writers and may safely be passed over in silence here. On this point indeed the language of Josephus is not quite explicit. He says (*Ant.* xviii. 1. 5) that, though they send offerings (ἀναθήματα) to the temple, they perform no sacrifices, and he assigns as the reason their greater strictness as regards ceremonial purity (διαφορότητι ἁγνειῶν ἃς νομίζοιεν), adding that 'for this reason being excluded from the common sanctuary (τεμενίσματος) they perform their sacrifices by themselves (ἐφ' αὑτῶν τὰς θυσίας ἐπιτελοῦσι).' Frankel therefore supposes that their only reason for abstaining from the temple sacrifices was that according to their severe notions the temple itself was profaned and therefore unfit for sacrificial worship. But if so, why should it not vitiate the offerings, as well as the sacrifices, and make them also unlawful? And indeed, where Josephus is vague, Philo is explicit. Philo (II. p. 457) distinctly states that the Essenes being more scrupulous than any in the worship of God (ἐν τοῖς μάλιστα θεραπευταὶ Θεοῦ) do not sacrifice animals (οὐ ζῶα καταθύοντες), but hold it right to dedicate their own hearts as a worthy offering (ἀλλ' ἱεροπρεπεῖς τὰς ἑαυτῶν διανοίας κατασκευάζειν

The avoidance of sacrifices is not accounted for.

The notices of Josephus and Philo considered.

[1] *Monatsschr.* 64.

ἀξιοῦντες). Thus the greater strictness, which Josephus ascribes to them, consists in the abstention from shedding blood, as a pollution in itself. And, when he speaks of their substituting private sacrifices, his own qualifications show that he does not mean the word to be taken literally. Their simple meals are their sacrifices; their refectory is their sanctuary; their president is their priest[1]. It should be added also that, though we once hear of an Essene apparently within the temple precincts (*B. J.* i. 3. 5, *Ant.* xiii. 11. 2)[2], no mention is ever made of one offering sacrifices. Thus it is clear that with the

Their statements confirmed by the doctrine of Christian Essenes.

Essene it was the sacrifices which polluted the temple, and not the temple which polluted the sacrifices. And this view is further recommended by the fact that it alone will explain the position of their descendants, the Christianized Essenes, who condemned the slaughter of victims on grounds very different from those alleged in the Epistle to the Hebrews, not because they have been superseded by the Atonement, but because they are in their very nature repulsive to God; not because they have ceased to be right, but because they never were right from the beginning.

It may be said indeed, that such a view could not be maintained without impugning the authority, or at least disputing the integrity, of the Old Testament writings. The sacrificial system is so bound up with the Mosaic law, that it can only be rejected by the most arbitrary excision. This violent process however, uncritical as it is, was very likely to have been adopted by the Essenes[3]. As a matter of fact, it did recommend itself to those Judaizing Christians who reproduced many of the Essene tenets, and who both theologically and historically may be regarded as the lineal

The Clementine Homilies justify this doctrine by

descendants of this Judaic sect[4]. Thus in the *Clementine Homilies*, an Ebionite work which exhibits many Essene features, the chief spokesman St Peter is represented as laying great stress on the duty of distinguishing the true and the false elements in the current

---

[1] *B. J.* ii. 8. 5 καθάπερ εἰς ἅγιόν τι τέμενος παραγίνονται τὸ δειπνητήριον: see also the passages quoted above p. 89, note 3.

[2] See below, p. 379.

[3] Herzfeld (II. p. 403) is unable to reconcile any rejection of the Old Testament Scriptures with the reverence paid to Moses by the Essenes (*B. J.* ii.

8. 9, 10). The Christian Essenes however did combine both these incongruous tenets by the expedient which is explained in the text. Herzfeld himself suggests that allegorical interpretation may have been employed to justify this abstention from the temple sacrifices.

[4] See *Galatians*, p. 322 sq.

Scriptures (ii. 38, 51, iii. 4, 5, 10, 42, 47, 49, 50, comp. xviii. 19). The saying traditionally ascribed to our Lord, 'Show yourselves approved money-changers' (γίνεσθε τραπεζῖται δόκιμοι), is more than once quoted by the Apostle as enforcing this duty (ii. 51, iii. 50, xviii. 20). Among these false elements he places all those passages which represent God as enjoining sacrifices (iii. 45, xviii. 19). It is plain, so he argues, that God did not desire sacrifices, for did He not kill those who lusted after the taste of flesh in the wilderness? and, if the slaughter of animals was thus displeasing to Him, how could He possibly have commanded victims to be offered to Himself (iii. 45)? It is equally clear from other considerations that this was no part of God's genuine law. For instance, Christ declared that He came to fulfil every tittle of the Law; yet Christ abolished sacrifices (iii. 51). And again, the saying 'I will have mercy and not sacrifice' is a condemnation of this practice (iii. 56). The true prophet 'hates sacrifices, bloodshed, libations'; he 'extinguishes the fire of altars' (iii. 26). The frenzy of the lying soothsayer is a mere intoxication produced by the recking fumes of sacrifice (iii. 13). When in the immediate context of these denunciations we find it reckoned among the highest achievements of man 'to know the *names of angels*, to drive away demons, to endeavour to heal diseases by charms (φαρμακίαις), and to find incantations (ἐπαοιδάς) against venomous serpents (iii. 36)'; when again St Peter is made to condemn as false those scriptures which speak of God swearing, and to set against them Christ's command 'Let your yea be yea' (iii. 55); we feel how thoroughly this strange production of Ebionite Christianity is saturated with Essene ideas[1].

The arbitrary excision of the Scriptures.

Essene features in this work.

---

[1] Epiphanius (*Hær.* xviii. 1, p. 38) again describes, as the account was handed down to him (ὡς ὁ εἰς ἡμᾶς ἐλθὼν περιέχει λόγος), the tenets of a Jewish sect which he calls the Nasareans, αὐτὴν δὲ οὐ παρεδέχετο τὴν πεντάτευχον, ἀλλὰ ὡμολόγει μὲν τὸν Μωϋσέα, καὶ ὅτι ἐδέξατο νομοθεσίαν ἐπίστευεν, οὐ ταύτην δέ φησιν, ἀλλ' ἑτέραν. ὅθεν τὰ μὲν πάντα φυλάττουσι τῶν Ἰουδαίων Ἰουδαῖοι ὄντες, θυσίαν δὲ οὐκ ἔθυον οὔτε ἐμψύχων μετεῖχον, ἀλλὰ ἀθέμιτον ἦν παρ' αὐτοῖς τὸ κρεῶν μεταλαμβάνειν ἢ θυσιάζειν αὐτούς. ἔφασκον γὰρ πεπλάσθαι ταῦτα τὰ βιβλία καὶ μηδὲν τούτων ὑπὸ τῶν πατέρων γεγενῆσθαι. Here we have in combination all the features which we are seeking. The cradle of this sect is placed by him in Gilead and Bashan and 'the regions beyond the Jordan.' He uses similar language also (xxx. 18, p. 142) in describing the Ebionites, whom he places in much the same localities (naming Moab also), and whose Essene features are unmistakeable: οὔτε γὰρ δέχονται τὴν πεντάτευχον Μωϋσέως ὅλην ἀλλά τινα ῥήματα ἀποβάλλουσιν. ὅταν δὲ αὐτοῖς εἴπῃς περὶ ἐμψύχων βρώσεως κ.τ.λ. These parallels will speak for themselves.

(ii) Nor again is Frankel successful in explaining the Essene prayers to the sun by rabbinical practices[1]. Following Rapoport, he supposes that Josephus and Philo refer to the beautiful hymn of praise for the creation of light and the return of day, which forms part of the morning-prayer of the Jews to the present time[2], and which seems to be enjoined in the Mishna itself[3]; and this view has been adopted by many subsequent writers. But the language of Josephus is not satisfied by this explanation. For he says plainly (*B. J.* ii. 8. 5) that they addressed prayers to the sun[4], and it is difficult to suppose that he has wantonly introduced a dash of paganism into his picture; nor indeed was there any adequate motive for his doing so. Similarly Philo relates of the Therapeutes (*Vit. Cont.* 11, II. p. 485), that they 'stand with their faces and their whole body towards the East, and when they see that the sun is risen, holding out their hands to heaven they pray for a happy day (εὐημερίαν) and for truth and for keen vision of reason (ὀξυωπίαν λογισμοῦ).' And here again it is impossible to overlook the confirmation which these accounts receive from the history of certain Christian heretics deriving their descent from this Judaic sect.

Epiphanius (*Hær.* xix. 2, xx. 3, pp. 40 sq., 47) speaks of a sect called the Sampsæans or 'Sun-worshippers[5],' as existing in his own time in Peræa on the borders of Moab and on the shores of the Dead Sea. He describes them as a remnant of the Ossenes (i.e. Essenes), who have accepted a spurious form of Christianity and are neither Jews nor Christians. This debased Christianity which they adopted is embodied, he tells us, in the pretended revelation of the Book of Elchasai, and dates from the time of Trajan[6]. Elsewhere (xxx. 3, p. 127) he seems to use the terms Sampsæan, Ossene, and Elchasaite as synonymous (παρὰ τοῖς Σαμψη-νοῖς καὶ Ὀσσηνοῖς καὶ Ἐλκεσσαίοις καλουμένοις). Now we happen to know something of this book of Elchasai, not only from Epiphanius himself (xix. 1 sq., p. 40 sq., xxx. 17, p. 141), but also from Hippo-

lytus (*Hær.* ix. 13 sq.) who describes it at considerable length. From these accounts it appears that the principal feature in the book was the injunction of frequent bathings for the remission of sins

---

[1] *Zeitschr.* p. 458.

[2] See Ginsburg *Essenes* p. 69 sq.

[3] *Berakhoth* i. 4; see Derenbourg, p. 169 sq.

[4] See above, p. 87, note 1.

[5] See above, p. 83.

[6] *Galatians* p. 324 sq. See also below, p. 407.

(Hipp. *Hær.* ix. 13, 15 sq.). We are likewise told that it 'anathematizes immolations and sacrifices (θυσίας καὶ ἱερουργίας) as being alien to God and certainly not offered to God by tradition from (ἐκ) the fathers and the law,' while at the same time it 'says that men ought to pray there at Jerusalem, where the altar was and the sacrifices (were offered), prohibiting the eating of flesh which exists among the Jews, and the rest (of their customs), and the altar and the fire, as being alien to God' (Epiph. *Hær.* xix. 3, p. 42). Notwithstanding, we are informed that the sect retained the rite of circumcision, the observance of the sabbath, and other practices of the Mosaic law (Hipp. *Hær.* ix. 14; Epiph. *Hær.* xix. 5, p. 43, comp. xxx. 17, p. 141). This inconsistency is explained by a further notice in Epiphanius (l. c.) that they treated the Scriptures in the same way as the Nasaræans[1]; that is, they submitted them to a process of arbitrary excision, as recommended in the Clementine Homilies, and thus rejected as falsifications all statements which did not square with their own theory. Hippolytus also speaks of the Elchasaites as studying astrology and magic, and as practising charms and incantations on the sick and the demoniacs (§ 14). Moreover in two formularies, one of expiation, another of purification, which this father has extracted from the book, invocation is made to 'the holy spirits and the angels of prayer' (§ 15, comp. Epiph. *Hær.* xix. 1). It should be added that the word Elchasai probably signifies the 'hidden power'[2]; while the book itself directed that its mysteries should be guarded as precious pearls, and should not be communicated to the world at large, but only to the faithful few (Hipp. *Hær.* ix. 15, 17). It is hardly necessary to call attention to the number of Essene features which are here combined[3]. I would only remark that the value of the notice is not at all diminished, but rather enhanced, by the uncritical character of Epiphanius' work; for this very fact prevents us from ascribing the coincidences, which here reveal themselves, to this father's own invention.

Its Essene peculiarities.

---

[1] See p. 372, note 3.

[2] *Galatians* p. 325, note 1. For another derivation see below, p. 407.

[3] Celibacy however is not one of these: comp. Epiphan. *Hær.* xix. 1 (p. 40) ἀπεχθάνεται δὲ τῇ παρθενίᾳ, μισεῖ δὲ τὴν ἐγκράτειαν, ἀναγκάζει δὲ γάμον.

In this respect they departed from the original principles of Essenism, alleging, as it would appear, a special revelation (ὡς δῆθεν ἀποκαλύψεως) in justification. In like manner marriage is commended in the Clementine Homilies.

In this heresy we have plainly the dregs of Essenism, which has only been corrupted from its earlier and nobler type by the admixture of a spurious Christianity. But how came the Essenes to be called Sampsæans? What was the original meaning of this outward reverence which they paid to the sun? Did they regard it merely as the symbol of Divine illumination, just as Philo frequently treats it as a type of God, the centre of all light (e.g. *de Somn.* i. 13 sq., I. p. 631 sq.), and even calls the heavenly bodies 'visible and sensible gods' (*de Mund. Op.* 7, I. p. 6)[1]? Or did they honour the light, as the pure ethereal element in contrast to gross terrestrial matter, according to a suggestion of a recent writer[2]? Whatever may have been the motive of this reverence, it is strangely repugnant to the spirit of orthodox Judaism. In Ezek. viii. 16 it is denounced as an abomination, that men shall turn towards the east and worship the sun; and accordingly in *Berakhoth* 7 *a* a saying of R. Meir is reported to the effect that God is angry when the sun appears and the kings of the East and the West prostrate themselves before this luminary[3]. We cannot fail therefore to recognise the action of some foreign influence in this Essene practice—whether Greek or Syrian or Persian, it will be time to consider hereafter.

Doubtful bearing of this Sun-worship.

The practice repugnant to Jewish orthodoxy.

(iii) The dépréciation of marriage not accounted for.

(iii) On the subject of marriage again, talmudical and rabbinical notices contribute nothing towards elucidating the practices of this sect. Least of all do they point to any affinity between the Essenes and the Pharisees. The nearest resemblance, which Frankel can produce, to any approximation in this respect is an injunction in Mishna *Kethuboth* v. 8 respecting the duties of the husband in providing for the wife in case of his separating from her, and this he ascribes to Essene influences[4]; but this mishna does not express any approval of such a separation. The direction seems to be framed entirely in the interests of the wife: nor can I see that it is at all inconsistent, as Frankel urges, with Mishna *Kethuboth* vii. 1 which allows her to claim a divorce under such circumstances. But however this may be, Essene and Pharisaic opinion stand generally in the sharpest contrast to each other with respect to marriage. The talmudic

---

[1] The important place which the heavenly bodies held in the system of Philo, who regarded them as animated beings, may be seen from Gfrörer's *Philo* I. p. 349 sq.

[2] Keim I. p. 289.

[3] See Wiesner *Schol. zum Babyl. Talm.* I. pp. 18, 20.

[4] *Monatsschr.* p. 37.

writings teem with passages implying not only the superior sanctity, but even the imperative duty, of marriage. The words 'Be fruitful and multiply' (Gen. i. 28) were regarded not merely as a promise, but as a command which was binding on all. It is a maxim of the Talmud that 'Any Jew who has not a wife is no man' (אינו אדם), *Yebamoth* 63 *a*. The fact indeed is so patent, that any accumulation of examples would be superfluous, and I shall content myself with referring to *Pesachim* 113 *a*, *b*, as fairly illustrating the doctrine of orthodox Judaism on this point[1]. As this question affects the whole framework not only of religious, but also of social life, the antagonism between the Essene and the Pharisee in a matter so vital could not be overlooked.

(iv) Nor again is it probable that the magical rites and incantations which are so prominent in the practice of the Essenes would, as a rule, have been received with any favour by the Pharisaic Jew. In Mishna *Pesachim* iv. 9 (comp. *Berakhoth* 10 *b*) it is mentioned with approval that Hezekiah put away a 'book of healings'; where doubtless the author of the tradition had in view some volume of charms ascribed to Solomon, like those which apparently formed part of the esoteric literature of the Essenes[2]. In the same spirit in Mishna *Sanhedrin* xi. 1 R. Akiba shuts out from the hope of eternal life any 'who read profane or foreign (i.e. perhaps, apocryphal) books, and who mutter over a wound' the words of Exod. xv. 26. On this point of difference however no great stress can be laid. Though the nobler teachers among the orthodox Jews set themselves steadfastly against the introduction of magic, they were unable to resist the inpouring tide of superstition. In the middle of the second century Justin Martyr alludes to exorcists and magicians among the Jews, as though they were neither few nor obscure[3]. Whether these were a remnant of Essene Judaism, or whether such practices

(iv) The Essene practice of magic still a difficulty.

---

[1] Justin Martyr more than once taunts the Jewish rabbis with their reckless encouragement of polygamy. See *Dial.* 134, p. 363 D, τοῖς ἀσυνέτοις καὶ τυφλοῖς διδασκάλοις ὑμῶν, οἵτινες καὶ μέχρι νῦν καὶ τέσσαρας καὶ πέντε ἔχειν ὑμᾶς γυναῖκας ἕκαστον συγχωροῦσι· καὶ ἐὰν εὐμορφόν τις ἰδὼν ἐπιθυμήσῃ αὐτῆς κ.τ.λ., *ib.* 141, p. 371 A, B, ὁποῖον πράττουσιν οἱ ἀπὸ τοῦ γένους ὑμῶν ἄν-

θρωποι, κατὰ πᾶσαν γῆν ἔνθα ἂν ἐπιδημήσωσιν ἢ προσπεμφθῶσιν ἀγόμενοι ὀνόματι γάμου γυναῖκας κ.τ.λ., with Otto's note on the first passage.

[2] See above, p. 91, note 2.

[3] *Dial.* 85, p. 311 C, ἤδη μέντοι οἱ ἐξ ὑμῶν ἐπορκισταὶ τῇ τέχνῃ, ὥσπερ καὶ τὰ ἔθνη, χρώμενοι ἐξορκίζουσι καὶ θυμιάμασι καὶ καταδέσμοις χρῶνται.

had by this time spread throughout the whols body, it is impossible to say; but the fact of their existence prevents us from founding an argument on the use of magic, as an absolutely distinctive feature of Essenism.

General result. Other divergences also have been enumerated[1]; but, as these do not for the most part involve any great principles, and refer only to practical details in which much fluctuation was possible, they cannot under any circumstances be taken as crucial tests, and I have not thought it worth while to discuss them. But the antagonisms on which I have dwelt will tell their own tale. In three respects more especially, in the avoidance of marriage, in the abstention from the temple sacrifices, and (if the view which I have adopted be correct) in the outward reverence paid to the sun, we have seen that there is an impassable gulf between the Essenes and the Pharisees. No known influences within the sphere of Judaism proper will serve to account for the position of the Essenes in these respects; and we are obliged to look elsewhere for an explanation.

Frankel has failed in establishing his point. It was shown above that the investigations of Frankel and others failed to discover in the talmudical writings a single reference to the Essenes, which is at once direct and indisputable. It has now appeared that they have also failed (and this is the really important point) in showing that the ideas and practices generally considered characteristic of the Essenes are recognised and incorporated in these representative books of Jewish orthodoxy; and thus the hypothesis that Essenism was merely a type, though an exaggerated type, of pure Judaism falls to the ground.

Affinities between Essenes and Phari- sees con- fined to the Judaic side. Some affinities indeed have been made out by Frankel and by those who have anticipated or followed him. But these are exactly such as we might have expected. Two distinct features combine to make up the portrait of the Essene. The Judaic element is quite as prominent in this sect as the non-Judaic. It could not be more strongly emphasized than in the description given by Josephus himself. In everything therefore which relates to the strictly Judaic side of their tenets and practices, we should expect to discover not only affinities, but even close affinities, in talmudic and rabbinic authorities. And this is exactly what, as a matter of fact, we do

[1] Herzfeld, II. p. 392 sq.

fiud. The Essene rules respecting the observance of the sabbath, the rites of lustration, and the like, have often very exact parallels in the writings of more orthodox Judaism. But I have not thought it necessary to dwell on these coincidences, because they may well be taken for granted, and my immediate purpose did not require me to emphasize them.

And again; it must be remembered that the separation between Pharisee and Essene cannot always have been so great as it appears in the Apostolic age. Both sects apparently arose out of one great movement, of which the motive was the avoidance of pollution[1]. The divergence therefore must have been gradual. At the same time, it does not seem a very profitable task to write a hypothetical history of the growth of Essenism, where the data are wanting; and I shall therefore abstain from the attempt. Frankel indeed has not been deterred by this difficulty; but he has been obliged to assume his data by postulating that such and such a person, of whom notices are preserved, was an Essene, and thence inferring the character of Essenism at the period in question from his recorded sayings or doings. But without attempting any such reconstruction of history, we may fairly allow that there must have been a gradual development; and consequently in the earlier stages of its growth we should not expect to find that sharp antagonism between the two sects, which the principles of the Essenes when fully matured would involve. If therefore it should be shown that the talmudical and rabbinical writings here and there preserve with approval the sayings of certain Essenes, this fact would present no difficulty. At present however no decisive example has been produced; and the discoveries of Jellinek for instance[2], who traces the influence of this sect in almost every page of *Pirke Aboth*, can only be regarded as another illustration of the extravagance with which the whole subject has been treated by a large section of modern Jewish writers. More to the point is a notice of an earlier Essene preserved in Josephus himself. We learn from this historian that one Judas, a member of the sect, who had prophesied the death of Antigonus, saw this prince 'passing by through the temple[3],' when his prophecy was on the point of fulfilment

The divergence of the Essenes from the Pharisees gradual.

Hence the possibility of their appearing in the records of orthodox Judaism.

---

[1] See above, p. 355 sq.
[2] *Orient* 1849, pp. 489, 537, 553.
[3] *B. J.* i. 3. 5 παριόντα διὰ τοῦ ἱεροῦ.

In the parallel narrative, *Ant.* xii. 11. 2, the expression is παριόντα τὸ ἱερόν, which does not imply so much;

(about B.C. 110). At this moment Judas is represented as sitting in the midst of his disciples, instructing them in the science of prediction. The expression quoted would seem to imply that he was actually teaching within the temple area. Thus he would appear not only as mixing in the ordinary life of the Jews, but also as frequenting the national sanctuary. But even supposing this to be the right explanation of the passage, it will not present any serious difficulty. Even at a later date, when (as we may suppose) the principles of the sect had stiffened, the scruples of the Essene were directed, if I have rightly interpreted the account of Josephus, rather against the sacrifices than against the locality[1]. The temple itself, independently of its accompaniments, would not suggest any offence to his conscience.

The approbation of Philo and Josephus is no evidence of orthodoxy. Nor again, is it any obstacle to the view which is here maintained, that the Essenes are regarded with so much sympathy by Philo and Josephus themselves. Even though the purity of Judaism might have been somewhat sullied in this sect by the admixture of foreign elements, this fact would attract rather than repel an eclectic like Philo, and a latitudinarian like Josephus. The former, as an Alexandrian, absorbed into his system many and diverse elements of heathen philosophy, Platonic, Stoic, and Pythagorean. The latter, though professedly a Pharisee, lost no opportunity of ingratiating himself with his heathen conquerors, and would not be unwilling to gratify their curiosity respecting a society with whose fame, as we infer from the notice of Pliny, they were already acquainted.

What was the foreign element in Essenism? But if Essenism owed the features which distinguished it from Pharisaic Judaism to an alien admixture, whence were these foreign influences derived? From the philosophers of Greece or from the religious mystics of the East? On this point recent writers are divided.

Theory of Neopythagorean influence. Those who trace the distinctive characteristics of the sect to Greece, regard it is an offshoot of the Neopythagorean School grafted on the stem of Judaism. This solution is suggested by the statement of Josephus, that 'they practise the mode of life which among

but the less precise notice must be interpreted by the more precise. Even then however it is not directly stated that Judas himself was within the temple area.

[1] See above, pp. 89, 371 sq.

the Greeks was introduced (καταδεδειγμένῃ) by Pythagoras[1].' It is
thought to be confirmed by the strong resemblances which as a
matter of fact are found to exist between the institutions and practices of the two.

This theory, which is maintained also by other writers, as for Statement
instance by Baur and Herzfeld, has found its ablest and most per- of the theory by
sistent advocate in Zeller, who draws out the parallels with great Zeller.
force and precision. 'The Essenes,' he writes, 'like the Pythagoreans,
desire to attain a higher sanctity by an ascetic life; and the absten-
tions, which they impose on themselves for this end, are the same
with both. They reject animal food and bloody sacrifices; they
avoid wine, warm baths, and oil for anointing; they set a high value
on celibate life: or, so far as they allow marriage, they require that
it be restricted to the one object of procreating children. Both wear
only white garments and consider linen purer than wool. Washings
and purifications are prescribed by both, though for the Essenes they
have a yet higher significance as religious acts. Both prohibit oaths
and (what is more) on the same grounds. Both find their social
ideal in those institutions, which indeed the Essenes alone set themselves to realise—in a corporate life with entire community of goods,
in sharply defined orders of rank, in the unconditional submission
of all the members to their superiors, in a society carefully barred
from without, into which new members are received only after a
severe probation of several years, and from which the unworthy are
inexorably excluded. Both require a strict initiation, both desire
to maintain a traditional doctrine inviolable; both pay the highest
respect to the men from whom it was derived, as instruments of
the deity: yet both also love figurative clothing for their doctrines,
and treat the old traditions as symbols of deeper truths, which they
must extract from them by means of allegorical explanation. In
order to prove the later form of teaching original, newly-composed
writings were unhesitatingly forged by the one as by the other,
and fathered upon illustrious names of the past. Both parties pay
honour to divine powers in the elements, both invoke the rising
sun, both seek to withdraw everything unclean from his sight, and
with this view give special directions, in which they agree as well
with each other as with older Greek superstition, in a remarkable

[1] *Ant.* xv. 10. 4.

way. For both the belief in intermediate beings between God and the world has an importance which is higher in proportion as their own conception of God is purer; both appear not to have disdained magic; yet both regard the gift of prophecy as the highest fruit of wisdom and piety, which they pique themselves on possessing in their most distinguished members. Finally, both agree (along with the dualistic character of their whole conception of the world...) in their tenets respecting the origin of the soul, its relation to the body, and the life after death[1]...'

Absence of distinctive Pythagorean features in the Essenes.

This array of coincidences is formidable, and thus skilfully marshalled might appear at first sight invincible. But a closer examination detracts from its value. In the first place the two distinctive characteristics of the Pythagorean philosophy are wanting to the Essenes. The Jewish sect did not believe in the transmigration of souls; and the doctrine of numbers, at least so far as our information goes, had no place in their system. Yet these constitute the very essence of the Pythagorean teaching. In the next place several of the coincidences are more apparent than real. Thus

The coincidences are in some cases only apparent,

for instance the demons who in the Pythagorean system held an intermediate place between the Supreme God and man, and were the result of a compromise between polytheism and philosophy, have no near relation to the angelology of the Essenes, which arose out of a wholly different motive. Nor again can we find distinct traces among the Pythagoreans of any such reverence for the sun as is ascribed to the Essenes, the only notice which is adduced having no prominence whatever in its own context, and referring to a rule which would be dictated by natural decency and certainly was not peculiar to the Pythagoreans[2]. When these imperfect and (for the purpose) valueless resemblances have been subtracted, the only basis on which the theory of a direct affiliation can rest is withdrawn. All the remaining coincidences are unimportant. Thus the respect paid to founders is not confined to any one sect or any one age. The reverence of the Essenes for Moses, and the reverence of the

---

[1] Zeller *Philosophie der Griechen* Th. iii. Abth. 2, p. 281.

[2] Diog. Laert. viii. 17; see Zeller l. c. p. 282, note 5. The precept in question occurs among a number of insignificant details, and has no special prominence given to it. In the

Life of Apollonius by Philostratus (e.g. vi. 10) considerable stress is laid on the worship of the sun (Zeller l. c. p. 137, note 6); but the syncretism of this late work detracts from its value as representing Pythagorean doctrine.

Pythagoreans for Pythagoras, are indications of a common humanity, but not of a common philosophy. And again the forgery of supposititious documents is unhappily not the badge of any one school. The Solomonian books of the Essenes, so far as we can judge from the extant notices, were about as unlike the tracts ascribed to Pythagoras and his disciples by the Neopythagoreans as two such forgeries could well be. All or nearly all that remains in common to the Greek school and the Jewish sect after these deductions is a certain similarity in the type of life. But granted that two bodies *and in others do not suggest any historical connexion.* of men each held an esoteric teaching of their own, they would secure it independently in a similar way, by a recognised process of initiation, by a solemn form of oath, by a rigid distinction of orders. Granted also, that they both maintained the excellence of an ascetic life, their asceticism would naturally take the same form ; they would avoid wine and flesh ; they would abstain from anointing themselves with oil ; they would depreciate, and perhaps altogether prohibit, marriage. Unless therefore the historical conditions are themselves favourable to a direct and immediate connexion between the Pythagoreans and the Essenes, this theory of affiliation has little to recommend it.

And a closer examination must pronounce them to be most unfavourable. Chronology and geography alike present serious obstacles to any solution which derives the peculiarities of the Essenes from the Pythagoreans. *Twofold objection to this theory.*

(i) The priority of time, if it can be pleaded on either side, must be urged in favour of the Essenes. The Pythagoreans as a philosophical school entirely disappear from history before the middle of the fourth century before Christ. The last Pythagoreans were scholars of Philolaus and Eurytus, the contemporaries of Socrates and Plato[1]. For nearly two centuries after their extinction we hear nothing of them. Here and there persons like Diodorus of Aspendus are satirised by the Attic poets of the middle comedy as 'pythagorizers,' in other words, as total abstainers and vegetarians[2]; but *(i) Chronological facts are adverse.* *Disappearance of the Pythagoreans.*

---

[1] Zeller l. c. p. 68 (comp. i. p. 242). While disputing Zeller's position, I have freely made use of his references. It is impossible not to admire the mastery of detail and clearness of exposition in this work, even when the conclusions seem questionable.

[2] Athen. iv. p. 161, Diog. Laert. viii. 37. See the index to Meineke *Fragm. Com.* s. vv. πυθαγορικός, etc. The words commonly used by these satirists are πυθαγορίζειν, πυθαγοριστής, πυναγορισμός. The persons so satirised were probably in many cases not more

the philosophy had wholly died or was fast dying out. This is the
universal testimony of ancient writers. It is not till the first century
before Christ, that we meet with any distinct traces of a revival.
In Alexander Polyhistor[1], a younger contemporary of Sulla, for the
first time we find references to certain writings, which would seem
to have emanated from this incipient Neopythagoreanism, rather than
from the elder school of Pythagoreans. And a little later Cicero
commends his friend Nigidius Figulus as one specially raised up to
revive the extinct philosophy[2]. But so slow or so chequered was
its progress, that a whole century after Seneca can still speak of the

Priority of Essenism to Neopythagoreanism. school as practically defunct[3]. Yet long before this the Essenes
formed a compact, well-organized, numerous society with a peculiar
system of doctrine and a definite rule of life. We have seen that
Pliny the elder speaks of this celibate society as having existed
'through thousands of ages[4].' This is a gross exaggeration, but it
must at least be taken to imply that in Pliny's time the origin of the
Essenes was lost in the obscurity of the past, or at least seemed so to
those who had not access to special sources of information. If, as
I have given reasons for supposing[5], Pliny's authority in this passage
is the same Alexander Polyhistor to whom I have just referred,
and if this particular statement, however exaggerated in expression,
is derived from him, the fact becomes still more significant. But
on any showing the priority in time is distinctly in favour of the
Essenes as against the Neopythagoreans.

The Essene tenets developed more than the Neopythagorean. And accordingly we find that what is only a tendency in the
Neopythagoreans is with the Essenes an avowed principle and a
definite rule of life. Such for instance is the case with celibacy, of
which Pliny says that it has existed as an institution among the
Essenes *per sæculorum millia*, and which is a chief corner-stone of

---

Pythagoreans than modern teetotallers
are Rechabites.

[1] Diog. Laert. viii. 24 sq.; see Zeller
l. c. p. 74—78.

[2] Cic. *Tim.* i 'sic judico, post illos
nobiles Pythagoreos quorum disci-
plina *extincta est* quodammodo, cum
aliquot sæcula in Italia Siciliaque vi-
guisset, hunc exstitisse qui illam *reno-
varet.*'

[3] Sen. *N. Q.* vii. 32 'Pythagorica
illa invidiosa turbæ schola præcep-

torem non invenit.'

[4] *N. H.* v. 15. The passage is quoted
above p. 85, note 3. The point of time,
at which Josephus thinks it necessary
to insert an account of the Essenes as
already flourishing (*Ant.* xiii. 5. 9), is
prior to the revival of the Neopythagorean school. How much earlier the
Jewish sect arose, we are without data
for determining.

[5] See p. 83, note 1.

their practical system. The Pythagorean notices (whether truly or not,
it is unimportant for my purpose to enquire) speak of Pythagoras as
having a wife and a daughter[1]. Only at a late date do we find the
attempt to represent their founder in another light; and if virginity
is ascribed to Apollonius of Tyana, the great Pythagorean of the first
Christian century, in the fictitious biography of Philostratus[2], this
representation is plainly due to the general plan of the novelist, whose
hero is perhaps intended to rival the Founder of Christianity, and
whose work is saturated with Christian ideas. In fact virginity can
never be said to have been a Pythagorean principle, though it may
have been an exalted ideal of some not very early adherents of the
school. And the same remark applies to other resemblances between
the Essene and Neopythagorean teaching. The clearness of conception and the definiteness of practice are in almost every instance
on the side of the Essenes; so that, looking at the comparative
chronology of the two, it will appear almost inconceivable that they
can have derived their principles from the Neopythagoreans.

(ii) But the geographical difficulty also, which this theory of
affiliation involves, must be added to the chronological. The home
of the Essene sect is allowed on all hands to have been on the
eastern borders of Palestine, the shores of the Dead Sea, a region
least of all exposed to the influences of Greek philosophy. It is
true that we find near Alexandria a closely allied school of Jewish
recluses, the Therapeutes; and, as Alexandria may have been the
home of Neopythagoreanism, a possible link of connexion is here
disclosed. But, as Zeller himself has pointed out, it is not among
the Therapeutes, but among the Essenes, that the principles in
question appear fully developed and consistently carried out[3]; and
therefore, if there be a relation of paternity between Essene and
Therapeute, the latter must be derived from the former and not
conversely. How then can we suppose this influence of Neopythagoreanism brought to bear on a Jewish community in the south-
eastern border of Palestine? Zeller's answer is as follows[4]. Judæa
was for more than a hundred and fifty years before the Maccabean
period under the sovereignty first of the Egyptian and then of the

[1] Diog. Laert. viii. 42.
[2] *Vit. Apol.* i. 15 sq. At the same time Philostratus informs us that the conduct of his hero in this respect had been differently represented by others.
[3] l. c. p. 288 sq.
[4] l. c. p. 290 sq.

Syrian Greeks. We know that at this time Hellenizing influences did infuse themselves largely into Judaism : and what more natural than that among these the Pythagorean philosophy and discipline should have recommended itself to a section of the Jewish people? It may be said in reply, that at all events the special locality of the Essenes is the least favourable to such a solution : but, without pressing this fact, Zeller's hypothesis is open to two serious objections which combined seem fatal to it, unsupported as it is by any historical notice. First, this influence of Pythagoreanism is assumed to have taken place at the very time when the Pythagorean school was practically extinct : and secondly, it is supposed to have acted upon that very section of the Jewish community, which was the most vigorous advocate of national exclusiveness and the most averse to Hellenizing influences.

The foreign element of Essenism to be sought in the East,

It is not therefore to Greek but to Oriental influences that considerations of time and place, as well as of internal character, lead us to look for an explanation of the alien elements in Essene Judaism. And have we not here also the account of any real coincidences which may exist between Essenism and Neopythagoreanism? We should perhaps be hardly more justified in tracing Neopythagoreanism directly to Essenism than conversely (though, if we had no other alternative, this would appear to be the more probable solution of the two) : but were not both alike due to substantially the same influences acting in different degrees? I think it will hardly be denied

to which also Pythagoreanism may have been indebted.

that the characteristic features of Pythagoreanism, and especially of Neopythagoreanism, which distinguish it from other schools of Greek philosophy, are much more Oriental in type, than Hellenic. The asceticism, the magic, the mysticism, of the sect all point in the same direction. And history moreover contains indications that such was the case. There seems to be sufficient ground for the statement that Pythagoras himself was indebted to intercourse with the Egyptians, if not with more strictly Oriental nations, for some leading ideas of his system. But, however this may be, the fact that in the legendary accounts, which the Neopythagoreans invented to do honour to the founder of the school, he is represented as taking lessons from the Chaldeans, Persians, Brahmins, and others, may be taken as an evidence that their own philosophy at all events was partially derived from eastern sources [1].

---

[1] See the references in Zeller I. p. 218 sq.; comp. III. 2, p. 67.

But, if the alien elements of Essenism were borrowed not so much from Greek philosophy as from Oriental mysticism, to what nation or what religion was it chiefly indebted? To this question it is difficult, with our very imperfect knowledge of the East at the Christian era, to reply with any confidence. Yet there is one system to which we naturally look, as furnishing the most probable answer. The Medo-Persian religion supplies just those elements which distinguish the tenets and practices of the Essenes from the normal type of Judaism. (1) First; we have here a very definite form of dualism, which exercised the greatest influence on subsequent Gnostic sects, and of which Manicheism, the most matured development of dualistic doctrine in connexion with Christianity, was the ultimate fruit. For though dualism may not represent the oldest theology of the Zend-Avesta in its unadulterated form, yet long before the era of which we are speaking it had become the fundamental principle of the Persian religion. (2) Again; the Zoroastrian symbolism of light, and consequent worship of the sun as the fountain of light, will explain those anomalous notices of the Essenes in which they are represented as paying reverence to this luminary[1]. (3) Moreover; the 'worship of angels' in the Essene system has a striking parallel in the invocations of spirits, which form a very prominent feature in the ritual of the Zend-Avesta. And altogether their angelology is illustrated, and not improbably was suggested, by the doctrine of intermediate beings concerned in the government of nature and of man, such as the Amshaspands, which is an integral part of the Zoroastrian system[2]. (4) And once more; the magic, which was so attractive to the Essene, may have received its impulse from the priestly caste of Persia, to whose world-wide fame this form of superstition is indebted for its name. (5) If to these parallels I venture also to add the intense striving after purity, which is the noblest feature in the Persian religion, I do so, not because the Essenes

Marginal notes: Resemblances to Parsism. (i) Dualism. (ii) Sun-worship. (iii) Angel-olatry. (iv) Magic. (v) Striving after purity.

---

[1] Keim (*Geschichte Jesu von Nazara* I. p. 303) refers to Tac. *Hist.* iii. 24 'Undique clamor; et *orientem solem* (ita in Syria mos est) tertiani salutavere,' as illustrating this Essene practice. The commentators on Tacitus quote a similar notice of the Parthians in Herodian iv. 15 ἅμα δὲ ἡλίῳ ἀνίσχοντι ἐφάνη Ἀρτάβανος σὺν μεγίστῳ πλήθει στρατοῦ· ἀσπασάμενοι δὲ τὸν ἥλιον, ὡς ἔθος αὐτοῖς, οἱ βάρβαροι κ.τ.λ.

[2] See e.g. *Vendidad* Farg. xix; and the liturgical portions of the book are largely taken up with invocations of these intermediate beings. Some extracts are given in Davies' *Colossians* p. 146 sq.

might not have derived this impulse from a higher source, but because this feature was very likely to recommend the Zoroastrian system to their favourable notice, and because also the particular form which the zeal for purity took among them was at all events congenial to the teaching of the Zend-Avesta, and may not have been altogether free from its influences.

Other coincidences accidental. I have preferred dwelling on these broader resemblances, because they are much more significant than any mere coincidence of details, which may or may not have been accidental. Thus for instance the magi, like the Essenes, wore white garments, and eschewed gold and ornaments; they practised frequent lustrations; they avoided flesh, living on bread and cheese or on herbs and fruits; they had different orders in their society; and the like[1]. All these, as I have already remarked, may be the independent out-growth of the same temper and direction of conduct, and need not imply any direct historical connexion. Nor is there any temptation to press such resemblances; for even without their aid the general connexion seems to be sufficiently established[2].

The destruction of the Persian empire not adverse But it is said, that the history of Persia does not favour the hypothesis of such an influence as is here assumed. The destruction of the Persian empire by Alexander, argues Zeller[3], and the subsequent erection of the Parthian domination on its ruins, must have been fatal to the spread of Zoroastrianism. From the middle of the third century before Christ, when the Parthian empire was established, till towards the middle of the third century of our era,

---

[1] Hilgenfeld (*Zeitschrift* x. p. 99 sq.) finds coincidences even more special than these. He is answered by Zeller (III. 2, p. 276), but defends his position again (*Zeitschrift* xi. p. 347 sq.), though with no great success. Among other points of coincidence Hilgenfeld remarks on the axe (Jos. *B. J.* ii. 8. 7) which was given to the novices among the Essenes, and connects it with the ἀξινομαντεία (Plin. *N. H.* xxxvi. 19) of the magi. Zeller contents himself with replying that the use of the axe among the Essenes for purposes of divination is a pure conjecture, not resting on any known fact. He might have answered with

much more effect that Josephus elsewhere (§ 9) defines it as a spade or shovel, and assigns to it a very different use. Hilgenfeld has damaged his cause by laying stress on these accidental resemblances. So far as regards minor coincidences, Zeller makes out as good a case for his Pythagoreans, as Hilgenfeld for his magians.

[2] Those who allow any foreign Oriental element in Essenism most commonly ascribe it to Persia: e. g. among the more recent writers, Hilgenfeld (l. c.), and Lipsius *Schenkel's Bibel-Lexikon* s. v. Essäer p. 189.

[3] l. c. p. 275.

when the Persian monarchy and religion were once more restored[1], its influence must have been reduced within the narrowest limits. But does analogy really suggest such an inference ? Does not the history of the Jews themselves show that the religious influence of a people on the world at large may begin just where its national life ends ? The very dispersion of Zoroastrianism, consequent on the fall of the empire, would impregnate the atmosphere far and wide ; and the germs of new religious developments would thus be implanted in alien soils. For in tracing Essenism to Persian influences I have not wished to imply that this Jewish sect consciously incorporated the Zoroastrian philosophy and religion as such, but only that Zoroastrian ideas were infused into its system by more or less direct contact. And, as a matter of fact, it seems quite certain that Persian ideas were widely spread during this very interval, when the Persian nationality was eclipsed. It was then that Hermippus gave to the Greeks the most detailed account of this religion which had ever been laid before them[2]. It was then that its tenets suggested or moulded the speculations of the various Gnostic sects. It was then that the worship of the Persian Mithras spread throughout the Roman Empire. It was then, if not earlier, that the magian system took root in Asia Minor, making for itself (as it were) a second home in Cappadocia[3]. It was then, if not earlier, that the Zoroastrian demonology stamped itself so deeply on the apocryphal literature of the Jews themselves, which borrowed even the names of evil spirits[4] from the Persians. There are indeed abundant indications that Palestine was surrounded by Persian influences during this period, when the Persian empire was in abeyance.

but favourable to the spread of Parsism.

Indications of its influence during this period.

Thus we seem to have ample ground for the view that certain

---

[1] See Gibbon *Decline and Fall* c. viii, Milman *History of Christianity* II. p. 247 sq. The latter speaks of this restoration of Zoroastrianism, as 'perhaps the only instance of the vigorous revival of a Pagan religion.' It was far purer and less Pagan than the system which it superseded ; and this may account for its renewed life.

[2] See Müller *Fragm. Hist. Graec.* III. p. 53 sq. for this work of Hermippus περὶ Μάγων. He flourished about B.C. 200. See Max Müller *Lectures on*

the *Science of Language* 1st ser. p. 86.

[3] Strabo xv. 3. 15 (p. 733) Ἐν δὲ τῇ Καππαδοκίᾳ (πολὺ γὰρ ἐκεῖ τὸ τῶν Μάγων φῦλον, οἳ καὶ πύραιθοι καλοῦνται· πολλὰ δὲ καὶ τῶν Περσικῶν θεῶν ἱερά) κ.τ.λ.

[4] At least in one instance, Asmodeus (Tob. iii. 17); see M. Müller *Chips from a German Workshop* I. p. 148 sq. For the different dates assigned to the book of Tobit see Dr Westcott's article *Tobit* in Smith's *Dictionary of the Bible* p. 1525.

Are Bud-
dhist in-
fluences
also per-
ceptible?

alien features in Essene Judaism were derived from the Zoroastrian religion. But are we justified in going a step further, and attributing other elements in this eclectic system to the more distant East? The monasticism of the Buddhist will naturally occur to our minds, as a precursor of the cenobitic life among the Essenes; and Hilgenfeld accordingly has not hesitated to ascribe this characteristic of Essenism directly to Buddhist influences[1]. But at the outset we are obliged to ask whether history gives any such indication of the presence of Buddhism in the West as this hypothesis requires.

Supposed
Buddhist
establish-
ment at
Alexan-
dria.

Hilgenfeld answers this question in the affirmative. He points confidently to the fact that as early as the middle of the second century before Christ the Buddhist records speak of their faith as flourishing in Alasanda the chief city of the land of Yavana. The place intended, he conceives, can be none other than the great Alexandria, the most famous of the many places bearing the name[2].

The au-
thority
misinter-
preted

In this opinion however he stands quite alone. Neither Köppen[3], who is his authority for this statement, nor any other Indian scholar[4], so far as I am aware, for a moment contemplates this identification. Yavana, or Yona, was the common Indian name for the Græco-Bactrian kingdom and its dependencies[5]; and to this region we naturally turn. The Alasanda or Alasadda therefore, which is here mentioned, will be one of several Eastern cities bearing the name of the great conqueror, most probably *Alexandria ad Caucasum.*

---

[1] *Zeitschrift* x. p. 103 sq.; comp. xi. p. 351. M. Renan also (*Langues Sémitiques* iii. iv. 1, *Vie de Jésus* p. 98) suggests that Buddhist influences operated in Palestine.

[2] x. p. 105 'was schon an sich, zumal in dieser Zeit, schwerlich Alexandria ad Caucasum, sondern nur Alexandrien in Aegypten bedeuten kann.' Comp. xi. p. 351, where he repeats the same argument in reply to Zeller. This is a very natural inference from a western point of view; but, when we place ourselves in the position of a Buddhist writer to whom Bactria was Greece, the relative proportions of things are wholly changed.

[3] *Die Religion des Buddha* i. p. 193.

[4] Comp. e.g. Weber *Die Verbindungen Indiens mit den Ländern im Westen* p. 675 in the *Allgem. Monatsschr.*

f. *Wissensch. u. Literatur*, Braunschweig 1853; Lassen *Indische Alterthumskunde* ii. p. 236; Hardy *Manual of Budhism* p. 516.

[5] For its geographical meaning in older Indian writers see Köppen l. c. Since then it has entirely departed from its original signification, and Yavana is now a common term used by the Hindoos to designate the Mohammedans. Thus the Greek name has come to be applied to a people which of all others is most unlike the Greeks. This change of meaning admirably illustrates the use of Ἕλλην among the Jews, which in like manner, from being the name of an alien nation, became the name of an alien religion, irrespective of nationality; see the note on Gal. ii. 3.

But indeed I hardly think that, if Hilgenfeld had referred to the original authority for the statement, the great Buddhist history *Mahawanso*, he would have ventured to lay any stress at all on this notice, as supporting his theory. The historian, or rather fabulist (for such he is in this earlier part of his chronicle), is relating the foundation of the Mahá thúpo, or great tope, at Ruanwelli by the king Dutthagámini in the year B.C. 157. Beyond the fact that this tope was erected by this king the rest is plainly legendary. All the materials for the construction of the building, we are told, appeared spontaneously as by miracle—the bricks, the metals, the precious stones. The dewos, or demons, lent their aid in the erection. In fact

> the fabric huge
> Rose like an exhalation.

Priests gathered in enormous numbers from all the great Buddhist monasteries to do honour to the festival of the foundation. One place alone sent not less than 96,000. Among the rest it is mentioned that 'Maha Dhammarakkito, théro (i.e. senior priest) of Yóna, accompanied by 30,000 priests from the vicinity of Alasaddá, the capital of the Yóna country, attended[1].' It is obvious that no weight can be attached to a statement occurring as part of a story of which the other details are so manifestly false. An establishment of 30,000 Buddhist priests at Alexandria would indeed be a phenomenon of which historians have shown a strange neglect.

Nor is the presence of any Buddhist establishment even on a much smaller scale in this important centre of western civilisation at all reconcilable with the ignorance of this religion, which the Greeks and Romans betray at a much later date[2]. For some centuries after the Christian era we find that the information possessed by western writers was most shadowy and confused; and in almost every instance we are able to trace it to some other cause than the actual presence of Buddhists in the Roman Empire[3]. Thus Strabo,

Side notes: and wholly untrustworthy in itself.

General ignorance of Buddhism in the West.

Strabo.

---

[1] *Mahawanso* p. 171, Turnour's translation.

[2] How for instance, if any such establishment had ever existed at Alexandria, could Strabo have used the language which is quoted in the next note?

[3] Consistently with this view, we may allow that single Indians would visit Alexandria from time to time for purposes of trade or for other reasons, and not more than this is required by the rhetorical passage in Dion Chrysost. *Or.* xxxii (p. 373) ὁρῶ γάρ ἔγωγε οὐ μόνον Ἕλληνας παρ' ὑμῖν......ἀλλὰ καὶ Βακτρίους καὶ Σκύθας καὶ Πέρσας καὶ

who wrote under Augustus and Tiberius, apparently mentions the Buddhist priests, the *sramanas*, under the designation *sarmanæ* (Σαρμάνας)[1] ; but he avowedly obtains his information from Megasthenes,

'Ινδῶν τινάς. The qualifying τινάς shows how very slight was the communication between India and Alexandria. The mission of Pantænus may have been suggested by the presence of such stray visitors. Jerome (*Vir. Ill.* 36) says that he went 'rogatus ab illius gentis legatis.' It must remain doubtful however, whether some other region than Hindostan, such as Æthiopia for instance, is not meant, when Pantænus is said to have gone to India: see Cave's *Lives of the Primitive Fathers* p. 188 sq.

How very slight the communication was between India and the West in the early years of the Christian era, appears from this passage of Strabo xv. 1. 4 (p. 686); καὶ οἱ νῦν δὲ ἐξ Αἰγύπτου πλέοντες ἐμπορικοὶ τῷ Νείλῳ καὶ τῷ Ἀραβίῳ κόλπῳ μέχρι τῆς Ἰνδικῆς σπάνιοι μὲν καὶ περιπεπλεύκασι μέχρι τοῦ Γάγγου, καὶ οὗτοι δ' ἰδιῶται καὶ οὐδὲν πρὸς ἱστορίαν τῶν τόπων χρήσιμοι, after which he goes on to say that the only instance of Indian travellers in the West was the embassy sent to Augustus (see below p. 394), which came ἀφ' ἑνὸς τόπου καὶ παρ' ἑνὸς βασιλέως.

The communications between India and the West are investigated by two recent writers, Reinaud *Relations Politiques et Commerciales de l'Empire Romain avec l'Asie Centrale*, Paris 1863, and Priaulx *The Indian Travels of Apollonius of Tyana and the Indian Embassies to Rome*, 1873. The latter work, which is very thorough and satisfactory, would have saved me much labour of independent investigation, if I had seen it in time.

[1] Strabo xv. 1. 59, p. 712. In the MSS it is written Γαρμάνας, but this must be an error either introduced by Strabo's transcribers or found in the copy of Megasthenes which this author used. This is plain not only from the Indian word itself, but also from the parallel passage in Clement of Alexandria (*Strom.* i. 15). From the coin-

cidences of language it is clear that Clement also derived his information from Megasthenes, whose name he mentions just below. The fragments of Megasthenes relating to the Indian philosophers will be found in Müller *Fragm. Hist. Graec.* II. p. 437. They were previously edited by Schwanbeck, *Megasthenis Indica* (Bonnæ 1846).

For Σαρμᾶναι we also find the form Σαμαναῖοι in other writers; e.g. Clem. Alex. l. c., Bardesanes in Porphyr. *de Abstin.* iv. 17, Orig. *c. Cels.* i. 19 (I. p. 342). This divergence is explained by the fact that the Pali word *sammana* corresponds to the Sanskrit *sramana*. See Schwanbeck, l. c. p. 17, quoted by Müller, p. 437.

It should be borne in mind however, that several eminent Indian scholars believe Megasthenes to have meant not Buddhists but Brahmins by his Σαρμάνας. So for instance Lassen *Rhein. Mus.* 1833, p. 180 sq., *Ind. Alterth.* II. p. 700: and Prof. Max. Müller (Pref. to Rogers's *Translation of Buddhaghosha's Parables*, London 1870, p. lii) says; 'That Lassen is right in taking the Σαρμᾶναι, mentioned by Megasthenes, for Brahmanic, not for Buddhist ascetics, might be proved also by their dress. Dresses made of the bark of trees are not Buddhistic.' If this opinion is correct, the earlier notices of Buddhism in Greek writers entirely disappear, and my position is strengthened. But for the following reasons the other view appears to me more probable: (1) The term *sramana* is the common term for the Buddhist ascetic, whereas it is very seldom used of the Brahmin. (2) The Ζάρμανος (another form of *sramana*), mentioned below p. 394, note 2, appears to have been a Buddhist. This view is taken even by Lassen, *Ind. Alterth.* III. p. 60. (3) The distinction of Βραχμᾶνες and Σαρμᾶναι in Megasthenes or the writers following him corresponds to the dis-

who travelled in India somewhere about the year 300 B.C. and wrote a book on Indian affairs. Thus too Bardesanes at a much later date gives an account of these Buddhist ascetics, without however naming the founder of the religion ; but he was indebted for his knowledge of them to conversations with certain Indian ambassadors who visited Syria on their way westward in the reign of one of the Antonines [1]. Clement of Alexandria, writing in the latest years of the second century or the earliest of the third, for the first [2] time mentions Buddha by name; and even he betrays a strange ignorance of this Eastern religion [3].

Bardesanes.

Clement of Alexandria.

---

tinction of Βραχμᾶνες and Σαμαναῖοι in Bardesanes, Origen, and others ; and, as Schwanbeck has shown (l. c.), the account of the Σαρμᾶναι in Megasthenes for the most part is a close parallel to the account of the Σαμαναῖοι in Bardesanes (or at least in Porphyry's report of Bardesanes). It seems more probable therefore that Megasthenes has been guilty of confusion in describing the dress of the Σαρμᾶναι, than that Brahmins are intended by the term.

The Pali form, Σαμαναῖοι, as a designation of the Buddhists, first occurs in Clement of Alexandria or Bardesanes, whichever may be the earlier writer. It is generally ascribed to Alexander Polyhistor, who flourished B.C. 80—60, because his authority is quoted by Cyril of Alexandria (c. Julian. iv. p. 133) in the same context in which the Σαμαναῖοι are mentioned. This inference is drawn by Schwanbeck, Max Müller, Lassen, and others. An examination of Cyril's language however shows that the statement for which he quotes the authority of Alexander Polyhistor does not extend to the mention of the Samanæi. Indeed all the facts given in this passage of Cyril (including the reference to Polyhistor) are taken from Clement of Alexandria (Strom. i. 15; see below n. 3), whose account Cyril has abridged. It is possible indeed that Clement himself derived the statement from Polyhistor, but nothing in Clement's own language points to this.

[1] The narrative of Bardesanes is given by Porphyry de Abst. iv. 17. The Buddhist ascetics are there called Σαμαναῖοι (see the last note). The work of Bardesanes, recounting his conversations with these Indian ambassadors, is quoted again by Porphyry in a fragment preserved by Stobæus Ecl. iii. 56 (p. 141). In this last passage the embassy is said to have arrived ἐπὶ τῆς βασιλείας τῆς Ἀντωνίνου τοῦ ἐξ Ἐμισῶν, by which, if the words be correct, must be meant Elagabalus (A.D. 218—222), the spurious Antonine (see Hilgenfeld Bardesanes p. 12 sq.). Other ancient authorities however place Bardesanes in the reign of one of the older Antonines ; and, as the context is somewhat corrupt, we cannot feel quite certain about the date. Bardesanes gives by far the most accurate account of the Buddhists to be found in any ancient Greek writer ; but even here the monstrous stories, which the Indian ambassadors related to him, show how little trustworthy such sources of information were.

[2] Except possibly Arrian, Ind. viii. 1, who mentions an ancient Indian king, Budyas (Βουδύας) by name; but what he relates of him is quite inconsistent with the history of Buddha, and probably some one else is intended.

[3] In this passage (Strom. i. 15, p. 359) Clement apparently mentions these same persons three times, supposing that he is describing three different schools of Oriental philosophers. (1) He speaks of Σαμαναῖοι Βάκτρων (comp. Cyrill. Alex. l. c.); (2) He distinguishes two classes of Indian gymno-

Still later than this, Hippolytus, while he gives a fairly intelligent,
though brief, account of the Brahmins[1], says not a word about the
Buddhists, though, if he had been acquainted with their teaching,
he would assuredly have seen in them a fresh support to his theory
of the affinity between Christian heresies and pre-existing heathen phi-
losophies. With one doubtful exception—an Indian fanatic attached
to an embassy sent by king Porus to Augustus, who astonished the
Greeks and Romans by burning himself alive at Athens[2]—there

sophists, whom he calls Σαρμᾶναι and
Βραχμᾶναι. These are Buddhists and
Brahmins respectively (see p. 392, note
1); (3) He says afterwards εἰσὶ δὲ
τῶν Ἰνδῶν οἱ τοῖς Βούττα πειθόμενοι
παραγγέλμασιν, ὃν δι' ὑπερβολὴν σεμ-
νότητος εἰς [ὡς?] Θεὸν τετιμήκασι.
Schwanbeck indeed maintains that Clement here intends to describe the same
persons whom he has just mentioned
as Σαρμᾶναι; but this is not the natural
interpretation of his language, which
must mean 'There are also among
the Indians those who obey the precepts of Buddha.' Probably Schwanbeck is right in identifying the Σαρμᾶναι with the Buddhist ascetics, but
Clement appears not to have known
this. In fact he has obtained his information from different sources, and
so repeated himself without being aware
of it. Where he got the first fact it is
impossible to say. The second, as we
saw, was derived from Megasthenes.
The third, relating to Buddha, came,
as we may conjecture, either from
Pantænus (if indeed Hindostan is
really meant by the India of his missionary labours) or from some chance
Indian visitor at Alexandria.

In another passage (*Strom.* iii. 7,
p. 539) Clement speaks of certain Indian celibates and ascetics, who are
called Σεμνοί. As he distinguishes
them from the gymnosophists, and
mentions the pyramid as a sacred
building with them, the identification
with the Buddhists can hardly be
doubted. Here therefore Σεμνοί is a
Grecized form of Σαμαναῖοι; and this
modification of the word would occur
naturally to Clement, because σεμνοί,
σεμνεῖον, were already used of the ascetic

life: e.g. Philo *de Vit. Cont.* 3 (p.
475 M) ἱερὸν ὃ καλεῖται σεμνεῖον καὶ
μοναστήριον ἐν ᾧ μονούμενοι τὰ τοῦ
σεμνοῦ βίου μυστήρια τελοῦνται.

[1] *Haer.* i. 24.

[2] The chief authority is Nicolaus of
Damascus in Strabo xv. 1. 73 (p. 270).
The incident is mentioned also in Dion
Cass. liv. 9. Nicolaus had met these
ambassadors at Antioch, and gives an
interesting account of the motley company and their strange presents. This
fanatic, who was one of the number,
immolated himself in the presence of
an astonished crowd, and perhaps of
the emperor himself, at Athens. He
anointed himself and then leapt smil-
ing on the pyre. The inscription on
his tomb was Ζαρμανοχηγὰς Ἰνδὸς ἀπὸ
Βαργόσης κατὰ τὰ πάτρια Ἰνδῶν ἔθη
ἑαυτὸν ἀπαθανατίσας κεῖται. The tomb
was visible at least as late as the age
of Plutarch, who recording the self-
immolation of Calanus before Alexander (*Vit. Alex.* 69) says, τοῦτο πολλοῖς
ἔτεσιν ὕστερον ἄλλος Ἰνδὸς ἐν Ἀθήναις
Καῖσαρος συνὼν ἐποίησε, καὶ δείκνυται
μέχρι νῦν τὸ μνημεῖον Ἰνδοῦ προσαγο-
ρευόμενον. Strabo also places the two
incidents in conjunction in another
passage in which he refers to this
person, xv. 1. 4 (p. 686) ὁ κατακαύσας
ἑαυτὸν Ἀθήνῃσι σοφιστὴς Ἰνδός, καθάπερ
καὶ ὁ Κάλανος κ.τ.λ.

The reasons for supposing this person to have been a Buddhist, rather
than a Brahmin, are: (1) The name
Ζαρμανοχηγὰς (which appears with
some variations in the MSS of Strabo)
being apparently the Indian *sramana-
karja*, i.e. 'teacher of the ascetics,'
in other words, a Buddhist priest;
(2) The place Bargosa, i.e. Barygaza,

is apparently no notice in either heathen or Christian writers, which points to the presence of a Buddhist within the limits of the Roman Empire, till long after the Essenes had ceased to exist[1].

And if so, the coincidences must be very precise, before we are justified in attributing any peculiarities of Essenism to Buddhist influences. This however is far from being the case. They both exhibit a well-organized monastic society: but the monasticism of the Buddhist priests, with its systematized mendicancy, has little in common with the monasticism of the Essene recluse, whose life was largely spent in manual labour. They both enjoin celibacy, both prohibit the use of flesh and of wine, both abstain from the slaughter of animals. But, as we have already seen, such resemblances prove nothing, for they may be explained by the independent development of the same religious principles. One coincidence, and one only, is noticed by Hilgenfeld, which at first sight seems more striking and might suggest a historical connexion. He observes that the four orders of the Essene community are derived from the

The alleged coincidences prove nothing.

Monasticism.

Asceticism.

Four orders and four steps.

where Buddhism flourished in that age. See Priaulx p. 78 sq. In Dion Cassius it is written Ζάρμαρος.

And have we not here an explanation of 1 Cor. xiii. 3, if ἵνα καυθήσομαι be the right reading? The passage, being written before the fires of the Neronian persecution, requires explanation. Now it is clear from Plutarch that the 'Tomb of the Indian' was one of the sights shown to strangers at Athens: and the Apostle, who observed the altar ΑΓΝΩϹΤΩΙ ΘΕΩΙ, was not likely to overlook the sepulchre with the strange inscription ΕΛΥΤΟΝ ΑΠΑΘΑΝΑΤΙϹΑϹ ΚΕΙΤΑΙ. Indeed the incident would probably be pressed on his notice in his discussions with Stoics and Epicureans, and he would be forced to declare himself as to the value of these Indian self-immolations, when he preached the doctrine of self-sacrifice. We may well imagine therefore that the fate of this poor Buddhist fanatic was present to his mind when he penned the words καὶ ἐὰν παραδῶ τὸ σῶμά μου...ἀγάπην δὲ μὴ ἔχω, οὐδὲν ὠφελοῦμαι. Indeed it would furnish an almost equally good illustration of the text, whether we read ἵνα

καυθήσομαι or ἵνα καυχήσωμαι. Dion Cassius (l. c.) suggests that the deed was done ὑπὸ φιλοτίμιας or εἰς ἐπίδειξιν. How much attention these religious suicides of the Indians attracted in the Apostolic age (doubtless because the act of this Buddhist priest had brought the subject vividly before men's minds in the West), we may infer from the speech which Josephus puts in the mouth of Eleazar (B. J. vii. 8. 7), βλέψωμεν εἰς Ἰνδοὺς τοὺς σοφίαν ἀσκεῖν ὑπισχνουμένους ... οἱ δὲ ... πυρὶ τὸ σῶμα παραδόντες, ὅπως δὴ καὶ καθαρωτάτην ἀποκρίνωσι τοῦ σώματος τὴν ψυχήν, ὑμνούμενοι τελευτῶσι...ἆρ᾽ οὖν οὐκ αἰδούμεθα χεῖρον Ἰνδῶν φρονοῦντες;

[1] In the reign of Claudius an embassy arrived from Taprobane (Ceylon); and from these ambassadors Pliny derived his information regarding the island, N. H. vi. 24. Respecting their religion however he says only two words 'coli Herculem,' by whom probably Rama is meant (Priaulx p. 116). From this and other statements it appears that they were Tamils and not Singalese, and thus belonged to the non-Buddhist part of the island; see Priaulx p. 91 sq.

four steps of Buddhism. Against this it might fairly be argued that such coincidences of numbers are often purely accidental, and that in the present instance there is no more reason for connecting the four steps of Buddhism with the four orders of Essenism than there would be for connecting the ten precepts of Buddha with the Ten Commandments of Moses. But indeed a nearer examination will show that the two have nothing whatever in common except the number. The four steps or paths of Buddhism are not four grades of an external order, but four degrees of spiritual progress on the way to nirvana or annihilation, the ultimate goal of the Buddhist's religious aspirations. They are wholly unconnected with the Buddhist monastic system, as an organization. A reference to the Buddhist notices collected in Hardy's *Eastern Monachism* (p. 280 sq.) will at once dispel any suspicion of a resemblance. A man may attain to the highest of these four stages of Buddhist illumination instantaneously. He does not need to have passed through the lower grades, but may even be a layman at the time. Some merit obtained in a previous state of existence may raise him *per saltum* to the elevation of a rahat, when all earthly desires are crushed and no future birth stands between him and nirvana. There remains therefore no coincidence which would suggest any historical connexion between Essenism and Buddhism. Indeed it is not till some centuries later, when Manicheism[1] starts into being, that we find for the first time any traces of the influence of Buddhism on the religions of the West[2].

Buddhist influences seen first in Manicheism.

[1] Even its influence on Manicheism however is disputed in a learned article in the *Home and Foreign Review* III. p. 143 sq. (1863), by Mr P. Le Page Renouf (see *Academy* 1873, p. 399).

[2] An extant inscription, containing an edict of the great Buddhist king Asoka and dating about the middle of the 3rd century B.C., was explained by Prinsep as recording a treaty of this monarch with Ptolemy and other successors of Alexander, by which religious freedom was secured for the Buddhists throughout their dominions. If this interpretation had been correct, we must have supposed that, so far as regards Egypt and Western Asia, the treaty remained a dead letter. But later critics have rejected this interpretation of its purport: see Thomas's edition of Prinsep's *Essays on Indian Antiquities* II. p. 18 sq.

III.

ESSENISM AND CHRISTIANITY.

IT has become a common practice with a certain class of writers to call Essenism to their aid in accounting for any distinctive features of Christianity, which they are unable to explain in any other way. Wherever some external power is needed to solve a perplexity, here is the *deus ex machina* whose aid they most readily invoke. Constant repetition is sure to produce its effect, and probably not a few persons, who want either the leisure or the opportunity to investigate the subject for themselves, have a lurking suspicion that the Founder of Christianity may have been an Essene, or at all events that Christianity was largely indebted to Essenism for its doctrinal and ethical teaching[1]. Indeed, when very confident and sweeping assertions are made, it is natural to presume that they rest on a substantial basis of fact. Thus for instance we are told by one writer that Christianity is 'Essenism alloyed with foreign elements'[2]: while another, who however approaches the subject in a different spirit, says; 'It will hardly be doubted that our Saviour himself belonged to this holy brotherhood. This will especially be apparent, when we remember that *the whole Jewish community* at the advent of Christ was divided into three parties, the Pharisees, the Sadducees, and the Essenes, and that *every Jew had to belong to one of these sects.* Jesus who in all things conformed to the Jewish law, and who was holy, harmless, undefiled, and separate from sinners, would therefore naturally associate Himself with that order

The theory which explains Christianity as an outgrowth of Essenism

---

[1] De Quincey's attempt to prove that the Essenes were actually Christians (*Works* VI. p. 270 sq., IX. p. 253 sq.), who used the machinery of an esoteric society to inculcate their doctrines 'for fear of the Jews,' is conceived in a wholly different spirit from the theories of the writers mentioned in the text; but it is even more untenable and does not deserve serious refutation.

[2] Grätz III. p. 217.

of Judaism which was most congenial to His nature[1].' I purpose
testing these strong assertions by an appeal to facts.

For the statements involved in those words of the last extract
which I have underlined, no authority is given by the writer himself; nor have I been able to find confirmation of them in any
quarter. On the contrary the frequent allusions which we find to
the vulgar herd, the ἰδιῶται, the ẹam haarets, who are distinguished
from the disciples of the schools[2], suggest that a large proportion of
the people was unattached to any sect. If it had been otherwise, we
might reasonably presume that our Lord, as one who 'in all things
conformed to the Jewish law,' would have preferred attaching Himself to the Pharisees who 'sat in Moses' seat' and whose precepts
He recommended His disciples to obey[3], rather than to the Essenes
who in one important respect at least—the repudiation of the temple
sacrifices—acted in flagrant violation of the Mosaic ordinances.

This preliminary barrier being removed, we are free to investigate the evidence for their presumed connexion. And here we are
met first with a negative argument, which obviously has great
weight with many persons. Why, it is asked, does Jesus, who so
unsparingly denounces the vices and the falsehoods of Pharisees and
Sadducees, never once mention the Essenes by way of condemnation,
or indeed mention them by name at all? Why, except that He
Himself belonged to this sect and looked favourably on their
teaching? This question is best answered by another. How can
we explain the fact, that throughout the enormous mass of talmudical and early rabbinical literature this sect is not once mentioned by name, and that even the supposed allusions to them, which
have been discovered for the first time in the present century, turn
out on investigation to be hypothetical and illusory? The difficulty
is much greater in this latter instance; but the answer is the same
in both cases. The silence is explained by the comparative insignificance of the sect, their small numbers and their retired habits.
Their settlements were far removed from the great centres of political
and religious life. Their recluse habits, as a rule, prevented them
from interfering in the common business of the world. Philo and
Josephus have given prominence to them, because their ascetic

Marginal notes:
tested by facts.

Our Lord need not have be-longed to any sect.

The argu-ment from the silence of the New Testa-ment an-swered.

---

[1] Ginsburg *Essenes* p. 24.   [3] Matt. xxiii. 2, 3.
[2] See above, p. 366.

practices invested them with the character of philosophers and interested the Greeks and Romans in their history; but in the national life of the Jews they bore a very insignificant part[1]. If the Sadducees, who held the highest offices in the hierarchy, are only mentioned directly on three occasions in the Gospels[2], it can be no surprise that the Essenes are not named at all.

As no stress therefore can be laid on the argument from silence, any hypothesis of connexion between Essenism and Christianity must make good its claims by establishing one or both of these two points : *first*, that there is direct historical evidence of close intercourse between the two; and *secondly*, that the resemblances of doctrine and practice are so striking as to oblige, or at least to warrant, the belief in such a connexion. If both these lines of argument fail, the case must be considered to have broken down.

The positive arguments for a connexion may be twofold.

1. On the former point it must be premised that the Gospel narrative does not suggest any hint of a connexion. Indeed its general tenor is directly adverse to such a supposition. From first to last Jesus and His disciples move about freely, taking part in the common business, even in the common recreations, of Jewish life. The recluse ascetic brotherhood, which was gathered about the shores of the Dead Sea, does not once appear above the Evangelists' horizon. Of this close society, as such, there is not the faintest indication. But two individuals have been singled out, as holding an important place either in the Evangelical narrative or in the Apostolic Church, who, it is contended, form direct and personal links of communication with this sect. These are John the Baptist and James the Lord's brother. The one is the forerunner of the Gospel, the first

1. Absence of direct historical evidence of a connexion.

Two individual cases alleged.

---

[1] This fact is fully recognised by several recent writers, who will not be suspected of any undue bias towards traditional views of Christian history. Thus Lipsius writes (p. 190), 'In the general development of Jewish life Essenism occupies a far more subordinate place than is commonly ascribed to it.' And Keim expresses himself to the same effect (I. p. 305). Derenbourg also, after using similar language, adds this wise caution, 'In any case, in the present state of our acquaintance with the Essenes, which

is so imperfect and has no chance of being extended, the greatest prudence is required of science, if she prefers to be true rather than adventurous, if she has at heart rather to enlighten than to surprise' (p. 461). Even Grätz in one passage can write soberly on this subject : 'The Essenes had throughout no influence on political movements, from which they held aloof as far as possible' (III. p. 86).

[2] These are (1) Matt. iii. 7; (2) Matt. xvi. 1 sq.; (3) Matt. xxii. 23 sq., Mark xii. 18, Luke xx. 27.

herald of the Kingdom; the other is the most prominent figure in the early Church of Jerusalem.

(i) John the Baptist

(i) John the Baptist was an ascetic. His abode was the desert; his clothing was rough; his food was spare; he baptized his penitents. Therefore, it is argued, he was an Essene. Between the premisses and the conclusion however there is a broad gulf, which cannot very easily be bridged over. The solitary independent life, which

not an Essene.

John led, presents a type wholly different from the cenobitic establishments of the Essenes, who had common property, common meals, common hours of labour and of prayer. It may even be questioned whether his food of locusts would have been permitted by the Essenes, if they really ate nothing which had life (ἔμψυχον [1]). And again; his baptism as narrated by the Evangelists, and their lustrations as described by Josephus, have nothing in common except the use of water for a religious purpose. When therefore we are told confidently that 'his manner of life was altogether after the Essene pattern [2],' and that 'he without doubt baptized his converts into the Essene order,' we know what value to attach to this bold assertion. If positive statements are allowable, it would be more true to fact to say that he could not possibly have been an Essene. The rule of his life was *isolation;* the principle of theirs, *community* [3].

External resemblances to John in Banus,

In this mode of life John was not singular. It would appear that not a few devout Jews at this time retired from the world and buried themselves in the wilderness, that they might devote themselves unmolested to ascetic discipline and religious meditation. One such instance at all events we have in Banus the master of Josephus, with whom the Jewish historian, when a youth, spent three years in the desert. This anchorite was clothed in garments made of bark or of leaves; his food was the natural produce of the earth; he bathed day and night in cold water for purposes of purification. To the careless observer doubtless John and Banus would appear to be men of the same stamp. In their outward mode of life there was perhaps not very much difference [4]. The conscious-

---

[1] See above p. 86.

[2] Grätz III. p. 100.

[3] τὸ κοινωνητικόν, Joseph. *B. J.* ii. 8. 3. See also Philo *Fragm.* 632 ὑπὲρ τοῦ κοινωφελοῦς, and the context.

[4] Ewald (VI. p. 649) regards this

Banus as representing an extravagant development of the school of John, and thus supplying a link between the real teaching of the Baptist and the doctrine of the Hemerobaptists professing to be derived from him.

ness of a divine mission, the gift of a prophetic insight, in John was the real and all-important distinction between the two. But here also the same mistake is made; and we not uncommonly find Banus described as an Essene. It is not too much to say however, that the whole tenor of Josephus' narrative is opposed to this supposition [1]. He says that when sixteen years old he desired to acquire a knowledge of the three sects of the Jews before making his choice of one; that accordingly he went through (διῆλθον) all the three at the cost of much rough discipline and toil; that he was not satisfied with the experience thus gained, and hearing of this Banus he attached himself to him as his zealous disciple (ζηλωτὴς ἐγενόμην αὐτοῦ); that having remained three years with him he returned to Jerusalem; and that then, being nineteen years old, he gave in his adhesion to the sect of the Pharisees. Thus there is no more reason for connecting this Banus with the Essenes than with the Pharisees. The only natural interpretation of the narrative is that he did not belong to any of the three sects, but represented a distinct type of religious life, of which Josephus was anxious to gain experience. And his hermit life seems to demand this solution, which the sequence of the narrative suggests.

Of John himself therefore no traits are handed down which suggest that he was a member of the Essene community. He was an ascetic, and the Essenes were ascetics; but this is plainly an inadequate basis for any such inference. Nor indeed is the relation of his asceticism to theirs a question of much moment for the matter in hand; since this was the very point in which Christ's mode of life was so essentially different from John's as to provoke criticism and to point a contrast [2]. But the later history of his real or supposed disciples has, or may seem to have, some bearing on this

(margin, top right:) who was not an Essene.

(margin:) General result.

---

[1] The passage is so important that I give it in full; Joseph. *Vit.* 2 περὶ ἑκκαίδεκα δὲ ἔτη γενόμενος ἐβουλήθην τῶν παρ' ἡμῖν αἱρέσεων ἐμπειρίαν λαβεῖν. τρεῖς δ' εἰσὶν αὗται· Φαρισαίων μὲν ἡ πρώτη, καὶ Σαδδουκαίων ἡ δευτέρα, τρίτη δὲ ἡ Ἐσσηνῶν, καθὼς πολλάκις εἴπαμεν. οὕτως γὰρ ᾠόμην αἱρήσεσθαι τὴν ἀρίστην, εἰ πάσας καταμάθοιμι. σκληραγωγήσας γοῦν ἐμαυτὸν καὶ πολλὰ πονηθεὶς τὰς τρεῖς διῆλθον. καὶ μηδὲ τὴν ἐντεῦθεν ἐμπειρίαν ἱκανὴν ἐμαυτῷ νομίσας εἶναι, πυθόμενός τινα Βανοῦν ὄνομα κατὰ τὴν ἐρημίαν

διατρίβειν, ἐσθῆτι μὲν ἀπὸ δένδρων χρώμενον, τροφὴν δὲ τὴν αὐτομάτως φυομένην προσφερόμενον, ψυχρῷ δὲ ὕδατι τὴν ἡμέραν καὶ τὴν νύκτα πολλάκις λουόμενον πρὸς ἀγνείαν, ζηλωτὴς ἐγενόμην αὐτοῦ. καὶ διατρίψας παρ' αὐτῷ ἐνιαυτοὺς τρεῖς καὶ τὴν ἐπιθυμίαν τελειώσας εἰς τὴν πόλιν ὑπέστρεφον. ἐννεακαίδεκα δ' ἔτη ἔχων ἠρξάμην τε πολιτεύεσθαι τῇ Φαρισαίων αἱρέσει κατακολουθῶν κ.τ.λ.

[2] Matt. ix. 14 sq., xi. 17 sq., Mark ii. 18 sq., Luke v. 33, vii. 31 sq.

investigation. Towards the close of the first and the beginning of the second century we meet with a body of sectarians called in Greek *Hemerobaptists*[1], in Hebrew *Tovle-shacharith*[2], 'day' or 'morning bathers.' What were their relations to John the Baptist on the one hand, and to the Essenes on the other? Owing to the scantiness of our information the whole subject is wrapped in obscurity, and any restoration of their history must be more or less hypothetical; but it will be possible at all events to suggest an account which is not improbable in itself, and which does no violence to the extant notices of the sect.

(a) We must not hastily conclude, when we meet with certain persons at Ephesus about the years A.D. 53, 54, who are described as 'knowing only the baptism of John,' or as having been 'baptized unto John's baptism[3],' that we have here some early representatives of the Hemerobaptist sect. These were Christians, though imperfectly informed Christians. Of Apollos, who was more fully instructed by Aquila and Priscilla, this is stated in the most explicit terms[4]. Of the rest, who owed their fuller knowledge of the Gospel to St Paul, the same appears to be implied, though the language is not free from ambiguity[5]. But these notices have an important bearing on our subject; for they show how profoundly the effect of John's preaching was felt in districts as remote as proconsular Asia, even after a lapse of a quarter of a century. With these disciples it was the initial

---

The Hemerobaptists.

(a) Their relation to John the Baptist.

John's disciples at Ephesus.

---

[1] The word ἡμεροβαπτισταὶ is generally taken to mean 'daily-bathers,' and this meaning is suggested by *Apost. Const.* vi. 6 οἵτινες, καθ᾽ ἑκάστην ἡμέραν ἐὰν μὴ βαπτίσωνται, οὐκ ἐσθίουσιν, *ib.* 23 ἀντὶ καθημερινοῦ ἐν μόνον δοὺς βάπτισμα, Epiphan. *Haer.* xvii. 1 (p. 37) εἰ μή τι ἄρα καθ᾽ ἑκάστην ἡμέραν βαπτίζοιτό τις ἐν ὕδατι. But, if the word is intended as a translation of *Toble-shacharith* 'morning bathers,' as it seems to be, it must signify rather 'day-bathers'; and this is more in accordance with the analogy of other compounds from ἡμέρα, as ἡμερόβιος, ἡμεροδρόμος, ἡμεροσκόπος, etc.

Josephus (*B. J.* ii. 8. 5) represents the Essenes as bathing, not at dawn, but at the fifth hour, just before their meal. This is hardly consistent either with the name of the *Toble-shacharith*,

or with the Talmudical anecdote of them quoted above, p. 369. Of Banus he reports (*Vit.* 2) that he 'bathed often day and night in cold water.'

[2] See above, p. 368 sq.

[3] The former expression is used of Apollos, Acts xviii. 24; the latter of 'certain disciples,' Acts xix. 1.

[4] This appears from the whole narrative, but is distinctly stated in ver. 25, as correctly read, ἐδίδασκεν ἀκριβῶς τὰ περὶ τοῦ Ἰησοῦ, not τοῦ κυρίου as in the received text.

[5] The πιστεύσαντες in xix. 1 is slightly ambiguous, and some expressions in the passage might suggest the opposite: but μαθητὰς seems decisive, for the word would not be used absolutely except of Christian disciples; comp. vi. 1, 2, 7, ix. 10, 19, 26, 38, and frequently.

impulse towards Christianity; but to others it represented a widely different form of belief and practice. The Gospel of St John was written, according to all tradition, at Ephesus in the later years of the first century. Again and again the Evangelist impresses on his readers, either directly by his own comments or indirectly by the course of the narrative, the transient and subordinate character of John's ministry. He was not the light, says the Evangelist, but came to bear witness of the light[1]. He was not the sun in the heavens: he was only the waning lamp, which shines when kindled from without and burns itself away in shining. His light might well gladden the Jews while it lasted, but this was only 'for a season[2].' John himself lost no opportunity of bearing his testimony to the loftier claims of Jesus[3]. From such notices it is plain that in the interval between the preaching of St Paul and the Gospel of St John the memory of the Baptist at Ephesus had assumed a new attitude towards Christianity. His name is no longer the sign of imperfect appreciation, but the watchword of direct antagonism. John had been set up as a rival Messiah to Jesus. In other words, this Gospel indicates the spread of Hemerobaptist principles, if not the presence of a Hemerobaptist community, in proconsular Asia, when it was written. In two respects these Hemerobaptists distorted the facts of history. They perverted John's teaching, and they misrepresented his office. His baptism was no more a single rite, once performed and initiating an amendment of life; it was a daily recurrence atoning for sin and sanctifying the person[4]. He

Professed followers at a later date.

The facts of history distorted by them.

---

[1] John i. 8.

[2] John v. 35 ἐκεῖνος ἦν ὁ λύχνος ὁ καιόμενος καὶ φαίνων κ.τ.λ. The word καίειν is not only 'to burn', but not unfrequently also 'to kindle, to set on fire', as e.g. Xen. *Anab.* iv. 4. 12 οἱ ἄλλοι ἀναστάντες πῦρ ἔκαιον; so that ὁ καιόμενος may mean either 'which burns away' or 'which is lighted'. With the former meaning it would denote the *transitoriness*, with the latter the *derivative character*, of John's ministry. There seems no reason for excluding either idea here. Thus the whole expression would mean 'the lamp which is kindled and burns away, and (only so) gives light'. For an example of two verbs or participles joined together, where the second describes a

result conditional upon the first, see 1 Pet. ii. 20 εἰ ἁμαρτάνοντες καὶ κολαφιζόμενοι ὑπομενεῖτε...εἰ ἀγαθοποιοῦντες καὶ πάσχοντες ὑπομενεῖτε, 1 Thess. iv. 1 πῶς δεῖ περιπατεῖν καὶ ἀρέσκειν Θεῷ.

[3] See John i. 15—34, iii. 23—30, v. 33 sq.: comp. x. 41, 42. This aspect of St John's Gospel has been brought out by Ewald *Jahrb. der Bibl. Wissensch.* iii. p. 156 sq.; see also *Geschichte* vii. p. 152 sq., *die Johanneischen Schriften* p. 13. There is perhaps an allusion to these 'disciples of John' in 1 Joh. v. 6 οὐκ ἐν τῷ ὕδατι μόνον, ἀλλ' ἐν τῷ ὕδατι καὶ ἐν τῷ αἵματι· καὶ τὸ πνεῦμα κ.τ.λ.; comp. Acts i. 5, xi. 16, xix. 4.

[4] *Apost. Const.* vi. 6; comp. § 23. See p. 402, note 1.

himself was no longer the forerunner of the Messiah; he was the
very Messiah[1]. In the latter half of the first century, it would

Spread of
Hemero-
baptist
principles.
seem, there was a great movement among large numbers of the
Jews in favour of frequent baptism, as the one purificatory rite
essential to salvation. Of this superstition we have had an instance
already in the anchorite Banus to whom Josephus attached himself
as a disciple. Its presence in the western districts of Asia Minor
is shown by a Sibylline poem, dating about A.D. 80, which I have
already had occasion to quote[2]. Some years earlier these sectarians
are mentioned by name as opposing James the Lord's brother and
the Twelve at Jerusalem[3]. Nor is there any reason for questioning
their existence as a sect in Palestine during the later years of the
Apostolic age, though the source from which our information comes
is legendary, and the story itself a fabrication. But when or how
they first connected themselves with the name of John the Baptist,
and whether this assumption was made by all alike or only by one
section of them, we do not know. Such a connexion, however false
to history, was obvious and natural; nor would it be difficult to
accumulate parallels to this false appropriation of an honoured name.

A wrong
use made
of John's
name.
Baptism was the fundamental article of their creed; and John was
the Baptist of world-wide fame. Nothing more than this was
needed for the choice of an eponym. From St John's Gospel
it seems clear that this appropriation was already contemplated,
if not completed, at Ephesus before the first century had drawn
to a close. In the second century the assumption is recognised
as a characteristic of these Hemerobaptists, or Baptists, as they are
once called[4], alike by those who allow and those who deny its

---

[1] *Clem. Recogn.* i. 54 'ex discipulis
Johannis, qui...magistrum suum veluti
Christum praedicarunt,' *ib.* § 60 'Ecce
unus ex discipulis Johannis adfirmabat
Christum Johannem fuisse, et non Jesum; in tantum, inquit, ut et ipse
Jesus omnibus hominibus et prophetis
majorem esse pronuntiaverit Johannem etc.'; see also § 63.

[2] See above, p. 96.

[3] *Clem. Recogn.* l. c. This portion
of the Clementine Recognitions is apparently taken from an older Judaizing
romance, the *Ascents of James* (see

Galatians pp. 330, 367). Hegesippus
also (in Euseb. *H. E.* iv. 22) mentions
the Hemerobaptists in his list of Jewish
sects; and it is not improbable that
this list was given as an introduction
to his account of the labours and martyrdom of St James (see Euseb. *H. E.*
ii. 23). If so, it was probably derived
from the same source as the notice in
the Recognitions.

[4] They are called Baptists by Justin
Mart. *Dial.* 10, p. 307 A. He mentions
them among other Jewish sects, without however alluding to John.

justice [1]. Even in our age the name of 'John's disciples' has been given, though wrongly given, to an obscure sect in Babylonia, the Mandeans, whose doctrine and practice have some affinities to the older sect, and of whom perhaps they are the collateral, if not the direct, descendants [2].

(b) Of the connexion between this sect and John the Baptist we have been able to give a probable, though necessarily hypothetical account. But when we attempt to determine its relation to the Essenes, we find ourselves entangled in a hopeless mesh of perplexities. The notices are so confused, the affinities so subtle, the ramifications so numerous, that it becomes a desperate task to distinguish and classify these abnormal Jewish and Judaizing heresies. One fact however seems clear that, whatever affinities they may have had originally, and whatever relations they may have contracted

(b) Their relation to the Essenes.

They were at first

---

[1] By the author of the *Recognitions* (l. c.) who denies the claim; and by the author of the *Homilies* (see below, p. 406, note 3), who allows it.

[2] These Mandeans are a rapidly diminishing sect living in the region about the Tigris and the Euphrates, south of Bagdad. Our most exact knowledge of them is derived from Petermann (*Herzog's Real-Encyklopädie* s. vv. Mendäer, Zabier, and *Deutsche Zeitschrift* 1854 p. 181 sq., 1856 p. 331 sq., 342 sq., 363 sq., 386 sq.) who has had personal intercourse with them; and from Chwolson (*die Ssabier u. der Ssabismus* I. p. 100 sq.) who has investigated the Arabic authorities for their earlier history. The names by which they are known are (1) *Mendeans*, or more properly *Mandeans*, מנדייא *Mandāyē*, contracted from מנדא דחייא *Mandā děchāyē* 'the word of life.' This is their own name among themselves, and points to their Gnostic pretentions. (2) *Sabeans, Tsabiyun*, possibly from the root צבע 'to dip' on account of their frequent lustrations (Chwolson I. p. 110; but see *Galatians* p. 325), though this is not the derivation of the word which they themselves adopt, and other etymologies have found favour with some recent writers (see Petermann *Herzog's Real-Encykl.* Suppl. XVIII. p. 342 s. v.

Zabier). This is the name by which they are known in the Koran and in Arabic writers, and by which they call themselves when speaking to others. (3) *Nasoreans*, נצורייא *Nātsōrāyē*. This term is at present confined to those among them who are distinguished in knowledge or in business. (4) 'Christians of St John, or Disciples of St John' (i.e. the Baptist). This name is not known among themselves, and was incorrectly given to them by European travellers and missionaries. At the same time John the Baptist has a very prominent place in their theological system, as the one true prophet. On the other hand they are not Christians in any sense.

These Mandeans, the true Sabeans, must not be confused with the false Sabeans, polytheists and star-worshippers, whose locality is Northern Mesopotamia. Chwolson (I. p. 139 sq.) has shown that these last adopted the name in the 9th century to escape persecution from the Mohammedans, because in the Koran the Sabeans, as monotheists, are ranged with the Jews and Christians, and viewed in a more favourable light than polytheists. The name however has generally been applied in modern times to the false rather than to the true Sabeans.

distinct,
if not anta-
gonistic.

afterwards with one another, the Hemerobaptists, properly speaking, were not Essenes. The Sibylline poem which may be regarded as in some respects a Hemerobaptist manifesto contains, as we saw, many traits inconsistent with pure Essenism[1]. In two several accounts, the memoirs of Hegesippus and the Apostolic Constitutions, the Hemerobaptists are expressly distinguished from the Essenes[2]. In an early production of Judaic Christianity, whose Judaism has a strong Essene tinge, the Clementine Homilies, they and their eponym are condemned in the strongest language. The system of syzygies, or pairs of opposites, is a favourite doctrine of this work, and in these John stands contrasted to Jesus, as Simon Magus to Simon Peter, as the false to the true; for according to this author's philosophy of history the manifestation of the false always precedes the manifestation of the true[3]. And again, Epiphanius speaks of them as agreeing substantially in their doctrines, not with the Essenes, but with the Scribes and Pharisees[4]. His authority on such a point may be worth very little; but connected with other notices, it should not be passed over in silence. Yet, whatever may have been their differences, the Hemerobaptists and the Essenes had one point of direct contact, their belief in the moral efficacy of lustrations. When the temple and polity were destroyed, the shock vibrated through the whole fabric of Judaism, loosening and breaking up existing societies, and preparing the way for new combinations. More especially the cessation of the sacrificial rites must have produced a profound effect equally on those who, like the Essenes, had condemned them already, and on those who, as possibly was the case

But after
the de-
struction
of the
Temple

---

[1] See p. 96 sq.

[2] Hegesipp. in Euseb. *H. E.* iv. 22, *Apost. Const.* vi. 6. So also the Pseudo-Hieronymus in the *Indiculus de Haeresibus* (*Corp. Haeres.* I. p. 283, ed. Oehler).

[3] *Clem. Hom.* ii. 23 Ἰωάννης τις ἐγένετο ἡμεροβαπτιστής, ὃς καὶ τοῦ κυρίου ἡμῶν Ἰησοῦ κατὰ τὸν τῆς συζυγίας λόγον ἐγένετο πρόοδος. It is then stated that, as Christ had twelve leading disciples, so John had thirty. This, it is argued, was a providential dispensation—the one number represents the solar, the other the lunar period; and so they illustrate another

point in this writer's theory, that in the syzygies the true and the false are the male and female principle respectively. Among these 30 disciples he places Simon Magus. With this the doctrine of the Mandeans stands in direct opposition. They too have their syzygies, but John with them represents the true principle.

[4] *Haer.* xvii. 1 (p. 37) ἴσα τῶν γραμματέων καὶ Φαρισαίων φρονοῦσα. But he adds that they resemble the Sadducees 'not only in the matter of the resurrection of the dead, but also in their unbelief and in the other points.'

with the Hemerobaptists, had hitherto remained true to the orthodox ritual. One grave obstacle to friendly overtures was thus removed; and a fusion, more or less complete, may have been the consequence. At all events the relations of the Jewish sects must have been materially affected by this great national crisis, as indeed we know to have been the case. In the confusion which follows, it is impossible to attain any clear view of their history. At the beginning of the second century however this pseudo-baptist movement received a fresh impulse from the pretended revelation of Elchasai, which came from the farther East[1]. Henceforth Elchasai is the prominent name in the history of those Jewish and Judaizing sects whose proper home is east of the Jordan[2], and who appear to have reproduced, with various modifications derived from Christian and Heathen sources, the Gnostic theology and the pseudo-baptist ritual of their Essene predecessors. It is still preserved in the records of the only extant people who have any claim to be regarded as the religious heirs of the Essenes. Elchasai is regarded as the founder of the sect of Mandeans[3].

there may have been a fusion.

(ii) But, if great weight has been attached to the supposed connexion of John the Baptist with the Essenes, the case of James the Lord's brother has been alleged with still more confidence. Here, it is said, we have an indisputable Essene connected by the closest family ties with the Founder of Christianity. James is reported to have been holy from his birth; to have drunk no wine nor strong drink; to have eaten no flesh; to have allowed no razor to touch his head, no oil to anoint his body; to have abstained from using the bath; and lastly to have worn no wool, but only fine linen[4]. Here we have a description of Nazarite practices at least and (must it not be granted) of Essene tendencies also.

(ii) James the Lord's Brother

invested with Essene characteristics.

But what is our authority for this description? The writer, from whom the account is immediately taken, is the Jewish-Christian his-

---

[1] See *Galatians* p. 324 sq. on this Book of Elchasai.

[2] See above, p. 374.

[3] See Chwolson I. p. 112 sq., II. p. 543 sq. The Arabic writer En-Nedim, who lived towards the close of the tenth century, says that the founder of the Sabeans (i.e. Mandeans) was *El-chasaich* (الكساىح) who taught the doctrine of two coordinate princi-

ples, the male and female. This notice, as far as it goes, agrees with the account of Elchasai or Elxai in Hippolytus (*Haer.* ix. 13 sq.) and Epiphanius (*Haer.* xix. 1 sq.). But the derivation of the name Elchasai given by Epiphanius (*Haer.* xix. 2) δύναμις κεκαλυμμένη (חיל כסי) is different and probably correct (see *Galatians* p. 325).

[4] Hegesippus in Euseb. *H. E.* ii. 23.

torian Hegesippus, who flourished about A.D. 170. He cannot therefore have been an eye-witness of the facts which he relates. And

But the
account
comes
from
untrust-
worthy
sources.

his whole narrative betrays its legendary character. Thus his account
of James's death, which follows immediately on this description, is
highly improbable and melodramatic in itself, and directly contradicts the contemporary notice of Josephus in its main facts[1].
From whatever source therefore Hegesippus may have derived his
information, it is wholly untrustworthy. Nor can we doubt that he
was indebted to one of those romances with which the Judaizing
Christians of Essene tendencies loved to gratify the natural curiosity of
their disciples respecting the first founders of the Church[2]. In like
manner Essene portraits are elsewhere preserved of the Apostles Peter[3]
and Matthew[4] which represent them as living on a spare diet of
herbs and berries. I believe also that I have elsewhere pointed out
the true source of this description in Hegesippus, and that it is taken
from the 'Ascents of James[5],' a Judæo-Christian work stamped,
as we happen to know, with the most distinctive Essene features[6].
But if we turn from these religious novels of Judaic Christianity
to earlier and more trustworthy sources of information—to the

No Essene
features in
the true
portraits
of James
or of the
earliest
disciples.

Gospels or the Acts or the Epistles of St Paul—we fail to discover
the faintest traces of Essenism in James. 'The historical James,'
says a recent writer, 'shows Pharisaic but not Essene sympathies[7].'
This is true of James, as it is true of the early disciples in the mother
Church of Jerusalem generally. The temple-ritual, the daily sacrifices,
suggested no scruples to them. The only distinction of meats, which
they recognised, was the distinction of animals clean and unclean as
laid down by the Mosaic law. The only sacrificial victims, which
they abhorred, were victims offered to idols. They took their part in
the religious offices, and mixed freely in the common life, of their
fellow-Israelites, distinguished from them only in this, that to their
Hebrew inheritance they superadded the knowledge of a higher truth

---

[1] See *Galatians* p. 366 sq.

[2] See *Galatians* p. 324.

[3] *Clem. Hom.* xii. 6, where St Peter
is made to say ἄρτῳ μόνῳ καὶ ἐλαίαις
χρῶμαι, καὶ σπανίως λαχάνοις; comp.
xv. 7 ὕδατος μόνου καὶ ἄρτου.

[4] *Clem. Alex. Paedag.* ii. 1 (p. 174)
σπερμάτων καὶ ἀκροδρύων καὶ λαχάνων
ἄνευ κρεῶν μετελάμβανεν.

[5] See *Galatians* p. 367, note.

[6] Epiphanius (*Haer.* xxx. 16) mentions two points especially, in which
the character of this work is shown:
(1) It represented James as condemning the sacrifices and the fire on the
altar (see above, pp. 371—373): (2) It
published the most unfounded calum-
nies against St Paul.

[7] Lipsius, *Schenkel's Bibel-Lexicon*,
p. 191.

and the joy of a better hope. It was altogether within the sphere of orthodox Judaism that the Jewish element in the Christian brotherhood found its scope. Essene peculiarities are the objects neither of sympathy nor of antipathy. In the history of the infant Church for the first quarter of a century Essenism is as though it were not.

But a time came, when all this was changed. Even as early as the *Essene influences visible before the close of the Apostolic age.* year 58, when St Paul wrote to the Romans, we detect practices in the Christian community of the metropolis, which may possibly have been due to Essene influences[1]. Five or six years later, the heretical teaching which threatened the integrity of the Gospel at Colossæ shows that this type of Judaism was already strong enough within the Church to exert a dangerous influence on its doctrinal purity. Then came the great convulsion—the overthrow of the Jewish polity and nation. This was the turning-point in the relations between Essenism and Christianity, at least in Palestine. The Essenes were *Consequences of the Jewish war.* extreme sufferers in the Roman war of extermination. It seems probable that their organization was entirely broken up. Thus cast adrift, they were free to enter into other combinations, while the shock of the recent catastrophe would naturally turn their thoughts into new channels. At the same time the nearer proximity of the Christians, who had migrated to Peræa during the war, would bring them into close contact with the new faith and subject them to its influences, as they had never been subjected before[2]. But, whatever may be the explanation, the fact seems certain, that after the destruction of Jerusalem the Christian body was largely reinforced from their ranks. The Judaizing tendencies among the Hebrew Christians, which hitherto had been wholly Pharisaic, are henceforth largely Essene.

2. If then history fails to reveal any such external connexion *2. Do the resemblances favour the theory of a connexion?* with Essenism in Christ and His Apostles as to justify the opinion that Essene influences contributed largely to the characteristic features of the Gospel, such a view, if tenable at all, must find its support in some striking coincidence between the doctrines and practices of the Essenes and those which its Founder stamped upon Christianity. This indeed is the really important point; for without it the external connexion, even if proved, would be valueless. The question is not whether Christianity arose amid such and such circumstances, but how far it was created and moulded by those circumstances.

---

[1] Rom. xiv. 2, 21. [2] See *Galatians* p. 322 sq.

(i) Observ-
ance of the
sabbath.   (i) Now one point which especially strikes us in the Jewish
historian's account of the Essenes, is their strict observance of
certain points in the Mosaic ceremonial law, more especially the
ultra-Pharisaic rigour with which they kept the sabbath. How far
their conduct in this respect was consistent with the teaching and
practice of Christ may be seen from the passages quoted in the
parallel columns which follow :

'Jesus went on the sabbath-day
through the corn fields; and his disciples began to pluck the ears of corn and
to eat[1]. ...But when the Pharisees saw
it, they said unto him, 'Behold, thy
disciples do that which it is not lawful
to do upon the sabbath-day. But he
said unto them, Have ye not read what
David did...The sabbath was made
for man, and not man for the sabbath.
Therefore the Son of Man is Lord even
of the sabbath-day...'
  'It is lawful to do well on the sab-
bath-days' (Matt. xii. 1—12; Mark ii.
23—iii. 6; Luke vi. 1—11, xiv. 1—6.

'And they avoid...touching any work
($\dot{\epsilon}\phi\acute{a}\pi\tau\epsilon\sigma\theta a\iota$ $\ddot{\epsilon}\rho\gamma\omega\nu$) on the sabbath-day
more scrupulously than any of the Jews
($\delta\iota a\phi o\rho\acute{\omega}\tau a\tau a$ $'Iov\delta a\acute{\iota}\omega\nu$ $\dot{a}\pi\acute{a}\nu\tau\omega\nu$); for

[1] Grätz (III. p. 233) considers this
narrative an interpolation made from
a Pauline point of view ('eine pau-
linistische Tendenz-interpolation').
This theory of interpolation, interposing wherever the evidence is unfavourable, cuts up all argument by the
roots. In this instance however Grätz
is consistently carrying out a principle which he broadly lays down elsewhere. He regards it as the great
merit of Baur and his school, that
they explained the origin of the Gospels by the conflict of two opposing
camps, the Ebionite and the Pauline.
'By this master-key,' he adds, 'criticism was first put in a position to test
what is historical in the Gospels, and
what bears the stamp of a polemical
tendency (was einen tendentiösen po-
lemischen Charakter hat). Indeed
by this means the element of trustworthy history in the Gospels melts
down to a minimum' (III. p. 224). In
other words the judgment is not to be
pronounced upon the evidence, but

the evidence must be mutilated to suit
the judgment. The method is not new.
The sectarians of the second century,
whether Judaic or anti-Judaic, had
severally their 'master-key.' The
master-key of Marcion was a conflict
also—the antagonism of the Old and
New Testaments. Under his hands
the historical element in the New Testament dissolved rapidly. The master-key of the anti-Marcionite writer
of the Clementine Homilies was likewise a conflict, though of another
kind—the conflict of fire and water, of
the sacrificial and the baptismal systems. Wherever sacrifice was mentioned with approval, there was a
'Tendenz-interpolation' (see above,
p. 372 sq.). In this manner again the
genuine element in the Old Testament
melted down to a minimum.
  [2] Grätz however (III. p. 228) sees a
coincidence between Christ's teaching
and Essenism in this notice. Not to
do him injustice, I will translate his
own words (correcting however several

See also a similar incident in Luke xiii. 10—17).

'The Jews therefore said unto him that was cured; It is the sabbath-day; it is not lawful for thee to carry thy bed. But he answered them, He that made me whole, the same said unto me, Take up thy bed and walk.... Therefore the Jews did persecute Jesus and sought to slay him, because he did these things on the sabbath-day. But Jesus answered them, My Father worketh hitherto, and I work, etc. (John v. 10—18; comp. vii. 22, 23).'

'And it was the sabbath-day when Jesus made the clay, and opened his eyes......Therefore said some of the Pharisees, This man is not of God, because he keepeth not the sabbath-day (John ix. 14, 16).'

they do not venture so much as to move a vessel[2], nor to perform the most necessary offices of life (B. J. ii. 8. 9).'

(ii) But there were other points of ceremonial observance, in which the Essenes superadded to the law. Of these the most remarkable was their practice of constant lustrations. In this respect the Pharisee was sufficiently minute and scrupulous in his observances; but with the Essene these ablutions were the predominant feature of his religious ritual. Here again it will be instructive to compare the practice of Christ and His disciples with the practice of the Essenes.

(ii) Lustrations and other ceremonial observances.

'And when they saw some of his disciples eat bread with defiled (that is to say, unwashen) hands; for the Pharisees and all the Jews, except they wash their hands oft (πυγμῇ), eat not...The Pharisees and scribes asked him, Why walk not thy disciples according to the tradition of the elders

misprints in the Greek): 'For the connexion of Jesus with the Essenes compare moreover Mark xi. 16 καὶ οὐκ ἤφιεν ὁ Ἰησοῦς ἵνα τις διενέγκῃ σκεῦος διὰ τοῦ ἱεροῦ with Josephus B. J. ii. 8. 9 ἀλλ' οὐδὲ σκεῦός τι μετακινῆσαι θαρροῦσιν (οἱ Ἐσσαῖοι).' He does not explain what this notice, which refers solely to the scrupulous observance of the sabbath, has to do with the profanation·of the temple, with which the passage in the

'So they wash their whole body (ἀπολούονται τὸ σῶμα) in cold water; and after this purification (ἁγνείαν)... being clean (καθαροί) they come to the refectory (to dine)......And when they have returned (from their day's work) they sup in like manner (B. J. ii. 8. 5).'

Gospel is alone concerned. I have seen Grätz's history described as a 'masterly' work. The first requisites in a historian are accuracy in stating facts and sobriety in drawing inferences. Without these, it is difficult to see what claims a history can have to this honourable epithet: and in those portions of his work, which I have consulted, I have not found either.

......But he answered...Ye hypocrites, laying aside the commandment of God, ye hold the tradition of men....'

'Not that which goeth into the mouth defileth the man; but that which cometh out of the mouth, this defileth the man......Let them alone, they be blind leaders of the blind...'

'To eat with unwashen hands defileth not the man (Matt. xv. 1—20, Mark vii. 1—23).'

'And when the Pharisee saw it, he marvelled that he had not first washed before dinner (τοῦ ἀρίστου). And the Lord said unto him: Now do ye Pharisees make clean the outside of the cup and the platter...Ye fools...behold all things are clean unto you (Luke xi. 38—41).'

'After a year's probation (the novice) is admitted to closer intercourse (πρόσεισιν ἔγγιον τῇ διαίτῃ), and the lustral waters in which he participates have a higher degree of purity (καὶ καθαρωτέρων τῶν πρὸς ἁγνείαν ὑδάτων μεταλαμβάνει, § 7).'

'It is a custom to wash after it, as if polluted by it (§ 9).'

'Racked and dislocated, burnt and crushed, and subjected to every instrument of torture ... to make them eat strange food (τι τῶν ἀσυνήθων)... they were not induced to submit (§ 10).'

'Exercising themselves in...divers lustrations (διαφόροις ἁγνείαις...ἐμπαιδοτριβούμενοι, § 12).'

Avoidance of strangers. Connected with this idea of external purity is the avoidance of contact with strangers, as persons who would communicate ceremonial defilement. And here too the Essene went much beyond the Pharisee. The Pharisee avoided Gentiles or aliens, or those whose profession or character placed them in the category of 'sinners'; but the Essene shrunk even from the probationers and inferior grades of his own exclusive community. Here again we may profitably compare the sayings and doings of Christ with the principles of this sect.

'And when the scribes and Pharisees saw him eat with the publicans and sinners they said unto the disciples, Why eateth your Master with the publicans and the sinners...' (Mark ii. 15 sq., Matth. ix. 10 sq., Luke v. 30 sq.).

'They say...a friend of publicans and sinners (Matth. xi. 19).'

'The Pharisees and the scribes murmured, saying, This man receiveth sinners and eateth with them (Luke xv. 2).'

'They all murmured saying that he was gone to be a guest with a man that is a sinner (Luke xix. 7).'

'And after this purification they assemble in a private room, where no person of a different belief (τῶν ἑτεροδόξων, i.e. not an Essene) is permitted to enter; and (so) being by themselves and clean (αὐτοὶ καθαροί) they present themselves at the refectory (δειπνητήριον), as if it were a sacred precinct (§ 5).'

'Behold, a woman in the city that was a sinner...began to wash his feet with her tears, and did wipe them with the hairs of her head and kissed his feet......Now when the Pharisee which had bidden him saw it, he spake within himself, saying, This man, if he had been a prophet, would have known who and what manner of woman this is that toucheth him; for she is a sinner (Luke vii. 37 sq.).'

'And they are divided into four grades according to the time passed under the discipline: and the juniors are regarded as so far inferior to the seniors, that, if they touch them, the latter wash their bodies clean (ἀπολούεσθαι), as if they had come in contact with a foreigner (καθάπερ ἀλλοφύλῳ συμφυρέντας, § 10).'

In all these minute scruples relating to ceremonial observances, the denunciations which are hurled against the Pharisees in the Gospels would apply with tenfold force to the Essenes.

(iii) If the lustrations of the Essenes far outstripped the enactments of the Mosaic law, so also did their asceticism. I have given reasons above for believing that this asceticism was founded on a false principle, which postulates the malignity of matter and is wholly inconsistent with the teaching of the Gospel[1]. But without pressing this point, of which no absolutely demonstrative proof can be given, it will be sufficient to call attention to the trenchant contrast in practice which Essene habits present to the life of Christ. He who 'came eating and drinking' and was denounced in consequence as 'a glutton and a wine-bibber[2],' He whose first exercise of power is recorded to have been the multiplication of wine at a festive entertainment, and whose last meal was attended with the drinking of wine and the eating of flesh, could only have excited the pity, if not the indignation, of these rigid abstainers. And again, attention should be directed to another kind of abstinence, where the contrast is all the more speaking, because the matter is so trivial and the scruple so minute.

(iii) Asceticism.

Eating and drinking.

'My head with oil thou didst not anoint (Luke vii. 46).'
'Thou, when thou fastest, anoint thy head (Matt. vi. 17).'

'And they consider oil a pollution (κηλῖδα), and though one is smeared involuntarily, he rubs his body clean (σμήχεται τὸ σῶμα, § 3).'

And yet it has been stated that 'the Saviour of the world...... showed what is required for a holy life in the Sermon on the Mount by a description of the Essenes[3].'

But much stress has been laid on the celibacy of the Essenes;

[1] See above, p. 87.   [2] Matt. xi. 19, Luke vii. 34.
[3] Ginsburg *Essenes* p. 14.

Celibacy. and our Lord's saying in Matt. xix. 12 is quoted to establish an identity of doctrine. Yet there is nothing special in the language there used. Nor is there any close affinity between the stern invectives against marriage which Josephus and Philo attribute to the Essene, and the gentle concession 'He that is able to receive it, let him receive it.' The best comment on our Lord's meaning here is the advice of St Paul[1], who was educated not in the Essene, but in the Pharisaic school. Moreover this saying must be balanced by the general tenour of the Gospel narrative. When we find Christ discussing the relations of man and wife, gracing the marriage festival by His presence, again and again employing wedding banquets and wedded life as apt symbols of the highest theological truths, without a word of disparagement or rebuke, we see plainly that we are confronted with a spirit very different from the narrow rigour of the Essenes.

(iv) Avoidance of the Temple sacrifices. (iv) But not only where the Essenes superadded to the ceremonial law, does their teaching present a direct contrast to the phenomena of the Gospel narrative. The same is true also of those points in which they fell short of the Mosaic enactments. I have already discussed at some length the Essene abstention from the temple sacrifices[2]. There can, I think, be little doubt that they objected to the slaughter of sacrificial victims altogether. But for my present purpose it matters nothing whether they avoided the temple on account of the sacrifices, or the sacrifices on account of the temple. Christ did neither. Certainly He could not have regarded the temple as unholy; for His whole time during His sojourns at Jerusalem was spent within its precincts. It was the scene of His miracles, of His ministrations, of His daily teaching[3]. And in like manner it is the common rendezvous of His disciples after Him[4]. Nor again does He evince any abhorrence of the sacrifices. On the contrary He says that the altar consecrates the gifts[5]; He charges the cleansed lepers to go and fulfil the Mosaic ordinance and offer the sacrificial offerings to the priests[6]. And His practice also is

---

[1] 1 Cor. vii. 26—31.

[2] See p. 371 sq.

[3] Matt. xxi. 12 sq., 23 sq., xxiv. 1 sq., xxvi. 55, Mark xi. 11, 15 sq., 27, xii. 35, xiii. 1 sq., xiv. 49, Luke ii. 46, xix. 45, xx. 1 sq., xxi. 37 sq., xxii. 53,

John ii. 14 sq., v. 14, vii. 14, viii. 2, 20, 59, x. 23, xi. 56, xviii. 20.

[4] Luke xxiv. 53, Acts ii. 46, iii. 1 sq., v. 20 sq., 42.

[5] Matt. xxiii. 18 sq.: comp. v. 23, 24.

[6] Matt. viii. 4, Mark i. 44, Luke v. 14.

conformable to His teaching. He comes to Jerusalem regularly to Practice of Christ and His disciples. attend the great festivals, where sacrifices formed the most striking part of the ceremonial, and He himself enjoins preparation to be made for the sacrifice of the Paschal lamb. If He repeats the inspired warning of the older prophets, that mercy is better than sacrifice[1], this very qualification shows approval of the practice in itself. Nor is His silence less eloquent than His utterances or His actions. Throughout the Gospels there is not one word which can be construed as condemning the sacrificial system or as implying a desire for its cessation until everything is fulfilled.

(v) This last contrast refers to the ceremonial law. But not (v) Denial of the resurrection of the body. less wide is the divergence on an important point of doctrine. The resurrection of the body is a fundamental article in the belief of the early disciples. This was distinctly denied by the Essenes[2]. However gross and sensuous may have been the conceptions of the Pharisees on this point, still they so far agreed with the teaching of Christianity, as against the Essenes, in that the risen man could not, as they held, be pure soul or spirit, but must necessarily be body and soul conjoint.

Thus at whatever point we test the teaching and practice of our Some supposed coincidences considered. Lord by the characteristic tenets of Essenism, the theory of affinity fails. There are indeed several coincidences on which much stress has been laid, but they cannot be placed in the category of distinctive features. They are either exemplifications of a higher morality, which may indeed have been honourably illustrated in the Essenes, but is in no sense confined to them, being the natural outgrowth of the moral sense of mankind whenever circumstances are favourable. Or they are more special, but still independent developments, which owe their similarity to the same influences of climate and soil, though they do not spring from the same root. To this latter class belong such manifestations as are due to the social conditions of the age or nation, whether they result from sympathy with, or from repulsion to, those conditions.

Thus, for instance, much stress has been laid on the aversion to Simplicity and brotherly love. war and warlike pursuits, on the simplicity of living, and on the feeling of brotherhood which distinguished Christians and Essenes alike. But what is gained by all this? It is quite plain that

[1] Matt. ix. 13, xii. 7.　　　　[2] See above, p. 88.

Christ would have approved whatever was pure and lovely in the morality of the Essenes, just as He approved whatever was true in the doctrine of the Pharisees, if any occasion had presented itself when His approval was called for. But it is the merest assumption to postulate direct obligation on such grounds. It is said however, that the moral resemblances are more particular than this. There is

Prohibition of oaths. for instance Christ's precept 'Swear not at all...but let your communication be Yea, yea, Nay, nay.' Have we not here, it is urged, the very counterpart to the Essene prohibition of oaths[1]? Yet it would surely be quite as reasonable to say that both alike enforce that simplicity and truthfulness in conversation which is its own credential and does not require the support of adjuration, both having the same reason for laying stress on this duty, because the leaders of religious opinion made artificial distinctions between oath and oath, as regards their binding force, and thus sapped the foundations of public and private honesty[2]. And indeed this avoidance of oaths is anything but a special badge of the Essenes. It was inculcated by Pythagoreans, by Stoics, by philosophers and moralists of all schools[3]. When Josephus and Philo called the attention of Greeks and Romans to this feature in the Essenes, they were simply asking them to admire in these practical philosophers among the 'barbarians' the realisation of an ideal which their own great men had laid down. Even within the circles of Pharisaism language is occasionally heard, which meets the Essene principle half-way[4].

Community of goods. And again; attention has been called to the community of goods in the infant Church of Christ, as though this were a legacy of Essenism. But here too the reasonable explanation is, that we have

[1] Jos. *B. J.* ii. 8. 6 πᾶν τὸ ῥηθὲν ὑπ' αὐτῶν ἰσχυρότερον ὅρκου· τὸ δὲ ὀμνύειν αὐτοῖς περίσταται, χεῖρόν τι τῆς ἐπιορκίας ὑπολαμβάνοντες· ἤδη γὰρ κατεγνῶσθαί φασι τὸν ἀπιστούμενον δίχα Θεοῦ, Philo *Omn. prob. lib.* 12 (II. p. 458) τοῦ φιλοθέου δείγματα παρέχονται μυρία...τὸ ἀνώμοτον κ.τ.λ. Accordingly Josephus relates (*Ant.* xv. 10. 4) that Herod the Great excused the Essenes from taking the oath of allegiance to him. Yet they were not altogether true to their principles; for Josephus says (*B. J.* ii. 8. 7), that on initiation into the sect the members were bound by fearful oaths (ὅρκους φρικώδεις) to fulfil certain

conditions; and he twice again in the same passage mentions oaths (ὀμνύουσι, τοιούτοις ὅρκοις) in this connexion.

[2] On the distinctions which the Jewish doctors made between the validity of different kinds of oaths, see the passages quoted in Lightfoot and Schöttgen on Matt. v. 33 sq. The Talmudical tract *Shebhuoth* tells its own tale, and is the best comment on the precepts in the Sermon on the Mount.

[3] See e.g. the passages in Wetstein on Matt. v. 37.

[4] *Baba Metsia* 49 a. See also Lightfoot on Matt. v. 34.

an independent attempt to realise the idea of brotherhood—an attempt which naturally suggested itself without any direct imitation, but which was soon abandoned under the pressure of circumstances. Indeed the communism of the Christians was from the first wholly unlike the communism of the Essenes. The surrender of property with the Christians was not a necessary condition of entrance into an order ; it was a purely voluntary act, which might be withheld without foregoing the privileges of the brotherhood[1]. And the common life too was obviously different in kind, at once more free and more sociable, unfettered by rigid ordinances, respecting individual liberty, and altogether unlike a monastic rule.

Not less irrelevant is the stress, which has been laid on another point of supposed coincidence in the social doctrines of the two communities. The prohibition of slavery was indeed a highly honourable feature in the Essene order[2], but it affords no indication of a direct connexion with Christianity. It is true that this social institution of antiquity was not less antagonistic to the spirit of the Gospel, than it was abhorrent to the feelings of the Essene ; and ultimately the influence of Christianity has triumphed over it. But the immediate treatment of the question was altogether different in the two cases. The Essene brothers proscribed slavery wholly ; they produced no appreciable results by the proscription. The Christian Apostles, without attempting an immediate and violent revolution in society, proclaimed the great principle that all men are equal in Christ, and left it to work. It did work, like leaven, silently but surely, till the whole lump was leavened. In the matter of slavery the resemblance to the Stoic is much closer than to the Essene[3]. The Stoic however began and ended in barren declamation, and no practical fruits were reaped from his doctrine.

Moreover prominence has been given to the fact that riches are decried, and a preference is given to the poor, in the teaching of our Lord and His Apostles. Here again, it is urged, we have a distinctly Essene feature. We need not stop to enquire with what limitations this prerogative of poverty, which appears in the Gospels, must be interpreted; but, quite independently of this question, we may

Prohibition of slavery.

Respect paid to poverty.

---

[1] Acts v. 4.
[2] Philo *Omn. prob. lib.* § 12 (II. p. 458) δοῦλός τε παρ' αὐτοῖς οὐδὲ εἷς ἐστιν ἀλλ' ἐλεύθεροι πάντες κ.τ.λ., *Fragm.* II.

p. 632 οὐκ ἀνδράποδον, Jos. *Ant.* xviii. 1. 5 οὔτε δούλων ἐπιτηδεύουσι κτῆσιν.
[3] See for instance the passages from Seneca quoted in *Philippians* p. 307.

fairly decline to lay any stress on such a coincidence, where all other indications of a direct connexion have failed. The Essenes, pursuing a simple and ascetic life, made it their chief aim to reduce their material wants as far as possible, and in doing so they necessarily exalted poverty. Ascetic philosophers in Greece and Rome had done the same. Christianity was entrusted with the mission of proclaiming the equal rights of all men before God, of setting a truer standard of human worth than the outward conventions of the world, of protesting against the tyranny of the strong and the luxury of the rich, of redressing social inequalities, if not always by a present compensation, at least by a future hope. The needy and oppressed were the special charge of its preachers. It was the characteristic feature of the 'Kingdom of Heaven,' as described by the prophet whose words gave the keynote to the Messianic hopes of the nation, that the glad tidings should be preached to the poor [1]. The exaltation of poverty therefore was an absolute condition of the Gospel.

The preaching of the Kingdom wrongly ascribed to the Essenes.

The mention of the kingdom of heaven leads to the last point on which it will be necessary to touch before leaving this subject. 'The whole ascetic life of the Essenes,' it has been said, 'aimed only at furthering the *Kingdom of Heaven* and the *Coming Age*.' Thus John the Baptist was the proper representative of this sect. 'From the Essenes went forth the first call that the Messiah must shortly appear, *The kingdom of heaven is at hand*'[2]. 'The announcement of the kingdom of heaven unquestionably went forth from the Essenes'[3]. For this confident assertion there is absolutely no foundation in fact ; and, as a conjectural hypothesis, the assumption is highly improbable.

The Essenes not prophets, but fortune-tellers.

As fortune-tellers or soothsayers, the Essenes might be called prophets ; but as preachers of righteousness, as heralds of the kingdom, they had no claim to the title. Throughout the notices in Josephus and Philo we cannot trace the faintest indication of Messianic hopes. Nor indeed was their position at all likely to foster such hopes [4]. The Messianic idea was built on a belief in the resur-

---

[1] Is. lxi. 1 εὐαγγελίσασθαι πτωχοῖς, quoted in Luke iv. 18. There are references to this particular part of the prophecy again in Matt. xi. 5, Luke vii. 22, and probably also in the beatitude μακάριοι οἱ πτωχοὶ κ.τ.λ., Matt. v. 3, Luke vi. 20.

[2] Grätz Gesch. III. p. 219.

[3] ib. p. 470.

[4] Lipsius *Schenkel's Bibel-Lexikon* s. v. Essäer p. 190, Keim *Jesus von Nazara* I. p. 305. Both these writers express themselves very decidedly against the view maintained by Grätz. 'The Essene art of soothsaying,' writes Lipsius, 'has absolutely nothing to do

rection of the body. The Essenes entirely denied this doctrine. The Messianic idea was intimately bound up with the national hopes and sufferings, with the national life, of the Jews. The Essenes had no interest in the Jewish polity; they separated themselves almost entirely from public affairs. The deliverance of the individual in the shipwreck of the whole, it has been well said, was the plain watchword of Essenism[1]. How entirely the conception of a Messiah might be obliterated, where Judaism was regarded only from the side of a mystic philosophy, we see from the case of Philo. Throughout the works of this voluminous writer only one or two faint and doubtful allusions to a personal Messiah are found[2]. The philosophical tenets of the Essenes no doubt differed widely from those of Philo; but in the substitution of the individual and contemplative aspect of religion for the national and practical they were united; and the effect in obscuring the Messianic idea would be the same. When therefore it is said that the prominence given to the proclamation of the Messiah's kingdom is a main link which connects Essenism and Christianity, we may dismiss the statement as a mere hypothesis, unsupported by evidence and improbable in itself.

They had no vivid Messianic expectations.

with the Messianic prophecy.' 'Of all this,' says Keim,' 'there is no trace.'

[1] Keim *l. c.*

[2] How little can be made out of Philo's Messianic utterances by one who is anxious to make the most possible out of them, may be seen from Gfrörer's treatment of the subject, *Philo* I. p. 486 sq. The treatises which bear on this topic are the *de Praemiis et Poenis* (I. p. 408, ed. Mangey) and the *de Execrationibus* (I. p. 429). They deserve to be read, if only for the negative results which they yield.

ADDENDA.

THE following collation of the text of the Epistle to the Laodiceans in the *La Cava* MS (see p. 282) was made by the Rev. J. Wordsworth, Fellow of Brasenose. It reached my hands too late for insertion in its proper place (p. 287 sq).

Explicit ad colossenses incipit aepistola ad laudicenses.
1 Apostolus] *om.*   Laodiciae] laudiciae.   3 orationem omnem] homnem horationem.   in operibus eius] *om.*   in diem] in diae. 4 neque destituant etc.] neque destituit vos quorundam vaniloquentia insinuantium hut vos evertant.   a me] ha me.   5 ut qui...profectum] hut qui sunt ex me perveniant ad profectum.   operum etc.] hoperumque salutis aeternae (*om.* vitae).   6 quibus] in quibus.   7 factum etc.] fletum orationibus vestris est. administrante etc.   8 vivere] vere vita.   9 ut] hut.   unanimes] hunanimes.   10 Ergo etc.] ergo dilectissimi hut audistis praesentiam mei (*om.* ita) retinete.   11 operatur in vos] hoperatur in vobis.   13 reliquum] *om.*   sordidos etc.] sordidos in lucro homines. sint petitiones.   15 amabilia] *add.* sunt.   16 Et quae] quae (*om.* et). 19 Domini Jhesu] domini nostri jhesu christi.   20 colosensibus et] *om.* Colosensium] colossensium.

The capitula of 1 Thessalonians follow immediately.

p. 338 sq.   The note on πρεσβύτης.
In an inscription given in Wood's *Ephesus*, Inscr. vi. 1. p. 24, l. 72, πρεσβευτέροις is engraved for πρεσβυτέροις. This example has the highest value as an illustration of St Paul, since the inscription belongs to the age of Trajan.

INDEX.

NOTES

Notes